KU-266-494

Jordan

THE ROUGH GUIDE

There are more than one hundred and fifty Rough Guide titles
covering destinations from Amsterdam to Zimbabwe

Forthcoming titles include

Argentina • Croatia • Ecuador • Money Online • Switzerland

Rough Guide Reference Series

Classical Music • Drum 'n' Bass • English Football • European Football
House • The Internet • Jazz • Music USA • Opera • Reggae
Rock Music • Techno • World Music

Rough Guide Phrasebooks

Czech • Dutch • Egyptian Arabic • European Languages • French
German • Greek • Hindi & Urdu • Hungarian • Indonesian
Italian • Japanese • Mandarin Chinese • Mexican Spanish • Polish
Portuguese • Russian • Spanish • Swahili • Thai • Turkish • Vietnamese

Rough Guides on the Internet

www.roughguides.com

ROUGH GUIDE CREDITS

Text editor: Paul Gray
Series editor: Mark Ellingham
Editorial: Martin Dunford, Jonathan Buckley, Samantha Cook, Jo Mead, Amanda Tomlin, Kate Berens, Ann-Marie Shaw, Chris Schüler, Helena Smith, Kieran Falconer, Judith Bamber, Olivia Eccleshall, Orla Duane, Ruth Blackmore, Sophie Martin, Jennifer Dempsey, Sue Jackson, Geoff Howard (UK); Andrew Rosenberg, Andrew Taber (US)
Production: Susanne Hillen, Andy Hilliard, Link Hall, Helen Ostick, James Morris, Julia Bovis, Michelle Draycott

Cartography: Melissa Flack, Maxine Burke, Nichola Goodliffe
Picture research: Eleanor Hill
Online editors: Alan Spicer, Kate Hands (UK); Geronimo Madrid (US)
Finance: John Fisher, Celia Crowley, Neeta Mistry
Marketing & Publicity: Richard Trillo, Simon Carloss, Niki Smith, Katherine Allen (UK); Jean-Marie Kelly, SoRelle Braun (US)
Administration: Tania Hummel, Alexander Mark Rogers

ACKNOWLEDGEMENTS

At Rough Guides, Paul Gray was a pleasure to work with, patient, insightful and with a superb eye for detail. Thanks also to Maxine Burke, Eleanor Hill and Helen Ostick; Jennifer Speake; Alison Cowan; Nick Thomson; Sam Cook; and to Martin Dunford for supporting me from the beginning.

In Jordan, more than a year of research brought me into contact with warmth, openhearted generosity and support from people all over the country. At the Ministry of Tourism, many thanks to HE Aqel Biltaji, Akram Massarweh, Habeeb F. Habash, Suha Battikhi, Khaled Alnsour and the unsung Bekr Habahbeh; at the Jordan Tourism Board, Marwan H. Khoury; at the RJGC Mahmoud Malkawi; at TURAB Basel Haddadin; an unnamed town-planner at the Petra Regional Council; and at the Royal Society of Fine Arts HRH Princess Wijdan and Dirar-Adnan Kanaan. At BMed/BA, Mark Hodson and Saad Jaber, and Dawn Essai in London, were swift, friendly and professional. The staff of the RSCN went well beyond the call of duty for me, in particular Qusay Ahmad and Chris Johnson; Tariq Abul Hawa, Abdul-Razzaq Khawaldeh and Saleh Mahasneh; and Othman Mirza, Ahmed Zoubi and Ahmed Sha'alan. Thanks also to Alison McQuitty; Alan

Rowe; Prof. Dr Abdel-Hamid Hamam; Samer Mouasher and Jad Younis; Waleed Hazbun; Ahmed al-Qatawneh and Osama Twal. The hospitality of Abdullah Qassem at Umm Qais; Deeb Hussein at Pella; and Ali Hillawi and Atta at Rum was always a joy. Abu Suleiman and Samer made the *Cliff* a home-from-home for three long months, and, in a few hours behind the wheel at a tough time, Maydullah Muhammad Atieeg quietly but memorably lifted a cloud. Last but by no means least, without Ammar Khammash's inspiration, this book would be much less than it is.

Thanks are also due to Daniel Jacobs; Mark Sleath and Lara Madge; Dr Barrett at MASTA; Roel Meijer; Isam al-Khafaji; and, for contributing pieces, Anna Hohler, Karinne Keithley and Michelle Woodward. Finally, I couldn't have started out on this project without Micha's support, encouragement and love. However, although it wasn't what I wanted, this book marked an ending. For listening to me when I needed to talk, I owe more than I can say to – in particular – Amanda, Samer, Peter, Suhail, Diala, Anna, Malijn and Kate. This book is dedicated to Alisa, and to Madian.

PUBLISHING INFORMATION

This first edition published November 1998 by Rough Guides Ltd, 62–70 Shorts Gardens, London WC2H 9AB. Reprinted May 2000
Distributed by the Penguin Group:
Penguin Books Ltd, 27 Wrights Lane, London W8 5TZ
Penguin Books USA Inc., 375 Hudson Street, New York 10014, USA
Penguin Books Australia Ltd, 487 Maroondah Highway, PO Box 257, Ringwood, Victoria 3134, Australia
Penguin Books Canada Ltd, 10 Alcorn Avenue, Toronto, Ontario, Canada M4V 1E4
Penguin Books (NZ) Ltd, 182–190 Wairau Road, Auckland 10, New Zealand
Typeset in Linotron Univers and Century Old Style to an original design by Andrew Oliver.
Printed in England by Clays Ltd, St Ives PLC.
Illustrations in Part One and Part Three by Edward Briant.
Illustrations on p.1 & p.305 by Henry Iles.

© Matthew Teller 1998.
No part of this book may be reproduced in any form without permission from the publisher except for the quotation of brief passages in reviews.
400pp – Includes index
A catalogue record for this book is available from the British Library.
ISBN 1-85828-350-7

The publishers and authors have done their best to ensure the accuracy and currency of all the information in *The Rough Guide to Jordan*. However, they can accept no responsibility for any loss, injury or inconvenience sustained by any traveller as a result of information or advice contained in the guide.

Jordan

THE ROUGH GUIDE

written and researched by

Matthew Teller

THE ROUGH GUIDES

THE ROUGH GUIDES

TRAVEL GUIDES • PHRASEBOOKS • MUSIC AND REFERENCE GUIDES

 We set out to do something different when the first Rough Guide was published in 1982. Mark Ellingham, just out of university, was travelling in Greece. He brought along the popular guides of the day, but found they were all lacking in some way. They were either strong on ruins and museums but went on for pages without mentioning a beach or taverna. Or they were so conscious of the need to save money that they lost sight of Greece's cultural and historical significance. Also, none of the books told him anything about Greece's contemporary life – its politics, its culture, its people, and how they lived.

So with no job in prospect, Mark decided to write his own guidebook, one which aimed to provide practical information that was second to none, detailing the best beaches and the hottest clubs and restaurants, while also giving hard-hitting accounts of every sight, both famous and obscure, and providing up-to-the-minute information on contemporary culture. It was a guide that encouraged independent travellers to find the best of Greece, and was a great success, getting shortlisted for the Thomas Cook travel guide award,

and encouraging Mark, along with three friends, to expand the series.

The Rough Guide list grew rapidly and the letters flooded in, indicating a much broader readership than had been anticipated, but one which uniformly appreciated the Rough Guide mix of practical detail and humour, irreverence and enthusiasm. Things haven't changed. The same four friends who began the series are still the caretakers of the Rough Guide mission today: to provide the most reliable, up-to-date and entertaining information to independent-minded travellers of all ages, on all budgets.

We now publish 100 titles and have offices in London and New York. The travel guides are written and researched by a dedicated team of more than 100 authors, based in Britain, Europe, the USA and Australia. We have also created a unique series of phrasebooks to accompany the travel series, along with an acclaimed series of music guides, and a best-selling pocket guide to the Internet and World Wide Web. We also publish comprehensive travel information on our Web site:

www.roughguides.com

HELP US UPDATE

We've gone to a lot of effort to ensure that *The Rough Guide to Jordan* is accurate and up to date. However, things change – places get "discovered", opening hours are notoriously fickle, restaurants and rooms raise prices or lower standards. If you feel we've got it wrong or left something out, we'd like to know, and if you can remember the address, the price, the time, the phone number, so much the better.

We'll credit all contributions, and send a copy of the next edition (or any other Rough Guide if you prefer) for the best letters. Please mark letters: "Rough Guide Jordan Update" and send to:
Rough Guides, 62–70 Shorts Gardens, London WC2H 9AB or Rough Guides, 375 Hudson St, 9th floor, New York NY 10014.
Or send email to: mail@roughguides.co.uk
Online updates about this book can be found on Rough Guides' Web site at www.roughguides.com

THE AUTHOR

Matthew Teller's first visit to the Middle East was in 1980 at the age of eleven, when he kept nagging to be taken back to Jerusalem's spice market to smell the smells. He's since travelled extensively throughout the eastern Mediterranean but, despite long periods living and working in Cairo, Jerusalem and Amman, he's still not entirely clear about the difference between *baba ghanouj* and *moutabbel*.

CONTENTS

Introduction ix

PART ONE   BASICS   1

Getting there from Britain and Ireland 3
Getting there from North America 8
Getting there from Australia & New Zealand 11
Getting there from neighbouring countries 13
Red tape and visas 16
Health 18
Travel insurance 22
Travellers with disabilities 23
Information and maps 25
Money and costs 29

Getting around 33
Accommodation 39
Food and drink 41
Post, phones and email 50
The media 53
Behaviour and attitudes 56
Police and trouble 63
Work and study 64
Directory 66

PART TWO   THE GUIDE   69

• CHAPTER 1: AMMAN AND AROUND   71–126

Some history 71
Orientation and information 74
Arrival 78
City transport 83
Accommodation 85
Downtown 90
Jebel al-Qala'a 94
The rest of the city 96
Eating and drinking 99

Nightlife and entertainment 104
Shopping 106
Moving on from Amman 108
Listings 115
Wadi Seer and Iraq al-Amir 118
Fhays 120
Salt 121
The Dead Sea 123
Travel details 126

• CHAPTER 2: JERASH AND THE NORTH   127–161

Jerash 130
Ajloun 142
Dibbeen National Park 144
Irbid 145
Umm Qais 149

Himmeh 154
Abila 155
Pella 157
South of Pella 159
Travel details 161

• CHAPTER 3: THE EASTERN DESERT
162–188

Khirbet as-Samra 165
Qasr Hallabat 166
Umm al-Jimal 167
The Hawran 169
Burqu 172

Azraq 173
Qusayr Amra 182
Qasr Hraneh 185
Qasr Mushatta 187
Travel details 188

• CHAPTER 4: THE KING'S HIGHWAY
189–224

Madaba 192
Mount Nebo 202
Hammamat Ma'in 204
Mukawir 205
Umm ar-Rasas 206
Wadi Mujib 208
Karak 210

Bab adh-Dhraa and Lot's Cave 216
Khirbet Tannur 218
Hammamat Afra and Tafileh 219
Dana Nature Reserve 219
Shawbak 223
Travel details 224

• CHAPTER 5: PETRA
225–270

Some history 225
Wadi Musa 232
Information and admission 241
The approach to the city 244
The High Place of Sacrifice 252
The East Cliff 255

The city centre 256
The Monastery 263
Southwest of Petra 265
Northeast of Petra 267
Siq al-Berid and Baydha 269
Travel details 270

• CHAPTER 6: THE SOUTHERN DESERT AND AQABA
271–304

The Desert Highway 273
Wadi Rum 277
Aqaba 285

The Wadi Araba road 302
Travel details 304

PART THREE CONTEXTS
305

The historical framework 307
Islam 331
Modern art 336
Writing from Jordan 340

Books 351
Language 360
Glossary 366

Index 369

LIST OF MAPS

Jordan	x–xi	**The King's Highway**	190–191
Chapter divisions	1	Madaba	193
Amman and around	72	Karak	211
Amman	76–77	Dana Nature Reserve	220
Aman: Downtown	80–81	**Petra/Wadi Musa area**	226–227
Salt	121	Wadi Musa	234–235
Jerash and the north	128	Petra	242–243
Jerash	132–133	Petra city centre	257
Irbid	146	**The Southern desert and Aqaba**	272
Umm Qais	150	Ma'an	275
The eastern desert	162–163	Wadi Rum	275
Umm al-Jimal	168	Aqaba	286–287
Azraq	174	Aqaba downtown	290
Qusayr Amra Frescoes	183		

MAP SYMBOLS

═══ Road	− − Ferry route	⊞ Hospital
ⅠⅠⅠⅠⅠⅠ Steps	✗ Airport	ⓘ Tourist office
- - - - Path	★ Bus or *service* stop	ⓒ Telephone office
—— Wall	▣ Restaurant	⊠ Post office
━━ Railway	◉ Accommodation	▮ Building
— — - Chapter division boundary	◆ Point of interest	✚ Church
▬ ▬ ▬ Undisputed International border	ⴲ Mosque	▦ Park
—·— Other border	⋏⋏ Mountain range	▦ Beach
—— Waterway	▲ Mountain peak	

INTRODUCTION

Western travellers have been exploring the Middle East for well over a century, but **Jordan** remains a newcomer to tourism, welcoming only a fraction of the numbers who visit its near neighbours. The country's popular image abroad encompasses not much more than proud desert nomads ruled by a wise king, and almost nothing is known of Jordan's mountains and beaches, castles and ancient churches, the urbanity of its people and richness of its culture. However, in the last decade the country has woken up to marketing its spectacular assets to the world. Tourist facilities are now well advanced, and for the curious few, there is no better time to visit.

Although surrounded by instability, Jordan is the safest country in the Middle East by quite a long way, a comforting fact which allows you to switch your concentration away from suspicious packages towards the stunning **landscapes** around you. The country is largely desert, but this one bland word covers a multitude of scenes, from the dramatic red sands and towering cliffs of the far south to the endless stony plains of volcanic basalt in the east. Also packed into this tiny wedge of land are the lush olive-rich hills of the north, teetering over the plunging rift of the Jordan Valley, which in turn runs down to the Dead Sea, lowest point on earth. The centre of the country is carpeted with tranquil fields of wheat, which are cut through by expansive canyons and bordered by arid, craggy mountains. At the southernmost tip of the country, beaches fringe the warm waters of the Red Sea, harbouring some of the most spectacular coral reefs in the world.

Jordan is part of the land bridge linking Europe, Africa and Asia, and has seen countless armies come and go – Greeks, Romans, Muslims, Christian Crusaders and more – all of whom have left evidence of their conquests. There are literally thousands of **ruins** and **archeological sites** from all periods in every corner of the country. In addition, Israel and Palestine, Jordan's neighbours to the west, have no monopoly on **biblical history**: Lot sought refuge from the fire and brimstone of the Lord in Jordan; Moses, Aaron and John the Baptist all died in Jordan; and Jesus may well have been baptized here. Even the Prophet Muhammad passed through.

And yet the country is far from being stuck in the past. Amman is a thoroughly modern capital, and Jordan's respectable economic growth means that grinding poverty is the rare exception rather than the rule. Kids may sell you cigarettes or offer to shine your shoes, but more desperate begging goes on in the streets of any European or

---

FACTS AND FIGURES

The Hashemite Kingdom of Jordan, as it's officially known, covers an **area** of 96,188 square kilometres (a little bigger than Portugal and a little smaller than Kentucky), about three-quarters of which is desert. Some 41 percent of the country's total **population** of 4.6 million is below the age of 15. Jordan's population has increased eight-fold since 1952, and its current growth rate of 4.4 percent, the highest in the Arab world, means it will hit 7 million by 2010. The country is desperately water-poor: current per capita consumption of **water** is about 200 cubic metres annually, compared with 1800 in Syria, 7700 as the world average, and 110,000 in North America. Almost a third of the water used in the country comes from non-sustainable or non-renewable sources.

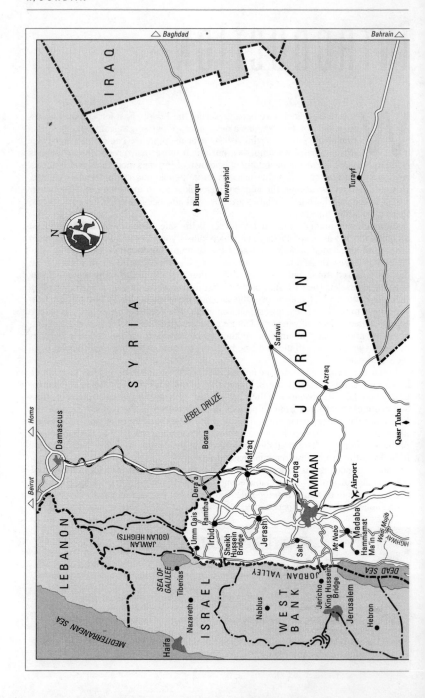

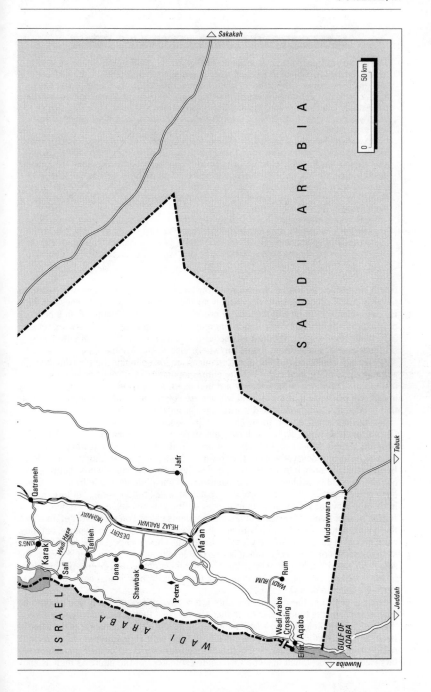

TRANSLITERATION OF ARABIC WORDS

There's no standard system of **transliterating** Arabic into English. Many sounds in Arabic have no equivalent in English, and any attempt to render them in English script is bound to be imprecise – you're certain to come across Arabic words and proper names in this book that don't match transliterations given elsewhere. **Place names** are the biggest sources of confusion, varying from map to map and often from sign to sign – you'll see roadsigns to Wadi Seer, Wadi El Sseir, Wadi Alsear and Wadi as-Sir, all referring to the same place.

We've tried throughout to stick to a phonetically helpful, common-sense system, making the English transliteration read (as much as possible) as the Arabic sounds, while also staying recognizably close to existing English renderings (exceptions are monuments which are known by a non-Arabic name). The **definite article** "al" has been removed from all place names other than compound ones: al-Aqaba and the elided ar-Ramtha and as-Salt have all been shortened (Aqaba, Ramtha, Salt), but Umm al-Jimal and Shuneh al-Janubiyyeh stay as they are.

World-renowned scholars have broken their heads over transliterating Arabic into English, yet it remains a complete dog's breakfast. The best way to deal with it is just to practise a little lateral thinking: if you want to go to Shawbak and you see a sign to Alshobak, followed by one to ash-Shaubek, you know you're heading in the right direction.

North American city than in the whole of Jordan. Government is stable, with leanings towards full democracy, and, due largely to the unique political astuteness of King Hussein, manages to be simultaneously pro-Western, pro-Arab, founded on a bedrock of Muslim authority and dedicated to ongoing peace with Israel. Domestic extremism is virtually non-existent. **Women** are better integrated into positions of power in government and business than almost anywhere else in the Middle East, military conscription was abolished in 1991, and Jordanians are exceptionally highly educated – at any one time, more than a third of the entire population is enrolled at an educational institution. Traditions of **hospitality** are ingrained, and taking up some of the many invitations you'll get to tea or a meal will expose you to an outlook among local people that is often as cosmopolitan and world-aware as anything at home.

Jordan has small ethnic minorities of **Circassians** and **Chechens**, as well as a **Christian Arab** minority, but well over ninety percent of the country's population are **Muslim Arabs**. Most people take great pride in their ancestry, and whether they're present or former desert-dwellers (**bedouin**) or from a settled farming tradition (**fellaheen**), most are born into a sub-clan of one of the dozens of **tribes** whose lands spread out over the entire Middle East in a patchwork of sheikhdoms. Aside from representing a noble heritage, tribes also wield a great deal of institutional power in Jordan, and, in theory, serve as community mouthpieces on the national stage – most members of Jordan's lower house of parliament are independents elected on a tribal ticket. In effect, the system seems shot through with nepotism, serving to muffle local voices, but most rural people in particular still stay loyal to their tribe above political considerations. The **king**, as sheikh of sheikhs, commands heartfelt loyalty among many people and, as the sole Arab world statesman, deep respect among most of the rest; people pin his photo up everywhere, but unlike in Syria or Iraq, there's no compulsion – spoken or unspoken – for them to do so.

Even if you're in the country for only a few days, it's quite likely you'll come up against perhaps the thorniest issue in modern Jordan – that of national identity. Due to the upheavals in neighbouring Israel and Palestine since the foundation of the State of Israel in 1948, Jordan has been perennially flooded with **Palestinians** either seeking refuge from conflict or thrown out of their homes. A majority of Jordan's population see themselves as Palestinian in some way; some estimates put the figure as high as sixty percent. Many people from tribes resident in Jordan before 1948 resent this overbalancing of the country's demography, and the fact that Palestinians, with their urbanized, entrepreneurial culture, have come to dominate private-sector business. Jordanians of Palestinian origin for their part, even in the second and third generations, hold out hopes for one day being able to return to their homeland on the West Bank of the River Jordan, but in the meantime many resent the "East Bank" Jordanians' grip on power in government and the public sector. All are Jordanian citizens, but citizenship tends to mean less to the Palestinian majority than their national identity, and less to many East Bankers than their tribal affiliation. Large numbers of long-stay guest workers from Egypt muddy the issue still further. "Where are you from?" – a simple enough question in most countries – is in Jordan the cue for a life story.

Where to go

The prime attraction in Jordan is **Petra**, an unforgettably dramatic 2000-year-old city carved out of a red sandstone valley in the south of the country. Hidden away from view behind mountain peaks, its numinous atmosphere and extraordinary architecture defy summary.

However, Jordan has a wealth of **historical sites** aside from Petra, outstanding among them the exceptionally well-preserved Roman city of **Jerash**, but also including **Umm Qais**, set on a dramatic promontory overlooking the Sea of Galilee, and **Pella**, where Jerusalem's Christians fled Roman persecution in the first century AD. **Madaba**, which became an important Christian town and regional centre for mosaic art during the Byzantine period, houses the oldest known map of the Middle East, made up of millions of tesserae laid on the floor of a church. After the Muslim conquest, the Umayyad dynasty built for themselves a series of retreats in the Jordanian desert, now dubbed the "Desert Castles". Most notable among them are the bath-house of **Qusayr Amra**, which features a unique set of naturalistic and erotic frescoes, and **Qasr Hraneh**, perhaps the most atmospheric ancient building in the country. Centuries later, the Crusaders established a heavy presence in southern Jordan, most impressively with the huge castles at **Karak** and **Shawbak**. The Arab resistance to the Crusader invasion left behind a no less impressive castle at **Ajloun** in the north.

Even though Jordan lost the holy sites of East Jerusalem, Bethlehem and Hebron to Israel in 1967, it has continued to market itself as the "Holy Land" for its handful of **religious sites**, most importantly **Mount Nebo**, from where Moses looked over the Promised Land and where he died. Of the many sites along the banks of the Jordan River where John the Baptist is claimed to have baptized Jesus, the most likely – and the focus for Jordan's millennium celebrations – is near **Shuneh al-Janubiyyeh** west of Amman. John eventually met his death at Herod's hilltop palace of **Machaerus** after Salome's demand for his head on a platter, and nearby are **Bab adh-Dhraa**, one of the leading contenders for the site of biblical Sodom, and the **cave** where **Lot** and his family sought refuge from the destruction of Sodom and Gomorrah. Jordan is also crammed full of Muslim religious sites, premier among them the **tomb of Haroun** at Petra and the sites dedicated to the prophets Lut (Lot) and Musa (Moses) outlined above. However, there are literally dozens more shrines and tombs in every corner of the country – we've covered the most notable in the Guide, but if you thirst for more exhaustive details, surf to *accessme.com/turab*.

However, probably your most abiding memories of a visit will be of Jordan's varied and beautiful **environment**. With its sheer cliffs and red desert sands, **Wadi Rum** – where David Lean filmed *Lawrence of Arabia* – is probably the country's most captivating natural site, where you can embark on camel treks of anything from an hour to a week. Way out in the east of the country, in the furnace of the Black Desert, lies a small dammed lake at **Burqu**, one of the most rewarding birdwatching sites in the entire Middle East. Both Wadi Rum and Burqu are planned as future nature reserves by the highly active and dedicated Royal Society for the Conservation of Nature, which currently maintains five reserves around the country. Pristine and tranquil **Dana**, in the rocky southern mountains, is breathtaking; **Mujib** (a fast-flowing gorge), **Shaumari** (oryx and ostrich), **Azraq** (a wetland habitat) and **Zubia** (virgin woods) are less developed but all have their own attractions for rough hiking or wilderness camping. Jordan also has some surprisingly watery pursuits for a desert land, most significantly some of the world's best diving and snorkelling in the coral-fringed Red Sea off **Aqaba**. The inland lake known as the **Dead Sea** is too buoyant to swim in, but you can instead float away a day supported by nothing more than the density of the salty water.

You'd be unwise to come to Jordan looking for **urban** excitement: the cities are all of modern construction and, almost without exception, mundane. The appeal of the capital, **Amman**, comes simply from its location, spread out over a series of precipitous hills, the friendliness of its people and the tranquillity of its life.

When to go

In theory, the tourist high seasons are April, May, September and October, but Western tourism to Jordan is still relatively low-key, and only the main path at Petra gets unpleasantly crowded at peak times. The weather should have more impact on your decision when to visit. Despite the small size of the country, you'll find wide variations in **climate** whenever you arrive – the same January day could have you throwing snowballs in Ajloun or topping up your tan on Aqaba's beaches.

Far and away the best time to visit is **spring** (March–May), when temperatures are toasty but not scorching, wildflowers are out everywhere (even the desert is carpeted), and the hills and valleys running down the centre of the country are lush and gorgeously colourful. The worst of the rain is over by March (it doesn't entirely peter out in Amman and the hills until late April), although Dana, at 1500m, stays blustery into May. Humidity is pleasant everywhere, and low, clear sunlight draws a spectacular kaleidoscope of colour and texture from the desert rocks. There's only one drawback – a desert wind, loaded with dust and grit, which blows regularly each spring. It's known as the *khamseen* after the fifty days it traditionally persists (although it rarely lasts longer than a week), and can darken the sky and raise the temperature by 10°C, coating everyone and everything in a layer of sand.

In **summer** (roughly June–Sept), Amman can sizzle – even up to 45°C in Downtown – and you'll find little respite in the rest of the country, although the hills around Ajloun catch some cooler breezes. Temperatures at the Dead Sea and Aqaba have been known to top a sticky 50°C, with Aqaba in particular suffering from an intolerable hot wind that makes you feel like you're basting in a fan-assisted oven. High, hazy light flattens the brown landscape and bleaches any beauty out of the desert, and you'll find it's too uncomfortably hot countrywide to do any walking or sightseeing between noon and 4pm. Typical **autumn** weather pretty much passes Jordan by, with only a few weeks marking the shift out of high summer – if you catch it, this can be a lovely time to visit. The first rains fall in early or mid-October, making the parched countryside briefly bloom again and the torrid temperatures drop to more manageable levels. In **winter** (roughly Dec–March), Amman can be desperately chilly, with biting winds sweeping through the valleys, annual falls of snow and plenty of cold rain, although the sun is still never far away. With short days and freezing nights, visits to Petra can be taxing; exceptional lows of -8°C have been recorded. Rum is more temperate, but Aqaba is the only retreat, with sunshine and warmth even in the depths of January. Winter, too, has the added disincentive in forthcoming years of the month-long daytime fast for Ramadan (see p.49).

Average Dead Sea and Red Sea **water** temperatures vary little either side of a balmy 24°C all year.

JORDAN'S CLIMATE

The table shows elevation, average minimum and maximum temperatures and average rainfall for the month.

	Jan	April	July	Oct
Amman	3°C	9°C	18°C	14°C
(800m)	12°C	23°C	32°C	27°C
	64mm	15mm	0mm	7mm
Aqaba	9°C	17°C	25°C	20°C
(sea level)	21°C	31°C	39°C	33°C
	5mm	4mm	0mm	1mm
Dead Sea	11°C	19°C	27°C	22°C
(400m below	21°C	31°C	40°C	33°C
sea level)	13mm	7mm	0mm	1mm
Irbid	5°C	10°C	19°C	15°C
(600m)	13°C	22°C	31°C	27°C
	111mm	51mm	0mm	14mm
Petra	4°C	11°C	18°C	14°C
(1100m)	12°C	22°C	36°C	24°C
	43mm	14mm	0mm	2mm
Rum	4°C	12°C	19°C	13°C
(950m)	15°C	25°C	36°C	29°C
	19mm	7mm	0mm	2mm

GETTING THERE FROM BRITAIN AND IRELAND

The fastest and most comfortable way to get to Jordan is, of course, to fly. Flights leave daily from London non-stop to Amman, with services from regional British and Irish airports feeding into London or major European hubs for onward connections. Aside from Amman, Jordan's other major airport is at Aqaba, well served by daily short-hop flights from the capital but with only sporadic international traffic. Specialist-interest packages and tours are also worth considering.

FLIGHTS

Flying to Amman (AMM) from Britain, you're presented with few choices. The only non-stop services are out of London Heathrow, taking around five hours; from elsewhere in the British Isles, you'll have to change planes either in London or – often more economically – in Paris or Amsterdam. **Fares** on routes into most Middle Eastern airports – including Amman – are notoriously pricey and rarely discounted, and you'll find that deals on tickets into Tel Aviv (Israel) can quite often save you substantial amounts. However, if you intend travelling in the region beyond Jordan, you should bear in mind the tricky bureaucracy regarding Israeli entry and exit stamps (see note on p.114).

All flights from Britain and Ireland to Jordan are **scheduled** services, with no charter flights currently in operation; tour companies instead either charter planes to Eilat or Ovda in Israel (just over the border from Aqaba) or nearby Sharm el-

Sheikh in Egypt, or use scheduled services. Being forced into the arms of the big European airlines has its advantages though (aside from the quality of the food): flights to Amman rarely depart chock-a-block full, and the three-, six- or even twelve-month tickets offered by the big carriers are generally quite flexible, with no particular requirements for advance booking, plus either free or inexpensive date-changes permitted.

Although very few international flights operate direct into **Aqaba** (AQJ), domestic shuttles arrive daily from Amman, and you can request an Amman–Aqaba add-on at the time of booking your international flight for a bargain £15–20 or so one-way, around half what you'd pay in Jordan.

FROM LONDON

Royal Jordanian flies non-stop from **Heathrow** to Amman five days a week, while British Mediterranean, a franchisee of British Airways, operates circular routes from Heathrow to the Levant and back – on certain days, you may have to wait on the ground in Damascus for an hour or more before your final hop to Amman. High-season round-trip fares (March–May, September, October and around Christmas) on either are around £360–420, although it's easier to find lower fares on RJ than on BMed. Flying in the low season can knock more than £100 off.

If you're prepared to surrender the luxury of direct service and change planes at a European hub, it's possible to save as much as forty percent. Rock-bottom prices on Tarom Romanian Airline's once-weekly jaunt from London to Amman via Bucharest can drop as low as £220 in the high season, while discount flight agents such as STA can throw up a high-season fare on Olympic of around £265 via Athens. For a little bit more comfort and convenience, fares on Austrian via Vienna, Air France via Paris or KLM via Amsterdam hover around £320–350. If you prefer **Gatwick**, Alitalia fly three times a week from there to Amman via Rome, but fares are high. KLM's lower fares make their flights out of **Stansted** (five times a week) or **London City** (six times a week) – both connecting with the onward Amman flight in Amsterdam – much more attractive.

MAJOR AIRLINES IN BRITAIN AND IRELAND

Air France, 10 Warwick St, 1st floor, London W1R 5RA (☎0181/742 6600; *www.airfrance.fr*); 29–30 Dawson St, Dublin 2 (☎01/844 5633). *Four times a week from Paris CDG non-stop to Amman. Connections into Paris from London and regional British airports such as Birmingham, Manchester and Newcastle.*

Alitalia, 4 Portman Square, London W1H 9PS (☎0171/602 7111; *www.alitalia.it*); 4–5 Dawson St, Dublin 2 (☎01/677 5171). *Three times a week from Rome non-stop. Codesharing with British Midland ensures good connections from many British and Irish airports.*

Austrian Airlines, 10 Wardour St, London W1V 4BJ (☎0171/434 7350; *www.aua.com*). *Three daytime flights a week from London Heathrow to Amman via Vienna.*

British Airways, 156 Regent St, London W1R 5TA; 101 Cheapside, London EC2V 6DT; Victoria Place, Victoria Station, London SW1W 9SJ; plus offices in Aberdeen, Belfast, Birmingham, Bristol, Edinburgh, Glasgow and Manchester (all UK enquiries ☎0345/222111; Ireland enquiries ☎1800/626747; *www.british-airways.com*). *Services to Amman operated by the franchisee, British Mediterranean. Six flights weekly from London Heathrow to Amman, four of which are non-stop.*

Cyprus Airways, Unit 5, The Exchange, Brent Cross Gardens, London NW4 3RJ (☎0181/359 1333). *Three flights weekly from London Heathrow, with six hours' connection time in Larnaca.*

EgyptAir, 29–31 Piccadilly, London W1V 0PT (☎0171/734 2395). *None of their daily flights London–Cairo connects with their daily flights Cairo–Amman, but not a bad option for combining an exploration of Egypt and Jordan without the long land-and-sea journey between the two.*

El Al, UK House, 180 Oxford St, London W1N 0EL (☎0171/957 4100; *www.elal.com*). *Much the*

same story as EgyptAir, with none of their London–Tel Aviv flights arriving in time to hook up with the Tel Aviv–Amman hop.

KLM uk (UK enquiries ☎0990/074074; Ireland enquiries ☎01/844 4747; *www.klmuk.com*). *KLM (Royal Dutch Airlines) fly daily from Amsterdam to Amman, including three non-stop flights a week. KLM recently bought Air UK, and the new KLM uk flies to Amsterdam from Aberdeen, Belfast, Birmingham, Bristol, Cardiff, Dublin, East Midlands, Edinburgh, Glasgow, Guernsey, Humberside, Jersey, Leeds-Bradford, London (City, Gatwick, Heathrow and Stansted), Manchester, Newcastle, Norwich, Sheffield and Teesside to connect with the Amman flight.*

Middle East Airlines (MEA) (Lebanese), 45 Albemarle St, London W1X 3FE (☎0171/493 5681). *Six flights weekly London–Beirut, and daily evening flights from there to Amman.*

Olympic Airways, 11 Conduit St, London W1R 0LP (☎0171/409 3400). *Four flights a week from London Heathrow to Amman via Athens.*

Royal Jordanian, 32 Brook St, London W1Y 1AG (☎0171/878 6300; *www.rja.com.jo*); Lancaster Buildings, 3rd floor suite 3, 77 Deansgate, Manchester M3 2BZ (☎0161/832 4847); 5 Clyde Rd, Ballsbridge, Dublin 4 (☎01/842 3144). *Daily morning flights from Heathrow to Amman; five are non-stop, two make intermediate stops in Europe. Dublin–London connections are on a different carrier.*

Tarom Romanian Airline, 27 New Cavendish St, London W1M 7RL (☎0171/224 3693). *Once a week from London Heathrow to Amman via Bucharest.*

Turkish Airlines, 125 Pall Mall, London SW1Y 5EA (☎0171/766 9300; *www.turkishairlines.com*). *Three flights a week from London Heathrow via Istanbul.*

FROM THE REST OF BRITAIN AND IRELAND

The lowest fares on flights to Amman from the rest of Britain and Ireland tend to be with Air France or KLM, with changing planes at their hubs in Paris or Amsterdam a necessity.

From Birmingham, Manchester and Newcastle, the most convenient option is on **Air France**, whose early-morning flights arrive at Paris CDG with enough time to connect with the

four afternoon flights a week from there to Amman. From elsewhere around the British Isles, you're generally restricted to either **Alitalia** (who have a code-sharing agreement with British Midland) or **KLM**; both have three non-stop evening flights a week from their hubs at Rome and Amsterdam to Amman (on the other four days, KLM has flights which stop first in Damascus or Beirut). These depart late enough to allow enough time for connections to arrive from

FLIGHT AGENTS IN BRITAIN

Campus Travel, 52 Grosvenor Gardens, London SW1W 0AG (☎0171/730 8111); 541 Bristol Rd, Selly Oak, Birmingham B29 6AU (☎0121/414 1848); 61 Ditchling Rd, Brighton BN1 4SD (☎01273/570226); 37 Queen's Rd, Clifton, Bristol BS8 1QE (☎0117/929 2494); 5 Emmanuel St, Cambridge CB1 1NE (☎01223/324283); 53 Forest Rd, Edinburgh EH1 2QP (☎0131/225 6111, telesales 668 3303); 122 George St, Glasgow G1 1RS (☎0141/553 1818); 166 Deansgate, Manchester M3 3FE (☎0161/833 2046, telesales 273 1721); 105 St Aldates, Oxford OX1 1BU (☎01865/242067). *Student/youth travel specialists, with branches also in YHA shops and on university campuses all over Britain.* Website: *www.campustravel.co.uk*

Council Travel, 28a Poland St, London W1V 3DB (☎0171/437 7767). *Flights and student discounts.* Website: *www.ciee.org*

Destination Group, 41 Goswell Rd, London EC1V 7EH (☎0171/490 8800). *Good discount fares.*

Flightbookers, 177 Tottenham Court Rd, London W1P 0LX (☎0171/757 2444); Gatwick Airport, South Terminal inside the British Rail station (☎01293/568300). *Low fares on an extensive offering of scheduled flights; extended opening hours at the Gatwick branch.*

The London Flight Centre, 131 Earls Court Rd, London SW5 9RH (☎0171/244 6411); 47 Notting Hill Gate, London W11 3JS (☎0171/727 4290); Shop 33, The Broadway Centre, Hammersmith tube, London W6 9YE (☎0181/748 6777). *Long-established agent dealing in discount flights.*

North South Travel, Moulsham Mill Centre, Parkway, Chelmsford, Essex CM2 7PX (☎01245/492882). *Friendly, competitive travel agency, offering discounted fares worldwide – profits are used to support projects in the developing world, especially the promotion of sustainable tourism.*

STA Travel, 86 Old Brompton Rd, London SW7 3LH; 117 Euston Rd, London NW1 2SX; 38 Store St, London WC1E 7BZ; 11 Goodge St, London W1P 1FE (enquiries ☎0171/361 6262); 38 North St, Brighton (☎01273/728282); 25 Queens Rd, Bristol BS8 1QE (☎0117/929 4399); 38 Sidney St, Cambridge CB2 3HX (☎01223/366966); 184 Byres Rd, Glasgow G1 1JH (☎0141/338 6000); 88 Vicar Lane, Leeds LS1 7JH (☎0113/244 9212); 75 Deansgate, Manchester M3 2BW (☎0161/834 0668); 9 St Mary's Place, Newcastle-upon-Tyne NE1 7PG (☎0191/233 2111); 36 George St, Oxford OX1 2OJ (☎01865/792800); and branches on many university campuses. *Worldwide specialists in low-cost flights and tours for students and under-26s, though other customers welcome.* Website: *www.statravel.co.uk*

Tradewings, Morley House 1st floor, 320 Regent St, London W1R 5AG (☎0171/637 0555). *Rock-bottom prices on Tarom Romanian Airlines.*

Trailfinders, 42–50 Earls Court Rd, London W8 6FT (☎0171/938 3366); 194 Kensington High St, London W8 7RG (☎0171/938 3939); 215 Kensington High St, London W6 6BD (☎0171/937 5400); 22 The Priory Queensway, Birmingham B4 6BS (☎0121/236 1234); 48 Corn St, Bristol BS1 1HQ (☎0117/929 9000); 254–284 Sauchiehall St, Glasgow G2 3EH (☎0141/353 2224); 58 Deansgate, Manchester M3 2FF (☎0161/839 6969). *One of the best-informed and most efficient agents for independent travellers.*

Travel Bag, 52 Regent St, London W1R 6DX; 373–375 The Strand, opposite the Savoy Hotel, London WC2R 0JF; 12 High St, Alton, Hants GU34 1BN (☎0171/287 5556). *Discount flights.*

The Travel Bug, 125 Gloucester Rd, London, SW7 4SF (☎0171/835 2000); 597 Cheetham Hill Rd, Manchester M8 5EJ (☎0161/721 4000). *Large range of discounted tickets.* Website: *www.travel-bug.co.uk*

Travel Cuts, 295 Regent St, London W1 (☎0171/255 2082). *Established in Canada in 1974, Travel Cuts specialize in budget, student and youth travel.* Website: *www.travelcuts.co.uk*

---

just about any airport in the British Isles, but on the downside, they all deposit you in Amman in the middle of the night. Of the two, KLM has the broader network and is always less expensive. You can buy through tickets from Dublin to Amman with **Royal Jordanian**, but they don't actually fly from Dublin; instead, you'll be shuttled in the early morning on Aer Lingus or British Midland into Heathrow to pick up the RJ flight to Amman.

Fares are generally about £30 higher out of southern England and Midlands airports than on the same carrier out of London, about £50 higher if you're flying from Manchester or northern England, and about £60 higher from Scotland and Northern Ireland. From the Irish Republic, it

FLIGHT AGENTS IN IRELAND

Aran Travel, 58 Dominick St, Galway (☎091/562595).

Co-op Travel Care, 35 Belmont Rd, Belfast 4 (☎01232/471717).

Fahy Travel, 3 Bridge St, Galway (☎091/563055).

Joe Walsh Tours, 34 Grafton St, Dublin 2 (☎01/671 8751); 69 Upper O'Connell St , Dublin 2 (☎01/872 2555); 8–11 Baggot St, Dublin 2 (☎01/676 3053); 117 St Patrick St, Cork (☎021/277959). *General budget fares agent.*

Lee Travel, 23 Princes St, Cork (☎021/277111).

Liffey Travel, 12 Upper O'Connell St, Dublin 1 (☎01/878 8322). *Package tour specialists.*

McCarthy Travel, 56 Patrick St, Cork (☎021/270127).

Thomas Cook, 11 Donegal Place, Belfast (☎01232/242341); 118 Grafton St, Dublin 2

(☎01/677 1721). *Package holiday and flight agent, with occasional discount offers.*

Trailfinders, 4–5 Dawson St, Dublin 2 (☎01/677 7888). *Competitive fares out of all Irish airports, as well as deals on hotels, insurance, tours and car rental worldwide.*

Twohigs, 8 Burgh Quay, Dublin 2 (☎01/677 2666); 13 Duke St, Dublin 2 (☎01/670 9750).

USIT, Fountain Centre, College St, Belfast BT1 6ET (☎01232/324073); 10 Market Parade, Patrick St, Cork (☎021/270900); 33 Ferryquay St, Derry (☎01504/371888); 19 Aston Quay, Dublin 2 (☎01/602 1700); Victoria Place, Eyre Square, Galway (☎091/565177); Central Buildings, O'Connell St, Limerick (☎061/415064); 36 Georges St, Waterford (☎051/872601). *Student and youth specialists.*

shouldn't be hard to find fares to Amman starting from around IR£420 in the high season. If you have the stamina for two changes of plane, flying from Dublin to London, to pick up a cheap Tarom or Olympic ticket from there, costs around IR£85.

OPEN-JAW AND ROUND-THE-WORLD TICKETS

If you're looking to travel overland through the region but don't want the hassle of making your way from Britain or Ireland by bus or train across Europe, you might consider flying into one airport, travelling overland, then flying home out of a different airport. These "open-jaw" tickets can save you endless backtracking, and if you choose a discounted airline and two airports that see a lot of traffic, you may actually save money on a normal point-to-point ticket between London and Amman.

The two regional airports most likely to produce the lowest fares are **Istanbul** and **Cairo**: it's not hard to get an open-jaw for these two cities from London through a specialist discount flight agent for little more than £250 (Czech Airways and Olympic are prime choices for carrier). Most other airports in the Middle East aren't as cheap; flying London–Damascus or London–Beirut on the first leg can add as much as £100 onto the Istanbul option.

As Amman is not a discount destination, trying to slot it into a longer **round-the-world** (RTW) jaunt is fraught with expense. Your best bet for incorporating the Middle East into a RTW journey is to make Cairo, a popular RTW hub, one of your stops; an overland journey from there into Jordan – and even into Israel/Palestine, Syria, Lebanon and back – beats shelling out as much as £250 for a Cairo–Amman–Cairo add-on to your RTW ticket.

ORGANIZED TOURS

The vast majority of **organized tours** which pass through Jordan slot a few days in the country into a longer international itinerary, often based in Israel or taking in Syria as well. If all you want from your visit is to be chaperoned around Petra, Amman and Jerash, it shouldn't be hard to find a Jordan add-on to an Israel-based tour from any number of mainstream high-street tour operators. The advantage of these packages is that they get you a good-value deal on flight-plus-accommodation; by booking a tour in advance you can end up staying in extremely comfortable places paying bargain prices. The disadvantage, of course, becomes clear if you fancy an extra day or two on your own to explore Petra once you get there.

However, where fixing up an organized tour ahead of time really comes into its own is if you

SPECIALIST TOUR OPERATORS IN BRITAIN

Andante Travels, The Old Telephone Exchange, Winterbourne Dauntsey, Salisbury SP4 6EH (☎01980/610555). *Small-scale, personalized, expert-led archeological/historical tours of the whole of Jordan – ten days for around £1250.*

Aquatours, Charter House, 26 Claremont Rd, Surbiton, Surrey KT6 4QU (☎0181/255 8050). *Jordan diving specialist, which tags itself as offering "adventures for the thinking diver": full tours around the country from £840 for 12 days.*

Bales Tours, Bales House, Junction Rd, Dorking, Surrey RH4 3EJ (☎01306/885991). *Family-owned company offering high-quality escorted tours, as well as tailor-made itineraries. Standard eight-day tour starts from £850, rising to £1800 for the full works; combination options with Jerusalem, Syria or Egypt available.*

Cox & Kings, Gordon House, 10 Greencoat Place, London SW1 1PH (☎0171/873 5000). *Highly respected and long-established company offering gilt-edged tours to Jordan, alone or in combination with Syria and/or Lebanon. Prices start from £1200.*

Destination Red Sea, 125 East Barnet Rd, New Barnet, Herts EN4 8RF (☎0181/440 9900, website *www.redsea.co.uk*). *Principally a Sharm el-Sheikh (Egypt) beach operator, but also offers seven-night B&B packages to Aqaba starting from around £400, Amman from around £500. Also runs tours of Jordan.*

Dragoman, 97 Camp Green, Debenham, Stowmarket, Suffolk IP14 6LA (☎01728/861133, website *www.dragoman.co.uk*). *Extended overland journeys in purpose-built expedition vehicles; itineraries such as London–Kathmandu (12 weeks), Istanbul–Cairo (5 weeks), Damascus–Delhi (6 weeks) and Kathmandu–Harare (25 weeks) pass through Jordan. Prices for these examples range from £800 to £5000-plus.*

Exodus, 9 Weir Rd, London SW12 0LT (☎0181/675 5550; brochure requests 673 0859, website *www.exodustravels.co.uk*). *Adventure tour operators, taking small groups on specialist programmes including walking and biking. Two-week tour of Jordan and Syria, from £700. Jordan also fits into their nine-, fifteen- and thirty-week overland tours from London to India, Nepal and Bali, which cost from £1500 to £5000.*

Explore Worldwide, 1 Frederick St, Aldershot, Hants, GU11 1LQ (☎01252/319448, brochure requests 344161, website *www.explore.co.uk*). *Big range of small-group tours. Few supplements for single travellers; accommodation in small local hotels or Bedouin tents. Ten-day tours to Jordan (around £700), or 16 days with either Israel or Syria included (around £1000).*

Goodwood Travel, St Andrew's House, Station Rd East, Canterbury CT1 2RB (☎01227/763336). *Extraordinarily lavish five-star tours of Jordan, starting and ending on Concorde, and in between, everything from a private cocktail party aboard your own steam-train to a barbecue with musical accompaniment on the shores of the Dead Sea. Five nights around £3000.*

Guerba Expeditions, Wessex House, 40 Station Rd, Westbury, Wilts BA13 3JN (☎01373/826611). *Trips long and short overlanding through Jordan on the way from Europe into Africa or Asia.*

Hayes & Jarvis, Hayes House, 152 King St, London W6 0QU (☎0181/748 5050). *Specialists in long-haul holidays; particularly good on diving destinations. Exotic weddings organized.*

Martin Randall Travel, 10 Barley Mow Passage, London W4 4PH (☎0181/742 3355). *Small-group cultural tours: experts on art and archeology lead travellers on week- or ten-day-long tours of Jordan alone or Jordan with Syria. Prices from £1250.*

Naturetrek, Chautara, Bighton, nr Alresford, Hants SO24 9RB (☎01962/733051, website *www.naturetrek.co.uk*). *Acknowledged leaders in birdwatching and botanical holidays worldwide, with sympathetic, expert guidance, small groups and regular tours to Jordan. The spring tour (15 days for £1400) covers every nook and cranny for birders in the country, from Burqu to the Aqaba sewage works; the nine-day winter tours (£1200) cover less ground.*

Regal Holidays, 22 High St, Sutton, Ely, Cambridgeshire CB6 2RB (☎01353/778096). *Experienced Red Sea diving operator, concentrating on Hurghada and Sharm but also running seven-night tours to Aqaba from around £500.*

Roadrunner International, 64 Mount Pleasant Ave, Tunbridge Wells, Kent TN1 1QY (☎01892/512700). *Small-group hostelling treks in Jordan and Israel.*

have a particular kind of holiday in mind. If you want to know all there is to know about Jordan's wealth of archeology, take a concentrated diving course, or if you have your heart set on sighting a Sinai rosefinch or Tristram's serin, specialist tour operators can sell you ready-made all-in packages or tailor a particular tour to suit your requirements. See also the list of Jordanian specialist tour operators on p.39.

GETTING THERE FROM NORTH AMERICA

Although there are no non-stop flights from North America to Amman, quite a few airlines fly direct from the US and Canada with one stop at a European hub. Many travellers, though, weave Jordan into a longer journey around the Middle East, and it's easier to find less expensive deals on flights into other Middle Eastern airports, particularly Cairo or Tel Aviv, with a view to proceeding overland from there.

SHOPPING FOR TICKETS

Barring special offers, the cheapest of the airlines' published fares is usually an **Apex** ticket, although this will carry certain restrictions: you will, most likely, have to book – and pay – 21 days before departure, spend at least seven days abroad (maximum stay three months), and you tend to get penalized if you change your schedule.

You can normally cut costs further by going through a **specialist flight agent** – either a **consolidator**, who buys up blocks of tickets from the airlines and sells them at a discount, or a **discount agent**, who in addition to dealing with dis-

---

AIRLINES IN NORTH AMERICA

Air France (US ☎1-800/237-2747; Canada ☎1-800/667-2747). *Flights from Toronto and Montréal to Paris, connecting to Amman four times a week.*

Alitalia (US ☎1-800/223-5370 or 212/582-8900; Canada ☎1-800/361-8336). *Flights to Rome with four connections weekly to Amman from New York, Boston, Miami, Chicago; and three times weekly from LA.*

British Airways (US ☎1-800/247-9297; Canada ☎1-800/668-1059). *Flights to London from many US and Canadian cities with connecting flights to Amman six days in the week.*

EgyptAir (☎1-800/334-6787 or 212/315-0900). *Flights to Cairo with connections to Amman three times a week from New York, and twice a week from LA.*

El Al (☎1-800/223-6700). *Six flights a week from New York to Tel Aviv.*

Northwest/KLM (US ☎1-800/374-7747; Canada ☎1-800/361-5073). *Daily flights (via Amsterdam) from most major cities in the US and Canada.*

Royal Jordanian Airlines (☎1-800/223-0470 or 1-800/RJ-JORDAN; regional offices ☎212/949-0050; ☎312/236-1702; ☎313/271-6663; ☎310/215-9627; ☎305/599-0800; ☎202/857-0401; ☎514/288-1655). *Direct flights (via Amsterdam) from New York five times a week; from Chicago twice a week; and, in conjunction with TWA, flights from plenty of other North American cities.*

DISCOUNT AGENTS, CONSOLIDATORS AND TRAVEL CLUBS IN NORTH AMERICA

Air Brokers International, 150 Post St #620, San Francisco, CA 94108 (☎1-800/883-3273 or 415/397-1383; www.airbrokers.com). *Consolidator and specialist in RTW tickets.*

Council Travel, Head Office, 205 E 42nd St, New York, NY 10017 (☎1-800/226-8624 or 888/COUNCIL or 212/822-2700). Other offices at: 530 Bush St #700, San Francisco, CA 94108 (☎415/421-3473); 10904 Lindbrook Drive, Los Angeles, CA 90024 (☎310/208-3551); 3300 M St NW, 2nd floor, Washington, DC 20007 (☎202/337-6464); 1153 N Dearborn St, Chicago, IL 60610 (☎312/951-0585); 273 Newbury St, Boston, MA 02116 (☎617/266-1926); and more. *Nationwide US organization specializing in, but not restricted to, student travel.*

High Adventure Travel, 353 Sacramento St #600, San Francisco, CA 94111 (☎1-800/350-0612 or 415/912-5600; www.highadv.com). *Round-the-world tickets. Website features interactive database that lets you build and price your own RTW itinerary.*

New Frontiers/Nouvelles Frontières, 12 E 33rd St, New York, NY 10016 (☎1-800/366-6387 or 212/779-0600); 1001 Sherbrook East #720, Montréal, PQ H2L 1L3 (☎514/526-8444). *French discount travel firm. Other branches in LA, San Francisco and Quebec City.*

STA Travel, 10 Downing St, New York, NY 10014 (☎1-800/777-0112 or 212/627-3111); 7202 Melrose Ave, Los Angeles, CA 90046 (☎213/934-8722); 51 Grant Ave, San Francisco, CA 94108 (☎415/391-8407); 297 Newbury St, Boston, MA 02115 (☎617/266-6014); 429 S Dearborn St, Chicago, IL 60605 (☎312/786 9050); and more. *Worldwide specialists in independent travel.*

Travac, 989 6th Ave, New York NY 10018 (☎1-800/872-8800). *Consolidator, with a branch in Orlando, FL.*

Travel Avenue, 10 S Riverside #1404, Chicago, IL 60606 (☎1-800/333-3335). *Discount travel company.*

Travel Cuts, 187 College St, Toronto, ON M5T 1P7 (☎1-800/667-2887 or 416/979-2406; call ☎888/238-2887 from US). Also at: 180 MacEwan Student Centre, University of Calgary, Calgary, AB T2N 1N4 (☎403/282-7687); 12304 Jasper Ave, Edmonton, AB T5N 3K5 (☎403/488-8487); 1613 Rue St Denis, Montréal, PQ H2X 3K3 (☎514/843-8511); 555 W 8th Ave, Vancouver, BC V5Z 1C6 (☎888/FLY CUTS or 604/822-6890); University Centre, University of Manitoba, Winnipeg MB R3T 2N2 (☎204/269-9530); and more. *Well-respected Canadian student travel organization.*

Unitravel, 11737 Administration Drive, St Louis, MO 63146 (☎1-800/325-2222 or 314/569-0900). *Consolidator.*

counted flights may also offer special student and youth fares and a range of other travel-related services such as travel insurance, car rentals, tours and the like. Remember, though, that these companies make their money by dealing in bulk – don't expect them to answer lots of questions. If you travel a lot, **discount travel clubs** are another option – the annual membership fee may be worth it for benefits such as cut-price air tickets and car rental.

Don't automatically assume that tickets purchased through a travel specialist will be cheapest – once you get a quote, check with the airlines and you may turn up an even better deal. Be advised also that the pool of travel companies is swimming with sharks – exercise caution and *never* deal with a company that demands cash up front or refuses to accept payment by credit card.

Regardless of where you buy your ticket, **fares** will depend on the season. Royal Jordanian have a fairly straightforward pricing policy in this respect, with their low season running from November 1 to December 14, and December 25 to March 31; shoulder season from April 1 to May 31, August 1 to October 31, and December 15 to December 24; and their high season June 1 to July 31. Other airlines operate more arcane systems. Note also that while flying on weekends ordinarily adds $50–70 to a round-trip fare, most carriers servicing Jordan don't seem to make this distinction.

If Jordan is only one stop on a longer journey, you might want to consider buying a **round-the-world** (RTW) ticket. Some travel agents can sell you an "off-the-shelf" RTW ticket that will have you touching down in about half-a-dozen cities, though these rarely include Amman – they would probably have to customize one for you, at considerably greater expense. Your best bet, in fact, for incorporating the Middle East into a RTW journey is to make Cairo, a popular RTW hub, one of your stops; from there you could travel overland to Jordan.

All prices quoted below are round-trip, exclude taxes and are subject to availability and change.

FLIGHTS FROM THE US

Royal Jordanian offers probably the most convenient service **from the US to Amman**, although not necessarily the cheapest. However, flying with them does give you the option to fly on to Aqaba at no extra cost. Although the following fares are not strictly Apex – they don't require advance booking – they do have Apex-type restrictions, such as a seven-day minimum, three-month maximum stay. From New York, fares (low/shoulder/high) are: $1019/$1219/$1369.

From Chicago add $180 onto all of these, and from LA add $400. The actual flying time (not including stops) to Amman is roughly 13 hours from New York, 15 hours from Chicago and 16 from LA.

For the most part, you won't find a great disparity between these fares and those of the other carriers listed below, but there are certain exceptions. For instance, at the time of writing, Northwest/KLM quote considerably lower fares for their New York–Amman flights: you could find $613/$793/$1219 without too much trouble. And while EgyptAir's current fares from New York are no bargain they do have a special high-season LA–Amman fare of only $1299. Finally, a discount travel agent may be able to track down heavily discounted fares: New York–Amman high-season for around $1120 isn't unheard of.

Another option would be to pick up a cheap flight to **Tel Aviv** (Israel) with an add-on (for around

---

TOUR OPERATORS IN NORTH AMERICA

Basic tour packages usually include trips to Petra, Wadi Rum, Jerash, Karak and the Dead Sea, sometimes with activities such as camel trekking, desert camping and snorkelling thrown in. All prices quoted below exclude taxes and are subject to change; where applicable, round-trip flights are from New York.

Abercrombie & Kent (☎1-800-323-7308; www.abercrombiekent.com). *Six days for $1985 (land only).*

Adventure Center (☎1-800/227-8747). *"Lawrence's Arabia" – ten days in Jordan from $1095 (land only).*

Adventures Abroad (☎1-800/665-3998 or 604/303-1099). *A wide range of tours offering Jordan either alone (1 week from $2111 by land/air) or in combination with Syria, Egypt, Israel, Yemen or the Gulf States.*

Archeological Tours (☎212/986-3054). *16-day tour in Jordan and Syria (with optional extension to Israel) led by professor of archeology plus local guides. From $4450 (land/air).*

Cox & Kings (☎1-800/999-1758). *Customized tours to Jordan and the Middle East.*

Elderhostel (☎617/426-8056). *Specialists in educational and activity programs, cruises and homestays for senior travellers (companions may be younger). "Israel and Jordan: Historic Crossroads" tour, three weeks from $3842 (land/air).*

Himalayan Travel (☎1-800/225-2380). *Eight days in Jordan from $865, or fifteen days*

through Jordan and Syria from $1695 (both land only).

Insight International Tours (☎1-800/582-8380). *Fifteen days in Jordan and Israel from $1675 (land only).*

International Gay Travel Association (☎1-800/448-8550). *Trade group with lists of gay-owned or gay-friendly travel agents, accommodations and other travel businesses.*

Journeys (☎1-800/255-8735; www.journeys-intl.com). *Customized tours and short trips mostly offered as add-ons to Africa or Egypt itineraries. Four-day Desert Camping Safari from $750 (land only).*

Roadrunner Worldwide Hosteling Treks (☎1-800/864-0335). *Fifteen-day tour of Jordan and Israel from $1299 (land only).*

Royal Jordanian Airlines (☎212/949-0060). *City breaks. Six days (plus two in-flight) for around $1750 (land/air).*

Safaricenter (☎1-800/223-6046). *Eight days from $725 (land only).*

Wilderness Travel (☎1-800/368-2794 or 510/558-2488; www.wildernesstravel.com). *Seventeen days in Jordan and Syria from $2995 (land only).*

$135 round-trip) covering the Tel Aviv–Amman leg. At the time of writing, El Al has a New York–Tel Aviv fare of $799 (low season) or $1219 (high).

FLIGHTS FROM CANADA

Flying **from Canada** to Jordan, you don't have quite so many options as from the US. It shouldn't be hard, though, to pick up a round-trip flight from Montréal (low/shoulder/high) for around C$1785/C$1870/C$1980; and from Vancouver for about C$2200/C$2290/C$2400. Actual flying times (not including stops) to Amman are approximately 13 hours from Montréal and Toronto and 16 from Vancouver.

GETTING THERE FROM AUSTRALIA & NEW ZEALAND

There are no non-stop flights from Australasia to Jordan, so your only option is to fly via Asia or Europe. **The Middle Eastern and Asian airlines, plus Alitalia, tend to offer the best deals, though some of the routings via Europe can result in a painfully long flight time.**

Flying from Australia, Gulf Air (via Singapore and Bahrain), Emirates (via Dubai) and EgyptAir (via Cairo) offer some of the most direct routes. Royal Jordanian and Kuwait Airways both team up with Ansett Australia, Qantas, Malaysian, Singapore and Thai to cover various sectors. From Auckland, Air New Zealand flies to most Asian and European capital cities, from where you can pick up services on to Amman. Given that you'll have to touch down anyway, it might be worth looking at some of the good-value **stopover deals** on offer with most of the Asian and Middle Eastern airlines. Flying with EgyptAir, for example, you can spend two nights (three days) in

---

AIRLINES IN AUSTRALIA AND NEW ZEALAND

Air New Zealand, 5 Elizabeth St, Sydney (☎13 2476); 139 Queen St, Auckland (☎09/357 3000).

Alitalia, 32 Bridge St, Sydney (☎1300/653747); 6/229 Queen St, Auckland (☎09/379 4457).

Ansett Australia, 19 Pitt St, Sydney (☎13 1414); 2/50 Grafton Rd, Auckland (☎09/379 6409).

British Airways, 26/201 Kent St, Sydney (☎02/9258 3300); 154 Queen St, Auckland (☎09/356 8690).

EgyptAir, 630 George St, Sydney (☎02/9267 6979).

Emirates, 456 Kent St, Sydney (☎02/9267 3955).

Gulf Air, 64 York St, Sydney (☎02/9321 9199).

Kuwait Airways, 15/31 Market St, Sydney (☎02/9264 8277).

Malaysia Airlines, 16 Spring St, Sydney (☎13 2627); 12/12 Swanson St, Auckland (☎09/373 2741).

Qantas, 70 Hunter St, Sydney (☎13 1211); 154 Queen St, Auckland (☎09/357 8900 & 0800/808767).

Royal Jordanian Airlines, 20/44 Market St, Sydney (☎02/9262 6133).

Singapore Airlines, 17 Bridge St, Sydney (☎13 1011); cnr Albert St & Fanshawe St, Auckland (☎09/379 3209).

Thai Airways, 75 Pitt St, Sydney (☎13 1960); 22 Fanshawe St, Auckland (☎09/377 3886).

Cairo for around A\$250, including transfers, accommodation and day-tours to the Pyramids.

SHOPPING FOR TICKETS

Whatever kind of **ticket** you're after, first call should be one of the travel agents listed in the box, who can fill you in on all the latest fares and any special offers. If you're a student or under 26, you may be able to undercut some of the prices given here; STA is a good place to start. All the fares quoted below are for travel during low or shoulder seasons; flying during high season (April to end Aug & Dec) can add substantially to these prices. The least expensive return fares to Jordan you're likely to find are around A\$1750 from the eastern states, A\$1815 from Western Australia. With code-share arrangements involving the ritzier airlines such as British Airways and Qantas you'll definitely be looking at fares in excess of A\$2000. From New Zealand, fares start at NZ\$2400, rising to NZ\$2800 or more during high season.

ROUND-THE-WORLD TICKETS

Given the excessive fares on normal point-to-point tickets and their awkward routings, **round-the-world** tickets that take in the Middle East are worth considering, especially if you have the time to make the most of some stopovers. Although few itineraries take in Amman specifically, several offer a stop in Cairo, Istanbul or Rome, from where you can take a side-trip to Jordan. Ultimately, your choice of route will depend on where else you want to visit, but starting from Sydney, you could fly to Hong Kong, Singapore, Cairo, and travel overland to London, before flying on to Chicago, Denver, Los Angeles and back to Sydney, with the whole deal starting at A\$2259. From New Zealand, one possible route would take you from Auckland to Los Angeles, Rome, London, Bangkok and Melbourne, before returning to Auckland, for roughly NZ\$2600.

PACKAGES AND TOURS

Package deals from Australia and New Zealand are pretty flexible, and most specialist agents can do anything from booking a few nights' accommodation in Amman for when you first arrive to arranging a fully escorted tour. Adventure World, for example, offer two nights' twin-share hotel accommodation, transfers and daily sightseeing for around A\$330–420 per person. Most tour companies offer a range of itineraries that take in the major sights, many with the option of spending a few days in Egypt or Israel as well. For example, Adventure World's six-day tours of Jordan, taking in Amman, Petra, Aqaba and Wadi Rum, start from A\$924, including all transport and accommodation with breakfast (but not flights from Australia). Middle Eastern specialist Ya'lla Tours can also make private tour arrangements in Jordan, with prices starting at A\$1003 for five days. The more adventure-orientated operators such as The Imaginative Traveller offer small-group escorted tours ranging from eight days (from A\$960) to 15 days

FLIGHT AGENTS IN AUSTRALIA AND NEW ZEALAND

Anywhere Travel, 345 Anzac Parade, Kingsford, Sydney (☎02/9663 0411).

Brisbane Discount Travel, 260 Queen St, Brisbane (☎07/3229 9211).

Budget Travel, 16 Fort St, Auckland, plus branches around the city (☎09/366 0061 & 0800/808040).

Destinations Unlimited, 3 Milford Rd, Auckland (☎09/373 4033).

Flight Centres, Australia: 82 Elizabeth St, Sydney, plus branches nationwide (☎13 1600). New Zealand: 205 Queen St, Auckland (☎09/309 6171), plus branches nationwide.

Northern Gateway, 22 Cavenagh St, Darwin (☎08/8941 1394).

STA Travel, Australia: 702 Harris St, Ultimo, Sydney; 256 Flinders St, Melbourne; other offices in state capitals and major universities (for your nearest branch call ☎13 1776, fastfare telesales ☎1300/360960). New Zealand: 10 High St, Auckland (☎09/309 0458, fastfare telesales 366 6673), plus branches in Wellington, Christchurch, Dunedin, Palmerston North, Hamilton and at major universities. Website: *www.statravelaus.com.au.*

Trailfinders, 8 Spring St, Sydney (☎02/9247 7666).

The Travel Specialists, 80 Clarence St, Sydney (☎02/9290 1500; website *www.travel.com.au).*

TOUR OPERATORS IN AUSTRALIA AND NEW ZEALAND

Adventure World, 73 Walker St, North Sydney (☎02/9956 7766 & 1800/221931), plus branches in Brisbane and Perth; 101 Great South Rd, Remuera, Auckland (☎09/524 5118). *Tour operators and agents for many international travel companies.*

Padi Travel Network, 4/372 Eastern Valley Way, Chatswood, Sydney (☎02/9417 2800 or 1800/678100). *Diving specialists.*

Peregrine Adventures, 258 Lonsdale St, Melbourne (☎03/9663 8611), plus offices in

Brisbane, Sydney, Adelaide and Perth. *Agent for tours run by The Imaginative Traveller.*

Pro Dive Travel, Dymocks Building, 428 George St, Sydney (☎02/9232 5733). *Diving specialists.*

Sun Island Tours, 92 Goulburn St, Sydney (☎02/9283 2144). *All Middle Eastern travel arrangements.*

Ya'lla Tours, 1st Floor, West Tower, 608 St Kilda Rd, Melbourne (☎03/9510 2844). *Holidays to Syria, Israel, Egypt and Jordan.*

(from A$2000). Their no-frills tours aimed at budget travellers are good value, especially for longer stays: a 22-day trip combining Jordan and Syria starts at A$1995. Again, all these prices exclude flights. For New Zealand travellers, a

nine-day tour of the major sights will set you back around NZ$1375 excluding international flights, while land-only itineraries (including a few days across the border in Syria) start from NZ$2380 for 15 days.

GETTING THERE FROM NEIGHBOURING COUNTRIES

Jordan is easily accessible from surrounding countries: land borders are open from all its neighbours, there's a regular, swift boat service from nearby Egypt, and Amman is closely linked into air routes around the Middle East.

FROM SYRIA

Many travellers arrive in Jordan on an overland Middle Eastern odyssey between Istanbul and

Cairo, and routes into the country from the Syrian capital **Damascus** (barely 100km from the Jordanian frontier) are plentiful and undemanding.

The easiest and fastest way is to travel by **service**, or shared taxi. All such cars bound for Jordan depart 24 hours a day from the *Karaj al-Urdun* (Jordan Garage), a chaotic open car-park next to the Karnak bus station in central Damascus. You're only allowed into this car-park through the front gates and your bags will be searched as you enter. Despite what drivers may claim, prices to all destinations are fixed and are posted (in Arabic only) on a black notice-board near the front gates. Currently, a seat in a *service* to **Amman** is S£382 (US$8 or JD5.500), to **Irbid** S£226 (US$5 or JD4). *Services* also run to the less useful destination of Zerqa, and sometimes also to Mafraq. If you're in a hurry or prefer some privacy, the price for the whole car is five times the per-person rate. Once you agree on a price, your passport will be spirited away to enable the driver to get a slip from the police permitting him to leave.

Cars bound for Amman use the newly opened border-post **between Nasib and Jaber**, where formalities are dealt with swiftly and efficiently; you'll only use the old border **between Dera'a and Ramtha** if you're heading for Irbid. Both border crossings have 24-hour banks as well as useful Jordanian tourist information offices (daily 7am–6pm), which offer free maps and can make hotel bookings. The usual *service* terminus in Amman is Abdali station, in Irbid the New Amman station; however, for a few extra dollars the driver can drop you off anywhere you want in those cities. Journey times to Amman can be as little as three hours, half-an-hour less to Irbid.

As an alternative, comfortable Karnak and JETT **buses** leave from the Karnak bus station in Damascus daily at 7am and 3pm for Amman; the fare is either US$5 or JD4 (you can't pay in Syrian pounds). Journey times are about three or four hours, and buses terminate next to the JETT External Lines office, about 500m uphill from Abdali station. It's wise to book seats one day ahead.

For a more peaceful journey, once-weekly **trains** – sometimes pulled by vintage steam engines – depart from the Hejaz station in Damascus every Sunday at 7am for a ten-hour meander to Amman. The fare is a rock-bottom S£160 (US$3).

Most **flights** from Damascus to Amman are awkward early-morning or late-night departures, prohibitively expensive and not worth bothering with. Time spent at both ends getting to and from the airports (both are 35km out of the city) plus an hour in the air adds up to a longer journey than by road.

FROM JERUSALEM AND THE WEST BANK

No public transport runs directly between Jerusalem (or any West Bank city) and Amman: the only way to go is with a combination of bus, taxi and/or *service*. All traffic is funnelled towards the single border crossing open to the public (Mon–Thurs & Sun 7.30am–midnight, Fri & Sat 7.30am–2pm), known to the Palestinians and the Jordanians as the **King Hussein Bridge** (in Arabic: *jissr al-Malek Hussein*) and to the Israelis as the Allenby Bridge (in Hebrew: *gesher Allenby*). On a good day, the journey can take as little as two hours; on a bad day, or after dark, it can be more than five.

A diplomatic anomaly left over from pre-peace-treaty days is that Jordan does not issue any **visas** on entering the country via this bridge.

Despite the peace treaty with Israel and despite Jordan's recognition of Palestinian autonomy, a complex piece of official doublethink leads to the bridge not being viewed as an international border: the government line is that the West Bank is still somehow part of Jordan. The most noticeable upshot of this is that no Jordanian flags fly over the bridge, and if you don't hold a Jordanian visa in advance, you'll be turned back by Israeli passport control at the bridge terminal.

From the Central Bus Station in **West Jerusalem**, it costs 18 Israeli shekels (NIS) to take bus #961, #963 or #964 towards Tiberias (Mon–Thurs & Sun 7am–7.30pm, Fri 7am–3pm; every 30–45min), which reach the Allenby turnoff on the Jordan Valley highway fifty minutes later, where you must wait for a passing taxi for the three-kilometre ride to the bridge terminal (NIS20). Cheaper, considerably faster and more convenient, though, are the *services* departing frequently from **East Jerusalem** direct to the bridge – the two most efficient companies are Abdo (☎02/628-3281), opposite Damascus Gate, and Star (☎02/627-6699), down an alley just beyond the bus station. It's advisable to book places at least a couple of hours ahead, but you may find that there are no *services* after mid-afternoon. The standard *service* fare is NIS30 or JD6 per person; when there are no *services*, a taxi for around NIS120 is the only option. If you're starting from elsewhere in the **West Bank**, *services* and dirt-cheap Palestinian buses run to the bridge from most towns, including Bethlehem, Ramallah and Jericho.

Once you're at the bridge terminal, signs will direct you to a small bank where you pay the crippling Israeli **departure tax**, currently NIS107 or JD24.500 or US$33 – make sure you get a receipt. If you intend using your passport for overland travel beyond Jordan, be sure to tell the Israeli and Jordanian passport officials not to stamp your passport; see p.114 for more. You'll be directed to wait for a bus for which you must pay JD1.500 (in dinars only), which will make the short drive across no-man's-land and the bridge itself to the Jordanian arrivals terminal. Once you're through the formalities, loitering *service* drivers will nab you for the one-hour ride direct to Abdali station in Amman (JD2 per person). If you turn left from the *service* stand, left again through an unmarked door into the locals' arrivals hall, then left through the glass doors, you'll discover another *service* and bus stand – occasional buses from here take about twice as long as the *service* for the uphill grind to Abdali (JD1.500), while others head for Zerqa and Salt.

There are no **flights** from Jerusalem or any West Bank cities to Jordan.

FROM ISRAEL

There are two land crossing-points between Israel and Jordan. Buses from Tel Aviv, Haifa and Nazareth run through to Irbid and Amman via the **Sheikh Hussein Bridge** (Mon–Thurs & Sun 6.30am–10pm, Fri & Sat 8am–8pm), located near the northern Israeli town of Bet She'an, where a hefty Israeli **departure tax**, currently NIS56, is levied.

From **Tel Aviv**, bus #333 departs from the fourth floor of the Central Bus Station (Mon–Fri & Sun 2.30pm; NIS70 or US$20). From **Haifa**, departures are from a hut outside the Merkaz train station (Mon–Fri & Sun 7.30am & 2.30pm; NIS53 or US$15; ☎04/862-4871), also picking up from the offices of Nazarin Tours on Paul VI Street in Lower **Nazareth** (same days 8.30am & 3.30pm, also Sat 3.30pm; NIS53 or US$15; ☎06/601-0458). All these buses drop off in Irbid at the office of the Trust International Transport Company near Sports City, and terminate at the Trust office in Amman next to the Royal Jordanian building off 7th Circle.

The other crossing-point from Israel is in the south, between the Red Sea resort towns of Eilat and Aqaba, known as the **Arava crossing** (Mon–Thurs & Sun 6.30am–10pm, Fri & Sat 8am–8pm). From **Eilat** Central Bus Station, take city bus #16 (NIS4) or simply walk 2km to the border. If you're arriving from Jerusalem or Tel Aviv and want to avoid Eilat town, ask to be dropped off on the highway at the border turnoff. There's a NIS56 Israeli **departure tax**. Once you're through the formalities, *service*s do the five-kilometre run into central Aqaba for JD1 per person.

It can save a great deal of time to **fly** from Tel Aviv's Ben Gurion Airport to Amman (no flights Sat), and this also offers the extra lure of flying low over superb scenery. Choose between Royal Jordanian (☎03/516-5566) and El Al (☎03/972-2333). Prices on either are US$80 one-way, US$135 for a one-month return, US$160 for a year's open return. All flights take about thirty minutes to reach Queen Alia Airport, south of Amman, although one RJ flight continues to Marka Airport near Amman's downtown. At the time of writing, there were no flights between Tel Aviv and Aqaba.

FROM EGYPT

Buses do run from **Cairo** all the way through to Amman, though you'd have to have masochistic tendencies to embark on such a long ride voluntarily. Jordanian JETT and Egyptian SuperJet buses make the 21-hour trek on Saturdays and Tuesdays, departing at 6am from the Arab Union Bus Company office (☎02/290-9013) in Midan Almaza, Heliopolis. The fare, which includes the ferry crossing, is US$66, payable in dollars only.

However, the time-honoured method of getting from Egypt to Jordan involves a leisurely few days or more spent exploring the Sinai, from where there are two possibilities for crossing into Jordan. The town of **Nuweiba**, 70km north of Dahab, is linked to Aqaba by a daily ferry and catamaran service operated by the Arab Bridge Maritime Company (☎02/356-2670), which run to an unreliable timetable. Although there are myriad ticket outlets in Cairo and elsewhere, it's perfectly safe to wait to buy your ticket until you get to the port, some 8km south of Nuweiba town. The slow **ferry** (April–Sept Mon, Tues, Fri & Sat noon & 6pm, Sun, Wed & Thurs 3pm; Oct–March daily 3pm) takes up to three hours to do the crossing, and costs US$32 or £E109 in ordinary class, or US$42 or £E142 in first class. Grotty A/C cabins are available for an extra US$5/10. The **catamaran** (daily 12.30pm & 4.30pm) takes an hour, and costs US$42 or £E142. All prices include the Egyptian departure tax. Once you're through the formalities at Aqaba port, *service*s stand poised to whisk you the 9km into town for JD1 per person.

An alternative option from the Sinai is to go **overland** through the Israeli resort of Eilat; this involves more bureaucracy than the boat but much less hanging around, and can be considerably cheaper too. **Taba**, on the Egyptian side of the border, is well served by transport from Nuweiba, Dahab and Cairo. The border itself is open 24 hours daily, but it's almost impossible to find any transport inside Israel during the Jewish *shabbat*, so avoid crossing after 2pm on Fridays or any time on Saturdays. There's no Egyptian departure tax, and most nationalities are routinely issued with free Israeli visas on arrival. Once in Israel, local city bus #16 (NIS4) runs directly to the Jordanian border (*hagvul ha-yardeni* in Hebrew), via Eilat's Central Bus Station. Shared taxis (*sheroot* in Hebrew) will also do the trip. For details of the Israeli departure tax and crossing procedures, see p.115. The journey from Taba to Aqaba need not take more than three or four hours. However, although the Israelis and the Jordanians will stamp you in and out on a loose sheet, the Egyptians won't – and this evidence in your passport will disqualify you from later entering Syria, Lebanon and most other Middle Eastern countries.

If you have limited time and can afford the extra expense, catching one of the daily **flights** from Cairo to Amman on either Royal Jordanian or EgyptAir is a viable option. Reasonably regular charter flights also link Amman and Aqaba with Luxor, Hurghada and Sharm el-Sheikh.

RED TAPE AND VISAS

Of all the countries in the region, Jordan has one of the least Kafka-esque bureaucracies, though visitors expecting Western standards of efficiency and service will get very frustrated very quickly. Overstaffed offices, demotivated clerks and endless rounds of signature-hunting characterize even the simplest procedures; try anything more complicated than a visa extension and you may find that things take literally days to complete. However, patience and good humour are vital – nothing will slow things down more assuredly than an argument.

VISAS

All visitors to Jordan must hold passports that are valid for at least **six months** beyond the proposed date of entry to the country. Everyone other than nationals of certain Arab countries must also have a **visa** to enter Jordan.

Single- and multiple-entry visas are available in advance from Jordanian embassies and consulates abroad. Single-entry visas are also issued to EU, Canadian, US, Australian and New Zealand nationals at all land, sea and air borders except the King Hussein (Allenby) Bridge. If you plan to enter Jordan for the first time via this bridge, you must already hold a visa; if, however, you left Jordan via this bridge and are returning the same way, you don't need to buy another visa as long as your current one is still valid.

Visa **fees** vary dramatically and, although it's infinitely less hassle just to buy a visa when you arrive, applying in advance can work out considerably cheaper for some nationalities. From a Jordanian consulate abroad, single- or multiple-entry visas for Australians are generally free; those for New Zealanders and Irish (in whose countries Jordan has no consulates – apply to Canberra and London, respectively) are the equivalent of around US$10 in local currency; those for Americans are $44 and for Canadians C$65; and Britons pay £27/48 for single-/double-entry visas. The fees for single-entry visas on arrival are: Australians JD16, Canadians JD36, Irish JD11, New Zealanders JD16, Britons JD23, US citizens JD33. Note that at the time of writing the whole system of visa fees was being re-examined, and prices at the embassies abroad may in future be brought into line with prices at the borders. Visa fees and departure taxes are not charged to **groups** of five or more people whose journey has been arranged by a travel agent and who intend to stay in Jordan for at least four nights – your travel agent should confirm this in advance with the authorities.

JORDANIAN EMBASSIES AND CONSULATES ABROAD

Australia 20 Roebuck St, Redhill, Canberra, ACT 2603 (☎02/6295 9951, fax 6239 7236).

Canada 100 Bronson Ave #701, Ottawa, ON, K1R 6G8 (☎613/238-8091, fax 232-3341).

Egypt 6 Jahini St, Doqqi, Cairo (☎02/349-9912, fax 360-1027).

Israel Beit Oz building, 10th floor, 14 Abba Hillel St, Ramat Gan, Tel Aviv (☎03/751-7722, fax 751-7713).

Lebanon Elias Helou Ave, Baabda town, southeast of Beirut (☎01/922500, fax 922502).

Syria Jalaa St, Abu Rummana, Damascus (☎011/333 4642, fax 333 6741).

Turkey Cinnah Cad 54/10-11-12, Ankara (☎312/440-2054, fax 440-4327).

UK 6 Upper Phillimore Gardens, London W8 7HB (☎0171/937 3685, fax 937 8795, recorded information ☎0891/171261).

USA 3504 International Drive NW, Washington DC 20008 (☎202/966-2861, fax 686-4491). Consulates at: 866 UN Plaza #554, New York, NY 10017 (☎212/752-0135); 972 Mission St, 4th floor, San Francisco, CA 94103 (☎415/546-1111); PO Box 3727, Houston, TX 77253 (☎713/224-2911); 5423 W 95th St, Oak Lawn, IL 60453 (☎708/422-9733); 28551 Southfield Rd #203, Lathrup Village, MI 48076 (☎248/557-4377).

VISA EXTENSIONS

All Jordanian tourist visas – whether single- or multiple-entry – are initially valid for a stay of **fifteen days** only. If you leave Jordan within that period, you needn't do anything. However, if you're planning to stay longer than that, you must **register with the police** some time before the fifteen days are up – a simple, free, five-minute procedure which, in effect, alters your status to that of "temporary resident" and simultaneously extends your visa to three months from the date of entry. Although in theory you can do this at any police station, in practice it's far more likely to go smoothly in Amman than anywhere else – see p.118 for details. You'll be asked a few simple questions, your passport will be stamped, and you should hang on to any bits of paper they give you. If you entered Jordan from the West Bank or Israel, and chose to keep your passport free of stamps, you must register at the Directorate of Residency and Borders in Amman. If you don't register, the **fine** is JD1 per day over the allotted fifteen, charged in full when you depart. Multiple-entry visa holders must re-register each time they enter the country.

CUSTOMS REGULATIONS

You're permitted to buy 200 cigarettes, one litre of spirits and two litres of wine **duty-free** on arrival. Personal items such as a camera are also exempt. Customs may take an interest in more expensive goods (such as a video-camera), but they'll only charge you duty if they think you plan to sell whatever it is in Jordan; otherwise, they'll enter a description of the item in your passport, meaning that you'll be charged duty when you leave if you don't have it with you. In theory, ordinary music CDs are liable for duty as well, so pack them deep.

In addition to any duty-free purchases at the airport or borders on arrival, you can also buy alcohol, cigarettes and luxury goods at the Duty Free Shop (daily except Fri 9am–6pm) in Royal Jordanian's City Terminal building below 7th Circle, but only within the first two weeks of your arrival in the country.

PASSPORTS AND CHECKPOINTS

Once in Jordan, you should always carry your **passport** with you – aside from security considerations, you'll need it to check in to hotels and occasionally to change money. It's also a wise precaution to photocopy the pages of your passport recording your personal details and keep them separately.

In moving around the country, random army **checkpoints** are rare, but not unheard-of, especially after dark. There are permanent checkpoints along the length of the Jordan Valley road and on all roads leading down from the hills beside the Valley, as well as at Umm Qais, along the Yarmouk Gorge road, the Dead Sea coast road, the Wadi Araba road, all roads joining them and on the Wadi Yitm entry road into Aqaba. Unpleasantness – or any questioning beyond "Where you go?" – is extremely unlikely at any checkpoint, but the single most authoritative symbol of your unthreatening tourist status is a foreign passport. Note that the checkpoints along the Baghdad Highway east of Safawi and on many small roads near the Syrian border east of Mafraq are a little more serious; depending on the outlook of the local bigwig, you might find yourself smilingly but firmly turned back.

HEALTH

No immunizations or vaccinations are required before you can enter Jordan, though you'll need a yellow fever certificate if you're arriving from equatorial Africa. However, it's strongly recommended that you be up-to-date before you leave home with a few standard immunizations.

JABS

It's advisable to make sure you're up to date with **immunizations** against the following five major diseases: **hepatitis A**, **polio**, **tetanus** (lockjaw), **tuberculosis** and **typhoid fever**. You should consult a doctor at least two months in advance of your departure date as several immunizations can't be given at the same time, and some take a while to become effective. In the UK, most general practitioners can give advice and certain vaccines on prescription, though they may not administer some of the less common jabs; since only some are free under the NHS, you may have to go to a specialist travel clinic, which can cost between £10 and £26.50 a shot.

TRAVELLERS' DIARRHOEA

Despite the warnings below, a bout of **diarrhoea** is the only medical problem you're at all likely to encounter in Jordan. No one, however cautious, seems to avoid it altogether, largely because the bacteria in Jordanian food are different from, and more numerous than, bacteria in the West. An attack of the runs is just your stomach's natural reaction to unfamiliar bacteria.

For this reason, instant recourse to **drugs** such as Imodium or Lomotil that plug you up (in fact, what they do is paralyze your gut so it can't work to rid itself of infection) is inadvisable; you should only use them if you absolutely must travel (eg if you're flying). The best thing to do when diarrhoea strikes is to wait up, eat nothing for at least 24 hours and let it run its course, while constantly replacing the fluids and salts that you're flushing away. In hot conditions you lose so much water through diarrhoea that you can go from normal to seriously dehydrated in a matter of hours, and maintaining fluid intake (even if it all rushes out again) is vitally important. **Rehydration solutions** such as Dioralyte or Electrosol are widely available in Jordan and the West, sold in sachets for dissolving in a glassful of clean water (they're often mistakenly marketed as being for babies only), and these will make you feel better and stronger than any other treatment. If you can't get the sachets, make up your own solution with one heaped teaspoon of salt and twelve level teaspoons of sugar added to a 1.5-litre bottle of mineral water. Even when chilled this will taste absolutely disgusting, and may make you retch, but you should keep downing it, whether or not the diarrhoea is continuing – at least one bottle of the stuff in a day interspersed with two more bottles of fresh water. Bouts of diarrhoea rarely last longer than 24–48 hours, but note that they can render the contraceptive pill ineffective.

DIARRHOEA COMPLICATIONS

If watery diarrhoea lasts longer than four days, seek medical advice. Nasty but easily treatable diseases such as giardiasis and amoebiasis must be tested for by a stool examination.

If there is at any time blood in your diarrhoea, you've most likely got dysentery – this is rare, but far from unheard-of among travellers in the Middle East. The most important thing is to get a stool sample to a doctor to find out which of the two main kinds you've got (although whichever it is, maintaining hydration levels is essential). **Bacillary dysentery** (shigella) is bacterial, and symptoms are cramping abdominal pains, fever, fatigue and lethargy. You'll eventually get over it, and, for all but the most serious cases, rehydration is far more important than treatment with drugs. **Amoebic dysentery** is far nastier, and

HEALTH AND MEDICAL CONTACTS

For up-to-the-minute information, make an appointment at a **travel clinic**. These clinics also sell travel accessories, including first-aid kits.

BRITAIN
British Airways Travel Clinic, 156 Regent St, London W1R 6LB (☎0171/439 9584), and at Flightbookers, 177 Tottenham Court Rd, London (☎0171/757 2504): walk-in service or by appointment at both. Appointment-only branches in London at 101 Cheapside (☎0171/606 2977); and at the BA terminal in Victoria Station (☎0171/233 6661). BA also operates around forty regional clinics throughout the country, including at Gatwick and Heathrow airports: call ☎01276/685040 for the one nearest to you or consult *www.britishairways.com.*
Hospital for Tropical Diseases Travel Clinic, St Pancras Hospital, 4 St Pancras Way, London NW1 0PE (☎0171/388 9600). Consultations by appointment, and a recorded Health Line (☎0839/337733; 49p per min) which gives tips on hygiene and illness prevention, as well as listing appropriate immunizations.
MASTA (Medical Advisory Services for Travellers Abroad), PO Box 14, Lee on Solent, Hants PO13 9LQ (☎01705/553933, fax 553936). Operates under the auspices of the London School of Hygiene and Tropical Medicine. Has a pre-recorded Travellers' Health Line (☎0891/224100; 49p per min) for information, and to order a comprehensive written "Health Brief" tailored to your journey.
Trailfinders travel agency runs walk-in immunization clinics at its 194 Kensington High Street branch in London (☎0171/938 3999) and its Glasgow branch at 254–284 Sauchiehall St (☎0141/353 0066).

IRELAND
Travel Medicine Services, PO Box 254, 16 College St, Belfast 1 (☎01232/315220).

Tropical Medical Bureau, Grafton St Medical Centre, 34 Grafton St, Dublin 2 (☎01/671 9200).
Tropical Medical Bureau, Dun Laoghaire Medical Centre, 5 Northumberland Ave, Dun Laoghaire, Co. Dublin (☎01/280 4996).

NORTH AMERICA
Canadian Society for International Health, 170 Laurier Ave W #902, Ottawa, ON K1P 5V5 (☎613/230-2654). Distributes a free pamphlet "Health Information for Canadian Travellers", containing an extensive list of travel health centres in Canada.
Centers for Disease Control, 1600 Clifton Rd NE, Atlanta, GA 30333 (☎404/639-3311; *www.cdc.gov*). Publishes outbreak warnings, suggested inoculations, precautions and other background information for travellers. Website is the best readily accessible source of information about travel health matters.
Travel Medicine, 351 Pleasant St #312, Northampton, MA 01060 (☎1-800/872-8633). Sells first-aid kits and other health-related travel products.
Travelers Medical Center, 31 Washington Square, New York, NY 10011 (☎212/982-1600). Consultation service on immunizations.

AUSTRALIA AND NEW ZEALAND
Auckland Hospital, Park Rd, Grafton, Auckland (☎09/379 7440).
Travellers' Medical and Vaccination Centre, 7/428 George St, Sydney (☎02/9221 7133); 3/393 Little Bourke St, Melbourne (☎03/9602 5788); 6/29 Gilbert Place, Adelaide (☎08/8212 7522); 6/247 Adelaide St, Brisbane (☎07/3221 9066); 1 Mill St, Perth (☎08/9321 1977). Website *www.tmvc.com.au.*

can recur over many years if left untreated, with abscesses forming in the liver. This is caused by a parasite, transmitted by tiny eggs left on food, and leads to bloody, slimy diarrhoea, fever, sweating and chills. You should be certain of the diagnosis – which can only be done by stool examination – before embarking on a course of metronidazole (sold as Flagyl). You should also see your doctor as soon as you get home to make sure you're entirely cured.

OTHER MALADIES, BITES AND STINGS

Top of the list of other maladies, well ahead of Jordan's worst creepy-crawlies, is **dehydration**. This is a major threat to health, and can work insidiously over days and weeks to weaken you to the point of exhaustion without your ever showing any signs of illness. From day one in the Middle East you should be drinking at least three litres of water per day; two or even three times as much if you're exerting yourself. It's something of a matter of pride among the desert bedouin not to drink water in front of foreigners, but if you copy them you're likely to make yourself ill quite quickly. Drinking to quench your thirst just isn't enough in a hot climate, since the combination of the sun's evaporation and your own sweating can pull water out of your system far quicker than your body can deliver thirst messages to your brain: you must drink well beyond thirst-quenching if you're to head off the lethargy and splitting headaches – and potentially serious physical and mental incapacity – caused by dehydration. It's also worth remembering that both **alcohol** and **caffeine** exacerbate the effects of dehydration. The best way to check your hydration levels is to check your urine output. If you have to go reasonably frequently and your urine is pale and straw-coloured, you're OK; if you only go once or twice a day and it's dark yellow and acidic, you're not drinking enough. Paradoxically, as well as drinking extra water, you should also be adding an extra sprinkle of **salt** to your food, in order to return to your body the salts you lose through sweating.

HEAT EXHAUSTION AND SUNSTROKE

Next up, and related, is **heat exhaustion**. You can't expect to arrive from cool or temperate climes and plunge straight into exertive Middle Eastern travel in the heat without ill effects. Forty-eight hours is the minimum acclimatization period to hot conditions, although you may not be entirely yourself for up to fourteen days. The Jordanian sun can be scorchingly intense, and – obvious though it sounds – you should do all you can to avoid exposure to it, especially if you're travelling in high summer (between May and September). Some kind of head protection is essential, although your fashion sense may stop short of the "hat with a brim of at least 8cm" recommended by the medical profession. Lightweight light-coloured 100-percent cotton clothes that protect your skin from the sun – such as long-sleeved shirts, and long trousers or ankle-length skirts – will allow air to circulate close to your skin to keep you cool and limit both sunburn and dehydration. Frequent periods of rest, adequate intake of salt and water (see above) and avoidance of excessive heat and direct sunlight are all important.

Sunstroke causes the normal bodily processes of temperature control to break down, making you feel very hot, dizzy and faint but without sweating. If you're gentle about breaking yourself into the heat, you're unlikely to succumb. If you do succumb you'll probably need medical assistance. Get out of the sun immediately, and into air-conditioning and/or a cold bath as soon as possible; at the least, douse yourself and your clothes with water.

BITES AND STINGS

Although malaria is a small risk in a few areas of Egypt, Syria and Saudi Arabia, it's not present in Jordan, so the local **mosquitoes** may be annoying but they're not life-threatening. Normal precautions, such as DEET-impregnated wrist- and ankle-bands, sprays and roll-ons, will keep the critters away; for sensitive skins, citronella is a good substitute.

Sandfly bites can lead to fevers and a flu-like illness with painful eyes and muscles that lasts three or four days: alarming but not serious. Treatment is with paracetamol or aspirin to lower temperature and relieve headache, and plenty of bed-rest. Sandflies are tiny, and can only fly short distances (up to 200m) from their breeding places in rubbish heaps, stone walls and animal dens. DEET can repel them, and covering exposed skin after dark can limit the risk of bites.

The likelihood of tangling with anything worse is very small. **Snakes** are frightened of humans, and to see one you'll have to search stealthily; if you crash around making slow, noisy movements and treading heavily, any snakes present will slither away. Jordan is home to a handful of dangerous **scorpions**; to avoid them, never walk barefoot, especially in the dark, and if you're camping always shake out your shoes and clothes before wearing them. There are also a few dangerous species of **spider**, found under stones, in bunches of fruit and in outside toilets.

If you've been bitten or stung you must get to a doctor fast. It's very important to be able to identify what bit you, preferably by killing it and bringing it with you. You should immobilize the affected limb using a splint and wind a crepe bandage over and above the bite/sting. Tourniquets, cutting around the wound, and trying to suck out poison have all been medically proved to be either worthless or positively dangerous.

PREVENTING ILLNESS – FOOD AND WATER

The most obvious and effective way to **prevent** yourself getting ill while in Jordan is to avoid eating contaminated food. If you've already been travelling in Egypt or Syria, it's quite likely you'll already have gone through travellers' diarrhoea, and so will be acclimatized to the lower levels of hygiene than at home. If you haven't, or if you arrive in Jordan directly from the West or Israel, you should give your stomach a chance to get used to the conditions; lay off the street food for a few days and spend a little extra to eat in posher, but cleaner, restaurants. Everywhere from the diviest diner upwards has a sink somewhere with soap for washing your hands.

Throughout your time in the Middle East, you should always thoroughly **wash** all fruit, salad and vegetables in clean water before eating – some cautious souls even stick to the rule that "if you can't peel it, don't eat it". **Undercooked** or raw meat, fish or shellfish are major sources of disease and you should definitely send food back if it's anything less than well done. Unpasteurized **milk** is another danger; but unless you're out with the bedouin – who drink milk fresh from the goat/camel – this is unlikely to come up.

Although Jordanians drink **water** freely from the tap, you might do better not to; tap-water is chlorinated enough not to do you any harm (it just tastes bad), but the pipes it runs through add a quantity of rust and filth you could do without. Bottles of local **mineral water** are available in all corners of the country.

TREATMENT IN JORDAN

Every town, large and small, has at least one **pharmacy** (*saydaliyyeh*), generally staffed by Western-trained, fluent English-speaking professionals. Unless you're obviously a hospital case, these are where you should head first, since a pharmacist charges nothing for a "consultation", and can either prescribe a remedy on the spot or refer you to a local doctor. If you're given a medicine, find out explicitly from the pharmacist what the dosage is, since printed English information on the box might be sketchy.

If you need a **doctor** (*doktor*) in Amman, you should ask your embassy to recommend one. Elsewhere, either ask a pharmacist for a recommendation or take your chances by popping into a surgery from the street. All medical training in Jordan is in English, and so all doctors are fluent; many also received training in hospitals in the UK or the US. If you're in real trouble, aim for the emergency room of a **hospital** (*moostashfa*); all large towns have them. If you need to be hospitalized for anything more than overnight, call the emergency helpline of your embassy and ask for advice. Standards of medical hygiene in giving injections and blood transfusions are as scrupulously high as in the West. Consultation fees and medical costs are much lower than back home, but you should still get signed **receipts** for everything in order to claim money back from your insurance company when you return.

TRAVEL INSURANCE

Most people will find it essential to take out a good travel insurance policy. Before you buy, however, check what level of cover you have already. North Americans, in particular, may find that they're already covered for medical expenses and loss of or damage to valuables while abroad. Bank and credit cards (particularly American Express) often have certain levels of medical or other insurance included, especially if you use them to pay for your trip.

Note also that very few insurers will arrange on-the-spot payments in the event of a major expense or loss; you will usually be reimbursed only after going home. In all cases of loss or theft of goods, you will have to contact the local police to have a report made out so that your insurer can process the claim.

If you plan to dive, parachute, sand-ski or do some serious hiking while in Jordan, you'll probably have to pay an **extra premium**. Check carefully that any insurance policy you are considering will cover you in case of an accident – treatment in Aqaba's recompression chamber after a diving accident can cost thousands.

BRITISH AND IRISH COVER

Most travel agents and tour operators will offer you insurance when you book your flight or holiday, and some will insist you take it. These policies are usually reasonable value, though, as ever, you should check the small print. If you feel the cover is inadequate, or you want to compare prices, any insurance broker or bank should be able to help. If you have a good "all risks" home insurance policy it may well cover your possessions against loss or theft even when overseas, or you can extend cover through your household contents insurer. Many private medical schemes also cover you when abroad – make sure you know the procedure and the emergency helpline number.

Some insurance companies refuse to cover travellers over 65, or stop at 69 or 74 years of age, and most that don't charge hefty premiums. The best policies for **older travellers**, with no upper age limit, are offered by Age Concern (☎01883/346964).

In **Britain**, standard cover costs from around £26.50 a month for Europe, £50 worldwide. Some companies' "Europe" policies cover all countries bordering the Mediterranean including, somehow, Jordan (but rarely Syria), others don't: check before you buy. Cover varies, but a standard policy will cover the cost of cancellation and curtailment of flights, medical expenses, travel delay, accident, missed departures, lost baggage, lost passport, personal liability and legal expenses. Good-value policies are issued by Campus Travel or STA (see box on p.5 for addresses); Columbus Travel Insurance, 17 Devonshire Square, London EC2M 4SQ (☎0171/375 0011); Worldwide, The Business Centre, 1–7 Commercial Rd, Tonbridge, Kent TN12 6YT (☎01892/833338); Endsleigh Insurance, Cranfield House, 97–107 Southampton Row, London WC1B 4AG (☎0171/436 4451); and Marcus Hearne & Co Ltd, 65–66 Shoreditch High Street, London E1 6JL (☎0171/739 3444).

In **Ireland**, travel insurance is best obtained through a travel specialist such as USIT (see box on p.6). Their policies cost IR£31 for one month in Europe and IR£63 for one month worldwide. Discounts are offered to students of any age and anyone under 35.

NORTH AMERICAN COVER

Canadian provincial health plans typically provide some overseas medical coverage, although they are unlikely to pick up the full tab in the event of a mishap. Holders of official **student/teacher/youth cards** are entitled to accident coverage and hospital in-patient benefits – the annual membership is far less than the cost of comparable insurance. **Students** may also

TRAVEL INSURANCE COMPANIES IN NORTH AMERICA

Access America (☎1-800/284-8300).
Carefree Travel Insurance (☎1-800/323-3149).
Desjardins Travel Insurance – Canada only (☎1-800/463-7830).
STA Travel Insurance (☎1-800/781-4040).
Travel Assistance International (☎1-800/821-2828).
Travel Guard (☎1-800/826-1300).
Travel Insurance Services (☎1-800/937-1387).

find that their student health coverage extends during the vacations and for one semester beyond the date of last enrolment. **Homeowners' or renters' insurance** often covers theft or loss of documents, money and valuables while overseas.

After exhausting these possibilities, you might want to contact a **specialist travel insurance company**; your travel agent can usually recommend one, or see the box above. Travel insurance policies vary: some are comprehensive while others cover only certain risks. In particular, ask whether the policy pays medical costs up front or reimburses you later, and whether it provides for

medical evacuation to your home country. For policies that include lost or stolen luggage, check exactly what is and isn't covered, and make sure the per-article limit will cover your most valuable possession. Note that most North American travel policies apply only to items lost, stolen or damaged while in the custody of an identifiable, responsible third party – hotel porter, airline, luggage consignment, etc.

The best **premiums** are usually to be had through student/youth travel agencies – STA policies, for example, cost $48–69 for fifteen days (depending on level of coverage), $85–110 for a month, $149–207 for two months, $510–700 for a year.

AUSTRALIAN AND NEW ZEALAND COVER

Travel insurance is available from most travel agents or direct from insurance companies, for periods ranging from a few days to a year or even longer. A typical policy for Europe (including Jordan) will cost A$170/NZ$190 for one month, A$250/NZ$275 for two months. In **Australia**, check out Cover More, 9/32 Walker St, North Sydney (☎02/9202 8000 or 1800/251881); or Ready Plan, 141 Walker St, Dandenong, Melbourne (☎03/9791 5077 or 1800/337462). In **New Zealand**, Ready Plan is at 10/63 Albert St, Auckland (☎09/379 3208).

TRAVELLERS WITH DISABILITIES

Jordan makes few provisions for its own citizens who have limited mobility, and this is obviously reflected in the negligible facilities for tourists. By far the best option is to plump for an organized tour – sightseeing is liable to be complicated enough that leaving the practical details to the professionals will most likely take a huge weight off your mind.

There are **organized tours and holidays** specifically for people with disabilities – the contacts in the box on p.24 will be able to put you in touch with any specialists organizing trips to Jordan. If you want to be more **independent**, it's important to know where you'll need to be self-reliant and where you may expect help, especially regarding transport and accommodation. It is also

vital to be honest – with travel agencies, insurance companies and travel companions. Know your limitations and make sure others know them. If you don't use a wheelchair all the time but your walking capabilities are limited, remember that you are likely to need to cover greater distances while travelling in Jordan (invariably over rougher terrain and in hotter temperatures) than you are used to at home. If you use a wheelchair, have it serviced before you go and carry a repair kit.

Read your travel **insurance** small print carefully to make sure that people with a pre-existing medical condition are not excluded. And use your travel agent to make your journey simpler: airline or bus companies can cope better if they are expecting you, with a wheelchair provided at airports and staff primed to help. A **medical cer-**

CONTACTS FOR TRAVELLERS WITH DISABILITIES

BRITAIN

Access Travel, 16 Haweswater Ave, Astley, Lancs M29 7BL (☎01942/888844, fax 891811). *Tour operator that can arrange flights, transfer and accommodation; everything is checked out personally before recommendation.*

Holiday Care Service, 2nd floor, Imperial Building, Victoria Rd, Horley, Surrey RH6 7PZ (☎01293/774535, fax 784647; Minicom ☎01293/776943). *Provides free lists of accessible accommodation abroad. Information on financial help for holidays available.*

RADAR (Royal Association for Disability and Rehabilitation), 12 City Forum, 250 City Rd, London EC1V 8AF (☎0171/250 3222; Minicom ☎0171/250 4119). *A good source of advice on holidays and travel abroad. They produce a guide for long-haul holidays (£5 inc. p&p) in alternate years.*

Tripscope, The Courtyard, Evelyn Rd, London W4 5JL (☎0181/994 9294, fax 994 3618). *This registered charity provides a national telephone information service offering free advice on international transport and travel for those with limited mobility.*

IRELAND

Disability Action Group, 2 Annadale Ave, Belfast BT7 3JH (☎01232/491011).

Irish Wheelchair Association, Blackheath Drive, Clontarf, Dublin 3 (☎01/833 8241, fax 833 3873; email *iwa@iol.ie*).

NORTH AMERICA

Directions Unlimited, 720 N Bedford Rd, Bedford Hills, NY 10507 (☎1-800/533-5343). *Travel agency specializing in custom tours for people with disabilities.*

Mobility International USA, PO Box 10767, Eugene, OR 97440 (voice and TDD: ☎541/343-1284). *Information and referral services, access guides, tours and exchange programs. Annual membership $25 (includes quarterly newsletter).*

Society for the Advancement of Travel for the Handicapped (SATH), 347 5th Ave #610, New York, NY 10016 (☎212/447-7284; *www.sittravel.com*). *Non-profit travel-industry referral service that passes queries on to its members as appropriate; allow plenty of time for a response.*

Travel Information Service (☎215/456-9600). *Telephone information and referral service.*

Twin Peaks Press, Box 129, Vancouver, WA 98666 (☎360/694-2462 or 1-800/637-2256). *Publisher of plenty of titles, including the Directory of Travel Agencies for the Disabled, listing more than 370 agencies worldwide.*

AUSTRALIA AND NEW ZEALAND

ACROD (Australian Council for Rehabilitation of the Disabled), PO Box 60, Curtin, ACT 2605 (☎02/6282 4333).

Disabled Persons Assembly, 173–175 Victoria St, Wellington (☎04/811 9100).

---

tificate of your fitness to travel, provided by your doctor, is also extremely useful; some airlines or insurance companies may insist on it. Make sure that you have extra supplies of drugs – carried with you if you fly – and a prescription including the generic name in case of emergency. Carry spares of any clothing or equipment that might be hard to find; if there's an association representing people with your disability, contact them early in the planning process.

If you have limited mobility, it's hard to envisage how the situation for travelling could be less accommodating than it is in Jordan. Throughout the country – from Amman's richest neighbourhoods to the tiniest rural villages – pavements are either narrow and broken or missing altogether, kerbs are high (sometimes over half-a-metre), stairs are ubiquitous and wheelchair access to hotels, restaurants and public buildings is pretty much non-existent. Hotel staff and tourism officials, although universally helpful and sympathetic, are generally poorly informed about the needs and capabilities of tourists with mobility limitations. You'll need patience and low expectations to get the most from a visit; travelling with an able-bodied helper and being able to shell out for things like a rental car (or a car-plus-driver) and a medium or high grade of accommodation will make things considerably less fraught.

All Jordan's **ancient sites** are accessible only by crossing rough and stony ground for at least some short distance, and sometimes for 200m or more. Scrambling around the rubble at sites such as Jerash or Hallabat is hard enough for those with full mobility; for those without, a visit represents a major effort of energy and organization.

Amra, Hraneh and the castles at Karak, Ajloun, Azraq and elsewhere are easier, but still involve rocky ground and/or steep stairs. Petra, strangely enough, though locked away behind rugged mountains, has better access: with advance planning, you could arrange to rent a horse-drawn cart to take you the entire distance from the ticket gate through to the Qasr al-Bint, from where – with written permission obtained ahead of time

from the tourist police – you could be picked up in a car and driven back via the Wadi Turkmaniyyeh road and through a checkpoint to your hotel. At Rum, if you can sit in a bouncing jeep, you can get to see – from a distance – just about anything you want with no restrictions. Some of Madaba's church mosaics and the Resthouse and viewing platform at Dana are made unnecessarily difficult to access by rampless stairs.

INFORMATION AND MAPS

Decent, up-to-date information on Jordan is hard to come by outside the country. Even within Jordan itself, there's very little available of any substance.

Around the world, the offices of the national airline, Royal Jordanian, double as **tourist information** centres, dispensing photo-leaflets, posters and largely inaccurate maps, although their official *Visitors' Guide* has some useful information. There are Jordan Information Bureau offices in London and Washington DC, but these work more as press and media liaison offices than anything else. Once in Jordan, the Downtown Visitors' Centre in Amman (see p.78) is the only source of reliable information about the country's tourist sites.

JORDANIAN TOURIST INFORMATION ABROAD (RJ OFFICES)

Australia 403 George St, Sydney, NSW 2000 (☎02/9321 9222).
Canada 45 St Clair Ave West, Toronto, ON, M4V 1K9 (☎416/962-3955); 1801 McGill College Ave #1050, Montréal, PQ, H3A 2N4 (☎514/288-1655).
Egypt Zamalek Sporting Club, 26th July St, Mohandiseen, Cairo (☎02/303-5537).
Ireland 3 Clyde Rd, Ballsbridge, Dublin 4 (☎01/842 3144).
Israel 5 Shalom Aleichem St, Tel Aviv (☎03/516-5566).
Lebanon Royal Air Services, Bliss St, near AUB, Beirut (☎01/863793).
New Zealand Manchester Courts #6c, 160 Manchester St, Christchurch (☎03/365 3910).

Syria 29 Ayyar St, Damascus (☎011/2211267).
Turkey Merkez Apt #163, 2nd floor, Elmadag, Istanbul (☎212/230 4074).
UK 32 Brook St, London W1Y 1AG (☎0171/878 6333); Lancaster Buildings, 3rd floor suite 3, 77 Deansgate, Manchester M3 2BZ (☎0161/832 4847).
USA 3504 International Drive NW, Washington DC 20008 (☎202/966-2664 ext 116). Nationwide enquiries ☎1-800/RJ-JORDAN. Offices at: 535 Fifth Ave, New York, NY 10017 (☎212/949-0060); 6 N Michigan Ave #803, Chicago, IL 60602 (☎312/236-1702); 6033 W Century Blvd #760, Los Angeles, CA 90045 (☎310/215-9627); and in Detroit, Houston, Miami and Washington DC.

USEFUL WEBSITES

JORDAN

accessme.com/JordanTimes
The last seven days of Jordan's major English-language newspaper

star.arabia.com
All issues of *The Star*, an English-language weekly

arabia.com/JordanToday
Feature articles on tourism and entertainment

mota.mota.gov.jo
The Ministry of Tourism and Antiquities homepage

arabia.com/DesertLand
Fascinating site devoted to bedouin culture, with long, erudite articles on mythology, shamanism and tribal genealogies

daratalfunun.org
Image-rich site presenting Darat al-Funun, an Amman arts centre

accessme.com/turab
Homepage of TURAB, a charitable foundation, giving details of all the Muslim and Christian holy sites in Jordan

britac3.britac.ac.uk/institutes/biaahhp/index.html
The British Institute at Amman for Archeology and History

198.62.75.1/www1/ofm/fai/FAlmain.html
The Franciscan Archeological Institute, Mount Nebo

www.go.com.jo/QNoorjo
Queen Noor's homepage

www.JordanView.net/princess/jnfwmain.htm
The Jordanian National Forum for Women

www.nic.gov.jo/jncw/jncw_index.html
The Jordanian National Committee for Women

www.JordanView.net/princess/pbwrcm.htm
The Women's Resource Centre

www.wam.umd.edu/~madanat/karak.html
A personal site devoted to Karak

www.intellicast.com/weather/amm
Amman's weather over the next four days

www.divernet.com/redseaaz/redsea1.htm
The A–Z of the Red Sea

www.arab.net/camels
The A–Z of camels

THE ARAB WORLD AND ISLAM

arabia.com
Premier source of Arab World news, information and culture

almashriq.hiof.no
Quirky overview of Levantine culture from Fairouz to falafel

www.birzeit.edu
Superb one-stop site for Palestinian politics, culture and happenings

islam.org
"IslamiCity" – clear, calm, intelligent and informative; with one of the many online versions of the Quran at *islam.org/mosque/default.htm*

www.1001sites.com
Arab World Internet directory

One of the best places to get hold of background information and practical details about Jordan before you leave home is the **World Wide Web**. There are dozens of sites devoted to Jordan, from the *Jordan Times* newspaper to the A–Z of camels. Any good search-engine (look for "Jordan *NOT* Michael") will turn up plenty of browsing possibilities; see the box for a list of the more interesting sites at the time of writing.

For official information, all governments publish security advisories for their citizens travelling abroad. Although these invariably err on the side of extreme caution, you might like to check out what your government believes Jordan to be like before you go. Either contact your Foreign Ministry (the State Department in the US), or check the web: the British Foreign Office travel advisories are at *www.fco.gov.uk*, the US ones at *travel.state.gov*. Searches at both Amnesty International (*www.amnesty.org/ailib*) and Human Rights Watch (*www.hrw.org*) will turn up recent illuminating reports on the state of human rights in Jordan.

As far as the international press goes, the only English-language **journal** to concentrate exclusively on Jordan is *Jordanies*, published quarterly in Amman by the French research centre CERMOC (email *cermoc@nets.com.jo*); a French/English review of politics and society, it's more for serious academics than the casual reader. More digestible are the high-quality international **magazines** that cover contemporary political, social and economic conditions in the Middle East as a whole. *Middle East Report*, a quarterly left-leaning analysis of social and political trends (*www.merip.org*), is the most intelligent, but the biweekly *Middle East International* (email *business@meiuk.u-net.com*) is a livelier, newsier read. *The Middle East* magazine (*www.africasia.com/icpubs*) features detailed monthly analysis of politics and society in the region, while the weekly *Middle East Economic Digest* (aka MEED) is dedicated to business-oriented comment. *Rive* is a weighty, photo-rich glossy published quarterly in separate English, French and Italian editions by the University of the Mediterranean in Rome (*www.uniroma1.it/unimed*) which explores cultural interaction between the countries of southern Europe, North Africa and the Levant. *Arabies Trends* is the new English edition of a long-established French magazine (*www.arabies.com*) commenting on culture and society in the Arab World.

MAPS

For all general purposes, our **maps** should be more than adequate. All the main map publishers cover Jordan in one way or another, but none of their offerings has close detail and many omit newer roads or mark villages or archeological sites inaccurately. The widely available GeoProjects 1:730,000 map (Third Edition or later) leaves out some detail but is probably the best of the lot, especially since it also has excellent plans of Amman, Aqaba, Jerash and Petra on the back, including blown-up detail of Amman city centre. The general *Jordan Tourist Map* produced by the Royal Jordanian Geographic Centre is the most accurate map covering the whole country, incorporating every village and most roads, but their fuzzy colour reproduction leaves a lot to be desired. However, this and the smaller RJGC maps to all the major sites are almost the only maps available in Jordan itself, at around JD2.500 each – there are 1:5000 maps for Petra, Rum, Jerash, Karak and Ajloun, a very ropey 1:10,000 map for Aqaba and a good 1:20,000 one for Amman. The Aqaba Region Authority produces a much better 1:10,000 map of its domain, on free giveaway in Aqaba itself.

MAP OUTLETS WORLDWIDE

LONDON

Daunt Books, 83 Marylebone High St, W1M 3DE (☎0171/224 2295); 193 Haverstock Hill, NW3 4QL (☎0171/794 4006).
National Map Centre, 22 Caxton St, SW1H 0QU (☎0171/222 2466).

Stanfords, 12 Long Acre, WC2E 9LP (☎0171/836 1321); in Campus Travel, 52 Grosvenor Gardens, SW1W 0AG (☎0171/730 1314); and in the British Airways offices, 156 Regent St, W1R 5TA (☎0171/434 4744).
The Travel Bookshop, 13 Blenheim Crescent, W11 2EE (☎0171/229 5260).

THE REST OF BRITAIN

Blackwell's Map and Travel Shop, 53 Broad St, Oxford OX1 3BQ (☎01865/792792).
Heffers Map Shop, 3rd Floor, in Heffers Stationery Department, 19 Sidney St, Cambridge, CB2 3HL (☎01223/568467).
James Thin Melven's Bookshop, 29 Union St, Inverness, IV1 1QA (☎01463/233500).
John Smith and Sons, 57–61 St Vincent St, Glasgow, G2 5TB (☎0141/221 7472).

Latitude, 34 The Broadway, Darkes Lane, Potters Bar, Herts EN6 2HW (☎01707/663090).
The Map Shop, 30a Belvoir St, Leicester LE1 6QH (☎0116/247 1400).
The Map Shop, 15 High St, Upton-upon-Severn, Worcs WR8 0HJ (☎01684/593146).
Newcastle Map Centre, 55 Grey St, Newcastle-upon-Tyne NE1 6EF (☎0191/261 5622).
Stanfords, 29 Corn St, Bristol BS1 1HT (☎0117/929 9966).

Continued over

IRELAND

Easons Bookshop, 40 O'Connell St, Dublin 1 (☎01/873 3811).

Fred Hanna's Bookshop, 27 Nassau St, Dublin 2 (☎01/677 1255).

Hodges Figgis Bookshop, 56 Dawson St, Dublin 2 (☎01/677 4754).

Waterstones, Queens Bldg, 8 Royal Ave, Belfast BT1 1DA (☎01232/247355); 7 Dawson St, Dublin 2 (☎01/679 1415); 69 Patrick St, Cork (☎021/276522).

USA

Adventurous Traveler Bookstore, PO Box 1468, Williston, VT 05495 (☎1-800/282-3963).

The Complete Traveler Bookstore, 199 Madison Ave, New York, NY 10016 (☎212/685-9007).

Phileas Fogg's Books & Maps, #87 Stanford Shopping Center, Palo Alto, CA 94304 (☎1-800/533-FOGG).

Rand McNally, 444 N Michigan Ave, Chicago, IL 60611 (☎312/321-1751); 150 E 52nd St, New York, NY 10022 (☎212/758-7488); 595 Market St,

San Francisco, CA 94105 (☎415/777-3131). Call ☎1-800/333-0136 (ext 2111) for other locations and for maps by mail order.

Sierra Club Bookstore, 6014 College Ave, Oakland, CA 94618 (☎510/658-7470).

Travel Books & Language Center, 4931 Cordell Ave, Bethesda, MD 20814 (☎1-800/220-2665).

Traveler's Bookstore, 22 W 52nd St, New York, NY 10019 (☎212/664-0995).

CANADA

Open Air Books and Maps, 25 Toronto St, Toronto, ON M5R 2C1 (☎416/363-0719).

Ulysses Travel Bookshop, 4176 St-Denis, Montréal, PQ H2W 2M5 (☎514/843-9447).

World Wide Books and Maps, 736 Granville St, Vancouver, BC V6Z 1E4 (☎604/687-3320).

AUSTRALIA AND NEW ZEALAND

Bowyangs, 372 Little Bourke St, Melbourne (☎03/9670 4383).

The Map Shop, 16a Peel St, Adelaide (☎08/8231 2033).

Perth Map Centre, 891 Hay St, Perth (☎08/9322 5733).

Specialty Maps, 58 Albert St, Auckland (☎09/307 2217).

Travel Bookshop, Shop 3, 175 Liverpool St, Sydney (☎02/9261 8200).

Worldwide Maps and Guides, 187 George St, Brisbane (☎07/3221 4330).

MONEY AND COSTS

By Western standards, Jordan is generally an inexpensive and good-value destination. In comparison with neighbouring Middle Eastern countries, most tourist essentials are more expensive in Jordan than in Syria or Egypt, but much less so than in Israel. The most significant dent in your budget is liable to come from a visit to Petra, where the tourist boom has arrived with vengeance and hotels and services are much pricier than in the rest of the country.

CURRENCY

The Jordanian unit of currency is the **dinar**, abbreviated to JD. Its exchange rate is pegged to the dollar at US$1=JD0.709; the current rate against sterling is £1=JD1.170.

You probably won't hear many people using the name "dinar"; *jaydee* is far more common, and another popular name is *lira*. Confusingly enough, it has two subdivisions: one dinar comprises either 1000 **fils** or 100 **piastres** (*qirsh*). In practice, locals always think of prices in piastres; they only use fils when talking to foreigners. In verbal exchanges, you'll also find that people quite often leave the denomination off the end of prices; if they say something costs "*ashreen*" (twenty), it's up to you to decide whether they mean 20 fils, 20 piastres (ie 200 fils) or JD20. Nicknames also pop up: 100 fils is often called a *barizeh* and 50 fils is a *shilin*. Written or printed hotel and restaurant bills are always in the form "14.650", meaning 14 dinars and 650 fils.

To avoid any more confusion than necessary, throughout the guide we've only indicated prices in dinars and fils.

Banknotes in circulation are JD20, JD10, JD5, JD1 and JD0.5, all with Arabic on one side and English on the other. If you can, try not to get lumbered with too many JD10 and JD20 notes – this is a lot of money to most Jordanians, and many ordinary places won't be able to give you change. Even when you do get change, trying to figure out the **coinage** is a real headache. Large seven-sided gold one-dinar, half-dinar and quarter-dinar coins were introduced recently to replace some of the paper money; however, for some reason they're all similar sizes, and even locals have to squint hard to see which one they're holding. Thick, seven-sided silver half-dinar coins and big, round silver quarter-dinars also do the rounds occasionally. Otherwise, the most common coins are 100 fils and 50 fils, and – worth exactly the same – ten piastres and five piastres, all of which are silver. Tiny 25 fils and two-and-a-half piastre coins, and copper ten fils and one piastre coins, are virtually worthless. All coins state their value on them somewhere in tiny English words.

CHANGING AND CARRYING MONEY

Although few banks in the West keep Jordanian dinars on hand, you should be able to order them with a few days' notice, and it's a good idea to bring a small supply with you, to cover visa and transportation costs on arrival and a night or two in a hotel – there are no restrictions on bringing in and taking out as much foreign or Jordanian currency as you like. Unlike other Middle Eastern countries, merchants prefer to use the local money, and in most situations it's impossible to pay for goods or services in dollars.

All major Western currencies are freely convertible in Jordan, as are Israeli shekels. However, New Zealand dollars and Irish punts aren't, and you may also encounter problems with Scottish and Northern Irish banknotes. For **changing cash**, every town has a welter of banks, with no difference in exchange rates between them; all generally offer fast service. If you want to change money outside the rather limited bank opening hours, though, you may have to sacrifice a few fils and hunt down an **exchange bureau**. Amman's Downtown is crammed with these, all of which are authorized and have comparable rates, a fraction lower than the banks' – but to get the best out of them you'll have to shop around and bargain hard. Other large towns generally have a few bureaux. High-denomination bills are always preferable: a single $100 bill will get you a better bureau exchange rate than a hundred $1 bills. Also make sure that the notes you're carrying are as crispy and new as possible, since some bureaux automatically reject older bills as possible forgeries. There's no black market in money exchange.

As far as **security** goes, wads of cash are entirely safe in your pocket. Whether on a crowded rush-hour bus or at 2am in a dark alley, you're in very little danger of being mugged, conned or pickpocketed. It's still prudent to split your resources between the convenience of cash and the security of either travellers' cheques or plastic.

TRAVELLERS' CHEQUES

If you're buying **travellers' cheques** it pays to get a selection of denominations. Make sure to keep the purchase agreement and a record of cheque serial numbers safe and separate from the cheques themselves. In the event that cheques are lost or stolen, the issuing company will expect you to report the loss immediately to their office in Amman; most companies claim to replace lost or stolen cheques within 24 hours. American Express are the most widely accepted brand in the Middle East, but you should have few problems with other major brands. Although the US dollar is king throughout the region, in Jordan – unlike Egypt or Syria – travellers' cheques in British pounds and major European currencies are universally acceptable.

In Jordan, all banks will change travellers' cheques in major currencies, but their procedures can be long-winded and they sometimes charge **commissions** or insist on seeing the cheques' proof of purchase; most exchange bureaux in Amman, Petra and Aqaba will deal with cheques with considerably less hassle. Bear in mind also that you'll get a slightly worse exchange rate for travellers' cheques than for cash.

CARDS AND CASH MACHINES

Most Jordanian hotels, shops and restaurants above the cheapest budget quality accept some form of plastic in payment (most often Visa). Many banks provide over-the-counter service for **cash advances** on credit and debit cards – the British Bank and the Jordan National Bank accept Mastercard only, the Housing Bank accepts Visa only, but the Union Bank accepts both. Easiest of all, though, is to use the **cash machines/ATMs**, which are found at banks in Amman and larger towns (though they don't all accept foreign cards); check with your card issuer that your PIN number will work overseas. Thoroughly reliable English-language ATMs attached to the British Bank accept cards with Visa, Mastercard, Global Access, Plus and Cirrus symbols on them, as do plenty of other banks' ATMs. Your bank will probably impose a handling charge (even up to £3/$5 per transaction), making it more economical to withdraw higher amounts of dinars less often. You may have a daily withdrawal limit of JD100 or JD300. American Express card-holders can get cash and travellers' cheques and draw on personal cheques at the Amex office in Amman (see box below).

One recent innovation – a sort of electronic version of travellers' cheques – is **Visa TravelMoney** (*www.visa.com*), a disposable prepaid debit card which you can access from over

---

LOST OR STOLEN CARDS AND TRAVELLERS' CHEQUES

American Express International Traders, opposite *Ambassador Hotel*, Shmaysani, Amman (daily except Fri 8am–6pm; ☎06/560 7075). Outside these times, call regional head office in Bahrain (☎00973-208088).

Mastercard Jordan National Bank, 3rd Circle, Jebel Amman (daily 24hr; ☎06/465 5863 or 465 4891).

Thomas Cook Space Tourism/American Airlines, opposite Sultan café, Shmaysani, Amman (Mon–Thurs & Sat 9am–1pm & 3–6pm, Sun 9am–1pm; ☎06/566 8069). Outside these times, call international head office in the UK (☎0044-1733-318950); they'll call you back.

Visa Jordan Payment Services, 3rd floor, Housing Bank Centre, Shmaysani, Amman (daily 24hr; ☎06/568 0554 or 568 0574).

WIRING MONEY

PHONE ENQUIRIES AT HOME

MoneyGram UK ☎0800/894887. Republic of Ireland ☎1800/555696. US ☎1-800/926-9400. Canada ☎1-800/933-3276. Australia ☎1800/230100. New Zealand ☎09/379 8243.
Thomas Cook UK ☎01733/318922. Republic of Ireland ☎01/677 1721. US and Canada

☎416/359-3764. Australia ☎02/9248 6100. New Zealand ☎09/379 3920.
Western Union UK ☎0800/833833. Republic of Ireland ☎1800/395395. US and Canada ☎1-800/325-6000. Australia ☎1800/649565. New Zealand ☎09/302 0143.

AGENTS IN JORDAN

MoneyGram Contact the tourism company International Traders that acts as the local agent for Amex to find out which of the Amex/MoneyGram partner banks you can best pick your money up from (there's a JD3 charge). "Traders" has three branches: opposite *Ambassador Hotel*, Shmaysani, Amman (daily except Fri 8am–6pm; ☎06/560 7075); *Silk Road Hotel* building, near Petra gate, Wadi Musa (daily except Fri 8am–1pm & 4–7pm; ☎03/215 7711); near *Ali Baba* restaurant, Aqaba (same times; ☎03/201 3757).
Thomas Cook Funds can be wired to the British Bank (enquiries daily except Fri

8.30am–12.30pm; ☎06/560 7471 ext 112), with branches in Amman only. You can pick up your money in JDs or other major currencies for a JD3 charge.
Western Union Funds can be wired to the Cairo-Amman Bank (enquiries daily except Fri 8.30am–12.30pm; ☎06/463 0030), with a branch in most towns. The sender need not specify a particular branch, since whichever one the recipient is waiting in will call and fax Amman headquarters for confirmation of the transaction. You can pick up your money in JDs or US dollars, without charges.

40,000 Visa/Plus ATMs in 115 countries with a PIN which you select yourself. When your funds are depleted, you simply throw the card away (it's recommended you buy at least a second card as back up in case your first is lost or stolen, and up to nine cards can be bought to access the same funds – useful for couples/families travelling together). In the UK, many Thomas Cook outlets sell the card, or contact IPS (☎0171/937 5507) for more details.

WIRING MONEY FROM ABROAD

Having money **wired** from home is fast but never cheap, and should be considered only as a last resort. All companies have an elaborate security system of passwords and code numbers which have to be agreed privately between sender and recipient before the transaction can be okayed; unless you've worked something out in advance, this will mean at least one phone call home to agree on a password. Once the transaction has been made, the money should be available for collection – on production of **your passport** – from the company's local agent within fifteen minutes of being sent via Western Union or MoneyGram; both charge on a sliding scale, so sending larger amounts is better value. Thomas

Cook – as well as acting as a MoneyGram agent – have their own Telegraphic Transfer service, which has a much cheaper flat-rate charge but which takes two working days for the money to arrive. Bank-to-bank transfers tend to be slower and involve more bureaucracy, but can be less expensive. Check with your bank before travelling to see if they have reciprocal arrangements with any banks in Jordan, and what information they need before making a transfer.

From **Britain**, places where you can wire funds via MoneyGram include Thomas Cook offices, Eurochange, all post offices and, for Amex card-holders, American Express offices. Rates for sending £100, £500, £1000 and £2000 are £12, £33, £44 and £70 respectively. Western Union's slightly higher charges are £14, £37, £47 and £75; you can wire money from any of their agents (which include Going Places travel agents and some newsagents and chemists), or, for an extra £3–7 charge, you can wire money down the phone off a credit card up to a maximum of £1500 (this takes up to an hour to clear). Thomas Cook's Telegraphic Transfer service costs £15 plus one percent of the amount to be sent (with a minimum charge of £25). They can also credit foreign bank accounts for the same fee. All the same facilities are available from **Ireland**; charges across the board are generally within IR£2–5 of the equivalent sterling fees. Thomas Cook's Telegraphic Transfer – for which you must visit their Dublin or Cork offices – has a flat-rate charge of IR£25.

From the **US and Canada**, agents of Western Union and MoneyGram vary from city to city. Wiring $500 to Jordan will cost about $30, or $2000 will cost about $100. From **Australia and New Zealand**, International Money Transfers can be made from any local bank to a nominated bank abroad for around A$25/NZ$30, but can take days or weeks to clear. The wire services are about twice as expensive.

SOME BASIC COSTS

You'll find Jordan an inexpensive place to visit; if you have the heart to bargain a little, prices that are low to start with will plummet through the floor. Almost nowhere in the country are discounts offered to students.

Amman's cheapest **accommodation** – a bed in a shared room – can be had for about £2/$3, plus 50p/80c for a shower; a cosier budget double might still only be twice that per person. About £20/$32 buys a comfortable, if small-ish, double room with an en-suite bathroom and some form of air conditioning. Five-star luxury hotels have been known to sell off double rooms for as little as £65/$105 with a little encouragement, although £100/$160 is nearer their mark. Bear in mind, though, that prices around the country can be a little higher than this, specifically in Aqaba and – especially – Petra.

Food is extremely inexpensive. If you're prepared to eat one or other of the basic staples at every sitting, you could get by paying as little as £2.50/$4 for three reasonably nutritious meals. If you include one high-quality meal plus a vitamin-supplementing fresh juice, food costs would still stay below £5/$8 a day. Even at the top end of the scale, a very reasonable £22/$35 covers a lavish buffet breakfast, a light lunch, and dinner (plus wine) in a good restaurant.

Entry to sites is a mixed bag. Most places around the country are free, or £1–3/$2–5 or so.

The unmissable Petra is the only exception, with a one-day pass costing a controversially high £17.50/$28.

If you're looking to cover all corners of the country independently, the one thing that can really push costs up is **transport**. Jordan's public transport system leaves quite a lot to be desired, although within Amman shared taxis whisk you around town for pennies and even a crosstown ride in a metered taxi is rarely as much as £1/$1.60. Travelling between urban centres is inexpensive (eg Amman–Aqaba £3/$5), but the more remote and interesting corners of the country are poorly served by public transport – if at all – and getting to them can involve more significant expense, either hiring a taxi for the day, renting a car or chartering a four-wheel-drive vehicle to go across country. Prices obviously vary, but £25/$40 generally covers a major full-day excursion in a car or 4x4.

HIDDEN COSTS AND TIPPING

Above a certain quality threshold, all hotels and restaurants automatically add a ten percent **government tax** and a ten percent **service charge** to all bills; they are legally obliged to state this somewhere, although it can be as surreptitious as a simple "++", as in "Double Room JD40++". On larger sums, this can obviously represent a hefty hike, but often, if you try to bargain, you'll find the "++" suddenly disappearing from view. In a good restaurant, even when a service charge is included, it's customary to round the bill up slightly as well. Occasionally, restaurants will add ten percent for tax but leave the service charge up to you; your meal would have to have been really awful to merit anything less than a ten percent tip. Budget local diners don't expect tips and will never press you for anything.

In most everyday situations, 100 fils is a perfectly satisfactory indication of your appreciation for a service, such as a porter loading your bags onto a bus or taxi. Taxi drivers deserve at least the same. For a bellboy in a four- or five-star hotel who brings your bags up to your room, half-a-dinar is nearer the mark.

GETTING AROUND

Jordan's public transport – of which there isn't much, other than buses – is a hotch-potch. Bus routes cover what's necessary for the locals: there is little or no provision for budget travellers wishing to visit out-of-the-way places, and it's impossible to get from one end of the country to the other without making at least two or three changes of bus. With some highly visitable places inaccessible by public transport, the best way to see the whole of Jordan is to rent a car for at least part of your stay.

BUSES AND *SERVICES*

The most common way of getting between cities is by **bus**, most of which are small, privately owned fifteen- or eighteen-seater minibuses. There are a few big old government-owned rattletrap buses and a handful of modern air-conditioned tour-buses serving as public transport, but they're rare. Throughout the guide, we've used "bus" as a catch-all term; in most cases, minibuses are the only transport option available, but we've only resorted to the term "minibus" when the distinction needs to be made between them and big buses. Virtually no timetables are in operation, and buses tend to depart only when they're full. This means that, on less-travelled routes especially, you should factor in sometimes quite considerable waiting time. However, once you get going, journeys are rarely arduous – roads are good; and the longest single journey in the country, from Amman to Aqaba, is unlikely to take more than four hours.

Bus **fares** are very low. As a guide, a half-hour hop between towns costs 100–150 fils.

Longer journeys – Amman to Jerash, or Zerqa to Azraq – are in the order of 400–500 fils; Amman to Karak is 750 fils. Fares tend to be a little inflated travelling to and from the major tourist sites of Petra and Wadi Rum, but the most you'll ever pay for a single bus ride – from Amman to Aqaba – is JD3. Minibuses always have someone employed to ride up front to keep the driver company and deal with letting people on and off; at some point during the journey, he'll come round to collect fares.

The only times you'll find a choice of bus possibilities is on a handful of long-distance runs, and even then, only two companies operating big **air-con buses** give an alternative to the ubiquitous minibuses. Jordan Express Tourist Transport, or JETT, has daily timetabled services from Amman to Aqaba, Petra and Hammamat Ma'in, while Hijazi operates between Amman and Irbid (mainly for students attending Yarmouk University). These offer the advantages of comfort and speed over the minibuses, and JETT even allows you to book in advance (in person only).

On most inter-city routes, shared taxis (universally known as ***services***, pronounced the French way as "ser-VEECE") tout for business alongside the buses. These are often vintage seven- or eight-seater Mercedes – generally white, but not always – which offer, at a slightly higher price, the single advantage of speed over the same journey by bus. However, being squashed into the back seat of a suspension-challenged heap on a long journey can counter in discomfort what might be gained in time. *Services* also operate the system of departing when full, but because there are fewer seats, they leave more often than buses. If you're carrying bulky or heavy luggage, you may well find that *service*, and some minibus, drivers will charge you for the space your bags occupy, whether or not they take up seating space.

For getting around **within cities**, only Amman and Irbid are too big to walk across; details of public transport provisions in these cities are in the relevant chapters. Although most other towns have their own systems of short-hop buses and *services*, all are small enough that you can easily walk between sights. The long, steep hills of Wadi Musa prompt most visitors to resort to taxis for getting to and from the Petra ticket gate.

Bus and *service* **etiquette** says that men should sit next to men and women next to women (except for husbands and wives or brothers and sisters), and you should stick to this rule when you can. No one will be mortally offended if circumstances force you to sit next to a Jordanian of the opposite sex, but – especially for a close-quarters *service* journey – other passengers may shuffle themselves around to make a more acceptable space for you.

HITCH-HIKING

Although public transport can usually get you where you want to go, in certain circumstances **hitching** is normal practice. However, the first rule of hitching in Jordan – apart from foreign women never hitching alone – is that you should always be prepared to **pay something**, even if your money is refused when offered. Rightly or wrongly, foreigners are seen as able to pay their bus fares, and trying to freebie your way around the country will inspire contempt rather than sympathy.

Travellers who decide to hitch should do so always in pairs. The risks of assault (or worse) attached to hitching in Europe or elsewhere in the world are minuscule in Jordan, but nonetheless do exist; women should never sit next to men, and spontaneous offers of hospitality on the part of drivers should be accepted only with extreme caution, if at all. On a more prosaic note, **water** and **a hat** are vital hitching accoutrements: out on the road, you're in more danger from dehydration than anything else.

Hitching a ride on well-travelled routes such as Amman to Irbid will likely take you hours, since drivers won't have a clue why you can't just get the bus like everyone else. However, in areas where buses may be sporadic or non-existent – the eastern desert, the southern portions of the King's Highway (south of Qadsiyyeh), the link road from the Desert Highway into Wadi Rum, or just from one village to the next on quiet country roads – all moving vehicles are fair game for hitching; local drivers stick to a well-established countryside protocol about picking people up if they have space. The generally accepted way to indicate you're hitching is to lazily hold out your arm and loosely flap your index finger.

DRIVING

Compared with Egypt or Syria, **driving** in Jordan is a breeze; compared with the West, it's a night-

mare. Cities, highways, backroads and *pistes* each pose a challenge to drivers' skills and nerve, and, apart from driving on the right and always obeying a policeman, **rules of the road** have individual interpretations. Overtaking on both sides is normal – always accompanied by a blast or two on the horn – as is pulling out into fast-moving traffic without looking. There is no universally accepted pattern of right-of-way. It's wise to follow the locals and sound your **horn** before many types of manoeuvre; out in the sticks, you should look out for kids playing on the hard shoulder and give a warning honk from a long way back. In general, **traffic lights** are always respected – except in the countryside where there's obviously nothing coming – as are most **one-ways**, although people do sometimes drive slowly the wrong way down a highway, searching for a place to U-turn. Right-of-way on roundabouts goes to whoever's moving fastest. Road surfaces are generally very good, although there are lots of unmarked **speed bumps** and rumble strips in unexpected places (including main highways). Look out also for drifting sand on roads in the desert: if you're going too fast when you hit a patch of sand, you can easily be spun off the road before you know what's happened. Speed limits are posted regularly, and are generally 100kmh on highways, dropping to 40kmh or so within towns, with a few police radar traps here and there. Spot fines for speeding are in the order of JD5. **Night driving** is a little more scary, since it's common – if inexplicable – practice on dark country roads to flip to main beam when you see somebody coming, effectively dazzling them blind. In addition, slow-moving trucks and farm vehicles often chug along in the dark without lights to save on headlight bulb usage. Most people flash their headlights to say "get out of the way", but some do it to say "OK go ahead" – you must make up your own mind at the time which it is.

On major roads, **directional signs** are plentiful and – when not plastered with old election posters – informative; most have English as well as Arabic. A new series of large white-on-brown signs has been set up across the country specifically to direct tourists to major sites, superseding older, idiosyncratically spelled white-on-blue ones. On unsigned back roads, the only failsafe method of finding the right direction is to keep asking the locals.

Although a normal **driving licence** from home is good enough, an International Driving

CAR RENTAL AGENCIES ABROAD

UK AND IRELAND

Avis UK	☎0990/900500
Republic of Ireland	☎01/874 5844
Budget UK	☎0800/181181
Republic of Ireland	☎0903/24668
Hertz UK	☎0990/996699
Republic of Ireland	☎01/676 7476
Thrifty UK	☎0990/168238
Republic of Ireland	☎01/679 9420

US AND CANADA

Avis US and Canada	☎1-800/331-1084
Budget US and Canada	☎1-800/527-0700

Hertz US	☎1-800/654-3001
Canada	☎1-800/263-0600
Thrifty US and Canada	☎1-800/367-2277

AUSTRALIA AND NEW ZEALAND

Avis Australia	☎1800/225533
NZ	☎0800/655111
Budget Australia	☎13 2727
NZ	☎09/375 2222
Hertz Australia	☎13 3039
NZ	☎09/309 0989
Thrifty Australia	☎02/9360 4055
NZ	☎09/275 6666

Permit can be useful, since it has an Arabic translation; these are available very inexpensively from the AA in Britain, or equivalent organizations in your home country. Without a Jordanian driving licence, you're only permitted behind the wheel of rental cars (yellow-on-green plates) and foreign-registered vehicles; to drive the regular black-on-white-plated cars you must hold a local licence.

RENTING A SELF-DRIVE CAR

For reaching all corners of the country at your own pace, a **rental car** is a worthwhile – sometimes essential – investment. The rental market is huge, with more than 150 different companies nationwide, competition being based on price rather than quality. Local operators tend to cater much more to Jordanians' own visiting friends and family than to Westerners, and many of these tiny outfits are no more than a guy with a phone renting out old cars on the cheap with no insurance, no papers and no service. Reliable companies in Amman or Aqaba, all of which take major credit cards, are recommended in the relevant chapters of the guide.

It is possible to arrange car rental **before you arrive** but, although this buys you peace of mind, prices quoted for international reservations are invariably higher than those quoted to walk-in customers, sometimes by as much as fifty percent. In addition, all local agencies can match or undercut the big agencies' walk-in rates, some maintaining equivalent levels of quality and service. The one possibility for true discounts before

you arrive comes if the airline you're flying with has signed an agreement with a rental agency; if they have, a **fly-drive** deal arranged in advance can be very good value. Whether you book in advance or on arrival, international agencies can generally bring a car to you at any border crossing or airport for free; local operators may add a surcharge. With two locations in Amman, plus others in Petra, Aqaba, Queen Alia Airport and at the Dead Sea, Hertz offers the best coverage and service, if not the best value for money.

Trustworthy businesses charge about JD28–31 a day, for a one- or two-year old manual car (automatic transmission costs more) comfortable for four people, including unlimited mileage and full insurance. A "subcompact", comfortable for two, is JD3–4 less. Some form of collision damage waiver (CDW) covering all but the first JD200–300 of damage might cost a few dinars more, but, considering the Jordanian driving style, is eminently worth it. Only the international agencies offer optional extras such as zero-deductible cover, personal accident insurance (PAI) and theft protection (TP) – the last truly an option too far. Before moving off, you'd do well to check that the car has a pumped-up spare tyre and a full toolkit and jack.

A couple of agencies in Amman, and a few more in Aqaba, rent out reliable **four-wheel drive** vehicles (universally called "four-by-fours") from about JD35 a day upwards. These are essential for getting to a handful of out-of-the-way archeological sites and quiet spots in Wadi Rum, but you should have some familiarity with 4x4 driving – and a local guide – before you set off into the desert. For all but the most dedicated adventurers, a normal car is fine.

DRIVING YOUR OWN CAR

It's quite feasible – and not overly foolhardy – to **drive from Europe** to the Middle East, although the expense and the amount of necessary preparation is enough to put off all the but most committed. Many British **car insurance** policies cover taking your car into the EU, but none will cover a journey beyond Turkey or Cyprus. Check with your insurer while planning your trip for full details of what is and isn't covered, but whatever the answer is, you'd be well advised to take out extra cover for motoring assistance in case your car breaks down abroad. In the UK, look into the RAC's European Cover (☎0800/550055) or the AA's Five-Star Europe cover (☎0800/444500). If you're driving a car abroad and you are already a member of the AA or the RAC in Britain, you can use the standard services of any affiliated motoring organization worldwide, including roadside assistance.

The major bind is that to drive outside Europe you need a **carnet de passage**, an internationally recognized customs document entitling you to temporarily import a vehicle duty-free into countries which normally require a deposit to be paid against import charges. The amount of money it costs in order to get a *carnet* is staggering. The actual *carnet* itself is £55 (for ten countries) or £65 (for 25 countries). However, on issuing a *carnet*, a motoring organization (such as the RAC or AA) becomes directly responsible for the payment of customs duties and taxes should you infringe any particular country's regulations, and in order to take on this responsibility, they'll require you to meet a number of conditions, including giving a bank guarantee or **indemnity** with an insurance company and a **cash deposit**. It's these sums –worked out for each individual application depending on the vehicle itself and the countries you intend to drive through – which can run into thousands, and even tens of thousands. Once you return home, and it's ascertained that there are no customs charges outstanding on your *carnet*, your deposit will be returned, along with fifty percent of the premium you paid on the indemnity. Miss a stamp at any point in your journey, and you'll be held liable for a list of customs duties as long as your arm.

The most common route from Europe into the Middle East is overland through **Turkey and Syria**, although it's equally possible to hop a ferry from Greece to Cyprus and another from there to **Israel**. Turkey and Israel are both pretty picky about *carnet*s, but many travellers have reported entering and exiting Syria – and even Jordan – without one. Beyond Jordan, you can take the ferry into Egypt, or – with sufficient visa organization in advance – head overland through Saudi Arabia to Yemen or the Gulf coast. Many drivers visit Jordan as part of a journey towards India, but the only way to get around Iraq is to return north to Turkey in order to cross into Iran.

You can drive into Jordan in a private, foreign-registered car at all land-border crossing-points *except* the King Hussein (Allenby) Bridge from the West Bank (only Jordanian- and Israeli-registered cars can cross here). Buying **third-party insurance** when you cross is obligatory, and all insurance companies in Jordan are under an umbrella organization which eliminates price competition. Costs vary depending on the vehicle (they're posted on the wall in English): for one month/three months, insurance for a small car costs JD33/50, for a motorbike JD16/22. Also obligatory when you cross is purchase of a licence to drive in Jordan, at JD7. You must present your *carnet* when you cross, but if you're entering Jordan from Israel and want to travel on to Syria or Saudi Arabia (which refuse entry to those bearing evidence of a visit to Israel), you can request both your passport and your *carnet* not to be stamped; exit customs are aware of these rule-bendings.

PETROL AND BREAKDOWNS

The Jordan Petroleum Refinery Company Ltd – with its distinctive red snowflake logo – has a monopoly on **petrol** sales around the country, with most towns having at least one small, filthy petrol station. All of them have attendants to do the work for you – either hand over your dinars before he starts, or just ask for "full". Low-octane regular (*benzeen*, aka *aadi*) is a standard 221 fils per litre, high-octane super (*soober*, aka *khas*) 301 fils, almost always cash only (barely a handful of stations take Visa). Most rental agencies will tell you to fill up with *soober*, but it's rarely found outside Amman; Wadi Musa, Aqaba and the Amman–Irbid road are the only places you can rely on it. Diesel (*deezel*) is available only rarely, and there are, in theory, five stations in Jordan selling unleaded (*khal min ar-rasas*), most reliably near 8th Circle in Amman.

Virtually all towns, big and small, have some form of **repair workshop**; entire neighbourhoods devoted to vehicle repairs can be found in Amman (especially on the truck routes to the south and east), Irbid (on the road to Umm Qais), Aqaba (northeast sector of town) and Azraq (everywhere). Toyota, Nissan, Hyundai and Mercedes are the best-known brands, though people drive everything from Beetles to Buicks and mechanics will attempt to fix anything. Parts can generally be ordered if not in stock (or if the mechanic can't jerry something together), and labour charges are significantly cheaper than in the West. In the case of an **accident**, you'll need a full written report from the police and from the first doctor on the scene who treated any injuries in order to claim costs back from the insurance company.

TAXIS AND CHAUFFEUR-DRIVEN CARS

All **taxis** in Jordan are yellow with green panels in Arabic on both front doors, and they'll go anywhere if the price is right. Inexpensive and quite often essential within Amman, their good value declines the further afield you want to go; renting a taxi to cover the transport-thin eastern desert, for instance, will cost you almost twice as much as if you drove there yourself in a rental car. As far as **fares** go, other than within Amman city limits you'll have to negotiate with the driver before setting off. Ballpark figures for particular routes are given in the guide, but where you're inventing your own itinerary, you'd do well to ask the advice of a disinterested party (such as a hotel receptionist) beforehand. Jordanian **women** would never get in the front seat next to the driver (there's just one female taxi-driver in the whole country), and foreign women should follow suit.

Most rent-a-car agencies can provide a **driver** for the day for about JD15 on top of the price of the rental; on a longer trip, JD35 a day should cover his food and accommodation costs. For something a little different, check out Najla International's (☎ & fax 06/412 6379) fleet of brand-new black **London cabs** – much more comfortable and roomy in the back than most cars, fitted with air conditioning and mobile phones and driven by English-speaking chauffeurs. Their understandably high charges are JD15 per hour, JD95 for an eight-hour day, or JD145 per day on a longer trip around the country.

TRAINS

The only usable passenger **train** tracks in Jordan are the remnants of the Hejaz Railway (see p.82), running from the Syrian border through Mafraq, Zerqa and Amman, and on into the desert via Qatraneh to Ma'an. The single regular service is a once-weekly train from Amman to Damascus. South of Amman, the unguarded line runs through open desert and the resident bedouin tend to rip up the rails for building joists when no one's looking; the only services into the desert are occasional steam trains chartered by visiting enthusiasts or tour groups. For your very own fully equipped steam locomotive pulling a comfortable carriage or two, prices start as low as JD200, rising the further you want to go. Call Ali Hassan Jehdullah (☎06/895413), Traffic Manager at the Hejaz Jordan Railway offices in Amman, for details of chartering your own train.

PLANES

Royal Wings (a subsidiary of Royal Jordanian) operates the single domestic passenger **air** route, between Amman and Aqaba. At JD30 one-way, this is not prohibitively expensive, and means you can travel from city centre to city centre in barely more than an hour, compared with more than four bumpy hours overland. In addition, the airborne views over the desert, the Dead Sea and the Petra mountains are worth the fare in themselves – make sure you're sitting on the right-hand side of the plane heading south.

The Royal Jordanian Gliding Club (☎06/874587), based at Marka Airport in Amman, can take you up for a unique view of the capital from above in either a free-flying or motorized glider, at around JD15/hr. For considerably more – up to JD150/hr – and with 24 hours' notice, they can provide a proper light aircraft for four passengers to fly to (or over) anywhere in Jordan.

BICYCLES

Propelling yourself around the country by **bicycle** is a very pleasant way to travel, although barely a handful of locals cycle – mostly in the flat Jordan Valley – and you're quite likely to be regarded as completely potty if you try. There are no bike rental firms in Jordan, so you must bring your own; you should also make arrangements for receiving advice and spare parts while on the road from a specialist back home.

Around the country, the roads are empty enough that much of the time you'll probably have the tarmac to yourself. Even Amman's traffic is low-key enough that you could negotiate the city with relatively little hassle. The major problem, though, comes in the terrain – coping with the one-in-six or -seven hills of the King's Highway while battling the prevailing westerly winds trying to sweep you into the ravine is no joke. The south of the country is particularly taxing: from Ras an-Naqb to Aqaba is down all the way, but then to return north you either have to struggle your way 80km back up to the plateau, or alternatively pedal against the strong northerly winds blowing down the funnel of the flat Wadi Araba. Winter rains and summer heat throughout Jordan can both be deadly, and you should ideally plan a cycling tour for the three spring months of March to May.

CAMELS

Most visitors from the West come to Jordan never having laid eyes on a **camel**, yet almost all arrive full of all kinds of ideas about the creatures; myths about the simplicity of desert life, the nobility of the bedouin and the Lawrence-of-Arabia-style romance of desert culture all seem to be inextricably bound up in Western minds with the camel. Jordanian bedouin, of course, long since gave up using camels either as means of transport or as beasts of burden – Japanese pick-ups are faster, sturdier, longer-lived and less bad-tempered than your average dromedary. However, some tribes still keep a few camels (mostly for nostalgic reasons and the milk), and the bedouin that live in or close to touristed areas such as Petra and Rum have small herds of them to rent out for walks and desert excursions.

If you're in any doubt about whether to take the plunge and have a **camel ride**, then rest assured that it's still a great experience. There's absolutely nothing to compare with the gentle, hypnotic swaying and soft shuffle of riding camelback in the open desert. Wadi Rum is the best place in Jordan to try it out, with short and long routes branching out from Rum village all over the southern desert, as far as Aqaba, Ma'an or Petra; these are hefty multi-day excursions, but then again anything less than a couple of hours' riding isn't really worth it.

As a beginners' tip, the key to not falling off a camel is to hang on to the pommel between your legs; they get up from sitting with a bronco-style triple jerk, and if you're not holding on as soon as your bottom hits the saddle, you're liable to end up in the dust. Once up and moving, you have a choice of riding your mount like a stirrupless horse, or copying the locals and cocking one leg around the pommel.

ORGANIZED TOURS

Although not a budget option, taking an **organized tour** once you arrive in Jordan can actually turn out to be the most rewarding way to get to some of the more isolated attractions in the hinterland. If all you want is to be taken around Amman, Jerash and Petra quickly and without hassle, you'd do far better to book a package deal from your home country in advance (see pp.7, 10, 13). Longer-stay special-interest holidays – such as bird-watching or diving – are also much better organized from home. However, it's significantly more complicated to try and organize from home camping overnight in Burqu, for instance, or a two-day hike through Wadi Mujib than it is to sort things out face-to-face with the relevant people once you arrive.

There are around 500 Amman **tour operators** dealing with incoming tourism but only a handful can take you off the beaten track. For exploring the wilder reaches of the Dana reserve, Wadi Mujib and the Zubia woodland reserve near Ajloun – and for any enquiries about getting out into Jordan's nature, guided or solo – you should talk first with the Ecotourism Unit at the Royal Society for the Conservation of Nature (RSCN). They can also direct you to particular individuals or companies that can help you get to where you want to go. Professional and reputable companies such as Discovery and Jordan Eco-Tours tend to specialize in incentive travel, but are more than happy to set up a customized itinerary at short notice for individuals or small groups, whether your bent is archeology or ecology. On a more historical note, the Friends of Archeology society runs monthly tours of major and minor archeological sites throughout the country, led by the most authoritative experts. They can also put you in contact with specialist archeological guides for customized trips.

SPECIALIST TOUR OPERATORS IN JORDAN

Discovery, PO Box 3371, Amman 11181 (☎06/569 7998, fax 569 8183, email *discovery @nets.com.jo*, website *www.discovery1.com*). A softly-softly approach to tourism, coupled with an encyclopedic knowledge of natural and cultural attractions in all seven corners of Jordan.

Friends of Archeology, PO Box 2440, Amman 11181 (☎ & fax 06/593 0682, email *foa@nets.com.jo*). First stop for anything archeology-oriented. Publishes a monthly newsletter giving details of upcoming trips.

International Traders, PO Box 408, Amman 11118 (☎06/560 7014, fax 566 9905, email *sahar@traders.com.jo*). The oldest and biggest tourism company in the country, but it has managed to move with the times into an environmentally-aware approach.

Jordan Eco-Tours, PO Box 183764, Amman 11118 (☎06/553 3526, fax 553 6964, email *jordanecotours@go.com.jo*, website *www.*

jordanecotours.com). Recommended for what their name might suggest.

Neptune, PO Box 183494, Amman 11118 (☎06/465 1780, fax 465 1779, email *info@neptune-tours.com*, website *www.neptune-tours.com*). Specialists in walking tours of the south.

Petra Moon, PO Box 129, Wadi Musa 71810 (☎03/215 6665, fax 215 6666, email *petram@go.com.jo*, website *www.petramoon.com*). The best of the many tour operators based in Wadi Musa, and unique in offering low-impact jeep trips into the remote countryside around Petra. Can set you up with good local guides for hikes and camel rides further afield.

Royal Society for the Conservation of Nature, PO Box 6354, Amman 11183 (☎06/533 7931, ecotourism unit 533 4610, fax 534 7411, email *rscn@nets.com.jo*). First stop for anything nature-oriented.

ACCOMMODATION

Accommodation in Jordan runs the gamut from the cheapest fleapit dives all the way up to international-standard luxury five-star hotels. Amman, Petra and Aqaba have a wide choice covering most price brackets, but other towns are restricted to a few, uninspiring options, almost exclusively at the bottom end of the market.

Most of Jordan's budget **hotels** are still unused to Westerners; its mid-range hotels are geared primarily towards group package tourists; and most of the expensive ones cater almost exclusively to business people. The country's hoteliers are adapting only very slowly to the growth in independent travel, and the room rates quoted at hotels above budget quality to walk-in arrivals are always more expensive than rates for pre-bookers. If times are hard, you may find reception clerks knocking a few percent off the rack rate for you, but booking ahead will always pay. Although the tourist **high season** officially runs from March to October, the hot midsummer months – June, July and August – are in fact pretty slow; spring and autumn are when you could find it hard to get a room to fit your budget without pre-booking.

Jordan has its own system for hotel **classification** that bears little resemblance to standards used elsewhere. The Ministry of Tourism grades all hotels from one to five stars, with so-called "unclassified" hotels off the bottom end of the

---

HOTEL PRICE CODES

Throughout the guide, hotels are categorized according to the price codes given below, which indicate the normal price for the cheapest double room in a particular establishment during the high season, excluding tax and service charge (see below). Single rooms can cost anything between seventy and a hundred percent of the double-room rates. Where a hotel offers beds in a shared room, the price to share has been given; if a price code has also been included, this indicates that some private rooms are available.

① under JD10   ④ JD30–40   ⑦ JD65–80
② JD10–20   ⑤ JD40–50   ⑧ JD80–95
③ JD20–30   ⑥ JD50–65   ⑨ over JD95

---

scale, and a new grade – "inn" – just introduced in 1998. As the criteria for star-rating seem to concentrate more on the range of communal facilities than on the quality of rooms or service, a hotel deemed to be four stars in Jordan might scrape only three according to international criteria.

All hotels above ③ in our price-coding system tack ten percent **government tax** onto their quoted prices and some also add another ten percent **service charge** (often indicated by "++", or "plus-plus"). **Standards** vary widely within each price bracket and sometimes within each hotel – if the room you're shown isn't good enough, ask to see others. Things to look out for are either **air conditioning** or a ceiling fan in summer and **heating** in winter – both are essential almost everywhere (although you're unlikely to need a heater in Aqaba, even in January) and worth paying for. South- or west-facing rooms that receive direct sunshine are liable to become ovens on summer afternoons and so stay uncomfortably hot during the night.

There are no **youth hostels** in Jordan and the tiny number of **campsites** are all privately run and not affiliated to international organizations.

BUDGET AND MID-RANGE HOTELS

Budget and mid-range hotels –covering the ① to ④ or ⑤ price brackets – comprise the vast majority of hotels in Jordan, and range from a handful of homely, good-value options to a whole bunch of generic, poorly equipped hotels knocked together in the last few years to cash in on the projected tourist boom that never came after peace was signed with Israel.

The bottom end of the market consists of cheap **dosshouses** in the centres of all towns

that cater to Egyptian, Syrian and Iraqi men come to Jordan to labour. These are universally filthy dives that are best avoided: washing facilities are likely to be spartan or non-existent, and there might easily be only one squat toilet to share between everybody. Slightly up from these – though still well inside the ① bracket – are **budget** establishments aimed either exclusively at Westerners, or at both locals and Westerners; often the latter will have some means of separation, like reserving one whole floor for locals only and another for Westerners only. Quite often you'll find a choice of shared or private rooms, housing two, three or four beds, with many places also offering a choice of some en-suite rooms as well. Whatever the outward appearance of the decor, though, you'd be advised to check things out before you commit yourself: seeing if the sheets are clean, the bed is stable, the flyscreens on the windows are intact, the ceiling fan works, the water in the bathroom is hot (or at least lukewarm), the toilets don't smell too much, and so on, are all completely acceptable things to do before agreeing to pay. Once you've checked in, most places won't bother with holding on to your **passport**, but nonetheless it's a good rule to insist on keeping your passport with you at all times.

Women travelling alone or together will have to play things by ear most of the time, although we've given some pointers in the guide on places that are OK for foreign women. In general – although not always – ① hotels that are geared towards Western backpackers will be safe and welcoming for women; ① hotels that are for locals only should be avoided. However, even if you're watching every fils, it has to be said that the security and privacy on offer in slightly more pricey places have obvious advantages over coping with inquisitive late-night doorknob-rattlings or finding peeping toms in the communal showers.

Breakfast is never included in ① and ② hotels, and – counting as an optional extra – provides some bargaining leverage in hotels of ③ and above.

Mid-range hotels – in the ③, ④ and ⑤ brackets – are all generally clean and comfortable. However, Jordan has no grand, fading colonial-age piles to fall back on for a night or two of nostalgia; Amman's old *Philadelphia Hotel*, built in the 1920s, was bulldozed a decade or so back for redevelopment. Instead, a handful of ageing, well-worn and more or less characterless places compete with generic hordes of glitzy, shiny new establishments aimed squarely at visiting Arab families. Most of these mid-range places are in the ③ bracket; there are very few ④ and ⑤ options nationwide.

LUXURY HOTELS

Although there are plenty of ⑥ hotels dotted around the country catering mostly to groups (and so distinctly inflexible when it comes to independent travellers), the **luxury** end of the market is where value for money begins to reappear. An over-concentration of ⑦, ⑧ and ⑨ hotels nationwide means that, with prudent advance booking (which can bring you bed and breakfast for less than the room-only rack rate), you could quite easily bring the cost of a five-star splurge down to mid-four-star levels. Amman, in particular, has more five-star beds than it knows what to do with, although the city's hotels themselves are rather underwhelming: this is prime bargaining territory, but if money is truly no object and you want outstanding luxury at any price, you should consider eschewing Amman altogether for the *Petra Mövenpick* or *Taybet Zaman* (see p.238), both well ahead of anything the capital can offer.

FOOD AND DRINK

Arab tradition values home cooking much more than eating out, and consequently the bulk of Jordan's restaurants are simple places serving straightforward fare. Excellent restaurants do exist, but must be sought out; unadventurous travellers can easily find themselves stuck in a rut of low-quality *falafel* and kebabs, departing the country never having tasted the best of what's on offer. An incorrigible Palestinian sweet-tooth ensures a steady supply of sweets and pastries, and fresh fruit and vegetables – grown in the natural hothouse of the Jordan Valley – are luscious and tasty year-round.

More often than not, you'll be eating with your fingers. Since the **left hand** is used for toilet purposes, Jordanians instinctively always eat only with the **right**. Using your left hand while eating from a communal platter in someone's house would be considered unhygienic and possibly rude (see p.62 for more on this kind of etiquette), but in restaurant situations no one will be mortally offended if you use your left hand for a tricky shovelling or tearing manoeuvre. In most budget diners, the only **cutlery** you'll find will be a spoon, used for rice and soupy stews. Even where there is cutlery, flaps or pockets of flat bread count as knife and fork, for dipping, mopping up sauces and tearing meat off the bone.

Unlike other Middle Eastern countries, **hygiene** is rarely a problem in Jordan. Nowhere in the country can you avoid **tobacco smoke**, least of all in cafés and restaurants.

WHERE AND WHEN TO EAT

Where you choose to eat depends partly on your budget and partly on your expectations. The easiest way to escape the endless budget round of *hummus*, chicken and *falafel* – aside from plumping for cheap burgers-and-shakes – is to take refuge in big-hotel food, more often than not a reasonable set-price buffet with a range of salads and hot dishes. The sole restaurant in more out-of-the-way places might be a nameless, dingy den with a couple of pots of meat stew in the back and a chicken roastery on the street. Larger towns generally have a choice of restaurants serving the ubiquitous basic staples; Amman, Madaba and Petra are where you're most likely to find variety, and quality.

As far as **timing** goes, simple breakfasts are generally finished with by 8am. Lunches are eaten between 1 and 3pm, and you may come across many locals taking a break around 6pm for coffee and sweet pastries. The main meal of the day is eaten late, rarely before 8pm; in Amman and the north of the country, restaurants may not even start to fill up until 9.30 or 10pm. In keeping with the bedouin tradition of eating only at home, you'll find that even quite large towns in the bedouin heartland of southern Jordan (such as Madaba or Karak) have a bare handful of unim-

pressive, often empty restaurants that do a roaring trade in early-evening takeaways and close up by 8 or 9pm.

Throughout the guide, we've included **phone numbers** for restaurants where it's a good idea to book.

BREAKFAST AND STREET SNACKS

The traditional Jordanian **breakfast** is a bowl of hot *fuul* (boiled fava beans mashed with lemon juice, olive oil and chopped chillis), mopped up with fresh-baked *khobbez* (flat bread) – guaranteed to keep you going for hours. *Hummus*, a cold dip of boiled chickpeas blended with lemon juice, garlic, sesame and olive oil, is slightly less heavy, but harder to find first thing in the morning. Both *fuul* and *hummus* can be ordered to take away (*barra*) in plastic pots. Bakeries that have an open oven (*firin*) usually offer a whole selection of savoury pastries, including *khobbez bayd* (a kind of small egg pizza) and a range of bite-sized pastry triangles (*fttayer*) filled with cheese (*jibneh*), spinach (*sabanegh*), potato (*batata*) or meat (*lahmeh*). Larger bakeries also have a wide range of chunky breadsticks, sesame-seed bread rings (*kaak*), thick slabs of crunchy toast (*garshella*) and rough brown bread (*khobbez baladi*). Along with some olives (*zaytoon*) and yoghurt – either runny (*laban*) or creamy (*labneh*) – it's easy to put together a picnic breakfast. Where breakfast is included in budget **hotel** prices, you generally get

EATING DURING RAMADAN

For the whole month of **Ramadan** (see also p.48) Muslims are forbidden by both religious and civil law from **smoking** and from **eating or drinking** anything – including water, and, in strict interpretations, even saliva – during the hours of daylight. This is taken seriously enough that Jordanians who flagrantly break the fast in public can expect to be jailed until the end of the month. Throughout Ramadan, all restaurants and coffee-houses nationwide stay closed until dusk, and many choose to take the whole month off for renovations; any that do business, though, often stay open from sunset until the early hours. Markets, groceries and supermarkets, however, are open, with slightly truncated hours; they close for an hour or two around dusk to allow their staff to break the fast at home. It is illegal for supermar-

kets or restaurants to sell alcohol for the entire month. Businesses operated by Christians adopt the same practices.

For **foreigners**, nothing serious will happen if you inadvertently light up a cigarette in public, but the locals will not thank you for walking down the street munching a sandwich. All four- and five-star hotels serve both food and soft drinks to foreigners during daylight and also alcohol after dark, although you may find that they'll only do so in places out of public view; lobby or terrace coffee-shops may not serve you. If you're travelling on a tight budget and are buying picnic food for both breakfast and lunch, you'll need to exercise a good deal of tact during the day in eating either behind closed doors or out of sight in the countryside.

pretty poor fare, but larger hotels offer more substantial buffet choices.

The staple **street snack** in the Middle East is *falafel*, small balls of a spiced chickpea paste deep-fried and served stuffed into *khobbez* along with some salad, a blob of *tahini* (sesame-seed paste) and optional hot sauce (*harr*). You'll also find up and down the country *shwarma* stands, with a huge vertical spit outside to tempt in customers. *Shwarma* meat is almost always lamb (only occasionally chicken), slabs of it compressed into a distinctive inverted cone shape and topped with chunks of fat and tomatoes to percolate juices down through the meat as it cooks. When you order a *shwarma*, the cook will dip a *khobbez* into the fat underneath the spit and hold it against the flame until it crackles, then fill it with thin shavings of the meat and a little salad and hot sauce.

Prices are nominal. All over the country, bowls of *fuul* and *hummus* cost 280–300 fils and small baked nibbles 100–200 fils. Bread is sold by weight, with a kilo of large *khobbez* (about five pieces) 200 fils, small *khobbez* (about 11 pieces) 280 fils. *Falafel* sandwiches are 120–150 fils, *shwarma* sandwiches 250–280 fils.

RESTAURANT MEALS

The cheapest budget **diners** will generally only have one or two main dishes on view – roast chicken or *fuul* or stew with rice – but you can almost always get *hummus* and salad to fill out the meal. In better-quality **Arabic restaurants**, the usual way to eat is to order a whole variety of small starters (*mezze*), followed by either a selection of main courses to be shared by everyone, or a single, huge dish.

Good restaurants might have thirty different choices of **mezze**, from simple bowls of *hummus* or *labneh* up to dishes of fried chicken liver (*kibdet dajaj*) or wings (*jawaneh*). Universal favourites are *tabbouleh* (parsley salad), *fattoush* (salad garnished with squares of crunchy fried bread), *warag aynab* (vine leaves stuffed with rice, minced vegetables and often meat as well) and spiced olives. *Kibbeh* – the national dish of Syria and Lebanon and widely available at better Jordanian restaurants – is a mixture of cracked wheat, grated onion and minced lamb pounded to a paste; it's usually shaped into oval torpedoes and deep fried, though occasionally you can find it raw (*kibbeh nayeh*), a highly prized delicacy.

Portions are small enough that two people could share four or five *mezze* as a sizeable starter or, depending on your appetite, a complete meal. Bread and a few pickles are always free. *Mezze* are the best dishes for **vegetarians** to concentrate on, with enough grains, pulses and vegetables to make substantial and interesting meat-free meals that cost considerably less than standard meaty dishes. Virtually all of the *mezze* salads are **vegan**, as are filling dishes such as *mujeddrah* (lentils with rice and onions) and *mahshi* (cooked vegetables stuffed with rice).

Main courses are almost entirely meat-based. Any inexpensive diner can do half a chicken (*nuss faroodj*) with rice and salad. Kebabs are also ubiquitous (the chicken version is called *shish tawook*). Lots of places also do lunchtime meaty stews with rice; the most common is with beans (*fasooliyyeh*), although others feature potatoes or a spinach-like green called *mulukhayyah*. Jordan's national speciality is the traditional bedouin feast-dish of *mensaf* – chunks of boiled lamb or mutton served on a bed of fatty rice, with pine-nuts sprinkled on top and a tart, yoghurt-based sauce on the side to pour over. You'll also find some delicious Palestinian dishes, including *musakhan* (chicken steamed with onions and a sour-flavoured red berry called *sumak*) and *magloobeh* (essentially chicken-with-rice). A few places mainly in Amman and the north do a high-quality Syrian *fatteh* (meat or chicken cooked in an earthenware pot together with bread, rice, pine-nuts, yoghurt, herbs and *hummus*, with myriad variations). Good fish (*samak*) is rare in Jordan, most of it imported frozen from Yemen; Aqaba's few fish restaurants can't match the St Peter's fish served at the Pella Resthouse fresh from the River Jordan. Pork is forbidden under Islam and only appears at expensive Chinese restaurants in Amman.

We've given rough per-person **prices** for each restaurant listed in the guide, but in general, diners serving chicken, stew or kebabs won't charge you more than JD1.500 or so for a stomach-filling, if not a gourmet, experience. Plenty of Arabic and foreign restaurants in Amman and other corners of the country serve high-quality meals for JD5–8 per person. It's easily possible to dine sumptuously on *mezze* at even the most expensive restaurants in the country for less than JD10 per person, although meaty main courses and wine at these places can rapidly torpedo a bill into the JD30s per head without too much effort.

SWEETS

Inexpensive eateries rarely offer desserts. The traditional Jordanian way to round off a meal is with fresh fruit, but if you fancy something sweet, all large towns have plenty of patisseries for **Arabic sweets** (*halawiyyat*), where, if they have a seating area, you can also get a coffee. It's not unknown to take a few choice sweets away in a box to munch at a nearby coffee-house. However, a Western-bred, naughty-but-nice sweet-tooth lags well behind the heavy-duty Palestinian variety: most *halawiyyat* are packed with enough sugar, syrup, butter and honey to give a nutritionist the screaming horrors.

There are three broad categories of sweets: large round trays of hot, fresh-made confections, often **grain-based**, which are sliced into squares and drenched in hot syrup; piles of pre-prepared, bite-sized honey-dripping **pastries** and cakes; and stacks of dry sesame-seed or date-filled **biscuits**. The best of the hot sweets made in trays is *k'naffy*, a heavenly Palestinian speciality of buttery shredded filo pastry layered over melted goat's cheese. *Baglawa* – layered flaky pastry filled with pistachios or other nuts – is available in any number of different varieties. Juice-stands often lay out tempting trays of *hareeseh*, a syrupy semolina almond-cake, sliced into individual portions. Of the biscuits, you'd have to go a long way to beat *maamoul*, buttery, crumbly rose-scented things with a date or nut filling. Everything is sold by weight, and you can pick and choose a mixture: a quarter-kilo (*wagiyyeh*) – depending on your choice but rarely more than JD1.500 – is plenty for two.

Large restaurants and some patisseries also have **milk-based** sweets, often flavoured deliciously with rosewater and no less sweet than anything else. King of these is *mahalabiyyeh*, a semi-set almond cream pudding served in individual bowls, but the Egyptian speciality *Umm Ali* – served hot, sprinkled with nuts and cinnamon – runs a close second.

For seasonal treats, extra-sweet, curiously elastic **ice-cream** is a summer standard around the country; Aqaba has the best range and quality. A common sight during Ramadan is for bakeries and patisseries to make stacks of fresh *gatayyif* – traditional **pancakes** – on hotplates set up on the street; locals buy dozens of them for stuffing at home with nuts and syrup.

FRESH FRUIT AND PICNIC FOOD

Street markets all over the country groan with stacks of **fresh fruit** year-round, including apples from Shawbak and oranges, mandarins and bananas from Gaza and the Jordan Valley. Local bananas are smaller, blacker and sweeter than the giant baseball-bat clones imported from Latin America. In the late spring, Fhays produces boxes of luscious peaches. Local grapes – green, red and black but none seedless – come from the Balqa and Palestine. Jordan is also one of the principal markets for exquisite Iraqi dates, which are available stoned and packed all year. The best time to look out for fresh dates is in late autumn, when you'll also see mountains of small, yellow-orange fruit often still on the branch; these are *balah*, sweet, crunchy unripe dates that never make it to the West. Around the same time, pomegranates appear everywhere, while spring and summer are the season for local melon and watermelon. As far as picnic **vegetables** go, carrots, tomatoes and cucumbers are year-round staples.

For picnic supplements, most towns have a good range of stalls or mobile vendors selling **dried fruit** and roasted **nuts and seeds**. Raisins, sultanas, dried figs and dried apricots can all be found cheaply everywhere. The most popular kind of seeds are *bizr* (dry-roasted melon, watermelon or sunflower seeds), the cracking of which in order to get at the minuscule kernel is an acquired skill. Local almonds (*luz*) – at around JD2 per quarter-kilo – are delectable. Pistachios and roasted chickpeas are locally produced; peanuts, hazelnuts and cashews are imported. It's often possible to buy individual **hard-boiled eggs** from neighbourhood groceries, and varieties of the local salty white **cheese** are available everywhere.

TEA, COFFEE AND OTHER DRINKS

The main focus of every Jordanian village, town and city neighbourhood is a **coffee-house**, where friends and neighbours meet, gossip does the rounds and a quiet moment can be had away from the family. The musicians, poets and storytellers of previous generations have been replaced everywhere by taped music and football on the TV, although a genial, sociable ambience survives. However, all are exclusively male domains and bastions of social tradition; foreign women will always be served without hesitation, but sometimes might feel uncomfortably watched.

The national drink, lubricating every social occasion, is **tea** (*shy*), a strong, dark brew served scalding hot and milk-less in small glasses. The traditional method of tea-making is to boil up loose leaves in a pot together with several spoons of sugar to allow maximum flavour infusion. In deference to foreign taste-buds, you may find the sugar being left to your discretion, but the tannins in steeped tea are so lip-curlingly bitter that you'll probably prefer the Jordanian way. Coffee (*gah-weh*), another national institution, has two broad varieties. **Turkish coffee** is what you'll come across most often. Made by boiling up cardamom-flavoured grounds in a distinctive long-handled pot, then letting it cool, then re-boiling it several times (traditionally seven, though in practice two suffices), it's served in small cups along with a glass of water as chaser. Sugar is added before-hand, so you should request your coffee unsweet-ened (*saada*), medium-sweet (*wassat*) or syrupy (*helweh*); let the grounds settle before sipping, and leave the last mouthful, which is mud, behind. The best coffee comes rich and pitch-black from the twin silver pots of mobile vendors, found on street corners and highway shoulders nationwide. **Arabic coffee** – also known as bedouin coffee – is an entirely different, almost greenish liquid, unsweetened and pleasantly bit-ter, traditionally made in a long-spouted brass pot set in hot embers. Public coffee-houses don't have it, and you'll only be served it in a social sit-uation by bedouin themselves.

Coffee-houses also serve soft drinks and a wide range of **herbal teas**, including –depending on the season –mint, fennel, fenugreek, thyme, sage and camomile. In colder seasons, you'll also come across the winter-warmer **sahleb**, a thick milky drink made from a ground orchid tuber and served very hot sprinkled with nuts, cinnamon and coconut. A coffee-house is also the place to try a tobacco-filled water-pipe, known by different names around the Arab world but most familiarly in Jordan as a "**hubbly-bubbly**", *arjileh* or *argileh*. The unadulterated tobacco is pretty rough, but most places do sweeter varieties flavoured with apple or honey.

Bottles of local **mineral water** are available in all corners of the country (see p.21 for advice on tap water). All brands have the price printed on the bottle, a standard 1.5-litre size costing 290 fils (although you pay a premium in out-of-the-way places – as much as JD1 inside Petra). Check that the seal is unbroken before you buy. Inexpensive diners always have jugs of tap-water (*my aadi*) on the table, but in restaurants waiters will quite often bring a bottle of mineral water (normally JD1) to your table with the menu – which you're quite entitled to reject.

FRESH JUICE AND SQUASH

Benefiting from the wealth of local fresh fruit, most Jordanian towns have at least one stand-up **juice-bar**; these are great places for supple-menting a meagre breakfast or just replenishing your vitamin C. Any fruit in view can be juiced or puréed. Sugar (*sukkr*) and ice (*taj*) are automati-cally added to almost everything; however, con-sidering ice blocks are generally wheeled in filthy trolleys along the roadside and broken up with a screwdriver, you might like to give it a miss – if so, request your juice *bidoon taj*. "Without sugar" is *bidoon sukkr*. Most fresh-squeezed juices, and each stall's own juice cocktail, cost 300–350 fils for a "small" glass (actually quite big), double for a pint. Exceptions are mango, strawberry and other exotic fruit, which cost a little more.

More popular – and thus easier to find – are much cheaper ready-made **fruit squashes**. Dark-brown *tamarhindi* (tamarind, tartly refreshing) and *kharoub* (carob, sweet-but-sour), or watery *limoon* (lemon squash) are the best bets; other, less common, choices include *soos* (made from liquorice root, also dark brown, supposedly medi-cinal and horribly bitter) and *luz* (sickly sweet white almond-milk). All are 50 fils a glass.

Juice-bars are happy to fill an empty 1.5-litre plastic bottle with any quantity of juice or squash to take away.

ALCOHOL

Alcohol is forbidden under Islam, and yet for a 94-percent Muslim country, led by a royal dynasty tracing its lineage from the Prophet Muhammad himself, it's surprisingly easy to get a drink in Jordan. Having said that, you have to look for it: the market streets and diners of most towns in the country show no evidence of the stuff at all. Apart from those in big hotels, the only **restau-rants** to offer alcohol are upscale establishments in Amman and Aqaba (Arabic and non-Arabic), resthouses at archeological sites nationwide and a couple of divey joints in Petra. You'll generally be able to find **liquor stores** only in Amman, Aqaba, Madaba and Fhays.

A FOOD AND DRINK GLOSSARY

Basic stomach-fillers

khobbez	flat, round bread	hummus	dip of chickpeas mashed with *tahini*, lemon juice, garlic and olive oil
falafel	spiced chickpea mixture, deep fried; stuffed into *khobbez* with salad to make a *sandweedj* (sandwich)	mana'eesh zaatar	small round of dough sprinkled with olive oil and *zaatar* (a mixture of dried thyme, marjoram, salt and sesame seeds), and baked until crispy
shwarma	shreds of lamb or chicken in *khobbez*		
fuul	spiced fava beans, mashed with lemon juice, olive oil and chopped chillis; side dishes include raw onion (*basal*), fresh mint and/or pickled vegetables	batatas	potatoes; by extension, french fries
		tahini	sesame-seed paste
		rooz	rice
fuul masri	blander Egyptian-style *fuul*; without chilli but served with a dollop of *tahini* instead		

Restaurant appetizers (*mezze*)

shorba(t addas)	(lentil) soup	labneh	thick set yoghurt, similar to sour cream
s'laata	salad; chopped tomato and cucumber, invariably without lettuce	shanklish	goat's cheese chopped with onion and tomato
tabbouleh	parsley and tomato salad with cracked wheat	warag aynab	stuffed vine leaves
fattoush	Lebanese dish: salad with chopped parsley and squares of crispy fried bread	kibbeh	ovals of spiced minced meat and cracked wheat
		sujuk	fried spicy mini-sausages
		mahshi	"stuffed"; by extension, a selection of stuffed vegetables such as peppers and aubergines
baba ghanouj	dip made from roasted mashed aubergine		
moutabbel	*baba ghanouj* with added *tahini*	makdoos	pickled aubergine

The main course

mensaf	boiled lamb or mutton on rice with a tangy yoghurt-based sauce, pine-nuts and spices	kebab halaby	Syrian speciality: spiced minced meat char-grilled like a kebab
musakhan	chicken steamed with onions, *sumak* (a lemon-flavoured berry) and pine-nuts, served on flat bread	shish tawook	marinated chicken kebab
		fatteh	spiced meat or chicken baked with rice, *hummus*, pine nuts, yoghurt or bread
magloobeh	literally "upside-down": Palestinian dish of chicken on steamed rice with strips of grilled vegetables	mulukhayyah	lamb or chicken stewed with a spinach-like vegetable
		fasooliyyeh	bean stew, often with chunks of meat or in a meat broth
(nuss) faroodj	(half-) chicken; usually spit-roasted	mujeddrah	Palestinian dish of lentils, rice and onions
kebab	pieces of lamb or chicken chargrilled on a skewer with onions and tomatoes	Daoud Pasha	meat balls stewed with onions and tomatoes
		lahmeh	meat

jadj	chicken-meat	samak	fish
kharouf	mutton or lamb	khootdar	vegetables
idjel	beef	zayt	oil
khanzir	pork	melleh	salt
kibdeh	liver	filfil	pepper
kelaawy	kidney		

Arabic sweets (halawiyyat)

k'naffy	shredded-wheat squares filled with goat cheese, smothered in hot honey syrup	Umm Ali	slice of corn cake soaked in milk, sugar, raisins, coconut and cinnamon, served hot
baglawa	layered flaky pastry with nuts	maamoul	rose-scented biscuits filled with dates or nuts
gatayyif	pancakes filled with nuts and drenched in syrup	barazik	thin sesame biscuits
fttayer	triangles of flaky pastry with different fillings	awameh	syrup-coated deep-fried balls of dough
hareeseh	syrupy almond and semolina cake	asabya zaynab	syrupy figs
		mushabbak	crunchy honey-coated pastries
mahalabiyyeh	rose-scented almond cream pudding	karabeedj halaby	sugar-coated curlies
		rooz b'laban	rice pudding with yoghurt
		halwa	dense, flaky sweet made from sesame

Drinks and fruits (fawakeh)

my	water	tfah	apple
gahweh	coffee	njas	pear
shy	tea	grayfroot	grapefruit
naana/yansoon	mint/fennel (tea)	jezer	carrot
zaatar/helbeh	thyme/fenugreek (tea)	manga	mango
marrameeya	sage (tea)	jowaffah	guava
babbohnidj	camomile (tea)	dourrag	peach
sahleb	thick, sweet, milky winter drink	limoon	lemon (also drink)
		aynab	grapes
haleeb	milk	karaz	cherries
tamarhindi	tamarind drink	rumaan	pomegranate
kharoub	carob drink	mishmish	apricot
soos	liquorice-root drink	teen	fig
luz	sweet almond-milk	battikh	watermelon
aseer/koktayl	juice/juice cocktail	shimmam	melon
mooz	banana	balah	crunchy unripe dates
boordan	orange	tamar	soft ripe dates

Nuts, seeds and simple provisions

foustoug	peanuts	zaytoon	olives
foustoug halaby	pistachios	jibneh	cheese
boondoog	hazelnuts	laban	yoghurt
luz	almonds	zabadi	high-fat yoghurt with cream
kashoo	cashews	zibdeh	butter
bizr	dry-roasted seeds	assal	honey
zbeeb	raisins	marrabeh	jam
bayd	eggs		

Drinking alcohol in public – which includes on the street, in cafés or coffee-houses, in hotel lobbies, on the beach or even in the seemingly empty desert or countryside – is completely unacceptable and will cause great offence to local people. Places to drink are limited to your own hotel room, areas such as poolsides within hotel precincts, and restaurants or bars that offer alcohol on the menu.

The predominant local **beer** is Amstel, brewed under licence and very palatable; local Henninger is better but rarer. Both come in 650ml bottles, for which liquor stores charge around JD1 (200 fils of which is a returnable deposit), Amman's upmarket bars as much as JD3. There's quite a range of Jordanian and Palestinian **wines**, both marketed as "Holy Land". The best in both red and white comes from Latroun, although Bethlehem's Crémisan runs a close second. Mount Nebo whites, although winning no prizes, have a certain chilled appeal. The best local wines are generally JD4–6, imported European bottles much more. As for **spirits**, the top local choice is anis-flavoured *araq*, much like Turkish *raki* and generally drunk with water over ice during a meal. A bottle of high-quality Lebanese *araq* will set you back JD13 or so, more than most imported whiskies, gins and vodkas.

BUSINESS HOURS AND PUBLIC HOLIDAYS

In common with all Arab countries, Jordan has a six-day working week, with all offices and many shops closed on Fridays. If somebody tells you a particular attraction is open "every day", quite often they mean every day except Friday. Some Christian-run businesses also close on Sundays.

Normal **shop** opening-hours are roughly 8 or 9am to 8 or 9pm; in more out-of-the-way districts they often close around 6pm. Some places might close for two or three hours in the middle of the afternoon, and it can be hard to find anything open for the hour or two either side of midday prayers on Fridays. Prime shopping hours in town-centre **markets** tend to be from 6pm onwards, and most of them are open and bustling on Fridays. For advice on café and restaurant mealtimes, see p.42.

Banks tend to be open from 8.30am to about 12.30pm; some also open again from about 4 to 5.30pm. All banks are closed on Fridays, except one in the airport. Normal **post office** hours are from 7 or 8am until 6 or 7pm, and quite often between 8am and 1pm on Fridays as well. **Government departments** keep standard hours of 8am to 2pm, closed on Fridays.

Where **archeological sites** have controlled opening hours, these are generally from 8am to dusk, seven days a week. Many sites, though, either have open access or are watched over by a *haris* (guardian), who will live on or close to the site and will open up as you approach. Government-run **museums** tend to open daily except Tuesday and Friday from 9am to 5pm; some, though, open on Fridays from 10am to 4pm.

All **transport services** operate seven days a week.

During **Ramadan**, the Muslim holy month of fasting, everything changes. Shops, museums and offices open from 9am to about 2 or 3pm (closed on Fridays), while street markets do business

FIXED PUBLIC HOLIDAYS

January 15	Tree Day
March 22	Arab League Day
May 1	Labour Day
May 25	Independence Day
June 10	Army Day (also celebration of the Arab Revolt)
August 11	King Hussein's Accession
November 14	King Hussein's Birthday
December 25	Christmas Day

PUBLIC HOLIDAYS

Jordan's **secular national holidays** tend to be low-key affairs, involving either limited local celebrations or military parades in the capital; although government offices are closed, shops and businesses quite often open as normal and you could easily not notice the holiday at all.

The handful of **Islamic religious holidays**, based on the Hijra calendar, are another matter, though, and are marked by widespread public observance. All shops and offices are closed and non-essential services are liable to be suspended. Jordan's **Christians** are mostly Orthodox and follow the Julian calendar, which varies from the Gregorian calendar used in the West by a couple of weeks. Nevertheless, the different Christian communities have all agreed to celebrate Christmas Day together on December 25, and since 1994 that date has been marked as a national public holiday (although Muslim shops and businesses are open as normal). See p.331 for more information about Islamic religious holidays.

every day but close up about half-an-hour before sunset. Banks and government departments may only be open for two or three hours in the morning. Some large supermarkets and a few shops might also open again for a couple of hours after dark. Large archeological sites such as Petra keep more or less normal hours, but guardians of smaller sites will want to lock up and get home an hour or so before sunset. Similarly, famished bus and *service* drivers take time off around sunset to break the fast.

FORTHCOMING ISLAMIC HOLIDAYS

The following dates are very approximate, since each holiday is announced only when the moon has been seen clearly by an authorized cleric from Jordan's Ministry of Islamic Affairs – each date could vary by several days in practice. If you're travelling close to these dates and want more detailed information, the most reliable source is your local mosque.

	1998	1999	2000	2001
Ramadan begins (30 days)	Dec 20	Dec 10	Dec 1	Nov 21
Eid al-Fitr begins (3 days)	–	Jan 19	Jan 9 & Dec 31	Dec 21
Eid al-Adha begins (4 days)	–	March 27	March 17	March 7
Ras as-Senneh (Muslim New Year)	–	April 18	April 8	March 29
Mowlid an-Nabawi (birthday of the Prophet Muhammad)	–	June 28	June 18	June 8

POST, PHONES AND EMAIL

In the last couple of years, Jordan's communications have improved dramatically. Post abroad is generally reliable, although it may take weeks to reach its destination. You can in theory dial internationally from most touristed parts of the country, but connections are neither guaranteed nor reliable outside Amman, and charges are sky-high. The capital also has a handful of cybercafés offering Internet access and email capability.

POST

Airmail **letters and postcards** can take anything up to two weeks to reach Western Europe from Jordan, a month to the USA or Australasia. Asking someone to write the destination country in Arabic can help avoid things going astray. It's safest to ignore the street post-boxes and instead send your mail from larger post offices, all of which have a box for airmail (*barid jowwy*) marked in English. To Europe, stamps (*tawabe'a*) for postcards currently cost 200 fils, for letters up to 10g 300 fils; to North America and Australasia postcards are 300 fils, letters 400 fils. If you're unlucky enough to have to send anything larger than a letter, you should come financially well-prepared. Sending a **small packet** of 1kg to Europe costs JD6.800, to North America or Australasia JD9. **Parcel post** is horribly expensive: 2kg to the UK costs JD12.900, to North America JD16.500 and to Australasia a mighty JD20.900.

Incoming mail (at least to Amman) is somewhat faster than outgoing – things can arrive in a matter of days from Europe. Mail addressed to you at "Poste Restante, Amman 11118" will drop into the little tray outside window 11 at the Downtown post office – you're free to riffle through the tray whenever you like. Mail addressed to you at "Poste Restante, Aqaba 77110" might get through … but then again it might end up in Amman instead. Poste restante to any other town is unlikely to show up. Bulky envelopes or packets sent to a poste restante address will be stored out of sight, with a small slip with the addressee's name left in the tray instead; show the slip (and your passport) to collect your package. The Amex office in Amman (see p.30) will keep mail for Amex customers (ie you only have to be holding Amex travellers' cheques) sent to PO Box 408, Amman 11118.

International **courier** firms are well represented in Jordan, most of them with offices in Amman and Aqaba. Prices are sky-high (for example, JD45 for 500g to the US), but there's no danger of items going astray.

PHONES

Since the first concrete steps were taken to privatize the Jordan Telecommunications Company (JTC) in 1994, **phone** service and connections have improved slightly, but JTC currently still retains a monopoly over land-lines, and prices are outrageously high. Although mobile phone calls are also overpriced, going to an unofficial "international communications bureau" that uses mobile phones can occasionally save dinars on official JTC rates. All towns and cities have a **telephone office** from which you can call abroad, and some have unofficial bureaux too (generally close by), but you're much more likely to get a reasonable connection and reasonable prices from Amman than from anywhere else. There's quite likely to be some hanging around wherever you try, unless you opt for the convenience of public **cardphones**, of which there are currently two types. Phones operated by Alo are all over most towns; JPP ones are less common. Phonecards are generally sold at nearby shops, but can't be used interchangeably, so it's generally better to stick to the more widespread Alo.

USEFUL NUMBERS IN JORDAN

International operator	☎0132
International directory enquiries	☎0135
Domestic operator	☎0131
Domestic directory enquiries	☎121 or
	☎06/464 0444

The **dialling tone** is a familiar low-pitched buzz or hum. If, after you dial, you get three persistent rising tones, a steady series of even-pitched tones, a continuous whine, a crackly message or silence, it means your number was **unobtainable** for some reason. Check the number is right and dial again: connections are hit-and-miss enough that you could quite easily get through next time.

INTERNATIONAL CALLS

Most of the time, if you make a call from an official JTC office or an unofficial bureau, you just write down the number you want and the clerk dials for you. If you need to **dial** an international call yourself, first dial the international access code – 00 – and the relevant country code: 44 for the UK; 1 for Canada and the US; 61 for Australia; 64 for New Zealand; 353 for Ireland. Connections can take up to thirty seconds to come through, so hang on until you get some kind of result.

Official JTC offices have four **price brackets**: during the day, one minute to Europe, the USA or Canada currently costs JD1.480; to Australasia and Africa JD1.650; to Arab countries 770 fils; and to Syria, Saudi Arabia or Iraq 550 fils. A **cheap-rate** period on international calls operates from 10pm to 8am and all day on Fridays, when prices drop to JD1.040, JD1.155, 539 fils and 385 fils respectively. However, you should bear in mind that all JTC offices have a three-minute minimum charge; it's only the unofficial places that allow you to pay by the minute, and you can shop around between them to get a good deal. From a hotel, connections are no more guaranteed than from a phone in the street, but you could quite easily find a 100 percent – or higher – surcharge slapped on top of the official rates.

You can dial anywhere in the world direct from Alo **phone booths**, but you need a JD15 card to do it (the JD3 ones are good for domestic calls only). Pressing the button marked i switches the display from Arabic to English.

It is impossible to make any kind of reverse-charge call, credit-card call or "home country direct" call from Jordan. Since the peace treaty you can dial direct between Jordan and the 972 country code which covers Israel and Israeli- and Palestinian-administered territories.

DOMESTIC CALLS

It can quite often be easier to call around the world than to call long-distance within Jordan – and line-clarity can often be better too. Every town apart from remote outposts can be dialled direct – Azraq is the largest town where all calls must first be routed through local operators.

Although the new Alo cardphone booths are proving popular, the time-honoured method of making public calls in most places in Jordan is with rotary-dial phones connected to **coin-boxes** – even the smallest town will most likely have at least one of these contraptions, probably in a restaurant or grocery shop. The first thing is to ask somebody what kind of coin it takes; some take only the old-style 100 fils coins, others take only the new-style ten piastre coins. Whichever it is, it generally buys you a three-minute local call, with long-distance calls (if they're even possible) proportionately more. There'll be silence when you lift the handset; to work these machines, first you have to rest your coin in the round hole and slide the slider along in order to get a dialling tone (you won't lose your coin). The domestic **ringing tone** is similar to the US – one-second bursts of tone separated by four seconds of silence. If there's no reply, just slide the slider back again and retrieve your coin. If someone does answer, you have to hit the red button (which knocks the coin down into the coin-box) in order to be heard.

With no particular rhyme, reason or speed, the domestic phone system is currently being **re-numbered** district by district: you may find that some phone numbers listed in this guide will have changed by the time you visit Jordan. At the time of writing, most (but not all) phone numbers in Amman, Aqaba, Petra and the north have seven digits, although Madaba, Karak, Irbid and other towns around the country still have six digits, and all mobile numbers (prefix ☎079) have five digits. Messages in English and Arabic let you know if the number you're trying to reach has been updated; if it has, dial domestic directory enquiries (see the box above) to ask for the new number.

CALLING JORDAN FROM ABROAD

First dial your **international access code** (00 from the UK, Ireland and New Zealand; 011 from the US and Canada; 0011 from Australia), followed by **962** for Jordan, then the Jordanian area code minus its initial zero, then the five-, six- or seven-digit subscriber number.

FAXES, TELEGRAMS AND TELEXES

Fax machines are widespread and knowledge of them is pretty good, but whether you can get a clear enough line for international fax transmission is a different story. Official JTC offices don't have the facilities for sending or receiving faxes; instead, you should go to the unofficial communications bureaux, who often charge a small surcharge per page on top of the usual phone rates. It's also worth checking out computer offices, many of whom offer an **email-to-fax** service at a fraction of paper rates.

Larger JTC offices have facilities for sending **telegrams**, which cost around 100 fils per word, depending on the destination country. JTC offices and five-star hotels generally also have the capacity to send and receive **telexes**.

EMAIL

The communications revolution is starting to be felt in Jordan: there are currently six Jordanian **Internet** service providers and – in the hipper urban centres at least – **email** and the Internet are becoming familiar.

Amman has well over a dozen cybercafés on top of the handful of impersonal business centres offering access. It's now also possible to connect from small computer offices in towns around the country: some ISPs have local nodes nationwide, which can keep prices reasonable, but quite often you'll find that you have to dial Amman to get online, which pushes up hourly rates quite significantly. Even in Amman, prices to connect are much higher than in the West, and connections much slower. PCs are everywhere; Macs are rarer than hen's teeth. None of the large international providers, such as CompuServe or America Online, currently has points of presence in Jordan.

Even if you're carrying your own **laptop** or palmtop and have all the necessary paraphernalia to connect, you might still encounter some problems. The most striking will be suspicion of such technology: reading about the Internet in the newspaper is one thing, but seeing a foreigner pull out a black box and a bunch of wires is too sinister for many ordinary people to take, and if you do so without warning in a phone office full of Iraqis and Syrians you may find the room emptying around you. Aside from that, phone bureaux, cybercafés and even the five-star hotels' business centres quite often rely on incomprehensible tangles of phone-wire spaghetti culminating in **hard-wired** wall connections, which leave you nowhere to plug in (Amman's *Inter-Continental Hotel* is an honourable exception). Before you travel, check out the website *kropla.com* for invaluable information on how to proceed. Where there are sockets, you'll generally find either a US-style **RJ-11** or Jordan's own style of two-pin socket. Adaptors to allow you to use an RJ-11 plug can be easily had, but ones for the wider British-style phone plug are more elusive. More significant technical problems may come in getting your modem to recognize the low-pitched Jordanian **dialtone**: you may need to get advice before you leave home on how to disable your modem's dialtone recognition facility so that it will dial without requiring recognition. The website *www.road-news.com* has general information for laptop-carrying travellers.

FREE EMAIL

The following websites are of a selection of companies which provide individuals with free, secure email addresses in return for their putting up with a lot of advertising. Email sent to these addresses can be picked up via the World Wide Web in Jordan, and some of these companies can also automatically divert email to any named account.

www.backpackers.com	*www.hotmail.com*	*www.rocketmail.com*
www.bigfoot.com		*mail.yahoo.com*

THE MEDIA

With the widespread use of English in public life, you'll have relatively good access to news and information while in Jordan. International newspapers and magazines all pass through the hands of the censor but tend to survive largely unscathed, and local English-language offerings are readable if a little over-worthy. Satellite TV is fairly widespread throughout the country.

FOREIGN AND LOCAL PRESS

In Amman at least, **foreign newspapers** and news magazines are widely available – from the Jordan Distribution Agency, *Books@Café* and all big hotels. The *International Herald Tribune* (JD1.250) and all British dailies (JD1.500–2) and Sundays (JD2.500–4) are generally one or two days late. Enough **magazines** are available – from *Cosmopolitan* to *The Economist* – to satisfy most tastes (the marker-pen scribble you'll discover obliterating photos of nudity is the work of the official censor). Outside Amman, foreign newspapers and magazines are available only in Aqaba.

Amongst the conservative and often state-owned **Arabic press**, Jordan's newspapers, all of which are independently owned, have – or had – a reputation for well-informed debate and relative outspokenness; had, that is, until a controversial 1997 amendment to the press law, passed by royal decree just months before an election, which effectively forced all the wackier opposition tabloid weeklies out of business, leaving only the government line to survive on the newsstands. Early in 1998 – handily enough, just after the election – the Supreme Court ruled the amendment to be unconstitutional, and some of the tabloids resurfaced, but frequent arrests of journalists, media blackouts on sensitive court cases and continuing pressure from the Ministry of Information not to present Jordan in a bad light significantly limit press freedom. The two biggest **dailies**, *ad-Dustour* ("Constitution") and *al-Ra'i* ("Opinion"), are both centrist regurgitators of government opinion. *al-Arab al-Yom* ("Arabs Today"), which was launched in 1997, is more populist and free-thinking, prepared, unlike the biggies, to back the opposition where necessary. *al-Aswaq* ("Markets") serves the business and financial

community. Of the **weeklies**, one of the most popular is the satirical *Abd Rabbo* ("Slave of His God"), the editor of which is often thrown in jail. *Shihan* is a hugely popular and sensationalist tabloid weekly. Amongst a plethora of other rags, Islamist opinion is expressed most cogently in *al-Sabeel* ("Path"), the unofficial mouthpiece of the Muslim Brotherhood.

As far as **local English-language press** goes, the choice is not wide. The establishment *Jordan Times* is published daily except Fridays and features several pages of agency reports, mingled with local news and rather ropily written conservative comment; the outstanding exceptions are the weekly columns of political analysis and occasional features on Jordan's archeological heritage written by leading journalist Rami Khouri. The paper is also a useful source of what's-on information, emergency phone numbers and flat-hunting ads. *The Star* – published every Thursday – tends to be more independently minded than the *Times* and is often a better read. The best English-language paper in the Arab World, regularly featuring the likes of Edward Said and Naguib Mahfouz, is *Al-Ahram Weekly*, published in Cairo and available only at the Jordan Distribution Agency. Other than that, there's only the monthly *Jordan Today* worth bothering with, a free pocket-sized guide for visitors with a few feature articles and some useful information. Of all of these, only the *Jordan Times* is available outside Amman, in a handful of outlets in Aqaba, Irbid and Wadi Musa.

TV AND RADIO

Jordanian TV – recently freed from state control – isn't up to much, and is regularly slated in the press for its appalling programming. Channel 1 is all in Arabic and relies heavily on reports of the king's official engagements and grippingly dramatic bedouin soaps (all glaring eyes, bushy beards and hands-on-daggers). The turgid English-language Channel 2 features mostly US shows – kids' stuff, light soaps and generic TV movies – with the main nightly news in English at 10pm. A new Channel 3 started up in 1998, concentrating on sport and cultural events. Most aerials will also pick up Syrian and Egyptian TV, for what they're worth, as well as a channel or two of glitzy Israeli TV, often showing watchable American movies and British drama.

Many hotels – large and small – have **satellite TV**, but whereas *CNN* can be had almost everywhere, most of the other available channels are not in English. *Dubai TV* features some English news. Other Arab, Turkish, French and German channels fill up the rest of the buttons, although it's occasionally possible to find *MTV India* airing the latest videos out of Mumbai, or D-list celeb interviews on *NBC Europe*. *BBC World TV* – although in theory available throughout Jordan – in practice never turns up anywhere outside the British Council in Amman.

As for **radio**, *Radio Jordan*'s English station is on 855kHz medium wave nationwide and 96.3FM (Amman) or 99FM (Aqaba), but features an unrelieved diet of pop music and diabolically bad DJs. English news is at 7am, 2pm, 7pm and 10pm. The taxi-drivers' favourite is *MBC* –a Saudi station

based in London – which has excellent Arabic music on 106.7FM (Amman); also check out *Radio Monte Carlo* on 97.4FM (Amman). *Radio Jordan*'s French service has classical music on 90FM (Amman). Israeli Army Radio on 576kHz MW plays hours of classic rock after midnight; and the Israeli music station *Reshet Gimel* pumps cool tunes to Aqaba on 100.5FM. After dark, medium wave is crammed with all shades of Arabic music out of Amman, Jerusalem and Cairo.

BBC World Service can be difficult to pick up in Amman's deep valleys; elsewhere it's generally pretty clear. Find it between 6am and 2am on 1323kHz medium wave; also on short wave at 9.410, 12.095, 15.575 or 17.640MHz. The BBC's Arabic service is on 103.1FM (Amman) and 639kHz MW. *The Voice of America* broadcasts on short wave at 15.205 in the morning and 9.760 in the evening. *Radio Australia* is on short wave at 15.530 and 17.880 in the morning and 7.330 in the evening.

SHOPPING FOR CRAFTS

Unlike Syria, Palestine and Egypt, the trading history of Jordan mostly revolves around goods passing through rather than being produced; no city within the boundaries of modern Jordan has ever come close to matching the craftsmanship on display in the workshops and bazaars of Aleppo, Damascus, Jerusalem and Cairo. Traditionally, people in Jordan have simply made whatever they needed for themselves – carpets, jugs, jewellery – without their skills being noticed or valued by outside buyers. Today, although a handful of individual outlets (almost exclusively in Amman) sell local and imported crafts, Jordan has no craft bazaars. You may come across items of aesthetic value here and there, but your chances of picking up bargain antiques are very small, and any that you might come across almost certainly originate from outside Jordan. For the record, Jordanian law forbids the purchase of any item dating from before 1700.

EMBROIDERY AND WEAVING

The field where Transjordanian people have the strongest tradition is in **hand-embroidered tex-**

tiles, although up to a few decades ago, such fabrics tended to stay within the confines of the town producing them and generally never came onto the open market. Embroidered jackets, dresses and cushion-covers are now available everywhere, in both traditional and modern styles, but relatively few are high-quality, hand-made items.

Wool and goat- and camel-hair have been used since time immemorial to **weave** tents, carpets, rugs, cushions, even food-storage containers, for family use. For the past couple of decades or so, local and international development projects – Save The Children among them – have been involved in nurturing traditional bedouin weaving; by doing so, and by establishing retail outlets in Amman and elsewhere for the sale of woven items, they have managed to rejuvenate a dying craft, and simultaneously create extra sources of income for the weavers, mostly rural women. The quality of **carpets**, **rugs** and home furnishings produced under these various projects is first-rate, although prices are concomitantly very high. The older, more traditional colours – deep reds, navy blues, greens, oranges and blacks – as well as the traditional styles of stripes and diamonds, are being augmented these days by brighter, chemically dyed colours and more modern patterns, to appeal to a new, Western-inspired clientele.

A more affordable woven craft is **weaving with straw**, bamboo or palm-fronds to produce baskets, trays, mats and wall-hangings.

JEWELLERY, METALWORK, WOOD AND GLASS

Many Jordanians have inherited their parents' and grandparents' preference – stemming partly from previous generations' nomadic existence, and partly from a rural mistrust of urban institutions – for investing their money in **jewellery** rather than in banks. Until very recently, bedouin brides wore their personal wealth in silver jewellery, and retained the right throughout their married lives to do with it what they wanted, husband's wishes notwithstanding. Owning jewellery was – and still is – something of a safety net for women against the possibility of abandonment, divorce or widowhood.

Traditionally, the bedouin much prefer **silver** to gold – indeed, it's just about impossible to find genuine old gold in Jordan. The **Gold Souq** –a collection of tiny modern jewellery shops all huddled together in a few Downtown Amman alleys – is slick and soulless, geared entirely towards serious local buyers and with very limited browsing potential; here, prices on gold and silver are much lower than in the West (they sell by weight), but everything is imported and of mostly uninspired generic modern design.

If you're after more distinctive jewellery, you should be aware that, although there are a few Jordanian designers producing new, hand-made items, practically all the new jewellery you'll see in craft shops has been imported from Turkey, India or Italy. Chunky **bedouin jewellery** that looks old generally turns out to have been made no more than sixty years ago, and much old "silver" is in fact a mix of eighty percent silver and twenty percent copper. Practically all the "old" necklaces on offer were strung relatively recently on nylon thread using stones and silver beads from long-dispersed older originals. However,

none of this detracts from the fact that beautiful and unique items are available; especially striking are necklaces that combine silver beads with beads of coloured glass, **amber** or semi-precious stones. Different stones have different significances: blue stones protect the wearer from the evil eye, white stones stimulate lactation during breastfeeding, and so on. You might also find rare Circassian **enamelwork**, dramatically adding to a silver bracelet or necklace's charm. However, note that all non-antique **precious stones** in Jordan are imported, mostly from Turkey. Jordan's own colourful **sandstone** is only used for sand-in-bottle novelties, sold at practically every souvenir shop and gift stall in the country.

In Amman, **copper** and **brass** items, such as coffee-pots, candlesticks, embossed or inlaid platters and the like, are generally unimpressive mass-produced Indian and Pakistani pieces, not to be compared to what's on offer in the Coppersmith's Bazaar in Cairo. Distinctive curved silver **daggers**, still carried by some bedouin in the south, are still being made by a workshop in Irbid, though older Yemeni or Iraqi daggers are much more ornate and generally of better quality. Since antiquity, **wood** has been a scarce resource in Jordan, and although you may dig out some Jordanian-carved pieces – simple cooking implements, mostly, from the local oak and pistachio – practically all the elegant wooden furniture you'll come across, wardrobes, chairs, beautiful inlaid chests and the like, originates (and is much cheaper) in Syria.

It's worthwhile remembering, too, that the line between what does and doesn't count as Jordanian is not an easy one to draw. Even if you're on the lookout for strictly local items only, the links between **Palestinian** craftspeople working in the West Bank and the retail craft-shops in Amman are strong, and many people make no distinction between the two. Prices in Amman for **olive-wood** or **mother-of-pearl** pieces from Bethlehem or the famous **blown glass** of Hebron (now also made in Na'ur, just outside Amman) can be half what you might pay in Jerusalem.

BEHAVIOUR AND ATTITUDES

Veterans of travel in Egypt or Morocco will be pleased to learn that, as far as hassle from the locals goes, Jordan is a breeze: your experience of Jordanian people is likely to be that they are, almost without exception, decent, honest, respectful and super-friendly. However, if you want to get the most out of a visit, it seems only right that you should return some of that respect in compliance with some basic tenets of Jordanian, Arab and Muslim culture.

DRESS CODES

Outward appearance is the one facet of interaction between locals and Western tourists most open to misunderstandings on both sides. A lot of tourists, male and female, consistently flout simple **dress codes** unaware of just how much it demeans them in the eyes of local people: clothes that are respectable at home can come across in Jordan as being embarrassing, disrespectful or offensive. Jordanians and Palestinians place a much greater emphasis on personal grooming and style of dress than people tend to in the West, and dressing down is unthinkable. For those locals who can afford it, anything less than every hair in place, a freshly ironed shirt or top, cologne or perfume, sharp trouser-creases or skirt-pleats, and shiny shoes simply won't do – and that's just for taking a walk. In addition, for reasons of **modesty**, Muslim men and women expose as little skin as possible. Sleeves are long and necklines high for both sexes. Men always wear long trousers, women either voluminous neck-to-ankle robes or calf-length skirts and loose tops.

If you want to come across as being someone worth talking to, you'll have to conform at least a little to this conservatism or run the risk of being dismissed either as a joke or an annoyance. Walking around in shorts and a T-shirt will cause shock and offence, and this kind of rejection of local values by women also reinforces the sex-object stereotypes that underpin many locals' attitudes to Western women.

MALE DRESS CODES

You'll never see local men wearing **shorts** in public in Jordan. Western men who break this code give roughly the same impression that they would

wandering around Bournemouth or Baltimore in their underpants. If you were to wear shorts, no doubt you'd be served in shops and restaurants – since to refuse would be disrespectful – but everyone would be rolling their eyes and tutting, and you'd be the butt of countless behind-your-back sniggers. **Long trousers** are essential in the city, the country and the desert, whatever the weather; clean and respectable light cotton or canvas ones (not the flimsy, brightly patterned beach-style ones) demonstrate normality and conformity – attributes high on the Jordanian social agenda. The single exception to the shorts rule is central Aqaba in the summer, which is so absurdly hot that even some locals cool their knees.

T-shirts are more problematic, since younger men do wear them; however, any garment that doesn't cover your shoulders and upper arms is also liable to tag you as an underwear-flaunting loony. Loose **button-down shirts** are far more common than anything else and, in general, you'll be received more respectfully by more people if you wear a tucked-in shirt than a tucked-out T-shirt. Jordanian men never, in any situation, walk around topless.

FEMALE DRESS CODES

To interact as a Western woman in Jordanian society with some degree of mutual respect, you'll probably have to go to even greater lengths than men to adjust your normal style of dress, although it is possible to do so without compromising your freedom and individuality too much. **Loose-fitting, opaque clothes** that cover your legs, arms and chest are a major help in allowing you to relate normally with local men. If **shorts** appear ridiculous on men, on women they appear flagrantly sexual and provocative, as do lycra leggings. The **nape of the neck** is considered particularly erotic and so is best covered, either by a high collar or a thin cotton scarf.

Hair is another area where conservatism helps deter unwanted attention. Jordanian women who don't wear a headscarf rarely let long hair hang over their shoulders; you might like to follow suit and clip long hair up. Walking around with **wet hair** is – for some reason – a general indication that you've just had sex, and thus may not be the kind of signal you wish to broadcast. If your hair is **blonde**, you must unfortunately resign yourself to a great deal more inquisitive, and sexualized, attention than is really your fair share to have to put up with – simply because of the novelty.

FOREIGN WOMEN: SEXUAL HARASSMENT

The biggest problem **women travellers** face in Jordan is the perceptions that local men have of them. Unless dressed modestly and accompanied by a husband, women tourists are often seen as being both morally loose and overtly contemptuous of Arab and Islamic values. The large numbers of Western women visitors who ignore dress codes and local norms of social contact unfortunately reinforce these perceptions. Even more unfortunately, local men thus often see foreign women as fair game for **harassment**, the level of which is lower than in Egypt or Morocco but much higher than you're likely to be used to at home.

To appreciate why harassment happens, it helps to understand that most young unmarried Jordanian men – the source of nearly all harassment – have very little chance to meet women and relate to them "normally" (in Western eyes). Dating is almost non-existent, since the pressure on women to retain a flawless reputation for moral behaviour is intense, and most simply can't afford to be seen in public consorting with strange men; dozens of women are killed each year in Jordan by their brothers, husbands or fathers for "bringing dishonour on the family name". Womens' pre-marital virginity is an almost universal requirement, leading many to shun personal contact with men until the big day, which may not come until their thirties. All this amounts to a religiously inspired social segregation that limits personal contact between men and women to an absolute minimum. As might be expected, this can lead to a deep-seated sexual frustration, which acts as a spur to many encounters between local men and foreign women. Add some stereotypes garnered from the media of Western women as being sexually available, and mix in the desire among young men to marry a foreigner and so get a visa to work in a rich country, and it becomes more understandable why the sight of a Western tourist walking down the street in a halter-top and lycra shorts can cause such an extreme, and offensive, reaction.

The single most effective way to stop harassment is to **dress modestly** (see above); the harsh truth is that, in Jordan, the onus is on you. Although men freely look at women – and, indeed, **staring** long and hard carries none of the implications of threat that it does in the West – all local women scrupulously avoid **eye-contact** with men on the street. A woman looking a man in the eyes will be interpreted as inviting him to approach her. It's a sad and sorry situation, but also overt friendliness or gregariousness shown to men on the street (such as smiling, chatting, joking or gesturing) may also be misinterpreted either as sexual looseness or as romantic interest.

Most harassment never goes beyond the verbal, and unless you're sufficiently well versed in Arabic swear-words to respond in kind (worth it for the startled looks), is ignorable if tiresome. A tiny fraction of incidents are more blatant – but still usually pretty harmless – comprising the usual tedious and demeaning round of gropes, hisses, kissy noises and the like. If you take the fight to your harasser, however, by pointing at him directly, shouting angrily and slapping away his hand, you're likely to **shame** him to his roots in front of his neighbours. Accusing him of bringing himself and his country into public disrepute – *aayib!* is Arabic for "shame!" – is about the most effective dissuasive action you could take, and many onlookers will be embarrassed and apologetic for your having suffered harassment. Unmarried or unrelated men and women never touch each other in public (apart from possibly to shake hands in a formal setting), and any man who touches you, even on the elbow to guide you, has overstepped the mark and knows it.

More serious harassment – blocking your path or refusing to leave you alone – is less common still, and actual bodily assault is virtually unknown. In Jordan strangers are much more likely to help a foreigner in distress than might be the case at home, and you shouldn't hesitate to appeal directly for help to shopkeepers or passers-by, or to bang on the nearest front door in an emergency.

FOREIGN MEN: SEXUAL PROPRIETY

Male travellers have slightly more leeway when it comes to interacting with local women. In the larger cities, it's normally OK to be verbally friendly towards a woman – if she's willing to talk to you, which is rare – without breaking any

FROM A WOMAN'S PERSPECTIVE – SOME SAMPLE EXPERIENCES

"During my time in Jordan there was just no way to hide that I was a tourist. And no way to hide that I was a woman. But most important of all, there was no way to prepare myself for everything that happened: not by reading any amount of books before leaving home, not even by listening to all my female friends' experiences of travel in the Middle East. For sure, sooner or later, you'll be surprised, as I was, by people's reactions – my best preparation was just to head out with self-confidence, curiosity and a sense of humour.

It's easy for women to travel alone in Jordan. People are extremely willing to help, and almost everyone invited me for tea – a boy selling table-cloths, taxi drivers, even the guardian in the museum. It surprised me that, although a man's presence could sometimes give more assurance to explore cafés and other places where women normally didn't venture, travelling for a time with a male friend felt somehow a little unreal. Suddenly, people stopped talking to me and paid attention only to him. Although this was probably due much more to respect for me than condescension, I couldn't help being a little upset. Self-confidence or no self-confidence, though, I wasn't there to be the centre of attention, and anyway (I told myself) such a cold shoulder put me in the best position to indulge my curiosity and observe events.

It was vital to be able to laugh at myself, for instance after having been followed by a bunch of teenage boys for at least an hour through the whole of Salt. They'd had a great time, running around and making jokes, and it'd been impossible to leave them behind; the only way out was to head for the bus station – they could tell that I was about to leave, and the game was over. Younger children I ran into, though, were rather obstinate; my mistake was to try and get away. I should've stayed and talked to them, lived up to my role and – best of all – taken a picture. They'd have loved that."

Anna Hohler, journalist, Lausanne

"One day in Karak, I decided to do some exercises in my hotel room. The door was locked, the shades were down. Handstands against the wall, then jogging in place. I can imagine the sound would've been intriguing from outside: *thud thud thud* (gasp) *thud* (sigh) *thud thud*. After about twenty minutes, I happened to glance up. Above the closet there was a small set of windows (hadn't noticed them before), and, in the window, a man's face, quickly disappearing.

The following morning, when I saw Mr Peeper in the lobby, he stared right at me without an

---

taboos, although touching is strictly forbidden and many women will refuse even to shake hands. In smaller towns and rural communities, although everything might appear fine at the time, her family might take her hanging out with a foreigner as a breach of morality, and possibly give her a hard time later. If you do talk with women in these circumstances, you should make sure that you're never alone together, and that you remain in full public view the whole time – preferably on the street rather than hidden in a café. You're extremely unlikely to become an object of affection, but if you choose to follow up any romantic interest, you'll have to be extremely discreet in your choice of venue. Although it's a criminal offence for a Jordanian woman to share a hotel room with a man not related to her, the legal sanctions pale into insignificance beside what her family might do to her if they find out.

COUPLES: DISPLAYING AFFECTION

If you're visiting Jordan with your (straight) partner, you should be aware of how social attitudes can also impact on **visiting couples** travelling together. Unlike in the hinterlands of Syria, no Jordanian hotelier will demand to see wedding rings before renting out a double-room. Nonetheless, **public displays of affection** between men and women are not acceptable behaviour. Even if you're married, walking arm-around-waist or arm-over-shoulder, touching each other's face or body or giving a fond peck on the lips are all seen as immoral and deeply distasteful. It is possible occasionally in Amman to see husbands and wives walking hand-in-hand, but it's rare. Relationships tend to symbolize something entirely different in Jordanian culture from what they do in the West, and for most Jordanian couples public expression of intimacy is unthinkable.

ounce of shame. Being peeped at is no surprise in any culture, but his lack of shame was a cultural lesson for me – not about relations between men and women in Jordan (because I think Jordanian women command a great deal of respect), but rather about the general perception of American women, primarily informed by porno flicks and B-movies. I was not assumed to have inviolable bodily boundaries. I was not assumed to question the rights of men over my body.

Nonetheless, you can regulate the respect you receive according to the way you dress. Complying with the standards of the place you're travelling in relieves you from harassment. It also signals your intention to understand. The assumptions about Western women are so image-based that changing your image will change your reception. It's as simple as that."

Karinne Keithley, dancer, New York

"Living and working in Jordan was rewarding and very comfortable, if trying at times; in the end, life being easy or difficult often came down to my own attitudes. Accepting the conservative nature of Jordanian culture and modifying my dress and behaviour to match social norms helped immensely. I don't mean I made radical changes to fit in. Just wearing loose clothes and long-sleeved shirts made me feel more confident and relaxed, especially in more traditional areas, and allowed local people to take me seriously.

Avoiding looking into men's eyes and maintaining a serious expression and demeanour made walking around alone mostly hassle-free. Being friendly with men I didn't know inevitably got me in trouble, since they interpreted it as flirting: I tried never to smile at men on the street and to keep my interactions with waiters and shopkeepers on a reserved and businesslike footing. This doesn't mean I didn't get stared at – I did. But I came to accept that as a foreigner I was an exotic sight to be seen, as much as Jordanian people are exotic to visitors.

The flipside of avoiding men's stares and comments was that I could smile and look freely at women. Since most women adopt a serious, frozen expression on the street to deal with male attention it was a great surprise, smiling tentatively at a woman passerby or exchanging a few words of greeting, to see her face light up with a broad smile in response. I had an immediate, spontaneous connection which surpassed words and cultural differences.

My time in Amman was also made much more enjoyable by cultivating a few places as refuges from conservative and male-centred culture. Darat al-Funun, and cafés like *Books@Café* and *el-Farouki's* were relaxing places to read, write, talk with friends or meet like-minded Jordanians."

Michelle Woodward, photographer,
San Francisco

GAY AND LESBIAN JORDAN

Amman has a small underground **gay** scene, with nothing of the pizzazz of Cairo, Tel Aviv or Beirut. For the most part, gay life in the city remains invisible to outsiders (and most locals as well), with a bare handful of uptown bars serving as gay meeting-places, and shady cruising going on at the Roman Theatre in Downtown. Nationwide, social disapproval of an overtly gay lifestyle is strong: dalliances between young, unmarried men are sometimes understood as "letting off steam", but they are accepted – if at all – only as a precursor to the standard social model of marriage and plenty of kids. Although local women form very strong bonds of friendship with each other to the exclusion of men, public perception of **lesbianism** is almost non-existent, although again Amman has a small, word-of-mouth scene. No surveys have ever been done of opinions on homosexuality within

Jordan, but locals in the know talk of some large majority of Jordan's gays and lesbians – especially those living outside the capital – being unhappily married, and either in denial or unable to come out for fear of social and familial isolation. Almost nobody actually considers themself gay, with only the most cosmopolitan Ammanis sheltering at best behind a self-identification as "bi". To make contact with the local scene, your first port of call should be *Books@Café*. There are no specifically gay or lesbian bars, but both gay and straight Ammanis pack out the Thursday dance nights at the Irish Pub.

A by-product of the strict social divisions between men and women, though, is that visiting gay or lesbian couples can feel much freer about limited **public displays of affection** than straight couples: cheek-kissing, eye-gazing and hand-holding between same-sex friends in public is normal and socially acceptable.

SOCIAL INTERACTIONS

Quite aside from issues of sex and sexuality, **social interaction** in Jordan is replete with all kinds of seemingly impenetrable verbal and behavioural rituals, most of which can remain unaddressed by foreigners with impunity. A few things are worth knowing, however.

The energy which Jordanians put into social relationships can bring shame to Westerners brought up on reticence and icy propriety. Total strangers greet each other like chums and chat happily about nothing special, passers-by ask each other's advice or exchange opinions without a second thought, and old friends embark on five-minute volleys of salutations and cheek-kisses, joyful arm-squeezing or back-slapping, and earnest enquiries after health, family, business and news. Foreigners more used to avoiding strangers and doing business in shops quickly and impersonally can come across as cold, uninterested and even snooty; learning one or two of the

standard forms of greeting (see box on p.361) and taking the time to exchange pleasantries will bring you closer to people quicker than anything else.

One stumbling block for many Westerners is the number of **questions** they face from Jordanians, questions which at home would seem overly personal. Aside from "what's your name?" and "where are you from?", absolutely everybody wants to know whether you're **married**. A couple answering "We're just good friends" – even if truthful – is likely to bring the conversation to an abrupt stop, since that means very little to Jordanians and merely highlights the cultural divide. Being able to point to a wedding/engagement ring – even if you have no plans – makes things instantly clear and understandable. For a woman alone, a ring, indicating an absent husband, is a powerful signifier of respectability. The next question is inevitably about **children** – how many, what are their names, why don't you have more, and so on. *Lissa* ("later") or *masha'allah*

GESTURES AND BODY LANGUAGE

There's a whole range of **gestures** used in Arab culture which will either be new to you or which carry different meanings from the same gesture in your home country. Rather than nodding, **yes** is indicated by inclining your head forwards and closing your eyes. **No** is raising your eyebrows and tilting your head up and back, often accompanied by a little "tsk" noise (which *doesn't* indicate impatience or displeasure). Shaking your head from side to side means **I don't understand**. A very useful gesture, which can be used a hundred times a day in all kinds of situations, is **putting your right hand over your heart**: this indicates genuineness or sincerity, and can soften a "no thanks" to a street-seller or a "sorry" to a beggar, or reinforce a "thank you very much" to someone who's helped you. Many people in the south of Jordan will instinctively touch their right hand to their heart after shaking hands.

One hand held out with the palm upturned and all five fingertips pressed means **wait**. A side-to-side wrist-pivot of one hand at chest level, palm up with the fingers curled, means **what do you want?** If someone holds their flat palm out to you and draws a line across it with the index finger of the other hand, they're asking you for whatever **document** seems relevant at the time – a bus ticket or passport. You can make the same gesture

to ask for the bill (check) in a restaurant. **Pointing** at someone or something directly with your index finger, as you might do at home, in Jordan casts the evil eye; instead you should gesture imprecisely with two fingers, or just flap your whole hand in the direction you mean. **Beckoning** with your palm up has cutesy and overtly sexual connotations; instead you should beckon with your palm facing the ground and all four fingers together making broom-sweeping motions towards yourself.

In all Arab cultures, knowingly showing the **soles of your feet or shoes** to someone is a direct insult. Foreigners have some leeway to err, but you should be aware of it when crossing your legs while sitting: crossing knee-over-knee leaves your sole pointing unobtrusively at the floor, but crossing ankle-on-knee means your sole is showing to the person sitting next to you. Equally, sitting on the floor requires some foot-tucking to ensure no one is in your line of fire. Putting your feet up on chairs or tables is not done.

Another major no-no is **picking your teeth** openly with your fingers; you'd cause less social discomfort if you were to snort, spit into a plastic bag, jiggle a finger in your ear and pick your nose. Most diners and restaurants offer tooth-picks, which should be used surreptitiously behind your palm.

("according to God's will") are two respectful, comprehensible ways to say you have none. Having a few snaps to pass around of parents, brothers, sisters, nephews and nieces can break the ice (if any ice needed breaking), and locals will happily show you their family pictures in return. People **shake hands** in Jordan much more than in the West, and even the merest contact with a stranger is normally punctuated by at least one or two handshakes to indicate fraternity.

WORDS OF WELCOME

Ahlan wa sahlan is the single phrase you'll hear most often in Jordan. Everyone says it, in all situations, often repeated like a mantra in long strings. As a visitor, you needn't actually ever say it yourself, but you'll have to field torrents of them from the locals. *Ahlan wa sahlan* is most commonly rendered as "welcome", but translates directly as "family and ease", and so might come out better in English along the lines of "relax and make yourself at home [in my house/shop/city/country]". With hospitality a fundamental part of Arab culture, there's no warmer or more openhearted phrase in the language. The proper response is *ahlan feek* or *ahlan beek* (*feeki* or *beeki* if you're talking to a woman), or you can just acknowledge the proffering of hospitality with a *shukran* ("thank you").

One rebound of the simplistic translation of *ahlan wa sahlan* is that you'll constantly be assailed on all sides with snippets of English along the lines of "welcome!" or "welcome to Jordan!", from kids and adults alike. Some of these welcomes are intended to convey a formal *ahlan wa sahlan*, but Jordanians also use *ahlan* on its own to mean "hello", and most of the welcomes you hear are simply people saying "hi!". The best response to these is *ahlayn!* (double-hello!).

The catch-all word used to invite someone – whether welcoming an old friend into your home or inviting a stranger to share your lunch (surprisingly common) – is **itfuddal**, often said together with *ahlan wa sahlan*. Translations of *itfuddal* (*itfuddalee* to a woman, *itfuddaloo* to more than one person) can vary, depending on circumstance, from "come in" to "go ahead" to "can I help you?" to "here you are, take it".

PERSONAL SPACE

Personal space is treated rather differently in Arab cultures from in the West: for all intents and purposes, it doesn't exist. There's an apocryphal Arab saying which sums up the attitude: "Hell is where there are no people." **Queuing** is a concept only just starting to catch on, and in many situations hanging back deferentially is an invitation for other people to move in front. Jordanians also relate to the **natural environment** rather differently from Westerners. Sitting alone or with a friend in even the remotest and most perfectly tranquil spot, you may well find someone coming up to you blocking the sunset and eager for a chat; it can be difficult, if not impossible, to convey your desire to be alone.

INVITATIONS

It's inevitable that during your time in Jordan you'll be **invited** to drink tea with someone, either in their shop or their home, and it's quite likely too that at some point you'll be invited for a full meal at someone's house. Jordanians take hospitality very much to heart, and are honestly interested in talking to you and making you feel comfortable, so it's a good idea to take at least a few people up on their offer. However, offers tend to flow so thick and fast that it would be very difficult to agree to every one, and yet people are often so eager it can also be difficult – and potentially rude – to refuse outright.

First and foremost – whether you're interested or not – is to take the time to chat civilly; nothing is more offensive than walking on without a word or making an impatient gesture, even if they're the twentieth person that day to stop you. If you're invited and you don't want to accept, a broad smile with your head lowered, your right hand over your heart and "*shukran shukran*" ("thank you, thank you") is a clear, but socially acceptable, no. You may have to do this several times – it's all part of the social ritual of polite insistence. Adding "*marra thaani, insha'allah*" ("another time, if God wills it") softens the "no" still further, indicating that you won't forget their kind offer *and* throwing in a reference to Allah, which is always a good thing.

BEFORE THE MEAL

If you're invited to eat with someone **at home** and you choose to accept, the first thing to consider is how to **repay your host's hospitality**. Attempting to offer money would be deeply offensive, but it is nonetheless entirely appropriate to bring some token of your appreciation. A kilo or two of sweet pastries handed to your host as you arrive will be immediately ferreted away out of sight and never referred to again; the gesture, however, will have been appreciated. Otherwise, presenting gifts directly to the adults of the family will generally cause embarrassment, since complex social etiquette demands that such a gift be refused several times before acceptance. Instead, you can acknowledge your appreciation by giving gifts to the small children – pens, small toys, sweets, even picture-postcards of your home country will endear you to your hosts much more than might appear from the monetary value of such things. It's worth pointing out too that you should be much more sparing and – above all – generalized in praising your host's home and decor than you might want to, since if you show noticeable interest in a particular piece, big or small, your host is obliged to give it to you. Whole minefields of complex verbal jockeyings to maintain dignity and family honour then open up if you refuse to accept the item in question. Many people keep their reception rooms relatively bare for this reason.

If you're a **vegetarian**, you would be quite within social etiquette to make your dietary preferences clear before you accept an invitation; especially in the well-touristed areas of Petra and Wadi Rum, vegetarianism is accepted as a Western foible and there'll be no embarrassment on either side. Elsewhere, it can help to clarify what seems an extraordinary and unfamiliar practice by claiming it to be a religious or medical obligation. All their best efforts notwithstanding, though, veggies may have to prepare themselves to sit down in front of a steaming dish of fatty meat stew and tuck in, while still looking like they're enjoying it.

DURING AND AFTER THE MEAL

This section outlines some of the things which may happen once you **sit down to eat** with a family. It may all seem too daunting for words to try and remember everything here; the bottom line is, you don't – you'd have to act truly outrageously to offend anyone deeply. Your host would never be so unhospitable as to make a big deal about some social blunder anyway.

Once you arrive for a meal, you'll probably be handed a thimbleful of bitter **Arabic coffee** as a welcoming gesture; down it rapidly, since everyone present must drink before sociabilities can continue. Handing the cup back with a jiggle of your wrist indicates you don't want any more. The meal – often a *mensaf* – may well be served **on the floor** if you're in a tent, generally with the head of the household, his adult sons and any male friends sit-ting cross-legged around a large communal platter; Western women count as males for social purposes and will be included in the circle. Even if wives and daughters are present, they almost certainly won't eat with you, and indeed you may find that they all stay out of sight in another part of the tent or house. If they do, it would be grossly impertinent to enquire after them.

Once the food appears (generally served by the women), you should confine yourself to eating – strictly with your right hand only – from that part of the platter directly in front of you; your host may toss over into your sector choice bits of meat such as the **tongue** – and, as an outside possibility, the eyes – which, if they land in front of you, it would be inexplicable to refuse. Quite often, everyone present will share a single **glass of water**, so if the only glass visible is put in front of you, it's not a cue for you to down it. While eating, locals will be careful not to **lick their fingers**, instead rolling their rice and meat into a little ball one-handed and popping it in from a short distance; however, it takes ages to learn how to do this without throwing food all over yourself, and you'll have enough social leeway to subtly cram in a fistful as best you can. It's no embarrassment – in fact, it's almost obligatory – to make a horrible greasy mess of yourself. You'd be well advised to stop or slow down **before you're full**, partly because as soon as you stop eating you'll be tossed more food; partly because no one will continue eating after you – the guest of honour – have stopped (so if you sit back too soon you'll be cutting the meal short); and partly because whatever doesn't get eaten by the men counts as dinner for the women and children. Never finish all the food in front of you, since not only does this tag you as greedy, it's also a direct insult to your host, who is obliged always to keep your plate well-stocked. When you've **finished**, your right hand over your heart and the words "*al-hamdulil-lah*" ("thank God") make clear your satisfaction.

After everyone has washed hands and face, **fresh coffee** will be served; you should take at least three before you return the cup with a jiggle of the wrist. There'll then be endless **tea**, along with bonhomie, conversation and possibly an *arjileh* or two. It's your host's unspoken duty to keep the tea flowing whatever happens, so after you've had enough – one or two glasses at least – the best way to stem the tide is to say "*da'i-man*" ("may it always be thus") and then simply to ignore your full glass.

POLICE AND TROUBLE

As a tourist and a foreigner, the chance of your coming into contact with any criminal activity while in Jordan is remote. The sense of honour and hospitality to guests embedded deep within Arab culture, coupled with a respect for others, means that you're very unlikely to be robbed, mugged, conned or pickpocketed on holiday in Jordan. Unfortunately, these values are more often applied to men than to women, and relatively minor but tiresome sexual harassment of foreign women is an ongoing problem; see p.57 for more.

Along with the ordinary police, Jordan maintains a force of **tourist police** – identifiable as such by armbands with English lettering – most of whom speak good English and all of whom are the height of courtesy. Posted at all tourist sites nationwide, they can deal with requests, complaints or problems of harassment by unofficial guides or hangers-on. Any representation by a foreigner, whether to the tourist police or the ordinary local police, will generally have you ushered into the presence of senior officers, sat down and plied with coffee, with your complaint taken in the utmost seriousness. The nationwide police emergency number is ☎199; phone numbers for the police in larger towns are given in the relevant chapters of the guide.

DRUGS

Drugs are nothing like as prevalent in Jordan as they are in Egypt or Lebanon, and it's highly unlikely, even if you go looking for it, that you'll come across any hashish, let alone anything more powerful. The country is principally a transit route for drugs rather than a consumers' market: desert smuggling routes lead from Syria through Jordan into the lucrative drug markets of Israel, Egypt and the Gulf states.

If you choose to seek out and use drugs while in Jordan, be aware that there's no tradition of smoking hash in Jordanian culture, as there is (or was) in Egypt – use of the stuff, and all other drugs, is unquestionably beyond the pale, officially, legally and in popular thinking. By indulging, you expose yourself to the exceptionally severe penalties that exist for possession, use or trafficking, and should expect no quarter from the authorities or your embassy if you're caught. Jordanian jails are notoriously unpleasant, even for the Middle East.

TERRORISM

Terrorism and civil disorder are about as common in Jordan as they are in Western countries – that is, extremely rare. In spring 1998, for example, while the world prepared to go to war with Saddam, and clashes on the West Bank grew more violent, and Egypt tried to pick up the pieces after the tourist massacre in Luxor, life in Jordan, sandwiched between the three, continued entirely as normal – except that the usual tide of Western tourists was down to a trickle as group cancellations poured in daily. In sharp contrast to Egypt, Israel, Lebanon, Turkey, France, Spain or the UK, no violently active group exists that holds any grievances against Jordan, its people, government or tourism policy, and the political and religious make-up of Jordanian society – as well as the invisible grip of the security services – makes domestic terrorism unlikely.

Nonetheless, super-aware both of the extremist attacks on tourists in Egypt, and of the tensions in Israel and Palestine that occasionally sweep innocent bystanders up in their violence, Jordan maintains forces of protective **armed police** in high-profile evidence at all major tourist sites. If you're staying in the country longer than a month or so, you might like to register your presence with your embassy in Amman – every one keeps a list of its nationals resident in the country. These precautions notwithstanding, though, and regardless of the impression journalists might like to give, you'd be no safer sitting on your own front doorstep than travelling in Jordan.

WORK AND STUDY

The chances for either work or study in Jordan aren't that great; in many ways Cairo is a much better bet. There are only a couple of decent language schools in Amman for English teachers to try their hand with, and although picking up work in other fields – specifically journalism and computer-aided design – isn't beyond the bounds of possibility, options are pretty slim and you'd be wise not to rely on anything. Jordan isn't a bad place to study Arabic, though, with two universities and a handful of other places offering casual and intensive courses, and the quantity of archeology being done around the country offers good possibilities to volunteer on a dig.

TEACHING ENGLISH

Amman's top two **language schools**, the British Council and the American Language Center (which doesn't restrict itself to hiring native American-English speakers), are bustling hives of activity, with continuous programmes of English teaching at all levels. Both mainly recruit their teachers outside Jordan, but vacancies do occasionally arise at short notice, so if you hold both a university degree and the RSA TEFL certificate (or equivalent), you've got nothing to lose by asking.

The handful of smaller language schools aren't really worth bothering with, but the huge demand for English has led to a thriving scene in private tutoring, for which qualifications only matter if

your student requires them; the noticeboards in all cultural centres are plastered with names and numbers of tutors, any of whom could probably give you an idea of how to set up.

STUDYING ARABIC

The main thing to determine before you start checking out Arabic courses is whether you want to learn **Modern Standard Arabic** (MSA; see p.360) or the **colloquial dialect** of Jordan and Palestine, since different courses teach different kinds of Arabic.

The highest-prestige courses for foreign students are the semester- and year-long MSA programmes at Amman's University of Jordan and Irbid's Yarmouk University, which are valid for transferable credits at most American and some British universities. However, by all accounts, teaching standards at either institution are not high. Colloquial Arabic – far more useful for the interested traveller – is taught on a more casual basis at a handful of cultural centres in Amman, principally the British Council and the French Cultural Centre; courses at the latter are taught by trilingual Arabic/French/English teachers, mostly in English but with occasional lapses into French. Prices for a one-semester (four-month) part-time course are around JD100. There's also any number of better- and worse-qualified **private tutors** in Amman, many of whom will be willing to do a deal teaching you Arabic in exchange for you teaching them English; check the noticeboards in cultural centres for leads. It has to be said, though, that by far the best structured courses to be had in the region in both MSA and colloquial Arabic are just across the border at Birzeit University, near Ramallah on the West Bank; see their superb website *www.birzeit.edu* for details.

ARCHEOLOGICAL WORK

There are good opportunities for amateur **archeologists** to get involved on a dig in Jordan, although you'll need to plan a long time in advance (six months or more) and be prepared to have to shell out for transport and living expenses for the privilege of being allowed to

USEFUL CONTACTS

ACOR (American Center for Oriental Research), PO Box 2470, Amman 11181 (☎06/534 6117, fax 534 4181, email *acor@go.com.jo*). A pillar of Jordan's academic establishment, which, in addition to conducting archeological investigations of its own – principally at Madaba, Petra, Aqaba, Karak and Rum – publishes books, pamphlets and newsletters on Jordan's heritage.

American Language Center, near 8th Circle, PO Box 676, Amman 11118 (☎06/585 9102, fax 585 9101, email *info@alc.edu.jo*, website *www.alc.edu.jo*).

Archeological Institute of America (AIA), 135 William St, New York, NY 10038. Publishes an annual compendium every January of opportunities for fieldwork throughout the Middle East, available from the publisher Kendall/Hunt (☎1-800/228-0810).

British Council, Rainbow St near 1st Circle, PO Box 634, Amman 11118 (☎06/463 6147, fax 465 6413, website *www.britcoun.org/jordan*). The head office, at 10 Spring Gardens, London SW1A 2BN (☎0171/930 8466), produces a free leaflet detailing study opportunites abroad. The Council's Central Management Direct Teaching (☎0171/389 4931) recruits TEFL teachers for posts worldwide (check *www.britcoun.org/english/engvacs.htm* for a current list of vacancies); they also publish an annual *Working Holidays* book (£9.99) available direct or from bookshops in the UK.

Council for British Research in the Levant (formerly British Institute at Amman for Archeology and History), PO Box 519, Jubayha, Amman 11941 (☎06/534 1317, fax 533 7197, email *biaah@nets.com.jo*, website *britac3.britac.ac.uk/institutes/biaahhp/index.html*). UK contact office: 29 The Walk, Southport, Lancs, PR8 4BG (☎ & fax 01704/569664, email *cm@biaahuk.demon.co.uk*). Very active in archeology around Jordan, with the jewel in their crown being the five separate digs under way at and near Faynan. Digs at Jerash and Pella are also continuing.

French Cultural Centre (Centre Culturel Français et de Cooperation Linguistique), PO Box 9257, Amman 11191 (☎06/463 7009, fax 463 0061, email *cccljor@nets.com.jo*).

German Protestant Institute of Archeology in Amman, PO Box 183, Amman 11118 (☎06/534 2924, fax 533 6924, email *gpia@go.com.jo*). A much smaller concern, and under threat of closure during 1999 due to budget cuts. The principal focus of energy over the years has been Umm Qais, but the institute has also undertaken other projects, notably at Petra and Azraq.

IFAPO (Institut Français d'Archéologie du Proche Orient), PO Box 5348, Amman 11183 (☎06/461 1872, fax 464 3840, email *ifapo-jor@nets.com.jo*). Large and long-established organization attached to the French government, with ongoing projects in Jerash, Iraq al-Amir, Wadi Musa and Wadi Rum.

work onsite. You'll be in more demand if you know the region well, have worked on digs before, or have particular skills such as photography or technical drawing to offer. In the first instance, you should write to the big archeological institutes in Amman who then, if opportunities are available, can put you in contact with the directors of specific projects.

DIRECTORY

ADDRESSES Jordan has no street addresses, and any nameplates you happen to see on street corners are there purely for the benefit of map-makers and foreigners – locals have their own names for streets and navigate by locating themselves in relation to prominent buildings or landmarks, or by asking passers-by. Mail is delivered only to PO boxes at post offices, and international courier companies deliver only to their own main offices, where parcels are held for collection.

BARGAINING There are only three rules of bargaining: firstly, never to start the process unless you want to buy; secondly, never, even in jest, to let a price pass your lips that you're not prepared to pay; and thirdly, never to lose your temper. However, the lack of any tradition of bazaar-style haggling in Jordan results in a reluctance among Jordanian merchants even to embark on the process. In most everyday situations, you'll rapidly be brought up short against an unbudgeable last price – which, unlike in the Cairo or Damascus bazaars, really is the last price, take it or leave it.

CHILDREN Kids are universally loved in Jordan, and travelling with your family is likely to provoke spontaneous acts of kindness, gooey-ness and genuine hospitality from the locals. Children are central to Jordanian society – many couples have four or five, and double figures isn't uncommon. Middle-class extended families tend to take pleasure in spoiling kids rotten, allowing them to stay up late and play endlessly, but as a counterpoint, you'll also often see kids from low-income families out on the streets at all hours selling cigarettes. The streets are quite safe and even very young children walk to school unaccompanied.

Only the cheapest hotels will bar children; most will positively welcome them, as will all restaurants, although discounts may have to be negotiated. There are a few precautions, however, to bear in mind when travelling with children. First and foremost is the heat: kids should really be protected from the sun as much as possible, both in terms of clothing (especially brimmed hats and long sleeves) and gallons of sunblock. Heatstroke and dehydration can work much faster on children than on adults, and sun damage to sensitive skin early on in life seems to give rise to a greater susceptibility to cancers later on. Sunglasses are a good idea as well. Second is the food: aside from the usual questions of hygiene, the oil and chilli liberally used in Jordanian cooking may not appeal to kids' tastes (although the sweets probably will), and restaurants may not be entirely switched on to how to prepare blander meals for children. Kids are also obviously much more vulnerable than adults to stomach upsets, and you should definitely carry rehydration salts in case of diarrhoea. Other things to watch out for include the crazy traffic – especially for British kids who'll be used to traffic driving on the other side of the road – stray animals that may be disease carriers, and jellyfish and poisonous corals off Aqaba's beaches.

Having said that, kids will probably love taking camel-rides, and even Petra's threadbare donkeys may hold an appeal. Most of the archeological sites will probably be too rarefied to be of anything more than passing interest (aside, possibly, from the castles at Karak, Shawbak, Azraq and Ajloun); Shaumari's ostriches and oryx "safaris" may well be a better bet, and the pedalos on the Dead Sea and glass-bottomed boats at Aqaba are perennial favourites. Children born and brought up in urban environments will probably never have experienced anything like the vastness and silence of the open desert, and you may find they're transfixed just by the emptiness.

CIGARETTES AND TOBACCO SMOKE It's impossible to escape cigarette smoke anywhere in the country, except during Ramadan. The anti-smoking lobby in Jordan makes little headway, and a huge majority of Jordanians both smoke themselves and assume everybody else does: it's not uncommon for locals to blithely light up in a crowded taxi, then close the window against the draught. Jordan's own tobacco industry is small, with local brands (around 700 fils) less rough than Egyptian or Syrian varieties, but familiar Western brands (around JD1.200) taste much better, even if they might have higher tar and nicotine content than back home.

CONTRACEPTIVES Imported brand-name condoms and lubricant are reliably available in pharmacies in Amman, Wadi Musa and Aqaba. If you use other methods, you should carry enough supplies to last the duration of your trip.

DEPARTURE TAX Payable as you leave in JD only: JD10 by air, JD6 by sea or JD4 by land.

ELECTRICITY 220v AC, 50Hz (the same as in Europe); supply is pretty steady in most areas and blackouts are rare. Plug style is a real mish-mash, though. Many new buildings have British-style square three-pin sockets. Older buildings tend to have one or other of two different styles of two-pin socket: thicker-pronged (round plugs) and thinner-pronged (flat plugs). For more information, visit the website *kropla.com* before you go. If you're having trouble, all electrical stores are well-stocked with inexpensive adaptors and convertors; in Amman, go to Khalil Snobar, next to the Downtown post office. American equipment will also need a 220-to-110 transformer.

PHOTOS Amman and Aqaba have a handful of trustworthy outlets to buy colour negative and slide film; elsewhere, film may be long past its use-by date and/or have been sitting for years in the desert sun. If you can, bring enough film with you from home. For developing, you'd probably do better to get your film developed at home by someone you trust. Jordanian knowhow and technical standards cover the simplest holiday snaps, but anything more valuable or complicated may not come out as you might wish; the only completely reliable labs for colour negative and slide film are in Amman (see p.117 for details). Prices of both film and processing are higher than in Europe.

SPORTS AND OUTDOOR PURSUITS The chances for engaging in participatory sports while in Jordan are pretty limited, mostly because vigorous exercise is not high on most locals' agenda, and facilities are few and far between. Swimming, snorkelling and diving in Aqaba – central to most travellers' itineraries – are covered in Chapter 6, along with the bare handful of watersports possibilities. Rock-climbing opportunities in Rum are outstanding, but are only for experienced pros. Otherwise, you're generally limited to rough hiking – there is no system of marked trails – or novelty pursuits such as sand-skiing (dunes east of Jafr are renowned), paragliding or parachuting, but you'll need a tour operator or the RSCN to set you up for these; see p.39 for further details. If you're in trim, you might fancy the annual Amman–Dead Sea 50-km Ultra-Marathon, run every April; find details at *www.deadseamarathon.com*.

TAMPONS AND PADS Local women generally prefer to use pads, and both Jordanian and imported European brands are widely available at pharmacies and supermarkets, although you may not get the choice of styles you have at home. Tampons are available – most reliably in pharmacies in Amman's uptown neighbourhoods – but might be a little harder to find.

THINGS TO BRING Jordan is not the back of beyond, and most normal travel items can be found in the flashier parts of Amman (if not elsewhere). However, it pays to bring with you a few choice bits and bobs to ease the way. The following are some ideas, ranked in order of importance:

• Anything to keep the sun off your head and neck: hat, headscarf, even a collapsible umbrella. In the intense heat of Petra or Rum, soaking your hat/scarf in water and then sticking it on your head is a great way to cool off.

• Lightweight light-coloured cotton clothes that protect your skin from the sun (long-sleeved shirts, long trousers, ankle-length skirts). These keep you much cooler than a T-shirt and shorts, and also inspire less ridicule. Bear in mind, though, that the desert at night can be chilly and that, outside the high summer months, nights in Amman, Petra and Dana can be positively bitter: a sweater is a necessity whenever you arrive. If you're in Jordan between November and March, you'll need proper warm and waterproof winter gear.

• Water bottle or canteen (or carry plastic mineral-water bottles for refilling). A cool bottle is also handy to keep juice or water at refreshing temperatures in the desert.

- Total sunblock, sweatproof (you'll still tan, even through Factor 40).
- Mosquito repellent (Rum has no mozzies, Petra and Aqaba a few, Amman enough in summer to be annoying).
- Talcum powder (to ease sweaty chafing).
- Multi-vitamin and mineral tablets (*fuul* and *falafel* only go so far).
- Torch/flashlight (for exploring ruins and camping in the desert).
- Sheet sleeping bag (or proper sleeping bag in winter).
- Whistle and pocket mirror (in case you need to attract attention in remote spots).

TIME Jordan is usually two hours ahead of Britain, seven hours ahead of New York and eight hours behind Sydney. Daylight Saving Time operates from the beginning of April to the end of October, although dates for the changeover aren't fixed and there can be an awkward overlap between Jordanian DST and European and Israeli summer times: for a week or two in spring, Amman runs three hours ahead of London and an hour ahead of Jerusalem; and, for a week or two in autumn, one hour ahead and one hour behind respectively.

TOILETS Public ones – if you can find any – tend not to be too bad, since they almost always have a caretaker, who'll give you some toilet paper if there isn't any visible. Fifty fils is a normal tip. Quite often you get a choice between hole-in-the-ground squat toilets and Western-style sit-down ones. Whichever you use, you should never put used paper down the hole, since it's likely to block the pipes; instead, drop it in the omnipresent little basket. A working toilet will always also have a working tap and a plastic jug, since the local way is to wash yourself clean using your left hand (there are no guidelines about drying off afterwards). Squat toilets almost never flush; instead, empty a jug or two down the hole. The proper Arabic word for toilet is *hammam*, but most people will understand *twalet*.

TOURIST GUIDES Within Jordan, the government monitors all official tourist guides and gives accreditation in three categories based on an annual written exam. Guides who have been awarded Category A status are deemed to be knowledgeable enough to guide visitors around all sites nationwide. Category B implies specialist knowledge of certain major sites only, while Category C guides are permitted to give information only about one particular site. The Downtown Visitors' Centre in Amman keeps the official Ministry of Tourism list of all registered guides in the country, with accreditation details and contact phone numbers. All guides must show their laminated photo-ID card at all times, and all of them also carry a "Tourist Guide Licence" showing expiry date and accreditation category, which they must produce on demand. The upshot of this rigorous system is effectively to eliminate hustlers from tourist sites, ensuring that someone who holds official ID and claims to be a guide does genuinely know his stuff – some guides hold advanced university degrees in ancient history, most speak two or three languages, and virtually all have put in time on archeological digs in Jordan or elsewhere.

Payment, though, is entirely negotiable. The going rate for a Category A guide to accompany you around the country is JD30–35 a day, excluding transport (negotiable) and his meals and accommodation (which amount to another JD25 or so). A local guide (who may be Category A anyway) hired once you arrive at a site should be paid at least JD4/hr. The standard rate at Amman and Jerash is about JD5/hr, at Petra JD8/hr. Tips are always optional.

WEIGHTS AND MEASURES Jordan uses the metric system in most everyday situations, with all roadsigns marked in kilometres, all fresh produce sold by the kilogramme, and mineral water in 1.5-litre bottles.

CHAPTER ONE

AMMAN AND AROUND

C onsistently overlooked and underrated by travellers to the Middle East, **AMMAN** stands in marked contrast to its raucous neighbours, with none of the grand history of Damascus, not a whiff of Jerusalem's tension and a tiny fraction of Cairo's monuments. It's a civilized, genteel place – Paul Theroux was led to dismiss it in a single sentence as "repulsively spick-and-span" – which can yield some quiet and undramatic charms.

Amman is a thoroughly twentieth-century invention, which was no more than an unregarded, muddy farming village when Emir Abdullah chose it to be his new capital in 1921. The consequent sense of Amman being a village-made-good is highlighted when you spend some time on the Downtown streets. Here the weight of history that is a constant presence in the heart of most Middle Eastern cities is manifestly lacking, replaced instead by a quick-witted, self-reliant dynamism that is entirely people-oriented. This energy stems in large part from displacement, with a huge majority of Ammanis identifying themselves as originating somewhere else: Circassians, Iraqis and above all Palestinians have arrived in the city in large numbers, voluntarily or forcibly exiled from their homelands, and they've brought with them distinctive cultures which are still jostling for living space with the culture of the native Transjordanian bedouin. Indeed, scratching beneath Amman's amiable surface reveals a whole cluster of multiple personalities jockeying for supremacy – Western-educated millionaire business-people flaunt their riches cheek-by-jowl with poverty-stricken refugees, Christians live next door to Muslims, Jordanians of Palestinian origin assert their identity in the face of nationalistic tendencies among "true" Jordanians, and so on. What it is to be Ammani is an ongoing dispute that shows no signs of resolution.

All this means that, for the time-pressed ruin-hunter, there's little more than an afternoon's sightseeing to be done; however, if you're on a long, slow journey of familiarity you could easily spend days exploring the slopes of Amman's towering hills, getting under the city's skin while seeing nothing in particular. The capital's impressive **Roman Theatre** and eighth-century **Umayyad palace** are the only significant monumental attractions, augmented by the country's major **archeological museum**, but of equal, if not greater, interest is contemporary Amman's burgeoning arts scene. The arts centre of **Darat al-Funun**, the **National Gallery** and regular music events can add a surprising perspective to your experience of the city's life. The principal day-trip out of Amman is to the unmissable **Dead Sea**, but distances in Jordan are tiny and **Madaba** (see Chapter 4) and the Roman ruins at **Jerash** (see Chapter 2) are both within easy reach.

Some history

The first known settlement near Amman dates from over nine thousand years ago, a Neolithic farming town near the **Ain Ghazal** spring in the hills to the

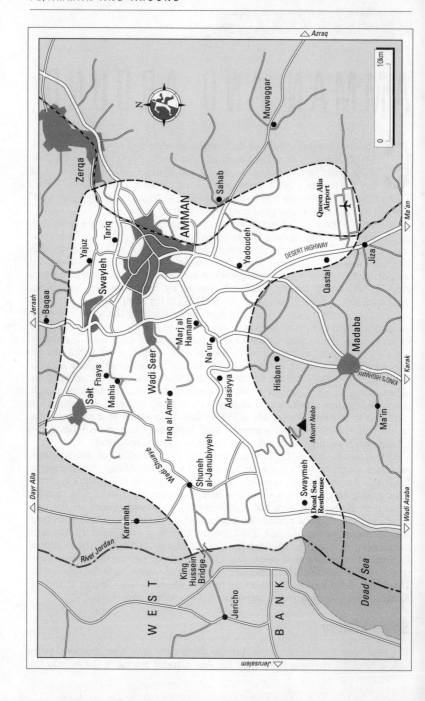

northeast of the modern city, which is one of the largest discovered in the region, three times bigger than contemporary Jericho. Artisans from amongst its two thousand inhabitants produced strikingly beautiful human busts and figurines in limestone and plaster, some of the earliest statuettes ever discovered (now on display in the Amman museum).

Around 1800 BC, during the Bronze Age, the hill now known as **Jebel al-Qala'a** which overlooks the central valley of Amman was fortified for the first time. According to Genesis, the area was inhabited by giants before the thirteenth-century BC arrival of the **Ammonites**, mythical descendants (along with the Moabites) of the drunken seduction of Lot by his own two daughters. By 1200 BC, the citadel on Jebel al-Qala'a had been renamed **Rabbath Ammon** (Great City of the Ammonites) and was capital of an amply defended area which extended from the Zerqa to the Mujib rivers. Rabbath – or Rabbah – is mentioned many times in the Old Testament; the earliest reference, in Deuteronomy, reports that, following a victory in battle, the city had seized as booty the great iron bed of King Og, last of the giants. Later, the book of Samuel relates that, around 1000 BC, the Israelite **King David** sent messengers to Rabbah with condolences for the death of the Ammonite king. Unfortunately, the Ammonites suspected the messengers were spies: they shaved off half their beards, cut their clothes away at the back and sent them home in ignominy. In response to such a profound insult, David sent his entire army against Rabbah, although he himself stayed behind in Jerusalem to develop his ongoing friendship with Bathsheba, who soon became pregnant. On David's orders, her husband Uriah was placed in the front line of battle against Rabbah and killed. David then travelled to Rabbah, butchered some Ammonites, burned others alive and returned home to marry the handily widowed Bathsheba. Their child was named Solomon, later to become king of Israel.

The feud between Ammon and its neighbours to the west simmered for centuries, with Israel and Judea coveting the wealth gathered by Ammon and its southern neighbours, Moab and Edom, from lucrative north–south trade routes. In the absence of military or economic might, Israel resorted to the power of prophecy. "The days are coming," warned Jeremiah in the sixth century BC, "that a trumpet blast of war will be heard against Rabbah of Ammon." The city was to become "a desolate heap" with fire "destroying the palaces". In a spitting rage at the Ammonites' celebration of the Babylonian conquest of Jerusalem in 587 BC, Ezekiel went one better, prophesying that Rabbah was to be occupied by bedouin and to become "a stable for camels".

After Alexander the Great conquered the region in 332 BC, his successor Ptolemy II Philadelphus rebuilt Rabbah and named it **Philadelphia**, the "city of brotherly love". Turmoil reigned following the Seleucid takeover in 218 BC until the Romans restored order by creating the province of Syria in 63 BC. Philadelphia was at its zenith as the southernmost of the great Decapolis cities (see p.129), and benefited greatly from improved trade and communications along the **Via Nova Traiana**, completed in 114 AD by Emperor Trajan to link the provincial capital Bosra with the Red Sea. The Romans completely replanned Philadelphia and constructed grand public buildings, among them two theatres, a nymphaeum, a temple to Hercules and a huge forum, all of which survive.

In Byzantine times, Philadelphia was the seat of a bishopric and was still a regional centre when the Arabs conquered it in 635; the city's name reverted to **Amman** under the Damascus-based Umayyad dynasty who oversaw an expansion of the city's influence. It became capital of the area and, around 720, the Umayyad governor of Amman developed and expanded the Roman buildings surviving on Jebel al-Qala'a into an elaborate palatial complex, which promptly collapsed in the great earthquake of 747. Following the Abbasid takeover shortly afterwards, power shifted east to Baghdad, and Amman's influence began to wane, although it continued to serve as an important stop for pilgrims on the way south to Mecca. Over the next centuries, travellers mention an increasingly desolate town; Amman had ceded regional prominence to Karak and by the time **Circassian** refugees were settled here by the Ottomans in the 1870s, Amman's hills served only as pasture-land for the local bedouin – Ezekiel's furious prophecy come true. The Circassians, however, revived the city's fortunes, and when the **Emirate of Transjordan** was established in 1921, Emir Abdullah chose Amman to be its capital.

Modern Amman

Since then the city has seen a remarkable growth in both wealth and size. Up to 1948, Amman comprised only a village of closely huddled houses in the valleys below Jebel al-Qala'a, with a handful of buildings on the lower slopes of the surrounding hills. But in that year, floods of **Palestinians**, escaping or ejected from the newly established State of Israel, doubled the city's population in just two weeks. Makeshift camps to house the refugees were set up on the outskirts, and, following another huge influx of Palestinian refugees from the West Bank, occupied by Israel in 1967, creeping development began to merge the camps with the city's sprawling new suburbs.

A fundamental shift in the city's fortunes came with the outbreak of the **Lebanese civil war** in 1975. Before then, Beirut had been the financial, cultural and intellectual capital of the Middle East, but when hostilities broke out, many financial institutions relocated their regional headquarters to the security of Amman. Most subsequently departed to the less parochial Gulf, but they nonetheless brought with them money and with the money came style (specifically Western style): today there are parts of West Amman indistinguishable from upscale neighbourhoods of American or European cities, with broad leafy avenues lined with mansions, and fast multi-lane freeways swishing past strip malls and black-glass office buildings. A third influx of Palestinians – this time expelled from Kuwait following the 1991 **Gulf War** – again bulged the city at its seams, squeezing ever more urban sprawl along the roads out to the northwest and southwest.

When King Hussein signed a **peace treaty** with Israel in 1994, many Ammanis hoped for the opening of a new chapter in the city's life; Amman's intimate links with Palestinian markets and its generally Western-oriented business culture led many to believe wealth and commerce – not to mention Western aid – would start to flow. However, although building development has burgeoned across the city, many of the new hotels and office buildings are white elephants, and Amman has so far seen very little economic comeback from political rapprochement with Israel. Nonetheless, with the city's carefully nurtured international image as the moderate and hospitable face of the modern Arab world – an image that rings true for visitors – Amman today enjoys a greater influence in the region and the world than at any time since the Romans.

Orientation and information

Amman is a city of hills and any map of the place can give only half the story. Although distances may look small on paper, the reality is that traffic and people are funnelled along streets either laid on valley-beds or clinging to the side of steep hills: to reach any destinations above Downtown you'll generally have to zig-zag up sharp gradients.

The area known in English as **Downtown**, in Arabic as *il-balad* (literally "the city"), is the historical core of Amman; Roman Philadelphia lies beneath its streets and as late as the 1940s this small area comprised virtually the whole of the city. Downtown forms a slender T-shape nestling in the valleys between six hills. At the joint of the T, and the heart of the city, is the imposing **Husseini Mosque**, which faces down **King Faysal Street**, commercial centre of Downtown and home to most of its cheap hotels. The other main thoroughfare of Downtown – Hashmi Street and King Talal Street, together forming the cross-piece of the T — runs in front of the mosque, passing to the west most of Amman's bustling street markets and, to the east, the huge **Roman Theatre**. Towering over Downtown is **Jebel al-Qala'a**, "Citadel Hill", site of a partly restored **Umayyad Palace** and the country's principal **Archeological Museum**.

Most of Amman's explosive growth in the last fifty years has been concentrated in respectable and upscale **West Amman**; other districts to the north, south and east are much poorer, though more populous. The various neighbourhoods of **Jebel Amman** form the heart of the city's rich western quarter; running along its crest is **Zahran Street**, the city's main east–west traffic artery, punctuated by numbered intersections known as **circles** (though not all of them are roundabouts). 1st Circle is closest to Downtown, while 8th Circle marks the western city limits.

STREET NAMES

Street names in Amman are a relatively recent innovation: some streets still have no name at all, some have had names assigned to them that no one knows but the mapmakers, and others have names that are entirely different from those published on maps or signposted on street corners. There is no system to this at all, and the only way to deal with it is to get used to it; newcomers have no way of knowing, for instance, that the street marked on all maps and signs as *sharia Abu Bakr as-Saddeeq* is one and the same as the universally known Rainbow Street. Common alternative names are given below; our maps use whichever name is in everyday usage.

OFFICIAL NAME	*COMMON NAME*
Downtown	
Quraysh Street	Saqf Sayl
Jebel Amman	
Abu Bakr as-Saddeeq Street	Rainbow Street
Omar bin al-Khattab Street	Mango Street
Jebel al-Lweibdeh and Shmaysani	
Khalaf Circle	Lweibdeh Circle
Jamal Abdul-Nasser Intersection	Interior Circle (*duwaar al-dakhliyyeh*)
Suleiman an-Nabulsi Street	Mukhabarrat Street
Arar Street, Ibn Seena Street, and Sharif Nasser bin Jameel Street	Wadi Saqra Street
Wasfi at-Tall Street	Gardens Street

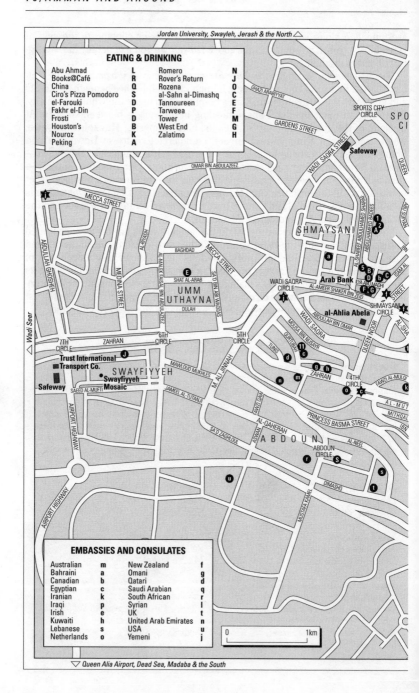

Jordan University, Swayleh, Jerash & the North △

EATING & DRINKING

Abu Ahmad	L	Romero	N
Books@Café	R	Rover's Return	J
China	Q	Rozena	O
Ciro's Pizza Pomodoro	S	al-Sahn al-Dimashq	C
el-Farouki	D	Tannoureen	E
Fakhr el-Din	P	Tarweea	F
Frosti	D	Tower	M
Houston's	B	West End	G
Nouroz	K	Zalatimo	H
Peking	A		

SPORTS CITY CIRCLE

SPO CI

Safeway

GHAZI ARABIYYAT

GARDENS STREET

OMAR BIN ABDULAZEEZ

WADI SAQRA STREET

QUEE

ABDULHAMED SHARAF

MECCA STREET

SHMAYSANI

1
2
A

AL-SHAREEF ABDULHAMED SHARAF

ISAM A

AL-RIYADH

BAGHDAD

MECCA STREET

ABDULLAH GHOSHEH

MEDINA STREET

AL-AMEER FAISAL

SA'D BIN ABI WAQQAS

SHAT AL-ARAB

E

UMM UTHAYNA

DULAH

WADI SAQRA CIRCLE

Arab Bank

5
B
D
b c

IYA ABU MADHI

AL-AMEER SHAKER BIN ZEID

F G

SHMAYSANI

△ Wadi Seer

ABDULLAH BIN OMAR

al-Ahlia Abela

SHMAYSANI CIRCLE

AL-SHA

7TH CIRCLE

ZAHRAN

6TH CIRCLE

5TH CIRCLE

MOUSA BIN NUSAYR

WADI SAQRA

QUEEN NOOR

Trust International
Transport Co.

J

MAWLOUD MUGHLES

TUNIS

QURTUBAH

11
c
d

g h

n m

ZAHRAN

4TH CIRCLE

FAWZ AL-MULQI

K

SWAYFIYYEH

Swayfiyyeh
Mosaic

Safeway

SAEED AL-MUFTI

JAMEEL AL-TUTANJI

M. AL JINNAH

FAWZ ID?W

o
c

AL-MUT

MITHQAL

IBN

PRINCESS BASMA STREET

AIRPORT HIGHWAY

SA'D ZAGHLOUL

AL-QAHERAH

ABDOUN

AL-NEEL

ASWAN

ABDOUN CIRCLE

r

S

s

DIMASHQ

u

t

AIRPORT HIGHWAY

MUSTAFA KAMEL

EMBASSIES AND CONSULATES

Australian	m	New Zealand	f
Bahraini	a	Omani	g
Canadian	b	Qatari	d
Egyptian	c	Saudi Arabian	q
Iranian	k	South African	r
Iraqi	p	Syrian	l
Irish	e	UK	t
Kuwaiti	h	United Arab Emirates	n
Lebanese	s	USA	u
Netherlands	o	Yemeni	j

0   1km

▽ Queen Alia Airport, Dead Sea, Madaba & the South

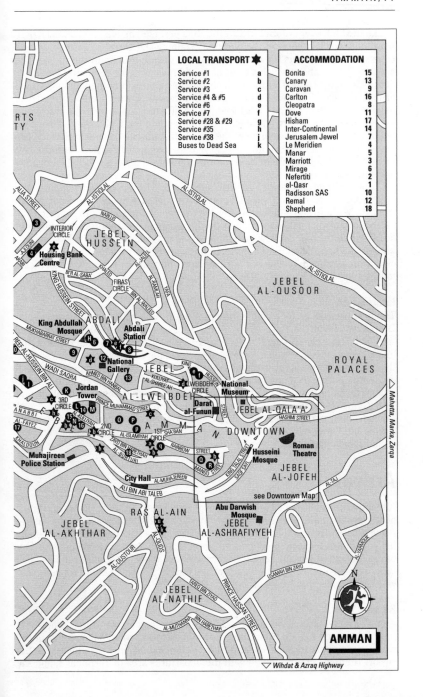

LOCAL TRANSPORT ★

Service #1	a
Service #2	b
Service #3	c
Service #4 & #5	d
Service #6	e
Service #7	f
Service #28 & #29	g
Service #35	h
Service #38	j
Buses to Dead Sea	k

ACCOMMODATION

Bonita	15
Canary	13
Caravan	9
Carlton	16
Cleopatra	8
Dove	11
Hisham	17
Inter-Continental	14
Jerusalem Jewel	7
Le Meridien	4
Manar	5
Marriott	3
Mirage	6
Nefertiti	2
al-Qasr	1
Radisson SAS	10
Remal	12
Shepherd	18

AMMAN

△ Mahatta, Marka, Zerqa

▽ Wihdat & Azraq Highway

The next hill over is **Jebel al-Lweibdeh**, a peaceful, monied residential neighbourhood which is home to the **National Gallery** and **Darat al-Funun**, an arts centre. Lweibdeh abuts the district known as **Abdali**, best known for its big bus and taxi station, above which a steep slope culminates in the distinctive landmark of the **Housing Bank Centre**, with shaggy foliage muffling the building's modernistic terraces. This marks the edge of **Shmaysani**, formerly one of the ritziest neighbourhoods of the city but these days a little worse for wear. Beyond here, the northwestern suburbs dribble on for miles out to the **University of Jordan**. South of Shmaysani, **Swayfiyyeh**, the city's most upscale shopping district, lies below 5th and 6th Circles – fittingly close to the lavish mansions of **Abdoun**, residence of most of Jordan's millionaires and night-time playground for the Porsche-and-sunglasses set.

Within spitting distance of Abdoun's tennis courts, the pungent drain of the Wadi Abdoun marks a division between rich West Amman and poor South Amman. **Muhajireen** and **Ras al-Ain** are the two districts of South Amman closest to Downtown; further south, beyond the mountainous **Jebel al-Ashrafiyyeh**, lies **Wihdat**, a dusty, rundown neighbourhood at the far end of which is another big bus and taxi station. East and North Amman are the least inviting areas of the city, with a ribbon of low-key development hugging the highway northeast towards Jordan's second city, **Zerqa**.

Information

The best place to go for reliable **information** in Amman is the government-run Downtown Visitors' Centre (daily: April–Oct 9am–7pm, Nov–March 9am–5pm; ☎06/464 6264), close to the Roman Theatre. As well as giving out all kinds of free maps, they can reserve you a room in any hotel in the country, rent you a car from the company of your choice, phone embassies for the latest visa information, call the tourist police, recommend an official guide or book a full-blown tour. Free literature includes the slick *Visitors' Guide*, which has some useful information, and *Your Guide to Amman*, which doesn't. The Jordan Tourism Board (daily except Fri 8am–4pm; ☎06/464 7951), on the second floor of the Kalbouni Building opposite Jordan Tower below 3rd Circle, can give you all the same free paperwork, but no more help than that.

Arrival

Although Amman is not a big city, points of **arrival** are rather far-flung, and you'll nearly always have a frustratingly involved onward journey across the city to reach a hotel. However, one thing you can almost always count on is a generally helpful attitude from bystanders. The worst that will happen to you on your first day in Amman will be an over-abundance of offers of help or a slightly inflated taxi fare – real rip-offs are very rare, and, at any time of the day or night, robbery with violence is entirely unheard-of.

By air

Amman has two international airports, but all intercontinental traffic comes into the pocket-sized **Queen Alia International Airport**, some 35km south of the city. Two separate terminals, identical in design and facilities – setting aside the airport **medical centre**, which is in the departures area of Terminal 2, and the

post office (daily 8am–7.30pm) in Terminal 1 – occupy opposite halves of a single, H-shaped building; the following information applies to arrival at either terminal. If you haven't got a **visa** in advance, the procedure for getting one is straightforward and the varying costs (in dinars only) are clearly posted near the relevant windows in front of the arrival gates – see p.16 for details. There's a range of **banks** near the visa windows, with more or less identical rates and services; only get a small amount of dinars here, as you can find better rates in the city centre. After 10pm these banks – if you can find a clerk – normally only change cash, but there are also cash machines (ATMs) for Visa cards. You can make international **phone calls** and send faxes from a nearby window. Once you're through the formalities, you emerge at street level, where you'll find a sporadically staffed **information desk**.

Plenty of meterless but officially sanctioned **taxis** wait just outside both terminals' arrival halls. The fare from the airport direct to anywhere in the city centre should not be more than JD13–15; resist any demands for extra payments for baggage. You can ignore taxi-drivers' claims that there are no **buses** from the airport into town: large, comfortable Airport Express buses leave from marked points directly outside the arrival halls. One runs to the Raghadan station (see p.82) in Downtown Amman (daily, hourly from 7.15am to 9.15pm; journey time 45min); the other to Abdali station (see below) via Shmaysani (daily, every 30min from 6am to 10pm, then every 2hr from 11pm to 5am; 45min). The fare on either is JD1, plus 250 fils for each large bag or suitcase; check your change carefully and hang on to the tickets.

The only commercial flights in and out of **Marka Airport** (otherwise known as Amman Civil Airport), a tiny airfield barely 5km east of Downtown, are short hops from Israel and Egypt operated by Royal Wings. **Visas** and formalities on arrival are all simple and obvious. Once you're outside, **taxis** should be waiting (about JD1 to Downtown, JD2 to Shmaysani); otherwise, if you walk 200m right out of the airport precincts to the roundabout on the main road, you can flag down *service* #17 heading left to the Raghadan station in Downtown.

By bus or *service*

Amman has a number of different termini scattered all over the city for local and international arrivals by bus or *service* – where you end up depends partly on where you're coming from, and partly on what form of transport you're using.

Abdali station (pronounced *Ub-d'lee*, with stress on the first syllable) is the most important point of arrival. A noisy, chaotic place, it's simply a big V-shaped island in the middle of King Hussein Street, pointing the way down the steep slope towards Downtown. Buses, minibuses and *service*s from most Jordanian towns north and west of Amman – including Jerash, Irbid and Ramtha – arrive here, as well as buses and *service*s from Damascus and the King Hussein Bridge (from the West Bank and Jerusalem). There are a few hotels near the station (see p.87), but most travellers head straight for Downtown, a thirty-minute walk away. If you can't face the hike, it's easy to grab any taxi heading downhill, while cheaper *service*s tend to line up and wait for a full car before departing.

Scheduled Karnak and JETT buses from Damascus terminate at the **JETT depot**, some 500m uphill from Abdali. JETT buses from Aqaba and Petra drop off not in the bus parking area itself, but a few metres away on the street outside the company's office; from here, *service* #6 runs to Downtown.

The other main transport terminus in Amman is the **Wihdat station**, some 5km south of Downtown, an open car-park with a scattering of fast-food stalls.

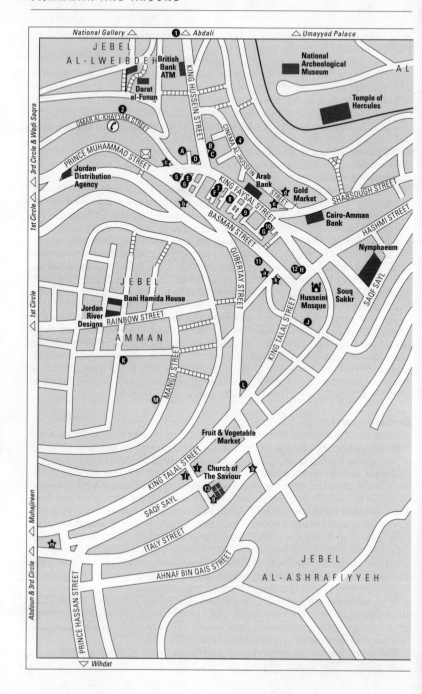

National Gallery △ ❶ △ Abdali △ Umayyad Palace

JEBEL
AL-LWEIBDEH

British
Bank
ATM

Darat
al-Funun

National
Archeological
Museum

Temple of
Hercules

AL

KING HUSSEIN STREET

OMAR AL-KHAYYAM STREET ❷

PRINCE MUHAMMAD STREET

Jordan
Distribution
Agency

CINEMA AL-HUSSEIN STREET

❹

Ⓐ Ⓑ Ⓒ
Ⓒ Ⓓ

Arab
Bank

Gold
Market

SHABSOUGH STREET

❺ Ⓔ
❻
Ⓕ
❼
❽
❾

KING FAYSAL STREET

Ⓖ

Cairo-Amman
Bank

HASHMI STREET

Ⓑ

BASMAN STREET

❿
Ⓖ

Nymphaeum

3rd Circle & Wadi Saqra

1st Circle

1st Circle

⓫
Ⓖ

⓬ Ⓗ

QUBERTAY STREET

JEBEL

Bani Hamida House

Jordan
River
Designs

RAINBOW STREET

AMMAN

Ⓚ

MANGO STREET

Ⓜ

Husseini
Mosque

Souq
Sukkr

Ⓙ

SAQF SAYL

KING TALAL STREET

Ⓛ

Fruit & Vegetable
Market

KING TALAL STREET

Church of
The Saviour

⓭
Ⓙ

SAQF SAYL

ITALY STREET

Muhajireen

Abdoun & 3rd Circle

PRINCE HASSAN STREET

AHNAF BIN QAIS STREET

JEBEL
AL-ASHRAFIYYEH

▽ Wihdat

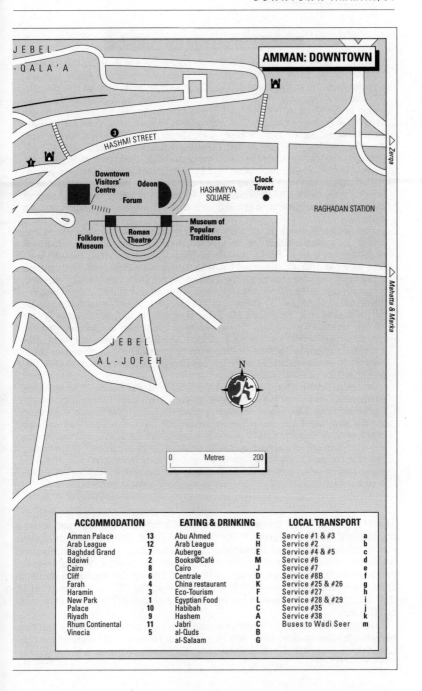

AMMAN: DOWNTOWN

JEBEL
-QALA'A

HASHMI STREET

Downtown
Visitors'
Centre

Odeon

Forum

Roman
Theatre

Folklore
Museum

Museum of
Popular
Traditions

HASHMIYYA
SQUARE

Clock
Tower

RAGHADAN STATION

▷ Zerqa

▷ Mahatta & Marka

JEBEL
AL-JOFEH

N

0   Metres   200

ACCOMMODATION		EATING & DRINKING		LOCAL TRANSPORT	
Amman Palace	13	Abu Ahmed	E	Service #1 & #3	a
Arab League	12	Arab League	E	Service #2	b
Baghdad Grand	7	Auberge	H	Service #4 & #5	c
Bdeiwi	2	Books@Café	M	Service #6	d
Cairo	8	Cairo	J	Service #7	e
Cliff	6	Centrale	D	Service #8B	f
Farah	4	China restaurant	K	Service #25 & #26	g
Haramin	3	Eco-Tourism	F	Service #27	h
New Park	1	Egyptian Food	L	Service #28 & #29	i
Palace	10	Habibah	C	Service #35	j
Riyadh	9	Hashem	A	Service #38	k
Rhum Continental	11	Jabri	C	Buses to Wadi Seer	m
Vinecia	5	al-Quds	B		
		al-Salaam	G		

THE HEJAZ RAILWAY

A plan for a **railway** to facilitate the Muslim pilgrimage was touted in the Ottoman capital, Istanbul, from the mid-nineteenth century onwards, and finally received approval from the sultan in the 1890s. At that time, a camel caravan covering the 1300km from Damascus to the holy cities of Medina and Mecca, in the Hejaz region of Arabia, took the best part of two months, a difficult journey through harsh country that left the pilgrims vulnerable to exhaustion, disease and bandits; the train would cut this down to three days. The route chosen for the rail line (and the adjacent **Desert Highway** that came later) followed almost exactly the pilgrimage route in use since the sixteenth century. By 1908, with goodwill funds pouring in from all over the Islamic world, modern, comfortable carriages, a luxury Pullman car and even a rolling mosque complete with two-metre minaret were running three times a week along the full length of the line to **Medina**, bringing new wealth and sophistication to towns such as Zerqa, Amman and Ma'an along the route.

During World War I, in an attempt to undermine Ottoman influence in the Middle East, Britain offered to back Arab claims for independence. Faysal and Abdullah, the sons of Sherif Hussein of Mecca, and the British colonel T. E. Lawrence ("of Arabia"), organized the **Arab Revolt** in the Hejaz, and slowly moved north up the rail line, harassing the Turkish supply lines, blowing up trains and eventually taking Damascus. After the war and the collapse of the Ottoman Empire, the dream of pilgrimage by Pullman was as ruined as the track itself and, amidst the political turmoil, money could be found to rebuild the line only as far as Ma'an. Its holy *raison d'être* negated, the railway lay semi-dormant for decades, and the only passenger services – between Damascus and Amman – came and went, subject to fluctuations in diplomatic relations. In 1982, a three-nation, three-year feasibility study on renovating the entire line came up with a projected cost of US$5 billion ... and the plan was abandoned.

In 1992, a British advertising company hit on the idea of filming an ad for extra-strong mints on the old Hejaz steam locomotives, paying the railway handsomely for the privilege. More enquiries came in, and since then profits from passenger service have paled into insignificance beside the flood of requests for **special charters** from diplomats and train buffs wanting nostalgic rides into the desert, and from film crews and tour operators capitalizing on the legend of Lawrence. Five-star package tours to Jordan now regularly include an afternoon of champagne and caviar on a steam-drawn Pullman, with the added "surprise" of a mid-desert Lawrence-style raid on the train by mounted bedouin warriors.

This is where all buses, minibuses and *service*s from the south of Jordan arrive – principally the towns of Aqaba, Petra, Ma'an and Karak (minibuses from Madaba run to either Wihdat, Abdali or Raghadan stations). Taxi-drivers generally meet arrivals, or you could take one of the three *service*s which depart from outside the *Merna* snack-bar. The most useful is #19, which runs to the Raghadan station in Downtown (see below); long queues form for both the #27, which drops off on Italy Street off the Saqf Sayl in the city centre, and the #27J to Abdali station via 3rd Circle.

Just next to the Roman Theatre in the heart of Downtown is the huge and rambling **Raghadan station**, filled with noise, dirt and fumes at all hours, which comprises three separate, clearly defined areas, for *service*s (closest to the amphitheatre), then minibuses, then big buses. It's no more than a ten-minute walk to the budget hotels from here, but only transport from Zerqa, Salt, Madaba, and in and around Amman uses this station.

If you're arriving on an Israeli or Jordanian bus direct **from Tel Aviv** or **Haifa** (the latter via Nazareth), you'll end up in an office estate off the Airport Highway below 7th Circle, way out in West Amman. There are no useful minibuses or *services* within reach, but plenty of metered taxis shark for business nearby. Scheduled JETT and SuperJet buses direct **from Cairo** drop off at the JETT office in Marka, northeast of the centre; take *service* #17 or a taxi to reach Downtown.

By train

Only one passenger **train** operates in Jordan, a single weekly departure from Damascus every Sunday at 7am, taking ten hours or so to meander into Amman's dinky **Hejaz station** in Mahatta, to the east of the centre. *Service* #17 to Raghadan runs outside, or you should be able to flag a taxi down for the short ride into the centre – Downtown is to your right, under the bridge.

City transport

Due to its geography and the unplanned nature of its expansion, Amman doesn't have a properly integrated **transport** system. Its city buses, jam-packed hulks that serve outlying neighbourhoods with no route information available in English, will be of little or no use to travellers. Far more useful are Amman's *services*, whose routes tend to radiate from various points in Downtown – crossing from one uptown neighbourhood to another without first passing through Downtown is virtually impossible without a taxi. Traffic can be horrendous, with relief coming after about 10pm, when things ease up until the rush hour begins again at 7.30am, and on Fridays, when streets can remain quiet most of the day. Walking, although essential for exploring Downtown, isn't really an option in the extended uptown districts.

By *service*

*Service*s (shared taxis) are essential for getting quickly and easily up the hills surrounding Downtown. They operate like small buses, with between four and six passengers cramming in and everyone paying a flat fare; you can get in and out wherever you like on the set route. All Amman's city *service*s are **white** all over, with black stencilled panels in Arabic on both front doors stating the general district they're going to, as well as two Arabic numbers on top of each other – the top one is the route number (very important) and the bottom one is the car number (utterly irrelevant). The cars tend to form long nose-to-tail lines at the bottom of the Downtown hills; the first passengers in the queue pile into the last car in line, which then pulls out and grinds its way past all the others up the hill and away. All the rest then roll backwards one place and the same thing happens again.

Throughout this chapter, *service*s are identified by their **route number**, although, if you ask them, Ammanis will quite often have no idea about which number is which, instead identifying *service*s by the district they go to. No official information or route maps exist, but if you want to pick up a *service* partway along its route, a bunch of people forming themselves into a queue on the kerbside is a sure sign of a stop. When you want to **get out**, "*allah yaatik al-afyeh*"

MAJOR *SERVICE* ROUTES	
All city *service*s have a little white sign somewhere on the dashboard stating the **fare** in Arabic. Fares are 90 or 100 fils per person, apart from #38 (170 fils), #27J (160 fils) and Abdali–Gardens St (160 fils).	
1	Basman St, opposite Husseini Mosque–Prince Muhammad St–1st Circle–2nd Circle–3rd Circle.
2	Basman St, behind *Cliff Hotel*–Rainbow St–Mango St–Buhtari St–2nd Circle–3rd Circle.
3	Basman St, opposite Husseini Mosque–Prince Muhammad St–Jordan Tower–3rd Circle–4th Circle.
4 & 5	Behind Downtown Post Office–Lweibdeh Circle–Jebel al-Lweibdeh–Muntazah Circle.
6	Cinema al-Hussein St–King Hussein St–Abdali–JETT–Interior Circle.
7	Cinema al-Hussein St–King Hussein St–Abdali–King Abdullah Mosque–Mukhabarrat St–Arab Bank Shmaysani.
8B	Shabsough St, junction of Hashmi St–King Hussein St–Abdali.
9	Shabsough St, behind Cairo Amman Bank–Jebel al-Qala'a–Jebel Hussein.
17	Raghadan Station–Hejaz Station–Marka Airport.
19	Raghadan Station–Wihdat Station.
25 & 26	Saqf Sayl, near Fruit and Vegetable Market–Jebel al-Ashrafiyyeh.
27	Saqf Sayl, near Fruit and Vegetable Market–Wihdat Station.
27J	Abdali Station–3rd Circle–Wihdat Station.
28 & 29	Saqf Sayl, opposite *Amman Palace* hotel–al-Quds St (Ras al-Ain).
35	Saqf Sayl, opposite *Amman Palace* hotel–Muhajireen St–Wadi Abdoun–3rd Circle.
38	Basman St, opposite Husseini Mosque–Prince Muhammad St–Wadi Saqra–Mecca St–Abdullah Ghosheh St.
Unnumbered	Abdali Station–Interior Circle–Gardens St.

("God give you strength" [in your work]) will have the driver veering over to the kerb for you.

As for **operating hours**, the first *service*s start running daily at 5.45 or 6am. From 7.30 to 9am, the Downtown queues can be 200m long, with correspondingly lengthy waiting times. In the evening, things start to wind down after 8pm; by 10pm there are long gaps between *service*s, and after 11.30pm any you find will probably be operating as unmetered taxis.

By taxi

Roughly a quarter of all cars in Amman are **taxis**; the metered fares are cheap and they can whisk you to places that might take hours to get to by any other means. Unless you're starting from a remote neighbourhood, or are planning a journey in the middle of the night, enough will be roaming the streets for you never to have to **phone** for one; if you do need to set a specific pick-up time, try Taxi al-Barq (☎06/464 1299). You should insist on the **meter** being switched on before you get going, though practically all drivers will do it anyway as a matter of course. The meters *always* work; if a driver claims it's broken and tries to negotiate a fixed fare with you, simply say *"ma'alesh"* ("forget it") and wait for another taxi to come along (note that although fares don't rise at night, the proportion of "broken" meters does). The **flagfall** is 150 fils, rising by a minuscule 10 fils every few seconds, so a ten-minute hop should cost something like 400 fils, with a long, crosstown journey hardly ever more than JD1; beware the favoured con of some drivers, which is to play on foreigners' misunderstanding of the currency and reinterpret the decimal point on the meter's readout.

Although most drivers know their way around pretty well, and are keen to be helpful and courteous, no Ammani relates to street names. Unless you're going somewhere obvious, like Abdali station or the Citadel, first give the name of the neighbourhood you're heading for, then, as you get closer, tell the driver which building you want, or maybe a nearby landmark – if he's not familiar with it, he'll quite likely just drive around asking passers-by for directions.

Walking

Walking in Amman is a mixed bag. It's absolutely the only way to get around Downtown, but once you venture further out, distances between sights lengthen and the uptown hills feel like mountain peaks.

You can walk from one end of **Downtown** to the other in about twenty or thirty minutes, staying on the flat the whole way. The trek from there to **Abdali** station, however, although not much more than 1km, is uphill and can take over thirty minutes; no local would consider walking it. **Jebel al-Lweibdeh** and the lower reaches of **Jebel Amman** (below 3rd Circle) are residential and can be explored on foot, but elsewhere, if you try to walk, you'll generally find yourself slogging along a broken kerbside beside streams of traffic in neighbourhoods designed for driving.

However, one of the most delightful discoveries of old Amman – largely ignored by visitors and locals alike – are the **flights of steps** which trace direct paths up and down the steep Downtown hills, dating from the days when hillside residences were otherwise inaccessible. Countless flights – most of them undocumented and unidentifiable, many weed-ridden and crumbling – criss-cross the area below 1st Circle on Jebel Amman, the nose of Jebel al-Lweibdeh, the flanks of Jebel al-Qala'a and the hills above the Roman Theatre, passing now and then through private backyards, beneath washing-lines or past once-grand deserted villas. If you're decorously dressed and sensitive to the fact that you're tramping through people's gardens – as well as to the possibility that the steps you happen to have chosen might not go anywhere – you're basically free to explore.

Accommodation

Amman has **accommodation** to suit all budgets, although much of it is not terribly inspiring, well maintained or conveniently located. Many hoteliers are beginning to tailor their services to the needs and expectations of Western, as opposed to Arab, tourists, but there are still plenty of places where the presence of Westerners is an unexpected novelty.

Although some **touting** for business at the main points of arrival does go on, it's fairly low-key and amiable; if you accept an offer of accommodation, it's unlikely you'll end up anywhere really awful. The only exception, of course, is if you're

---

HOTEL PRICE CODES

Throughout this guide, hotels have been categorized according to the **price codes** given below, which indicate the normal price for the **cheapest double room** in a particular establishment during the **high season** (excluding the ten-percent tax and ten-percent service charge levied in all hotels of ③ and above). **Single rooms** can cost anything between seventy and a hundred percent of the double-room rates. Where a hotel offers beds in **shared rooms**, the price per person to share has been given; if a price code has also been included, this indicates that private rooms are also available. For a fuller explanation, see p.39.

① under JD10	④ JD30–40	⑦ JD65–80
② JD10–20	⑤ JD40–50	⑧ JD80–95
③ JD20–30	⑥ JD50–65	⑨ over JD95

female, and the accommodation turns out to be in the tout's apartment – this, unfortunately enough, does happen.

In general, rooms on **higher floors** tend to be less dusty and less prone to excessive traffic noise and fumes. In the high season (April–October), many places across all price brackets fill up quickly – you'd be well advised to **book ahead**, even for the cheapest of the cheap. There are no **campsites** in or near Amman.

Inexpensive and mid-range hotels

At first glance, Downtown seems crammed with **inexpensive hotels**, lining all the main streets, but the huge majority of these places are dosshouses for itinerant labourers. Even if you're a bloke, with the lowest of standards and the tightest of budgets, you'd do well to steer clear of these dives; apart from the dirt, the bugs and the noise, many don't want the reputation of having foreigners hanging around. No harm will come to you if you choose to talk your way in, but there's little need to – Downtown has enough good-value inexpensive hotels that will welcome you.

Mid-range places tend to be located in the hills above Downtown, mainly Jebel Amman and Shmaysani. Here, you'll find quite a good range of small, reasonably comfortable hotels, ranging from the brisk and cheerful to the swish and elegant.

All hotels above ③ should be safe for everybody, but some ① and ② places are best avoided by **women** travelling singly or together. We've noted in the reviews below which inexpensive hotels offer women privacy and security.

Downtown

If you come in on *service* #6 or #7 from Abdali station, you'll be dropped on Cinema al-Hussein Street, in the thick of **Downtown** and within five minutes' walk of most of the hotels listed here. *Service* #19 from Wihdat station drops off at Raghadan station, next to the Roman Theatre; there are a couple of cheap options nearby, or you could walk 200m or so to the unmissable Husseini Mosque which faces up King Faysal Street, crammed with hotel possibilities.

Amman Palace, Saqf Sayl, near Church of the Saviour (☎06/464 6172, fax 465 6989). Pitched firmly at a respectable Arab clientele, this is the highest-quality hotel in Downtown, though not as clean as it should be. Rooms come with air con, phone and satellite TV. Accepts Visa and Mastercard. ③.

Arab League, King Faysal St, opposite the Husseini Mosque (☎06/462 3143). One of the best cheap hotels in the city, above the *Arab League* café. Friendly (excellent English spoken), with clean, spacious rooms and reliably hot water; showers cost 500 fils. The only problem is the proximity to the mosque and its prayer-blasting speakers. However, women travellers will feel comfortable. Free luggage storage. JD2 to share. ①.

Baghdad Grand, King Faysal St (☎06/462 5433). Another Downtown favourite: small rooms with street-side balconies or larger, quieter alternatives at the back. Showers are free and hot. ①.

Bdeiwi, Omar al-Khayyam St (☎06/464 3394, fax 464 3393). A friendly place, up the hill behind the post office, with spotless rooms, where women will feel welcome. Fans and hot showers are free and you can call and fax at discount rates. ①.

Cairo, King Faysal St, opposite the Arab Bank (☎06/463 8230). Basic Downtown dive, with some quiet hot-water en-suite doubles that aren't bad at all. JD2.500 to share. ①.

Cliff, unmarked entrance in an alley between Prince Muhammad St and Basman St, opposite Khalifeh Stores (☎06/462 4273). The best cheap hotel in the country and the closest you'll find to a travellers' hostel. Well run by a jovial and patient Jerusalemite with an inexhaustible supply of sound advice on how to get around. Excellent-value rooms are clean, all with cold-water sinks and fans, though those overlooking the next-door restaurant get a little noisy. Upstairs are cheaper, pokier rooms and the roof features a summer sleep-in. Hot showers cost 500 fils. Other features include free luggage storage and use of the kitchen, an airport pick-up service and tours to different parts of the country. Safe and comfortable for women. Book ahead or arrive early. JD3 to share. ①.

Farah, off Cinema al-Hussein St (☎06/465 1443, fax 465 1437). Glossy, brand-new cheapie on six floors (look for the big red signs), with hand-painted murals on every wall. Lift access, 24-hour hot water and fans in every room. One of the few places which takes Western visitors only. Safe for women and quiet. JD3.500 to share. ①.

Haramin, Hashmi St, almost opposite the Roman Theatre (☎06/465 5890). Brand-new, spotlessly clean and run by a friendly young student. Excellent rooms all have fans. Separate bathrooms for men and women are pristine. Recommended, despite the horrendous street noise. ①.

New Park, King Hussein St, opposite the law courts (☎ & fax 06/464 8145). A cut above its neighbours, with well-kept rooms all with TV and telephone. Safe for women, with very welcoming female staff. Clean, comfortable and good value, with breakfast included. Accepts Visa and Mastercard. ②.

Palace, King Faysal St, opposite the Gold Souq (☎06/462 4326, fax 465 0602). Take the lift up to an unexpected bit of quality in the heart of the bustle. Comfortable, top-floor rooms, each with two balconies and a spotless en-suite bathroom, are best. ②.

Rhum Continental, Basman St (☎06/462 3162, fax 461 1961). Four floors of plain, en-suite rooms, the best ones higher up. A lift, air con in every room and scrupulous cleanliness raise it well above its neighbours. ②–③.

Riyadh, King Faysal St (☎06/462 4260). Another good budget option on the main drag, with fans, hot water and understanding staff. JD3 to share. ①.

Vinecia, on an alley between Prince Muhammad St and Basman St (☎06/463 8895, fax 461 6825). Travellers' favourite right next to the *Cliff*, its gloomy ambience only partly offset by the friendliness of the staff. Rooms upstairs are quieter but hotter in summer and grimy, and the ancient bathrooms are in a real state. JD3 to share. ①.

Abdali and Jebel al-Lweibdeh

The main advantage of most of the following places is their proximity to **Abdali station**, useful if you arrive late at night from Jerusalem, Jerash or Damascus, or if you want an early start. However, traffic noise around the station is a major problem, and none offers particularly good value for money. **Jebel al-Lweibdeh**, the steep hill southeast of Abdali, is largely residential, with quiet, leafy streets and marvellous views from its peak over the whole of Amman.

Canary, opposite the Terra Sancta College, Jebel al-Lweibdeh (☎06/463 8353, fax 465 4353). Peaceful place, where clean, if basic, rooms come with TV, fan and breakfast ... and prices are negotiable. A perfect escape from the Downtown crush. *Service* #4 runs nearby. ③.

Caravan, Police College Rd, just off King Hussein St near King Abdullah Mosque (☎06/566 1195, fax 566 1196). Most rooms are clean and pleasant, all with fan and some with balcony, although the dawn call to prayer from the mosque is a drawback. Accepts major credit cards. Book well in advance as groups fill the place up. ③.

Cleopatra, King Hussein St, next to Abdali station (☎06/463 6959, fax 465 9953). Tatty, seedy and grimy, this is the only true budget option in the area. Bargain hard. ①.

Jerusalem Jewel, top floor of the building at the north end of Abdali station (☎06/461 3970, fax 461 5565). Clean, quiet and airy rooms are all en suite – go for the ones with fabulous views out over Abdali towards Downtown. Continental breakfast on the roof is included. ③.

Mirage, corner of King Hussein St and Mukhabarrat St (☎06/568 2000, fax 568 8890, email *mirageh@go.com.jo*). Spanking new, within spitting distance of Abdali station. Well-appointed rooms, with air con, TV and room service, as well as a parking area and rooftop barbecue, jacuzzi and sauna. Although all a little overblown, it's surprisingly affordable (credit cards accepted). The closest hotel of this quality to Downtown. ④.

Remal, just off King Hussein St, near the Police Directorate (☎06/463 0670, fax 465 5751). Quiet two-star place, safe for women; some rooms have double beds and a balcony, all are en suite with TV and fans. Mostly very clean, and set back from the main road – look for the sign on the downhill side of Abdali station. Takes credit cards. ②.

Jebel Amman

Hotels on **Jebel Amman** are almost all pricey, and many of them are a long distance from sights and nightlife; some, however, can offer a gentle ambience and a quality of service that's hard to find anywhere else in the country. Closest to Downtown, 1st Circle is a quiet and beautiful district with some elegant old stone buildings. The area around 2nd Circle is less characterful, while 3rd Circle is a tangle of tunnels pumping fast-moving traffic around the city, though its backstreets are quiet and pleasant. Beyond the leafy districts up to 4th Circle, shops, restaurants and local colour are non-existent. All these places accept major credit cards.

Bonita, on a side-street opposite *El-Yassmin Suites*, very close to 3rd Circle (☎06/461 5061, fax 461 5060, email *bonita@cns.go.com.jo*). Six rooms above a Spanish restaurant, small but en suite, clean and cosy. The street is leafy and quiet, the friendly staff laid-back. ⑤.

Carlton, directly opposite the *Inter-Continental Hotel*, between 2nd and 3rd Circles (☎06/465 4200, fax 465 5833). Clean rooms are bright and airy, with air con and heating, satellite TV and minibars. Service is good and the street-level restaurant cool and quiet. Book ahead as it's popular with groups. ⑥.

Dove, Qurtubah St, a side-street midway between 4th and 5th Circles (☎06/569 7683, fax 567 4676). A small hotel, way out on the fringes of the city proper, with cool breezes and nice views. Unremarkable rooms are spacious, some with balconies; prices will halve with a little encouragement. ④.

Hisham, just off Mithqal al-Fayez St near the French Embassy, between 3rd and 4th Circles (☎06/464 2720, fax 464 7540, email *hishamhotel@nets.com.jo*). Small, long-established residential hotel in the heart of the embassy quarter with an excellent reputation and unfailingly courteous and efficient staff. A peaceful terrace, pub, high-quality food and only 22 rooms make this the nearest thing to an English-style family hotel you'll find in Jordan. ⑥.

Shepherd, Zaid bin al-Harith St, midway between 1st and 2nd Circles (☎06/463 9197, fax 464 2401). Pristine and classy, the best choice in this price range citywide, and comfortably close to both the Downtown sights and the uptown restaurants. Rooms are pleasant and quiet, with a huge and affordable room service menu. ③–④.

Shmaysani

Once the most ostentatious neighbourhood in the city, **Shmaysani** is still home to many of Amman's richer inhabitants and a rump of underwhelming nightlife. Shops, late-night cafés, cinemas and restaurants are all clustered around the distinctive Housing Bank Centre and along the nearby streets, but Downtown is a twenty-minute taxi ride away.

Manar, Abdul Hamid Sharaf St (☎06/566 2186, fax 568 4329). Small, well-run place, right in the heart of the action. Comfortable, basic rooms are spotless, but you're paying well over the odds. ④.

Nefertiti, 26 al-Jahed St, close to the *Peking Restaurant* (☎06/560 3865). Simple, spartan rooms – the only remotely budget option in this part of town. ②.

al-Qasr, opposite the *Peking Restaurant* (☎06/568 9671, fax 568 9673). Cosy, quiet rooms are very light and bright, with direct-dial phones and all facilities. One of the top choices for business-people bored with five-star isolation. Credit cards accepted. ⑥.

Luxury hotels

Following a glut of hotel-building in the last year, Amman now boasts a full complement of international **luxury** names – and at the time of writing, a new *Hyatt Regency*, *Sheraton* and *Holiday Inn* were all in the final stages of completion. Since the tiny market for top-end accommodation in the city is now absurdly over-supplied, room prices are dropping rapidly; if you book in advance through a travel agent, you can slash the walk-in rates indicated below by up to a third. All these places accept major credit cards.

Inter-Continental, midway between 2nd and 3rd Circles, Jebel Amman (☎06/464 1361, fax 464 5217, email *ammha@go.com.jo*). One of the city's landmarks, with spacious, well-appointed rooms and packed with all kinds of diversions, from a crafts gallery to nightly bellydancing. Star features include the lobby café, one of the best bookshops in the city and an excellent – if pricey – Indian restaurant. Non-residents can use the comfortably big pool (daily 9am–5pm) for an uncomfortably big JD12. ⑧–⑨.

Le Meridien (formerly *Forte Grand*), adjacent to the Housing Bank Centre, Shmaysani (☎06/569 6511, fax 567 4261, email *meridien@go.com.jo*). As lavish as all the others, but somehow more dowdy too, and with less attention to detail. The minuscule pool is set right by the road and is shaded in the afternoon, and the terrace restaurant has an unappealing view of the Ministry of Industry and Trade opposite. ⑧–⑨.

Marriott, Issam al-Ajlouni Street, near Interior Circle, Shmaysani (☎06/560 7607, fax 567 0100, email *marriott@cns.go.com.jo*). Airy top-floor rooms have spectacular views; some pokier ones lower down are enticingly affordable. One highlight is the hotel's authentic and easy-going sports bar and burger joint *Champions*. Non-residents can use the pocket-sized outdoor pool, as well as the indoor pool, jacuzzi, exercise room and sauna, for JD12. ⑦–⑨.

Radisson SAS (formerly *Philadelphia*), Hussein bin Ali St, overlooking Wadi Saqra, Shmaysani (☎06/560 7100, fax 566 5160, email *ammzhres@go.com.jo*). Following a recent renovation, these are probably the best hotel rooms in Amman, exceptionally spacious and pleasant, with service to match. Some on lower floors remain unrenovated, and are less expensive. ⑧–⑨.

Long stays

Should you decide to stay for a while, you may be able to negotiate discounts at some of the inexpensive Downtown **hotels**: travellers' favourites such as the *Cliff*, *Vinecia*, *Arab League*, *Farah* and *Bdeiwi* are probably your best bets (in that order). In the long run, though, you'd do better to **rent** somewhere to live. One glance in the *Jordan Times* or the *Star* will turn up half-a-dozen ads for accommodation, most to move in immediately with little or no deposit. These are almost always mansions or huge penthouses in uptown districts such as Shmaysani, Abdoun, 4th Circle or distant suburbs near the University such as Tla'a al-Ali and Gardens. If you don't mind the impersonality of such neighbourhoods – and can afford monthly rents of JD350–400 plus – you could move in with little or no fuss.

Finding a cosy place in more congenial neighbourhoods such as Jebel al-Lweibdeh or 1st Circle takes a little more effort. Check the well-used **notice-boards** in all cultural centres, supermarkets and *Books@Café* first, but your best bet is to spread the word to English-speaking locals as quickly as possible. Wandering your favoured area chatting in shops and cafés, and sticking up your own "wanted" ad everywhere are good ploys. Space is not at a premium and once you get on the grapevine things can move rapidly. It's possible to find a good flat in a quiet neighbourhood for as little as JD180 a month furnished (*mafroush*) or JD140 unfurnished, less if you're prepared to share. The costs of water (*my*), electricity (*kahraba*) and gas (*gaz*) are negligible, heating oil (*solar*) less so. If the place has no phone, it'll cost you hundreds to get one installed; renting a mobile makes more sense.

Amman is a tenants' market: under Jordanian law, once you're in, the landlord cannot raise the rent until you leave, and neither hell nor high water can budge a tenant unwilling to go. For this reason, many landlords rent exclusively to foreigners, who can be expected to leave of their own accord eventually. If things aren't up to scratch, you have a sizeable degree of bargaining power: most landlords start out assuming that minor repairs are the responsibility of the tenant, but need little persuasion to relent. It's worthwhile checking the **rental contract** out with a lawyer or a translation bureau before you sign.

Downtown

Although it would be next-to-impossible to visit Amman without spending at least some time in **Downtown**, the cramped valleys between towering hills shelter comparatively few obvious sights; rather, Downtown is the spiritual and physical heart of the city and is unmissable for its street life. This is the district that most strongly resembles the stereotype of a Middle Eastern city – loud with traffic and voices, Arabic music blaring from tape stores, people selling clothes, coffee, cigarettes or trinkets on the street. The handful of Roman ruins that survive have been irreverently incorporated into the everyday bustle of the city. The banked seating of the huge **Roman Theatre** is always dotted with small groups of locals seeking refuge from the traffic noise, and the adjacent **forum** is filled with trees and cafés, a public meeting-place today as it was for the Romans.

The Roman Theatre and the forum

Dominating the centre of Downtown, the **Roman Theatre** (unrestricted access) is the best place to begin an exploration of Amman. This massive construction – endlessly plugged on posters, brochures and the back of every street-sweeper's overalls – was the centrepiece of Roman Philadelphia, and the initial focus for Amman's modern settlement late last century.

As you approach from the road, winding your way through the trees, a long Corinthian colonnade and some original Roman paving are the only physical remains of Philadelphia's **forum**, the marketplace which filled the gap between the theatre and the main street. What also survives, however, is the spirit of the place: this whole area is still the city's main hangout, as Ammanis crowd the dozens of little cafés, promenade up and down, guzzle ice-cream and sweets, meet friends and snooze on the grass.

Several nineteenth-century travellers to Amman reported seeing the remains of a large **propylaeum**, or ornamental gateway, on the edge of the forum; this still stood in 1911 but has since disappeared. If you stop in front of the theatre and look back towards the street, high on the summit of Jebel al-Qala'a opposite you'll spot the columns of the Temple of Hercules; originally, the propylaeum would have stood at the foot of a tremendous monumental staircase leading down from the temple, linking the religious and social quarters of the city.

Cut into the hillside, the **theatre** is impressively huge, and the view, as well as the ability to eavesdrop on conversations between ant-like people on the stage below, definitely repay the steep climb to the top. The structure was built between 169 and 177 AD, during the reign of Emperor Marcus Aurelius, for an audience of almost six thousand, and is still occasionally filled today for concerts. Above the seating is a small, empty **shrine** with niches; the dedication isn't known, although part of a statue of Athena was discovered during clearance work. Standing on the stage or in the orchestra – the semicircle in front of the stage – you can get a sense of the ingenuity of the theatre's design: the south-facing stage is flooded with sun throughout the day, while virtually every spectator remains undazzled and in cool shadow. To discover the incredible acoustics, stand in the middle of the orchestra and declaim at the seating, and your normal speaking voice will suddenly gain a penetrating echo; step off that spot and there's no echo. Furthermore, two people crouching down at opposite ends of the orchestra can mutter into the semicircular stone wall below the first row of seats and easily hear each other.

The museums of folklore and popular traditions

To the sides of the stage are two small museums, housed in vaults beneath the auditorium. On the right as you walk in, the **Folklore Museum** (Mon, Wed, Thurs, Sat & Sun 9am–5pm, Fri 10am–4pm; JD1) displays mannequins engaged in traditional crafts and a moderately interesting reconstruction of a sophisticated Ammani's living-room. Nothing is very well labelled, however, and it barely justifies the admission price. Much more worthwhile is the **Jordanian Museum of Popular Traditions** opposite (same hours and admission price), which deftly manages to enliven the well-worn theme of traditional clothing, jewellery and customs by rooting it firmly in the present-day life of ordinary people. The vaulted rooms are full of examples of national dress, with detailed notes and occasional photographs to set them in context. Other exhibits include pieces of antique bedouin jewellery and a fascinating range of stones used by the bedouin in healing, as well as mosaics downstairs gathered from Madaba and Jerash (and viewable up close).

The Odeon

Facing onto the forum area outside the theatre is the Roman **Odeon** (unrestricted access). Re-opened in 1997 after complete renovation, this free-standing theatre seating about five hundred dates from slightly earlier than the large theatre and was probably the venue for either parliamentary-style council meetings or small-scale drama. In antiquity, the whole building would probably have been roofed.

The Husseini Mosque and around

From Raghadan bus station and the theatre, lively **Hashmi Street** storms west past *shwarma* stands, juice bars, patisseries and cafés towards the commercial hub of Downtown and the focal, pink-and-white-striped **Husseini Mosque**. Like everything else in Amman, this is a relatively recent construction, although a mosque has stood here since 640 (and, before that, a Byzantine cathedral). Any remnant of the original building was erased when Emir Abdullah ordered the site cleared for construction of the current mosque in 1932. Renovated in 1987, it remains one of Amman's most important places of worship, and is often also the focus for political demonstrations. Although you're free to wander around the gates, whether or not you'll be allowed inside depends on the whim of the caretaker, who can normally be found sitting just inside the right-hand gate.

The area around the mosque is the heart of Amman's **bazaars**. To the east lies a bustling warren of alleys known as the **Souq Sukkr** (Sugar Market), where stalls sell everything from dates and spices to soap and mops. To the right of the mosque, the main street funnelling traffic south out of Downtown is **King Talal Street**, lined with stores selling ordinary household goods, fabric and bric-à-brac; a little way down on the left, hidden behind a row of shopfronts, is the city's main fruit and vegetable market.

The main street parallel to Talal Street follows exactly the course of the Roman *decumanus maximus*, which was formed by paving over the free-flowing stream beneath. The street is still known as the **Saqf Sayl** (Roof of the Stream), but these days the *sayl* is dry, having been tapped much further upstream to provide drinking water. This is the busiest and liveliest area of the city, with cobblers, tape-sellers and hawkers of soap and toothbrushes competing for space under the pavement colonnades with a dirt-cheap second-hand clothes market; there's also a small bus station here serving villages near Amman.

The Nymphaeum

On the Saqf Sayl behind the Husseini Mosque, excavation and renovation work on the Roman **Nymphaeum** has been going on for a year or more. It's very similar in design to the huge nymphaeum at Jerash which has been dated to 191 AD; at that time, Philadelphia too was at its zenith. You're free to wander about the site, though, apart from the immensity of the construction, there's not an awful lot to admire. Nymphaea – public fountains dedicated to water nymphs – were sited near rivers running through major cities throughout the Greco-Roman world. Philadelphia's, facing onto an open plaza at the junction of the two principal city streets, the east–west *decumanus* and the north–south *cardo*, was originally two storeys high and must have been quite a sight. Colonnades of Corinthian columns would have drawn even more attention towards the concave building, which was lavishly faced in marble, with statues of gods, emperors or city notables filling the niches all around.

King Faysal Street

The Husseini Mosque faces up **King Faysal Street**, modern Amman's oldest thoroughfare, occupying the valley between Jebel Amman to the south and Jebel al-Qala'a to the north. Although it follows exactly the course of the Roman *cardo*, any trace of the ancient past has been built over; the oldest buildings, with elegant arched windows and decorated stone balconies, date from the 1920s. There's little to grab your attention other than the **Souq al-Dahab**, the gold market, a series of minuscule jewellery shops clustered together next to the large Arab Bank building. Nearby is Shabsough Street, named after the Shabsough tribe of Circassians who first settled here (see box), from which stairs rise up to Jebel al-Qala'a.

THE CIRCASSIANS

The first people to settle in Amman in modern times were Muslim refugees from Christian persecution in Russia. The **Circassians**, who began arriving in the 1870s, trace their origins back to mountain villages above the eastern Black Sea, in the region of the **Caucasus** around present-day Georgia and Chechnya.

In the 1860s, Russian military offensives in the Caucasus forced 1.5 million people out of their homes into exile in Ottoman Turkish territory. Some headed west towards the fertile lands of the Balkans (establishing Muslim communities in the former Yugoslavia), while others drifted south into the Ottoman province of Syria. Stories began to filter back to those left behind of life in a Muslim land, and many Circassian and Chechen villages went *en masse* into voluntary exile. European governments lent their weight to the Ottoman policy of dumping the refugees on ships bound for distant Syria.

Meanwhile, Amman had been uninhabited for virtually a thousand years. In 1877, Selah Merrill, a visiting American archeologist, "spent part of one night in the great theatre ... The sense of desolation was oppressive. Kings, princes, wealth and beauty once came here to be entertained, where now I see only piles of stones, owls and bats, wretched *fellahin* [peasants] and donkeys, goats and filth." The first Circassian refugees arrived the following year, setting up home in the galleries of the theatre; others founded new villages in the fertile valley of Wadi Seer to the west and among the deserted ruins of Jerash to the north. The presence of settlers caused some conflict with local tribes, but the Circassians held their own in skirmishes with the bedouin, and soon a mutual respect and a formal pact of friendship emerged between them. After 1900, Circassian labour was central to the building of the Hejaz railway line, and Circassian farmers became famed for their industry. One of their great innovations was the reintroduction of the wheel – with no roads to speak of, wheeled transport hadn't been used in Transjordan for centuries.

When, in the 1920s, Emir Abdullah established a new state and chose Amman to be its capital, he bound the Circassian community into his new administration: loyal and well-educated families were the mainstay of both the officer corps and the civil service. Over the years, however, overt expressions of Circassian culture faded – Arabic became the *lingua franca*, the use of national dress died out and, with the rise in land prices following the influx of Palestinian refugees in 1948, many Circassians sold their inherited farmlands around Amman for the building of new suburbs. However, their internal identity remained strong, and Circassians today form an integrated minority of 25,000. Their historians are starting to re-examine the circumstances of the exile, and the **Circassian Community Centre** on Jebel Amman (☎06/582 5175) often hosts theatre and dance commemorating the homeland.

Jebel al-Qala'a

Jebel al-Qala'a has been a focus for human settlement since the Paleolithic Age, more than 18,000 years ago. Unfortunately, when the Romans moved in to occupy the area, they cleared away whatever they found, including the remains of the Ammonite city of Rabbath Ammon, and chucked it over the side of the hill – Bronze Age, Iron Age and Hellenistic pottery sherds have been found mixed up with Roman remains on the slopes below. Of the remains surviving today, the most impressive by far is a huge **Umayyad palace** complex on the upper terrace of the citadel, dating from the first half of the eighth century. On the middle terrace below and to the south lies the Roman **Temple of Hercules**, its massive columns dramatically silhouetted against the sky, and close by is Jordan's principal **archeological museum**. East of the temple, Roman fortifications protect the grassy lower terrace, which has no visible antiquities.

The easiest way to reach the summit is by **taxi** (500 fils from Downtown). **Service** #9 can drop you at the crossroads below the northern tip of the Citadel, but it's still a scramble to the top from there. For the ambitious who prefer to **walk**, the ascent is very steep: it might only take twenty minutes, but your legs will remember it long after. About 150m along Shabsough Street, and just past the second turning on the left (which has the line of #9 *service*s heading up), another side-street has a wide flight of steps leading left up the hillside. Turn right at the top, and head up from here any way you can – there are crumbling steps most of the way, often leading through private backyards. You'll eventually arrive at the wall below the Temple of Hercules.

The National Archeological Museum

The **National Archeological Museum** (Mon, Wed, Thurs, Sat & Sun 9am–5pm, Fri 10am–4pm; JD2) is the major repository for archeological finds from all periods and all parts of the country, though it's far too small for its collection. A visit to the cramped, badly organized building can be frustrating, but an attempt has been made to sort things into some coherent order, and what's on display is of the highest quality. English noticeboards supply well-written background information on everything, and you could easily browse for an hour or two.

The collection begins before you even get inside. At the top of the steps leading up to the door you'll see an enormous marble hand, discovered in the grounds of the Temple of Hercules nearby and presumed to be part of a statue of the god-hero himself. The complete figure would have been a fittingly gigantic 9m high.

Inside, you should turn right for a chronological tour of the collection. Staring eerily at you from its cabinet, a statuette discovered at the **Neolithic** settlement of Ain Ghazal is one of the earliest human figures ever discovered – though well over eight thousand years old, it displays a surprisingly expressive grace. Round the corner, a skull provides gruesome evidence of the failure of **Bronze Age** surgery techniques: this particular patient didn't just submit to having one hole drilled into his or her head (which healed up), but came back for three more – which conclusively halted the onset of any further disease.

Bypassing the Nabatean room, the tour continues with the **Iron Ages**, including a fabulous limestone statuette of Yerah Azar, king of Ammon, in a characteristically stiff regal pose clutching a lotus flower to his chest. Nearby cabinets hold plenty of coins, as well as a beautiful little **Hellenistic** jug in blue and yellow. Round near the entrance look out for a delightful **Byzantine** swan made from a seashell and carved ivory.

At this point, the chronological scheme begins to go haywire, with **Roman** figurines and glassware from Jerash dotted everywhere. At the back of the museum is an extensive collection of **Nabatean** art and pottery from Petra; its huge semi-circular centrepiece represents the goddess of vegetation, taken from the temple at Khirbet Tannur (see p.218). On the left wall is the earliest mural ever discovered, from Teleilat Ghassul (see p.308); the six thousand years since it was painted have taken their toll, but figures are still recognizable. In the small room to the right – as well as a copy of the Mesha Stele (see p.208) – is a collection of Dead Sea Scrolls.

Back in the main part of the museum, an **Islamic** room to the right displays ceramics and some wafer-thin gold dinars. At the back of this room, a doorway leads to two compelling Roman copies of Hellenistic statuary. Facing you is **Apollo**, beautifully slender and winsome, while in the corner stands the highlight of the whole museum – a grippingly intense **Daedalus**, reaching out to his doomed son Icarus (who has just flown too close to the sun and melted the wax holding his wings together).

Before you leave, make time for the bust of **Tyche** in the middle aisle of the main room. The equivalent of the patron saint of Philadelphia, she probably had a shrine down in the lower city, now lost.

The Temple of Hercules

The steps of the archeological museum look onto the Roman **Temple of Hercules**, built in the same period as the theatre below. The temple stands on a platform at the head of the monumental staircase which led up from the lower city – the blocks on the cliff edge near the temple's standing columns mark the position of the staircase, and afford a tremendous panoramic view over the city centre, particularly striking at sunset. The columns themselves, re-erected in 1993, formed part of a colonnaded entrance to the cella, or inner sanctum. Within the cella – these days often the scene of hard-fought football games among the local kids – a patch of bare rock is exposed, which, it's thought, may have been the sacred rock that formed the centrepiece of the ninth-century BC Ammonite Temple of Milcom on this spot. The Roman dedication to Hercules is not entirely certain but, given the quantity of coins bearing his likeness found in the city below, pretty likely.

The Umayyad Palace

Climbing the path to the upper terrace from the Temple of Hercules, you'll pass a small ruined **Byzantine church** on the right, dating from the fifth or sixth centuries, which reused many of the columns from the nearby temple. The church formed part of a Byzantine town which probably covered much of the hill and which is still being excavated; about 20m further north are a huge round cistern and the remains of an olive-pressing works.

The huge **Umayyad palace** complex stretches over the northern part of the hill. Part of the palace was built over pre-existing Roman structures, and an entire colonnaded Roman street was incorporated into it. Built between 720 and 747 AD, when Amman was a provincial capital, the complex probably combined the residential quarters of the governor of Amman with administrative offices. It was still in use during the Islamic Abbasid (750–969) and Fatimid (969–1179) periods, although much of the brand-new palace was never rebuilt following a devastating earthquake in 747.

The first building you come to, and the most impressive, is the **entrance hall**, reached by crossing the first of four plazas. Built over an earlier Byzantine building (which is why it's in the shape of a cross), the hall is decorated with stucco colonnettes and Persian-style geometric patterns, set off by foliage rosettes and a hound's-tooth zigzag. A great deal of renovation has been carried out here in recent years, not all of it very subtly – the sharp-edged 1990s stucco around the interior walls clashes rather nastily with the original work, and in 1998 a new dome was hastily constructed above the building, riding roughshod over the considerable archeological controversy about whether there ever was a dome here in antiquity. Between the entrance hall and the cistern is a small, newly excavated **baths**, although only a changing area and the "cold room" survive.

Beyond the entrance hall is the second large plaza, from which the **colonnaded street** leads ahead. This was the heart of the administrative quarter, surrounded by nine separate office or residential buildings (of which only four have been excavated), each in the typical Umayyad style of a self-contained *bayt* – small rooms looking onto a central courtyard. The *bayt*s were constructed within the pre-existing Roman enclosure, possibly a temple, whose exterior walls are still visible in places. To the west of the courtyard is "Building F", which may have been the site of official audiences, since it was of elegant design and situated close to the entrance hall; two large *iwan*s – audience rooms open on one side – with triple arcades give onto a central courtyard, from where a staircase led to an upper storey.

At the far end of the colonnaded street, a decorated doorway takes you through the Roman wall into the third plaza and the private **residential quarters** of the ruler of Amman. Rooms open from three sides, but the plaza is dominated by a huge *iwan*, which presages a domed, cruciform **throne room**, or *diwan*. According to Umayyad protocol, the ruler always stayed hidden behind a curtain during audiences – the tiny passageway between the *iwan* and the *diwan* could have served this purpose. To either side lie the largely unexcavated residential *bayt*s for the ruling household. At the back of the *diwan*, a doorway leads through to the fourth and final plaza – a private affair, looking north over the massive Roman retaining wall to the hills opposite.

The rest of the city

If you venture at all into the rest of the city, you're most likely to visit sprawling **West Amman**, one of the richest and most Western-oriented parts of the Arab world. It's here that you'll find practically all of Amman's nightlife, upmarket hotels and restaurants. Aside from a single, beautiful Byzantine **mosaic**, however, no antiquities are worth bothering with here, although the **National Gallery of Fine Arts** and **Darat al-Funun**, an arts centre, are worth a look. In general, West Amman is too large to attempt aimless exploratory rambling, though if you have a spare afternoon to fill, you might like to take a wander through the small neighbourhood below 1st Circle on Jebel Amman, particularly around the lower reaches of **Rainbow Street**; here you'll find many fine old 1920s villas and much leafiness – and the city's most attractive bookshop and Internet café – but no specific sights to aim for.

You're unlikely to have much reason to visit the low-income, populous neighbourhoods to the north, east and south of the city, other than to make a pilgrimage to the far-flung **Cave of the Seven Sleepers**.

Jebel al-Lweibdeh

Amman has a surprisingly active contemporary arts scene, and the two best galleries are within walking distance of each other in the neat, respectable neighbourhood of **Jebel al-Lweibdeh**, overlooking the hubbub of Downtown. The area has a relatively high proportion of Christian residents, and you'll find a tangibly different atmosphere from other parts of the city – many women are unveiled, there is less of a laid-back street life, and you may well hear the unfamiliar sound of church bells.

Darat al-Funun

If you're on foot, head for Omar al-Khayyam Street, which leads up behind the Downtown post office, and, turning right at the first hairpin, you'll soon come in sight of a high wall; head through the anonymous gate set into the wall on your left, which leads into the grounds of **Darat al-Funun** (daily except Fri 10am–7pm; ☎06/464 3251; free), a lush haven of tranquillity housing a centre for contemporary Arab art, about five minutes' walk (or 2min on *service* #4) from the post office. The "little house of the arts", as its name translates, comprises a set of three 1920s villas alongside the remains of a sixth-century Byzantine church. The "Blue House", at the very top of the steeply terraced complex, houses changing exhibitions, and its restored Circassian-style wooden porch serves as a tiny café – Amman's most beautiful and peaceful by far. On the same level is the former home of Emir Abdullah's court poet, now a private studio for visiting artists. Below, the former official residence of the British Commander of the Arab Legion sports a wonderful semicircular portico and has been superbly renovated to house well-lit galleries, studios and an excellent art library.

Exhibitions at Darat al-Funun vary from grand overviews of contemporary Arab art to small shows from local artists. There are also plenty of lectures and performances, often in the ruined church, and everything is free to the public. Even if art isn't your strong point, dropping in gives a sense of a flourishing side of Jordanian culture that's barely touched upon by most visitors.

Jordan National Gallery of Fine Arts

Leaving from the top gate of Darat al-Funun, it's a stiff five-minute climb past the Luzmila Hospital to the roundabout known as Lweibdeh Circle on top of the hill. Ten minutes or so from Lweibdeh Circle along quiet, shady Shari'a College Street, past the Terra Sancta religious academy, will bring you to Muntazah Circle, an oval expanse of green lined with elegant town-houses. One of these, on the right, is the newly refurbished **Jordan National Gallery of Fine Arts** (daily except Tues 9am–5pm; JD1), which is also accessible on *service* #4 from Downtown. At this, the premier establishment art showcase in Jordan, artists from Arab countries, the wider Islamic world and beyond are all represented in the fascinating 1500-work collection. Downstairs rooms feature a constantly changing selection of works from the permanent collection, while the upstairs extension features interesting temporary exhibitions. The small giftshop has a few prints and other knick-knacks for sale.

The Swayfiyyeh church mosaic

Way out in the sprawling western suburbs, hidden amongst the chi-chi boutiques and fast-food outlets of Swayfiyyeh, is almost the only **mosaic** to be seen in Amman. Discovered in the garden of a private house by chance in 1969 and now protected under a roofed shelter (daily except Fri 8am–2pm; free), the mosaic, of which only the left-hand portion survives, originally formed the floor of a late sixth-century Byzantine church and is in a very good state of preservation. Bordered with foliage and various animals, it features many bucolic vignettes – a red-tongued lion, a laden donkey and more. Special care was taken with the mens' faces, which are made up of tinier stones than the rest. In the corners, two striking white-bearded faces are probably personifications of the seasons.

To get there, take either a Wadi Seer **minibus** from Downtown (see p.118) or a **taxi** to 6th Circle. Turn left at the circle, take the first right, the second left and the fourth right, and continue past the *Boston Fried Chicken* joint. The small hangar housing the mosaic is then about 500m along opposite the *Liwan Hotel*.

South Amman

Perched over Downtown to the south is **Jebel al-Ashrafiyyeh**, the highest and steepest hill in the city, topped by the peculiar black-and-white-striped **Abu Darwish Mosque**. *Service* #25 or #26 from the Saqf Sayl will take you up to the gates of the mosque, which was built in 1961 by a Circassian immigrant. On the inside, it's utterly unremarkable, but outside, it's an Alice-in-Wonderland palace, complete with a row of black-and-white chess pawns atop its walls and multicoloured fairy lights after dark. The only other reason to come up here is for the **view**, yet there are no clear sightlines from street level; you'll have to – subtly – get onto the roof of one of the apartment buildings just down from the mosque. Any effort will be amply rewarded, though, especially early in the morning or after sunset: from this high up, the entire city is laid out like a relief map at your feet.

Behind Jebel al-Ashrafiyyeh lies **Wihdat**, a low-income neighbourhood that is almost entirely Palestinian. *Wihdat* are prefab housing units, and this is where many refugees settled in camps of temporary accommodation following their flight from Israel in 1948. To this day, the UN provides aid to many Palestinian families still resident here in their *wihdat*, fifty years on.

The Cave of the Seven Sleepers

Southeast of Wihdat, tucked away in the run-down suburb of Abu Alanda, the **Cave of the Seven Sleepers** (daily 8am–5pm; free) – known in Arabic as *Ahl al-Kahf* – is a pilgrimage site associated with a story recorded in the Quran about seven young Christian men who escaped Roman religious persecution by hiding in a cave. God put them to sleep for hundreds of years and when they awoke, their attempts to buy food with ancient coins aroused incredulity. The youths were taken to the – by then – Christian governor, who realized that a miracle had occurred, and ordered celebrations. Their work of enlightenment done, the men returned to the cave where God put them to sleep for good.

The atmospheric cave, one of many Byzantine rock-cut tombs nearby, is set into the hillside next to a modern mosque, built to service the tide of devout Muslims who come to pay their respects. In antiquity, a small church was built literally on top of the cave – the *mihrab* of its later conversion into a mosque is directly overhead. The decorated entrance, shaded by an ancient olive tree, is topped by five medallions, one of which is a cross. Inside are alcoves with four sarcophagi, one of which has a much-worn hole through which you can peek at an eerie jumble of bones. The walls show remains of painted decoration, with a curious eight-pointed star recurring many times which looks much like a Jewish Star of David, though it is in fact a Byzantine Christian symbol.

To reach *Ahl al-Kahf* by car or **taxi** (JD1.500 from Downtown), turn left at a crossroads about 3km south of Middle East Circle and drive about 2km to where two roads join on the left; take the second of the two, which will bring you to a little roundabout in Abu Alanda itself. **Buses** from the Saqf Sayl can also drop you here. Turn right, and the cave is about 1km ahead.

Eating and drinking

Although Amman is a relatively small city, it has plenty of possibilities for **eating out**. There are some first-rate Arabic restaurants, as you might expect, but also affordable and surprisingly good Indian, Chinese and European food. If you're on a tight budget, Downtown has dozens of cheap diners, with American-style fast food universally popular. Ammanis also have an incorrigible sweet tooth, which they are constantly placating with visits to the city's many **patisseries**, for honey-dripping pastries and cakes, or its **coffee houses** and **cafés**, for syrupy-sweet tea and coffee (and soft drinks by the crateful).

Places where you can drink **alcohol** are scattered across the city, ranging from uptown Western-style bars and pubs, complete with satellite TV and imported beers, to covert liquor dens in Downtown back alleys.

Coffee houses, patisseries, cafés and juice bars

One of Amman's oldest **coffee houses** – which it's best to visit first to get a sense of the style of these places – is the *Arab League*, but there are more tucked away in every alley in Downtown. These traditional places are often shunned by hip young locals, however, who prefer instead to kill their hours in newer, Western-style pavement **cafés** in Shmaysani and other uptown neighbourhoods, where langorous people-watching is easy and where women can feel at least slightly more comfortable.

You'll also find **juice bars** (generally daily except Fri 7am–9pm or so) in every corner of Downtown. Two good places face each other on King Faysal Street opposite the entrance to the *Arab League* coffee-house, while the best *tamarhindi* in the city is to be had from the place at the end of Basman Street, opposite the Husseini Mosque. From here, walk towards the Roman Theatre, and a very friendly juice bar on the right has good *luz* (sweet almond-milk) as well as the best-tasting *kharoub* around.

Downtown

In addition to the places listed here, unnamed, less hectic coffee-houses can be found in the alleys surrounding the *Cliff Hotel* and the Cairo Amman Bank, as well as down dim staircases between shops on King Talal Street. The open cafés lining Hashmi Square near the Roman Theatre are less traditional, and a little more expensive.

Arab League, King Faysal St (entrance round the side), opposite the Husseini Mosque. This traditional, cavernous, bay-windowed palace is large and relaxed enough that discreet foreign women generally pass unnoticed. Choose a window table for one of the best Downtown street views you can get. Daily 7am–midnight.

Auberge, alley between Prince Muhammad St and Basman St (unmarked entrance). One floor below the *Cliff Hotel* and uncompromisingly male. However, the coffee is good and the tiny balcony a great place to watch the street go by. A small back room serving beer and arak adds to the air of dissipation. Daily 7am–midnight.

Centrale, King Hussein St, at the corner with King Faysal St (entrance shared with *Hilton Bar*). Completing the triumvirate of big Downtown coffee houses, the *Centrale* has never been the same since the glorious open-air terrace was ripped out for redevelopment a few years back. Until work begins, it remains one large room that soaks up the morning sun. Daily 7am–midnight.

Eco-Tourism Café (aka *al-Rasheed Courts*), in an alley off King Faysal St, opposite the Arab Bank. Downtown's newest, most relaxed and foreigner-friendly coffee-house, with a younger crowd than most. The balcony – Downtown's best – is a pleasant place to hang out and chat with local twenty-somethings. Daily 9am–1am.

Habibah, King Hussein St, near the corner with King Faysal St (Arabic sign only, but it's unmissably big, symmetrical blue-on-white). The best patisserie in the city, if not the country, piled high with every conceivable kind of sweetmeat, pastry and biscuit, all very affordable. There's a mixed-company café upstairs for eat-ins. Smaller pop-in branches are dotted around the city. All daily 7am–midnight.

Jabri, King Hussein St, close to *Habibah*. A slightly more dowdy outlet than the slick *Habibah* but with much the same stock, plus OK ice-cream. Also with a mixed upstairs café. Branches in Shmaysani and elsewhere. All daily 8am–10pm.

West Amman

As befits the clientele, most of the cafés in the richer parts of the city are pretty upscale places – more espresso-and-gateau than *shy*-and-*arjileh*.

Books@Café, Mango St, just off Rainbow St, below 1st Circle, Jebel Amman. A Californian atmosphere unlike anywhere else in Jordan, with a bookshop downstairs and gourmet coffee upstairs. Highlights, in addition to Internet access, are treats such as brownies, toasted sandwiches and free perusal of foreign newspapers. With Amman's uptown monied set for company, you could easily forget you were in the Middle East altogether. *Service* #2. Daily 9am–midnight.

Darat al-Funun, opposite the Luzmila Hospital, Jebel al-Lweibdeh. This gallery complex and centre for the arts has the quietest, most attractive little café in Amman (see p.97). *Service* #4. Daily except Fri 10am–7pm.

el-Farouki, opposite the landmark fast-food joint *Chili House*, Shmaysani. The best and most congenial of Shmaysani's hangouts, with good, fresh-roasted coffee and a relaxed back-room where women can puff in peace. Daily 10am–1am.

Frosti, beside *el-Farouki*, Shmaysani. Amman's finest ice-cream and frozen yoghurt, bar none. Daily 10am–1am.

Tower Restaurant, 23rd floor of Jordan Towers building, Prince Muhammad St, below 3rd Circle, Jebel Amman. A circular café-restaurant perched high above the city. Steep prices are worth it for the jaw-dropping views and to be able to sink into one of their deep leather armchairs. *Service* #3. The entrance is unsigned, directly opposite the *City Hotel*; walk to the back and you'll find the lifts. Daily 11am–midnight.

Zalatimo, upper end of Abdali station. Perhaps the best-loved name in the *halawiyyat* (Arabic sweets) business, with mountains of topnotch gloopy goodies at premium prices. Mon–Thurs, Sat & Sun 8am–8pm, Fri 8am–7pm.

Restaurants

Amman's **restaurants** cover a broad spectrum, from back-street canteens ladling meat stew to air-conditioned palaces serving international delicacies. Downtown restaurants – many of which congregate opposite the Roman Theatre – are almost exclusively basic Arabic-style diners offering roast chicken and kebabs, but there's plenty of opportunity for cheap and tasty snacking – *falafel* sandwiches and bowls of *fuul* or *hummus* are unbeatable, and street *shwarma* stands are everywhere (the best *shwarma*, however, is from the stall on 2nd Circle, at the corner heading towards 3rd). All the better restaurants, and virtually all the non-Arabic places, are located in uptown districts.

Western fast food is well established, with original chains and local imitators all over the city. *Service* #38 runs out to a host of junk-food outlets on Abdullah Ghosheh Street, while pricey *Pizza Hut* (☎06/464 4097), near 2nd Circle, does free home or hotel delivery. Swayfiyyeh is crammed with choices: everything from *Arby's* to *Dunkin' Donuts* to *I Can't Believe It's Yoghurt!* Amman's best quality of cheap food by miles, however, is available from *Snack Box* (takeaway only; see p.103).

Arabic: budget diners

Cairo, down a side-street behind the Husseini Mosque, Downtown. The most convivial of a trio of celebrated Downtown diners (the others are *al-Quds* and *Hashem* – see below), serving uncomplicated fare ranged in hot cabinets at the back. You'd have to stuff yourself to part with more than JD1.500; expect to share a tab. Daily 8am–11pm.

"Egyptian Food" (scrawled on the only English sign), King Talal St, opposite the vegetable market, Downtown. The only place in Amman serving *kushari*, a budget Egyptian stomach-filler comprising rice, pasta, lentils and tomato sauce topped with fried onions. Daily 9am–9pm.

Hashem, in an alley opposite *Cliff Hotel*, Downtown. A fast-paced outdoor diner that's been around since the Twenties, with tables set out all down the alley and just *fuul* or *hummus* to choose from. Tea-waiters periodically stride around shouting "*shy, shebab*" (tea anyone?) – grab a glass off the tray. To supplement your dish, the stand opposite sells bags of cheap *falafel* balls. Daily 24hr.

al-Quds, King Hussein St, next to *Habibah* patisserie, Downtown. The best restaurant in Downtown (which isn't saying much), serving a range of rather over-cooked Arabic specialities, including the celebrated bedouin speciality *mensaf* (mutton with rice and yoghurt). Prices are reasonable – a full meal needn't set you back more than JD2.500 or so – but the menu is in Arabic only. Lunchtimes are more congenial. Daily 7am–11pm.

al-Sahn al-Dimashq, Ilya Abu Mahdi St, near *Pizza Hut*, Shmaysani. Arabic sign only – look for the elaborate Damascene-style decoration. Solid fare at good prices, with the added attraction of half-a-dozen varieties of *fatteh* and *kebab halaby*. Celebrated, high-quality *shwarmas* too. Daily noon–midnight.

al-Salaam, King Faysal St, opposite the Gold Souq, Downtown. Simple diner with reasonable half-chickens (that's just about all they do). Rarely more than JD2. Daily 10am–10pm.

Tarweea, part of the Haya Cultural Centre, opposite *KFC*, Shmaysani. Surprisingly good Lebanese *fatteh*, stuffed *falafel* and fresh *mana'eesh*, served in airy, clean and calm surroundings at rock-bottom diner prices – a quality alternative to Shmaysani's junk-food fixation. Daily 24hr.

Arabic: mid-range and expensive restaurants

Abu Ahmad, two branches: the *Orient*, on Basman St next to the *Cliff Hotel*, Downtown; and the more formal *New Orient*, behind the *Inter-Continental Hotel*, near 3rd Circle, Jebel Amman (☎06/464 1879). Well-regarded places with pleasant garden terraces serving a welter of accomplished dishes. Around JD4 or so. Both daily 11am–midnight.

Fakhr el-Din, 40 Taha Hussein St, behind Iraqi Embassy, between 1st and 2nd Circle, Jebel Amman (☎06/465 2399). Amman's premier establishment, catering to the royal and diplomatic upper crust. Excellent food and impeccable service, yet judicious choices can keep the bill around JD10. Lunch special JD4. Reservations essential. Daily 1–3.30pm & 8pm–midnight.

Nouroz, on 3rd Circle, Jebel Amman. Small, easy-going kind of place, with a simple menu and good food, including beer. Rarely above JD4. Daily 11am–11pm.

Sahtain, at Kan Zaman, al-Yadoudeh village, on a hill 3km off the airport road at the Madaba exit (turn left, not right to Madaba), about 15km south of Amman (☎06/412 6449). At the high-profile tourist village of Kan Zaman (see p.107), the classy *Sahtain* restaurant seats 400 in subtly lit vaults and is a deeply atmospheric place to eat a superb buffet, but not cheap. Arabic music and dance nightly. Daily 1–4pm & 7pm–midnight.

Tannoureen, Shatt al-Arab St, Souq Umm Uthayna, near 6th Circle (☎06/551 5987). High-quality Lebanese cuisine in a cosy, arty setting. Not as wide a choice as might be expected, but exquisite *mezze* and a fantastic *shish tawook* (marinated chicken breast) make up for it. JD10 and upwards. Daily 1–4pm & 8–11pm.

Indian, Chinese and Japanese

Bukhara, at the *Inter-Continental Hotel*, midway between 2nd and 3rd Circles, Jebel Amman (☎06/464 1361). Very expensive but spectacularly good Indian food, with tandoori a speciality and plenty for vegetarians. Daily noon–3pm & 7–11.30pm.

China, just off Rainbow St, 100m from Bani Hamida, below 1st Circle, Jebel Amman (☎06/463 8968). Low-key place with a dedicated East Asian expat clientele. The food is good, and with careful selections it's easy to keep prices well inside single figures. Daily noon–3.30pm & 7pm–midnight.

China Town, at *Le Meridien Hotel*, adjacent to Housing Bank Centre, Shmaysani (☎06/569 6511). Top-quality Chinese meals, in a classy, comfortable ambience, for around JD10. Also has a *teppanyaki* bar with a pricey range of *sushi* and Japanese specialities. Daily 12.30–3.30pm & 7.30–11.30pm.

Peking, opposite *al-Qasr Hotel*, Shmaysani (☎06/566 0250). Superb Chinese restaurant, with a long and varied menu. Highlights include a wonderful "sour peppery soup" and *ma po* tofu wok-fried to perfection. Prices are high: a full meal could set you back JD20. Daily 1–3.30pm & 7–11.30pm.

European

Bonita, down a side-street opposite *El-Yassmin Suites*, very close to 3rd Circle, Jebel Amman (☎06/461 5061). The best Spanish restaurant in town, known for its superb fish and seafood, and three kinds of paella (one of them vegetarian). A full meal could reach JD15. Next door is a quiet tapas bar with Mexican beer and dozens of cheap nibbles. Restaurant daily noon–midnight; bar daily 7.30pm–midnight.

Ciro's Pizza Pomodoro, near *Café Moka*, just off Abdoun Circle, Abdoun (☎06/592 8515). Popular branch of an upmarket international chain, which is hard to spot: go round the side of an anonymous office building and down the stairs. Inside, it's dim and loud. A huge choice of good-quality pizzas go for roughly JD4.500 each, with a familiar array of salads, pasta dishes and beer to wash it down. Also has live music. Reservations essential. Daily 8pm–3am.

Pizza Reef, Medina St, 200m north of Duwaar al-Waha (the junction of Medina St and Gardens St), Tla'a al-Ali, suburban West Amman (no phone). The best pizza in the city, thin-crust, wood-fired fresh to order and not expensive (around JD2.500). They can make up anything you fancy, with or without meat or cheese – their unique *labneh* and rucola offering with extra rosemary is delectable. Nearby sister outlet *Pizza Rimini* (turn right off Gardens before the junction at the Best supermarket and go 100m; ☎079/20885), does takeaways. You'll need a taxi and a detailed map to find either. *Reef* daily except Sat noon–2pm & 5–10pm; *Rimini* daily except Tues noon–2pm & 5–10pm.

Romero, down a side-street almost opposite the *Inter-Continental Hotel*, near 3rd Circle, Jebel Amman (☎06/464 4227). One of the best restaurants in the country, and the best Italian by a long streak. Service is uniquely calm and friendly, and the food outstanding, but you could easily walk out with change from JD10. Daily 1–3pm & 8–11pm.

Rover's Return, beneath *Comfort Hotel*, Swayfiyyeh (two streets behind the mosque midway between 6th and 7th Circles). A thoroughly authentic, poky English pub, with loud music and excellent food – including steak-and-kidney pie and the best fish-and-chips in Jordan (JD3). Go early to get a seat. Daily 12.30pm–1.30am.

Rozena, down a side-street behind the Turkish Embassy, near 2nd Circle, Jebel Amman (☎06/461 3572). Calm, unassuming "piano bistro", where steaks and chicken dishes are supplemented by a handful of vegetarian options. Roughly JD10. Daily 12.30–3.30pm & 7pm–midnight.

North American

Champions, at the *Marriott Hotel*, Issam al-Ajlouni St, near Interior Circle, Shmaysani. A roomy, lively American diner-cum-sports-bar, crammed with TVs. Food includes nachos, burgers and apple pies, in enormous portions; wash it all down with a pitcher of beer. English football is shown live, as is every other conceivable sporting occasion. One final attraction: they serve alcohol during Ramadan. Daily noon–1am.

Houston's, 11th of Ab St, Shmaysani (☎06/562 0610). Casual Tex-Mex joint, crammed on weekend nights. Huge salads, draught beer and the best nachos around. Daily noon–midnight.

Mama Juanita, at the *Inter-Continental Hotel*, between 2nd and 3rd Circles, Jebel Amman (☎06/464 1361). Tacos, burritos and fajitas, pricey but generally well-prepared. Squeeze your way past the expense-account journos at the bar exchanging tales of Baghdad bravery. Daily 12.30–3.30pm & 7.30–11.30pm.

West End, above the landmark fast-food joint *Chili House*, Shmaysani (☎06/569 3053). Authentic American steakhouse, classy and expensive. Menu highlights include a humungous 14oz char-grilled T-bone with all the trimmings, and fresh apple-pie. The high-quality meat is all USDA-approved, pushing the bill towards JD20. Daily 12.30pm–midnight.

Buying your own food and drink

Putting together a picnic is easy. The main Downtown **fruit and vegetable market**, with everything from potatoes to persimmons, is in a well-hidden back-alley off King Talal St, and there are some good general **grocery shops** in the alleys around the *Cliff Hotel*. The uptown **supermarkets** (see below) not only often undercut Downtown prices on fresh produce, but are also the sole outlets for ham and luncheon meat.

Hashem's restaurant will give you superb **hummus** or **fuul** in plastic pots to take away – to avoid leakages, ask for it *bidoon zayt* (without oil) – and the excellent **kushari** from *Egyptian Food* on King Talal St is also available to carry out. For something more substantial, head for the *Snack Box* takeaway (☎06/566 2402; closed Fri), directly opposite the King Abdullah Mosque 200m uphill from Abdali station, which does cheap, top-quality **Western-style dishes** such as steak sandwiches and huge stir-fries (veggie or not), all cooked to order. Good **bakeries** can be found in every neighbourhood, all selling fresh *khobbez*, rolls and breadsticks;

for something different, try Abela supermarket's fresh baguettes and rye loaves. Exquisite Iraqi **dates** are available year-round in the Downtown Souq Sukkr, while Faraon Honey, on the second floor of the Housing Bank Centre, sells inexpensive home-potted **honey** from the north of Jordan.

For buying **alcohol** in Downtown, there are plenty of liquor stores selling cold beer, wine and harder stuff, both local and imported. *Sweiss* on Basman Street behind the *Cliff Hotel* is one of the best, and there's a good, nameless place on King Faysal Street opposite the Gold Souq. All uptown supermarkets apart from Abela stock alcohol. Note that many cheap and mid-range hotels will object strongly to your bringing alcohol onto the premises; see p.48 for more on this.

Supermarkets

al-Ahlia Abela Superstore, next to Jordan National Bank, Queen Noor St, Shmaysani, close to 4th Circle. A city landmark, universally known as Abela. Classier than Safeway, with a wider choice and especially good bread. Daily 7am–11pm.

Rainbow Market, Rainbow St, 100m from 1st Circle, Jebel Amman. Friendly little corner store, and easy to get to. Daily 8.30am–8.30pm.

Safeway, Wadi Saqra, near Sports City. Another landmark, which every taxi-driver knows. Huge and filled with familiar brands; after 11pm, it turns into one of the capital's hottest nightspots, as all kinds of dangerous liaisons take place behind the shelter of the canned soups. Upstairs is CyberTunnel Internet café and Music Box with plenty of tapes and CDs. Bigger branch behind the Royal Jordanian building at 7th Circle. Both daily 24hr.

Stop & Shop, on Lweibdeh Circle, Jebel al-Lweibdeh (☎06/462 5140). Reasonably sized and close to Downtown – though none too cheap. Free delivery to anywhere in the city. Daily 8am–8pm.

Nightlife and entertainment

Setting aside the handful of **drinking and dancing** venues on the social circuit of the city's affluent twenty-somethings, Amman has a surprising amount of cultural **entertainment** to indulge in, although information, unless you call the relevant venue or sponsor in advance, is not easy to come by. Most cultural events are advertised on noticeboards in cultural centres, supermarkets and embassies; the *Jordan Times* lists events for that evening, and the *Star* supposedly for the week ahead, but neither is totally reliable. Also worth looking out for are openings of art exhibitions at Darat al-Funun and elsewhere, some of which are accompanied by music or poetry readings.

Bars

For a Muslim capital, Amman has a surprisingly wide range of **bars**, from swish upmarket hotel pubs to dingy dives well hidden in back alleys. All those in Downtown are devoted to quiet, sedentary drinking, but quite a few of the uptown joints have ear-blasting sound systems and dinky dancefloors. Thursday is the big night out.

Your best bet for **Downtown** drinking dens is the web of alleys surrounding the *Cliff Hotel* – here you'll find the *Jordan Bar*, *Salamon Bar*, *Kit-Kat Bar* (round next to the cinema) and, further away on King Hussein St opposite *Jabri's*, the *Hilton Bar*. All are grungy places, with no attractions whatsoever other than the alcohol.

Women, whether accompanied or not, are likely to attract a good deal of attention from slimeball barflies. There's a slightly less grisly bar attached to the *Rhum Continental Hotel*, nearby on Basman St. Most of these places open some time in the afternoon and close around midnight; a beer is about JD1.200.

Uptown neighbourhoods offer the possibility of classier drinking and – though beers are more expensive (roughly JD2.500) – the added attractions of foreign imports and Amstel on draught everywhere you go. Modesty in dress for both men and women goes out the window in these places, and T-shirts, short skirts and the like are common. The English-style *Rover's Return* (see p.103) in Swayfiyyeh is one of the best and most popular pubs in town, while the *Irish Pub* (daily 6pm–2am), in the basement of the *Dove Hotel* between 4th and 5th Circles, does a good imitation of a British student bar and gets packed out on hectic Thursday nights by Amman's young dance crowd. Two contrasting alternatives are the young-and-loud *Saluté*, opposite *Fakhr el-Din* restaurant behind the Iraqi Embassy; and the darker, quieter *After Eight*, in the *Granada Hotel* near 1st Circle (both daily 6pm–1am). All four- and five-star hotels have their own bars, but most are pretty deadly; *Champions* (see p.103) in the *Marriott* is a lively exception.

Music, dance and theatre

There's a well-established performance scene in Amman, especially of Western **classical music** – orchestras and soloists often pass through, and students from the National Music Conservatory (☎06/568 7620) perform regularly. The various cultural centres (see p.116) frequently sponsor performances, but **Arabic music** pops up frustratingly rarely. **Folkloric dance** is well represented, with the National Jordanian Folklore Troupe (run by the Ministry of Culture) and the Royal Jordanian Folklore Troupe (sponsored by the airline) leading the way. The major **venue** for everything is the Royal Cultural Centre (☎06/566 1026) in Shmaysani, 300m beyond the *Regency Palace Hotel* off Interior Circle, although there are outdoor performances in summer at Darat al-Funun and, occasionally, the Roman Theatre. Although Arabic-language **theatre** – both comedy and drama – is well-catered for, performances in English are a rarity. For more information on the star-studded **Jerash Festival**, see the box on p.135.

Film

Although there are plenty of **cinemas** in Downtown, they're all limited to showing last year's Hollywood action blockbusters and 1970s soft porn, everything sliced to ribbons by the censor and often dubbed appallingly into Arabic; tickets are a rock-bottom JD1. Otherwise, the main cinemas for new releases (subtitled in Arabic and French, and more subtly censored) are the Philadelphia, next to the Jordan Towers building below 3rd Circle; the Concord, down a side-street opposite the Housing Bank Centre in Shmaysani; the Plaza, inside the Housing Bank Centre (all of which charge JD3.500); and the plush, big-screen Galleria, just off Abdoun Circle (JD5). All have five shows daily between noon and 10.30pm; check the *Jordan Times* for what's on.

In **other venues** around town, plenty of movie surprises are on offer – mostly on video, but all free of charge. The British Council and the American Center both have regular programmes of English-language films, and all the other cultural centres show films from their own countries, sometimes subtitled in English.

Darat al-Funun regularly shows documentary art films. The charitable Abdul Hameed Shoman Foundation (☎06/465 9154) shows some non-commercial films, in English or with English subtitles; their building is directly opposite the Iraqi Embassy between 1st and 2nd Circles (sign in Arabic only; look for the "Maraqa Commercial Center" and go up the stairs). **European film festivals** run every May and October in different cinemas around town, and there's also a Franco-Arab Film Festival every June; festival programmes are always announced in advance in the *Jordan Times*, or you could call the Shoman Foundation or the French Cultural Centre (☎06/463 7009) for details.

Shopping

Amman's **shops** are never going to set your pulse racing. Compared to Cairo, Jerusalem, Damascus and Aleppo, which all have centuries-old *souq*s and long traditions of craftsmanship, Amman is a modern lightweight, with no memorable *souq*s to explore. Where the city scores is in its range of **bedouin crafts** from Jordan and Palestine at prices a fraction of Jerusalem's.

Souvenirs and local crafts

There's only a handful of genuine **craft shops** in Amman, and they tend to be associated with projects to revive or nurture the skills of local craftspeople; prices are honestly high and you're certain to be purchasing quality goods. **Souvenir shops** which are simply sales outlets for local or imported merchandise are more numerous; here prices can be high without necessarily implying a matching quality. There are many of the latter within walking distance of **Lweibdeh Circle**, and if you want to get a sense of what's available, this is a good place to start. King Talal Street, next to the Husseini Mosque, is lined with shops selling **household goods** where you could browse for interesting everyday items; good buys include a Turkish coffee service (a tiny pot for boiling the grounds plus six handleless cups on a tray), decorative Islamic prayer-beads or an *arjileh*, often steel but occasionally brass (check the joints carefully for leaks). There are myriad outlets near the mosque where you could pick up a simple but attractive cotton-polyester *jellabiyyeh* (robe) for less than JD10, a *keffiyeh* (head-dress) for JD2.500. Unless indicated otherwise, all the shops listed below accept major credit cards.

al-Afghani, opposite the Husseini Mosque, Downtown. Daily except Fri 9am–6pm. Also two branches on Jebel al-Lweibdeh. Amman's most famous souvenir shops, originally founded in Palestine in 1862 by a merchant from Kabul and still in the same family. The Downtown shop is a wonderful little Aladdin's cave, crammed to the ceiling with everything from Bohemian glass to ornate Cairene Ramadan lamps; serious browsing is better undertaken at the branches on al-Lweibdeh.

al-Aydi (aka Jordan Craft Development Centre), behind the former Lebanese Embassy, just off 2nd Circle, Jebel Amman. Daily except Fri 9am–7pm. Far away the best place to buy locally produced handmade crafts, with a huge variety of textiles, jewellery, ceramics, wood and metalwork, both old and new. It has the biggest collection of carpets in the country – Jordanian, Iraqi and Kurdish, ranging from antique pieces to newly-mades.

Bani Hamida House, next to Jordan River Designs, just off Rainbow St, below 1st Circle, Jebel Amman. Mon–Thurs, Sat & Sun 8am–6pm, Fri 10am–6pm. The main outlet for superb carpets woven by women of the Bani Hamida tribe (see p.206). Although it's possible to pick up a tiny wall-hanging for JD20, reasonably sized small rugs start around JD50; big carpets can be JD400.

Beit al-Bawadi, Fawzi Qaw Street, Abdoun. Daily except Fri 8am–7pm. High-quality ceramics, carpets and bric-à-brac to adorn Abdoun's mansions.

The Gold Souq, a network of alleys between the Arab Bank and the Cairo Amman Bank, off King Faysal St, Downtown. Most shops daily except Fri 8.30am–7pm. Dozens of tiny shops all next to each other, selling modern gold jewellery at competitive prices.

The Green Branch, opposite the Centre Culturel Français, just off Lweibdeh Circle, Jebel al-Lweibdeh. Daily except Fri 9am–6pm. The least pushy of the Lweibdeh souvenir shops, with an impressive selection of hand-embroidered jackets and dresses. No credit cards.

Jordan River Designs, next to Bani Hamida, just off Rainbow St, below 1st Circle, Jebel Amman. Mon–Thurs, Sat & Sun 8am–7pm, Fri 10am–7pm. A project originally set up by Save The Children, selling simple, bright and pricey handmade home furnishings. In the same courtyard is a nice little shop (daily 9am–6pm) devoted to selling jewellery, dried herbs and organic olive oil from Dana, a village co-operative in southern Jordan (see p.221).

Kan Zaman, al-Yadoudeh village, 3km off the airport road at the Madaba exit (turn left, not right to Madaba), about 15km south of Amman. Daily 10am–midnight. Kan Zaman (Once Upon A Time) was formerly a farming estate, established in the nineteenth century, which has had a highly touristic reconstruction as an Ottoman village. Prices in the lavish antiques shop are sky-high. Another shop nearby sells glassware, jewellery and ceramics made by ArtiZaman (you can visit their workshops downstairs), although it's easy to find items of the same quality and design for much less elsewhere.

al-Yousour, next to al-Aydi, just off 2nd Circle, Jebel Amman. Daily except Fri 9am–6pm. Tiny showroom attached to a workshop, with jewellery, brass and glass decorated with Arabic calligraphy that's designed, made and sold on-site. No credit cards.

Books, newspapers and music

Dozens of places all over Amman call themselves "bookshop" or "library", but don't be fooled – somewhere along the line "stationer's" was mistranslated, for that's what all these places are, selling office supplies and nothing more literary than *Muscle Monthly*. Nonetheless, Amman does have some excellent, if well-hidden, outlets for English **books**. You can pick up the *Jordan Times* and *Star* **newspapers** from Downtown pavement stalls, and a wide range of slightly old international newspapers and magazines from all five-star hotels. There are good **music** stores for Arabic tapes in every neighbourhood in the city, but the widest selection of both Arabic and Western music on tape and CD is at Music Box, just off Abdullah Ghosheh Street a short walk down from *McDonald's* (branches also at both Safeways).

Amman Bookshop, Prince Muhammad St, opposite Citibank, just below 3rd Circle, Jebel Amman. Daily except Fri 8.30am–2.30pm & 3.30–6pm. The most accessibly located big selection, but everything's new and a little pricey. Art, design and fiction are especially well covered.

Books@Café, Mango St, just off Rainbow St, below 1st Circle, Jebel Amman. Daily 9am–midnight. See also p.100. An eclectic choice of new and used books on everything from architecture to showbiz, with plenty of classic and pulp fiction. Some women's literature and gay and lesbian issues – the latter the only selection of its kind in the country. Also international newspapers and magazines.

Inter-Continental bookshop, in the *Inter-Continental Hotel*, between 2nd and 3rd Circles, Jebel Amman. Daily 8am–9pm. A good, if small, selection of books on the Middle East, plus some fiction paperbacks and a wide choice of newspapers and magazines.

Jordan Distribution Agency, 9th of Sha'aban St, near the junction with Prince Muhammad St, 300m uphill from the Downtown post office. Daily except Fri 8am–5pm. The closest true bookshop to Downtown, but stronger on newspapers than books.

Philadelphia, opposite the mosque halfway along Gardens St, West Amman. Mon–Thurs, Sat & Sun 9am–7pm, Fri 9am–noon. Satisfyingly large, diverse and often discounted range, with emphases on politics and literature, and plenty of translated Arab fiction and poetry.

Sharbain, Rainbow St at 1st Circle, Jebel Amman. Mon–Thurs & Sat 8.30am–6pm, Sun 8.30am–1pm. Tiny place with a choice of classics and others.

Moving on from Amman

Amman is the centre of Jordan's **transport** network and its main link to the outside world. Where your onward transport leaves from depends partly on what your destination is and partly on how you want to get there.

If you're **flying** out of Amman (don't forget the JD10 departure tax), you'll probably be using **Queen Alia International Airport** (information ☎06/445 3200; see also p.78). On the way out, one of the Airport Express buses (☎06/465 3313) leaves from the clocktower at one side of Raghadan station (daily, hourly 6am–8pm) and runs via Middle East Circle in Wihdat; another leaves from beneath the distinctive square sign at the top end of Abdali station (daily, every 30min 6am–10pm, then midnight, 2am & 4am) and runs via the Housing Bank Centre and 7th Circle. Terminal 1 handles Royal Jordanian flights to Europe (not Amsterdam), the Middle East, North Africa and Pakistan, as well as some domestic departures to Aqaba; Terminal 2 across the road (stay on the bus another minute) handles RJ flights for Amsterdam, North America, India and Southeast Asia, and worldwide departures on all other carriers; both terminals have duty-free shops. If you're flying RJ, you can check your bags in, pay your departure tax and receive a boarding card any time within 24 hours of your

---

FLIGHT AGENTS AND AIRLINES IN AMMAN

There are no truly discounted tickets to be had from **flight agents** in Amman. The cheapest fares to Europe tend to be with Olympic and Austrian; on Middle Eastern routes, the lack of competition results in unavoidably inflated fares whomever you ask. Downtown travel agents, which can knock only a few dinars off airlines' prices, are concentrated along King Hussein Street, up the hill from *Jabri*. The best is Rainbow (☎06/462 1652), but it's worth comparing prices in Nahas (☎06/462 5535) and Pan Pacific (☎06/462 1688) on the same street. Beware of agents who take backhanders from certain airlines to promote their routes over others which may be cheaper and/or more convenient – it's worth asking around to get the full picture. One thing to look out for are specially reduced group fares (on EgyptAir and Turkish, among others): these vary, but can give discounts for "groups" of two or more people flying together.

The following **airlines** fly out of Amman: Aeroflot ☎06/464 1510; Air France ☎06/566 6055; Alitalia ☎06/462 5203; Austrian ☎06/569 4604; British Airways/British Mediterranean ☎06/582 8801; Cyprus ☎06/562 0115; EgyptAir ☎06/463 0011; El Al ☎06/562 2526; Emirates ☎06/464 3341; Gulf Air ☎06/465 3613; IranAir ☎06/463 0879; KLM ☎06/465 5267; Kuwaiti ☎06/569 0144; MEA (Lebanese) ☎06/463 6104; Olympic ☎06/568 2140; Pakistani ☎06/462 5981; Qatari ☎06/568 4576; Royal Jordanian ☎06/567 8321; Royal Wings ☎06/875201; Saudi Arabian ☎06/463 9333; Tarom (Romanian) ☎06/463 7380; Turkish ☎06/465 9102; Yemenia ☎06/462 4363.

departure at their City Terminal building at 7th Circle (daily 7am–8pm; ☎06/585 6855).

Royal Wings is the only carrier using the tiny **Marka Airport** (also known as Amman Civil Airport; information ☎06/875201; see also p.37), flying scheduled hops to Aqaba and Tel Aviv, as well as charters to Cyprus, Egypt and Turkey.

Within Jordan

Awkwardly enough, the three big bus-and-*service* stations – **Abdali**, **Raghadan** and **Wihdat** – are widely spaced across the city (see p.79). Aside from destinations south of Tafileh, all **fares** on non-JETT buses are below JD1, with fares to close-at-hand places such as Jerash and Madaba under 500 fils.

To Jerash and the north
Abdali is the departure point for all buses to destinations in the north of Jordan, including **Jerash**, **Irbid**, **Ajloun** and **Ramtha**. Most leave from the upper half of the station. There are also some *service*s, generally departing from the lower half of the station, to Irbid and Ramtha. Hijazi's big, comfortable air-con buses to Irbid are the only ones that run to a schedule (daily 6.15am–7.30pm, every 15min). For Umm Qais and the far north, change in Irbid.

To Azraq and the east
The only direct public transport between Amman and points east are buses from Abdali to **Mafraq**, where you should change for Umm al-Jimal and the far desert; and from Abdali or Raghadan to **Zerqa**, from where buses depart to Hallabat and Azraq. There is no public transport along the Amman–Azraq highway apart from a bus from Raghadan to **Muwaggar**, making it impossible to reach Qasr Hraneh and Qusayr Amra without your own transport – many travellers resort to hiring a taxi (see p.37).

To Petra and the south
Practically all transport heading for the south of Jordan leaves from Wihdat; departures are much more common in the morning (from 7am onwards) than the afternoon. Destinations covered by bus or *service* are **Aqaba**, **Karak**, **Ma'an**, **Shawbak**, **Tafileh** and **Wadi Musa/Petra**. For *service*s to most of these places, you'll be quoted prices higher than normal to start with. Some hopeful drivers to Petra start as high as JD5, although the real price is half that (or JD1.500 on the bus); the best tactic – since this isn't about bargaining – is simply to laugh it off and make it clear, calmly but firmly, that you know what the proper price is.

Bear in mind that there is no direct public transport from Amman along the picturesque **King's Highway**: all buses and *service*s from Amman use the Desert Highway (see p.192). **Madaba** is served by buses from Abdali, Raghadan and Wihdat. A few buses leave Wihdat in the mornings for Ma'in, some going on to **Hammamat Ma'in** – but you can find more reliable connections from Madaba (see p.204).

From the **JETT** office (☎06/566 4146) on King Hussein Street, 500m uphill from Abdali station, up to eight big, fast air-con buses depart daily to **Aqaba** (JD4), the first at 7am, the last at 4.30pm. For years JETT also had one departure, daily at 6.30am, to the Visitors' Centre at **Petra**, but this was axed in 1998 and it's uncertain whether it will be reinstated.

Royal Wings (☎06/875201) has two or three **flights** daily from Amman to **Aqaba** (JD30), generally from Marka Airport in the early morning and Queen Alia Airport in the evening, although occasionally there are useful mid-morning and mid-afternoon flights.

To the Jordan Valley

For the northern valley, **Dayr Alla** is served by direct buses from Abdali; change there for Pella. For the southern valley, it's relatively easy to reach **Shuneh al-Janubiyyeh** (see p.126), but the only buses south from there go to Swaymeh and no further.

To neighbouring countries

Getting to some of the international departure points in Amman can be tricky, so it's advisable to ask someone to write in Arabic the name and location of where you're going to show to taxi-drivers or passers-by in case of difficulty. The two most travelled routes – to **Damascus** and **Jerusalem** – can be complicated, and so are described in some detail; basic information is given for the others. All JETT (and foreign) bus departures detailed in this section – except where noted – leave from the JETT External Lines office (☎06/569 6151) in Abdali, round the corner from the normal JETT office.

Visas for neighbouring countries

Visas for **Israel** (free) and **Turkey** (Britons and Irish £10, Americans US$20, all others free) can be obtained on arrival in those countries. Jordan's other near-neighbours are a little more troublesome, and much prefer that foreigners apply for visas in their home capital. If you apply in Amman but don't hold full Jordanian residency, you're often obliged to buy a pricey letter of recommendation from your own embassy then wait up to two weeks while your application is scrutinized. For independent travellers, it's difficult to get a **Syrian** visa at the best of times, and in Amman it's almost impossible. **Iraq**, unsurprisingly, isn't issuing visas to independent Western travellers, and **Saudi Arabia** issues no tourist visas of any kind, only transit, business and Islamic *umrah* visas. On the other hand, Amman's **Lebanese** and **Egyptian** embassies are hectic but efficient. On application forms, it can sometimes cause major complications if you write anything other than "Tourism" under "What is the purpose of your visit?", or if you confess to being Jewish. All the countries listed here apart from Egypt officially refuse you entry if your passport shows **evidence of a visit to Israel**; see p.114 for more.

The embassies of the more important neighbouring countries for travellers are: **Egypt**, Qurtubah Street, next to *Dove Hotel*, between 4th and 5th Circles, Jebel Amman (☎06/560 5202). Visa applications daily except Fri 9am–noon; collection same day noon–2pm. One photo needed. One-month single-entry "tourist visas" cost JD12 for all nationalities. A one-month "Sinai-only" visa, valid only for travel along the east Sinai coast as far as Sharm el-Sheikh (including St Catherine's), is free. All these are extendable in Egypt, and they're also available at every airport and border (except Rafah) on arrival, but then you can pay only in US dollars or Egyptian pounds, and prices and validities may be different.

Iran, 50m from Syrian Embassy, Fawzi al-Mulqi St, between 3rd and 4th Circles, Jebel Amman (☎06/464 1281). Visa applications Sun & Tues 10am–noon. Two photos needed. Without a local sponsor, Iran is difficult for independent travellers to get into, but not impossible; however, the application form takes the biscuit, with 34 questions in Arabic, including "Are you a drug addict?" Number 34 is trickiest, a Hobson's Choice demand for what you already know about Iran; apparently, applications which have "geography" and "art" circled are least likely to be automatically rejected. If approval comes through from Tehran, all nationalities pay JD35 for a one-month visa.

Lebanon, Nile (pronounced *Neel*) St, near the British Embassy, Abdoun (☎06/592 9111). Visa applications Mon–Thurs & Sat 8–11am; collection next day 1.30–2pm. One photo needed. For all nationalities, one-month single-entry visas cost JD14, three-month multiple-entries JD28. No letter of recommendation needed. More expensive visas, payable in Lebanese pounds only, are granted on arrival at land, air or sea borders to Americans, Canadians, Australians (but not New Zealanders) and Western European nationals. Note that there is no Lebanese embassy in Damascus.

Syria, Hazza al-Majali St, behind Ministry of Foreign Affairs, between 3rd and 4th Circles, Jebel Amman (☎06/464 1076). Visa applications daily except Fri 9–11am; collection same day or next day 1.30–2pm. Two photos needed. Applications must be accompanied by a letter of recommendation from your embassy (not required by US citizens), and, even then, are often summarily rejected without reason. Answering anything other than "no" to the question "Have you visited Occupied Palestine?" or admitting that you're a journalist or student of politics are likely to rule you out. If you're planning to visit Lebanon and want to return to Syria, you should be sure to ask for a double-entry visa. Fees vary dramatically between nationalities; the following are prices for single-/double-/multiple-entry visas, all valid initially for two weeks: Americans JD44/55/67, Australians free/free/JD3, Britons JD37/57/57, Canadians JD40/77/77, Irish JD23/46/69, New Zealanders JD43/43/43.

Other embassies of neighbouring countries include:

Bahrain, Faris al-Khouri St, off Abdul Hamid Sharaf St, Shmaysani (☎06/566 4148).

Iraq, between 1st and 2nd Circles, Jebel Amman (☎06/462 3175).

Kuwait, 250m along Zahran St between 4th and 5th Circles, Jebel Amman (☎06/567 5135).

Oman, 300m along Zahran St between 4th and 5th Circles, Jebel Amman (☎06/568 6155).

Qatar, Zahran St, corner Tunis St, between 4th and 5th Circles, Jebel Amman (☎06/560 7311).

Saudi Arabia, Rainbow St at 1st Circle, Jebel Amman (☎06/463 0337).

United Arab Emirates, Bou Madyan St, behind Zahran St 200m before 5th Circle, Jebel Amman (☎06/593 4780).

Yemen, beside Syrian embassy, 3rd Circle, Jebel Amman (☎06/464 2381).

To Damascus

There are many ways to reach **Damascus** from Amman, varying wildly in cost, duration and comfort. However, before you embark on any of them, you must have a valid entry visa for Syria – contrary to travellers' rumours, it's impossible for citizens of non-Arab countries to buy Syrian visas at the border. There are now two crossing points, both open 24 hours daily: the old one at Ramtha–Dera'a, and a new one between Jaber (Jordan) and Nasib (Syria). The latter is on the fast Amman–Damascus highway just north of Mafraq, so journeys to Damascus can now take as little as three hours. Whichever method of transport you choose, you should remember to factor in the JD4 **departure tax**, levied as you cross.

The simplest method of reaching Damascus is by **service** from any of the private companies lining the road either side of Abdali station. The cars are roomy Seventies-vintage Chevrolets or Dodges, and the sign of a part-filled *service* waiting for passengers is an open boot (trunk). As soon as you approach, the driver will start touting for business with "Shum, Shum, Shum" (one of the Arabic names for Damascus). Although you may have to bargain, the real fare is JD5.500 per person, or JD27.500 for the whole car (seating five). *Service*s head out at all hours of the day and night, so you never have to wait too long, and – aside from the driver stashing a few bits and pieces on the way to sell in Syria – they go fast and direct. You can also book a *service* one day ahead and arrange a pick-up from your hotel; the best company for this is al-Saqer (☎06/462 5576). *Service*s with Jordanian number-plates terminate in central Damascus at the *Karaj al-Urdun* (Jordan Garage), next to the long-distance bus station; those with Syrian plates can drop you off where you like for a few dollars more.

Scheduled **buses** operated by JETT and Karnak, the Syrian state-owned bus company, are cheaper than *service*s but rarely as fast. Daily departures are at 7am (JETT) and 3pm (Karnak), with extra buses at 9am and 4pm in June, July and August. The fare is JD4.500.

The longest and least comfortable method is also the cheapest and most atmospheric: by **train**. A decrepit diesel leaves Amman's Hejaz Station (☎06/895413) every Monday at 8am for the ten-hour meander to the Hejaz Station in central Damascus. The fare is a rock-bottom JD2.500; turn up 30min early to buy your ticket. As an added incentive, it has been known for a steam engine to be hooked up for the beautiful journey from the Syrian border into Damascus.

Daily **flights** from Queen Alia Airport are operated by Royal Jordanian, Air France and KLM, all of them arriving in Damascus late at night and all disastrous value at around JD45.

To Jerusalem and the West Bank

As the crow flies, Amman and **Jerusalem** are only about 50km apart, but the Jordan Valley and a heavily fortified frontier bridge lie in the way, making the journey by road tortuously long and slow. No buses or *service*s run directly between the two cities. The only way to go is with a combination of buses and taxis/*service*s, changing at the only bridge between Jordan and the West Bank that's open to the public (Mon–Thurs & Sun 8am–midnight, Fri & Sat 8am–2pm); to the Jordanians and the Palestinians it's known as the **King Hussein Bridge** (*jissr al-Malek Hussein*), to the Israelis it's the Allenby Bridge (*gesher Allenby* in Hebrew).

The least arduous cheap way to go begins with a **service** from the southern end of Abdali station direct to the foreigners' – *not* the locals' – terminal near the bridge (about 1hr; JD2), where you'll pay your JD4 **departure tax**. You'll then have to sit and wait for anything up to two hours for a bus to fill up, which will cover no-man's-land on either side of the bridge and drop you at the Israeli terminal; the fare for this ten-minute ride is JD1.500.

An easier but pricier option is to take the **JETT bus** (daily 6.30am); you should book this ahead of time or turn up at their office no later than 6am to guarantee a

AMMAN–JERUSALEM: THE BUREAUCRACY

The contradictory **bureaucracy** surrounding the journey from Amman to Jerusalem is grotesque. The **Jordanians** still view the West Bank as intimately linked with Jordan: although you no longer need a permit from the Jordanian Ministry of the Interior to travel in the West Bank, if you have a single-entry Jordanian visa and cross the King Hussein Bridge to spend time in the West Bank or Israel, then return *the same way* to Jordan, the Jordanians don't see you as ever having left the country and you don't need to buy a new Jordanian visa, as long as your current one is still within its validity (bear in mind, though, the crippling cost of the Israeli departure tax – see p.14). You must buy a new Jordanian visa, however, if you return to the country having used another route out or in.

However, once you cross the King Hussein Bridge from Jordan into the West Bank, the **Israeli** authorities view you as arriving in Israel proper, and routinely issue free tourist visas on arrival, valid throughout Israeli- and **Palestinian**-administered West Bank territory and Israel itself. You'll be waved through any checkpoints on the "Green Line" between the West Bank and Israel proper (a border you'll find marked on Jordanian maps but not Israeli ones). Thus, on the West Bank you can feel as if you're in three countries simultaneously – sightseeing in Palestinian towns, having been granted entry to Israel and with a still-valid Jordanian visa in your passport.

seat. The JD6 fare takes you swiftly all the way through to the Israeli terminal, but doesn't include the JD4 departure tax. Beware the bus-driver taking the passports of all the passengers to give in a huge pile to the immigration officials for stamping; if you want yours to stay unsullied, insist on taking it in to them yourself.

At passport control at the **Israeli arrivals terminal**, you should be loud and clear in asking for your passport not to be stamped: many travellers have reported the Israeli immigration officials forgetting after being asked only once. After the formalities, there's a **bank** to change money (although Palestinian businesses throughout the West Bank accept Jordanian dinars). *Services* (called *sheroot* in Hebrew) wait just outside; the one-hour ride to **East Jerusalem**, dropping you at the Damascus Gate of the Old City, costs a fixed JD6 or 30 Israeli shekels (NIS). If you walk out of the bridge terminal and to your right, you'll find the exit area from the locals' building, where you can pick up dirt-cheap buses to **West Bank** destinations such as Jericho, Bethlehem and Ramallah – but not Jerusalem.

There are currently no **flights** from Amman to Jerusalem or West Bank cities, although the international airport at Gaza awaits only an Israeli say-so to begin operation. Meanwhile, the fledgling Palestinian Airways instead flies from Amman to the tiny airfield at al-Arish, in northern Sinai (Egypt), from where passengers are bussed into Gaza. Britons, Americans and Canadians need no visas for this journey (only patience); all other foreign nationals must apply in advance to both the Egyptian and Palestinian embassies in Amman.

To Tel Aviv, Haifa and Nazareth

Direct **buses** run from Amman to the Israeli cities of **Tel Aviv** (Central Bus Station; Mon–Fri & Sun 7am; JD14) and **Haifa** (Merkaz Train Station; Mon–Fri & Sun 7.30am & 2pm; JD10.500), the latter via Lower **Nazareth** (also JD10.500). The Trust International Transport Company, with an office next to the Royal Jordanian building off the Airport Highway near 7th Circle (☎06/581 3427), is the Jordanian

ISRAELI BORDER STAMPS

If you intend to visit Israel, the West Bank or the Gaza Strip as part of a longer journey in the region, you need to bear in mind that all Middle Eastern and North African countries except Egypt, Jordan, Tunisia and Morocco refuse entry to people with **evidence of a visit to Israel** in their passports. "Evidence" includes not only specifically Israeli stamps, but also entry or exit stamps from the Jordanian border-posts at the Sheikh Hussein Bridge, the King Hussein Bridge and the Aqaba–Eilat border, as well as those from the Egyptian border-posts at Taba (near Eilat) and Rafah (northern Sinai). Visas issued in Israel for travel to any country will also bar you, as will anything in Hebrew discovered in your belongings.

With a bit of ingenuity, it is just about possible to visit Israel and subsequently enter those countries which would otherwise be off-limits. Israeli and Jordanian immigration officials will routinely stamp you both in and out on a **piece of paper** if you ask, thus avoiding any permanent evidence of having been "on the other side" (as many travellers call Israel, to avoid detection by eavesdropping officials). However, if you enter Jordan from Israel at the Sheikh Hussein Bridge or Wadi Araba crossing without a visa, Jordanian officials must stamp a visa into your passport, which gives you away. Even if you enter at these crossing-points or the King Hussein Bridge with a visa bought in advance and ask for your entry stamp to be given on paper, if you then exit Jordan at, say, the Syrian border, the lack of a Jordanian entry stamp in your passport might well arouse the suspicions of the Syrian officials. The only foolproof method is to enter Jordan by air, sea or across the land borders from Syria, Iraq or Saudi Arabia (picking up an uncontroversial arrival stamp as you go), then use the King Hussein Bridge to cross from Jordan to the West Bank and back (picking up stamps on pieces of paper), while making sure your Jordanian visa does not expire. When you then leave Jordan for good, your passport will bear ordinary entry and exit stamps, with no evidence of the intervening visit to Israel.

It's a well-known ploy of travellers who have unwittingly acquired evidence of an Israeli visit to lose their passports deliberately in Egypt or Jordan and apply for new ones from their embassies. However, after several years of stamping visas into unsullied passports, Syrian consulates have finally cottoned on to the scam, and these days an unused passport issued in Cairo or Amman is as much evidence to them of a visit to Israel as a border stamp. Even if the loss of your old passport was genuine, you may still find yourself refused entry to Syria on this suspicion.

side of the operation. All buses leave from outside the office, and all of them avoid travelling through the West Bank, instead using the **Sheikh Hussein Bridge** between Irbid and the northern Israeli town of Bet She'an. There's an additional bus (Sat 7.30am) which goes to Nazareth only; all buses also pick up passengers in Irbid. You should arrive half-an-hour before stated departure times for police searches, and don't forget to add the cost of the JD4 departure tax onto all fares.

Royal Wings **flies** to Tel Aviv two or three times daily from both Marka Airport and the less convenient Queen Alia Airport; El Al flies six times weekly from Queen Alia. Fares on either are JD54 one-way, JD98 for a one-month return or JD110 for a year's open return.

To Cairo

Although there are direct **buses** between Amman and **Cairo**, they are neither very pleasant nor very economical. Unless speed is absolutely of the essence (in which case, you might consider flying), you'd do far better to break your journey in Aqaba and/or the Sinai along the way.

If you do choose the direct option, note that most Westerners need a full Egyptian visa, best obtained in advance (see p.110). JETT operates two weekly departures, on Saturday (a Jordanian bus) and Tuesday (an Egyptian SuperJet bus), both leaving at 7am from JETT's office in Marka (☎06/894872), 50m from the Marka Airport roundabout in East Amman. Buses go first to Aqaba port for customs formalities, then head onto the ferry for Nuweiba on Egypt's Sinai coast. The five-hundred-kilometre haul from Nuweiba terminates at the office of the Arab Union Bus Company at Midan Almaza in Heliopolis, still a long way from central Cairo. Total journey time is about 21 hours, and the fare, which includes the ferry, is a steep US$52, payable in dollars only; you'll also have to pay a JD6 departure tax at Aqaba. It's advisable to book up to a week ahead. Slightly cheaper buses run from Abdali though these are liable to take much longer; ask in the office just behind Hijazi.

Both Royal Jordanian and EgyptAir operate daily **flights** between Amman and Cairo; one-way fares on either are overpriced at JD85. There are also plenty of charter flights to other Egyptian airports, mainly Sharm el-Sheikh, Hurghada and Luxor; ask at travel agents or Royal Wings for details.

Listings

Banks and exchange bureaux For cash on credit/debit cards over-the-counter service in banks can take ages (the Union Bank is most efficient), and it's much easier to use a cash machine: the British Bank has thoroughly trustworthy ones that take Visa and Mastercard, with branches in Downtown (200m up from *Jabri's* on King Hussein St), Jebel Amman (just below 2nd Circle on Buhtari St), near Shmaysani (100m from Interior Circle on Istiqlal St) and on Abdoun Circle. Otherwise, for the best deals out of hours, head for King Faysal Street's exchange bureaux: all do cash, most take travellers' cheques, virtually none takes credit cards. Rates can vary so you should shop around, and you should also proceed cautiously with these sharp operators: check exactly how many dinars and fils you're going to get before handing over any money or signing your cheques, and explicitly confirm any commission.

Car rental Amman's best-value outfit by far is Reliable (☎ & fax 06/592 9676; email *reliable@nets.com.jo*); they have brand-new air-con cars with unlimited mileage, insurance and collision damage waiver from JD28 a day, less for longer periods. They'll bring the car to you, and you can drop it off for free at the airport or anywhere in Amman. However, for one-way rentals to Petra or Aqaba (minimum three days), Avis (☎06/569 9420, fax 569 9430) or Hertz (☎06/553 8958, fax 552 8406) are cheaper. Other quality local operators include: al-Barakeh (☎06/568 7988), Cruise (☎ & fax 06/553 0176) and al-Masy (☎06/553 5644, fax 553 1655). Other international agencies include: Budget (☎06/569 8131, fax 567 3312), EuroDollar (☎06/569 3399, fax 568 7233) and Payless (☎06/552 5180, fax 553 2525).

Children The Haya Centre (Mon, Wed, Thurs, Sat & Sun 8.30am–5pm; in summer, also Tues 8.30am–2pm; ☎06/566 5195), opposite *KFC* in Shmaysani, has plays, puppet theatre, music and loads of courses and activities for children. English-speaking families are welcome to use the facilities at any time – highlights include a safe and monitored sandy playground with an adjacent café for tired parents, a kids' library and a small planetarium (English summary-sheet available). Admission 500 fils (unaccompanied adults not admitted). The Luna Park (daily 10am–10pm), on Wadi Saqra Circle, has a great cable-car ride. Kids might also appreciate Amusement World (Mon–Thurs & Sat 3–9pm, Fri 10am–9pm; 300 fils), next to the British Council on Rainbow St, near 1st Circle, the bottom two floors of which are full of video games, bumper cars and choo-choo trains.

Cultural centres and libraries The library of the British Council (Rainbow St, 300m from 1st Circle; Mon–Wed, Sat & Sun 10am–6pm, Thurs 10am–2pm; ☎06/463 6147) is a bit frumpy, though the section on Jordan has many out-of-print gems. The American Center library (in the American Embassy, Abdoun; daily except Fri 8am–5pm; ☎06/592 0101) isn't bad, but difficult to get to. Both have newspapers and magazines. Other cultural centres with libraries include: Centre Culturel Français, just off Lweibdeh Circle, Jebel al-Lweibdeh (daily except Fri 11am–8pm; ☎06/463 7009); the Goethe Institut (German), off 3rd Circle, Jebel Amman (Mon–Wed & Sun 9am–1pm & 4–8pm, Thurs 8.30am–2pm; ☎06/464 1993); and the Instituto Cervantes (Spanish), behind the *Inter-Continental Hotel*, near 3rd Circle, Jebel Amman (Mon–Thurs & Sun 9am–1pm & 4–7pm; ☎06/461 0858). Darat al-Funun (see p.97) has a superb art library. The Royal Society for the Conservation of Nature, way out in Jubayha beyond the university (☎06/533 7931), has books and materials on environmental themes. Excellent historical libraries are run by the following: American Center of Oriental Research in Tla'a al-Ali (☎06/534 6117); CERMOC, a French research centre near 3rd Circle (☎06/461 1171); Council for British Research in the Levant, Jubayha (☎06/534 1317); Department of Antiquities behind 3rd Circle (☎06/464 4336).

Email, Internet and computer access The swiftest, most pleasant and convenient place by far to surf or check your email is Books@Café (see p.100). Slower competitors include CyberTunnel, located at Safeway, and Internet cafés opposite the University. All charge roughly JD1.250 for 15min. If you just need to type a letter and print it out, the Abdul Hameed Shoman Foundation (see p.106) charges nothing at all to use its computer room. If you're carrying a laptop with modem and need a phone line, most Downtown phone offices are unfamiliar with, and suspicious of, such technology; the business centres in the five-star hotels are your best bet, or try the *Bdeiwi Hotel*, up the hill behind the Downtown post office.

Embassies and consulates Australia, near Ministry of Social Development, between 4th and 5th Circles (☎06/593 0246); Canada, Philadelphia Investment Bank building, between *Pizza Hut* and *Chili House*, Shmaysani (☎06/566 6124); Ireland, near Ministry of Finance, King Hussein St, Downtown (☎06/462 5632); New Zealand, Khalaf building, 99 King Hussein St, above Downtown (☎06/463 6720); South Africa, behind Jordan Supermarket, off Abdoun Circle (☎06/592 2288); UK, Damascus St, Abdoun (☎06/592 3100); USA, Abdoun (☎06/592 0101). Most are open daily except Fri 10am–noon at the least. Letters of recommendation generally cost JD8–15; Britons pay JD24. Embassies of Jordan's neighbouring countries in Amman are listed on pp.110-11.

Emergencies Police ☎191; ambulance ☎193; fire ☎06/462 2090 or 461 7101; traffic police (in the city) ☎06/465 6390; traffic accidents ☎06/896390; highway police ☎06/534 3402.

Flight enquiries For information on arrivals and departures on Royal Jordanian call ☎06/445 3200; Royal Wings ☎06/875201; all other carriers ☎06/445 2700.

Galleries As well as the National Gallery and Darat al-Funun (see p.97), there are several excellent commercial art galleries around town with regular exhibitions by local and foreign artists. The best are the Baladna (Gardens St; ☎06/553 7598), the Gallery (in the *Inter-Continental Hotel*) and the Hammourabi (Gardens St; ☎06/553 6098). Shows are publicized in the *Jordan Times*.

Gliding For a paltry JD15/hr, the Royal Jordanian Gliding Club, based at Marka Airport, can take up one passenger at a time for a unique, silent view of Amman from above. They fly at limited times (Mon–Wed 2pm–sunset, Thurs & Fri 8.30am–sunset), and you should call ahead on ☎06/874587.

Laundry If your hotel can't help out, there are laundries dotted all over Downtown. One of the most reliable – though not exactly speedy – is *Alf Lown wa Lown* or "The Thousand and One Colours" (daily except Fri 8.30am–4.30pm); standing with the *Cliff Hotel* behind you, cross the street, head up the hill 10m, turn right and it's the third shop on the left. They can do a normal-sized load for about JD4, priced piece by piece, with ironing extra. Normal turnaround time is at least 24hr, but they do a good job.

Massage For JD18, a trained masseur at the *Inter-Continental Hotel*'s health club will lay you down and embark on a luxurious hour-long oiled Swedish massage and acupressure session – and you can also use their sauna and jacuzzi if you fancy.

Medical facilities and pharmacies The Khalidi Hospital (☎06/464 4281), near 4th Circle, is one of the best in Jordan, and has a 24hr emergency room. If you need a doctor, Dr Bashier (☎06/551 3640) comes recommended, as does the dentist Dr Bilemjian (☎06/553 5574). The most efficient pharmacy is Jacob's (daily 8.30am–midnight) on 3rd Circle. Names and numbers of doctors on night duty and 24hr pharmacies are listed daily in the *Jordan Times*.

Petrol stations 24hr stations are on all main roads: near Downtown on Prince Muhammad St; in West Amman at 7th and 8th Circles, on the airport highway, Gardens St, University St and near the *Regency Palace* hotel; and on the highways northeast to Zerqa and southeast to Azraq. All these have *soober*.

Phones and faxes There are dozens of Alo and JPP phone-booths all over town, with cards generally sold at nearby shops. The official phone office (daily 7.30am–midnight) is on Omar al-Khayyam St; go to the top of the hill directly behind the Downtown post office and it's 50m more on the left. Everything works quite efficiently although it can get very busy. The staff dial for you, a computer counts the seconds and you pay at the end; there's a three-minute minimum charge. Before you reach the official place you'll run into a plethora of private phone and fax offices on the same street, which sometimes offer cheaper rates and which all charge by the minute with no minimum. Those using mobile phones tend to be cheaper; some have cabins where you can talk in privacy; a couple claim 24hr service. If you can't face the hassle of shopping around, the *Bdeiwi Hotel* opposite the phone office is trustworthy, allows you privacy to talk and will also let you send and receive faxes for a small charge (they hold all faxes sent to 4647878 until claimed).

Photos Salbashian's Konica lab under the *Vinecia Hotel* in Downtown does adequate two-hour processing. Amman's only entirely trustworthy and professional lab is Kizirian's Petra Lab, 25 Hani al-Shaybani St (☎06/465 8025), just off Wadi Saqra below 3rd Circle, with slightly higher prices but much higher quality. If you must develop slide film, the lab that's least likely to scratch your pictures is the branch of Konica on Wadi Saqra near the Cairo-Amman Bank.

Police and complaints The courteous and efficient English-speaking tourist police are on duty inside the Roman Theatre (daily 8am–8pm), as well as up near the museum on the Citadel (daily 24hr; ☎06/464 1151); headquarters is at 8th Circle (☎06/586 1271). The Downtown police station is halfway along King Faysal Street, opposite the Arab Bank, a plain doorway leading up some stairs; there's also a police station opposite the *Inter-Continental Hotel*. In other areas, or if you're in real distress, tell any passerby that you want the *buleece* (police), and someone is bound to help; see also "Emergencies" above. Specific complaints about personal harassment or rip-offs, large or small, are best taken to the tourist police. Complaints about hotels or restaurants can also be registered with the Ministry of Tourism on ☎06/464 2311 or 560 5800.

Post offices and parcels The most convenient post office for everyday business is the big Downtown office (Mon–Thurs, Sat & Sun 7.30am–7pm, Fri 7.30am–1.30pm; hours slightly curtailed in winter) on Prince Muhammad St, 50m from the *Cliff Hotel* – the only sign on the building says "Postal Savings Bank". Street vendors sell paper and envelopes nearby. Inside, stamps are sold from windows 5 and 6. Poste restante mail is kept for several months in a box in front of window 11 and can be riffled through at will. To send a parcel (daily except Fri 7.30am–2pm) first take it unwrapped to be checked by the Customs Department, which is through an unmarked gateway on the left halfway up the hill behind the Downtown post office. Then take it across the street to the Parcels Office, seal it up, fill out a despatch form and pay the money. For sending valuables, you'd do better to trust international couriers such as Aramex (☎06/551 5111), DHL (☎06/585 8451) or FedEx (☎06/569 5415). Smaller branch offices, which keep the same hours as the Downtown post office, include: on 1st Circle (down the steps opposite the Saudi consulate); in the forecourt of the *Inter-Continental Hotel* between 2nd and 3rd Circles; under the Jordan Tower below 3rd Circle; a few doors down from the Centre Culturel Français off Lweibdeh Circle; and under the Housing Bank Centre in Shmaysani.

Religious services The following churches have services in English: Amman International (Protestant) Church (☎06/465 2526); Anglican (☎06/465 8383); Assemblies of God (☎06/463

2785); Latter-Day Saints (☎06/465 4932); Roman Catholic (☎06/461 4190). Other churches are listed in the *Jordan Times*, as are the exact Muslim prayer times. There is no Jewish community.

Swimming and sport Most of the big hotels charge JD12 per day for non-guests to use their pools; the *Inter-Continental*'s is best. The small pool at the *Manar Hotel* in Shmaysani costs JD3.500. Tenpin bowling occupies two floors of Amusement World (Mon–Thurs, Sat & Sun 3–11pm, Fri 10am–11pm), next to the British Council, at JD1.500 per person per game. Baize buffs should head for Amusement World's top floor (same hours) or a tatty room on the second floor of the Housing Bank Centre (daily 9.30am–11pm); both have pool and snooker for JD3/hr. The much classier Abdoun Snooker Centre (daily 2pm–2am; ☎06/593 2224) on Princess Basma St charges JD4 for professional tables. The ritzy, pricey Orthodox Club, also in Abdoun (☎06/592 0491), has swimming, tennis, squash and basketball.

Translation bureaux The following have solid reputations for Arabic–English translations: Abdel Nour Corporation, Batarseh building, Jebel Hussein (☎06/560 2838); al-Resheg, Diplomat building, 1st Circle (☎06/464 8644); an-Nahda, down an alley off King Hussein St, Downtown (☎06/462 2595).

Visa extensions If you intend to stay in Jordan for longer than fifteen days, you must extend your visa sometime before that period is up by registering with the police (see p.17). If you have entered Jordan from the West Bank or Israel and kept your passport free of stamps, you register at the Directorate of Residency and Borders on Mukhabarrat Street in Abdali, the clearly marked fifth gateway on the right on the long road up the hill past the King Abdullah Mosque; *service* #7 from Downtown runs outside. If you entered Jordan any other way, you must register at a police station. The relevant station if you're staying in Downtown is in Muhajireen – *service* #35 from opposite the *Amman Palace Hotel* on the Saqf Sayl can drop you almost at the junction of Ali bin Abi Taleb Street and Princess Basma Street, and the police station is the white building 150m away on the other side of the crossroads; when you enter the courtyard, the relevant office is through the door on the right. If you're staying uptown, register at the Zahran police station, virtually opposite the *Inter-Continental Hotel*. You're permitted a second three-month extension – issued only at the Directorate in Abdali – if an official AIDS test proves negative.

Around Amman

With the exception of the unmissable **Dead Sea**, day-trip destinations out of Amman are low-key and generally untouristed. The gentle hills which roll westward down to the Jordan Valley through the historic Balqa region – of which the graceful old town of **Salt** is capital – are laced with lush, beautiful valleys and dotted with pleasant towns such as **Wadi Seer** and **Fhays**, the latter with an appealing little crafts quarter. Near Wadi Seer is one of the few examples of Hellenistic architecture surviving in the Middle East – the impressive white palace of **Qasr al-Abd**, set in gorgeous countryside near an ancient cave system known as **Iraq al-Amir**. All these places are easily accessible on short bus rides from Amman.

Wadi Seer and Iraq al-Amir

Lying just beyond Amman's city limits to the west, the lush valley of **Wadi Seer** makes for an easy escape from urban claustrophobia; add to the natural beauty a couple of small-scale archeological gems and the area definitely merits an exploratory picnic, although, if you choose a Friday for your outing, you'll discover that most of Amman has had the same idea.

Though barely 12km from central Amman, the town of **WADI SEER** – small and peaceful, filled with trees and birdsong – has the atmosphere of a country village. **Buses from Amman** depart from Ali bin Abi Taleb Street, at the southern end of the Saqf Sayl in Ras al-Ain, and drop off at the town's bus station, perched above a roundabout in the centre. Originally settled by Circassian immigrants in the 1880s, Wadi Seer boasts many nineteenth- and early twentieth-century Ottoman stone buildings in the streets around the centre, including a mosque of yellowish limestone with a beautiful carved minaret. Tucked away on a back street close to the mosque, a nameless and sporadically open shop sells brightly coloured hand-woven carpets. However, the main reason to come out here is for the ten-kilometre **walk** from the town through the countryside to Iraq al-Amir, the road sloping gently downhill all the way, hugging the side of a fertile valley and passing through a series of tiny villages. The scenery is gorgeous, the valley thick with fig, olive, cypress and pomegranate trees and watered by a perpetually flowing stream; springtime sees a riot of poppies and wild iris. There are plenty of picnic spots and even a riverside café, *al-Yannabeea*, partway along. A few shops in Wadi Seer sell simple groceries and *falafel*, though if you're picnicking you should really bring food with you from Amman. At the bus station roundabout, with your back to the video store, the road leading down into the wadi is to the left. If you want a shorter walk, you might consider taking the **bus** that runs along the road from Wadi Seer to the Qasr al-Abd (see below) as far as the *Yannabeea* café and walking the 6km from there. A **taxi** from Wadi Seer to the *qasr* should cost about JD1 (JD3 or so if you get him to wait and take you back).

About 4km out of Wadi Seer town, the road reaches the valley floor and passes a **Roman aqueduct**; the *Yannabeea* **café** occupies a perfect spot on the grassy bank here (daily 7am–midnight) – you could do a lot worse than suck on a cold Pepsi with your feet dangling in the stream. Just before the café, a possible detour for the energetic leads steeply up to the left; after about 500m, a fork to the left gives some rough paths up the hillside. A short scramble will bring you to the two strange and rather eerie caves – out of sight from below – known as **ad-Dayr** (meaning "the monastery"), which has the appearance of a medieval pigeon-fanciers' den rather than a spiritual retreat. The large interiors are lined from floor to ceiling with hundreds of small triangular niches, and stone grilles are still in place over the cave windows. There's nothing really to make of the place, other than to speculate on whether the caves were in fact used for religious purposes; it's certainly more appealing to imagine every niche holding a flickering candle rather than a flapping bird.

Beyond the *Yannabeea* café, the road continues straight – apart from one left fork marked in English – for another 6km or so to **IRAQ AL-AMIR** (meaning "Caves of the Prince"). Just before you reach the rapidly expanding village, you'll spot the smoke-blackened **caves** high up to the right of the road. However, if you scramble up to them, you'll find very little to get excited about: most are malodorous, and there's nothing to see but the view across the fields and a single ancient Hebrew inscription, referring to the family who built the white palace visible down in the valley.

Qasr al-Abd

After passing through Iraq al-Amir village, the road ends about 1km further on at the gates of the **Qasr al-Abd**, a strikingly beautiful pre-Roman country villa set on a platform above the fields. The villa was begun in the years around 200 BC by Hyrcanus, a member of the powerful Tobiad family, as the centrepiece of a lavish, cultivated estate; its name, meaning "Palace of the Servant", derives from a fifth-century BC member of the clan, who is mentioned in the Old Testament as being a governor, or "servant", of Ammon. Hyrcanus died in 175 BC and the palace was never completed; indeed, for some reason the huge limestone building blocks – some up to 25 tonnes in weight – were originally laid precariously on their half-metre edges, and so dutifully collapsed at the first earthquake, in 365 AD. Since then, the building has been only sporadically occupied, possibly during the Byzantine period by Christian monks. It was only in the 1980s that the palace could be partially reconstructed by industrial cranes; before then, the fallen masonry was too heavy to be reassembled.

When you arrive, the guardian will probably materialize to unlock the gates. Inside, only foundations of internal walls survive, although picture-windows still ring the building and stairs lead up to a now-collapsed second storey. The main attractions, though, are outside. Around the walls are elegant carvings of wild animals, appropriate for such a rural setting although it's unlikely such beasts roamed the area even in antiquity. At ground level on both sides of the building are dolomite leopards doubling as fountains, and around the top of the walls are eagles and lions. The best of all, high up on a back corner, is a lioness – complete with mane for some reason – suckling her cubs.

Fhays

Set among rolling hills barely half-an-hour northwest of Amman, **FHAYS** is a prosperous but rarely visited small town with a delightful, partially restored old quarter of rooftop restaurants and sleepy craft shops. The town is also 95 percent Christian and boasts at least five churches, three of which date back to the nineteenth century. Its easy-going atmosphere – and, in summer, the best peaches in Jordan – makes Fhays a pleasant place to spend an afternoon; it has good bus connections and can easily be combined with a visit to Wadi Seer and/or Salt.

Once free of Swayleh on Amman's fringes, the road plunges into thick pine forest, passing the Royal Stables before entering Fhays. The town has two distinct halves. The first, known as **al-Allali** (with a huge calligraphic sculpture in the central roundabout), is newer and less attractive; make sure you carry on down the steep hill to the old part of town, known as **al-balad**. Between the two lies a vast cement factory, Jordan's biggest and Fhays's main claim to fame. Over seventy percent of the town is employed at the plant, but Allali in particular has suffered recently from clouds of cement dust and soaring rates of asthma. In a depressed economy, though, there's little the locals can do but grit their teeth and stage occasional sit-ins.

In *al-balad*, the web of lanes and hundred-year-old stone cottages now known as **al-Ruwaq** – between the bus terminus and the deep Wadi Rahwa – had long been slated for demolition when, in 1992, a local character opened an art gallery here; he then slowly bought up the cottages one by one and converted them into a self-contained arts-and-crafts neighbourhood (crafts shops open Mon & Wed–Sun 4–10pm). Although the crafts are a little uninspired, it makes for an interesting wander and the tiny lanes come into their own in the golden light of late afternoon. During August, there's an annual carnival of music and dance held in the village; details can be had from the Amman tourist office.

Practicalities

Buses run to Fhays from Amman's Abdali station. From Wadi Seer, regular buses drop you at the flyover at Swayleh, from where you can pick up the

Amman–Fhays buses on the corner to the left (the road is marked "One Way"). All buses run through al-Allali to *al-balad*. Tucked away in a renovated old house in the lanes of al-Ruwaq, barely 50m from the bus terminus, is an excellent and very reasonably priced Arabic **restaurant**, *Zuwwadeh* (daily 10am–midnight; ☎079/32413). The kebabs and *fatteh* are superb, but you could dine lavishly on *mezze* alone and part with little more than JD3. An alcoholic, arak-flavoured *arjileh* here – a speciality of the house – is likely to put an interesting spin on your journey back to Amman. Note that the last bus back to Abdali leaves around 8pm.

Salt

For many centuries, **SALT** was the only settlement of any size in Transjordan. A regional capital under the Ottomans, the town came into its own in the late nineteenth century when merchants from Nablus arrived to expand their trading base into Transjordan. Into what was then a peasant village of shacks boxed between precipitous hills, the merchants brought sophisticated architects and masons to work with the honey-coloured local limestone; buildings were put up in the ornate Nabulsi style to serve both as grand residences and merchandise centres. With

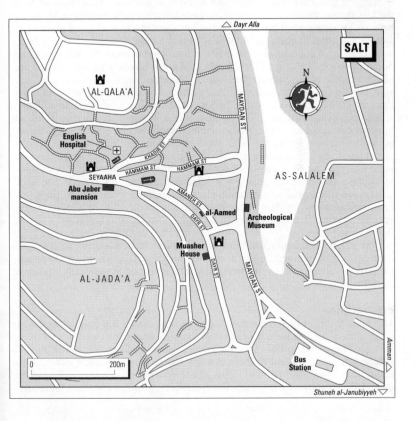

SALT BY NAME, SWEET BY NATURE

Salt's name apparently derives from the ancient Greek *saltos*, meaning "thick forest", and the town has been renowned since antiquity for its natural fertility. Indeed when Salt's own variety of small, pale, very flavourful and high-quality grapes were first dried, a whole new type of raisin resulted, known, with due deference to the town, as a **sultana**.

open trade to and from Palestine, Salt's boom continued into the 1920s; the new Emirate of Transjordan was formally proclaimed in 1921 in the town's main square, but by then the railway from Damascus had reached nearby Amman and Emir Abdullah chose the newer town to be his capital. As quickly as Salt had flourished, so it went into decline: superseded by Amman, it was cut off in 1948 from its traditional trade outlet to the Mediterranean at Haifa, then again in 1967 from its Palestinian twin, Nablus. Consequently, the town has seen none of the headlong modernization that has afflicted the capital, so much of the Ottoman architecture in the old centre has survived, as has peace and quiet, perfect for aimless exploration.

Standing under the huge eucalyptus at the road junction a short walk up from the bus station, you are surrounded by three towering hills: to your right are the bare rocky slopes of **al-Salalem**, to the left rises the tree-adorned peak of **al-Jada'a** and straight ahead is **al-Qala'a**, named for the Mamluke fortress on its summit which was demolished in 1840 and finally swept away recently by a white-domed mosque. Walking a little way along Maydan Street brings the arched and pillared facade of the **Salt Archeological Museum** (daily 8am–6pm; free) into view, but the displays of glass and pottery bits and bobs are much less impressive than the building housing them, the former stately home of the Touqan family (King Hussein's third wife, Queen Alia, was a Touqan). A few rooms off an upstairs courtyard have been rather unnecessarily turned into an ugly folklore museum. Turning left at the Arab Bank a few minutes further along Maydan Street leads you into a narrow market alley, Hammam Street (although the *hammam* itself was razed in the 1930s for lack of customers), lined with buildings – including a wonderful old mosque – which date from Salt's golden age. The street emerges at the **Seyaaha**, Salt's main plaza, dominated on one side by the graceful arched facade of the **Abu Jaber mansion** and on the other by a hideous modernistic mosque. Bending sharply to the right is tiny Khadir Street, with several flights of steps leading steeply up the face of **Jebel al-Qala'a**. Partway up you'll see the colonnaded honeystone **English Hospital**, locked and rusted gates still bearing an "EH" monogram. The view from the summit, bathed in afternoon sunshine, out over the town to the rolling Balqa hills beyond is worth any amount of leg-ache.

Practicalities

There are plenty of **buses** direct to Salt from both Abdali and Raghadan stations in Amman, as well as from the flyover at Swayleh (the same pick-up point as for buses to Fhays – see p.120). Buses from Salt also serve Dayr Alla and Shuneh al-Janubiyyeh in the Jordan Valley, and a few run to Zerqa. Meagre **information** about the town can be had from the Department of Antiquities office (☎05/555651) above the museum. For refreshment while wandering, there are a few **coffee-houses** dotted around; one of the best spreads itself over Dayr Street next to the white-domed mosque close to the museum. **Restaurants** are exclusively in the spit-and-sawdust category, and king among them is *al-Aamed*, which has been churning out quality shish-kebabs to the Salti cognoscenti since the days of Abdullah. It's on Amaneh Street (parallel to Dayr Street), with no sign in English or Arabic; spot it by the huge rusty pipe that sticks out of the wall above its entrance.

If you're **moving on** from Salt rather than heading straight back to the capital, it's worth knowing that the road down to Shuneh follows the beautiful and dramatic **Wadi Shuayb**, a perpetually flowing stream lush with undergrowth all year and carpeted with wildflowers in spring; this is a much more impressive route down to the valley floor than the highway from Amman. North of Salt, on the Dayr Alla road, the **Zai National Park** is perfect picnic territory, thick forest with rough trails and plenty of wild nooks.

The Dead Sea

Oppressively hot most of the year, smelly, desolate, and flanked by bone-dry, corrosively salty beaches, the **DEAD SEA** (*al-Bahr al-Mayit* in Arabic) is a surprisingly fun place to hang out – and swimming in it is a memorable experience, unlike anything else on the planet.

At 400m below sea level, the land-locked lake is **the lowest point on Earth**, lying on the Great Rift Valley, a deep geological cleft which can be traced from Turkey all the way into East Africa. It got its name in antiquity due to its uniquely salty water, which kills off virtually all marine life – seawater is about three or four percent salt, but Dead Sea water is over thirty percent. The lake is fed mainly by the River Jordan, flowing south from Galilee, but due to the geological upheavals, it has no outflow; instead, water evaporates off the surface at the rate of millions of litres a day, leading to continuous precipitation of salt onto the beach and a thick atmospheric haze overhead which dampens sound down to almost nothing – there's little to hear but lapping water anyway. The haze also filters out harmful UVB sunrays, handily allowing tanning but not burning. The major reason for a visit, though, is that the lake's high salinity makes the water so buoyant that it's impossible for swimmers to sink. Olympic swimmers and hopeless paddlers alike become bobbing corks, unable to do anything but relax and float. As you walk in, you'll find your feet are forced up from under you – you couldn't touch bottom if you tried and you ride too high in the water to swim. If you do try to stroke, you'll find you just splash ineffectually and are likely to get water in your eyes: not a pleasant experience. The salt will also make you very aware of every little cut and open blemish on your skin, and most people make for dry land after twenty itchy minutes. Nonetheless, the drama of floating completely unaided and silent on a flat, hot sea surrounded by hazy mountains is worth the discomfort.

Other diversions include covering yourself in the hot, sulphurous black **mud** which collects in pools on the beach; letting it dry in the sun before washing it off will leave you with tingling muscles and baby-soft skin. However, scorching temperatures (well over 40°C in summer) and exceptionally low humidity make **dehydration** a real danger, and you should be drinking twice or three times as much water as normal to compensate.

The only developed **beaches** along the eastern shoreline (the western shore is half in the West Bank and half in Israel) are at the lake's northeastern tip near

LIFE AND DEATH IN THE DEAD SEA

By far the highest proportion of visitors to the Dead Sea indulge in what's been called **therapeutic tourism**: both the waters and the mud have medically proven benefits, putting many severe skin diseases and joint problems into long-term remission. Calcium, magnesium, bromine, sulphur and bitumen – all with beneficial properties – are found in extremely high concentrations, and, in addition, the air is very highly oxygenated, due to the combination of high rates of evaporation, high temperatures, high atmospheric pressure and low humidity. Though well developed on the Israeli shore, therapeutic tourism is a relatively new field for Jordan, currently concentrated at the medical centre of the *Dead Sea Spa Hotel*, which is often booked solid for months ahead. Celebrated skin-care products from the Dead Sea can be bought all over the country.

Despite its name, there is life in the Dead Sea, though you won't lose your toes to it: only three species of **bacteria** and one of **algae** can withstand the concentrations of salt. The relationship between them is a neat adaptation to difficult circumstances, though human intervention is making things more difficult still. The bacteria are considerably more tolerant of high salinity levels than the algae, so when salinity in the lake rises, the algae vanish and the bacteria – which normally feed on them – are forced to rely on sunlight alone for nutrition. When salinity drops, the algae reappear and the bacteria thrive, their feeding turning the lake a beautiful purplish-pink colour. However, with the diversion of more and more water out of the Sea of Galilee and the River Jordan further upstream, the amount of sweet water reaching the lake has been dropping in recent decades and thus salinity has been steadily rising, keeping the algae away. The purplish bacterial bloom has occurred only three times since 1964, and looks increasingly unlikely ever to happen again.

Indeed, the whole future of the lake is in doubt. Since the 1960s, greater and greater inroads have been made into its **freshwater sources**, and today far more water evaporates from the lake than flows into it. At present, there are four dams across the River Jordan and three pumping stations; another twelve dams and eight pumping stations are planned. Both Israel and Jordan have also developed major mineral and potash industries at the southern end of the lake which depend on large-scale evaporation for production. In the 1950s, the lake's surface area was about one thousand square kilometres; today, it's less than seven hundred and still falling, representing a drop in the water level of 15m. Since the 1970s, Lynch's Strait, which formerly connected the northern and southern parts of the lake, has dried out, turning the Lisan Peninsula into a land-bridge. If things continue as they are – which is likely, unless a regional peace incorporating ecologically sound sharing of freshwater sources comes about – the Dead Sea will dry up in just four centuries.

Swaymeh, and get very crowded on Fridays. One thing to bear in mind is that you should take a dip near a place that supplies **freshwater showers**: Dead Sea water is thick and very slimy, and leaves an immensely uncomfortable layer of salt on your skin that you can't wash off quickly enough once you're out. Currently, Swaymeh is the only resort offering showers and a moderately sandy beach; jagged, salt-encrusted rocks line much of the shore elsewhere.

Practicalities

Buses for the Dead Sea from Amman leave from al-Quds Street, in the Ras al-Ain district south of Downtown (*service* #28 or #29 from the Saqf Sayl opposite the *Amman*

Palace Hotel will take you to the spot). A few of them run direct
stop short at **Shuneh al-Janubiyyeh** (South Shuneh) in the Jo
crossroads at Shuneh, frequent buses go on to Swaymeh, as wel
and Madaba. The last bus direct to Amman from Swaymeh depa
last from Shuneh around 6pm (both an hour or two earlier in win
these, you'd have to get to Salt, from where buses run later to Amn

The road from Amman to Swaymeh is the old Jerusalem highw ~~sec-
tion south of Shuneh was formerly an area controlled by the m.....ary; it's still
blocked by a **checkpoint** at the turnoff to the old King Abdullah Bridge, which
was damaged in the 1967 war and never rebuilt. You'll need your **passport** to get
through hassle-free.

After the checkpoint, buses pass first through Swaymeh village, then drop you
at the gates of the **Dead Sea Resthouse**, which has rather dowdy facilities down
on the shore (daily 8am–midnight; JD2; ☎05/572900). There are separate changing rooms for men and women (the latter with its own set of showers), and open
showers on the beach (until sunset). Lockers cost 500 fils, and the air-con **café-
restaurant** is unsurprisingly pricey – a bottle of water here is an outrageous 960
fils. An all-over mud pack costs JD2, and four-person pedalboats can be rented for
JD2 per quarter-hour. If you miss the bus back to civilization, you might be forced
to consider their accommodation – horrible, boxy little air-con **bungalows**
(June–Aug ③; Sept–May ⑤; normally book in advance on ☎06/568 1042, fax 568
1028). The only attraction of staying is the sunset.

If you walk 200m to the right of the Resthouse you'll come to the free-entry
public beach. Things are spartan – no cafés or shops – but changing facilities are
acceptable, and there are a couple of temperamental showers. The mud is the
same but free, and you can **camp** on the beach for nothing.

If you have your own transport, another possibility is the **Dead Sea Spa Hotel**
(☎08/546101; book rooms in advance on ☎06/560 1554, fax 568 8100), about 5km
south and unreachable on the bus. Using their swimming pool (daily 9am–6pm) and
patch of beach (daily 6am–11pm) costs JD7.500, and they can offer an equally pricey
buffet lunch and a hilariously incongruous Hawaiian-style beach-bar. Hotel **rooms**
(⑨) are large and comfortable, complete with satellite TV and all the trimmings, and
the building is air-conditioned (and soulless) throughout. Next to the *Spa* hotel, a
five-star *Dead Sea Mövenpick* is near completion, and a *Dead Sea Marriott* is scheduled for opening in late 1999. There are many proposals for developing Swaymeh
and the sleepy eastern shore of the lake for tourism – a total of 3200 new beds are
planned by the year 2000, with more to follow. Approval was controversially granted
in 1998 to pipe the waters of the Mujib river (see p.209) north to supply drinking
water to the area. Studies are currently under way to assess the impact of such development on the unique local environment, but at the time of writing it seems unlikely either that the proposed tourism facilities will be ecologically sound, or that the
barren lakeshore will be able to retain its atmosphere of wilderness for long.

South of Swaymeh

The Resthouse is at the beginning of a highway which runs south along the shoreline of the Dead Sea, entering the Wadi Araba (see p.302) and eventually arriving
at Aqaba 278km away. However, there's no public transport along here, and there
are only two turnings off the road – after 54km to Karak and 99km to Tafileh –
and one single petrol station at Safi, 76km south of Swaymeh. The scenery all the
way down is spectacular: aside from the deep blue of the Dead Sea, framed by the

ns opposite and speckled with white outcrops of salt, after 14km you'll
e to some hot springs at **Zara** where the Wadi Zerqa Ma'in flows into the lake,
nd 15km further a graceful bridge crosses the outflow of **Wadi Mujib**. Further
south – past Lot's Cave (see p.216) – lies Safi, at the head of the long **Wadi Araba**,
with drifting sand and wandering camels all the way down to Aqaba.

travel details

Since most buses and all minibuses and *services*
simply depart whenever they are full, regularity of
service is indicated only when a fixed timetable is
in operation.

Buses, minibuses and *services*

Amman (Abdali station) to: Ajloun (1hr 30min);
Dayr Alla (1hr); Fhays (35min); Irbid (New Amman
station; every 15min; 1hr 15min to 2hr); Jerash
(1hr); King Hussein Bridge (1hr); Madaba (30min);
Mafraq (Bedouin station; 1hr); Queen Alia Airport
(every 30min; 45min); Ramtha (2hr); Salt (35min);
Swayleh (15min); Zerqa (New station; 35min).

Amman (JETT office, Abdali) to: Aqaba (6–8
daily; 4hr); Hammamat Ma'in (1 daily; 1hr 30min);
King Hussein Bridge (1 daily; 1hr); Petra (1 daily;
3hr).

Amman (Raghadan station) to: Madaba
(30min); Muwaggar (30min); Queen Alia Airport
(hourly; 45min); Salt (40min); Wadi Seer (30min);
Zerqa (New station; 25min).

Amman (Ras al-Ain, Ali bin Abi Taleb Street)
to: Wadi Seer (25min).

Amman (Ras al-Ain, al-Quds Street) to:
Shuneh al-Janubiyyeh (1hr); Swaymeh (Dead Sea
Resthouse; 1hr 30min).

Amman (Wihdat station) to: Aqaba (4hr);
Hammamat Ma'in (2hr); Karak (2hr); Ma'an (2hr
30min); Madaba (30min); Shawbak (2hr 45min);
Tafileh (2hr 30min); Wadi Musa/Petra (3hr).

Fhays to: Amman (Abdali station; 35min);
Swayleh (20min).

Iraq al-Amir to: Wadi Seer (20min).

King Hussein Bridge to: Amman (Abdali station; 1hr).

Queen Alia Airport to: Amman (Abdali station;
every 30min; 45min); Amman (Raghadan station;
hourly; 45min).

Salt to: Amman (Abdali station; 35min); Amman
(Raghadan station; 40min); Dayr Alla (40min);

Shuneh al-Janubiyyeh (30min); Swayleh (20min);
Zerqa (New station; 45min).

Shuneh al-Janubiyyeh to: Amman (Ras al-Ain;
1hr); Dayr Alla (40min); Madaba (1hr); Salt
(30min); Swaymeh (Dead Sea Resthouse; 30min).

Swayleh to: Amman (Abdali station; 15min);
Wadi Seer (15min); Fhays (20min); Salt (20min).

Swaymeh (Dead Sea Resthouse) to: Amman (Ras
al-Ain; 1hr 30min); Shuneh al-Janubiyyeh (30min).

Wadi Seer to: Amman (Raghadan station;
30min); Amman (Ras al-Ain; 25min); Iraq al-Amir
(20min); Swayleh (15min).

Domestic flights

Amman (Marka Airport) to: Aqaba (1 daily; 50min).

Amman (Queen Alia Airport) to: Aqaba (1
daily; 50min).

International buses and *services*

Amman (Abdali station) to: Aleppo (10–18hr);
Baghdad (10–18hr); Beirut (8–12hr); Cairo
(15–28hr); Damascus (3–7hr); Dammam (36hr);
Istanbul (48hr); Jeddah (24hr); Riyadh (24hr).

Amman (JETT office, Abdali) to: Abu Dhabi (2
weekly; 36hr); Baghdad (3 weekly; 15hr);
Damascus (2 daily; 3hr 30min); Dammam (1 daily;
24–28hr); Dubai (2 weekly; 36hr); Jeddah (1 daily;
20–24hr); Riyadh (1 daily 20–24hr).

Amman (JETT office, Marka) to: Cairo (2 weekly; 20–24hr); Kuwait City (2 weekly; 24–28hr).

Amman (Mahatta, Army Street) to: Baghdad
(10–18hr).

**Amman (Trust office, 7th Circle, near Royal
Jordanian)** to: Haifa (12 weekly; 5hr); Nazareth
(1–2 daily; 4hr); Tel Aviv (6 weekly; 6hr).

International trains

Amman (Hejaz station) to: Damascus (1 weekly;
10hr).

CHAPTER TWO

JERASH AND THE NORTH

T he rolling hills of the **north** of Jordan hold some of the loveliest countryside in the whole Middle East, acres of olive and fig trees, patches of ancient pine forest and fields of wheat, interspersed with deep, fertile, cultivated valleys pointing the way west down to the immense Jordan Valley. This is the most densely populated part of the country, and every hill and wadi has its village; many of the local people are Jordanian, but plenty of towns also have a significant population of Palestinians, who continue to farm the East Bank of the Jordan much as they did the West Bank and Galilee before they were forced to flee in the wars of 1948 and 1967.

In biblical and classical times, this was the greater part of the area known as the **Decapolis**, and extensive ruins of important Roman cities survive, most notably at **Jerash**, to the north of Amman, and at **Umm Qais**, on the border overlooking the Sea of Galilee. West of Jerash, the fairytale ruins of an Arab-built Crusader-period castle dominate the hills above **Ajloun**. **Irbid**, the modern capital of northern Jordan, is a workaday university city; for travellers its highlight is by far the most engaging historical and craft museum in the country. The natural boundary between Palestine and Transjordan – still an international border today – is the swelteringly subtropical **Jordan Valley**, well under 200m below sea level, which carries the trickling River Jordan south to the Dead Sea and is today the scene of intensive year-round agricultural production. Ongoing excavations at the Decapolis city of **Pella**, which was built around a spring just above the valley floor,

---

HOTEL PRICE CODES

Throughout this guide, hotels have been categorized according to the **price codes** given below, which indicate the normal price for the **cheapest double room** in a particular establishment during the **high season** (excluding the ten-percent tax and ten-percent service charge levied in all hotels of ③ and above). **Single rooms** can cost anything between seventy and a hundred percent of the double-room rates. Where a hotel offers beds in **shared rooms**, the price per person to share has been given; if a price code has also been included, this indicates that private rooms are also available. For a fuller explanation, see p.39.

① under JD10	④ JD30–40	⑦ JD65–80
② JD10–20	⑤ JD40–50	⑧ JD80–95
③ JD20–30	⑥ JD50–65	⑨ over JD95

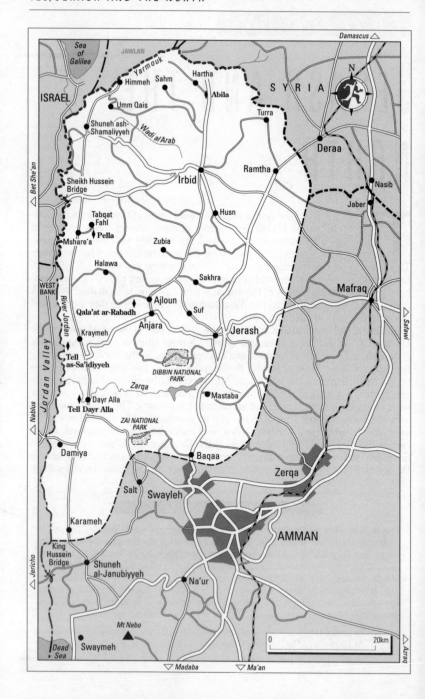

Abu Darwish mosque, Amman

Smoking a hubbly-bubbly, Amman

Downtown Amman

Beans and spices for sale, Amman

Salt

The Dead Sea shore

The cardo maximus at Jerash

The East Church, Pella

Fresco of a dancing girl, Qusayr Amra

Doorways at Qasr Hraneh

MICHELLE WOODWARD

The white camels of Umm al-Jimal

MICHELLE WOODWARD

الحدود العراقيه
IRAQI BORDERS
الرويشد
AL RUWAISHED-H4

Iraqi tankers on the Baghdad Highway

THE DECAPOLIS

From the time of Alexander the Great, a group of around ten important cities of the region began to be associated together. Bastions of urban Greek culture amidst a Semitic rural population, these cities were founded or re-founded during or following Alexander's consolidation of power in the Levant in the late fourth century BC. **Decapolis** means "ten cities" in Greek, but classical authors disagreed on both the number and identity of the ten: a reasonably authoritative list, from the first century AD, comprises, in modern-day Jordan, Philadelphia (Amman), Gadara (Umm Qais), Pella and Gerasa (Jerash); Damascus, Raphana, Hippos, Dion and Canatha (all in modern Syria); and Scythopolis (Israel). Although it's tempting to imagine the Decapolis cities working together in a formal league of co-operation, no records survive of such a pact, and it seems instead that the term was used simply to refer to the geographical area of northern Transjordan and southern Syria – the gospels of Matthew and Mark, for example, mention the Decapolis only as a region. All that can be said for sure is that the Decapolis cities shared a common history and culture.

After the Roman armies arrived in 63 BC, the area enjoyed a sizeable degree of both affluence and autonomy. The population within the cities – by this stage predominantly of Middle Eastern origin – spoke much more Greek than Latin (the latter was only used on formal occasions, in official documents and correspondence), and were almost certainly also fluent in Aramaic, the language spoken in the countryside. Even in its heyday, Jerash, for instance, remained at core a semitic society, its ancient local traditions overlaid with a thick veneer of Greco-Roman ideas and political structures.

By the second century, the Decapolis appears to have expanded; a list from this period names eighteen cities, including Abila (Qwaylbeh), Arbela (Irbid) and Capitolias (Bayt Ras, near Irbid). However, historical confusion between authors subsequently reigns supreme, with some indicating the Decapolis to be a part of Syria, others seeming to show that Syria was a part of the Decapolis, and still more including within the Decapolis cities that seem to have played no part in the common history and culture of the original ten. It was **Emperor Trajan** who effectively broke the cultural bonds in the Decapolis and sowed the seeds of this confusion. His Province of Arabia, newly created in 106 AD, included only some of the cities, but Pella and Scythopolis, for instance, remained within the Province of Syria. Bosra became the new provincial capital, and although Decapolis centres such as Jerash and Philadelphia subsequently experienced a golden age in culture and sophistication, Trajan's reorganization ensured that their horizons now encompassed more than merely their own region: they were bonded firmly into the greater Roman order. By the time of the division of empire into east and west under Diocletian at the end of the third century the notion of a special, parochial link between the cities of the Decapolis was dead.

are revealing continuous habitation for at least five thousand years even before the Romans arrived.

Transport links around the north are good, with **buses** linking all towns and –with less regularity – just about every village; on inter-city runs, a handful of *services* can cut down journey times, but distances are so small that the bus is no hardship. Jerash deserves at least a full day-trip, but with no hotels in the town itself (and nowhere to leave a heavy bag) you'll have to base yourself elsewhere: besides the *Olive Branch* – nearby but difficult to reach – and Amman, Irbid with its good transport connections makes most sense, although for peace and fresh air, Ajloun would be far preferable. A **car**, of course, would be a major boon, allowing you to explore backroads, and to get to more remote sites like Himmeh or Pella without having to rely on a sporadic bus service.

Jerash

One of the best-preserved, most dramatic and explorable Roman cities in the Middle East, set in the bowl of a well-watered valley just 50km or so from Amman, **JERASH** is the principal focus of a trip into northern Jordan. With its monumental and sophisticated public buildings tempered by charmingly human touches, the city is likely to inspire you even if you are on the jaded final leg of a ruin-hopping tour of the region.

Jerash is a huge site, and you could easily spend a full day here; if you have only a couple of hours, you could rapidly absorb the **Oval Plaza** buildings, the **Cardo** (the main thoroughfare), the **Sacred Way** leading up to the **Temple of Artemis** and the **North Theatre**, but without really doing the place justice. Even on a longer visit, the less energetic could skip entirely the northern reaches of the city and Birketayn, and even the maze of western churches, without missing out. With no hotels in immediate striking distance apart from the hard-to-reach *Olive Branch*, nowhere to leave heavy bags while you explore, and no buses departing after 6pm, you're most likely to want to treat Jerash as a day-trip from Amman, Irbid or Ajloun.

Note that, after Petra, the largest chunk of public and private money spent on Jordan's ancient sites is lavished on Jerash. Consequently, archeologists are working continuously at several different digs within the city, and facilities for visitors are being overhauled at a rapid rate, attracting busloads of tourists, both foreign and Jordanian. Especially in the mid-morning hours before lunch, the more accessible sights – the Oval Plaza area, and the Cardo up to the Temple of Artemis – can get overcrowded (school-trip day is Wednesday), but it takes only a minute's wandering off the beaten track to sidestep the hubbub. During late July and early August, the popular **Jerash Festival** occupies the entire city, with craft markets and an impressive line-up of evening performances (see the box on p.135).

Some history

Set in the fertile hills of **Gilead**, mentioned frequently in the Old Testament as being a populated and cultivated region, the Jerash area has attracted settlement since prehistory: Paleolithic and Neolithic implements have been uncovered nearby, and archeological investigation around the South Gate of the city has revealed evidence of settlement going back to the Middle Bronze Age (around 1600 BC).

Gerasa (the ancient name for Jerash) was founded during the 170s–160s BC, the relatively small city of the time focused around the Temple of Zeus and the low hill opposite. Very little evidence of this Hellenistic period survives today. It was at some point around this time that the idea of the **Decapolis** first emerged (see box on p.129). Gerasa and its Decapolis neighbours were "liberated" by the Romans under Pompey in 63 BC and granted autonomy under the higher authority of the **Province of Syria**. The century which followed saw unprecedented growth and stability in Gerasa, and it was during the first century AD that the basic town plan as it survives today was laid down: a colonnaded north–south axis cut by two colonnaded side streets, along with a temple to Zeus (built over the pre-existing temple) fronted by an oval plaza, expansion of the temple to Artemis and construction of the South Theatre.

In 106, when **Emperor Trajan** reorganized Roman authority in the region around his new Province of Arabia, Gerasa lost its autonomy and was governed from the provincial capital, Bosra. Gerasa gained a link by a branch road to Trajan's new highway running between Bosra and the Red Sea, while other main roads linked the city with Philadelphia and Pella. Suddenly, the city found itself not only close to the provincial capital but also astride the highly lucrative trade routes that had been jealously guarded by the Nabateans for so long. In 129–30, Gerasa briefly became the absolute centre of the Roman Empire, as Trajan's successor, **Hadrian**, wintered in the city; in his honour, the Gerasenes built a new monumental arch outside the city's southern walls, and embarked on major expansion works, including widening of the main street and renovation of temples and public buildings. Hadrian's visit ushered in a golden age for the city, and Gerasa's population may have hit 25,000 during the later second and early third centuries.

Civil disorder in Rome in the 190s heralded the end of the boom. Taxation increased to help cover greater military expenditure – which fuelled further resentment, as well as crippling inflation – and the **Sassanians** began to whittle away at the eastern flanks of the empire. Trade was seriously affected, and in Gerasa the lavish programme of public works was cut back.

By 359, Gerasa had embraced **Christianity**. During the fifth and sixth centuries, dozens of churches went up, though the Byzantine style of architecture was very different from the rigorously ordered Roman style preceding it; many pre-existing buildings were ransacked for stones and columns, giving a botched, make-do feel to many of Gerasa's churches. By the late seventh century, the city was literally crumbling under the twin blows of shoddy workmanship and lack of maintenance; at one point, even the water supply failed. **Persian** forces were able easily to occupy the once-grand metropolis for a dozen years or so from 614, their only legacy an adaptation of the hippodrome into a polo field.

After the Muslim victory over the Byzantines in 636, Gerasa – now arabized to Jerash – slipped into anonymous decline; a single, jerry-built **Umayyad mosque** and a handful of kilns are the only evidence from the Islamic period in the city. The cataclysmic earthquake of 747 finally brought the city to its knees, and for a thousand years Jerash lay deserted.

At the beginning of the nineteenth century, **European** explorers – including, on a four-hour visit, Burckhardt – were taken around the ruins by local bedouin, and news of the "discovery" of the ancient city of Gerasa spread rapidly to the West. Throughout the nineteenth century, and up until the present day, archeological investigation at Jerash has been continuous and wide-ranging, although vast areas still remain untouched beneath the grass. A new lease of life for the city, however, was to come from an unexpected quarter. In 1879, in the same process of migration and resettlement that brought **Circassian** settlers to the deserted ruins of Amman, the Ottoman authorities directed refugee Circassians to settle in the ruins of Jerash. They occupied what is believed to have been the Roman residential quarters, on the east bank of the river, and the bustling town which has since grown up there, now capital of its own governorate, still has Circassians in the majority.

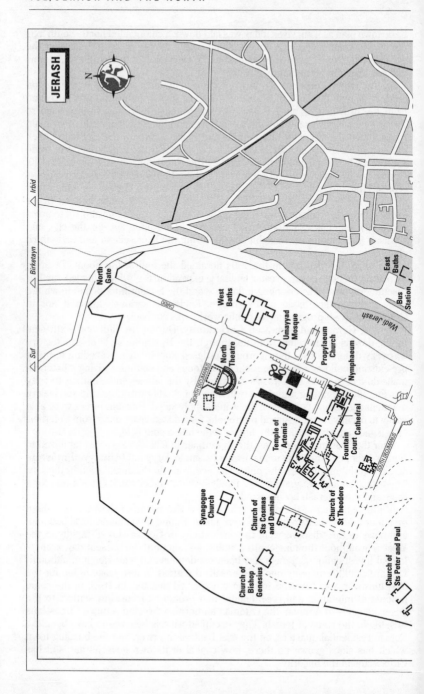

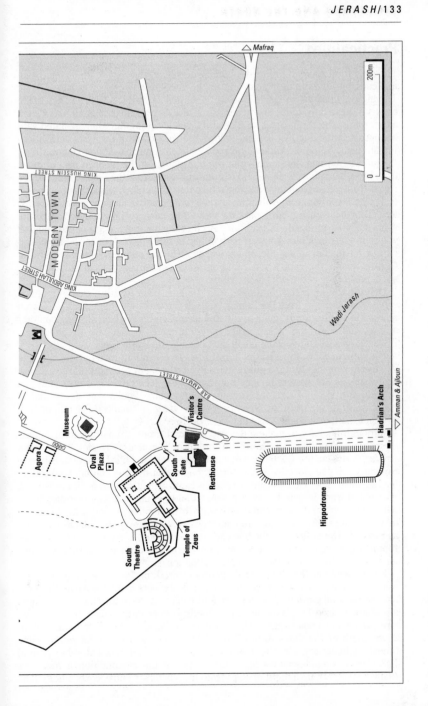

Practicalities

The road from Amman to Jerash plunges steeply off the Swayleh hills into beautiful countryside, with the Ajloun hills on the horizon snow-capped as late as April. The highway passes alongside **Baqaa**, the largest of Jordan's UN-run Palestinian camps – these days more of a breezeblock shanty town than a camp – and soon after crosses the River Zerqa, in a beautiful rustic setting but foully polluted with chemicals. A turning just beyond follows the west bank of the Wadi Jerash into Jerash itself. All public **buses** and *services* from Amman's Abdali station, Irbid, Ajloun, Mafraq and Zerqa **arrive** at the bus station in the modern part of town; from here, it's a short walk behind the mosque and across the South Bridge to the ruins. Note when planning your departure that all public transport out of Jerash ends by 5.30 or 6pm – after that time, you'll have to either hitch or negotiate a taxi fare. Tour buses use a large parking area – one corner of it crammed with souvenir stalls – to the side of Hadrian's Arch at the southern edge of the ruins. If you're in your own **car**, you can park either in this bus-park or in the small car-park a bit further along the main road next to the newly revamped **Visitors' Centre**. Inside the centre you'll find an office co-ordinating local guides, a gift shop, post office and model of the ruins.

Orientation on arrival is simple, with the lush Wadi Jerash dividing the modern town to the east from the Roman ruins to the west. The huge Hadrian's Arch marks the southernmost point of the Roman city and is the best starting-point for a visit, although the ticket office and entrance to the site proper (daily 7.30am–sunset; JD5) is 400m north, just outside the South Gate.

For **information**, the Visitors' Centre has free handout maps of the site, and you might consider hiring a **guide** to lead you personally around the ruins. These professionals are generally very knowledgeable (see p.68 for more), and can provide the kind of detailed running commentary books can never match. Authorized guides from the Visitors' Centre charge a standard flat rate of JD5, whether the tour actually takes one hour or three.

Although it's easy to make a day-trip to Jerash from Amman, Irbid or Ajloun, there are – incredibly – no **hotels** in the town. The nearest is the *Olive Branch* (☎079/23546, fax 06/582 6034; ④), some 8km away and hard to reach. Buses to **Suf** can drop you close by; make sure, though, that the bus you take is heading for Suf town, not Suf Palestinian refugee camp which lies on a different road. Some 6km from Jerash, before Suf, you should get out at a sign pointing left to Sakib. From here, it's a two-kilometre walk through olive groves to the hotel, set in a lovely, peaceful location with enormous views out over the hills as far south as Swayleh. Upper floors of the hotel are still being built, but the airy ground-floor rooms are en suite, comfortable and very clean. You can camp in their grounds for JD4, and they'll rent you a tent for JD1 on top.

Eating while in Jerash is equally poorly catered for. Picnics among the ruins aside, you might well favour one of the plain local diners in the town over the identikit Arabic food gardens that compete for business close to the ruins, all of which are characterized by plastic furniture, loudspeakers in the trees and mediocre fare. Acceptable choices among them are the *Lebanese House* (daily 10am–11pm), 200m south of Hadrian's Arch off the Ajloun road, and the *al-Khayyam* (same times), virtually opposite the Visitors' Centre, with solid meals at either around JD3. The meat-and-potatoes lunchtime buffet at the air-conditioned *Resthouse* (daily 8am–8pm), up a flight of steps from the Visitors' Centre, costs a hefty JD6,

THE JERASH FESTIVAL

Founded in 1980, the annual **Jerash Festival of Culture and Arts** has grown from insignificant beginnings to become one of the premier international show-cases for music, dance and poetry from the Arab world, and also includes perfor-mances by visiting troupes from Europe, the US and further afield. For several weeks before the festival – held during late July and early August – the ruins see feverish activity as the South and North Theatres are prepared for performances, and stages are set up on the steps of the Temple of Artemis, near the Oval Plaza and at other sites dotted amongst the stones and columns. Recent visitors to the festival have included orchestras from Eastern Europe, dance troupes from Japan and India, Britain's Original Shakespeare Company and a wealth of local perform-ers, including singers, poets and Circassian folkloric dancers. Top-flight perform-ers from the Arab world – principally Lebanon, Egypt and Iraq – attract audiences of thousands, who pack the theatres and public spaces much as the spectators of pagan festivals in antiquity must have done. All along the Cardo and in the Oval Plaza artisans from around Jordan and as far afield as Lebanon and North Africa set up shop to sell their crafts direct to the promenading visitors. Performances and celebrations start in the afternoon and continue late into the night; JETT lays on special daily buses to and from Amman throughout the festival. For more infor-mation, and a schedule of performances, you can either surf to *www.arabia.com/ jerashfest* or contact the festival administration in Amman on ☎06/567 5199. If you're in Jordan at the time, you should definitely not miss it.

or JD4 for *mezze* only – you're paying for the location. They also have an *à la carte* menu.

Hadrian's Arch and the Hippodrome

The first monument you see as you approach Jerash from Amman is the huge **Hadrian's Arch**, poised over the town's main roundabout. The eleven-metre-high triple-arched gateway, which originally stood to almost 22m, was built to hon-our the visit of the Roman emperor Hadrian to Jerash in 129–130 AD. The huge arches, which probably had wooden doors, are flanked by engaged columns unusually decorated with capitals at the bottom rather than the top. Seemingly out on a limb, over 400m from the city walls, the positioning and structure of the arch in fact point to a grandiose scheme for southward expansion of Jerash at the zenith of its power. It would appear that the municipal authorities were envision-ing the arch as an enormous city gate, since its side walls were left untrimmed to enable tight bonding with new perimeter walls. The plan remained unrealized, however, and when it became clear – maybe a century or so later – that Gerasa wasn't going to expand any more, two small side pavilions, with niches mirroring the arch's side entrances, were added.

On the west side of Hadrian's Arch, an array of small arches belongs to the recon-structed south wall of the **Hippodrome**, which is currently undergoing extensive renovation work. It's possible to climb up onto the wall just behind the arch to get an overview of the whole arena, though almost nothing remains of its original struc-ture. Some 260m long and seating up to 15,000 spectators, this was the scene of ancient Gerasa's sporting festivals and chariot races, although you'll need a vivid imagination these days to summon up *Ben Hur* from the jumbled stones.

Walking from the arch north towards the gleaming Visitors' Centre takes you past the small, ruinous Byzantine **Church of Bishop Marianos** on the right, built in 570 among Roman and Byzantine tombs on what was then the main Gerasa–Philadelphia road.

The southern part of the ancient city

Beyond the Visitors' Centre, the ticket office for the site stands opposite the reconstructed **South Gate**, the principal entry into the ancient city. It seems from the wheel ruts on the thresholds that the west door was reserved for wheeled traffic, and that the central and east doors were used principally by soft-footed pedestrians. Near the gate is a section of the three-metre-thick wall which originally ran for over 3.5km around the city, a fourth-century strengthening of the original, thinner first-century wall.

Beyond the gate, the split-level **South Street** runs between what is believed to be a Hellenistic settlement on the right and the restored vaults supporting the lower terrace of the Temple of Zeus complex to the left, and gives onto what is one of the most impressive pieces of Roman urban design in the world, the **Oval Plaza**. Comprising a large central paved area enclosed by two curving colonnades – both irregular bent ellipses and of different lengths – the Oval Plaza forms an elegant, smooth entry into the city proper, while deftly linking the east–west axis of the Temple of Zeus with the north–south axis of the main street, the Cardo. Approaching from the south, the shorter western arm of the colonnade draws your eye and your feet towards the opening of the Cardo, which may well originally have been marked by a triple arch. Beautiful stone paving swirls around the plaza following the curve of the Ionic colonnades; two slightly wider intercolumnar spaces on the west show where small side streets led in. The column in the centre of the plaza was put up recently to celebrate the Jerash Festival, but the podium it stands on is original and may have supported a statue instead. In the seventh century, a water tank was built around the podium, and pipes are still visible set into the paving.

The South Theatre

From the plaza a track climbs west up to the breathtaking **South Theatre**, the most magnificent of all Jerash's monuments and the largest of the city's three theatres. Recently extensively restored, it was built in the 90s AD to seat over three thousand, the cost of construction partly offset by contributions from wealthy Gerasenes. Inscriptions record such generosity, and lower seats on the shadier western side of the auditorium are numbered – notable citizens could presumably reserve these prime spots. You enter the theatre into the orchestra, and, as with all theatres, there are plenty of acoustic games to play; talking while standing at the midpoint of the orchestra gives an effect as good as a PA system, and if two people opposite each other stick their heads into the round indentations below the seats they can hear each other's mutters quite clearly. The stage has been restored in stone – it was probably wood originally – and the *scenae frons*, or backdrop, would have had another storey on top of the elaborate and beautifully carved detail that exists today.

The Temple of Zeus

Adjacent to the theatre on the same hill, the **Temple of Zeus** in its heyday must have towered over the city, and, like its sister temple of Artemis in the city centre, was intended to be visible from all parts of Jerash. Originally surrounded on all four sides by gigantic Corinthian columns 15m high – the three that are standing now were re-erected in 1982 in the wrong place – the temple was built in 162/3 AD on the foundations of a first-century predecessor, which itself replaced a temple from the second century BC. The inner sanctum is plain and simply decorated, and the massive front wall is 4.5m thick to accommodate stairs up to the roof. In front of the temple, huge dismembered columns have lain untouched since the day of some cataclysmic earthquake in antiquity; the slope they lie on, now covered with earth and overgrown, probably conceals a monumental staircase. From above, the layout of the *temenos*, or sacred terrace, below the temple is clear, with remains of an altar to the left; the far side of the *temenos* is supported on the restored vaults visible from South Street. What is also clear from here is the vast extent of ancient Gerasa: as well as the entire sweep of the ancient ruins, much of modern Jerash is visible. Behind a minaret in a distant space between buildings in the town you can spot a surviving remnant of the eastern city wall.

The ancient city centre

The colonnaded **Cardo**, the main boulevard of Jerash, leads north from the Oval Plaza into the city centre. Some 800m long, the street was originally laid out with Ionic columns, but at some point during the remodelling of the city in the second century, it was widened as far as the Temple of Artemis and the columns updated to the grander Corinthian order. Along the Cardo the columns supported a continuous architrave, and a wide covered pavement on both sides gave access to shops behind. Because of the gentle gradient, each column stands a few centimetres higher, and is slightly shorter, than the last; where the column height would have been too small to maintain strict architectural proportion, the architrave was halted, bracketed into the side of the next column and begun again at a higher level. The diagonal street paving is marked by deep grooves worn by centuries of metal-wheeled traffic, while round drain covers gave access to an underground sewerage system.

Four taller columns on the left mark the entrance to the **agora**, the ancient food market, an octagonal courtyard built around a central fountain and surrounded by small shops. Originally there were massive tables in four corners of the courtyard; strikingly carved supports survive in the farthest corner. Opposite the agora, steps lead up to the small site **museum** (daily: April–Oct 8.30am–5pm, Nov–March 8.30am–4pm), the garden of which is dotted with carved sarcophagi and chunks of statuary. Inside are exhibits tracing settlement of Jerash from Neolithic times, including a good display and explanation of ancient coinage.

A little way further, the Cardo meets the first of Jerash's two major cross-streets, the **South Decumanus**, at an intersection known as the **South Tetrakionion**. At the centre of this circular plaza are four free-standing podia, or *tetrakionia*, each of which was decorated with shell niches and held four columns topped by a square entablature; a statue probably stood between the four columns of each podium. This impressive structure would have turned a simple street junction into a grand meeting-point flanked with shops, without impeding traffic circulation from street to street. To the east, the South Decumanus crossed the river into what was probably Gerasa's residential neighbourhoods at the **South Bridge** – it's now restored, but a modern fence bars access.

The Nymphaeum

From the South Tetrakionion, the Cardo was expanded to its widest extent, and Byzantine raising of the pavement included the addition of small niches down at ankle level, either for small statues or, possibly, street lamps. Eight tall columns on the left mark the entrance to the Cathedral (which is best left for later in the visit – see p.140), and beyond, fronted by four even taller columns, is Gerasa's extraordinarily lavish **Nymphaeum**. Completed in 191 AD, and dedicated to the water nymphs, young daughters of Zeus who inspired ordinary people with dancing, music and poetry, it was nothing more than a huge and grandiose public fountain, but the sight and sound of water splashing in abundance from such a finely carved monument must have been delightful. Even today, dry, the carving which survives on the two-storey semicircular recess is impressive. Originally, the lower storey was faced in green marble, while painted plaster covered the upper storey – traces of the green and orange design survive in the topmost niche on the left. Concealing the holes in the lower niches, statues were probably designed to appear to be pouring water into the basin below, from which lion's-head fountains spat water into shallow basins at pavement level – one of Jerash's most endearing small details is the basin carved as four fish kissing, their eyes serving as drainage holes. The huge red granite laver is a Byzantine embellishment. Beyond the Nymphaeum, thirteen ordinary-sized columns presage four gigantic ones marking the entrance to the Temple of Artemis.

The Temple of Artemis complex

The most important edifice in the ancient city, the **Temple of Artemis** was approached via a long east–west **Sacred Way** which originated somewhere in the residential eastern quarters and cut across the Cardo at the point marked by the four huge columns. The best way to see the route is to pick a path to the east through the jumble of rubble opposite the four columns and stand on top of the apse of what is called the **Propylaeum Church**, ingeniously created from elements of the Roman street. In the sixth century, when the cult of Artemis had passed into historical memory, the Christian inhabitants of Gerasa sealed off the old Sacred Way with the apse you're standing on and used the colonnades of the street as the divisions between nave and aisles. Between the church and the Cardo, a plaza – decorated with beautiful spiral-twisted columns topped with a delicately carved architrave that now lies in chunks nearby – became the atrium of the new church. Down below the Propylaeum Church, a Roman bridge carrying the Sacred Way once spanned the river where buses now turn into Jerash's bus station; one of the few monuments of Gerasa to survive in modern Jerash is the huge East Baths building, which you can see plum in the middle of the bus station opposite.

Back on the west side of the Cardo, a portico leads you to the **Propylaeum** itself, a massive, ornately decorated gateway, which gives onto a monumental staircase of seven flights of seven steps. At the top – but still well below the temple proper – is a terrace with the foundations of a small **altar**; from here, another monumental staircase, originally over 120m wide, takes you up to the level of the sacred courtyard, or *temenos*, with a dramatic view of the temple.

The temple

The Temple of Artemis is set far back in a vast **courtyard** some 161m deep and 121m wide, which was originally lined on all four sides with a colonnade and is now cluttered with the ruins of Byzantine and Umayyad pottery kilns and workshops. The temple has clung onto its huge **portico**, whose clustered limestone columns have been burnt peachy bronze over the centuries. Inserting a long stick or a key between the drums of any of them (the fourth on the left is a favourite) demonstrates how these mammoth constructions, in order to absorb the effects of earth tremors and high winds, were designed to sway gently – and have been for almost two millennia without toppling. The **cella**, or inner sanctum, is today exposed, but would originally have been surrounded by a peristyle of six columns across each short side, eleven on each longer side; the capitals of those that stand are still in place, but some elements of the entablature have never been found, pointing to the possibility that the temple was never completed. The inner walls of the *cella* would have been richly decorated with slabs of marble supported on hooks fitting into the holes all round the walls, which were pilfered during the Byzantine period to adorn churches. At the back is the single focus of all this wealth of extraordinary architecture along the Sacred Way: the niche which once housed the image of Artemis, daughter of Zeus and goddess of the forests, who cared for women and brought fertility to all creatures.

The northern part of the ancient city

From the Temple of Artemis courtyard, a track leads north to the back of the restored **North Theatre**. Much smaller than its southern twin, this was originally constructed in the 160s AD to be a small performance space or council chamber; many of the seats in the lower rows are marked with Greek names, referring to tribes which voted in the city council. On the two ends of the semicircular orchestra wall, lovely little stone reliefs show women and boys dancing and playing different musical instruments. Upper rows of seats were constructed early in the third century to give a total capacity of around 1600, but by the fifth century the building seems to have gone out of use as a theatre. Much reconstruction and renovation work has been done here in the last decade or two, not least in the orchestra, with its beautiful marble flooring. The restored theatre saw its first public performance in more than 1500 years when, at the opening of the 1997 Jerash Festival, the hugely popular Palestinian writer Mahmoud Darwish gave a poetry reading in front of thousands.

In front of the theatre, work is proceeding on reconstruction of a **plaza**, with huge Corinthian columns on one side of the street, faced by an equally huge colonnade on the other that's flanked by unusual double columns ingeniously knitted into the walls of the theatre itself. To the right of the plaza, the **North Decumanus** meets the main Cardo at a junction known as the **North Tetrapylon**. Simpler than the South Tetrakionion, this dates from the late-second-century remodelling of Gerasa and comprises arches on all four sides leading into a small, possibly domed, central space.

On the eastern side of the Cardo here rise the huge arches of the **West Baths**, the building itself unexcavated and tangled with undergrowth. It's possible to scramble among the chest-high weeds through the different rooms – changing area, hot and cold baths – but the highlight is a room fronted by two columns on the northern edge of the complex which has somehow clung onto its marvellous domed roof. A fraction south of the baths, a small area of ruins close to the Cardo is an **Umayyad mosque** – the only mosque surviving in Jerash – with a reused Roman conch serving as a makeshift *mihrab*.

Beyond the tetrapylon, the northernmost section of the Cardo is the quietest and most intimate part of the city. Ignored during the city's second-century facelift, this part of the street retains its original, plain Ionic colonnade, and is the same width as when initially laid out in the first century AD. The peaceful walk ends after some 200m at the **North Gate**, dating from 115 AD, from which a road led on to Pella. The gate is a cleverly designed wedge shape, in order to present a square facade both to the Cardo and to the Pella road. From here, you can either continue your northerly progress for 1.5km to visit Birketayn (see p.141), or retrace your steps partway down the Cardo to explore the Cathedral and surrounding ruined churches.

The Cathedral and the western churches

Fifteen Byzantine **churches** have so far been uncovered in Jerash, and wending a path through the largely unexcavated southwestern quarter of the ruins to visit nine of them, starting with the Cathedral and ending up near the South Theatre, brings you out of the main crush of the central sights.

The **Cathedral Gateway**, marked by eight large columns on the Cardo just south of the Nymphaeum, is a large, elaborate construction which originally presaged a now-vanished second-century temple, thought to have been dedicated to Dionysus. During the fourth century, the old temple was converted by the Christian Gerasenes into the large church which survives today, at the head of a monumental **staircase**. The walls flanking the stairs originally supported high enclosed and roofed colonnades on both sides, but earthquakes toppled the lot. The old pagan temple probably faced west – as does the Temple of Artemis – but the new church was to face east: the Byzantine architects seem to have been less concerned about aesthetic harmony than their Roman predecessors, and calmly plonked the apse of the new church square across the head of the staircase. To provide some focus for the ascent, a small shell-niche **Shrine to Mary** was placed on the blank exterior wall of the apse. Originally dedicated to "Michael, Holy Mary and Gabriel", it's still possible to read the Greek for Gabriel in red paint along the band beneath the shell.

Left or right from the shrine, passages bring you round into the **Cathedral** itself, a shadow of its former self. Very little is known about this building, and its dedication or even the supposition that it was Gerasa's cathedral remain unconfirmed. Colonnades – of which only bits and pieces remain scattered about – divided the nave and the aisles, and the high side walls were decorated with elaborate glass mosaics. Although very little of the stone paving of the nave has survived, pale pink limestone flags remain in the aisles. To the south of the cathedral is a small **chapel**.

Immediately west of the cathedral, a portico beautifully paved in red and white octagons and diamonds leads into the atrium, known as the **Fountain Court** after the square fountain in its centre fed by water brought from the great reservoir at Birketayn. Roman historians, including Pliny, hinted that Gerasa held festivals to Dionysus (the god of wine) at which water miraculously turned into wine, and the idea must have been a tenacious one: after the Dionysian temple here had been converted into a church, it became the venue for festivals celebrating Jesus performing the same feat at Cana, at which, the historian Epiphanius records, the square fountain in this court miraculously began to flow with wine.

To the side of the paved portico is a small room known as the **Glass Court**, named for the enormous quantity of glass fragments discovered there during clearance work. The weeds and rubble carpeting its floor conceal beautiful mosaics, reburied for protection.

Left (west) of the Glass Court, a staircase leads up to the tiny **Sarapion Passage**, which runs beneath precarious lintels out to the **Stepped Street**. Turning left up the street brings you past the maze of tiny rooms forming the Byzantine **Baths of Placcus**, which date from an unusually late 455 AD, evidence that luxurious Roman bathing habits died hard. Dominating the baths to the left are the majestic twin colonnades of the **Church of St Theodore**, dating from 496. Nothing remains of the main superstructure of the building, the marble paving of the nave and aisles or the glass mosaics which covered both the interior walls and the semi-dome over the apse; all that does remain is the huge apse itself, dramatically nosing out above the Fountain Court one terrace below.

The western churches

A path from St Theodore's leads west over scrubby hillocks, reaching a group of three interconnected churches built between 529 and 533 AD after 150m. On the right, the **Church of SS Cosmas and Damian** houses the best of Jerash's viewable mosaics, although the only way to see it is to lean over the high wall around the church; the church doors are locked and covered in barbed wire. Cosmas and Damian were doctors, twin brothers born in Arabia in the late third century, who studied medicine in Syria and became famous for never charging a penny to their patients. Their church is floored with a large mosaic open to the elements, which shows birds and animals in a geometric grid of diamonds and squares. Just below the chancel screen, the dedicatory inscription is flanked by portraits of the donors of the church; to the left is Theodore swinging a censer in his official robes as a kind of church trustee, and to the right his wife Georgia, her hands upraised.

From here, it's possible to work your way back easily to the Resthouse through the adjacent circular **Church of John the Baptist** and **Church of St George**, both with fragments of floor mosaics surviving. Alternatively, you could make your way up to the high ground north of Cosmas and Damian, where stands the ruined **Synagogue Church**, invisible from below. A Jewish synagogue originally stood here, oriented westwards towards the Temple in Jerusalem, with a floor mosaic depicting the Flood and various Jewish ritual objects. On its conversion into a church in 530 or 531, during a period of Jewish persecution under Emperor Justinian, a new geometric mosaic was laid over the original, and the orientation of the building reversed, with an apse laid in what was formerly the synagogue's vestibule.

South of here, and west of Cosmas and Damian, lie the untended ruins of the **Church of Bishop Genesius**, built in 611 just three years before the Persian invasion and featuring a prominent benched apse. On a hill 300m south, tucked just inside the southwestern city walls not too far from the Southern Theatre, the **Church of SS Peter and Paul** and, close by, the **Mortuary Church** are slowly being reclaimed by Mother Nature.

Birketayn

Branching off the main route north to Irbid, two smaller roads pass in front of Gerasa's North Gate. The road on the left climbs towards Suf, but an easy 1.5-kilometre walk along the other, leading directly away from the gate, will bring you to

Birketayn (Arabic for "two pools"). Set in a beautiful shaded valley in a crook of the road, this is a Roman double reservoir – restored in the 1960s – which fed water into Gerasa. Birketayn was the venue for the notorious Maiumas festivals, nautical celebrations of ancient origin which involved, among other things, the ritual submersion of naked women. By the time of Gerasa's heyday, the festivals seem to have become thinly veiled excuses for open-air orgies, and were duly banned by the city's early Christian rulers. In 396 AD, the powers-that-be relented, and reinstated the festivals provided that they follow "chaste customs"; however, the pleasures of the flesh seem to have proved irresistible, since three years later the ban was reimposed. Some 130 years passed before the festival was again resurrected by the Gerasenes and incorporated into their Christian faith as a kind of harvest celebration, purged of sensuality.

Next to the reservoir stands the small, thousand-seat **Festival Theatre** and, beyond, a path leads through the trees to the ruined and atmospheric **Tomb of Germanus**, standing amid sown fields, some columns upright and others – along with the empty sarcophagus – entwined in thistles down the slope.

Around Jerash

Jerash is set amidst rolling, verdant hills cut through by countless lush valleys, and – even in the height of summer, when the hills are baked brown and dry – you'd miss a good deal of the beauty of Jordan if you neglected the chance for a trip into the countryside around the ruins. In ancient (and not-so-ancient) times, these hills were covered with thick forests of pine, oak and pistachio, which survived largely undamaged until the early 1900s, when large swathes of forest were felled to provide timber for the Hejaz Railway, both for track-building and for fuel. Enough forest has survived, though, in the areas around **Ajloun** and **Dibbeen** – both within half an hour of Jerash – to give plenty of walking and picnicking possibilities. Ajloun also has a strikingly photogenic Crusader-period castle, Qala'at ar-Rabadh, perched among olive groves on a hilltop west of the town.

Ajloun

A thriving market town, recently promoted to capital of its own governorate, **AJLOUN** has been a centre of population for a thousand years or more. Marking the centre of the town, 150m along the market street from the bus station, is a **mosque** that probably dates from the early fourteenth century. The square base of its minaret, as well as the simple prayer hall and carved Quranic inscriptions set into the walls, are original, and the guardian is quite willing to show you around inside.

Qala'at ar-Rabadh

The history of Ajloun is bound up in the story of the **Qala'at ar-Rabadh** which towers over it. A perfect location, with bird's-eye views over the whole of the surrounding countryside and over three major wadis leading to the Jordan Valley, the hill on which the castle sits, Jebel Auf, is said to have formerly been the site of an isolated Christian monastery, home to a monk named Ajloun. By 1184, in the midst of the Crusades, the monastery had fallen into ruin, and an Arab general and close relative of Salah ad-Din, **Azz ad-Din Usama**, took the opportunity to build a fortress on the ruins, partly to limit expansion of the Crusader kingdoms – Belvoir castle stands just across the Jordan to the west and the Frankish stronghold of Karak is ominously close – partly to protect the iron mines of the nearby hills, and partly to show a strong hand to the squabbling clans of the local Bani Auf tribe. Legend has it that, to demonstrate his authority, Usama invited the sheikhs of the Bani Auf to a banquet in the newly completed castle, entertained and fed them, then threw them all into the dungeons. The new castle also took its place in the chain of beacons which could transmit news by pigeon post from the Euphrates frontier to Cairo headquarters in twelve hours. From surviving records, it seems that Ajloun held out successfully against the Franks.

Expanded in 1214–15 by Azz ad-Din Aybak – who also worked on Qasr Azraq – Ajloun's castle was rebuilt by Baybars after being ransacked by invading Mongols in 1260. Ottoman troops were garrisoned here during the seventeenth and eighteenth centuries, but when the explorer Burckhardt came through in 1812, he found the castle occupied only by forty members of a single family. Severe earthquakes in 1837 and 1927 caused a great deal of damage, and major consolidation and preservation work on the surviving structures is ongoing.

These days, the castle (daily: April–Oct 8am–7pm, Nov–March 8am–5pm; JD1) is entered across a **moat bridge** into the east wall. A long, sloping passage leads up to an older, arched entrance, decorated with carvings of birds, and just ahead stands the original entrance to Usama's fortress. Although the warren of chambers and galleries beyond is perfect for scrambled exploration, with all the rebuilding over the centuries, it's very difficult to form a coherent picture of the castle's architectural development; there's even – in this Muslim-built, wholly Muslim-occupied castle – one block carved with a cross, presumably part of the monk Ajloun's monastery. However, a climb to the top of any of the **towers** gives breathtaking views over the rolling landscape, and these more than make up for any historical confusion.

Off to the side of the castle road, behind the *Bonita* restaurant (see below) and all around the castle itself are acres of olive groves, carpeted in spring with wildflowers and perfect **walking** territory.

Practicalities

Buses run to **Ajloun** from Amman, Irbid, Jerash and Kraymeh (in the Jordan Valley), but the road from Jerash is the most beautiful way to approach, loping over the hills among stands of pine and olive trees, with the castle in plain view silhouetted on the horizon for at least half the way. If you're driving, don't miss the right-hand turn to Ajloun in the town of Anjara. An infrequent **bus** makes the run between Ajloun bus station and **Qala'at ar-Rabadh** for pennies; the going rate for a **taxi** up is 500 fils, or JD2 for him to wait and bring you down again. If you fancy the stiff three-kilometre **climb**, start from the town-centre roundabout (topped with a kitschy model of the castle) near the old mosque, and head up the road with the minaret on your left.

There are two over-priced **hotels** on this quiet castle road, both of them gloomily empty and unwelcoming most of the time. The first is the *al-Rabad Castle* (☎02/642 0202, fax 06/463 0414; ③–④), with a lovely garden in front; all rooms are spotless, en suite and with balconies, and some have stunning castle views. A few hundred metres further up, the *Ajloun Hotel* (☎ & fax 02/642 0524; ③–④), with much the same style, throws in breakfast for free.

Restaurant options are limited either to basic diners clustered around the town-centre roundabout, or the *Bonita* (daily 11am–sunset), some 50m below the castle with an open-air balcony and superb views. The food at *Bonita*, however, is consistently disappointing, and you'd do well to eat elsewhere and enjoy the vistas over a drink instead. On Thursdays and Fridays, the *Bonita*, the slopes around the castle and the castle itself are all crowded with carloads of locals enjoying a day out – not a good time to find peace or solitude.

In the same building as the *Bonita* is Ajloun's **tourist office** (daily except Fri 8am–2pm; ☎02/642 0115), though they can't tell you much that isn't already in plain view.

Around Ajloun

For drivers, the major route down to the **Jordan Valley** from Ajloun is via Anjara and Kufranjeh, but there is a much more beautiful back way down between the hills. Turn off the castle road at the *al-Rabad Castle Hotel*, fork left after 4km and right 4km further. The rustic village of **Halawa** appears after another 7km, in the middle of which there's a steeply sloping fork; the road to the left (which runs past the post office) will eventually deliver you after 10km of gorgeous countryside around **Wadi al-Yabis** to the Jordan Valley highway. Another option for the fit is to take a bus to Halawa from Ajloun and walk the spectacular last leg down through the fig and pomegranate trees and past deserted waterfalls. If in any doubt of the way, follow signs – or ask the locals – for *aghwar* (valleys).

At **Zubia**, some 15km north of Ajloun off the Irbid road, the Royal Society for the Conservation of Nature has established a forest nature reserve, with protected herds of roe deer. Research is still being done into the scientific feasibility of the site and, although you can **camp** at a wilderness site within the reserve (by prior arrangement only; see box on p.39 for details), as yet there are no facilities for casual visitors.

Dibbeen National Park

A large, mostly untended area of fragrant pine-forested hillside southwest of Jerash, the **DIBBEEN NATIONAL PARK** is one of the most beautiful, and remote, getaways in the whole of the north, despite (or perhaps because of) the fact that there are virtually no facilities for visitors and no buses run even close. If you haven't got any transport, it's hard to justify the effort of getting to the park; with a rental car, of course, a visit is much easier. From Saturday to Wednesday, the forest is utterly peaceful, and you could wander for hours along dappled tractor tracks through Aleppo pine and evergreen oak, with huge views of the hills all around; Thursdays and Fridays – family outing days – see a major influx of barbecues, car radios and games of football.

With dreary **accommodation** and a **restaurant** of sorts, the institutional *Dibbeen Resthouse* (☎02/635 2413, fax 635 1146) sits walled off in the middle of the park, constantly blaring Arabic music to itself from megaphones in the trees. Dotted around its compound are horribly bare and rundown bungalows (③), worth putting up with only if you place a high value on early-morning walks in the forest. The resthouse is on a road which winds through the park, connecting at both ends eventually with the Jerash–Ajloun road. Coming from Jerash, a **taxi** is about JD4. If you're **driving** your own car, follow a sign for the park pointing left off the Ajloun road 100m from Hadrian's Arch in Jerash; this road continues straight, through the Ghazza Palestinian refugee camp and down into the gorgeous Wadi Haddada and the reforestation projects at Jamla. The park road branches right at a signpost 11km from Jerash; you could stop anywhere along here and take off into the trees. The resthouse is 2km further, but if you continue straight through the park, you'll eventually end up, after 14km or so, back on the Jerash–Ajloun road.

Irbid

Although **IRBID** has been inhabited since Chalcolithic times and has also been identified as the Decapolis city of Arbela, the *tell* rising above downtown – now home to a police station and flea market – is all that's visitable of the city's ancient past. Irbid today is unlikely to set your pulse racing, a humdrum city most often visited as a staging-post for journeys into the far north of the country or down into the Jordan Valley. On a campus well south of the town centre, **Yarmouk University** is one of Jordan's – and the Middle East's – best, and has generated around itself a funky quarter of cheap restaurants, music stores and Internet cafés. Savouring the lively student-ish atmosphere here beats hands down the rather depressing experience of mooching around the drab streets downtown.

Museum of Jordanian Heritage

The Yarmouk campus is the rather incongruous home to one of the best historical and archeological museums in Jordan. The small **Museum of Jordanian Heritage** (daily except Thurs & Fri 10am–5pm; free) is a superbly presented showcase of information fleshed out with a few, carefully chosen objects, where you can readily grasp the sequence of historical eras and the cultural trends that accompanied them – you could easily spend an engaging hour or more here exploring the displays. However, the museum isn't easy to spot. From the main gate of the university, continue straight ahead until the second roundabout, and it's the second building to the right, part of the Institute of Archeology and Anthropology.

The **ground floor** rooms are more or less chronological, beginning from prehistory (with some of the 9000-year-old statuettes discovered at Ain Ghazal near Amman), plus excellent informative background on such topics as Jordan's external relations in 2000 BC and the development of territorial states. All periods of Jordan's history, from the Bronze and Iron Ages, through the "forgotten" centuries of Jordan under the Mamlukes and Ottomans, up to the present day, are explained clearly, and subtly illustrated with interesting artefacts, including reconstructions of a traditional medieval apothecary's shop and a blacksmith's. **Upstairs**, displays are devoted to informative explanations of traditional crafts, such as pottery, glass and textiles, while the old stone-built rooms around the **courtyard** are filled with tools of rural life.

Practicalities

There's no tourist office in Irbid, and no city map in English available. Rudimentary **information** can be had from Public Relations on the second floor of the Municipality (*baladiyyeh*) building, on Hashmi Street at the foot of the *tell* downtown. The downtown **post office** (Mon–Thurs, Sat & Sun 7am–7pm, Fri 7am–1.30pm; hours curtailed slightly in winter) is on Baghdad Street, while Alo **cardphones** are all over the city.

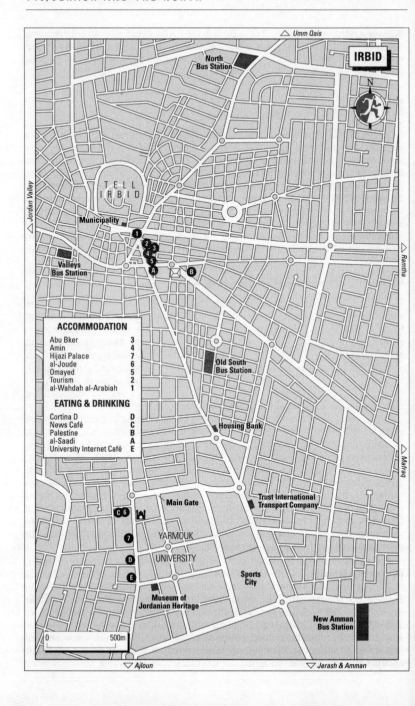

△ Umm Qais

IRBID

North
Bus Station

N

T E L L
I R B I D

△ Jordan Valley

Municipality

1

2 3
4
5

A B

**Valleys
Bus Station**

▷ Ramtha

✉

ACCOMMODATION

Abu Bker	3
Amin	4
Hijazi Palace	7
al-Joude	6
Omayed	5
Tourism	2
al-Wahdah al-Arabiah	1

**Old South
Bus Station**

EATING & DRINKING

Cortina D	D
News Café	C
Palestine	B
al-Saadi	A
University Internet Café	E

Housing Bank

▷ Mafraq

Main Gate

**Trust International
Transport Company**

C 6

7

YARMOUK

D

UNIVERSITY

E

**Sports
City**

**Museum of
Jordanian Heritage**

**New Amman
Bus Station**

0   500m

▽ Ajloun   ▽ Jerash & Amman

Accommodation

In keeping with the schizophrenic split between the city centre and the university district, Irbid's inexpensive **hotels** are all clustered together in the heart of downtown, while the two more upmarket choices are within metres of Yarmouk's campus.

Abu Bker, just off Orouba St (☎02/242695). On the second and third floors, so a little quieter than the competition, and spotlessly clean after its recent paint job. ①.

Amin, Orouba St (☎02/242384). Not bad as a stop-gap cheapie, but has nothing to recommend it over the *al-Wahdah*. ①.

Hijazi Palace, opposite Yarmouk University side gate (☎02/279500, fax 279520). The priciest hotel in the whole of the north, but singularly seedy and run-down. Better rooms and cheaper rates are to be had at the *al-Joude*. ⑤.

al-Joude (formerly *al-Razi*), hidden at the end of Manama St, a side alley behind *Quick Burger* opposite the university mosque (☎02/275515, fax 275517). Best value for money in town: spotlessly clean and spacious en-suite rooms, friendly service and the excellent *News Café* downstairs. ③.

Omayed, above Irbed Supermarket, Baghdad St (☎ & fax 02/245955). Cosy and comfortable rooms on the second floor with big windows; those at the back are quiet and have ceiling fans. ②.

Tourism, opposite *al-Wahdah al-Arabiah* (☎02/242353). Cheapest and nastiest of the cheap-and-nasties. Shower 500 fils. JD2 to share. ①.

al-Wahdah al-Arabiah, just off Hashmi St (☎02/242083). The best budget choice in town, friendly and comfortable for women. Shower 500 fils. ①.

Eating, drinking and the Internet

Downtown, you're restricted to plain Arabic fare, most easily had from the myriad nameless *falafel* and *shwarma* stalls on every street. Sit-down places range from basic diners that are often full to knife-and-fork places that are invariably empty. The *Palestine*, close to the post office on Baghdad Street, is the best of the former, and the gloomy *al-Saadi*, opposite the *Omayed* hotel, best of the latter. All are open for lunch, but most are closed by 9pm.

Better choices by far can be found on the honky-tonk strip outside the **University**, hopping during lunchtimes and until about 10pm. Virtually every establishment is an eating house of some kind, although many are plastic-tablecloth places indistinguishable from one another. The best food, in the biggest portions, is at the *News Café* under the *al-Joude* hotel just off the strip – as well as great espressos, MTV and a student clientele practising their cool, they also have beer, and you can walk out replete for only a couple of JDs. The Italian *Cortina D*, a little south of the *Hijazi* hotel, is calm and serious, though they can't stretch to more than pizza and pasta along the lines of *Pizza Hut* up the road. Pizza at the *Delicate* is cheaper but less good, and if the worst comes to the worst, you can always run for the security of *Planet Donuts*.

For **email and the Internet**, the relaxed *News Café* offers an hour of access plus a mug of gourmet coffee for JD2. A more intense, techie experience is to be had lining up with the other square eyes at one of the 23 terminals in the *University Internet Café* (JD1/hr), south of the *Hijazi* hotel.

Transport

Irbid has four **bus** stations, of which three serve destinations other than local villages. The **New Amman station** (*mujemma Amman al-jdeed*), 200m or so east of Sports City, has buses serving Amman's Abdali station (including the big, fast, air-

MOVING ON TO SYRIA OR ISRAEL

To move on from Irbid to **Syria**, plenty of *service*s run day and night from the New Amman station to **Dera'a** (JD2), **Damascus** (JD4) and points further afield (as well as some destinations in Lebanon); book at the office diagonally opposite the Hijazi ticket counter and be prepared to show your passport and Syrian visa. This is the simplest way to get there, but if you need to save every fils, you could take a bus from the same station to **Ramtha**, on the border some 20km east of Irbid (the new highway crossing at Jaber is further away and less easy to get to). *Service*s run regularly from Ramtha's bus station to Dera'a for JD2, but it's not hard to **hitch-hike** across the border: jump off the bus before you get to Ramtha bus station, at a roundabout on the outskirts of town, and stand on the road bearing right which bypasses the town and leads straight to the border, which is open daily 24hr; there's a departure tax of JD4.

By far the easiest way to get from Irbid into **Israel** is with the buses run by the Trust International Transport Company (☎02/251878), located on the approach road from Amman close to the Sports City stadium. Departures are to **Tel Aviv** (Mon–Fri & Sun 8.15am; JD14) and **Haifa** (same days 9.15am & 3pm; JD8.500). All Haifa buses drop off in **Nazareth** town centre (JD8.500), and there's an additional bus (Sat 9.15am) which goes to Nazareth only. All buses originate in Amman, so timings are subject to traffic conditions, and all cross via the Sheikh Hussein Bridge, where you pay a departure tax of JD4.

con Hijazi ones), Ajloun, Jerash, Mafraq, Ramtha and Zerqa. Off Palestine Street about 500m west of downtown, the **Valleys station** (*mujemma al-aghwar*) serves destinations in the Jordan Valley and the smaller valleys running down to it; the only places of interest here are likely to be Mshare'a (for Pella; only one or two buses go direct to Tabqat Fahl itself), the Sheikh Hussein Bridge, Shuneh ash-Shamaliyyeh and Kraymeh. Some 1.5km north of downtown on Fadl al-Dalgamouni Street is the **North station** (*mujemma ash-shomali*), with buses to Umm Qais, Himmeh and Hartha via Qwaylbeh.

For **transport around the city**, *service* minibuses link all of the bus stations, although unless you read Arabic it's impossible to tell these from intercity minibuses – you'll have to ask around for where you want to go in Arabic. Similar *service* minibuses and ordinary *service* taxis also serve the bus stations and the university from different points along Hashmi Street downtown. Plenty of (often meterless) taxis prowl all main streets and bus stations; a negotiated fare across the city shouldn't come to more than 500 fils.

The far north

The land hard up against the Syrian border in the **far north** of Jordan is hilly farming country, especially beautiful in springtime when a riot of colour covers the fields between groves of olives and figs. The ancient trees around the picturesque village of **Umm Qais**, perched on the very edge of the Transjordanian plateau, are famed for producing some of the choicest olives in the region, although the village is best known as the site of Gadara, one of the Decapolis cities. For its atmospheric ruins and its spectacular views, if not its olives, Umm Qais shouldn't be missed. The River Yarmouk joins the River Jordan just south of

CALLING THE NORTH

The communications revolution has yet to hit the north of Jordan. Currently, the only way to **telephone** into Umm Qais and Himmeh from outside is on a handful of lines into local post offices, where operators connect you manually to the extension you ask for (the only exception is the *Umm Qais Resthouse*, which has its own line). Needless to say, even if you can get hold of the operators – which is rare in itself – connections are more miss than hit. We've listed the exchange numbers and extensions you should ask for, but don't be surprised if you can't get through.

the Sea of Galilee, running west–east through a dramatic gorge below Umm Qais, which now marks the border between Jordan and the Israeli-occupied Jawlan (Golan Heights). Travel along the gorge is restricted, but nestled among palm trees and banana plantations below the Jawlan is **Himmeh**, graced with hot springs and a laid-back air that belies the Israeli watchtowers within shouting distance. Further east, tucked away in the peaceful Wadi Qwaylbeh north of Irbid, lie the part-excavated ruins of **Abila**, another of the Decapolis cities, featuring a hillside rock-cut cemetery decorated with some startlingly fresh Byzantine frescoes.

Umm Qais

Some 30km northwest of Irbid, tucked into the angle of borders formed by Jordan, Israel and the Jawlan, the windswept village of **UMM QAIS** is well worth the effort of a long journey, whether you visit on a day-trip from Irbid or stay overnight to relish the still twilight and fresh, chilly morning. The main attraction is exploring the remote, widespread ruins of the Decapolis city of Gadara, some of which are jumbled together with the striking houses of black basalt and white limestone of an abandoned Ottoman village.

Some history
After the death of Alexander the Great in 323 BC, Gadara was founded by the **Ptolemies** as a frontier station on their border with the Seleucids to the north. In 218 BC, the Seleucids took the city, but came under siege a century later from the Jewish Hasmoneans; when the Roman general **Pompey** imposed order throughout Syria in 63 BC, he personally oversaw the rebuilding of Gadara as a favour to one of his favourite freedmen, a Gadarene. The city won a degree of autonomy, and became a prominent city of the **Decapolis** (see the box on p.129).

Roman rule – particularly following Trajan's annexation of the Nabatean kingdom in 106 AD – brought stability and prosperity to the Decapolis; as at Jerash, Gadara saw large-scale public building works during a second-century **"golden age"**, including construction of the great baths at Himmeh. Literary sources describe Gadara at this time as a city of great cultural vitality, a centre for philosophy, poetry and the performing arts, where pleasure-seeking Romans came from all over the empire.

By 325 AD Gadara was the seat of a **bishopric**, but its proximity to the decisive battles at Pella and Yarmouk, when Muslim armies defeated the Christian Byzantines, led to the establishment of Muslim rule over the city well before the foundation of the Umayyad caliphate in Damascus in 661. However, a series of

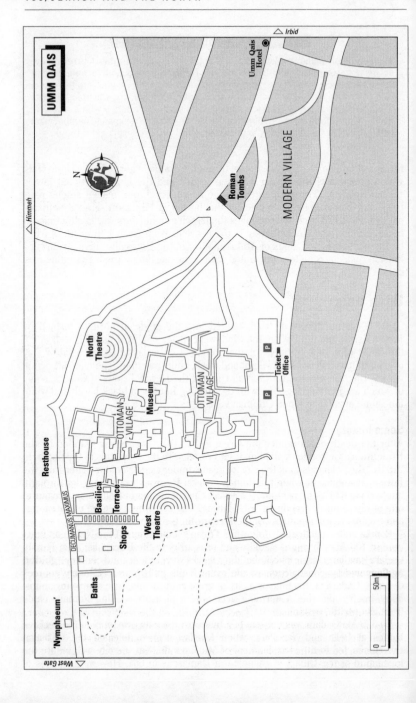

THE GADARENE SWINE

Gadara's main claim to fame centres on a story, recounted in the New Testament books of Matthew, Mark and Luke, of Jesus crossing the Sea of Galilee. The following version is at Matthew 8:28–32:

And when he came to the other side, to the country of the Gadarenes, two demoniacs met him, coming out of the tombs, so fierce that no one could pass that way. And behold, they cried out, "What have you to do with us, O Son of God? Have you come here to torment us before the time?" Now a herd of many swine was feeding at some distance from them. And the demons begged him, "If you cast us out, send us away into the herd of swine." And he said to them, "Go." So they came out and went into the swine; and behold, the whole herd rushed down the steep bank into the sea, and perished in the waters.

Needless to say, the pagan Gadarenes were distinctly uncomfortable at the sight of hundreds of pigs careering downhill for 8km and vaulting the wide Yarmouk gorge into the Sea of Galilee, and gathered to ensure this Jesus meddled no more in their city's affairs. Consequently, theologians have interpreted the story as both a demonstration of the supreme power of God – able to cast out evil with a word – and a literal illustration of the pigheadedness of unbelievers in rejecting divine miracles.

earthquakes not long afterwards destroyed much of Gadara's infrastructure, and the town went into rapid decline. At some point in the Middle Ages, its name changed from Gadara, originally a Semitic word meaning "fortification", to Umm Qais, possibly deriving from the Arabic *mkes* (frontier station) or *maqass* (junction).

In 1806, the German traveller Ulrich Seetzen identified the ruins as those of Gadara, and since then excavation and restoration work has proceeded slowly: Umm Qais has never had the kind of attention or funds that Jerash has commanded. During the 1890s, a small **village** grew up on the Roman ruins, the inhabitants reusing the pre-cut stones to build graceful courtyard-style houses. A modern village soon developed nearby, but people continued to occupy the Ottoman cottages right through until 1986, when the 1500 inhabitants accepted payment from the Ministry of Tourism to leave their homes, in order to enable archeologists to clear the site for excavation.

However, since then, not a single square of village land has been cleared. The ministry recently changed its tune, backing instead a project to convert the Ottoman cottages into a **tourist village** and chalet-style hotel. A handful of houses have been renovated – among them the buildings now housing the Resthouse and the Museum – but the work hasn't progressed far. Needless to say, the former residents are none too happy at having been ousted under false pretences, and have lodged claims to participate in the renovation work and share in any profits. Meanwhile, the abandoned village and its once-grand Roman neighbour stand ghostly quiet for the eleven months in the year that no archeological work is done, weeds growing higher and dust infiltrating the long narrow streets.

The site

The **site** (daily 7am–sunset; JD1) occupies a hill on the west side of the modern village of Umm Qais, with the **ticket office** in the car-park on the south side of the hill. On the way, in a hollow at the turnoff from the modern village, you'll pass two Roman **tombs**; the basalt doorways are beautiful, but, disappointingly, there's nothing to see inside.

MELEAGER, GADARENE POET

Born in Gadara in the first century BC, the Greek poet **Meleager** moved to Phoenician Tyre in his youth and spent time in different towns around Syria, ending his life on the Greek island of Kos. As well as writing satirical social criticism, he was one of the first authors to compile a poetry anthology, *The Garland*, comprising works from 41 poets (including himself), each of whom was compared with a different flower or plant. Meleager, however, is best known for his short, lyrical elegies on love and death, and his langorous nature poetry suits perfectly the atmosphere of a warm afternoon at his native Umm Qais (translated by W. R. Paton):

> *Noisy cicada, drunk with dew drops, thou singest thy rustic ditty that fills the wilderness with voice, and seated on the edge of the leaves, striking with sawlike legs thy sunburnt skin, thou shrillest music like the lyre's. But sing, dear, some new tune to gladden the woodland nymphs, strike up some strain responsive to Pan's pipe, that I may escape from Love and snatch a little midday sleep, reclining here beneath the shady plane-tree.*

Climbing the steps from the ticket office will bring you into the abandoned Ottoman village, where you can wander freely in and out of the weed-ridden courtyards and dusty alleys. Looming above is a crane, which has been poised over the **West Theatre** for a number of years, as archeologists slowly clear the site and reassemble the tumbled stones. The theatre is built entirely of basalt, and its three thousand spectators – including VIPs in free-standing high-backed power chairs – had a fine view west over the city (now a grassy hill dotted with olive trees). North of the theatre is Gadara's most dramatic space, the **Basilica Terrace**, cut into the bedrock on one side and supported by vaulted **shops** below on the other. Its main feature, closest to the theatre, is a square Byzantine church dating from the fifth or sixth century. A small narthex opens into an outer circular passageway, still paved with coloured geometric tiles, which encloses a central octagon demarcated by basalt columns which probably supported a dome. Within the octagon, a small depression and apse housed the altar, behind which stands a thin, pink marble column carved with a cross. On the north side of the terrace, the white limestone paving and columns of the atrium stand in stark contrast to the black columns of the church. The atrium gives onto Gadara's main, paved street, the **Decumanus Maximus**, the clear line of which can be traced east and west.

Above the terrace to the east rise the restored arches of the Resthouse (see below), but the rest of the city extends for the best part of a kilometre westward, largely unexcavated beneath the fields. About 100m west of the terrace, the building on the right was first thought to be a **nymphaeum**, but, after investigation of the plumbing, it seems that it served some other, unknown function. Opposite, fences enclose a **baths** complex, once excavated but now forlornly overgrown. Some 250m further you'll reach a colonnaded section of the street, and away to the left are the unexcavated remains of some unknown building to explore. After another 200m you'll spot a circular structure, foundations of the tower of a gate across the street, within which steps lead down into a locked underground mausoleum. Gadara's **West Gate**, with an exposed section of basalt street, is 200m further. Alongside the modern tarmac road (which formerly ran to Tiberias) are the remains of a **hippodrome**, culminating in a partly reconstructed **monumental**

gateway to the city, designed to impress visitors approaching from the Jordan Valley below. Looking back from here gives an idea of the enormous size of Gadara in its heyday, and the impossible archeological task of excavating it.

Back at the Basilica Terrace, following the Decumanus around the edge of the hill brings you to the grassy bowl of the **North Theatre**, its stones plundered to build the Ottoman cottages. Above is the site **museum** (daily except Tues: April–Oct 8am–5pm, Nov–March 8am–4pm), highlights of which include a headless marble statue of Tyche found in the West Theatre, mosaics from around the city and, adorning the lovely internal courtyard, carved sarcophagi and capitals. The museum caretaker can come with you to explore a chill, **underground aqueduct**, accessed down rickety stairs and just high enough to stand up in, which winds in a tortuous course beneath much of the city centre and emerges on the side of the hill. However, the most poignant relic of Gadara lies forgotten in a far corner of the museum courtyard, a three-line Greek inscription. "I'm talking to you, passerby," says the inhabitant of the mausoleum in which it was found. "As you are now, so I used to be; as I am now, so you will be. Treat life as a mortal should."

Practicalities

The only regular **buses** running to and from Umm Qais's main street serve Irbid's North station, and – although it's unlikely – you may need to show your passport along the way if there's a checkpoint.

The village's sole **accommodation** option is the *Umm Qais Hotel* (☎02/217210 ext 80, fax 242313; ①–②) – cosy, clean and with reliably hot water. Standard, shared-bath rooms are on the reception floor, while more comfortable en-suite rooms are up above.

There are excellent *fuul*-and-*falafel* **diners** either side of the hotel (the *fuul* up here, prepared with *sumak* and other spices, makes an interesting change from Amman-style), or you could throw together a hearty **picnic** in a two-minute stroll along the street. However, you shouldn't leave Umm Qais without sitting awhile on the terrace of the privately owned **Resthouse** (daily 10am–sunset; ☎02/217555) in the midst of the ruins. This gives without doubt the single best view in the country, a breathtaking, wind-exposed 180-degree sweep taking in the Jordan Valley, the Sea of Galilee (with the Israeli shore-side city of Tiberias in plain view), the Yarmouk gorge and, most impressive of all, the Jawlan, pointing the way north towards snow-capped Jebel ash-Sheikh (Mount Hermon), which is sometimes visible in the far distance. The food here, costing around JD6 a head, is very good; you should reserve on Thursdays and Fridays. Although the Resthouse normally closes around sunset, you can book ahead for dinner on the terrace after dark – a meal that, given the surroundings, you're unlikely to forget.

SEEN FROM AFAR

Since the foundation of the State of Israel in 1948, **Palestinians** who were expelled from or fled their homes have come to Umm Qais specifically to savour the views over their former homeland – the city of **Tabariyyeh** (the Arabic name for Tiberias), the dark waters of the lake, and the villages and lush countryside of the Galilee. Even today, many Palestinian Jordanians, who either refuse to travel into Israel on principle or who have been denied entry visas, still gather on the Resthouse terrace to look into the past and dream of the future.

Himmeh

In its day, Gadara's lavish baths complex, built around the seven hot springs at **HIMMEH**, was grand enough to bear comparison with the fabulous imperial Roman baths at Baiae, near Naples. Modern Himmeh – also known as **Mukhaybeh** – is a shadow of its former self, and has been divided by modern boundary-drawing: most Roman remains are now in fact in what the locals call "Syrian Himmeh", on the north bank of the Yarmouk in territory currently occupied by Israel. Hemmed in by mountains, and lying at some 200m below sea level, the tiny village is crowded with palm trees and giant banana plants that thrive year-round in the tropical conditions. In winter and spring, there's a weekly influx of local day-trippers and overnighters, come to dip in the warm, slightly sulphurous **waters** and gawp at the massive heights dwarfing the village. The rest of the year, Himmeh is swelteringly hot, making the prospect of a warm dip considerably less appealing, although the towering Jawlan – with its easily visible Israeli jeep patrols – is reason enough to visit.

Over ninety percent of the village land is owned by a single member of a wealthy Jordanian family, one Mamdouh Bisharat, whose private villa in the village – behind the tall blue gates – has its own spring and Roman pool; ask at the *Sah al-Noum* hotel to be shown around this gloriously lush and tranquil retreat. The village's tenant farmers, many of whom are of African descent and sport Egyptian-style robes and turbans, receive the standard wage of JD3 a day (for men, that is – women get half and working children a quarter), so buying some small item from the impromptu markets set up by the locals can help the village economy more than you might realize.

Practicalities

Irregular **buses** leave from Irbid's North station and pause to pick up in Umm Qais before heading down to Himmeh. Taxis do the run from Umm Qais for about JD2. At least one **checkpoint** bars the way, for which you'll need your passport. If you're driving, head straight over the crossroads at the foot of the Umm Qais hill; Himmeh is 4km further, and charges a **toll** of 300 fils per private car.

The first thing you come to is *al-Hameh Restaurant and Recreation*, a complex comprising a large **pool**, a nondescript air-con **restaurant** (both open daily 6am–8pm), and a **hotel** (☎02/249830 ext 5; ③) with worn three- or five-bed rooms, all with balcony, ceiling fan and air con. The rather grungy pool (entry JD1.100) operates on a two-hour shift system, alternating between men only and women only. Mixed groups of foreigners can rent an hour's exclusive dip-time for JD11. Bear in mind, though, that the pool is open and public: however much the management claims that Western-style swimsuits are acceptable, women wearing a costume any less modest than long shorts and a baggy T-shirt are likely to cause a stir. All in all, a much more genuine welcome is to be had at the *Sah al-Noum* hotel (☎02/249830 ext 10; ①) – wander left at the fork – where everything is very basic, rooms all equipped with ceiling fan and a private hole-in-the-ground bathroom. Out back, a channel holds a rushing flow of hot spring water, wide enough for dipping but not swimming.

Thursdays and Fridays are the big days here, when the spring and bedrooms at *Sah al-Noum* are generally full, and even the *al-Hameh* fills up fast. If you can, visit during the rest of the week, when the village is at its most peaceful.

The Yarmouk Gorge road

Himmeh is as far east along the Yarmouk that you're allowed to venture, but, if you're in your own car, you can drive west alongside a portion of the deep and dramatic **Yarmouk Gorge** (all buses go back up the hill to Umm Qais). There are checkpoints aplenty down here, and although you may be able to snatch a photo or two of the extraordinary scenery, or of the wrecked bridge, bombed in the 1967 war and still hanging twisted over the gorge, you may find the soldiers in the next watchtower objecting. The road eventually delivers you to the town of **Shuneh ash-Shamaliyyeh** (North Shuneh), at the head of the Jordan Valley, but you may also spot signs just before Shuneh to **"Baqoura Restored Lands"**. This tiny sliver, less than a kilometre square sandwiched between the Jordan and Yarmouk rivers at their confluence, was occupied by Israel in 1967 and returned to Jordan under the 1994 peace treaty. Popular as a local beauty spot, at the time of writing Baqoura was closed to non-Jordanians following the 1997 shooting there of seven Israeli schoolgirls by a Jordanian soldier. A rapid, high-profile trial (which had the effect of whipping up much public feeling against the treaty with Israel) convicted the soldier of murder, but his mental instability controversially saw the death penalty commuted to life with hard labour. Once some time has passed, it may again be possible to visit Baqoura, known, rather hollowly now, as the "Island of Peace".

Abila

Lying virtually unknown in the cradle of the lush Wadi Qwaylbeh, 12km north of Irbid, the ruins of the Decapolis city of **Abila** are, in themselves, rather unimpressive, and have only just begun to be excavated from the grassy fields. In sharp contrast, the city's Roman-Byzantine **cemetery**, comprising dozens of tombs cut into a neighbouring hillside, has to be explored to be believed: at least six tomb caves, each of which held dozens of bodies, are still adorned with their original frescoes, some patchy and damaged, some in startlingly fresh, near-perfect condition. The experience of stumbling across portraits of long-dead Abilenes gazing back into your torchlight from the rock-cut coffin that once held their bones is one to be remembered.

Buses running from Irbid's North station towards Hartha head left 11km north of Irbid at a quiet fork, which divides in front of an isolated domed mosque close to Wadi Qwaylbeh. The best way to approach Abila is to get out at the fork and follow the right-hand road for exactly 900m, then cut left straight across the fields. This will bring you to a dry stone wall, teetering over the steep flank of the Wadi Qwaylbeh. Prominent against the sky on a hilltop opposite is a columned seventh-century church, while the slope below the wall shelters Abila's necropolis. Very near the wall, but not immediately visible, are two of the beautifully painted **tomb caves**. It would be impossible to describe fully the locations of the others, scattered at different levels across the slope, and there are no signs to them; persistent exploration is required, but you'll find that those which hold frescoes generally have iron gates across them, invariably unlocked or pushed in. It's not impossible that a local shepherd might wander up and lead you around. Bear in mind, though, that aside from a torch, essential exploration equipment is a steady nerve: the caves – once filled with corpses – are all dank, pitch-dark, deathly quiet and very spidery. The **frescoes** themselves, however, are in remarkably good condition, delightful portraits of men and women, flowers and fruits, and one a spectacular scene of dolphins covering the ceiling.

Working your way north (right) along the cave-dotted slope will bring you, after about 2km, to a modern building which overlooks the original Roman **bridge** across the stream, leading into what was once the city centre. The site is currently being cleared for excavation, although you can easily make out the bowl of a **theatre** next to a section of basalt-paved Byzantine **street**. Exploration of Tell Abila, opposite the theatre, is barely worth it, and instead you should follow the track curling up the steep hill; after climbing over a barbed-wire fence, you'll be able to explore the hilltop **church**, with its alternating basalt and limestone columns, seen from the necropolis slope opposite. Olive groves conceal the Hartha road from the church; once on the road, you could hitch a ride back to Irbid, or wait for a bus.

The Jordan Valley

The deep cleft of the **Jordan Valley** carries the River Jordan south from the Sea of Galilee (some 200m below sea level) to the Dead Sea (400m below), only 104km as the crow flies though the meandering river twists and writhes for more than three times that length. Set down in a deep gorge flanked by a desolate flood plain (the *zor*), the river is never visible from the main road which sweeps south through the *ghor*, or cultivable valley floor, well to the east. Flanked by 900-metre-high mountains on both sides and enjoying a swelteringly subtropical climate of low rainfall, high humidity and scorching temperatures, the valley with its fertile alluvial soil is perfect for agriculture on a large scale: this vast open-air greenhouse can these days produce crops up to two months ahead of elsewhere in the Middle East and can even stretch to three growing seasons annually. Indeed as early as five thousand years ago, foodstuffs from the valley were being exported to nearby states, and irrigation systems and urban development progressed hand-in-hand soon after. Throughout the centuries since, agriculture has been at the heart of the valley economy, from the wheat, barley, olives, grapes and beans of the Bronze Age to an extensive sugar-cane industry under the Mamlukes. For three hundred years up to the late nineteenth century the valley was almost deserted, but since then rapid and concentrated development – and, in particular, the building of the King Abdullah Canal in the 1960s to irrigate the eastern *ghor* – has led to a burgeoning agricultural industry that supplies most of Jordan's tomatoes, cucumbers, bananas, melons and citrus fruits, as well as producing a surplus for export.

In contrast to the prosaic vistas of concrete piping, plastic greenhouses and farm machinery that characterize the area today, well over two hundred archeological sites have been catalogued in the valley, although – with the notable exception of the Roman-Byzantine remains at **Pella** – almost all of them are Neolithic or Bronze Age settlements on the summits of *tell*s, with very little to see other than one or two courses of stone foundations.

Transport in the valley is mostly restricted to buses shuttling north and south along the highway between the main hubs of Shuneh ash-Shamaliyyeh, Kraymeh, Dayr Alla and Shuneh al-Janubiyyeh, stopping at all points in between. Bearing in mind the excessive heat, and the lack of decent eating places, the best way to see the valley is to start from Irbid and devote either a half- or a full-day to the trip. After Pella, you could get to Ajloun and be back in Amman in little more than two hours.

Pella

For specialist archeologists, **PELLA**, comprising a large *tell* overlooking a well-watered valley protected by hills, is quite thrilling, possibly the most significant site in all of Jordan; evidence has been found of human activity in the area for nearly a million years, with extensive remains from almost all periods from the Paleolithic through to the Mamluke. The *tell* itself has been occupied for the last six thousand years almost without interruption. However, though it's worth a short detour from Irbid, Pella can appear rather underwhelming to non-archeologists, with – in effect – little more than three ruined Byzantine churches to divert attention from the beautiful hill-walking all around.

Some history

The reasons for Pella's long history have much to do with its location on the junction of major trade routes: north–south between Arabia and Syria, and east–west between the Transjordanian interior and the Mediterranean coast. With its positioning almost exactly at sea level – the Jordan Valley yawns below – the city has a comfortably warm climate and is watered both by the gushing springs in the bed of the Wadi Jirm and by a reasonable annual rainfall, all ensuring perfect conditions for agriculture. In addition, the city was surrounded in antiquity by thick oak forests – since felled – which at more than one point provided the backbone of the city's economy.

From artefacts discovered near Pella, it seems that **Stone Age** hunters roamed the area's forests and savannahs up to a million or so years ago, bagging native game such as elephants, deer and lions. By five thousand years ago, a **Neolithic** farming village was spread out above the springs in the main Wadi Jirm, and remains have been uncovered of a larger, terraced **Chalcolithic** settlement just below Jebel Sartaba, southeast of the *tell*. By the early third millennium BC, during the **Bronze Age**, there was a thriving city at Pella, extensive evidence of which has been excavated from the *tell*: pieces dating from at least four main periods of occupation around the sixteenth and fifteenth centuries BC include luxury items imported from Egypt, Syria and Cyprus – indicating well-established trade links – such as bronze pins, stylized sculpture, gold thread, alabaster bottles, cuneiform clay tablets and beautiful inlaid ivory boxes. In the thirteenth century BC, Pella was the principal supplier to pharaonic Egypt of wood for chariot spokes. **Iron Age** cities flourished on the *tell* up to the seventh century BC, but during the Persian period (539–332 BC), it seems that the area was abandoned.

The **Hellenistic** period is the first for which the name of Pella can be attested from historical records, and was a time of considerable affluence for the city. In 218 BC, the Seleucid king Antiochus captured Pella on a sweep through Palestine and Transjordan, and thereafter occupation of the site spread over the *tell*, the slopes of Tell Husn opposite, the so-called "Civic Complex" area on the valley floor and the peak of Jebel Sartaba.

In 83 BC, the Jewish **Hasmonean** leader Alexander Jannaeus crossed into Transjordan from Palestine and sacked pagan Pella and its neighbours Gadara, Gerasa and others. The arrival twenty years later of Pompey and the **Roman** army imposed order in Pella as elsewhere in the Decapolis region, and the city settled down to a period of stability, minting its own coins and embarking on a programme of building. However, one legacy of the city's location above a perpetually flowing spring is that, due to a rise in alluvium levels, it's been impossible to excavate in the valley bed. Consequently, virtually nothing of the Roman period apart from a small theatre survives, although coins show a nymphaeum, various temples, probably a forum, a baths and lavish public buildings dotted throughout the city.

A massacre of 20,000 Jews in a single hour at Caesarea in Palestine in 66 AD fuelled a widespread Jewish revolt against Roman rule, and amidst the turmoil the nascent **Christian** community of Jerusalem fled *en masse* to the relative safety of Pella – though by the time of the rebuilding of Jerusalem around 130 AD, they had returned. Pella reached its zenith during the **Byzantine** fifth and sixth centuries, with churches, houses and shops covering the slopes of the *tell* and Tell Husn, and pottery from North Africa and Asia Minor indicating significant international trade. However, by the seventh century, the city was again in decline; in 635, **Muslim** forces defeated the Byzantine army near Pella, and the city reverted to its pre-Hellenistic Semitic name of Fahl. The devastating earthquake of 747 destroyed most of Pella's standing structures, and the city lay abandoned for several centuries, small groups of farmers coming and going throughout the Abbasid and Mamluke periods.

The site

Although there may not be much romance left to Pella, it's certainly in a beautiful location. Sweet spring water cascades out of the ground on the floor of the Wadi Jirm; and the imposing bulk of the sheer Tell Husn to one side, the long, low *tell* on the other and Jebel Abu al-Khas between them (on which stands the modern, triple-arched Resthouse – see below) enclose the little valley with high slopes of green, leaving only the stunning vista westwards over the Jordan Valley. The abundant spring water, however, has proved irresistible to modern agriculture, and 100m beyond the antiquities stands a new pumping station serving a lush area of irrigated farmland. You may well find constantly chugging machinery coupled with a choking reek of agrichemicals limiting your appreciation of the natural and historical drama of the site.

Before you reach the main site, you'll see the remains of the **West Church** behind barbed wire on the edge of the modern village. The church was built in the late fifth or early sixth centuries, in Pella's prime, and – although overgrown and in a poor state of repair – is one of the largest Byzantine churches uncovered in the entire Middle East. There's a gate through the site fence a few hundred metres further on, which gives access to the rest of the ruins. The main valley is dominated by the standing columns of the **Civic Complex Church** on the edge of the bubbling spring. All the re-erected columns belong to the church's atrium; to the east, in front of a finely paved portico, are two exquisite columns of green swirling marble, one of which cracked in two as it fell in antiquity. The church itself, its columns collapsed like a house of cards, has three apses, and was originally decorated with glass windows, glass mosaic half-domes, stone mosaics on the walls and floor and chancel screens of marble. The **monumental staircase** in front was added in the seventh century, when the valley floor was some two or three metres below its current level. To one side of the church is the bowl of a small Roman **theatre**, built in the first century AD to seat about four hundred. Many of its stones were plundered to build the church staircase. Across the whole area of the modern springs, there may once have stretched a forum, with the stream channelled below through subterranean vaulting, some of which is still visible.

The **tell** itself is likely to excite only archeologists. Although several different excavations have revealed dozens of levels of occupation over millennia, all there is to see for the layperson are the criss-crossing foundations of coarser and finer walls at different levels and a couple of re-erected columns. Of most significant interest is a small **Mamluke mosque** close to the modern dighouse, with a plaque commemorating the decisive Battle of Fahl of 635.

Below the Resthouse and a little to one side stand the columns of the atmospheric **East Church**, built in the fifth century overlooking the lower city and originally accessed by a monumental staircase from below. The atrium has a small pool in the centre.

Longer exploration of the area around Pella can take the form of a combination of ruin hunting and adventure hiking. You'd have to be very keen to scale **Tell Husn** in order to poke around the sixth-century Byzantine fortress on its summit, but if you head past the East Church to curve behind the Resthouse, you'll find rough trails leading across the hills for an hour or more out to the peak of **Jebel Sartaba**; here stands a Hellenistic fortress, rather less dramatic in itself than the remoteness of the location and the stunning views across the hills and valleys west into Israel/Palestine and east towards Ajloun.

Practicalities

The ruins of Pella are situated close to the modern village of **Tabqat Fahl**, about 2km up a steep hill from **Mshare'a** on the valley-floor highway. There are one or two **buses** running direct to Tabqat Fahl village from Irbid's Valleys station, but departures from Irbid are much more frequent to Mshare'a, from where it should not be too hard to hitch or hike up the hill. Plenty of buses also ply the valley highway north from Dayr Alla (via Kraymeh) and south from Shuneh ash-Shamaliyyeh, stopping everywhere in between.

About 1km beyond the entrance gate to the site, on top of Jebel Abu al-Khas, the wonderfully cool and shady **Resthouse** (daily 8am–sunset; ☎079/74145) serves fresh orange juice, cold beers and, for a bargain JD6 including *mezze*, the best and freshest fish in Jordan. A new, subtly small hotel was going up just behind the Resthouse at the time of writing, but at least until it's ready, the Resthouse manager is operating a small **guesthouse** (②) in his home in Tabqat village, simple rooms with breakfast and genuine hospitality thrown in. It's him you should ask for directions about hiking and camping in the countryside around Pella.

South of Pella

Beyond Pella, the Jordan Valley road cuts a straight path through simple villages past huge swathes of farmland south to the Dead Sea. Points of interest are few and far between down here: the culture is all rural and agricultural, transport is limited to buses running up and down the main road, and the archeological sites – though plentiful – are strictly for scientists; barely one stone stands upon another in any of them.

Around 20km south of Mshare'a is the town of **Kraymeh**, served by buses from Ajloun as well as the valley villages north and south. A little beyond the town, opposite an isolated mosque with a stone minaret, a road branches west towards the huge mound of **Tell as-Sa'idiyyeh**, some 2km away. Occupied for a period in the Early Bronze Age, up to about 2800 BC, the *tell* was home to a large city during the Late Bronze Age, during the thirteenth and twelfth centuries BC. Halfway along the right-hand slope of the *tell*, a reconstructed Iron Age **stone staircase** leads up from a spring-fed **pool** to the summit; here a few excavation trenches display remnants of an Egyptian-style **public building** (Sa'idiyyeh may have been a northern outpost of the Egyptian empire) and a substantial **city wall**. The *tell* gives stunning views along the length of the valley, though the River Jordan itself, only a few hundred metres away, is still invisible in its gorge. The lower mound to the west, outside the walls, comprised a huge Late Bronze Age **cemetery**.

Some 9km further south, the large **Tell Dayr Alla** rises next to the road. Heading down the street hugging the south flank of the *tell* will bring you to a small research station (☎05/573136), centre for all archeological research in the Jordan Valley. As well as providing information and impromptu refreshment, the staff can unlock the small **museum** (daily except Fri 8am–1pm & 2–5pm; free), housing a collection of interesting bits and bobs from sites throughout the valley. The *tell* itself, punctured by deep excavation trenches exposing anonymous walls and rooms, is barely worth the effort of the climb. Dayr Alla town, 1km south, is served by buses from Amman, Salt and valley destinations.

Some 26km south of Dayr Alla lies the humdrum town of **Karameh**, best known today for its huge dam project, but still resonant in local minds as the location for one of the few military victories enjoyed by combined Jordanian-Palestinian forces over Israel. On March 21, 1968, the Israeli army – recent conquerors of the West Bank – launched a raid against Palestinian commandos in Karameh, and were repelled during a fierce battle in which Jordanian artillery and the Palestinian *fedayeen* worked side by side. Palestinian crowds that later went out onto the streets of Amman to celebrate marginalized the Jordanian army's role and claimed the victory entirely for their own cause, fuelling the fire that was to become Black September (see p.324).

A little way south of Karameh is the crossroads town of **Shuneh al-Janubiyyeh** (South Shuneh), from where main roads head to Amman (ignore roadsigns for Salt and continue instead through the centre of Shuneh to a major junction) and south to the Dead Sea and beyond. Between Shuneh and the Dead Sea, near the village of **Kafrayn**, is a small road leading down towards the Jordan which as yet is inaccessible to the public; in the small **Wadi Kharrar** a little before the river, in a militarily controlled zone, the site of an ancient church is thought to mark **Bethany-beyond-the-Jordan**, mentioned in the Gospel of St John as the place where John the Baptist baptized penitents and thus where it's presumed he **baptized Jesus Christ**. Competing sites on both banks of the river have attracted pilgrims since the fourth century, but since the 1967 war, when the river became an international ceasefire line, it's been impossible to visit the eastern bank. However, following the peace with Israel, work began early in 1998 to develop facilities here for tourists to be able to go right down to the river, both to commemorate the baptism of Jesus, re-enact the baptism ritual themselves, and, more prosaically, take advantage of the only opportunity to see and explore the river, its flora and fauna at first hand. Jordan is marketing itself for the millennium celebrations as "The Land and River of the Baptism", and the unveiling of the newly equipped baptism site at Wadi Kharrar is to be the focus of the country's plans. Until 2000 comes around, the closest you can get, though, is to surf to *198.62.75.1/www1/ofm/fai/FAIbapt.html* for plans, photos and information.

travel details

Since most buses and all minibuses and *services* simply depart whenever they are full, frequency of service is indicated only when a fixed timetable is in operation.

Domestic buses, minibuses and *services*

Ajloun to: Amman (Abdali station; 1hr 30min); Irbid (New Amman station; 45min); Jerash (30min); Kraymeh (30min); Qala'at ar-Rabadh (10min); Zerqa (Old station; 1hr 15min).

Dayr Alla to: Amman (Abdali station; 1hr); Kraymeh (10min); Mshare'a (30min); Salt (50min); Shuneh al-Janubiyyeh (40min); Shuneh ash-Shamaliyyeh (50min).

Himmeh to: Irbid (North station; 1hr); Umm Qais (15min).

Irbid (New Amman station) to: Ajloun (45min); Amman (Abdali station; every 15min; 1hr 15min–2hr); Jerash (35min); Mafraq (Fellahin station; 45min); Ramtha (20min); Zerqa (Old station; 1hr).

Irbid (North station) to: Himmeh (1hr); Qwaylbeh (20min); Umm Qais (45min).

Irbid (Valleys station) to: Mshare'a (45min); Sheikh Hussein Bridge (1hr); Shuneh ash-Shamaliyyeh (30min); Tabqat Fahl (1hr).

Jerash to: Ajloun (30min); Amman (Abdali station; 1hr); Irbid (New Amman station; 35min); Mafraq (Fellahin station; 40min); Zerqa (Old station; 40min).

Kraymeh to: Ajloun (45min); Dayr Alla (10min); Mshare'a (20min).

Mshare'a to: Dayr Alla (30min); Irbid (Valleys station; 1hr); Kraymeh (20min); Shuneh ash-Shamaliyyeh (20min); Tabqat Fahl (15min).

Qala'at ar-Rabadh to: Ajloun (10min).

Qwaylbeh to: Irbid (North station; 20min).

Ramtha to: Irbid (New Amman station; 20min); Mafraq (Fellahin station; 30min).

Sheikh Hussein Bridge to: Irbid (Valleys station; 1hr).

Shuneh ash-Shamaliyyeh to: Dayr Alla (50min); Irbid (Valleys station; 30min); Mshare'a (20min).

Tabqat Fahl to: Irbid (Valleys station; 1hr 15min); Mshare'a (15min).

Umm Qais to: Himmeh (15min); Irbid (North station; 45min).

International buses and *services*

Irbid (New Amman station) to: Damascus (2hr); Dera'a (50min).

Irbid (Trust office, near Sports City) to: Haifa (12 weekly; 4hr); Nazareth (1–2 daily; 3hr); Tel Aviv (6 weekly; 5hr).

Ramtha to: Damascus (1hr 40min); Dera'a (30min).

Sheikh Hussein Bridge to: Haifa (12 weekly; 3hr); Nazareth (1–2 daily; 2hr); Tel Aviv (6 weekly; 4hr).

CHAPTER THREE

THE EASTERN DESERT

or hundreds of kilometres east of Amman, the grey and stony **Eastern Desert** plains extend unbroken to the Iraqi border – and beyond, clear to Baghdad. This is the harshest and least populated part of the country, with a bare handful of roads linking small, dusty towns and frontier villages. The

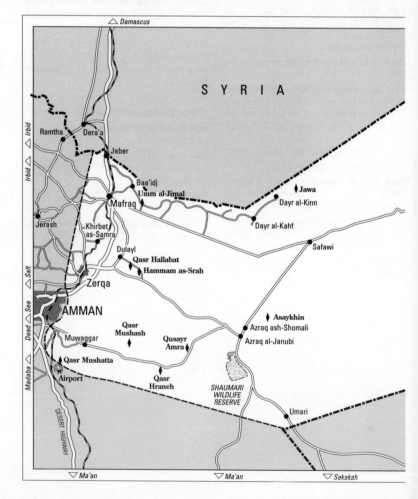

two exceptions are **Zerqa**, an industrial city and transport hub, and **Mafraq**, amiable but remote-feeling capital of the northeast. East of Mafraq, in the black basalt desert hugging the Syrian border, sit the stark ruins of **Umm al-Jimal**, enormously romantic in the cool evening. The plains east of Zerqa are dotted with a string of atmospheric early Islamic inns and hunting lodges, dubbed the "Desert Castles", at least one of which, **Qusayr Amra**, is unmissable. The highlight of a journey, though, is the castle and twin villages of **Azraq**, Lawrence of Arabia's chosen headquarters, set in a once-majestic oasis. For hard-bitten adventurers, **Qasr Burqu**, a ruined black castle on the shores of a lake, lies remote in the far desert, just 50km from the Iraqi border.

Transport in the desert is predictably thin. However, Zerqa and Mafraq have good connections with Amman and other northern towns, and both serve as the

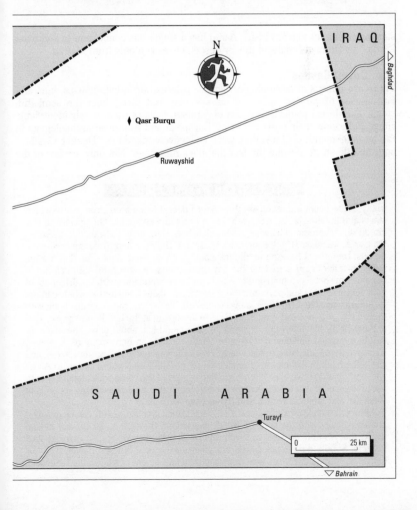

HOTEL PRICE CODES

Throughout this guide, hotels have been categorized according to the **price codes** given below, which indicate the normal price for the **cheapest double room** in a particular establishment during the **high season** (excluding the ten-percent tax and ten-percent service charge levied in all hotels of ③ and above). **Single rooms** can cost anything between seventy and a hundred percent of the double-room rates. Where a hotel offers beds in **shared rooms**, the price per person to share has been given; if a price code has also been included, this indicates that private rooms are also available. For a fuller explanation, see p.39.

① under JD10	④ JD30–40	⑦ JD65–80
② JD10–20	⑤ JD40–50	⑧ JD80–95
③ JD20–30	⑥ JD50–65	⑨ over JD95

starting points for journeys east. Azraq has a single bus connection to and from Zerqa. For Umm al-Jimal and the far desert, buses run only from Mafraq.

The "Desert Castles"

There are dozens of archeological sites – palaces, forts, bath-houses, inns and farmhouses of varying ages and sizes – scattered throughout the semi-arid, steppe-like desert plains to the east of Amman, most of them barely identifiable ruins. Following their rediscovery by European and American archeologists in the late nineteenth century, they were collectively tagged as **"Desert Castles"** and the title stuck, despite the fact that it's a misnomer. Not only are few of the

THE EASTERN DESERT CIRCUIT

Many of the major attractions in the eastern desert lie on a **circular route** which starts and finishes in Amman, with Azraq as its furthest point. On or close to this circuit lie, running clockwise, Qasr Hallabat, Hammam as-Srah, Qasr Azraq, Qusayr Amra, Qasr Hraneh and Qasr Mushatta. Only the first three are accessible by bus; the others have no public transport running even close. For this reason, many travellers **rent a taxi** for the day from Amman to cover the entire circuit in one go. Your hotel can help find one and conduct negotiations with the driver about your requirements and payment; the going rate is about JD40 for the whole car, not including a tip. The *Cliff Hotel* knows some reliable drivers, but you must book with them a day or two ahead (you don't have to be staying at the hotel); otherwise, Taxi al-Barq (☎06/464 1299) are trustworthy. You could just about cover the main circuit in a hurried half-day; diverting to Mushatta adds an hour or more. However, it's much more satisfying to start early, break the journey in and around Azraq, and aim to be back in Amman by nightfall. Other possibilities – going by bus to Azraq and renting a taxi there, or hitch-hiking all or part of the route – are detailed in the text. However, if you hold a driving licence, by far the most convenient option is to slash the taxi fare and **rent a self-drive car** for the day.

Although both Qasr Burqu (see p.172) and Qasr Tuba (see p.274) can be grouped archeologically with the sites on the desert circuit, they are so far off any beaten tracks that it's only possible to reach them with a local guide and an **offroad 4x4 vehicle**. Simple directional details are given in the text, but see *Basics*, p.38, for details of Amman operators who can organize a tour by 4x4 of sites in the far desert.

buildings true castles, but many were built on what was then the semi-fertile fringes of the desert; in the 1200 years since their abandonment, both **Qasr Hallabat** (which actually is a fortress) and **Qasr Mushatta** (a palace) have seen the desert encroach right up to their walls. Even the remote **Qusayr Amra** (a bath-house) had an area of well-watered agricultural land surrounding it to feed its permanent staff. In recent years, archeologists have suggested titles to replace "Desert Castles" – desert complexes, country estates, farmsteads – but none exactly fits the bill.

Zerqa and around

Some 20km northeast of Downtown Amman, and connected to the capital by a ribbon of suburbs, **ZERQA** is Jordan's second largest city and its principal industrial centre. Although some older buildings survive in the ugly breezeblock jungle, there's no reason to spend any time here except to pass between the **bus stations**, which are 1km apart, within walking distance of the clocktower in the centre of town. The **New Station** serves Amman – either Abdali or Raghadan – as well as Salt and southern destinations such as Madaba and Karak. A shuttle bus runs to the **Old Station** but you can walk the 1km easily: head left on the main road under the canopy for 500m and then aim for the clocktower. Most buses from the Old Station serve only nearby villages, including **Khirbet as-Samra**, with its Roman-Byzantine ruins, and **Hallabat**, with its fascinating castle, although there are other useful connections to Mafraq, Jerash, Irbid and Ajloun. Buses to Azraq leave from the very back of the station on the right, behind the row of vegetable stalls. If you feel the need to break your journey in Zerqa viable places to **eat**, apart from bus station *falafel* and *shwarma,* are within reach of the clocktower, though none could actually be recommended.

If you're **driving**, follow Hashmi Street east from Downtown Amman direct to the Zerqa clocktower. For Khirbet as-Samra, turning right 4km beyond the tower to Hashmiyya and right again after another 13km will bring you after 6km to Samra's train station. For Hallabat, the road straight past the clock tower goes through Dulayl after 22km; the *qasr* is 7km down the right-hand turn in Dulayl, the *hammam* 3km further.

Khirbet as-Samra

Aside from using Zerqa as a launching pad for a journey to Hallabat or possibly Azraq, you might take a couple of hours out to catch a bus to a small and forlornly isolated site about 20km northeast of the town. Decked in wildflowers in spring and baked brown in summer, the grassy hills surrounding the mud-and-breezeblock village of **KHIRBET AS-SAMRA** were once crossed by caravans travelling the Roman *Via Nova Traiana*, and the town – then named Hattita – was a major stop on the road for five hundred years or more. A Roman cohort was garrisoned here during the fourth century, and archeologists have uncovered eight Byzantine churches, all with mosaic floors.

Unfortunately, Hattita is better in the telling than the seeing: all the mosaics have either been removed or covered over for safekeeping, there's barely a discernible building amongst the rambling mess of rubble, and you'll probably enjoy the sense of countryfied isolation more than anything else. The bus can drop you at a gap in the wire fence around the ruins; walking left (south) will bring you to a large reservoir. From here, the **Church of St John** is about 50m north, a tiny place identifiable by its white limestone (instead of the otherwise ubiquitous black basalt) and paved floor, complete with a distinctive curved apse. Scramble 60m north and you'll find the foundations of the west wall of the original **Roman fort**, traceable around to the exposed **East Gate**, with the threshold and bases of flanking twin towers visible. The site guardian can take you to the blue Department of Antiquities building in the village and show you a map and photos from the French excavation team who spend a few weeks here each year, but there's little else to keep you.

Qasr Hallabat

The main reason for passing through Zerqa is to head for **Qasr Hallabat**. Perfectly situated on a small hill roughly 30km east of the town, Hallabat is one of the most elaborate of the "Desert Castles", but also the most ruinous. A black basalt Roman fort was built on this site in the second century to guard the Azraq road, and parts of it still survive, but much of the present remains date from an eighth-century Umayyad restoration in contrasting white limestone, when the beautiful mosque to one side was added and mosaic floors laid. Although jumbled and broken, Hallabat is far from a washout; it's exciting to scramble around and make sense of the place.

   HALLABAT village has two separate halves – Hallabat al-Gharbi (West) and Hallabat ash-Sharqi (East). There's virtually nowhere to eat or drink in either, so at the least bring plenty of water with you. Buses from Zerqa drop off at a road-sign 50m from the *qasr* gates in Gharbi. It's a 200-metre walk over stones from the gate (where the guardian hangs out in a bedouin-style tent) to the ruins. You first see the small **mosque**, just next to the fort, the patterned decoration cut into the arch over its doorway standing out a mile with the sky behind it. The renovated *mihrab* is to the left.

   The fort lies to the right of the mosque. A wobbly **entrance arch** – one shake and it'd be rubble – leads into the stone-flagged **courtyard**, full of reused inscribed blocks jammed higgledy-piggledy everywhere and lined in black and white; a path leads left across the courtyard into a room with a roughly carved basalt lintel filled with bits of Greek and Latin. A scramble to the highest point of the ruins will help orientate you; visible in the nearby walls are very old blocks from the tiny original **Roman fort** which occupied this corner. Opposite, a water channel runs under the stairs, carrying rainwater from the roof to cisterns under the courtyard and outside the walls. If you sweep away dust from the floors of nearby rooms, well-preserved fragments of the Umayyad mosaics peep out.

   The Umayyads also built a small bath-house, **Hammam as-Srah** ("The Desert Baths") about 3km from the fort in Sharqi. Smaller than Qusayr Amra, its *caldarium* (hot room) is nearest the road, followed by the *tepidarium* (warm room) with the hypocaust system of underfloor heating and terracotta flues in the walls. The *apodyterium* (changing room) is furthest away, next to the original entrance, where there's some decorative cross-hatching on the walls. Although these days it's a lonely refuge for birds and lizards, it's easy to imagine the *hammam* in its heyday, and the pleasure of a cool, quiet day spent here bathing, away from the hectic fort on the hill. If you're heading on to Azraq after exploring the *hammam*, turn right from here and the highway, where you can flag down a bus, is 2km away.

Mafraq and the Hawran

Barely 12km from the Syrian border lies the small, ramshackle town of **MAFRAQ**. Squeezed between it and the Jordan Valley, not 40km to the west, is the whole of the northern Jordanian agricultural and industrial heartland, but to the east yawns the open desert, and the mood within the town is of a tussle with the elements scarcely won. Dust fills the long, empty streets, the buildings are squat and ranged close together; many people wear the billowing robes of desert dwellers. Close by in southern Syria, and often visible, is the extinct volcano of Jebel Druze, rising to 1800m and surrounded for hundreds of kilometres in all directions by blisteringly hot plains of basaltic lava known as the **Hawran**. Around Mafraq, irrigated fields temper the monotony, but further east – and south as far as Azraq – the desert is shadowy and grimly blackish, stark bedrock overlaid by dark boulders and glassy basalt chips too hot to touch.

Mafraq, like Zerqa, has nothing in itself to tempt you, but it's the main staging-post for journeys east, and you may well find yourself having to change buses here. Frustratingly enough for a one-horse town, it has two **bus stations**, 1.5km apart. You're likely to arrive at the large, open **Bedouin station**, so called because it serves mostly desert destinations, from where buses depart to Umm al-Jimal, Dayr al-Kahf, Safawi and Ruwayshid, as well as Zerqa and Amman's Abdali station; occasional *service*s could get you to Zerqa more rapidly. Local *service*s can shuttle you to the **Fellahin station**, serving agricultural areas; buses from here run to Irbid, Jerash and Ramtha, and in theory, a few also go to Dera'a in Syria and Damascus – ask in an office against the far wall. Town life is centred on the Fellahin station, but you'll find little to **eat** beyond chicken and *hummus*.

Umm al-Jimal

In 1913, the American archeologist H. C. Butler wrote: "Far out in the desert, in the midst of the rolling plain, there is a deserted city all of basalt, [rising] black and forbidding from the grey of the plain." The romance and sense of discovery accompanying a visit to **UMM AL-JIMAL** (literally "Mother of Camels") today is still memorable, even though the plain is now irrigated, and a modern village with good roads has grown up around the ruins. At first glance a mass of rubble, the town has been well excavated and is actually very easy to explore – you could happily spend a couple of hours or more here, although the combination of sun and basalt can sometimes be intolerable. You should bring water and plan to visit either before 11am or after 4pm; the hours just before sunset are the best, with low light casting shadows among the warm stones.

As far as the town's **history** goes, Umm al-Jimal was occupied for seven hundred years up to about 750 AD. In the first part of its existence, it was a rural village that lived more or less undisturbed under Roman authority. Following Queen Zenobia of Palmyra's rebellion against Rome in the third century, the village was rebuilt as a military station on the fortified frontier of the Roman Empire. From the fifth century on, the town prospered as an agricultural and commercial centre, and a sixth-century conversion to Christianity resulted in fifteen churches going up. However, a 150-year onslaught of plague, war, the Muslim conquest and a massive earthquake led to the town's abandonment. For well over a millennium it lay deserted, until a community of Druze fleeing political upheavals in Syria

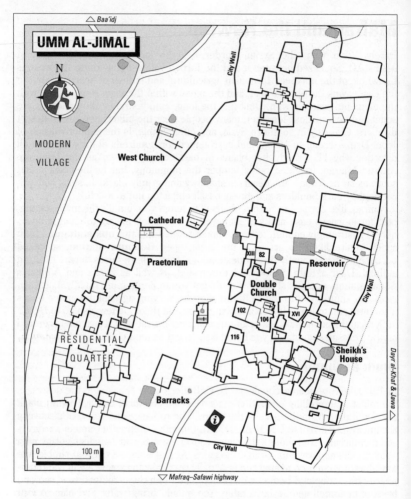

△ Baa'idj

UMM AL-JIMAL

N

City Wall

MODERN
VILLAGE

West Church

Cathedral

Praetorium

XIII 82

Reservoir

**Double
Church**

102
104 XVI

116

RESIDENTIAL
QUARTER

**Sheikh's
House**

Barracks

City Wall

0   100 m

Day al-Khaf & Jawa ▷

▽ *Mafraq–Safawi highway*

passed through in the 1920s, occupying the ghost town for a few years and
rebuilding here and there.

The appeal of Umm al-Jimal lies in its ordinariness. Although it is roughly contemporary with the grand city of Jerash only a day's ride westward, Umm al-Jimal
has no temples or monumental buildings and nothing impressive to commemorate
an emperor's visit. There's not even any evidence of the town's original Roman
name. The archeologist who excavated the ruins, Bert de Vries, perceptively
explained Umm al-Jimal's appeal as "a symbol of the real life of Rome's subjects".

The site

Where the modern road cuts through the ancient town walls, a rarely staffed
tourist information hut sits opposite a gap in the site fence, where the bus can

drop you. Umm al-Jimal is really far too big to explore in its entirety in one go, but you could start a one- or two-hour walking tour at the nearby **Barracks**, dating from the fifth century. In the eastern wall the basalt slab door, which still moves on its hinges, gives onto a courtyard. The late Byzantine **corner tower** is inscribed with crosses and the names of the four archangels: Gabriel, Raphael, Michael and Uriel.

Picking a path between Houses 102 and 116, and left around House 104 (see our map), will deliver you to the tumbled entrance to the **Double Church**, a private affair tucked into the houses around it, fronted by a small ablutions basin. Nearby House XVI's lockable double doors would have fitted together snugly, and inside is a good example of a corbelled ceiling, the strong basalt beams supporting a much greater load than limestone could. Back behind you, the **Sheikh's House** is outside on the left. Its large internal courtyard is one of the town's finest, with a cantilevered staircase on the left and two in front forming a V shape; stables were ranged around the courtyard, while bedrooms lay upstairs. Above you in the wall are two different lintel-relieving devices, one a window, the other a minuscule slot of an arch: both were designed to protect the lintels below by deflecting the weight of the heavy basalt wall onto the doorposts instead. You'll find such devices above doorways all over Umm al-Jimal; in a couple of places where they're missing, such as at the Double Church, the lintel has cracked under the strain. If you leave the courtyard through the gate, you'll spot a beautiful **double arched window** three storeys up.

From here, wandering north through a residential district strewn with loose, clinking basalt will bring you out to the huge **reservoir** – now fenced off – that was originally Roman. Umm al-Jimal's farmers lived in close proximity with their animals and, just west of the reservoir, a scramble through House 82 brings you into House XIII, with mangers and a superb interlocking stone ventilation screen – partially obscured by a Druze-built twentieth-century arch – dividing space for livestock within the house.

It's a 150-metre walk across town to the four graceful and strikingly silhouetted arches of the **West Church**. The structure that remains is the division between the nave and a side aisle, and beautiful Byzantine crosses are carved on the arches. A little way south the **Cathedral** sports a reused lintel stone mentioning Valens, Valentinian and Gratian, co-emperors in 371 AD. Close by is the **Praetorium**, currently being renovated, with a triple doorway. One of the rooms nearby has strings of barbed wire across its entrances and is now the pen for a herd of beautiful white camels belonging to the local sheikh. From here, your starting point at the Barracks is nearby, or you can go on to explore the dense southwestern **residential quarter** of the town.

Other Hawran sites

Either side of Umm al-Jimal, between the main Mafraq–Safawi road and the Syrian border, are a string of rural communities and a handful of ancient sites accessible only by **car**, one of them only by 4x4. A bus does occasionally run out here on the back roads from Mafraq, but it's barely worth the time and effort considering the inaccessibility and low-key nature of the sites.

A word of warning: because of the harshness of the country and its proximity to the Syrian border, the Hawran is one of the principal smuggling routes for

Lebanese hashish bound for Israel, Egypt and the Arabian Peninsula. There are many **checkpoints** on these back-country roads, and although the soldiers are very friendly, they'll be interested to know why you're cruising around the countryside. You should carry your passport and be prepared for lengthy jovial cups of tea.

West of Umm al-Jimal, a well-preserved stretch of the Roman *Via Nova Traiana* survives just outside the unpronounceable village of **BAA'IDJ**, pointing the way across the fields right towards Bosra and left towards Amman. The road was cambered, with a central spine and carefully laid kerb stones, and, originally, the rough stony surface would have been covered with earth beaten flat. Drivers aiming for Baa'idj should take the perimeter road around Umm al-Jimal to the West Church and fork left; after 7km, a left turn at a T-junction, right at a small roundabout and straight on at a bigger roundabout will bring you after 600m to the stretch of Roman road.

Way to the east lies a small basalt Roman fort, **Dayr al-Kahf**, dating from 306 AD; it was one of many situated on the *Strata Diocletiana*, a frontier road designed by Emperor Diocletian to link Bosra with Azraq. Well preserved, the walls of the fort are still standing, and remnants of carved columns have been dumped in the plastered cistern; one perfect arch survives in the far wall. A wander around the quiet, atmospheric courtyard reveals ground-floor stables and upper-level rooms. You can get to Dayr al-Kahf by driving 7km past the Umm al-Jimal information hut, turning left at the T-junction and right after 22km; the fort comes into view 26km further.

About 25km east of Dayr al-Kahf – and only accessible with a 4x4 – lie the bleak and mysterious ruins of **JAWA**, a town constructed five thousand years ago from the local basalt by an unknown people, occupied for only fifty years then abandoned. For archeologists specializing in the Chalcolithic Near East, the site, desolate on its rocky hill, is a goldmine; anybody else will probably find themselves in awe more of the spectacular surroundings of the Black Desert than of the ancient ruins: in these vast expanses of basalt, the silence and sense of ominous open space are overwhelming.

If you're aiming to drive to Jawa in your own vehicle, you'll need to find a guide before heading out: first choice is Mouaffaq, a guardian at Umm al-Jimal who speaks good English and knows the site. The road east from Dayr al-Kahf passes through **Dayr al-Kinn**, itself home to a crumbling Roman fort; 2km on, a rough track heads right off the road along the right-hand bank of the large Wadi Rajil for 5km into the desert. The substantial **walls** of Jawa are visible ahead, fortifying a craggy outcrop above the wadi. Divided into a lower and an upper town, the city has more **gates** than any other prehistoric settlement yet discovered – six inner and eight outer, many of which are still discernible. Closely packed **houses** – tiny, irregularly shaped one-room shacks – cram the city, and a complex system of **canals and reservoirs** originally diverted and stored the winter rains. The city was attacked very shortly after its construction, and was occupied either by the attackers or by the successful defenders for a brief period until the water system failed and the city was abandoned. Well over a thousand years later, during the Middle Bronze Age, a short-lived citadel of sorts was built in the upper town, presumably to serve as a caravanserai on the routes between Syria and Mesopotamia to the north and Palestine, Egypt and Arabia to the south.

The Baghdad Highway

The longest, straightest, dullest road in Jordan points like the barrel of a gun away from Amman into the pancake-flat open desert. This is the **Baghdad Highway** and the Iraqi capital is only about 800km away – a day's drive by car, or two days in the massive lumbering trucks and oil tankers which are the highway's principal traffic. There are only two towns out here, neither of which qualifies as anything more than a truck stop. However, the whole of Jordan's "panhandle" – from the boulder-strewn Black Desert out to the undulating limestone plateau and grasslands in the farthest corners of the country – is praised by ornithologists as one of the most fascinating and rewarding areas for birdwatching in the whole of Jordan. Although you'll probably have only limited satisfaction if you attempt to travel in the area alone, a handful of tour companies – both local and foreign – organize excellent **birdwatching and eco-tours** that can get you to all kinds of remote crannies, notably the lake at **Burqu**; see the "Getting There" sections and "Getting Around" in Basics for more details.

The major town out here, **SAFAWI**, 75km east of Mafraq, is an oil-stained, engine-roaring kind of place that's unlikely to inspire: patching tyres and roasting chickens for dinner are the sole entertainments. The main drag is guarded at one end by a police post – along the Baghdad Highway, even more than in the Hawran, you'll have to spend plenty of time sweet-talking your way through checkpoints, since camera-laden tourists are about as common as beach balls.

HIGHWAY HAZARDS

The highway from Amman to Baghdad is notorious as one of the most dangerous stretches of road in the world. On the Iraqi side, travellers must deal with roving **highwaymen** who regularly seize goods and passports from taxis and private cars. Before you even get out of Jordan, though, the stretch between Safawi and the Iraqi border is lined with burnt-out wrecks and shredded truck tyres, skid marks seared into the tarmac as testimony to dozens of horrific accidents. Unable due to UN sanctions imposed after the 1991 Gulf War to sell more than a fraction of its abundant oil, Iraq has been awash with **petrol** for most of the 1990s; in 1998, one litre cost the equivalent of two US cents, with the same quantity selling for 31 cents next door in Jordan. Desperately impoverished Iraqi truck- and taxi-drivers plying the highway have found that one way to bring in some extra income is to attach hidden tanks under their vehicle and smuggle cheap Iraqi petrol into Jordan to sell for profit. However, the scam is not so easy. Petrol may be cheap, but under the sanctions **tyres** and spare parts have become luxury commodities: unable to shell out five months' salary for a new truck tyre, drivers must instead rely on old ones, patching them up by hand and praying nothing goes wrong. With jerry-built tanks of petrol sloshing around under the chassis, fumes filling the cab, rigged-up spare parts holding the engine together, old, bald tyres and a cargo of crude oil – not to mention a hot, two-day drive along dead-straight roads – these Iraqi tankers are accidents waiting to happen … and, tragically, **fireballs** are a relatively common occurrence along this highway. Look out for these guys (Iraqi plates are white-on-blue and all Arabic), and, for your sake and theirs, give them a wide berth.

You may spot roadsigns to Safawi that include "H5" in brackets; this number refers to a pumping station along the route of an **oil pipeline** constructed in the 1930s, which prompted the later construction of the highway along its length. Only operational for fifteen years up until the declaration of the State of Israel in 1948, the pipeline originated in Kirkuk, Iraq, with one branch running through Syria to Tripoli in Lebanon and the other through Jordan to Haifa, now in Israel. All the pumping stations along the Haifa branch were numbered, with the prefix H: H4 is just before Ruwayshid, while H2 (over the border) became infamous during the 1991 Gulf War as the firing-point for Iraqi Scud missiles directed at Israel.

In the unlikely event that you are refused permission to continue east along the highway, you could instead branch southwest from Safawi to Azraq. Otherwise, the last settlement of any size in Jordan before the Iraqi border is **Ruwayshid**, even less prepossessing than its distant neighbour Safawi. Some 10km before the village, and 90km east of Safawi, a checkpoint at **Muqat** is the starting-point for a journey north into the roadless desert towards Burqu.

Burqu

The *qasr* at **BURQU** (pronounced along the lines of *Beurkah*) can be grouped – archeologically speaking – with the "Desert Castles" of Hallabat, Azraq and others, a small Roman fort occupied and expanded during the Islamic period. However, the ruins take a poor second place to Burqu's quite extraordinary natural environment, both on the offroad journey to reach the site and once you arrive: the *qasr* stands on the shores of **Ghadir Burqu**, a substantial lake some 2km long which is fabulous enough by itself, hidden in the depths of the desert, but which also serves as the lifeline and congregation point for an array of animals and local and migrating birds. Proposed to become a protected nature reserve under the aegis of the Royal Society for the Conservation of Nature (RSCN), Burqu is a wild and dramatic place, well worth the long and difficult journey.

The **dam** 2km north of the *qasr* (which led to the lake's formation) and the tower which still rises above the ruined walls of the castle are thought both to have been constructed in the third century, possibly to guard the water source for caravans travelling between Syria and Arabia. Inhabited continuously during the Byzantine period – possibly as a monastery – Burqu was expanded and fortified by Emir Walid in the year 700 AD; an inscription dated 1409 might indicate occupation up to that date. The entrance into the *qasr* is on the north wall, which gives access to two **inscriptions** – one naming Walid – above the lintel of the room in the far left-hand corner of the **courtyard**, next to a room with a pointed arch. In the opposite corner is a small, free-standing circular room with a cross carved into its lintel; next to it is the original **tower**, still standing to around 8m, with a tiny, easily defended door (now blocked) in one wall.

However, it's the enormous **lake** and its flora and fauna which most impress. The journey from the highway to Burqu crosses a large, flat *qa*, or depression, from which subterranean water rises to form the lake, full almost year-round and bordered in spring by poppies, iris and other wildflowers. The projected nature reserve is to be centred on this mirage-like apparition, which stands between two very different habitats. To the east is a vast expanse of *hammada*, or stony desert pavement, covered with bushes and grasses in winter. To the west sweeps the black *Harrat ash-Sham*, a moonscape of basalt rocks ranging in size from a few centimetres to a metre or more across. The rocks make the *harra* impassable even for 4x4 jeeps: hunters cannot penetrate the area, turning it into a perfect wildlife refuge. **Gazelles** roam the *harra*, the last few herds surviving in Jordan, in addition to hyenas, wolves, red foxes, wildcats, caracals and hares, all of which were logged in an RSCN survey of Burqu. Rumours, as yet unsubstantiated, persist among the locals of the presence of **cheetahs**. Birders, too, will be delighted: as well as regular sightings of sandpipers, larks, wheatears and finches, Burqu boasts herons, pelicans, storks and cranes, along with buzzards, owls, vultures and even the rare Verreaux's Eagle.

Practicalities

Buses from Mafraq drop off in the middle of Safawi, but once you've arrived, there's nowhere to go but back again; if you find yourself without a ride, you could quite legitimately ask the police to stop a Zerqa-bound oil tanker for you. The only way to get to Burqu itself is in a **4x4** and with a guide: some buses do go on to Ruwayshid, but even if you get through the checkpoints, your chances of managing to get out to Burqu independently – or getting back from it – are virtually nil. If you're intending to head to Burqu in your own 4x4, the RSCN's Ecotourism Unit in Amman may be able to sort out a guide for you – see p.39 for details, and for information about specialist **tour operators** in Jordan. Wilderness **camping** on the shores of the lake is possible, but should only be undertaken when accompanied, and is dangerous in autumn and winter when flash floods can strike. There are options for **eating** in Safawi, but you shouldn't consider driving around the desert without also carrying enough food and water to keep you going for several days.

Azraq and around

As in antiquity, **AZRAQ** is today a crossroads for international traffic. In the past, its location at the head of the Wadi Sirhan, the main caravan route from Arabia to Syria (known as the Wadi al-Azraq before its settlement by the bedouin Sirhan tribe), meant that Azraq was both a vital trading-post and a defensive strongpoint for the populated areas to the north and west. The focus of settlement was **Qasr Azraq**, originally built by the Romans and continuously renovated over the succeeding centuries; in 1917, the old castle was chosen by Lawrence of Arabia to be his headquarters.

Azraq means "blue" in Arabic, and the reason why it was such an essential caravan crossroads is that it used to be the only permanent **oasis** in thirty thousand square kilometres of desert. Fed by aquifers draining millions of cubic metres of filtered rainwater into a massive shallow basin, Azraq was surrounded by expansive freshwater pools and forests of palm and eucalyptus. Literally millions of migrating birds stopped off every year to recuperate in the highly improbable lushness on their long desert flights between Central Asia and Africa, and water buffalo and wild horses were common. Azraq was – and still is – protected under a global treaty safeguarding wetland habitats. A successful breeding programme at the **Shaumari Wildlife Reserve** to the south of town has produced large numbers of oryx and ostrich. However, after just twenty years of pumping from the aquifers to supply ever-growing Amman with drinking water, the oasis is today near collapse. Although ragged palms survive, the pools are stagnant, the buffalo

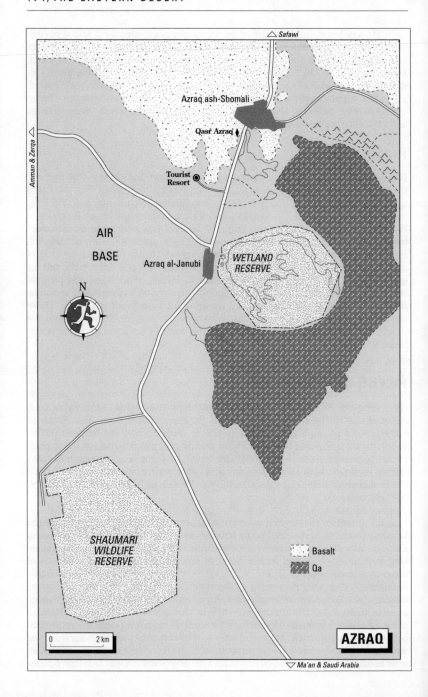

WINSTON'S HICCUP

Azraq is situated at the crook of the strange angle formed by Jordan's eastern border with Saudi Arabia, which zig-zags here for no apparent reason. Demarcating this border was the work of Winston Churchill, then British Colonial Secretary, who boasted of having created the new Emirate of Transjordan with a stroke of his pen one Sunday afternoon in 1921. A story grew up that, after a particularly liquid lunch that day, he had hiccuped while attempting to draw the border and – Winston being Winston – had refused to allow it to be redrawn. Thus the zigzag has been written into history as **"Winston's Hiccup"**. Unfortunately, on closer examination, the truth is rather less engaging: Churchill in fact carefully plotted the zigzag to ensure that the massive Wadi Sirhan – a long finger of a valley pointing a route between Damascus and Arabia, and a vital communications highway – ended up excluded from the territory of the new emirate.

---

are dead and migrating birds now head for Galilee instead. Dust storms are more common today than ever before. The underground reservoirs, exploited almost to exhaustion, are slowly turning brackish.

Lawrence wrote of Azraq's numinous power, of it being "magically haunted", but little, it seems, can now save this uncelebrated desert outpost from ecological breakdown. Visiting – and staying – is not easy, but can still be a rewarding experience in the short time left before the once-lush oasis becomes just another truck stop in the desert.

Some history

Large numbers of **Paleolithic** hand axes and flint tools have been discovered around Azraq oasis, indicating a substantial settlement up to 200,000 years ago; archeological work only began in earnest relatively recently and is ongoing. The **Romans** built a fort on the site of the present *qasr* in the third century, roughly when the nearby forts of Uwaynid and Asaykhin were also occupied, although archeologists have found milestones near Azraq dating from a hundred years earlier. Also used by the **Byzantines** and the **Umayyads**, the fort was rebuilt in 1237 by the **Ayyubid** governor Azz ad-Din Aybak, fifty years or so after the Ayyubid leader Salah ad-Din had expelled the main Crusader force from east of the Jordan. Still in use under the **Mamlukes** and the **Ottomans**, the castle was occupied during the winter of 1917–18 by **Lawrence** and the forces of the Arab Revolt; their final attack on Damascus, which saw the collapse of Ottoman power, was launched from here.

Just after World War I, wandering **Druze**, from Jebel Druze nearby in southern Syria, occupied the castle for a while, also founding the village outside the walls in the area of two large springs of sweet water. The volcanic plains spreading south from Jebel Druze engulf the castle, and their village was – and still is – dominated by hard black-grey basalt, very difficult to cut and dress, giving a lumpy, unfinished look to the older parts of the village. Although some Druze became farmers, most earned their livelihood from salt (see the box on p.179) and today, Azraq is home to half the Druze in Jordan.

Barely a decade later, **Chechens** arrived at Azraq following a great emigration in 1898 from Russian military and religious persecution in their homeland in the Caucasus. They settled some 7km south of the Druze village, on flat ground near three equally large springs feeding a huge area of wetland marsh. The basalt runs out in a remarkably clear line of scarps about 4km south of the Druze village and the new settlement instead lay in an area of limestone. Most of the Chechen emigres became farmers and fisherfolk, and, to differentiate between the two villages, the first became known as **Azraq Druze**, the second as **Azraq Shishan**.

In the 1950s, Palestinians and Syrians arrived in Azraq, blurring the clear ethnic boundaries between the two villages; recently, in an attempt to reflect the new mix, Azraq Druze officially renamed itself **Azraq ash-Shomali** (North Azraq) and Azraq Shishan became **Azraq al-Janubi** (South Azraq) – but the old names still survive in the minds of most locals. Today, the two Azraqs have a combined population of only about six thousand people, not including the large contingents of Jordanian and US air force personnel quartered at the huge airbase just outside the town. Although fishing died with the oasis, farming is still carried on here and there –and salt is still a major earner – but the town now mainly exists by serving the traffic on the international highways from Iraq, Saudi Arabia and Syria.

Practicalities

The roads from Zerqa and from Amman meet 9km west of Azraq. All traffic is then funnelled towards a T-junction, from where the restaurants of Azraq al-Janubi are visible to the right, extending for about 1km southwards. To the left, some 7km down the road, lie Qasr Azraq and the garages and workshops of Azraq ash-Shomali (and, 54km further, Safawi). **Buses** from Zerqa wander through Janubi first, then head for Shomali, dropping off here and there before terminating at the open area opposite the post office. If you tell the driver where you want to be dropped beforehand he'll take you to the door.

There is no public transport between the two halves of Azraq. Instead, the locals just flag down any vehicle heading in the right direction – a simple "Shomali?" or "Janubi?" to the driver suffices. The standard fare to offer, bus or not, is 100 fils.

A couple of banks at the north end of Shomali can **change money**, travellers' cheques and do Visa advances. There's a 24-hour English-speaking **pharmacy** – al-Sseddeeq – in Janubi, next door but one to an **international phone** bureau. There are two **post offices**: the Janubi branch (daily except Fri 8am–7pm) is behind the petrol station, while the other (Mon–Thurs, Sat & Sun 8am–7pm, Fri 8am–2pm) is on the Shomali crossroads.

Accommodation

Most tourists don't stop in Azraq, but the evenings and early mornings are by far the best times to enjoy the place. The problem is that the few **hotels** here get

---

PHONING AZRAQ

Azraq currently has no direct-dial phone service. Instead, all incoming and outgoing calls are routed through the post offices in each half of the town, each of which has two Amman lines and two Zerqa lines. To reach numbers in **Azraq ash-Shomali** from outside, call ☎06/464 7610–1 or ☎09/991974 or ☎09/901974, then ask for the extension. To reach numbers in **Azraq al-Janubi** from outside, call ☎06/464 7622–3 or ☎09/991973 or ☎09/901973, then ask for the extension. The stalwart operators – if you can get through – speak surprisingly good English.

most of their business from Saudi or Gulf families passing through, and tend to view Westerners as bringing down the tone – although it's easy to find a bed, you may feel a little out of place. The best deal, and the most memorable night, is to be had **camping** in the grounds of the Shaumari Wildlife Reserve (JD5); if you don't have a tent, the staff will rent you one for JD5, or you could sleep under the stars on top of their observation tower.

al-Sayad (aka *Hunter Hotel*), 500m south of Qasr Azraq, Azraq ash-Shomali (Shomali ☎94; or reserve in Amman ☎06/464 4988). An incongruously kitsch palace, with manicured gardens, fake-Islamic architecture and pristinely untouched rooms; the best overlook the (empty) pool. Every corner of the place is festooned with the owner's paintings – you may bump into her striding around the empty corridors. The restaurant menu seems to be a product of the same fanciful imagination that came up with the decor. ④.

Tourist Resort (aka *Government Resthouse*), southwest of Shomali, signposted west down a 1.5km-long avenue 2km north of the highway T-junction (Shomali ☎6; or reserve in Amman ☎06/568 1042, fax 568 1028). Comfortable enough chalet-style rooms around a pool, but difficult to reach without transport and a bit institutional. Prices are reasonable, considering they include a decent dinner and breakfast. ③.

al-Zoubi, behind the *Refa'i* restaurant at the southern end of Azraq al-Janubi (Janubi ☎12). The best budget choice in town. Simple rooms – all sleeping three or four – are clean and en suite, though the hard-nosed manager is rarely swayed by bargaining ploys. ②.

al-Zoubi, 23km south of Azraq al-Janubi, at the Jafr interchange. No phone. The most remote hotel in Jordan, reachable only by car. Huge photographic murals of blue seaside scenes and lush green gardens contrast comically with the barren views out of the window. Spartan rooms are large and clean. ②.

Eating and drinking
Janubi is lined with **restaurants**, most of them pretty basic and all serving standard truckers' fare of meat stew, chicken or *hummus*. As soon as you're spotted, you'll be beckoned in – the restaurants that don't call to you (and that don't have English signs) are probably better. There's a good *falafel* stand next to *Brown Chicken*.

Better but more expensive options are in **Shomali**. The dowdy *Government Resthouse* restaurant (daily 6am–midnight) seems mainly used as a residential

---

MOVING ON FROM AZRAQ ·

The **bus** from Azraq to Zerqa starts from the Shomali post office, cruises up and down in Shomali, then heads to Janubi and does the same; stop it at any point and jump on. The first one departs at 6am, the last at 5pm, and all go past the turnoff to Hallabat, from where you'll have to walk or hitch to Hammam as-Srah and Qasr Hallabat. Buses fill up quickly on Wednesday, the day off for the police and military.

No public transport serves Qusayr Amra (25km west of Azraq) or Qasr Hraneh (15km further). **Renting a taxi** in Azraq to see these two and bring you back will cost around JD10–15. Otherwise, you could **hitch** the whole way, or take a Zerqabound bus 9km west to where the Amman highway branches off and hitch from there. It's quite feasible to explore both sites and reach Amman (55km beyond Hraneh) in a day by hitching, although you should bring food and plenty of water with you.

The highway south of Janubi splits left to the Saudi border at Umari (the first big Saudi town is Sakakah, some 450km further); and right to Jafr and Ma'an the best part of 300km south. If you have a 4x4, it's possible to reach Qasr Tuba (see p.274) from this latter road, although you shouldn't attempt it without a local guide.

pub and nightspot by Saudis popping across the border – the menu has more alcohol than food. Nonetheless, they can do a frill-free meal for JD5 or so. Just north of the signpost to the *Resthouse*, the laid-back *Azraq Palace Tourist Restaurant* (daily 8am–11pm) has a poor-value JD6 buffet. The most atmospheric place in town to eat is the *al-Montazah Falls* (daily 10am–11pm); there's a sign just opposite the *qasr* pointing off the road, and it's the building at the first crossroads. Set amongst a grove of palms, with water tumbling through (when they turn on the tap), it's shady, cool and quiet, and is almost the only place left where you can get a sense of the former lushness and abundance of the oasis. North of the post office in Shomali are a couple of inexpensive diners; *al-Arez* is best.

Qasr Azraq

We hurried up the stony ridge in high excitement, talking of the wars and songs and passions of the early shepherd kings, with names like music, who had loved this place; and of the Roman legionaries who languished here as garrison in yet earlier times. Then the blue fort on its rock above the rustling palms, with the fresh meadows and shining springs of water, broke on our sight.

T. E. Lawrence, *The Seven Pillars of Wisdom*

Lawrence will be turning in his grave at the fate of his "blue fort", **Qasr Azraq**. Leaving aside the 1927 earthquake, which shook some height from the walls and towers, new apartment buildings now loom over the castle, the meadows have vanished and the "shining springs of water" have been diverted to keep Amman alive. Adding insult to injury, the main highway from Baghdad thunders past the walls, slicing the castle away from the oasis that inspired it, drowning out the rustling palms and masking the warm, dry breeze with motor oil. Nonetheless, the *qasr* is still a romantic and explorable place, with marvellous sunsets, and all the more poignant for its modest fame and the town's recent travails. A Druze family – currently in the third generation – have acted as guardians of the castle since the days of Lawrence and, as you approach, one or other of them will probably materialize to guide you round.

As you enter the dog-leg gatehouse, machicolation and an Arabic **inscription** commemorating the 1237 renovation of the castle are above your head. The massive basalt slab front door still swings on its hinges. Inside the gatehouse are carved stone images of animals found nearby (which are probably Umayyad), and Roman milestones and inscribed blocks; on one of them "Ioviorum" refers to the emperor Diocletian. Down at your feet, a double row of seven indentations in a threshold stone is for a gatekeeper's solitaire-type game using pebbles.

Inside the courtyard, the rooms immediately to the left were patched up with palm fronds either by Lawrence's men or by later Druze occupiers. Further around, the west wall is dominated by a massive **tower**, at the base of which is a three-tonne basalt slab door, barely swingable to and fro – Lawrence described the whole west wall trembling as it was slammed shut. The supposed **prison** in the northwest corner features a locking hole in the door-frame rubbed smooth and shiny by centuries of curious fingers. To the north are the smoke-blackened **kitchens** and the elegant **dining hall**, and, beside them, the **stables**, supported by oddly shaped arches. A seven-metre **well** in the east wall was filled with water until the mid-1980s, but is now dry; these days the water table has dropped way deeper. Sitting skewed in the middle of the courtyard is a remarkably graceful lit-

---

AZRAQ SALT

Much of the **table salt** used in Jordan, as well as that used in the surrounding Arab countries, comes from Azraq. Strangely enough for a freshwater oasis, Azraq has separate, extensive underground pockets of extremely salty water, which have provided the major source of income and employment for the village since the 1930s. Recently, a co-operative was set up, and today six hundred families are involved – virtually the entire town.

The salt season runs only from June to September. In the broiling heat of summer, locals head out to the **salt pans** east of the village and set up shanties where they'll stay for weeks. Wells are sunk to draw up the brine, much thicker and more concentrated than seawater, which is drained into shallow evaporating lagoons where the sun does the work. This is repeated several times until a thick crust of salt remains, which is raked over, collected and bagged. A single pan of 25m by 10m can yield more than 20,000 kilos of salt, and the only thing that can disturb production is rain; in 1994, an unexpected early September shower washed away 20,000 tonnes of harvestable salt.

---

tle three-aisle **mosque**, probably built during the Ayyubid renovations. The inevitable highlight, though, is the room above the gate you entered by: this was **Lawrence's room**, in a plum position to look out over the courtyard and the palms. In *Seven Pillars* he wrote:

In the evening when we had shut-to the gate, all guests would assemble ... and coffee and stories would go round until the last meal, and after it, till sleep came. On stormy nights, we brought in brushwood and dung and lit a great fire in the middle of the floor. About it would be drawn the carpets and the saddle-sheepskins, and in its light we would tell over our own battles, or hear the visitors' traditions. The leaping flames chased our smoke-ruffled shadows strangely about the rough stone wall behind us, distorting them over the hollows and projections of its broken face.

Azraq Wetlands Reserve

Spreading east of Janubi village is the **Azraq Wetlands Reserve**, a sadly depleted shadow of its former self. Before the oasis dried up (see box on p.180), this whole area of marshes and lakes, in the midst of Azraq's *qa*, or depression, was the scene of vibrant life. Well over a hundred water buffalo roamed the area, along with wild horses and small livestock. In the winter of 1967, a staggering 240,000 ducks landed here, along with 180,000 teals, 100,000 pintails, 40,000 coots, 20,000 wigeons and 2000 mallards. Insects, molluscs and hundreds of thousands of frogs thrived; there was even a particular species of fish endemic to Azraq's pools.

All this, though, is history. Today, there's little to see in the Wetlands Reserve, a grand name for what is now an area of more or less deserted reedbeds and low muddy pools. Down a side street opposite the petrol station in Janubi, past the small white mosque, you'll spot the fence around the reserve through the palms. A gate is generally open near the small pumping station on the edge of the pools; if you look down, you'll see the single pipe bringing fresh water back into the reserve – a drop in the thirsty desert. Some distance back into the reeds, there's a clearing where a visitors' centre is under construction. There's nothing to stop you wandering out as far as you like, but little to see or do.

DEATH OF AN OASIS

Before 1975, Azraq positively gushed with **water**, fed to the village from all points of the compass. Rain falling on Jebel Druze 80km or so to the north takes just a few years to filter through the basalt to Azraq: five springs, two in Shomali and three in Janubi, poured 34 million litres of water every day into Azraq's pools. In addition, a total of ten riverbeds feed into Azraq's *qa*, including the mighty Wadi Sirhan from the southeast and Wadi Rajil from the north, draining surface rainwater (entirely separate from the underground aquifers) towards Azraq. In rainy years, the entire *qa* – fifty square kilometres in the midst of a parched and burning desert – was flooded to a depth of a metre or more with sweet water.

The abundance was too tempting to resist. In September 1963, a small amount of **pumping** began from Azraq to Irbid; the oasis could replenish itself and no damage was done. But, following the 1967 war with Israel, the population of Jordan – and of Amman in particular – was swollen by hundreds of thousands of Palestinian refugees, and the national water infrastructure of the time couldn't cope. In 1975, large-scale pumping to Amman began, Azraq alone supplying a quarter of the city's water. In addition, Syria dammed the Wadi Rajil, depriving the *qa* of a third of its runoff water and severely damaging Azraq's ecosystem. To ensure that the quantity of water being pumped to Amman didn't drop, Jordan then tapped Azraq's aquifers again, deeper and this time fatally. While signing Azraq's death warrant with one hand, in 1977 Jordan signed with the other an international treaty protecting wetland habitats.

During the 1980s, Azraq gained a reputation as an attractive and fruitful place to farm: people began to move to the area and sank illegal, private **wells** to irrigate their fields. Whereas in previous years such wells needed to be only three metres or so deep, by this time drilling ten times deeper produced no water. In 1992, after just seventeen years of abuse, the fragile wetlands dried up. Seven years later, 25 million cubic metres of Azraq water is still being pumped annually to Amman – a city which, it's been claimed, loses 55 percent of its water through leaky pipes – while a further 20 million cubic metres is drawn off by local wells. Rainfall can only contribute under half of this amount, and at this rate the underground reservoirs have barely twenty more years' supply. Yet this shortfall is only one of Azraq's ticking timebombs. Normally, a natural balance in water pressure exists between the freshwater aquifers and the neighbouring salt pans. However, with the pumping, pressure has been dangerously lowered in the aquifers. **Seepage of salt** is already making creeping inroads into the freshwater supply, and is irreversible: once brackish, an aquifer stays brackish forever.

The problems of Azraq aren't going unregarded. For the last year or two, the Royal Society for the Conservation of Nature has managed to ensure that 1.5 million cubic metres of freshwater is returned to Azraq's pools in an attempt to replenish the loss. This is a start, but it's scant recompense. If things continue the way they are – which seems likely, unless politicians enforce regional water-sharing agreements – the dying oasis will be lost to the desert in a matter of years, not decades.

Shaumari Wildlife Reserve

Out on the baking desert south of Azraq, where the highest point of land for miles around – raised a bare metre or two above the dust – is the Saudi highway, you'll find **Shaumari Wildlife Reserve**, run by the RSCN (daily 8am–sunset; JD3, students 500 fils). However, before you approach the place, you should banish thoughts of embarking on dramatic safaris in a majestic wilderness: there are no breathtaking vistas here, no big game, no drama. Shaumari comprises just 22 square kilometres of the flat, bare desert and although there are some majestic animals, money for tourist development is running low, and there's not exactly a lot to do or see.

No public **transport** runs close to Shaumari: if you don't have a car, you can ask at any of the restaurants or shops in Janubi for a lift. The going rate is JD3, or more than twice that if you want someone to wait and bring you back. If you're driving, look for a sign about 7km south of Janubi pointing right; the reserve is 6km along a sometimes rough road.

Shaumari was officially designated a reserve in 1975 and selected as the reception area for returning **Arabian oryx** to the wild. Oryx had been extinct in Jordan since 1921, but a few had been saved from the wild before the last animal was shot by hunters in Oman in 1973; four years later, the World Wildlife Fund brought four oryx from San Diego Zoo to Shaumari for breeding. Unfortunately, it took six months before anyone realized they were all males; the following year four females were brought from San Diego, as well as three more from a zoo in Qatar in order to mix the genes of the herd, and the first foal was born in 1979. By 1983, there were 31 animals, and today the herd numbers 216 – too many, since the reserve was only designed for a maximum of 120. Plans are under way to release some oryx into the wild but, notwithstanding the danger from illegal hunting, the reaction of the local bedouin at having oryx mingling with their flocks of sheep and goats has yet to be assessed.

Also resident at Shaumari are **ostrich**. Wild Arabian ostrich were common in Azraq as late as the 1920s, but were also hunted to extinction. In 1986, two blue-necked ostriches were brought to Shaumari from Oklahoma Zoo, and eight of their offspring are still alive amongst Shaumari's total of seventeen blue-necked and three red-necked birds. The reserve also has a herd of ten **onagers** – a kind of wild ass – and five different species of **snake**, as well as sand rats, lizards and plenty of birdlife – kestrels, long-tailed eagles, marsh harriers and pied wheatears among others.

Just inside the gates, the kids' **Visitors' Centre** is kitted out with informational boards and models to explain the habitat and lifestyles of Shaumari's oryx, gazelle and ostrich. The reserve's dusty buildings are set amongst a small, recently planted grove of eucalyptus, which is a marvellously cool and peaceful escape from the merciless desert all around, and perfect for a shady picnic. The highlight of a visit, though, is a **"safari"** (JD20) – a 4x4 trip out into the reserve to get close to the oryx, check out any ostrich nests, and see what the desert flora looks like when not nibbled by hordes of sheep and goats. Back near the buildings is a complex of pens housing baby oryx, ostrich and gazelle, and on the edge of the trees is a ten-metre **observation tower**; the staff can lend you binoculars to search for oryx or do some eagle-spotting. The dauntingly huge and imperious adult ostriches roam around a wide area near the base of the tower.

Asaykhin

Some 15km or so north of Azraq ash-Shomali are the hilltop ruins of the Roman fort at **Asaykhin**, but they're only reachable by 4x4 with the help of a guide; you may be able to persuade someone on the staff at Shaumari to show you the way.

One of the string of fortified stations built along the road between Azraq and Bosra probably in the third century AD to protect the empire's exposed eastern frontier, Asaykhin occupies a commanding position over the desert landscape. After a rough ride east from the road (the hill is clearly visible from some distance away), and a steep scramble up to the summit, you'll find a series of small rooms built around a **courtyard**, with a **gatehouse** and some arched ceiling supports still standing in places. The **views** more than make up for the rather underwhelming ruins.

However, the real reason for embarking on a 4x4 trek out here is to be able to wander on foot in the extraordinary natural art gallery of the rugged basalt desert to the east of the hill. It seems as if almost every other boulder and rock here features some kind of prehistoric inscription or drawing, most of which are probably at least 10,000 years old: in this once-lush land, anonymous shepherds and farmers from past eras drew stylized people, camels and other animals, geometric patterns and random unknown markings on the only canvas they had available – basalt.

West from Azraq to Amman

Only completed in 1985, the major features of the **highway from Azraq to Amman** are that it's fast, more or less straight, and runs right past two of the best archeological sites in Jordan, **Qusayr Amra** and **Qasr Hraneh**. There's nothing else to detain you along this stretch – no public transport, no towns, no petrol stations; only the desert. For advice on getting to Amra and Hraneh from Azraq, see p.177; both sites have guardians who can help out if you run out of water. The huge and ruined **Qasr Mushatta**, although next to Queen Alia airport south of Amman, is impossible to reach by bus, and is best visited as an adjunct to a driving tour of the eastern desert circuit (see p.164). If you happen to be hitching the circuit anti-clockwise, you could start from **Muwaggar**, served by a bus from Raghadan station. You might find something simple to **eat** or **drink** in Muwaggar, but don't rely on it – if you're hitching, you'd do well to bring sustenance with you.

Qusayr Amra

If you're not ready for it, you might easily miss the squat shape of **Qusayr Amra** down in the low Wadi Butm just to the north of the highway. A small bath-house, Amra was built to capitalize on the waters of the wadi, named after the *butm* (wild pistachio) trees which formerly grew here in abundance and which in springtime still form a ribbon of fertility winding through the desert, now arbitrarily cleft by the highway. A short walk in the wadi-bed beyond Amra can transport you within minutes into total silence among the trees. However, what makes Amra unmissable is neither its natural environment nor the building itself, but the extensive **frescoes** covering every centimetre of the interior walls. Joyously human, vivid and detailed, they were painted as a celebration of the good things in life. Recently restored, they're in good condition, and you could easily spend an hour or more enjoying them.

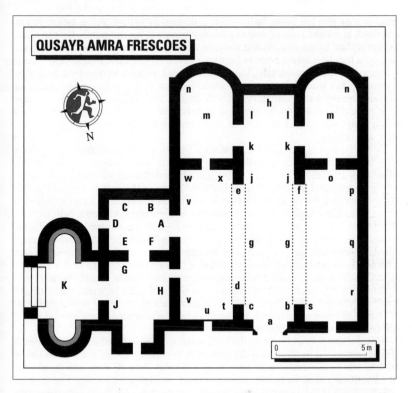

QUSAYR AMRA FRESCOES

Some history

Amra was probably built between 711 and 715 by the **Umayyad** caliph **Walid I**. In the few years before, Walid and his predecessors had overseen the construction of the Great Mosque in their capital Damascus and the majestic Dome of the Rock in Jerusalem, and were firmly established as the new defenders of the new Islamic orthodoxy. But a hard-pressed caliph needs some time to relax. Down in the desert, far from prying eyes in Damascus, Amra was where the Umayyad establishment came to let its hair down. In a hugely entertaining counterpoint to the gorgeous mosaics of the Great Mosque, which depict a heavenly paradise for the faithful, the apparently solemn and learned Umayyads instead had Amra's walls painted with an earthly paradise of luscious fruits and vines, naked women, cupids, musicians, hunters and the kings of the lands they'd just conquered. The first Islamic edict ordering the destruction of images came from one of Walid's successors, when Amra's frescoes were just five years old, but for some reason they were overlooked and have managed to survive 1300 years of fire and graffiti.

The frescoes

As you approach the building, what you see first is the water supply system – a cistern, a deep well and the *saqiya*, or turning circle (an ox or a donkey went round and round this circle to draw water up from the well). The main door opens southwards into the **main hall**, which is divided into three aisles; facing you at the back is a small suite of rooms probably reserved for the caliph. On the sides of the arches facing you, setting the tone of the place, are a topless woman holding up a fish [e – letters refer to locations keyed on our map] and a nude female dancer welcoming visitors[f]. Above the entrance is [a] a woman on a bed, with figures by her side, [b] a pensive woman reclining with a winged angel and [c] a female flautist, a male lute-player and a dancer, with [d] another nude woman. The central aisle that you're standing in mostly has [g] real or fantasized scenes from **court life**: aside from women, there are horsemen, archers and people sitting and talking.

At the far end of the right-hand (west) aisle, [o] a woman reclines on a golden couch beneath an awning, with a male attendant and a woman seated on the ground nearby; at the head of the couch is a **bearded man** who pops up in many of the murals and who might have been in charge of the bath-house. Above the figures are two peacocks and a Greek inscription referring to victory. Below is what looks like a walled city, and below that, a decorative geometric pattern runs at eye level around the room. Near the corner – and unfortunately very difficult to make out – are [p] **six kings**, all conquered by Walid: the Byzantine emperor, the last Visigothic king of Spain, the Persian emperor, the king of Abyssinia and two others, now obscured (the king of India, the emperor of China or the Turkish khan). Next to them is [q] a large and strikingly clear **nude female bather**, surrounded by onlookers, one of whom is the bearded man; he's also watching [r] male gymnastics. Above, wild asses, their ears pricked, are being driven into nets. Much of the rest is damaged, but round near the entrance, there are [s] some grapes and fragments showing curled toes.

If you move into the suite at the back – sometimes called the **throne room** – you'll first see [j] leopards and [k] fruit trees decorating the side walls. On either side of where the throne would probably have stood are [l] male and female figures with very clear faces, one, very pregnant, representing fertility. Dominating the back wall is [h] a **seated king**, possibly Walid; two attendants with fans or fly whisks keep him happy and there's a frieze of partridges around his head. On either side are presumably royal withdrawing rooms, with [m] mosaic floors and [n] murals of fat grapes, giant pomegranates, acanthus leaves and peaches or heart-shaped fruit.

Back in the main hall, the east aisle is mostly devoted to male pursuits. Starting near the entrance there's [t] a huge leaf design next to [u] **hunters** killing and disembowelling asses inside huge nets. The whole of the east wall is devoted to [v] a long hunting scene of saluki hounds chasing and capturing asses. At the far end are [w] the muses of History and Philosophy, alongside [x] Poetry. Dominating the aisle, though, are a series of very clear everyday scenes overhead depicting metalworkers, carpenters, blacksmiths, hodcarriers and jolly working camels.

The door in the east wall leads into the **baths**, which have a different style of decoration, probably the work of a different artist. The first room you come to is thought to have been a changing room (*apodyterium*) or a cool room (*frigidarium*); whichever it is, it was originally floored in marble and had benches on two sides. Above the door is [A] a luxuriantly reclining woman, gazed on by a stubbled admirer and a cupid. The south wall has a sequence of little figures in a diamond pattern, including [B] a monkey applauding [C] a bear playing the lute. Opposite the door is [D] a woman with a very Sixties hairdo; next to her are [E] a flautist and [F] a female dancer. On the ceiling overhead, blackened by smoke, is a fabulous sequence showing **the three ages of man**, with the very penetrating gaze of the same man in his twenties, forties and sixties. Next door is a *tepidarium*, with a plunge pool and a hypocaust system to allow warm air to circulate beneath the floor and up flues in the wall. Beside the door is [G] a tableau of three nude women, one of them holding a child; if you follow the picture round to the right, [H] a woman is pouring water and [J] is about to bathe the child.

The last room, a domed **steam room**, or *caldarium*, is next to the furnace; the holes in the wall all around supported marble wall slabs, and there are a couple of plunge pools. Above is [K] one of the earliest representations of the **sky** on a domed surface, although the constellations have been transposed: it seems like the artist copied them from a globe, where the sky is depicted from the "outside" looking down, rather than from a map of the sky, where the sky is seen from the Earth's surface looking up. Dead ahead you can easily identify Sagittarius, the centaur, with the tail of Scorpio to the left. Ophiucus the serpent-holder is above Scorpio and below an upside-down, club-wielding Hercules. From Scorpio, follow the red band left to Gemini, the twins, and Orion. The whole map is centred on the North Star; just to the left of it is the Great Bear. Above and at right angles is the Little Bear, and twisting between the two is Draco, the snake. Just to the right, Cepheus is shrugging his shoulders, next to Andromeda with outspread arms. Cygnus the swan is just by Andromeda's left hand.

Qasr Hraneh and beyond

Of all the inns, bath-houses and forts in the eastern desert, **QASR HRANEH** (often signposted in English as "Kharaneh" or "Kharana") was probably the one which gave rise to the misnomer "Desert Castles". Standing foursquare to the south of the highway – and visible for miles around – Hraneh looks like a fortress built for wholly defensive purposes, with round corner towers, arrow slits in the wall and a single, defendable entrance. However, at closer examination, you'll find that Hraneh's towers are solid – and thus unmannable – and that only three-metre giants with triple-length arms could fire anything out of the arrow slits. Rather, it seems most likely that Hraneh – positioned at the meeting-point of many desert tracks – was a kind of country **conference centre**, occasionally used by the Umayyad rulers of the day as a comfortable and accessible place to meet with local bedouin leaders, or even as a place where the bedouin themselves could meet on neutral ground to iron out tribal differences. The theory that Hraneh was a continually occupied inn or caravanserai is thrown into doubt by the fact that it only lies near – not on – a major trade route and that it has no obvious cisterns or forms of water storage to support passing caravans. Although the date of construction is unclear, the late seventh century seems most likely; a few lines of graffiti in an upper room were written on November 24, 710.

The qasr

Marvellously cool and perfectly still inside, the *qasr* is one of the most atmospheric and beautiful ancient buildings in Jordan. You could easily soak up the peace and quiet for a couple of hours or more.

Walking around the building to reach the entrance, the first thing you'll notice is the distinctive band of diagonal bricks up near the top of the walls, a decorative device still in use on garden walls all over Jordan today. If the guardian doesn't meet you to unlock the gate, he's probably relaxing in the small concrete hut about 200m away to one side. As you enter the *qasr*, to left and right are long, dark rooms probably used as stables. The **courtyard** is surprisingly small, and it's here you realize how deceptive the solid exterior is: the whole building is only 35m square, but its doughty towers and soaring entrance make it seem much bigger. An arched **portico** originally ran round the courtyard, providing shade below and a corridor above – when it was in place, virtually no direct sun could penetrate into the interior. All the rooms round the courtyard, including those upstairs, are divided into self-contained units, each called a *bayt*, comprising a large central room with many smaller rooms opening off it. This is typically Umayyad, and the same system was used in the palace at Amman, as well as at Mushatta and Tuba. Weaving in and out, you can explore your way around the deliciously musty and cool ground floor to get a sense of how the maze-like *bayt* system works. Presumably each *bayt* held a single delegation – the central, well-lit room used for meetings or socializing, the flanking, darker rooms for sleeping or storage. Hraneh had space for a total of eight delegations and their horses.

Of the two staircases, the left-hand one as you came in delivers you to the more interesting **upper western rooms**; at the top of the stairs, it's easy to see the springs of the portico arches below. The room immediately to your left upstairs is lined with **rosettes** very similar to those lying around in the rubble at Hallabat. Next door, an extremely ornate room holds the few lines of eighth-century **graffiti** which help to date the *qasr* (as well as many more modern examples). In black painted Kufic script in the far left-hand corner above a doorway, they say, simply enough, "Abd al-Malik the son of Ubayd wrote it on Monday three days from Muharram of the year 92". All around are graceful and elegant blind arcades and friezes of rosettes, with the semi-domed ceiling supported on squinches. The **northern bayts**, which are open to the sky, give onto the large **east room**, with a simple hound's-tooth design also used in the palace at Amman (you might also be lucky and spot the family of white owls which lives here). From the southeast corner there's a nice view along the whole width of the *qasr* through alternately lit and dark areas, and it's now clear that the so-called arrow slits couldn't be anything but thin windows to give ventilation and indirect light. The **southern room**, with a row of little arched windows over the courtyard, isn't part of a *bayt* and has the only large window, looking out above the entrance: this was either a watch-post or possibly a public reception area. One of the small, dark rooms on the south wall has a unique **cross-vaulted ceiling**, with decorated squares and diamonds not found elsewhere. Take the stairs up again to the **roof** to watch the dustdevils spinning across the flat, stony plain and to wonder in passing what on earth possessed the Jordanian government to build a major new highway, an electricity plant and a huge broadcasting station all within metres of a beautiful ancient monument – as if pressed for space in the desert.

West of Hraneh

Some 38km beyond Hraneh on the highway towards Amman – after a rather alarming stretch where the road widens out and has runway markings on it (to be used in an emergency if Queen Alia Airport is out of action) – you'll pass the small village of **MUWAGGAR** sitting on top of a hill. As you approach the village, on the left is a huge Umayyad reservoir, dating from the early 720s and still in use today; a ten-metre column, the capital of which is now in the Amman archeological museum, formerly stood in the reservoir to mark the water level. About 700m further, a sign points the way right to the tiny, ruined **Qasr Mushash**, 24km into the desert by 4x4 and truthfully not worth the effort. Sahab, a southern suburb of Amman and the end of the highway, is 17km beyond Muwaggar.

Qasr Mushatta

The largest of all the "Desert Castles", **Qasr Mushatta** (Arabic for "Winter Palace") may be the last thing you ever see in Jordan, or it may be the first: the high-arched palace lies just beyond the north runway of Queen Alia Airport and is clearly visible on both takeoff and landing. The howl of nearby jet engines does tend to detract from a visit, but you may be lucky and arrive in a lull in air traffic. The guardian, if you need him, lives in a hut at the back of the site.

Mushatta dates from later than both Hraneh and Hallabat – probably the 740s – and is moderately well preserved, although it was never finished. The site is enclosed by a square wall 144m along each side, with collapsed towers all round and portions of amazingly intricate classical-style **carving** surviving on the exterior. Similar pieces at one time covered all of the exterior, but as a sop to Kaiser Wilhelm of Germany before World War I, the Ottoman sultan Abdul Hamid II had most of them stripped off and presented to the Pergamon Museum in Berlin where they still lie. The whole site is littered with unfinished work, capitals and column drums; along with the carving, everything hints at a splendour of design and execution that was never fully realized.

As you walk in, remnants of a **mosque** lie to the right, its *mihrab* set into the external wall. The palace buildings themselves are massive, built of very unusual burnt brick above a stone base. The tripled-arched **entrance hall** has a colonnade of beautiful swirling greenish marble columns which are still standing, very striking against the reddish brick; ahead is the huge triple-apsed **reception hall**. All around are *bayt*s, some of which still have their high, barrel-vaulted ceilings in place; if you decide to explore, tread loudly and heavily to warn the resident snakes of your presence. Behind the impressive arched *iwan*s, at the back of the hall on both sides, ancient **toilets** stick out of the wall, complete with runoff drain.

Practicalities

The simplest way to reach **Mushatta** is to drive: follow signs to the airport and, just past the *Alia Gateway* hotel, there's a roundabout with a tiny sign pointing right. This is the perimeter road, and you must drive 11km around three sides of a square to reach the *qasr*. You'll have to go through several checkpoints, one of which will hold onto your **passport** until you return. If you have no transport, you might try taking an Airport Express bus from Abdali or Raghadan stations in Amman to the *Alia Gateway* and hitching from there, but the perimeter road is long and quiet. Otherwise, a taxi from the airport terminal would probably oblige at a price. Airport security won't let you walk the couple of kilometres from the terminal buildings.

travel details

No timetables are in operation – most buses, and all minibuses and *services* simply depart when they're full.

Buses and minibuses

Azraq to: Zerqa (Old station; 1hr 20min).

Dayr al-Kahf to: Mafraq (Bedouin station; 1hr).

Hallabat to: Zerqa (Old station; 40min).

Khirbet as-Samra to: Zerqa (Old station; 30min).

Mafraq (Bedouin station) to: Amman (Abdali station; 1hr); Dayr al-Kahf (1hr); Ruwayshid (2hr 30min); Safawi (1hr 15min); Umm al-Jimal (30min); Zerqa (Old station; 30min).

Mafraq (Fellahin station) to: Irbid (New Amman station; 45min); Jerash (40min); Ramtha (30min).

Muwaggar to: Amman (Raghadan station; 30min).

Ruwayshid to: Mafraq (Bedouin station; 2hr 30min); Safawi (1hr 15min).

Safawi to: Mafraq (Bedouin station; 1hr 15min); Ruwayshid (1hr 15min).

Umm al-Jimal to: Mafraq (Bedouin station; 30min).

Zerqa (New station) to: Amman (Abdali station; 35min); Amman (Raghadan station; 25min); Karak (2hr 30min); Madaba (1hr); Salt (45min).

Zerqa (Old station) to: Ajloun (1hr 20min); Azraq (1hr 20min); Hallabat (40min); Irbid (New Amman station; 1hr); Jerash (45min); Khirbet as-Samra (30min); Mafraq (Bedouin station; 30min).

International buses

Mafraq (Fellahin station) to: Damascus (2hr 30min); Dera'a (1hr 20min).

CHAPTER FOUR

THE KING'S HIGHWAY

A long, meandering squiggle of a road running through some of Jordan's loveliest countryside, the **King's Highway** – the grandiose translation of an old Hebrew term which probably only meant "main road" – has been the route of north–south trade through Transjordan and the scene of battles since prehistoric times. **Moses** was refused permission to travel on the King's Highway by the king of Edom, and later, the **Nabateans**, from their power base in **Petra**, used the highway to trade luxury goods between Arabia and Syria (although located on the highway, Petra is important enough to merit its own chapter, starting on p.225). When the Romans annexed the Nabatean kingdom, Emperor **Trajan** renovated the ancient road to facilitate travel and communications between his regional capital at Bosra, northeast of Mafraq, and Aqaba on the Red Sea coast. Early Christian pilgrims visited a number of sites on and off the road around **Madaba**, whose beautiful Byzantine mosaics still merit a pilgrimage today. The **Crusaders** used the highway as the linchpin of their Kingdom of Oultrejourdain, fortifying positions along the road at **Karak** and **Shawbak** – where extensive remains of castles survive – and also at Petra and Aqaba. However, with the development by the **Ottomans** of the faster and more direct *Darb al-Hajj* (Pilgrimage Route), from Damascus to the Holy Places through the desert further east – and the subsequent construction both of the Hejaz Railway and the modern Desert Highway along the same route – the King's Highway faded in importance. Only tarmacked along its entire length in the 1950s and 1960s, today it is a simple road, often rutted and narrow, which meticulously follows the contours of the rolling hills above the Dead Sea rift. Linking a series of springs, and also following the line of maximum hilltop rainfall, the road runs through intensively cultivated farmland, and travelling on it today – although not easy – can both give you a glimpse of the reality of rural life for many Jordanians,

HOTEL PRICE CODES

Throughout this guide, hotels have been categorized according to the **price codes** given below, which indicate the normal price for the **cheapest double room** in a particular establishment during the **high season** (excluding the ten-percent tax and ten-percent service charge levied in all hotels of ③ and above). **Single rooms** can cost anything between seventy and a hundred percent of the double-room rates. Where a hotel offers beds in **shared rooms**, the price per person to share has been given; if a price code has also been included, this indicates that private rooms are also available. For a fuller explanation, see p.39.

① under JD10	④ JD30–40	⑦ JD65–80
② JD10–20	⑤ JD40–50	⑧ JD80–95
③ JD20–30	⑥ JD50–65	⑨ over JD95

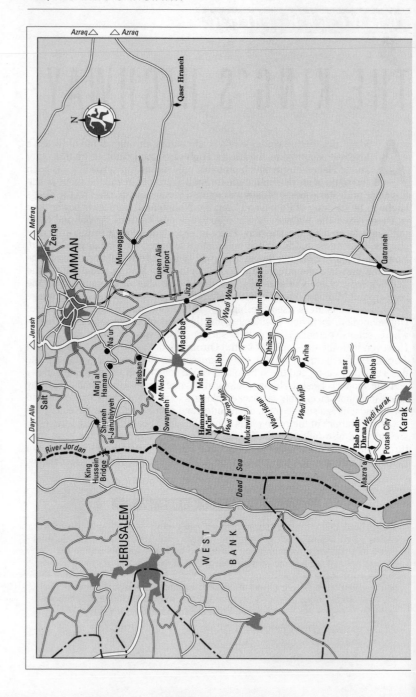

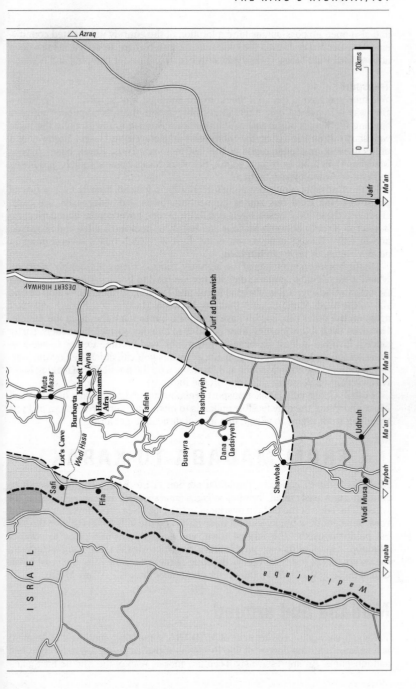

and also open up possibilities for exploration of the entirely untouristed country-side. One particular draw is the spectacular **Dana Nature Reserve**, set in a deep and isolated wadi below Qadsiyyeh, with good facilities for camping and hiking.

Transport

Whether you have a day or a week, by far the best way to travel on the King's Highway is by **rental car**, since, incredibly enough, there is no public transport running the length of the road. All buses from Amman to towns along the high-way start out on the faster, but thoroughly unpicturesque Desert Highway and only cut west on feeder roads at the last moment. Thus, Karak buses bypass Madaba, Tafileh buses bypass Karak, Shawbak buses bypass Tafileh, and buses to Petra or Aqaba bypass them all.

Public transport along the King's Highway is instead limited to a series of **point-to-point** local bus routes connecting towns and villages on the road. However, these local buses often don't run across governorate boundaries: no buses run directly between Madaba and Karak, or between Tafileh and Shawbak, and to make these journeys, you either have to switch buses several times in small villages, or resort to **hitching**.

On the northern stretches of the highway, transport runs reasonably frequent-ly and at manageable times of day: it's not too hard to hop a series of buses from Amman to Qadsiyyeh (via Madaba, Karak and Tafileh), although they stop on one rim of the Wadi Mujib canyon (halfway between Madaba and Karak) and start again on the other rim, so you have no choice but to hitch the bit in the middle. However, even if this journey were possible in one day – which is unlikely, partly since it involves at least six buses – you would have no time to stop to see any-thing on the way. **Overnighting** in Karak means you can at least enjoy the jour-ney; additional nights in Madaba and Dana open up the possibility of making high-ly rewarding exploratory side trips off the highway.

South of Qadsiyyeh, public transport is almost non-existent. From here to Wadi Musa and Petra, the only feasible option is to hitch, but there are enough pickups trundling from village to village that it's not difficult to get a ride.

FROM MADABA TO KARAK

Much as it did in antiquity, the initial portion of the King's Highway south of Amman runs past small farming villages interspersed among wide plains of wheat. The edge of the plateau overlooking the Dead Sea rift is never far from the road, and countless tracks lead off westwards into the hills teetering over the low-est point on earth. The largest town, and only worthwhile place to stay, is **Madaba**, capital of its own governorate. South of Madaba, the King's Highway meanders through several valleys draining rainwater off the hills; the most beau-tiful of these is **Wadi Wala**, the deepest and most dramatic, **Wadi Mujib**.

Madaba and around

The small, easy-going market town of **MADABA**, some 30km southwest of Amman, is best known for the dozens of fine Byzantine **mosaics** preserved in its churches and museums. An impressive sixth-century mosaic map of the Middle East takes

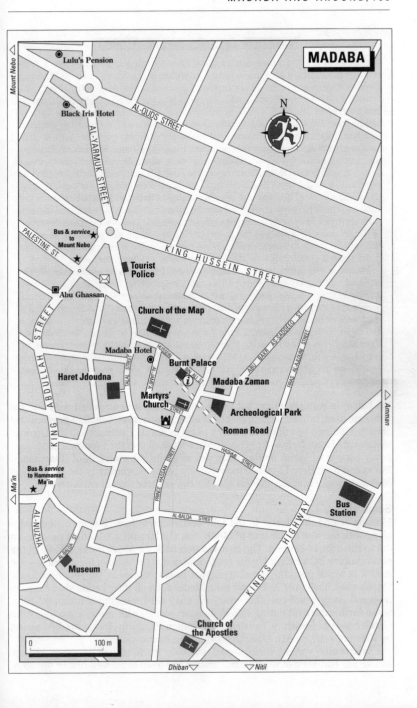

MADABA

N

Mount Nebo

Lulu's Pension

Black Iris Hotel

AL-QUDS STREET

AL-YARMUK STREET

PALESTINE ST

Bus & *service* to Mount Nebo

KING HUSSEIN STREET

Tourist Police

Abu Ghassan

ABDULLAH STREET

Church of the Map

Madaba Hotel

HUSSEIN STREET

TALAL STREET

AL-AMEA

Burnt Palace

Haret Jdoudna

Madaba Zaman

ABU BAKR AS-SADDEHO ST

RAS AL-AIOUN STREET

Martyrs' Church

STREET

Archeological Park

Roman Road

KING

HASHMI STREET

Bus & *service* to Hammamat Ma'in

PRINCE HASSAN STREET

Ma'in

AL-NUZHA ST

ALBALQA ST

AL-BALQA STREET

Bus Station

KING'S HIGHWAY

Amman

Museum

Church of the Apostles

0   100 m

Dhiban   Nitil

THE MOSAICS OF JORDAN

Hundreds of floor-laid **mosaics** in stone have survived in Jordan, from a first-century BC example at Herod's palace at Mukawir (now on display in Madaba) through to pieces from the eighth century AD, when Christian mosaicists were still at work under the Muslim caliphate. Specific styles were used for places of worship and for civilian buildings, whether public baths, private mansions or the palaces and hunting lodges of the Umayyads. During the reign of the Byzantine emperor Justinian, for example, a retro taste for classical motifs was popular: many secular buildings were decorated with scenes taken from **Greek and Roman mythology**, with the Jordanian mosaicists tending to work in small, demarcated panels rather than composing one tableau across an entire floor. Churches, of course, couldn't be decorated with the same pagan designs, but in addition to dedicatory inscriptions recording names of bishops and benefactors, and **Christian symbols** such as the lamb and the fish, classical-style **personifications** of the sea, the earth and the seasons appeared on church floors throughout Jordan. These church mosaics served to dazzle and awe visitors to the house of God and, in an age of almost universal illiteracy, to teach the events of the Bible pictorially; the many representations of buildings and great cities may also have served as a rudimentary atlas.

Mosaic artists throughout the empire worked from **pattern-books** compiled in regional cultural centres, above all Constantinople. One result of this common artistic heritage is the predominance of **pastoral** scenes – which, in provincial backwaters such as Transjordan, also represented the reality of daily agricultural life for many people. The regularly recurring watery vignettes of ducks, boats and fish were rooted in a classical taste for representations of life on the **Nile**, and **hunting** scenes, often featuring lions, leopards and other extraordinary creatures, grew out of the Roman practice of capturing wild beasts for amphitheatre sports. In addition, Jordanian mosaicists portrayed in detail a whole encyclopedia of **flora**

top billing in package tours, but the town's narrow streets, dotted with fine old Ottoman stone houses, lead to plenty of other, much more beautiful mosaics that are often ignored by visitors in a hurry to get to Karak. Excursions to the fabulous mosaics at **Mount Nebo** – from where Moses looked over the Promised Land – and newly uncovered **Umm ar-Rasas**, as well as to the hot waterfalls of **Hammamat Ma'in** and King Herod's ruined mountain-top palace perched over the Dead Sea at **Mukawir**, make Madaba an ideal base for two or three days of exploration.

Some history

Madaba is first mentioned in the Old Testament as having been conquered – along with the rest of the land of **Moab** – by the Israelites, who then parcelled it out to the tribe of Reuben. The city was won back for Moab in the middle of the ninth century BC by King Mesha (as proclaimed in the famous Mesha Stele – see p.208), at which point the Israelite prophet Isaiah stepped in, prophesying doom: "Moab shall howl over Nebo and over Medeba: on all their heads shall be baldness and every beard cut off … everyone shall howl, weeping abundantly." After some further turmoil during the Hellenistic period, with the city passing from Greek hands to Jewish to Nabatean, the Roman *Provincia Arabia* brought order; by the third century AD, Madaba was minting its own coins.

Christianity spread rapidly, and by 451, Madaba had its own bishop. Mosaicists had been at work in and around the town since well before the 390s,

and fauna, drawn from local experience, the tales of travellers (elephants, croco-diles and octopus), and the realms of imagination (sea monsters and phoenixes).

However, the controversy concerning the **depiction of people** which raged across Byzantium and Transjordan – then already in the control of the Muslim armies – in the eighth and ninth centuries led to many mosaics being disfigured. What was under attack, from **iconoclasts** both Byzantine and Umayyad, was, at heart, polytheism. For centuries, Christians in the East had been venerating reli-gious images in paint, stone and mosaic in a way that more ascetic elements in the Byzantine hierarchy considered too close for comfort to antique paganism. In 726 Emperor Leo III banned the use of icons in worship throughout his empire. In Transjordan, though, with the Umayyads in control, what had as much practical impact was a parallel movement within Islam. The Prophet Muhammad is report-ed to have taught that God is the only creator; interpreting this to imply that human "creation" of images of living creatures was blasphemous, the Umayyad caliph Yazid II (719–24) issued a directive to destroy all depictions of people – and, by extension, animals – throughout the Muslim empire. With unequivocal orders from the highest religious and civil authorities, Transjordan's mosaicists had no choice but to set to work to obliterate with blank stones all images of people and animals in existing mosaics, sometimes with care, often in a panic: many of Jordan's mosaics today feature only surreal clouds of haze hanging over what were once portraits. Some mosaics survived unscathed by having been buried in earlier years; others, laid after the order was given, avoided the issue by remaining stu-diously abstract. After 120 years of bitter controversy, the Christian ban was rescinded, but the Muslim injunction remained and still applies today.

As a footnote to Jordan's mosaic heritage, thousands of glass mosaic tiles have been uncovered in churches everywhere from Jerash to Madaba, testifying to the former existence of large and lavish wall mosaics in **coloured glass**, the glory of which can only be imagined.

---

but mosaic art really began to flourish in Madaba during the reign of Emperor Justinian (527–65). Towards the end of that century, Bishop Sergius oversaw a golden age of artistic accomplishment: surviving mosaics from the Cathedral (576), the Church of the Apostles (578), the Church of Bishop Sergius at Umm ar-Rasas (587), Madaba's Crypt of St Elianos and Church of the Virgin (both 595) and the Moses Memorial Church on Mount Nebo (597) – as well as, conceivably, the famed mosaic map of the Holy Land – all date from his period in office. When the **Persian** armies came through in 614, closely followed by the **Muslims**, Madaba surrendered without a fight and so retained its Christian identity and population; churches were still being built and mosaics laid for another hundred years or more. A mosaic discovered at Umm ar-Rasas mentions a bishop of Madaba as late as 785.

Madaba was abandoned during the **Mamluke** period and its ruins – by then strewn over a huge artificial mound, or *tell* – lay untouched for centuries. In 1879, conflict between Christian and Muslim tribes in Karak led to ninety Catholic and Orthodox families going into voluntary exile; they arrived at Madaba's uninhab-ited *tell* shortly after, laid claim to the surrounding land and began to farm. The **Ottoman** authorities in Damascus rubber-stamped the *fait accompli* but gave the settlers permission to build new churches only on the sites of previously existing ones. It was in 1884, during clearance work for a new church, that Madaba's fab-ulous **mosaic map of the Holy Land** was uncovered, closely followed by many more mosaics which lay in churches and houses all over the town. Scholars and archeologists arrived from all over the world to excavate in Madaba, and this continuous process still regularly uncovers mosaics and remnants of the past beneath the streets of the modern town centre.

Arrival, information and accommodation

Buses from Amman, Dhiban and elsewhere (there are no buses from Karak) arrive at the **bus station**, situated on the King's Highway about ten minutes' walk to the east of the town centre. The **tourist office** (daily except Fri 8am–5pm; ☎08/543376) is on Hussein bin Ali Street, in the same complex as the Burnt Palace, with free maps and helpful staff. The Arab Bank in the centre of town can change cash, travellers' cheques and give Visa cash advances; its ATM accepts foreign Visa and Plus cards. Opposite is the main **post office** (Mon–Thurs, Sat & Sun 7.30am–5pm, Fri 7.30am–1.30pm); you can make laborious international **phone calls** from here, but much easier *Alo* cardphones are all over the centre of town. The **tourist police** are generally always on duty outside St George's Church, and they also have an office about 100m north (☎08/541901; in emergency, dial ☎191).

Madaba currently has just three **hotels**, none of them strictly budget accommodation; all, though, have goodish breakfasts included in the room prices. The best is the cosy *Lulu's Pension* (☎08/543678, fax 547617; ②–③), a ten-minute walk north of the centre – look for the "JOLIFT" sign – with comfortable rooms, some en suite, plus a communal TV lounge and kitchen. Round the corner, the *Black Iris* (☎08/541959; ③) has spotlessly clean, spacious en-suite twins and doubles. The spartan *Madaba Hotel* (☎08/540643, fax 544367; ②), plum in the heart of town, offers plain rooms and shared bathrooms. You can **camp** in *Lulu's* garden for JD5 or so.

The Church of the Map

Madaba's prime attraction is a fabulous Byzantine **mosaic map** of the Holy Land, housed in the modern **St George's Church** (Mon–Thurs & Sat 8.30am–6pm, Fri & Sun 10.30am–6pm; JD1). Although hyped a little excessively – and thus suffering from well over a thousand whistle-stop visitors a day in the high season – the map is well worth seeing, notwithstanding the cramped space inside the church itself and the constant, echoing explications of tour guides.

THE MIRACLE OF THE BLUE HAND

St George's is the focus of Madaba's **Greek Orthodox** community, and services are held there every week, with carpets laid over the precious mosaic to protect it. One Sunday morning in 1976, during Mass, worshippers passed in front of one of the church's many icons as normal, looking at it and touching it. Later in the service, someone chanced to look at the icon again – a picture of the Virgin and Child, which had been in full public view for years – and noticed that it had suddenly "grown" a third, **blue hand**, unseen by the full congregation an hour or so before. No one had an explanation, and it was declared to be a miracle – the Virgin showing Madaba a helping hand. The celebrated icon, still with its blue hand, is now behind glass in the crypt; any one of the church guardians can take you down to see it and hear more of the story.

Although there is no evidence of a date of composition, or the identity of the artist, the map was undoubtedly laid some time in the second half of the sixth century, in a Byzantine church that stood on the same site as the modern one but was possibly much larger; two of the original columns survive outside in the churchyard. The map's size and style both mark it out as special. What survives today are just fragments of the original, which comprised over two million stones, measured an enormous 15.6m long by 6m wide and depicted virtually the entire Levant, from Lebanon in the north to the Nile Delta in the south and the Mediterranean coast to the open desert east of Karak. Other, simpler, mosaic renderings of cities and towns – and even mosaic maps – have been uncovered around the Mediterranean, but the Madaba map is unique in depicting the larger towns and cities with an oblique perspective, as if high above the city to the west: what you see of Jerusalem, Karak, Gaza and Nablus is the outside of the western city wall and the inside of the eastern one, with buildings inside shown accurately in 3D-style, as if the mosaicist intended to produce a city plan. Indeed, the whole, novel purpose of laying a map on the floor of the church may have been – in addition to glorifying God's works in the lands of the Bible – to better direct pilgrims to sites of biblical significance. Although there are some inaccuracies, the mapmaker has reproduced settlements and geographical features very precisely and, even by today's standards, the work is mostly cartographically correct.

Jerusalem

The map is oriented to the east, its front edge being the Mediterranean coast with north lying to the left. What you come to first, as you walk up the aisle of the church, is **Jerusalem**, the "centre of the world" and the map's largest city, oval-shaped and labelled in red Η ΑΓΙΑ ΠΟΛΙC ΙΕΡΟΥCΑ[ΛΗΜ] (The Holy City of Jerusalem). The six Byzantine gates of the city are shown in their exact locations and all survive to this day. At the northern edge of the city, marked by a tall column, is the Damascus Gate (in Arabic *Bab al-Amud*, or Gate of the Column); the long, colonnaded *cardo maximus* runs from here due south to the Zion Gate. In order to show detail within the city as accurately as possible, the mosaicist opened up the street, turning the western colonnade upside down. A second, parallel street runs from Damascus Gate under an arch – still present today – to the Dung Gate, almost indiscernible in the jumble of detail at the southern end of the city. A short street branches off to St Stephen's Gate in the eastern wall, next to which lies the Golden Gate. In the western wall of the city, the only breach is for the Jaffa Gate, from which the *decumanus* (today's David Street) runs east to join the *cardo*, with a dog-leg hooking south behind the Citadel. Of Jerusalem's many churches, the biggest is the Church of the Holy Sepulchre, a centrally located complex of buildings topped with a red roof and the Dome of the Resurrection. At the southern end of the *cardo* is the New Church of the Mother of God, with a double yellow doorway; this was consecrated on November 20, 542, which helps in dating the Madaba map. In the southwest corner of the city looms the huge basilica on Mount Zion, also with a double yellow doorway. Outside the walls to the southeast, a large patch of damage obscures everything up to the Dead Sea, but the four letters ΓΗΘC (GETHS) indicate the garden of **Gethsemane**.

The rest of Palestine

To the north of Jerusalem, the whole of the area outside the Damascus Gate is crammed with text identifying myriad biblical sites, including the portion of land allotted to the tribe of Benjamin following the Israelites' conquest of Canaan. A badly charred section conceals **Nablus**, identified as ΝΕΑΠΟΛΙC (Neapolis), seemingly as far north as the map shows; however, an isolated fragment between the pews against the left-hand wall of the church shows a patch of modern-day Lebanon, giving an idea of the full extent of the original map. To the east of Nablus, between the high ground and the sinuous curves of the River Jordan, lies **Jericho** (IEPIXW), shown face-on surrounded by palm trees. Nearby, exactly at the location of today's King Hussein Bridge, a small watchtower guards a ferry crossing, the boats hauled across the river by rope. A fish unknowingly swims downriver to a salty death in the Dead Sea, while another tries frantically to swim against the current. On the east bank, a gazelle is fleeing from a lion (obliterated in antiquity), showing the presence of considerably wilder wildlife in the Jordan Valley than survives today.

West of Jerusalem are crowded more place names and biblical references, including, outside the southwestern corner of the city, the "field of blood" (AKEΛ ΔAMA), bought with Judas Iscariot's thirty pieces of silver (Matthew 27). The nearest major town is the unwalled Lod (ΛWΔ); just below, in large red letters, is marked the allocation of land to the tribe of Dan ([KΛH]POC ΔAN). Below, and to the left of the patch of damage, is a tiny red-domed building, with the Mediterranean Sea beyond; this was one of the possible locations for **Jonah**'s being thrown up onto dry land out of the belly of the whale – TO TY ΑΓΙΥ ΙWΝΑ (The [sanctuary] of St Jonah). To the south, beyond the damaged area, lies **Ashdod** harbour, identified as AZWTOC ΠAPAΛO[C], with Ashdod town (ACΔW[Δ]) further inland.

To the south of Jerusalem, on the edge of the surviving mosaic, lies **Bethlehem** (BHΘΛEEM), shown surprisingly small compared to less important towns; the mosaicist chose only to show the Church of the Nativity, isolated on a circular plain. Due south is the land of Judah (IOYΔA). Hard up against the pillar of the church is the sacred tree of Abraham (Genesis 18), identified as H ΔPYC MAM[BPH] (The oak of Mambre); the small church just south of it lies over the Cave of the Makhpelah near **Hebron**. An isolated fragment of mosaic preserves part of the town of Ashkelon (ACKAΛW[N]) to the west.

The Dead Sea, Transjordan and the Nile

Central in the surviving fragments of the mosaic is the long, sausage-shaped **Dead Sea**, with shipping indicating trade links in antiquity. Of the two boats, the left one is being rowed (its sail is furled) with a cargo of what seems to be salt. The right one has an open sail and a yellowish cargo, which might be wheat. The detail of both crews, though, has been obliterated by iconoclasts. On the north-eastern shore of the sea are the hot springs of Callirhoë (ΘEPMA KAΛΛIPOHC) at the outflow of the Wadi Zerqa Ma'in, showing pools and flowing water. To the east, although the original map undoubtedly showed Philadelphia (Amman) and the mosaicist's hometown of Madaba, all that remains of Transjordan is a stretch of mountainous land reaching out as far as **Karak** ([XAP]AXMWB[A] or Kharakh-Moba, the fortress of Moab), fortified and isolated on its hilltop. The deep east–west valley to the south of Karak, labelled as [Z]APEΔ (Zared) is today called Wadi Hasa. On the southeastern tip of the sea, near Zoora (ZOOPA), is Lot's Cave (TO TY ΑΓΙΥ Λ[WT]), a church commemorating the site where Lot was drunkenly seduced by his two daughters. The four letters EPHM are the beginning of the Greek word for desert.

The final section of the map is the most difficult to relate to reality. Against the right-hand wall of the church curl the arms of the **Nile** delta; however, instead of flowing from south to north (as it does), the Nile is depicted as flowing from east to west. In order to squeeze the river onto his strictly rectangular map, and also so as to keep faith with the notion of all the Rivers of Paradise – the Nile being one of them – flowing from the east (Genesis 2), the mosaicist used artistic licence to twist things around. The major city of the region is **Gaza** ([Γ]AZA), on the westernmost edge of the surviving map, intricately depicted with walls, towers, streets and buildings. To the south of Gaza is a two-line text in red describing "the border between Egypt and Palestine", a border which survives to this day. Over a dozen villages surround Gaza, which comprised the land allotted to Simeon (ΚΛΗΡΟC CYME[WN]). Of all the towns marked in the Nile Delta, only Pelusium (TO ΠΗΛΟYCIN), near modern-day Port Saïd, is of any size.

The rest of the town

Although most visitors don't stop to look, Madaba is crammed with other mosaics, many of them more complete than the mosaic map and most far more aesthetically pleasing. Walking through the car-park behind St George's Church will bring you out on Hussein bin Ali Street near the **Burnt Palace** (behind the tourist office). A sixth-century patrician mansion, the palace was destroyed by fire early in the seventh century; its large mosaics, including an image of the Roman city-goddess Tyche and several hunting scenes, are currently covered by sand for protection, but this whole area, which includes a swathe of second-century **Roman road** and the **Martyrs' Church** (currently hidden behind a high wall), is scheduled to open to the public in 1999 as "Archeological Park 2".

The Archeological Park

Barely 100m southeast of the tourist office is the original, very impressive **Archeological Park** (daily: April–Oct 8am–7pm, Nov–March 8am–5pm; JD3 ticket also covers entry to the Church of the Apostles and the Madaba Museum). Comprising a linked complex of a large Byzantine mansion, a church and a small museum of mosaics, it houses some of the most striking mosaic images in the country and is well worth an hour or more. Left of the ticket office hangs a Hellenistic-period mosaic – the oldest discovered in Jordan – from Herod's palace at Mukawir. Walking right past more mosaics brings you to an open plaza; follow the catwalk over a stretch of diagonally paved Roman road (some two metres below the present road surface) to reach the well-worn mosaic floor of the ruined Church of the Prophet Elias, dated to 607/8, and, below it, the tiny Crypt of Elianos, from 595/6.

Cross over the Roman road again to the plaza and the marvellous **Hippolytus Hall** mosaic, housed beneath a well-designed protective hangar. Dating from the early sixth century, probably from the reign of Justinian, the mosaic lay on the floor of what must have been a breathtakingly lavish private house; less than a century later, though, the house was demolished and the mosaics buried to make way for the construction of the adjacent Church of the Virgin. Closest to the doorway is a diamond grid showing birds and plants. Next to this, and damaged by the foundations of an ancient wall, is a panel depicting the myth of Phaedra and Hippolytus; an almond-eyed Phaedra, sick with love for her stepson Hippolytus is supported by two hand-maidens and awaits news of him with a falconer in attendance (the image of Hippolytus himself has been lost). Above is a riotous scene. To the right, a bare-breasted Aphrodite, sitting on a throne next to Adonis, is spanking a winged cupid with a sandal; all around, the Three Graces and a servant girl have their hands full dealing with several more mischievous cupids, one of which is upsetting a basket of petals. Outside the lavish acanthus-leaf border of the main mosaic – itself decorated with hunting scenes of leopards, lions and bears – are three women, personifications of (from the left) Rome, Gregoria and Madaba, seated next to a couple of hideous sea-monsters.

The stepped catwalk leads you on to overlook the circular nave of the **Church of the Virgin**. Just discernible around the edge of the main mosaic are images of flowers dating from the construction of the church, some time at the end of the sixth century. Most of what is now visible, though, dates from an elaborate geometric reworking of the mosaic floor completed in 767, during the Muslim Abbasid period. Swirls, knots and endlessly twisting patterns encircle a central medallion, with an inscription urging the congregation to "purify mind, flesh and works" before looking on Mary. A second inscription says that the mosaic was laid "thanks to the zeal and ardour of the people who love Christ in this city of Madaba".

The catwalk delivers you to a small colonnaded courtyard next to the hangar, hung with more mosaics, some from nearby Ma'in. There are depictions of Hesban and Gadaron (Salt), but the most interesting piece is over in the far corner. A mosaic picture of an ox has been lovingly obliterated by a tree (all that remains are hooves and a tail); similar care was taken in disfiguring many of the mosaic images in and around Madaba, implying that a great deal of iconoclasm was effected by local artists working under orders, rather than by religious zealots charging through the town destroying whatever they saw.

The Church of the Apostles

At the corner of Nuzha Street and the King's Highway lies the **Church of the Apostles** (daily: April–Oct 8am–7pm, Nov–March 8am–5pm; JD3 combination entry ticket with the Archeological Park and the Madaba Museum), housed beneath enormous modern stone arches. The mosaics inside are currently being cleaned and restored, but can still be viewed.

The church itself was a huge 24m by 15m basilica with a couple of side chapels, dating to 578, the high point of the Madaba school of mosaic art. The centrepiece of the mosaic is a personification of the sea, a spectacular portrait of a composed, regal woman emerging from the waves, surrounded by jumping fish, sharks, sea-monsters and even an octopus. She holds a rudder up beside her face like a standard and is making a curious, undefinable hand gesture. The main body of the mosaic features pairs of long-tailed parrots; the acanthus-leaf border is filled with animals (a crouching cat, a wolf, a hen with her chicks) and boys at play. In the corners are distinctive, chubby foliate masks.

Madaba Museum

Just off Nuzha Street, to the southwest of the town centre, the small **Madaba Museum** (Mon, Wed, Thurs, Sat & Sun 9am–5pm, Fri 10am–4pm; JD3 combination entry ticket with the Archeological Park and the Church of the Apostles) is worth a quick look. Nestled in a residential courtyard, the museum buildings were formerly houses themselves and feature mosaics uncovered by the residents during modern renovation work. Next to the ticket office and down some steps is a partly damaged mosaic, featuring a naked satyr prancing in a Bacchic procession (although Bacchus himself is missing). Through an arch and to the right is the al-Masri house, with a mosaic showing a man's head and pairs of animals between fruit trees. Outside, steps lead down to the museum rooms, with pottery and coins discovered at local sites, but the most appealing exhibit is at the very back, the tiny chapel of the Twal house, laid with an exquisite mosaic floor featuring a lamb nibbling at a tree. Climb the steps back up to a quiet courtyard at the top, where there's a mosaic pavement from Hesban and peaceful open views across the roofs and fields.

Eating, drinking and shopping

The best **restaurant** in town – in fact, one of the best in the country – is the *Saraya* (daily 11am–3pm & 7pm–midnight; ☎08/548650), upstairs in the *Haret Jdoudna* craft complex, about 100m south of the Church of the Map; a mere JD7 or so will buy you a meal of superb Arabic food in a tasteful, atmospheric setting. Bookings are essential for Thursdays and Fridays. Downstairs, *Pizza Giordania* (daily noon–midnight) has great wood-fired pizzas for JD2. Both take credit cards. For simpler fare, *Abu Ghassan*'s excellent chicken, rice, *fuul* and *hummus* dishes, on King Abdullah Street near the Bank of Jordan are worth sampling, and their fresh *falafel* is up there with the best in the country. There are also strings of cheap diners along Nuzha Street near the museum and Yarmouk Street towards *Lulu's*. An excellent **bakery** is near the mosque on Prince Hassan Street, and, Madaba being an important Christian town, you'll also find **liquor stores** everywhere.

As well as mosaics, Madaba is known for its **carpets**. If you're in the market for such items, you'll find that prices are more reasonable, and quality often better, than in Amman. Many places in the town still weave carpets on traditional upright handlooms, although these days all the actual weaving is done by Egyptian employees. Just beside the *Madaba Hotel*, a local old-timer oversees a continuously active loom, although your best bets are the two trustworthy and reliable shops either side of the tourist office. For other local **crafts**, *Haret Jdoudna* has dozens of tiny shops that are worth wandering through, but the sterile and over-priced *Madaba Zaman* craft centre opposite the Archeological Park should be avoided like the plague.

MOVING ON FROM MABADA

Most **buses** depart from the bus station. From here, four routes run to different points in **Amman**: more or less direct to Abdali, Raghadan and Wihdat stations, and a long way round to the Saqf Sayl, via Hesban and Na'ur. The last departs around 9pm. You can also bypass Amman: plenty of buses run to **Zerqa**, from where there are connections for the Eastern Desert. For points south along the King's Highway, nearly all regular buses terminate in **Dhiban**, the last town before the dramatic gorge of Wadi Mujib. However, one bus a day runs from Madaba through Mujib and on to Muta University near Karak; the drawbacks are that it departs at around 6am and costs JD1 – ask around in the bus station the day before to get the lowdown. For getting to Mount Nebo, Hammamat Ma'in, Mukawir and Umm ar-Rasas, see the relevant paragraphs in each section below.

Mount Nebo

Northwest of Madaba, a series of peaks generally referred to collectively as
MOUNT NEBO (in Arabic, *Siyagha*) comprise the single most important biblical
site in Jordan, and one with a unique resonance for Jews, Christians and Muslims
alike. Having led the Israelites for forty years through the wilderness, Moses
finally saw – from this dizzy vantage point – the Promised Land that God had forbidden him to set foot in; after he died on the mountain, his successor Joshua
went on to lead the Israelites into Canaan. In Christian and Jewish tradition,
Moses was buried somewhere on (or in) Mount Nebo, but Muslims – to whom
Moses is a prophet of Allah – hold that his body was carried across the river and
placed in a tomb now lying off the modern Jericho–Jerusalem highway. The lack
of earthly remains on Nebo, though, doesn't temper the drama accompanying a
visit: the mountain, and the church on its summit, feel so remote – and the view
is so awe-inspiring – that the holiness of the place is almost tangible. And besides,
the marvellous mosaics on display in the church would be reason enough in
themselves to visit.

The Moses Memorial Church

The focus of a visit is the **Moses Memorial Church** (daily: April–Oct 7am–7pm,
Nov–March 7am–5pm; 500 fils). The first structure on this site may have dated
from classical times, but by 394 AD it had been converted into a triapsidal church
floored with mosaics. Major expansion work was undertaken during the sixth
century, and over the subsequent centuries the building was added to until it
became the focus for a large and flourishing monastic community; the monastery
is known to have been still thriving in 1217, but by 1564 it had been abandoned.
In 1933, the ruined site was purchased by Franciscans, who began excavating and
restoring the church and the surrounding area. Today, Siyagha (originally
Aramaic for "monastery") remains both a monastic refuge and the headquarters
of the energetic Franciscan Archeological Institute.

Entrance is at the back of the church, but you should spend a little time absorbing the view first. From a cliff-edge platform beneath a huge, stylized cross in the
form of a serpent – inspired by Jesus' words in John 3: "As Moses lifted up the serpent in the wilderness, so must the Son of Man be lifted up" – a panoramic view
of the Land of Milk and Honey takes in the northern shore of the Dead Sea, the
dark stripe of the River Jordan in its valley, Jericho on the opposite bank, and,
haze permitting, the towers on the Mount of Olives in Jerusalem amidst the hills
opposite.

As you enter the simple, stone-clad church, on your left, and a metre lower than
the rest of the church, is the **Old Baptistry**, which boasts the most entertaining of
all the mosaics in and around Madaba. Completed in August 531, it was rediscov-
ered in 1976, when the mosaic which had been laid over it during expansion work
in 597 (now hung on the wall) was removed for cleaning. The huge central panel
features four beautiful and intricately designed tableaux. At the top, a tethered zebu
is protected by a shepherd fighting off a huge lion, and a soldier lancing a lioness.
Two mounted hunters with dogs are spearing a bear and a wild boar. Below, things
are more peaceful, as a shepherd sits under a tree watching his goat and fat-tailed
sheep nibble at the leaves. Closest to the catwalk, a dark-skinned Persian has an
ostrich on a leash, while a boy next to him is looking after a zebra and an extraordinary creature that is either a spotted camel or a creatively imagined giraffe.

The main hall of the church is divided by columns into a nave and aisles, and mosaics are everywhere. In the aisles and between some of the columns survive fragments of the pieces laid in 597. To the right and left hang panels from the **Church of St George** at Mukhayyat (see below), showing peacocks, a lion, a harvester and other animals. One, featuring doves and a deer around a date palm, dates from 536 and has, on one side, the name Saola in Greek and, on the other, either the same name in old Aramaic script, or the word *bislameh* ("with peace") in Arabic; if the latter is correct, this is the earliest example of Arabic script found in Jordan, predating Islam by a full century.

In the far right-hand corner of the church, what was formerly a funerary chapel became the **New Baptistry** in 597. As you enter, a small mosaic panel to the right – originally laid on the threshold – wishes "Peace to All". Just next to the Baptistry is a small modern **altar** with space for votive candles, decorated by a simple and strikingly beautiful mosaic cross which hung in a room exactly in this location in the original fourth-century church.

As you leave, next to the door is a small display of books; to the left are notice-boards occupying part of the **Theotokos (Virgin Mary) Chapel**, which was added to the main building in the seventh century. Most of the floor is taken up with a mosaic carpet of plants and flowers, but the apse features a stylized representation of the Temple of Jerusalem, and, to the left, a perfect and endearingly bright-eyed gazelle, complete with a little bell around its neck.

Around Mount Nebo

About 1km back along the road towards Madaba from Mount Nebo, a clutch of dismal restaurants marks a left-hand turn leading steeply down the hillside to **Ayoun Musa**, the Springs of Moses, one of the reputed locations for Moses striking the rock and water gushing forth (the Ain Musa spring above Petra is another). The spring itself is overlooked by lush foliage, and is set in beautiful countryside – the vineyards nearby produce some of Jordan's best wine – but aside from a couple of tiny ruined churches about ten minutes' walk beyond the spring, you'll find little of specific interest. All the mosaics discovered in the churches down here were long ago removed to Siyagha.

Back on the main road, about 1km further brings you to the village of Faysaliyyeh, and a right-hand turn to **Khirbet al-Mukhayyat**, site of the biblical town of Nebo and home to five ruined churches and yet another outstanding mosaic. At the first fork, the older road (left) will bring you, after about 2km, to a small car-park at the foot of a small but steep hill; on the summit sits the **Church of SS Lot and Procopius**. A building was constructed in the 1930s to protect the large, almost perfectly preserved floor mosaic inside, featuring dozens of bunches of grapes, tableaux of vine-harvesting and musically accompanied grape-treading, along with rabbit-chasing and lion-hunting. The most entertaining pieces are in between the column stumps: nearest the door are a fisherman and a man rowing a boat either side of a church, and two peculiar fishtailed monsters, while opposite lie vignettes of geese and ducks in a pond full of fish and lily pads.

Visible on the hilltop beyond SS Lot and Procopius, the ruined **Church of St George** occupies the highest peak on the mountain. Its mosaics now adorn the church at Siyagha, but the view from St George is breathtaking. There are three more churches dotted around the valley nearby (the guardian can tell you where), but none has mosaics *in situ*.

Practicalities

Buses and **services** from outside the Bank of Jordan on Palestine Street in central Madaba normally only go as far as the village of **Faysaliyyeh**; there is no transport to either Ayoun Musa or Khirbet al-Mukhayyat and, to get to Siyagha, you may either have to walk 2km from Faysaliyyeh or hope the driver's willing to go the distance for 250 fils extra. From the church, it shouldn't be hard to hitch a ride back, or you could walk back to Faysaliyyeh for a bus or *service* (you'll pass the Mukhayyat turnoff 500m before the bus stop). Getting a taxi to take you from Madaba to Siyagha, wait, and bring you back shouldn't cost more than JD4–5, a little more if you include other sites.

Siyagha isn't the end of the road, though you wouldn't want anyone but a close friend behind the wheel for the death-defying journey off the back of the mountain, plunging 1200m in a series of switchbacks down to the Dead Sea shore near Swaymeh.

Hammamat Ma'in

Some 30km southwest of Madaba, at the end of possibly the steepest, most tortuous road in the country, the hot springs of **Hammamat Ma'in** make one of the best side trips off the King's Highway. Continuously dousing the precipitous desert cliffs of the **Wadi Zerqa Ma'in** with steaming water – varying between a langorous 40°C and a scalding 60°C – the springs are almost the only natural attraction in Jordan to have been deliberately turned into a touristic resort complex. The waters have been channelled to form two **hot waterfalls**, there are hot spa pools, natural and artificial saunas and overpriced accommodation, but it's still not too hard to escape the melee and find a quiet, steamy niche in the rock all to yourself. If you're feeling energetic, **hiking** some or all of the way down the deep gorge to the Dead Sea is an exhilarating counterpoint to lying around in hot water all day. Bear in mind when planning a visit, though, that spring and autumn Fridays see the entire valley crammed with people, from gangs of rambunctious young lads splashing around to respectable family groups, with veiled women ducking fully clothed under the waterfalls.

The road from Madaba passes first through fields and the small farming community of **MA'IN**; the village, perched on its *tell*, is mentioned in the Bible, and excavations in its Byzantine and Umayyad-period churches revealed many mosaics, now on display in the Madaba Archeological Park. Beyond Ma'in, the terrain dries out, and the road begins to heave and twist around the contours of land above the Dead Sea. Thin tracks off to the left give innumerable options for picnic spots on slopes perched high above cultivated sections of the Wadi Zerqa Ma'in; to the right, the views over the desert hills down to the fairytale Dead Sea, luminous blue in a valley of brown, are incredible. The road keeps coiling and recoiling in steep switchbacks until it finally enters the barren, yawning gorge of the lower Wadi Zerqa Ma'in; it's only once you approach the resort on the valley floor that the humid lushness of this isolated spot becomes apparent.

Practicalities

Virtually all local **buses** from Madaba, plus a few early-morning departures from Amman's Wihdat station, stop at Ma'in village, 8km from Madaba and some 21km short of Hammamat Ma'in itself; to go further, you'll have to cross the driver's palm with dinars. A JETT bus leaves Amman daily at 8am for the hot springs;

paying JD3.750 to go there and back is a good deal, but their JD10 ticket, which includes return transport, entry to the resort area, some form of lunch and dips in both a hot pool and an ordinary outdoor swimming pool, is not really a bargain. You can pick up this bus on its way through Madaba, but you need to book in advance. The going rate for a taxi from Madaba to Hammamat Ma'in and back, with a reasonable wait included, is around JD7. For returning, the easiest option is to take the 5pm (Nov–March 4pm) JETT bus back to Madaba (500 fils) or Amman (JD2). You might also find one or two *service*s touting for business around 5pm, but if you want to stay for sunset, try and fix up a ride ahead of time.

The whole area of the hot springs has only one road in, across which has been positioned the **main gate** (daily 24hr) where entrance costs an unavoidable JD2 per adult; paying JD3.850 also covers entry to the "Roman bath" (see below) and the swimming pool. From the main gate, the road winds on for 1km down to the hulk of the *Ashtar Hotel* (☎08/545500, fax 545550; ⑥), the only worthwhile **accommodation** option, featuring pleasant, en-suite rooms, all with balcony, air con and only the sound of the waterfalls to disturb you. Partway down, there are "chalets" – actually budget-style self-catering rooms, drab, cramped and none too clean (④) – and "caravans" – tiny sweatbox portakabins (③) – neither of which has working air con: if you can't afford the *Ashtar*, you'll need easy-going tastes to enjoy an overnight stay here. The main gate forbids you to bring in your own **food and drink**, but, absurdly, the only facilities for eating are at the hotel – an expensive restaurant buffet or unappealing coffee-shop fare. The Drop & Shop supermarket has nothing but cheeseballs, crackers and water.

The **hot waterfalls** tumble down off the cliffs to one side of the valley. The one next to the *Ashtar* is public, with unlimited free access. To the right of it is the fenced-off "family" waterfall (daily 8am–midnight; JD1), a much better option for women, whether solo or accompanied, although you may find decently long shorts and a baggy T-shirt still attracting wolf whistles. Both these waterfalls are equally hot and equally explorable, while near the mosque behind the hotel there's a smaller, less crowded public waterfall. In the middle of the resort is an ordinary swimming pool (daily 8am–4pm; JD2.200), or you can use the more secluded pool behind the hotel (same times; JD6). The hotel's treatment room (daily 8am–8pm; JD4.800) has two hot pools, a jacuzzi and specialists on hand to give massages and apply mudpacks; and up towards the main gate, the "Roman bath" (daily 8am–midnight; JD1.650) has separate hot pools and steam rooms for men and women. In case you were in any doubt, however, the hot waterfalls are all you need: everything else is eminently missable.

Hiking along the river to its outflow at ancient **Callirhoë** on the Dead Sea shore – where King Herod soothed his many ills – involves scrambling about 8km along the riverbed. It's not at all taxing to go part of the way, but to attempt the whole thing you'll need plenty of drinking water (temperatures can soar in the sweltering, breeze-less gorge), a change of clothes for the inevitable patches of wading and a ride back to civilization from the other end.

Mukawir

The King's Highway heads south from Madaba through quiet, picturesque farmland for 13km to Libb, where a well-signed road branches right for a long, slow 20km across the windblown hilltops to the small village of **MUKAWIR** (pronounced "*m-KAA-whirr*"), views yawning away in all directions. This whole area is the homeland of the **Bani Hamida** tribe, now well known in Jordan following the success of a highly publicized project to revive traditional weaving skills among the women of the tribe. At the far end of the village is the Bani Hamida centre (daily except Thurs & Fri 8am–3pm), sister outlet to the shop in Amman (see p.106), where you can watch the women weaving and buy beautiful rugs, wall-hangings and other knick-knacks.

However, the main reason for visiting is to make the short hike up to the isolated conical hill beyond the village, which is topped with the ruins of the **palace of Machaerus**. During the first century BC, the hill was a stronghold of the Jewish **Hasmonean** revolt against the Seleucids, based in Syria, and was fortified to be a buffer against Nabatean power further south. In the last decades of the century, **Herod the Great**, king of Judea, constructed a walled citadel at Machaerus and developed road access to the site from the Dead Sea port at Callirhoë, 8km west, although trade on the King's Highway – just 22km east – remained under the control of the Nabateans.

Shortly after, another Jewish revolt began, this time against **Roman** rule. In 66 AD the rebels seized Machaerus from the Roman garrison, and held it for seven years, eventually surrendering when faced by Roman forces preparing to assault the fortress; in an almost identical situation at **Masada**, west of the Dead Sea, a Jewish resistance force committed mass suicide rather than submit. The Romans immediately moved into Machaerus, razed the buildings, massacred the local civilian population and departed, and the hill has remained quiet since.

Today, a visit to Machaerus is more likely to inspire for the views and the beautiful, rolling countryside, carpeted with wildflowers in spring, than for the archeology. Kestrels wheel against the Dead Sea haze above a handful of gleaming modern columns which sprout from the part-excavated rubble on the hilltop. Of the palace ruins, a few rooms are discernible, as are the remains of the Roman **assault ramp** on the far slopes of the hill and the line of an **aqueduct** across the saddle. A **mosaic** – the oldest discovered in Jordan – once lay in the baths complex, but has been removed to Madaba for display. According to the Roman historian Josephus, it was at Machaerus that Salome danced for Herod Antipas and had the head of **John the Baptist** presented on a platter. Christian tradition holds that the Baptist was buried where he died, in a well-signposted **cave** near the hill, but Islam, according to which John was a prophet of Allah, keeps two shrines holy, one for his body (the same cave) and another in Damascus for his severed head, which was supposedly taken to that city and buried at the site of the Great Mosque.

Practicalities

Occasional **buses** run from Madaba to Mukawir, normally dropping off in the village. You may be able to persuade the driver to take you the extra 2km to the car-park opposite the hill; if not, it's a pleasant walk. From the car-park, a steep but easy fifteen-minute climb across the saddle and up some steps brings you to the hilltop ruins, known gloomily to the locals as *Qala'at al-Meshneqeh*, or the Citadel of the Gallows.

Umm ar-Rasas

A tiny farming village on a back road midway between the King's Highway and the Desert Highway, **UMM AR-RASAS** is a gem, well worth a couple of hours' detour. The village is the site of the Roman garrison town of Kastron Mefaa, which developed during the Byzantine and Umayyad periods into a relatively important city, and large and fabulously rich **mosaic** floors from two of its fifteen or so churches have been cleaned and protected for display.

Excavation work is ongoing, and if you join the local goats for a stumble through the ruins of the ancient city, only an arch or two poking through the acres of rubble give any indication of former urban splendour. The mosaics lie beneath a pale green shelter on the corner of the ruins furthest from the road. Entrance is to one side of the intricate mosaic floor of the **Church of St Stephen**, dated to 785, over 150 years after Muslim rule was established in Jordan. The apse has a dazzling kaleidoscopic diamond pattern swirling out from behind the altar, and the broad nave is framed by mosaic panels showing cities of the day: closest to the door is Jerusalem, with seven Palestinian cities below, including Nablus, Asqalan and, at the bottom, Gaza. On the far side are seven Transjordanian cities, headed by Kastron Mefaa itself, with Philadelphia (Amman), Madaba, Hesban, Ma'in, Rabba and Karak below. The central section is filled with scenes of fishermen, seashells, jellyfish and all kinds of intricate detail of animals, fruit and trees, although in antiquity iconoclasts blocked out virtually all representations of people. Against the far wall is an older mosaic belonging to the adjacent **Church of Bishop Sergius**, dated to 587. Its main feature is a rectangular panel in front of the altar featuring pomegranate trees and very wise-looking rams; on the other side of the catwalk, hard up against the exterior wall, a beautifully executed personification of one of the seasons survived the iconoclasts by having had a pulpit built over it at some point.

And yet, attractive though they are, Umm ar-Rasas's mosaics are only half the story; if you've taken the time to visit, you shouldn't leave without standing awhile at the foot of the village's peculiar square **tower**, a kilometre away from the ruins and represented on the church floor by Kastron Mefaa's own mosaicists as an obviously important identifying feature of their city. Desolate, windblown and mysterious, the fifteen-metre tower has defied explanation. It is solid, without internal stairs, yet at the top is a room with windows in four directions. Simple, almost rough crosses are carved on the three sides facing away from the city, but details of intricate and beautiful carving survive on the topmost corbels. Every indication would point to this being the Stylite tower of a Christian holy man – the fifth-century ascetic Simon Stylites spent 38 years atop a pillar near Aleppo, and a cult of pilgrimage grew up around him and later imitators who isolated themselves from worldly distractions in order to concentrate on their prayers. The foundations at the foot of the tower are of a roughly built church, and further away are cisterns and a three-storey building which may have been some kind of hostel for pilgrims come to pray in the presence of the Stylite. Today, almost wrenched apart by earthquakes, the sinister ruined tower is home only to pigeons and kestrels.

Practicalities

The only **buses** to Umm ar-Rasas run a few times daily from Madaba, on the back roads via Nitil. As they approach, they pass a small blue-domed mosque on the left. To visit the **tower**, ask to get off about 600m further, at the end of the row of buildings; from here, a road winds away to the left. The tumbled stones of the city, as well as the shelter housing the **mosaics**, are clearly visible about a kilometre's easy walk away. If you're **driving**, turn off the road from Nitil at the post office

500m before the village's main T-junction (from where the Desert Highway is 14km east, Dhiban 16km west). From the post office, a track winds for 500m alongside the ruined city walls to the shelter.

Along the highway south of Madaba

South of Madaba, the first of the series of large wadis slicing west–east across southern Jordan is the lush **Wadi Wala**, a little beyond Libb, pleasantly dotted with vineyards and shaded by groves of pine and eucalyptus. From the valley floor, you can follow the river west for some 15km into the quiet and beautiful **Wadi Hidan**; this road terminates in a dead end, but Hidan itself goes on to meet the Mujib river just before the Dead Sea. Back on the highway, when you reach the top of the southern slope of Wadi Wala, a stretch of the Roman *Via Nova Traiana* is visible on the valley floor behind. Some 10km further (33km south of Madaba), **Dhiban** is the terminus for buses from Madaba and the last town before the dramatic Wadi Mujib canyon.

Wadi Mujib and the road to Karak

Some 2km or so south of Dhiban, the vast canyon of the **Wadi Mujib** opens up spectacularly in front; just over the lip of the gorge is a small rest stop and viewing platform, with tourist police on duty and a souvenir stall tucked surreptitious-

---

THE MESHA STELE

These days a largely unregarded village, in the past **Dhiban** was a large and important city, capital of Moab and mentioned many times in the Old Testament. In around 850 BC, a man named **Mesha**, described as a "shepherd king", liberated Moab from Israelite aggression, built a palace in Dhiban and set about refortifying the King's Highway against future attack.

Almost three thousand years later, in 1868, a German missionary travelling in the wild country between Salt and Karak was shown by Dhibani bedouin a large basalt stone inscribed with strange characters. Unaware of its significance, he nonetheless circumspectly informed the German consul of his discovery, who then made quiet arrangements to obtain the stele on behalf of the Berlin Museum. However, a French diplomat in Jerusalem who heard of the discovery was less subtle; he travelled to Dhiban, took an imprint of the stele's text there and then and then offered the locals a large sum of money. Suddenly finding themselves at the centre of an international furore over a seemingly very desirable lump of rock, the bedouin refused his offer and sent him packing; they then did the obvious thing and devised a way to make more money. By placing the stone over a fire, then pouring cold water on it, they successfully managed to shatter it, and thus sell off each valuable fragment to the covetous foreigners one by one. Meanwhile, scholars in Europe were studying and translating the imprint of the text, which turned out to be Mesha's own record of his achievements, significant as the longest inscription in the Moabite language and one of the longest and most detailed original inscriptions from the biblical period yet discovered. The mostly reconstructed stele now sits in the Louvre in Paris; having become something of a symbol of national pride, copies of it are displayed in museums all over Jordan.

WADI MUJIB NATURE RESERVE

Most of the area between the King's Highway and the Dead Sea shore, as far north as Hammamat Ma'in and including almost the entire Mujib river, was made a protected **nature reserve** in 1987. During ecological surveys of the reserve, the Royal Society for the Conservation of Nature (RSCN) discovered four plant species never before recorded in Jordan and made sightings of the rare Syrian wolf, Egyptian Mongoose, Blanford's fox and large numbers of raptors. An enclosure in the mountains on Mujib's southern plateau established to breed twenty endangered **Nubian ibex** has resulted in more than a hundred adult animals, some of which are planned for future release into the wild.

However, problems are on the horizon, connected, as always, with the search for **fresh water**. In 1998, with little assessment either of environmental impact or of alternative water sources, the government approved plans to construct a weir across the lower Mujib, which would divert the river into a pipe system to supply agriculture and hotel construction on the Dead Sea shore further north. As well as significantly altering the river's upstream flow, oxygen levels, salinity and sediment levels, the plan would ensure that the riverbed below the weir would be dry for eighty percent of the year, effectively wiping out most of the indigenous flora and fauna.

For the moment, though, Wadi Mujib remains one of the most dramatic and unspoiled areas of natural beauty in Jordan, and is well worth the time and effort to experience. By booking ahead, **groups** of ten or more can be led by an RSCN guide along the valley floor from the King's Highway to the river's outflow at the Dead Sea, a taxing but exhilarating nine- or ten-hour **hike** with some rock scrambling and wading, only undertaken in the relatively temperate conditions of spring and early autumn. There are few such dramatic places left untouched in the Middle East, and the JD20 per person fee could hardly go to a more worthy cause. You can get more information on this trip, on other, shorter hikes in the reserve, and on the possibilities for wilderness **camping** from the RSCN's Ecotourism Unit in Amman (see p.39 for contact details).

ly out of sight. The dramatic canyon, some 500m in depth and 4km broad at the top, is an obvious natural focal point, and in biblical times, Arnon, as it was named, was the heartland of Moab; these days, it divides the governorates of Madaba and Karak. The sheer scale of the place is what takes your breath away, with vultures, eagles and kestrels wheeling silently on rising thermals all around and the valley floor to the right losing itself in the mistiness of the Dead Sea. The broad, flat plain of the wadi bed is noticeably hotter and creaks with frog calls; a small building off to one side here is well placed for the honour of most isolated post office in the world.

After snaking up Mujib's southern slope, the King's Highway emerges onto the flat Moabite plateau, fields of wheat stretching off in all directions. The first village on the southern rim, some 3km from the gorge, is **Ariha**, and from here the highway ploughs a straight furrow south through small farming communities to two towns nurturing minor remnants of a more glorious past. **Qasr**, 12km south of Ariha, boasts a Nabatean temple east of the town, while **Rabba**, 5km on, was a large and important Roman and Byzantine settlement – a fact celebrated by the authorities in the re-erection of ancient columns along the main street. The remains of a Roman temple sit gracefully to the west of the highway behind the modern bustle of the town.

Practicalities

The towns between Libb and Rabba are too small to warrant even a *falafel* stand, let alone a diner: on a journey through, your only choices are to have a hearty breakfast in Madaba and hold out for lunch in Karak, or to bring along a **picnic**.

Aside from the once-daily student **bus** from Madaba (see p.201), there is no public transport through Wadi Mujib, all southbound buses terminating at Dhiban. However, Dhibanis are well aware of foreigners' desire to travel through Mujib, and have a nice little earner going offering their pickups as taxis. Asking around at the handful of shops on Dhiban's central roundabout for a ride through the canyon will quickly bear fruit; the going rate for a full car to Ariha, the first village on the southern rim, is JD4, a little more if weather is bad. From Ariha, plenty of buses run along the King's Highway to Karak, picking up on the way in Qasr and Rabba.

Around Karak, the King's Highway describes a poorly signposted zigzag, and if you're **driving**, it's easy to get confused. At a T-junction 12km south of Rabba, turning left will eventually deliver you to the Desert Highway at Qatraneh, while turning right will lead you through hilly suburbs to another T-junction at the foot of Karak castle. From here, the King's Highway heads left to Tafileh, while a right turn brings you spiralling up into Karak town.

FROM KARAK TO PETRA

The southern stretches of the King's Highway pass through an increasingly arid landscape dotted with lushly watered settlements. **Karak**, the most important town of southern Jordan, still lies largely within its Crusader-era walls and boasts one of the best-preserved castles in the Middle East. The gaping canyon of **Wadi Hasa** to the south, overlooked by an extraordinary extinct volcano, runs a close second to Mujib for natural drama. From **Tafileh** a little beyond, the highway rises into the Shara mountains, well over 1500m above sea level (and considerably more above the deep Dead Sea rift to the west); up here are both the unspoiled **Dana Nature Reserve** and another Crusader castle at **Shawbak**. A little way south, the dry, jagged mountains conceal ancient Petra (see p.240).

Karak and around

A small but busy town atop an isolated hill still encircled by Crusader walls, **KARAK** is the unofficial capital of southern Jordan. Roughly midway between Amman and Petra, it's also a natural place to break a journey along the King's Highway. The 'huge and well-preserved Crusader **castle** which occupies the southern tip of the hill is one of the finest in the Middle East, second only to Syria's Crac des Chevaliers for explorability.

Some history

The hill on which Karak stands – with sheer cliffs on three sides and clear command over the Wadi Karak leading down to the Dead Sea – features both in the Old Testament and on Madaba's Byzantine mosaic map as a natural defensive stronghold. The **Crusaders** began building a fortress on a rocky spur atop the

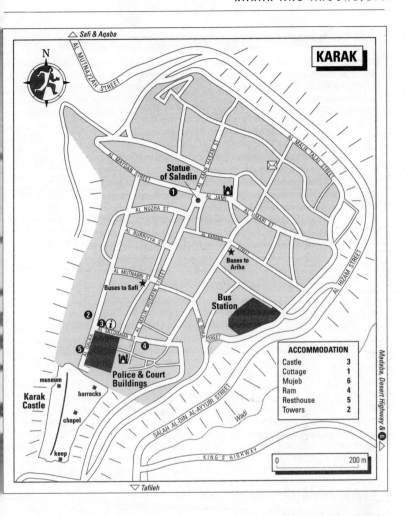

hill in 1142, boosting the natural advantages of the site by digging dry moats to the north and south and reinforcing the slopes with a paved *glacis*.

The castle's construction was initiated by the knights of the successful First Crusade, but its eventual downfall is inextricably linked with the personalities of those who came later, specifically **Reynald of Chatillon**. A ruthless warrior who arrived in the Holy Land in 1147 on the Second Crusade, Reynald was both vicious and unscrupulous, and it was specifically to avenge his treachery that the Muslim commander, **Salah ad-Din**, launched a campaign to expel the foreign invaders. In 1177, Reynald married Lady Stephanie, widow of the Lord of Oultrejourdain. Safely ensconced in Karak, he began a reign characterized by wanton cruelty: one of his more notorious pleasures involved encasing the heads of his prisoners in wooden boxes so that, when he flung them off the castle walls,

THE CRUSADERS IN TRANSJORDAN

Following an appeal from the Byzantine emperor for foreign military assistance to defeat the Seljuk Turks, it took only a few years from the Pope's first call to arms of 1095 for invading Christian European armies to seize **Jerusalem**. European-run statelets were set up in quick succession throughout the Levant – the Kingdom of Jerusalem, the Counties of Tripoli and Edessa and the Principality of Antioch. One of the Christian lords, **Baldwin**, was crowned King of Jerusalem on Christmas Day 1100, and it was under his rule that the Crusaders began to realize the benefit of controlling the Transjordanian land route from Syria into Egypt and Arabia, in order to stand between the Muslim power bases in Damascus and Cairo and to be able to harass Muslims making the pilgrimage to the Arabian holy places. In 1107, simply the threat of attack by Baldwin's army persuaded a Seljuk force to flee their stronghold in **Wadi Musa**, and persistent harrying over a decade or more in the area around **Ajloun** successfully played havoc with established trade patterns in the region. In 1115, Baldwin crossed the Wadi Araba from Hebron with the intention of fully incorporating Transjordan into the Crusader realms, and began construction of a large castle at modern **Shawbak**, which he named *Le Krak de Montreal*, or the Fortress of the Royal Mountain. Establishment of a string of Crusader possessions soon followed, at Aila (Aqaba) – including, possibly, a fortress on an island off Aqaba, which has not been conclusively dated – Wu'ayra near Wadi Musa, Habees within Petra, and Tafileh. However, the Lordship of Oultrejourdain, as it came to be known, was far from impregnable, and infiltration across the River Jordan by a Muslim raiding party in 1139 seems to have persuaded Paganus the Butler, by then the effective ruler, to move his power base northwards from Shawbak. Construction of the massive fortress at **Karak** began in 1142, and twenty years later, with the addition of another citadel at Ahamant (possibly Amman), Crusader-controlled territory in Transjordan extended from the River Zerqa to the Red Sea, and from the Jordan Valley to the desert.

Such power was short-lived, however. Between 1169 and 1174, the Karak headquarters underwent four sieges, managing to survive partly because the opposing Muslim armies were divided. By 1174, though, Salah ad-Din had united the Muslim forces under his own banner, and began methodically to oust the Crusaders from Transjordan. Karak withstood two more sieges during 1183, but the tide was turning: the Latin armies were much depleted, and their young king, Baldwin IV, was dying of leprosy. In 1187, at **Hattin** near Tiberias, they were roundly defeated by Salah ad-Din, who executed the lord of Karak, Reynald, and soon after took Jerusalem. Wu'ayra and the great prize, Karak itself, capitulated in late 1188, and Shawbak – the last Transjordanian possession – fell in the spring of 1189. The Europeans struggled on, but just a century later the entire Holy Land was once again under Arab rule.

he could be sure that they hadn't lost consciousness by the time they hit the rocks below. In 1180, he robbed a Mecca-bound caravan on the King's Highway in violation of a truce signed by King Baldwin and Salah ad-Din; Baldwin was unable to bring Reynald to heel, and Salah ad-Din was forced to swallow his anger until a suitable time for revenge could be found.

In November 1183, the wedding of Reynald's heir was celebrated within the walls of Karak castle at the very moment that Salah ad-Din and his army, having already invaded the town, were poised just beyond the north moat ready to attack. Lady Stephanie sent plates of food from the banquet to the Muslim army beyond the walls; in response, while his men were trying to bridge the moat and continuing to catapult rocks against the walls, Salah ad-Din enquired which tower the newly-weds were occupying. In an expression of his impeccable chivalry, he then ordered his army to direct their fire elsewhere.

Karak withstood that siege, but at the **Battle of Hattin** in 1187, the Crusaders, stymied by the strategic ineptitude of Reynald and others, suffered utter defeat. The victorious Salah ad-Din characteristically spared the king and the Crusader lords – all apart from Reynald, whom he personally decapitated. The besieged Crusader garrison at Karak held out for months; they sold their wives and children in exchange for food, and resorted to eating horses and dogs, but surrender was inevitable. Karak capitulated in November 1188.

Over the following centuries, Ayyubid and **Mamluke** occupiers of the castle rebuilt and strengthened its defences. Remote Karak ranked last among the Syrian provinces of the Mamlukes, and the castle was used mainly as a dumping ground for disgraced sultans and officers. Under the **Ottomans**, anarchy was the rule rather than the exception in the lands around Karak. During widespread rebellion in 1879, Karaki Christians abandoned their town, moving north to settle among the ruins of ancient Madaba. In 1894, troops finally imposed order in Karak and, to keep the town sweet, the Ottoman administration began to make monthly payments to the local sheikhs. However, official backhanders threatened the local tribal grip on power, and Karak's ruling families – among them the respected **Majali** clan – fomented rebellion. In 1908 they rallied a local force and stormed Karak's government buildings, forcing the Ottoman garrison to seek refuge in the castle. After eight days, troops arrived from Damascus to put down the revolt: five rebel leaders were publicly executed in Karak, and the Majalis were declared outlaws.

The Ottoman administration was swept away in the Arab Revolt of 1917–18, but Karak retained its reputation for political activism, and – a little ironically, considering the family history – the prime minister of Jordan up until mid-1998 was a Majali. Karak hit world headlines in 1996 when, under intense pressure from the IMF to reform economic policy, the then-prime minister Abdul Karim Kabariti ended government **subsidies** on grain. The result was an immediate doubling of bread prices. Discontent, especially strong in the poorer towns of the south, flared into open **rioting**. Government buildings in Karak were burned and looted, and tanks were deployed in an attempt to restore order. Curfews and broadcast appeals from King Hussein – to whom the rioters displayed unwavering loyalty throughout – eventually brought the situation under control, but the issues of economic liberalization and democratization were left largely unresolved. Karak remains both economically depressed and, with the continuing nationwide monopoly on power held by tribal notables, politically hamstrung.

Arrival, information and accommodation

Everything you need is within a few minutes' stroll of the castle, on the highest point of the hill and marked by a huge **communications tower** visible from all over the town. Here lie hotels cheap and not-so-cheap, diners and restaurants, and the moderately useful **tourist office** (daily except Fri 8am–2pm), next to the *Castle* hotel. However, it's not easy to find your way to the castle from the **bus station** – a dreary patch of open ground on a terrace below a residential neighbourhood – partly because there are no signs and partly because it involves climbing steep slopes. With or without heavy bags, you might want to do your legs a favour and take a taxi.

The centre of town has all the normal array of **banks** for changing cash and travellers' cheques and making ATM withdrawals. The main **post office** (Mon–Thurs, Sat & Sun 7.30am–5pm, Fri 7.30am–1pm) is behind the large city-centre mosque. Jammed *Alo* **cardphones** are all over the town, but the one outside the *Ram* hotel has an eye kept on it and so works most of the time. The tourist **police** are always on duty at the castle gates.

Accommodation

In a prime position halfway between Amman and Petra, Karak has long been an overnight stop for travellers, and yet the choice of **accommodation** is not exactly broad. Immediately after the peace treaty with Israel was signed, a handful of inexpensive hotels were flung up around the castle to meet the influx of visitors, and, unheard of elsewhere in Jordan, a small grocery even put up a sign in Hebrew welcoming Israeli tourists. However, the flood quickly slowed to a trickle and these days you could easily bargain a room for well below initial asking prices. One complicating factor, which rather undermines most bargaining ploys, is that the *Castle* (closed for renovation at the time of writing), *Ram* and *Towers* hotels, as well as the grocery with the Hebrew sign and the *Fida* and *Peace* restaurants, are all owned by the same man, who'll no doubt greet you happily when you arrive.

Cottage, near the statue of Salah ad-Din downtown (☎03/354359). Surprisingly OK rooms, clean and comfortable, with a cosy atmosphere. ①.

Mujeb, 4km east of Karak at the Desert Highway junction (☎03/386090, fax 386091). Impressively airy and well-designed building, spanking new and with good facilities. Pleasant and spotless rooms are all en suite, and the tourist-group trade ensures high-quality meals. However, you'll need your own transport. ③.

Ram, 100m east of the castle (☎03/353789, fax 351105). Spartan breezeblock kind of place, clean enough and unremarkable. Some rooms are shared (JD3.500 per person), others are with or without bathroom. ①–②.

Resthouse, next to the castle (☎03/351148, fax 353148). Small place, now in private hands, offering the most characterful rooms in town with amazing views down the Wadi Karak. Fans, heating and en-suite bathrooms are standard, and the breakfasts are the best you could hope for. Book ahead, though, as it's regularly full. Credit cards accepted. ④.

Towers, 50m from the Resthouse (☎ & fax 03/354293). The best of the inexpensive hotels. Cheaper rooms share a bathroom, while slightly more expensive en-suite ones boast Resthouse-style views. Nonetheless, pretty basic. ②.

Karak castle

Occupying a rocky spur on the southern edge of Karak town, the **castle** is first – and most impressively – visible on the approach from the east, its restored walls and *glacis* looming above the ravine below. From within the town, it's less easy to get a sense of the castle's bulk – until you make your way inside.

Entry (daily 8am–5pm; JD1) is through a gate a little way past the Resthouse. The castle has seven separate levels, some buried deep inside the hill, and the best way to explore is to take a **torch** and simply let your inquisitiveness run free: it's quite possible to spend two or three atmospheric hours poking into dark rooms and gloomy vaulted passageways.

A good place to start is by heading up the slope once you enter, then doubling back on yourself into a long, vaulted passageway along the inside of the huge north wall built by the Crusaders. Down here, close to the original entrance of the castle in the northeastern corner, are a **barracks** and, on the right, the **kitchens**, complete with olive press and, further within, a huge oven. You emerge along the **east wall**, close to the ruined **chapel**. Over the battlements the restored *glacis* heralds a dizzy drop, and facing you is the partly complete Mamluke **keep**, the best-protected part of the castle. It's not difficult to climb to the highest point, from where there are scarily vertiginous views in all directions. In a sunken area between the chapel and the keep lie the remains of a Mamluke **palace**, while at the bottom of some steps just behind the chapel's apse is a beautifully carved stone panel. Of the two rooms opposite the panel, the one on the right features some reused Nabatean blocks set into the wall; next door, Reynald's extensive and suitably dank **dungeons** head off into the hill. Back at the carved panel, a passageway to the left eventually brings you out, after passing another barracks, near the entrance. If you head down from here to the lower western side of the castle, you'll come across the small **museum** (daily except Tues 8.30am–4.30pm), featuring some glass and pottery bits and bobs. Much more interesting – if you can persuade the museum caretaker to unlock the door for you – is a restored Mamluke **gallery** nearby running virtually the length of the west wall at the lowest level of the castle.

Eating and drinking

Karak being largely a bedouin town, the locals tend to favour home cooking over restaurant dining, and the choice of **eating** places is limited and pretty uninspiring. Apart from the *Resthouse*, everything is open for breakfast but closed by 9pm. In plum position on the castle drag are the *Sewar*, *Peace* and *Fida* restaurants, all with similar kebab and chicken dishes that can be easily bettered in more interesting places a little further into town. The Syrian guy running the *Akbash* diner, just down from the *Fida*, is the height of friendliness and, although his simple fare is nothing to write home about, his cosy, cross-vaulted little den is an atmospher-

---

MOVING ON FROM KARAK

Buses for **Amman**'s Wihdat station, Ma'an and Zerqa (all via the Desert Highway), **Tafileh** (via the King's Highway) and **Aqaba** (via the Wadi Araba road) all operate out of the bus station, but only between 7am and about noon. You might be lucky and find a bus after that time, but don't rely on it. One or two buses might make the run past Tafileh to **Shawbak** on the King's Highway – but not after 8am. Buses north along the King's Highway, terminating in **Ariha**, leave from a side street in the middle of town. Buses to **Safi**, an industrial town on the Dead Sea shore, leave from a different street corner in town and run past Bab adh-Dhraa and the turning for Lot's Cave.

With the dearth of public transport to **Petra** – most travellers' next major port of call – Karak's taxi-drivers are more than willing to help out. JD35–40 is the exorbitant going rate for a full car to Wadi Musa via the King's Highway, a two-and-a-half hour ride that admittedly would take considerably longer by bus and thumb. The local entrepreneur who owns the *Ram* hotel (among others) can help in fixing up a taxi ride. The slow way of getting to Petra along the King's Highway involves a bus to Tafileh, another to Qadsiyyeh, hitching to Shawbak and a bus or *service* into Wadi Musa. A less picturesque, but faster, route is with a bus to Ma'an along the Desert Highway and a bus or *service* from there to Wadi Musa.

ic place to hang out. Next to the statue of Salah ad-Din, a Turkish restaurant and a *Mankal Chicken Tikka* dive are worth passing over for the much better *Alomara* restaurant down the street, with the best *shwarma* in town. At none of these places need you pay more than JD2–3 for a filling experience.

With an in-town monopoly on serving the better-heeled class of visitor, the *Resthouse* (daily noon–4.30pm & 7.30–11pm) offers lunch and dinner buffets at JD6 per person which are lavish in scope but pedestrian in flavour. Their **bar** helps divert attention to the views instead.

Bab adh-Dhraa and Lot's Cave

Two sites close to the Dead Sea shore west of Karak can be visited either as an excursion from the town or on a journey north or south along the Wadi Araba highway. Both are connected with the biblical story of the divine destruction of Sodom and Gomorrah: **Bab adh-Dhraa** is the site of a second-millennium BC town and cemetery, and the preferred location for the destroyed city of Sodom, while **Lot's Cave** features a small but dramatically situated Byzantine-period church clinging to the cliffs above the Dead Sea, where Abraham's nephew Lot is reputed to have taken refuge from the brimstone. The climate down here is much hotter and more humid than in the mountains above, and if you make a day-trip from the cool heights of Karak, come equipped with plenty of water and avoid scrambling around in the killing noonday sun.

Buses from Karak to Safi or Aqaba (the Safi ones run more often) drive straight past both Bab adh-Dhraa and the turnoff to Lot's Cave, but it also should not be too hard to **hitch** a ride in either direction. For more information on travelling up or down the Wadi Araba road, see p.302. You may be lucky and find a *falafel* sandwich to **eat** in Safi, but there's no guarantee, and you'd do better to stock up beforehand with picnic supplies.

Bab adh-Dhraa

Just 1km or so before the road from Karak emerges onto the Dead Sea shore, the Bronze Age *tell* of **Bab adh-Dhraa** rises to the right of the road. As far as archeological remains go, the site is far more exciting for specialists than ordinary visitors, although, after scrambling up the *tell*, anyone can make out a thick **city wall** and a handful of building foundations. However, the attraction of Bab adh-Dhraa isn't so much in investigating the ruins as in relating the place to a name. A large town which flourished around 2600 BC, with some graves in the huge **cemetery** across the road dating from as early as the fourth millennium, Bab adh-Dhraa is the leading candidate for the biblical city of **Sodom**, location of so much wickedness and depravity that God felt compelled to raze the city and rain brimstone and fire down on the heads of its inhabitants (see the box opposite). Standing on the *tell* today, amidst barren rocks on the hazy shores of a salt lake, you can only wonder what on earth the poor Sodomites must have been up to in these rooms to deserve such damnation.

Lot's Cave

Under continuous excavation since 1988, **Lot's Cave** is an extraordinarily rich archeological site that has thrown up evidence of Early and Middle Bronze Age habitation, as well as Nabatean pottery, Byzantine mosaics and the earliest example of carved wood yet discovered intact in Jordan, a door that dates from the seventh-century Umayyad period. It's a shame that many of the more

SODOM AND GOMORRAH

The tale in Genesis of how God punished the depravity of the inhabitants of **Sodom and Gomorrah**, and how **Lot** and his wife escaped, is one of the best-known biblical stories, though some of the details are unfamiliar and unusual. After arriving in Canaan (Palestine), Lot and his uncle Abraham began to bicker over grazing grounds. They separated, and Lot pitched his tents at the southeastern corner of the Dead Sea near Sodom, one of the five "cities of the plain" (the others were Gomorrah, Zoar, Admah and Zeboyim). "But," as Genesis warns, "the men of Sodom were wicked and sinners before the Lord exceedingly." One evening, Lot was visited by two angels, come to warn him of the city's impending divine destruction. Lot, his wife and two daughters fled and "the Lord rained upon Sodom and Gomorrah brimstone and fire." Every one of the five cities was destroyed, and every person killed. As they were fleeing, Lot's wife disobeyed a divine order not to look back at the destruction, and was turned into a pillar of salt.

Seemingly the last people left alive in the world, Lot and his daughters sought refuge in a cave in the mountains. Calculating that, with all potential mates vapourized, they were likely to die childless, the daughters hatched a plan to get their father so drunk he wouldn't be able to tell who they were, whereupon they would seduce him and thus preserve the family. Everything worked to plan and both daughters gave birth to sons; the elder named her child **Moab**, and the younger Ben-Ammi, or "father of **Ammon**".

The last of these bizarre biblical episodes has been commemorated for centuries, and possibly millennia, at a cave-and-church complex in the hills above Safi. Ruins within Safi itself – as well as at four other scanty Early Bronze Age sites nearby (Bab adh-Dhraa, Numayra, Fifa and Khanazir) – show evidence of destruction by fire, and these could possibly be the five "cities of the plain". The only fly in the ointment is that they were razed around 2350 BC, several hundred years before the generally accepted era of Abraham and Lot.

interesting archeological discoveries have either been covered over or put into temporary storage, pending the projected establishment of a nearby Museum of the Dead Sea and Jordan Valley, but nonetheless the location – not to mention the notion of standing in Lot's sandalprints – is dramatic enough to warrant a visit.

Some 22km south of the Karak turning on the Wadi Araba road, a sign points left to the site; 1km down this road you must head left steeply up the hillside for 2km to a shack. This is where the guardian hangs out, and he'll probably accompany you up steep stairs to the site itself. The first area you come to is a **court**, part of which has slipped down the hill, but which originally served to support the floor of the **church** above. The main **apse** has seating for the bishop and is slightly raised. Five **mosaics** – one dated April 606, another May 691 – are currently under renovation. The **narthex** was originally entered from the right, via a doorway from the court below; this ingenious piece of design enabled visiting Jewish and Muslim pilgrims to avoid stepping inside the church and instead head straight for the holy **cave**, the entrance to which is to the left of the apse. A beautifully carved **lintel** over the cave entrance presages an interior mosaic (now covered for protection beneath the dirt floor) which mimics the round stones embedded in the roof. All around the church was spread a **monastery**, with the remains of six or seven isolated cells dotted around the parched hillside. The views from the church over the Dead Sea and the nearby town of Safi are stunning.

South of Karak

The King's Highway floats along the wheat-sown plateau south of Karak for 10km before reaching **Muta**, best known today as the home of one of Jordan's leading universities, but also the scene, in 629 AD, of the first major battle between the Byzantine Empire and the nascent Muslim army on its first surge out of Arabia. On this occasion, the Muslims were routed, and its generals, including the Prophet Muhammad's adopted son Zaid bin Haritha and his deputy Jaafar bin Abi Talib were killed. Some 3km south of Muta, in the town of **Mazar**, a large, royally funded mosque is currently being constructed over the shrines of Zaid and Jaafar; the small **Islamic museum** (daily except Tues 8am–2pm; free) in the same building is only of passing interest. According to legend, on his march north to Muta, Jaafar rested beneath the lone pistachio tree which survives today well beyond Mazar, to the left of the highway some 5km south of Qadsiyyeh; locals still bedeck the holy tree with pieces of cloth as expressions of their faith.

Khirbet Tannur

A little way out of Mazar, two roads, old and new, descend past the cultivated fields of Ayna village into the vast **Wadi Hasa**, a natural boundary which marked the transition from Moab into the land of Edom. Dominating the wadi is a huge and elementally scary black mountain – actually an extinct volcano – which clashes so startlingly with the white limestone all around that it seems to be under a permanent, ominous cloud. The Nabateans (see p.228) clearly felt something similar, since they built, on the conical hill of Jebel Tannur directly opposite, a large temple complex, **Khirbet Tannur**, ruined today but still visitable.

As you rise out of the wadi bed, a broken concrete sign on the right side of the highway, 24km from Mazar, marks the track leading to Khirbet Tannur. This is passable for a little way by car, but eventually you'll have to get out and make the tough climb across a saddle and up the steep slope to the atmospheric ruins.

The temple area dates from the second century AD, although some form of altar may have been constructed here up to two centuries earlier. Unfortunately, excavations in the 1930s carted off virtually everything of any interest, and all the carving and statuary that used to adorn the site now gathers dust in museums in Amman and Cincinnati. But, however hard it is to imagine the complete structures which once stood here, the windswept isolation of this rugged summit is able to resurrect the numinous presence of the Nabatean gods more potently even than Petra's quietest cranny.

You arrive on the summit more or less where the Nabatean worshippers would have arrived: in front is a humped threshold, originally part of the entrance **gateway** to a paved courtyard. It's easy to make out the wall foundations of three **rooms** to the right, and although only random chunks of decorative carving survive, many of the courtyard's **flagstones** are still in place. Ahead is a raised platform on which stood the small **temple**, its entrance originally crowned with a large carved image of the goddess Atargatis bedecked with vines and fruit, now on display in the Amman museum. Within the holy of holies stood images both of Atargatis and the god Zeus-Hadad.

Hammamat Afra and Tafileh

Barely 2km from the Khirbet Tannur turning, the King's Highway is carried over Wadi Laban, a tributary of Wadi Hasa, on a small bridge; no buses follow the small turning off to the right side, but private transport can bring you some 13km further to the luxurious hot springs at **Hammamat Afra**, a perfect place to come back down to earth after Khirbet Tannur. Before you reach Afra, a small branch road after 7km leads down to the much smaller springs at **Burbita**, but there's only one rather smelly pool here under a tin roof above the reedbeds – you'd do far better to carry on to the new resthouse currently under construction overlooking Afra's well-maintained **pools** (four outdoor ones for men, one indoors for women). The water here is a striking rust-red colour from the high iron content, and genuinely hot: the last pool on the left – popularly known as the *megla*, or frying pan – is a broiling 52°C. The walls all along the narrow valley drip water, mineral reds and mossy greens daubing the white limestone. Splashing barefoot up or down the warm river here is as much pleasure as flopping around in the pools with everybody else. Without your own transport, the only way to get to Afra is by taxi; the going rate from Tafileh is about JD10 round-trip.

South of Wadi Hasa, the King's Highway begins to climb into the Shara mountains, eventually reaching a small plateau where a road branches east to the Desert Highway (if you're heading north along the King's Highway, the signposting at this junction is very bad and it's easy to lose the way). Near here occurred, in January 1918, the only fully fledged battle of the Arab Revolt, Faysal and Lawrence's armies sweeping away an Ottoman force only to be halted in their tracks by heavy snow.

Some 25km south of the Afra turning, the picturesque town of **TAFILEH** comes into view, spread along gently curving terraces, with orchards of fruit and olives blanketing the hillside below. Although a governorate capital and a sizeable town, Tafileh has no specific attractions to make for, and you'll probably find yourself stopping only to switch buses. Along the main drag in the centre of town, the rather purposeless tourist office (daily except Fri 8am–2pm) looks onto the **bus station**, from where you can depart, generally in the mornings only, to Amman and Ma'an (via the Desert Highway), Aqaba (via the Wadi Araba road) and Karak (via the King's Highway). Further along, above a reeking chicken butcher, stands Tafileh's single **hotel**, the *Afra* (☎03/341832; ①) – bug-lovers will relish a night here. Buses to Qadsiyyeh depart from the main street 100m further. A handful of nameless diners serve basic Arabic **food**; the best is opposite the Qadsiyyeh bus stop.

Dana Nature Reserve

Around 27km south of Tafileh, a steep road winds down to the tiny village of Dana, at the eastern edge of Jordan's flagship **DANA NATURE RESERVE**, which encompasses the breathtakingly beautiful Wadi Dana and stretches as far as the Wadi Araba in the west. The village itself has been the scene of an extraordinary – and successful – social experiment (see the box on p.221) conducted by the Royal Society for the Conservation of Nature to rejuvenate a dying community by protecting the natural environment. Clinging to the edge of the cliff below the King's Highway, Dana is the starting-point for a series of walks and hikes through one of Jordan's few protected areas of natural beauty, and it is well worth a day or two of your time.

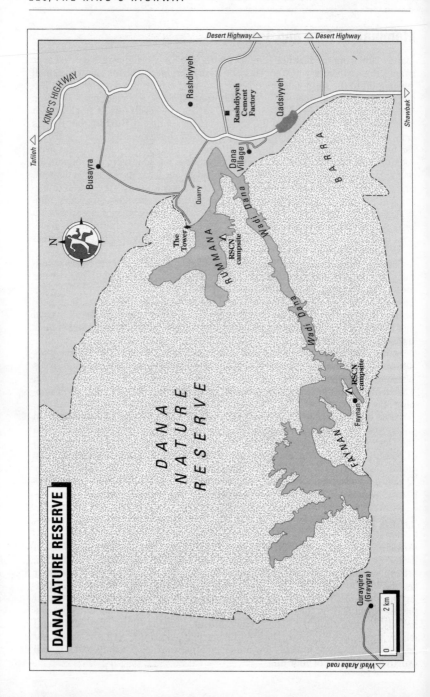

DANA NATURE RESERVE

DANA'S STORY

For most of the twentieth century **Dana** was a simple farming community thriving on a temperate climate, three abundant springs and good grazing; some inhabitants had previously left Tafileh specifically for a better life in the village. But as Jordan developed new technologies and the general standard of living rose, a growing number of villagers felt isolated in their mountain hamlet of Ottoman stone cottages. Some moved out in the late 1960s to found a new village, **Qadsiyyeh**, on the main Tafileh–Shawbak road, and the attractions of electricity and plumbing rapidly emptied primitive Dana. For many people, the construction of the huge Rashdiyyeh cement factory close by in the early 1980s was the last straw: with well-paid jobs for the taking, most locals saw the daily trek up from the village to the factory as pointless, and almost everyone moved to Qadsiyyeh.

Dana lay semi-abandoned for a decade or more, its handful of impoverished farmers forced to compete in the local markets with bigger farms using more advanced methods of production. This was what a group of twelve women from Amman discovered in the early 1990s as they travelled across the country to catalogue the remnants of traditional Jordanian culture. Realizing the deprivation faced by some of the poorest people in the country, these "**Friends of Dana**" embarked on a project to renovate and revitalize the fabric of the village under the auspices of the **Royal Society for the Conservation of Nature**. Electricity, telephones and a water supply were extended to the village and 65 cottages renovated. People started to drift back to Dana. The RSCN quickly realized the potential of the secluded Wadi Dana for scientific research, and, in a new $3.3 million project funded partly by the World Bank and the UN, turned the area into a protected **reserve**, built a small research station next to the village and, in 1994, launched a detailed ecological survey. Dana's small-scale agriculture was clearly no longer economically viable and thousands of domesticated goats, sheep and camels had overgrazed the wadi for decades; continued grazing couldn't be reconciled with the need for environmental protection and was banned, and studies were made into the feasibility of creating sustainable opportunities for villagers to gain a livelihood from the reserve without destroying it. The ingenious solution came in redirecting the village's traditional crops to a new market. Dana's farmers produced their olives, figs, grapes, other fruits and nuts as before, but, instead of going to market, they sold everything to the RSCN, who employed Dana villagers to process these crops into novelty products such as organically produced jams and olive-oil soap for direct sale to relatively wealthy, environmentally aware consumers. Medicinal herbs were introduced as a cash crop to aid the economic recovery; and the last Dana resident familiar with traditional pottery-making has been encouraged to teach her craft to a younger generation. Dana soon hit the headlines, and in 1996 the RSCN launched low-impact tourism to the reserve, with the traditional-style Guesthouse going up next to the research buildings. Local villagers – some of whom were already employed as research scientists – now also work as managers and guides.

Dana is unique in the Middle East, a positive, visionary programme combining scientific research, social reconstruction and sustainable tourism. The nurturing of traditional crafts and the rejuvenation of a village economy by creating an array of long-term jobs for local people have managed to proceed successfully hand-in-hand with active protection of the environment. Quite apart from its extraordinary natural beauty, Dana is worth visiting to see its remarkable achievements.

On the way down to the village, a small **viewing platform** gives a tremendous panorama of Wadi Dana and the roofs of the old stone cottages of the village below. Once you arrive, it's worth stopping in at the RSCN-run **Guesthouse** – whether you're staying there or not – for the views from their terrace and to get some first-hand information about the wildlife of the reserve from the experts. Dropping from 1500m above sea level at Dana to well below sea level west of Faynan, the geology of the reserve switches from limestone to sandstone to granite, ecosystems varying from lush, well-watered mountain slopes and open oak and juniper woodlands to scrubland and arid sandy desert. The list of flora and resident fauna is dizzying: a brief roundup includes various kinds of eagles, falcons, kestrels and vultures, cuckoos, larks, owls, wheatears, the Sinai rosefinch and Tristram's serin; wildcats, caracals, hyenas, foxes, wolves and porcupine; snakes, chameleons and lizards galore; and, so far, three plants new to science.

The village itself is also worth exploring, and the RSCN can set up a visit to the jewellery workshops and fruit-drying centres for you. Next to the Guesthouse is a small **shop** (daily 9am–4pm) selling local products. If you want to head into the **reserve** (daily dawn–dusk; JD5), the only way is on foot: cars are banned. The Guesthouse has leaflets on possible **walks** around and about, and can provide a trained **nature guide** for JD6–10 for short walks or JD30 for a full day; or you can strike out alone. Highly recommended is the three-hour hike on a reasonably level path around the head of the wadi to the campsite at **Rummana** (where ibex are frequent visitors). A guide lives on site at Rummana and can point you onto small and easy trails into the gorgeous countryside around the campsite. An exhilarating four- or five-hour trek from Dana along the floor of the wadi brings you to **Faynan**, site of another campsite and, in antiquity, an extensive copper-smelting settlement; British-led archeological investigations to discover more are ongoing. Another highly explorable area is **Barra**, a 15-minute drive south of the village, where lush woodlands give way to networks of canyons and gorges cutting into the mountainous landscape. If you arrive in summer, you'd be unwise to turn down the chance for an expert-guided **night walk** into the reserve, giving the chance to see the wadi come alive after dark with wildlife. Two- and three-day hikes within the reserve can be arranged with advance notice, and a four-day trail from Dana to Petra via Faynan and Baydha is currently being opened up.

Practicalities

The only **bus to Dana** shuttles regularly to and from Qadsiyyeh on the King's Highway above. Qadsiyyeh is connected by regular buses with Tafileh, but the section of the King's Highway to the south, between Qadsiyyeh and Shawbak, has no public transport at all. Hitching is one option, or a full **taxi** to Dana from Shawbak or Tafileh shouldn't cost more than JD5, from Wadi Musa JD10. If you're **driving**, you might easily miss the Dana turnoff, 3km south of the Rashdiyyeh cement factory: forget the brown roadsigns (which are confusingly far from the right place) and look out instead for a square black one at the junction. Away from the village, the RSCN's **Rummana campsite** (see below) is accessible by road: 22km south of Tafileh, just before the highway passes through a small grove of trees, turn right (the sign says "Ain Lahda"), and follow this bumpy dirt road past a huge quarry on the left and down a left turn. Some 800m beyond a lone roadside pistachio tree, Jordan's last three wild cypress trees are visible silhouetted on a hillside over your right shoulder. A little further, at the entrance to the reserve (daily 7.30am–dusk; JD5), is the "Tower" where you must park; a shuttle bus from here down to the campsite is free.

ACCOMMODATION AND EATING

Dana's **accommodation** – whether in a building or under canvas – isn't cheap but, considering what's been achieved in the village, is worth the extra and more. The lack of shops or diners means that, for **eating**, you must either take all meals in one of the two hotels, or bring in supplies for picnics and self-catering; in many ways, the latter is much preferable.

For the cosy atmosphere, simple comforts and an incredible silence, a night at the small RSCN-run *Guesthouse* (☎03/368497, fax 368499; ③–④) overlooking Wadi Dana is likely to be your most memorable in Jordan. Nine rooms are attractively furnished in spartan style, spotlessly clean and most with private balconies. You can pay less for no balcony, or more for an en-suite bathroom, but should always book well in advance. Prices include a good breakfast, and, with notice, they can lay on substantial lunches and dinners for JD6 extra per meal. The tiny, grubby *Dana Hotel* (☎ & fax 03/368537; ②) in the middle of the village – unconnected with the RSCN – has five basic rooms, spacious but dark and draughty, with shared outside bathrooms. Breakfast is JD2 extra, lunch and dinner JD4 each.

However, the great Dana outdoors is best experienced by **camping**. The RSCN has two campsites in the reserve, in the hills at Rummana (March–Oct only), reachable by walking or driving; and down where Wadi Dana meets Wadi Araba at Faynan (open all year; walking only from Dana, or by 4x4 from Wadi Araba – see p.303). Prices for both are the same, and won't cheer a miser's heart: apart from the JD5 to enter the reserve, you pay JD5 to hire a solid, roomy tent that sleeps four and comes with mattresses and blankets, plus JD5 per person. In order to control numbers in the reserve, you're not allowed to pitch your own tent. The Rummana campsite has excellent facilities, including separate, spotless toilet and cold-shower blocks and a proper kitchen; you can book meals ahead for JD3–5, or pay JD2 to cook your own food. Faynan has similar, but more basic facilities, shared with the archeologists. The only other option for camping is a less well-maintained site run by the *Dana Hotel* people near the Ain Kharrara spring in the wadi (they can drive you down there). Here, a two-person tent is JD20 all-in and there are cold showers and a simple kitchen. Women will experience no intrusive hassles at any of the campsites or hotels.

Shawbak castle

Perched dramatically like a ship on the crest of a hill, **Shawbak castle** was the first to be built by the Crusaders in Transjordan (see p.212 for some Crusader history). In a more ruinous state than Karak castle, and much rebuilt by Mamlukes and Ottomans, it's nonetheless well worth an exploratory detour, and entrance is free. The castle is 3km west of **SHAWBAK** town, which is itself some 22km south of Qadsiyyeh. Set in acres of lush orchards, Shawbak is Jordan's leading producer of apples, but this quiet farming village has also been trying for years to reap some benefit from the tourists heading south to Petra. Aside from the excellent *falafel* diners on the main drag, its numerous groceries beat those in Wadi Musa on both price and quality – if you intend to picnic in Petra, you might do well to stock up here in advance. No buses run up to the castle, so if you arrive in Shawbak without transport, you'll need to persuade a taxi-driver to take you or face a stiff climb.

As they are today, the **walls** and **towers** are Mamluke, and all the towers which stand have beautifully carved external calligraphic inscriptions dating from rebuilding work in the 1290s. As you enter, down and to the left is a small **chapel**, at the back of which are pools and channels of unknown usage. Below the chapel runs a long, dank and pitch-dark **secret passage**, which supposedly brings you out in the middle of the castle if you head right and outside the walls if you head left. To the left side of the **gatehouse**, two round wells presage a scarier secret passage – a dark and foul opening with, apparently, 375 broken and slippery steps leading down into the heart of the hill. Even archeologists only got to number 150 or so before giving up, but legend has it that this was the castle's main water supply: somehow the Crusaders knew that by digging down so far they'd eventually hit water. The gatehouse gives onto a street, at the end of which is a building with three **arched entrances**, one topped by a calligraphic panel; up until the 1950s the castle was still inhabited, and this building was the old village school. If you head through to the back and turn right, a long vaulted corridor leads you out to the north side of the castle, and a maze of abandoned **Ottoman cottages**, beneath which is an exposed **Ayyubid palace** complex, with a large reception hall and baths. Further round towards the entrance stand the beautiful arches of a **church**, beneath which is a small room filled with catapult balls and chunks of carved masonry.

travel details

No timetables are in operation – most buses, and all minibuses and *service*s simply depart when they're full.

Buses, minibuses and *service*s

Ariha to: Karak (40min).

Dana to: Qadsiyyeh (10min).

Dhiban to: Madaba (40min).

Faysaliyyeh (Mount Nebo) to: Madaba (15min).

Hammamat Ma'in to: Amman (JETT office; 1 daily; 1hr 45min); Madaba (1hr).

Karak to: Amman (Wihdat station; 2hr); Aqaba (3hr); Ariha (40min); Ma'an (2hr); Qasr (20min); Rabba (15min); Safi (40min); Tafileh (1hr); Zerqa (New station; 2hr 30min).

Madaba to: Amman (Abdali station; 30min); Amman (Raghadan station; 30min); Amman (Saqf Sayl; 45min); Amman (Wihdat station; 30min); Dhiban (40min); Faysaliyyeh (Mount Nebo; 15min); Hammamat Ma'in (50min); Ma'in village (15min); Mukawir (1hr); Umm ar-Rasas (50min); Zerqa (New station; 1hr).

Ma'in village to: Madaba (15min).

Mukawir to: Madaba (1hr).

Qadsiyyeh to: Dana (5min); Tafileh (40min).

Qasr to: Karak (20min).

Rabba to: Karak (15min).

Safi to: Aqaba (2hr); Karak (1hr).

Shawbak to: Amman (Wihdat station; 2hr 45min); Ma'an (30min); Wadi Musa/Petra (30min).

Tafileh to: Amman (Wihdat station; 2hr 30min); Aqaba (2hr 30min); Karak (1hr); Ma'an (1hr); Qadsiyyeh (40min).

Umm ar-Rasas to: Madaba (50min).

CHAPTER FIVE

PETRA

Petra is overwhelming. That anybody should even have the idea of carving ornate classical facades – hundreds of them – into the desert cliffs is surreal enough, but then actually to do it with such skill and assuredness simply beggars belief. Tucked away in a remote valley basin in the heart of southern Jordan's Shara mountains and shielded from the outside world behind an impenetrable barrier of rock, Petra cannot fail to instil a sense of mystery and drama. Today, it's almost as if time has literally drawn a veil over the once-great city, which grew wealthy enough on the caravan trade to challenge the might of Rome: two millennia of wind and rain have blurred the sharp edges of the facades and rubbed away at the soft sandstone to expose vivid bands of colour beneath. Since a Western adventurer stumbled on the fabled ancient city in 1812, Petra has fired imaginations, its crumbling grandeur and dramatic setting pushing it – like Palmyra and the Pyramids – into the realms of legend.

From where Petra sits, in a valley basin between two lines of jagged peaks, there's only one route in and out, and that passes through the modern town of **Wadi Musa**, on the eastern side of the mountains. Consequently, in the last few decades Wadi Musa has grown to serve the lucrative tourist trade to Petra, and has all the hotels, restaurants and services: there's nowhere to stay within the ancient city, and virtually nowhere to eat either. The single ticket gate into Petra is in humdrum Wadi Musa, but once you've crossed the ticket barrier, you're immediately thrown into the rocky landscape of the desert. Within Petra there is no urban development of any kind, and the local culture is all rural. Spending a few days here is a constant to-and-fro – down-at-heel Wadi Musa providing all the necessaries of life and majestic Petra all the historical and natural drama.

Some history

In prehistory, the Petra region saw some of the first experiments in farming. The hunter-gatherers of the Paleolithic Age gave way, over nine thousand years ago, to settled communities living in walled farming villages such as at **Baydha**, just north of Petra. Nomadic tribes passed through the Petra basin in the millennia following, but the spur to its development came with attempts at contact between the two great ancient powers of Mesopotamia and Egypt. The desert plateaux of Mesopotamia, to the east of the King's Highway, were sealed off by high mountains from the routes both across the Naqb (Negev) to Gaza and across the Sinai to Egypt; somehow a caravan route across the barrier had to be found if contact was to be made. Petra, where abundant springs tumble down into the Wadi Araba through a natural fault in the mountains, was prime choice, marking the spot on the north–south King's Highway where an east–west passage could connect the two empires.

The first significant mention of Petra is in the Old Testament, as the **Israelites** approached Edom after their forty years in the desert. Local legend – running

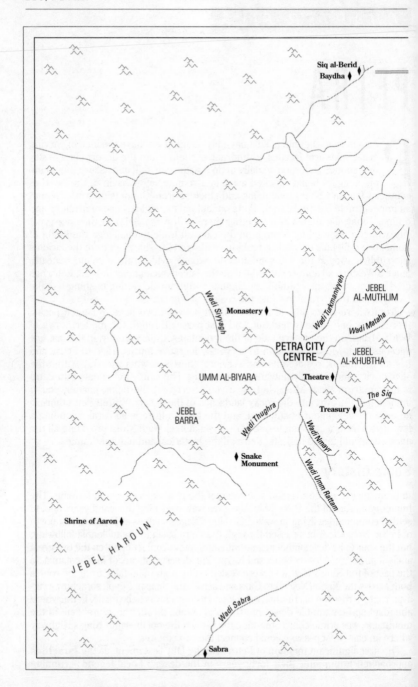

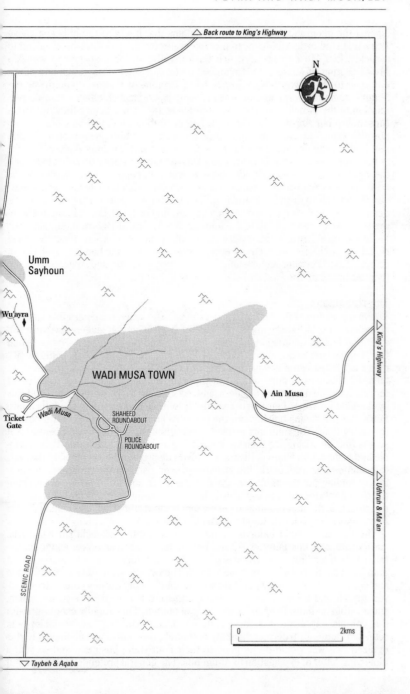

Back route to King's Highway

N

Umm
Sayhoun

Wu'ayra

WADI MUSA TOWN

Ain Musa

Ticket
Gate

Wadi Musa

SHAHEED
ROUNDABOUT

POLICE
ROUNDABOUT

King's Highway

Udhruh & Ma'an

SCENIC ROAD

0   2kms

Taybeh & Aqaba

against the geographical evidence – maintains that it was in the hills just above Petra that God ordered Moses to produce water for the Israelites by speaking to a rock; when Moses instead struck the rock, the spring that gushed was **Ain Musa** (Spring of Moses), today housed beneath a small domed building at the entrance to the town of Wadi Musa. **King Reqem** of Edom – Reqem was the Semitic name for Petra, and he was probably just a local chieftain – refused permission to the Israelites to pass through his territory, but before they departed, Moses' brother Aaron (Musa and Haroun in Arabic) died, and was buried supposedly on top of **Jebel Haroun** overlooking Petra. A white shrine atop the mountain is still a site of pilgrimage for Jews, Christians and Muslims alike.

Just after 1000 BC, the Israelite **King David** moved to take control of Petra and the whole of Edom – by now rich on the proceeds of copper production as well as trade. His son **Solomon** consolidated the Israelite grip on trade and technology, and for fifty years diverted Petra's profits into his own coffers. However, after his death, the Israelite kingdom collapsed and feuding erupted. Some Edomites withdrew to a settlement on top of the impregnable **Umm al-Biyara** mountain overlooking central Petra and to a village at **Tawilan** above Ain Musa. Fluctuations in regional power soon after led to Petra passing from Edomite hands to Assyrian to Babylonian to Persian: such instability left the way open for a new people to stamp their authority on the land and stake a claim to its future.

The Nabateans

The first mention of the **Nabateans** was in 647 BC, when they were listed as one of the enemies of Ashurbanipal, last king of Assyria; at that stage, they were still a tribe of bedouin nomads inhabiting northern and northwestern Arabia. When the Babylonians depopulated much of Palestine during the sixth century BC, many Edomites came down from Petra to claim the empty land to the west. In turn, the Nabateans migrated out of the arid Arabian desert to the lusher and more temperate mountains of Edom, and, specifically, to the well-watered and easily defended prize of Petra. Whereas the Edomites had occupied the hills above Petra, the Nabateans quickly saw the potential for developing the central bowl of the valley floor. The migrants arrived slowly, though, and for several centuries it seems that most stuck to their bedouin lifestyle, building little other than a temple and refuge atop Umm al-Biyara. However, displaying the adaptability that was to become their trademark, the Nabateans soon gave up the traditional occupation of raiding the plentiful caravans that passed to and fro in favour of charging the merchants for safe passage and a place to do business. It was probably around this time that the first organized, permanent trading emporium was established at Petra, and Edom became known as **Arabia Petrea**.

The Roman author Diodorus Siculus reports that the Seleucid ruler of Syria, **Antigonus**, attacked Petra in 312 BC, both to limit Nabatean power and to undermine Ptolemaic authority. His troops sneaked in under cover of darkness, and found that all the Nabatean men were away. The Greeks slaughtered a few women and children and hurriedly made off with as much booty as they could carry – silver, myrrh and frankincense. However, someone managed to raise the alarm, since within an hour, the Nabateans were in pursuit. They rapidly caught up with the complacent army, massacred all but fifty, recovered the valuables and returned home. In true merchant style, though, the Nabateans instinctively recognized that war would do no good to their flourishing business, and so sent a mollifying letter of explanation to Antigonus. The general pretended to accept, but was secretly fuming; he let some time pass before sending another army against Petra. The small garrison they encountered, however, was easily able to repel the attackers. Comfortably ensconced in their unassailable headquarters and with almost limitless resources of money, the Nabateans acted the wealthy tycoon: unruffled by the skirmish, they reached into their deep pockets to buy peace from the humiliated Greeks.

Over the following two centuries, the battling between Seleucid Syria and Ptolemaic Egypt for control of Alexander's empire enabled the Nabateans to fill the power vacuum in Transjordan and extend their kingdom far beyond Petra. By 80 BC they were in control of Damascus. The Nabatean capital grew fabulously wealthy on its profits from **trade**, standing at the pivots between Egypt, Arabia and Syria, and between East Asia and the Mediterranean. Traditional commodities such as copper, iron and Dead Sea bitumen, used for embalming in Egypt, were losing ground to spices from the southern Arabian coast – myrrh, balsam and frankincense, the last of which was central to religious ritual all over the Hellenistic world. Pepper, ginger, sugar and cotton arrived from India for onward distribution. Chinese documents even talk of imports of silk, glass, gold, silver, henna and frankincense from a place known as Li-Kan, taken to be a corruption of "Reqem". Nabatean power seemed limitless, and even when **Pompey** sent troops against Petra in 62 BC, the Nabateans were able to buy peace from the Roman Empire for the price of three hundred talents of silver. Petran prosperity grew and grew.

From then on Petra was at its zenith, with a settled population of perhaps as many as 30,000. The Roman author Strabo describes it as a wealthy, cosmopolitan city, full of fine buildings and villas, gardens and watercourses, with Romans and other foreigners thronging the streets, and a democratic king. "The Nabateans", reported Strabo, "are so acquisitive that they give honours to those who increase their possessions, and publicly fine those who lose them." However, the writing was on the wall. The discovery of the monsoon winds had begun to cause a shift in trade patterns: overland routes from Arabia were being abandoned in favour of transport by sea. In addition, Rome was sponsoring the diversion of inland trade away from the upstart Petra, instead directing it into Egypt and via the Wadi Sirhan into Syria, presaging the rise of Palmyra. Pressure on Nabatea to come to heel was inexorable. The last Nabatean king, Rabbel II, tried moving his capital from Petra north to Bosra, but eventually had to strike a deal with Rome. On his death in 106 AD the entire Nabatean kingdom passed peacefully into Roman hands.

The Roman, Byzantine and Crusader eras

Under the **Romans**, Petra became a principal centre of the new *Provincia Arabia*, and seems to have undergone something of a cultural renaissance, with the theatre and Colonnaded Street both being renovated. The city was important enough to be visited by Emperor Hadrian in 130, and possibly also by Emperor Severus in 199. However, the tide of history was turning, and by 300 Petra was in serious decline, with houses and temples falling derelict through lack of maintenance. Palmyra, an oasis entrepot in the eastern Syrian desert, was on the ascendant, and sea trade into Egypt was well established; Petra was stuck between the two, and there was no reason to keep it alive. Roman patronage began to drift away from the city, and, sensing the party was over, entrepreneurs and merchants followed.

Petra's decline was drawn out. **Christianity** was adopted as the official religion of the empire in 324, but for many decades after that the proud Nabateans mingled elements of the new faith with remnants of their own pagan heritage. The massive earthquake of 363, according to the contemporary bishop of Jerusalem, levelled half of Petra, although the city limped on for another couple of centuries. In 447, the **Urn Tomb** was converted into a huge church, and both the lavishly decorated **Petra Church** and plainer **Ridge Church** were built within the following century or so. Nonetheless, by the time of the seventh-century Islamic invasion, Petra was more or less deserted, and the earthquake of 747 probably forced the final stragglers to depart the crumbling city.

On their push through Transjordan in the early twelfth century, the **Crusaders** built small forts within Petra at **al-Habees** and **Wu'ayra**, though these were tiny outposts of their headquarters at nearby Shawbak and were abandoned less than a century later. In 1276, the **Mamluke** sultan Baybars – on his way from Cairo to suppress a revolt in Karak – entered Petra from the southwest and proceeded through the deserted city "amidst most marvellous caves, the facades sculptured into the very rock face". He emerged from the Siq on June 6, 1276, and, as far as records show, was the last person, other than the local bedouin, to see Petra for over five hundred years.

The modern era

On August 22, 1812, a Swiss scholar and explorer, Jean Louis **Burckhardt** (see the box below), entered the Siq in heavy Arab disguise in the company of a local guide.

"SHEIKH IBRAHIM" BURCKHARDT

Jean Louis Burckhardt was born in Lausanne in 1784, son of a colonel in the French army, and became a strong-willed and energetic teenager. He travelled to London when he was 22 and shortly after came under the wing of the Association for Promoting the Discovery of the Interior Parts of Africa, which offered him the mission of discovering the source of the River Niger. Burckhardt accepted. Then as now, Egypt was the gateway into Africa, and so he devised a plan to familiarize himself with Islam and Arab culture in preparation for the expedition. Journeys into the Middle East at this time were seen, with some justification, as extremely dangerous: the territory was virtually unknown and local people (few of whom had ever seen Europeans) were engaged in continuous tribal skirmishing and highly suspicious of outsiders. While still in England, Burckhardt embarked on crash courses in Arabic, astronomy and medicine, and took to sleeping on the ground and eating nothing but vegetables to toughen himself up.

On arrival in Aleppo in 1810, locals immediately questioned him about his strange accent. Burckhardt told his cover story: that he was a Muslim trader from India and his mother tongue wasn't Arabic but Hindustani. Suspicion persisted, and he was pressed to say something in Hindustani, whereupon he let loose a volley of fluent Swiss-German – which seemed to satisfy the doubters. Burckhardt spent over two years in Aleppo, adopting local customs, taking the name **Sheikh Ibrahim ibn Abdallah**, perfecting his Arabic and becoming enough of an expert in Quranic law that disputes were often brought to him for resolution.

In 1812, Burckhardt set off for Cairo, recording everything that he saw and experienced in a **secret journal** – had he been found out, no doubt he would have been killed as a spy. Around Karak, he heard the locals talking of an amazing ancient city locked away in the heart of an impenetrable mountain. His curiosity was aroused, but there was no way he could openly declare an interest without

His short visit, and the notes and sketches he managed to make in secret, brought the fable of Petra to the attention of the world once again. In May 1818, two commanders of the British Royal Navy, C. Irby and J. Mangles, spent some days sightseeing in the ancient city, but it was the visits of **Léon de Laborde** in 1826 and the British artist **David Roberts** in 1839 that brought plentiful images of Petra to the West. Laborde's engravings were often fanciful and cloyingly romanticized, but Roberts's drawings were surprisingly accurate. As well as helping to shape the legend of Petra in Western minds – **Burgon**'s oft-quoted line about the "rose-red city" (see the box on p.248) appeared within a few years – they also launched tourism to the place. The second half of the nineteenth century saw a steady trickle of earnest visitors, even though Petra was still a destination way off any beaten tracks, reached only with extreme hardship on horse or camel from Jerusalem. Serious archeological investigation began at the turn of the century, with specialists cataloguing all Petra's monuments in 1898 and producing the first accurate maps in 1925.

By this time, the Thomas Cook Travel Company had set up a camp near the Qasr al-Bint for European tourists, offering the choice of tent or cave accommodation; until a regular bus service from Amman began in 1980, facilities around the site were minimal. Wadi Musa town remained a backwater, despite the designation of Petra as a national park. In the early 1980s, after protracted but fruitless negotiations, the government ordered the **Bdul** tribe (see p.251), who had been resident in Petra's caves for as long as anyone could remember, to move out to

bringing suspicion onto himself: a genuine devotee of Islam would know that such ruins were the work of infidels and of no concern. Burckhardt made up a story that he had vowed to sacrifice a goat at the shrine of the Prophet Aaron atop Jebel Haroun near the ruins – an unimpeachably honourable motive for pressing on.

As he and his guide approached Wadi Musa (then known by its old name of Elji), they were stopped by the Liyathneh tribe, camped near Ain Musa, who tried to persuade them to sacrifice their goat there and then, with the white shrine in plain view on the distant summit. But Sheikh Ibrahim insisted on going on, much to the irritation of his guide. They went down the steep hill, on into the Siq, and soon came up to the Treasury. Burckhardt, concealing both his excitement and his journal, somehow managed to make detailed notes and a sketch of the facade, and they continued throughout the city in this way, Burckhardt writing and sketching in secret, his guide becoming ever more suspicious. They reached the foot of Jebel Haroun as dusk was falling, and Burckhardt finally submitted to his guide's insistence that they make the sacrifice and turn back. He had seen enough.

After Petra, Burckhardt's adventures continued: he arrived in Cairo to prepare for his great African expedition, but quickly got tangled in bureaucracy. While cooling his heels, he travelled deep into Nubia, crossed the Red Sea to Jeddah (and was probably the first Christian ever to enter Mecca, where he made a profound impression on the religious judge of the city with his Quranic learning), and explored Sinai, but back in Egypt in 1817, he contracted dysentery and died in eleven days, with his journey to the Niger not even begun. All Burckhardt's journals were published after his death, *Travels in Nubia* and *Travels in Arabia* overshadowed by the news of his rediscovery of Petra, published in 1822 in **Travels in Syria and the Holy Land**. His **grave**, bearing his pseudonym Sheikh Ibrahim, is still visitable in a Muslim cemetery in Cairo, and its existence shows that, far from being simply a game or ploy, Burckhardt's *alter ego* took on a genuine life of its own.

Umm Sayhoun, a purpose-built settlement of small breezeblock houses 4km from both Petra itself and the town of Wadi Musa. The prospect of electricity, running water, healthcare and better education for the kids proved irresistible, and, in dribs and drabs, the Bdul departed. Development of the site and archeological exploration took off, although some older folk live on in the Nabatean tombs that they see as their inheritance.

For some years before the peace treaty was signed with Israel in 1994, Petra had stood for young Israelis as a rite of passage: many sneaked across the highly militarized border to visit, collect a rock and return to a hero's acclaim (although some never made it home again). The treaty opened the floodgates, and 1995 was a boom season, with dozens of hotels going up in Wadi Musa to serve the busloads of Israelis come to see the legend with their own eyes. Since then, tourism has plummeted, and Wadi Musa was the first to feel the pinch, although Petra remains Jordan's top tourist draw by a long streak.

WADI MUSA

WADI MUSA is an anomaly, a southern Jordanian town much like any other given a strange new twist with lots of signs in English, a huge number of hotels and something of a gold-rush energy. This unpretentious little place overlooks the most lucrative source of tourist income in the country, and yet its stolid roots hold firm. Plagued by disastrously bad management of resources and town planning of the most tragically shortsighted kind, Wadi Musa is filled with a tawdry and rather sad air of powerlessness, a small agricultural community resigned to a collective free-for-all scrabbling at the whirlwinds of cash drifting through its fingers. It's a ramshackle place, not flashy at all, and for those locals who don't make their living serving tourists, utterly run-of-the-mill. Farmers and labourers walk on the broken streets, and the usual vegetable stalls, butchers and workshops crowd the humdrum centre of town. Only the final strip just before the Petra ticket gate – a self-consciously touristic quarter below the town, lined with pristine facades but straggling half-built up the hillside behind – lacks the usual mundane atmosphere.

Arrival and orientation

Considering the popularity of the place, **public transport** provision for Wadi Musa is diabolical. *Service*s and a few buses run from Amman's Wihdat station

---

IN THE PINK

Wadi Musa may not be flush financially, but these days there's a rosy glow to its cheeks. A few years back, after much deliberation, the joint forces of the municipality, the Petra Regional Council, the Governorate of Ma'an and the Ministry of Tourism, amongst other weighty bodies, came to the decision that all buildings in Wadi Musa, new and old, should be painted exactly the same shade of pink, in order to give the town a motif and to reflect Petra's "rose-red" reputation. Much of the town complied, but many buildings still obstinately remain white or, worse, grey: local people report wryly that pink paint is not cheap.

(via the Desert Highway) and Aqaba in the mornings only, and a single bus arrives in the early morning from Wadi Rum. More frequent buses arrive from Ma'an and Shawbak – but these towns are hardly high on most visitors' agendas. The JETT company (☎06/566 4146) ran a big, comfy air-con bus – with the pricey optional extra of a guided tour – from their Amman office to the Petra Visitors' Centre daily from 1980 until 1998, when a lack of custom forced them – temporarily they said – to axe the service. It's currently uncertain if it will be restarted, or on what basis.

All buses and *services* into Wadi Musa from north and south funnel along the main road past the **Ain Musa** spring in the hills to the east of Petra. From here, the whole of Wadi Musa town is strung along a four-kilometre-long road which eventually terminates at the Petra ticket gate. If you're on a bus, you'll probably be dropped at the **Shaheed Roundabout** in the middle of Wadi Musa (although there are no signs naming it), or you could ask to be let out at the hotel of your choice along the way. In theory, the same thing happens in a *service*, but you may well find that the driver "recommends" a particular hotel by taking you to the door. Feel free to accept or decline, but be aware that he only does this to earn a commission from the hotel, who will correspondingly charge you a little more for your room. Note that there are no buses operating within Wadi Musa, and the only means of town transport is **taxi** (see p.240).

If you have **private transport**, it's worth knowing that the two roads which meet at Ain Musa – the King's Highway from Shawbak and the Desert Highway feeder road from Ma'an via Udhruh – aren't the most scenic entries into the Petra area. Coming from **the north**, you'd do far better to take the right turn marked Abdalih 16km south of Shawbak, which takes you the back way through beautiful countryside, with fantastic views of Jebel Haroun and the Petra mountains; a left turn is signposted near Baydha, and once beyond Umm Sayhoun and Wu'ayra you're finally deposited at the *Mövenpick* hotel. Coming from **the south**, the left turn just as you crest the plateau at Ras an-Naqb is the southernmost stretch of the King's Highway and takes you across the rolling fields to the village of Taybeh; from here, the road, dubbed the "Scenic Road", clings to the cliffside with dramatic views over the whole of Petra until you arrive at the Police Roundabout (just up the hill from the Shaheed Roundabout) in Wadi Musa. This route from Taybeh has been under major reconstruction for several years and is slated for final resurfacing sometime in 1999 (though don't count on it); just dodge the bulldozers and keep going.

Accommodation

In keeping with Petra's status as Jordan's top attraction, Wadi Musa has **accommodation** to suit all budgets except the very tightest. At the last count there were 65 hotels, most of them drab mid-range places flung up in the good old days of 1994 to deal with the tide of Israelis flooding across the border. Mideast politics swiftly put paid to the boom, though, and these days dozens of hotels stand empty most of the year, many with whole floors half-built awaiting better days.

Wadi Musa's hotel prices are more open to **bargaining** than anywhere else in Jordan, especially in the low seasons of June to August and November to February. **En-suite bathrooms** are offered as standard in virtually all hotels, from budget upwards. Another feature of Wadi Musa is that all hotels have rates

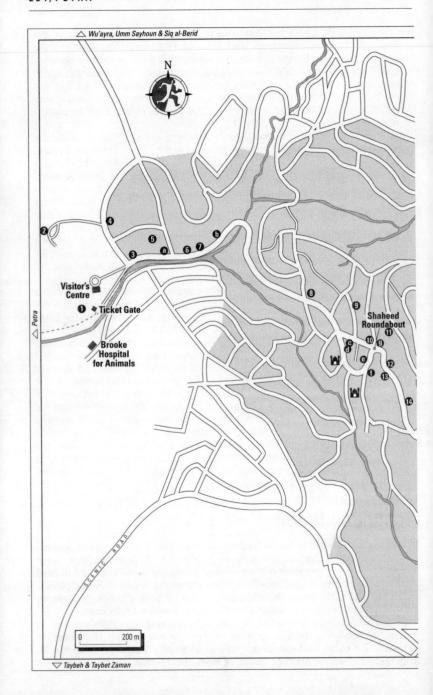

N

Wu'ayra, Umm Sayhoun & Siq al-Berid

Petra

Visitor's Centre

1 Ticket Gate

Brooke Hospital for Animals

Shaheed Roundabout

0   200 m

Taybeh & Taybet Zaman

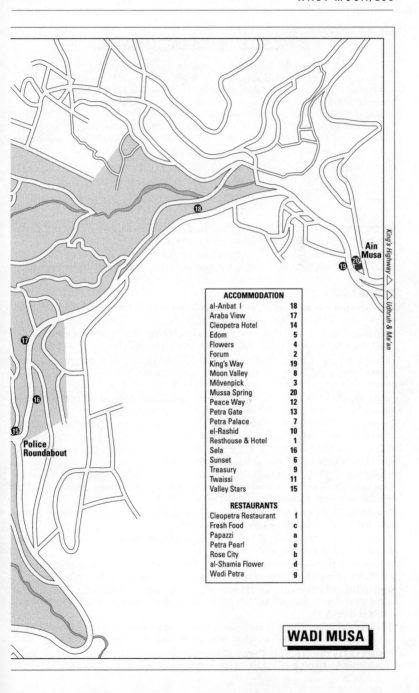

King's Highway ▷
▷ **Udruh & Ma'an**

**Ain
Musa**

**Police
Roundabout**

ACCOMMODATION

al-Anbat I	**18**
Araba View	**17**
Cleopetra Hotel	**14**
Edom	**5**
Flowers	**4**
Forum	**2**
King's Way	**19**
Moon Valley	**8**
Mövenpick	**3**
Mussa Spring	**20**
Peace Way	**12**
Petra Gate	**13**
Petra Palace	**7**
el-Rashid	**10**
Resthouse & Hotel	**1**
Sela	**16**
Sunset	**6**
Treasury	**9**
Twaissi	**11**
Valley Stars	**15**

RESTAURANTS

Cleopetra Restaurant	**f**
Fresh Food	**c**
Papazzi	**a**
Petra Pearl	**e**
Rose City	**b**
al-Shamia Flower	**d**
Wadi Petra	**g**

WADI MUSA

HOTEL PRICE CODES

Throughout this guide, hotels have been categorized according to the **price codes** given below, which indicate the normal price for the **cheapest double room** in a particular establishment during the **high season** (excluding the ten-percent tax and ten-percent service charge levied in all hotels of ③ and above). **Single rooms** can cost anything between seventy and a hundred percent of the double-room rates. Where a hotel offers beds in **shared rooms**, the price per person to share has been given; if a price code has also been included, this indicates that private rooms are also available. For a fuller explanation, see p.39.

① under JD10	④ JD30–40	⑦ JD65–80
② JD10–20	⑤ JD40–50	⑧ JD80–95
③ JD20–30	⑥ JD50–65	⑨ over JD95

for room only, **bed-and-breakfast**, and **half-board** (breakfast and dinner): make sure you confirm what you want when you check in.

All hotels listed below have been **keyed** by number, which corresponds to the map on pp.234-5; the higher the number, the further from the Petra ticket gate.

Budget hotels

The main thing to look out for in a **budget hotel** in Wadi Musa is heating: summer nights are cool enough that natural air conditioning is free, but all during winter and even as late as April, mornings and evenings can be very chilly. Most of these hotels have some double-bed rooms, but you won't find a soft mattress at any of them.

al-Anbat I [18] (☎03/215 6265, fax 215 6888). Great value, with friendly service, well-equipped rooms and a cosy atmosphere. Free transport to and from the ticket gate, a campground and a good restaurant add to the appeal. ①–②.

Araba View [17] (☎ & fax 03/215 6107). Simple rooms, with Wadi Musa's best views from the rear balcony. Good value, but lack of heating lets it down. ②.

Cleopatra [14] (☎ & fax 03/215 7090). One of the better cheapies, cleaner than most but a little overpriced. Free transport to and from the gate. ②.

Moon Valley [8] (☎03/215 6824, fax 215 7131). Excellent choice, with a reputation to uphold, good facilities and information, and friendly staff. ②.

Mussa Spring [20] (☎03/215 6310, fax 215 6910). Long-standing backpackers' favourite – clean rooms, good service and free transport to and from the gate. Rooms are shared-bath or en suite, or you can crash on the roof. JD4 to share. ①–②.

Peace Way [12] (☎ & fax 03/215 6963). Cosy and comfortable little place, with a nice personal touch. All rooms have reliable hot water. ②–③.

Petra Gate [13] (☎ & fax 03/215 6908). Funky and friendly hangout, with a pool table and solid dinners. JD2 to share. ①–②.

el-Rashid [10] (☎03/215 6800, fax 215 6801). Unmissable huge sign overlooking the central Shaheed roundabout, with very clean, cosy and quiet rooms. Excellent value. ②–③.

Sunset [6] (☎03/215 6579, fax 215 6950). The only remotely budget-like choice on the tourist strip close to the gate, but you pay for the location: rooms are small and grimy and dinner is JD5. ②.

Treasury [9] (☎ & fax 03/215 7274). Quiet place up dozens of stairs in a residential neighbourhood well off the main drag. Great views temper its characterlessness a little. ②.

Twaissi [11] (☎03/215 6423). Potentially one of the best budget hotels in the country, with a good location, meticulously clean rooms, books, videos, a rooftop sleep-in, sizeable meals and free transport to and from the gate. However, some women travellers have felt uncomfortable here. JD4 to share. ①–②.

Valley Stars [15] (☎03/215 6915, fax 215 6914). Small, spartan place that's eager to please. ①.

Mid-range and luxury hotels

There's a huge number of **mid-range** ④ and ⑤ hotels in Wadi Musa, almost all of them existing for tour-group business. Rates for individuals are always much higher but you can limit the damage by reserving well ahead; if you arrive without a reservation, it pays to shop around. Hotels close to the gate charge considerably more than those back in town. At the **luxury** end of the scale, the two best hotels in Jordan – the *Mövenpick* and *Taybet Zaman* – compete with a shower of nightmarish carbuncles flung up on the Scenic Road. All the places listed below accept major credit cards.

Edom [5] (☎03/215 6995, fax 215 6994, email *edom@go.com.jo*, website *www.fto.de/edom*). The best value by far in this price range, with comfort, good service and some style. Prices can halve in the off season. ⑤.

THE SCENIC ROAD AND TAYBET ZAMAN

Coiling through Wadi Musa and out onto a ridge overlooking Jebel Haroun and the Petra mountains, the so-called **Scenic Road** – aside from giving some breathtaking views – was the focus of much controversy during the 1990s. With the signing of the 1994 peace treaty with Israel, entrepreneurs saw tourist dollars carved into the rockface and quickly slapped a handful of luxury hotels onto the roadside, with little regard for the environment, the views, or basic engineering practice. Very soon it was realized that the road desperately needed consolidation before it slipped into the valley. Three years on, the work still continues, the sound of bulldozers and earth-movers echoing daily across the whole of Petra from on high. Meanwhile, development has been halted, but three very expensive blots on the landscape survive: the *Grand View* – whose swimming pool recently developed a huge crack, as the hotel begins its long slide down the hillside into oblivion – the *Petra Plaza* and the *Nabatean Castle*.

About 11km from Wadi Musa, the Scenic Road enters the quiet town of **Taybeh**, where plans were afoot for a new kind of hotel even before the peace treaty. Early in the 1990s, a Jordanian tourism company was looking for some old buildings to renovate for hotel conversion. In consultation with the village council, the mayor of Taybeh offered his town – mostly modern buildings but with a crumbling, Ottoman quarter on the hillside below – for the experiment on a profit-sharing basis. The residents of the old cottages were paid to depart, conversion began and **Taybet Zaman** was the incredible result, an environmentally-sound, open-air luxury hotel, built to recreate the atmosphere of a nineteenth-century Jordanian village. Each old cottage is now a self-contained single or double "room", tastefully furnished and fitted out to international five-star standard. There are no corridors – each room opens onto the cobbled street – and restaurants, bars, a pool, Turkish bath, shops and two heliports are tucked away in different corners of the "village", separated off from the rest of workaday Taybeh by a high perimeter wall. The only thing lacking, of course, is any kind of atmosphere, but certain things are impossible to recreate. Even if you don't stay, it's worth making it out here somehow, if only to savour a cold beer while marvelling at the audacity of it all. Local buses shuttle back and forth from Wadi Musa to Taybeh village for pennies; a taxi, depending on the road conditions, may only be JD2 or so.

Flowers [4] (☎03/215 6770, fax 215 6771). Small and simple rooms are overpriced, but with a great location the hotel is popular and often full. ④.

Forum [2] (☎03/215 6266, fax 215 6977, email *petrafh@nets.com.jo*). Close to the gate and very comfortable, even if the style's a little bland. Worth visiting to hang out on their poolside, perched in front of the rocky ravines, especially at night when floodlights illuminate the mountains. ⑨.

King's Way [19] (☎03/215 6799, fax 215 6796, email *resrv@kingsway-petra.com*). Classy choice way up at Ain Musa, with comfortable, spacious rooms and attentive service, although no free rides to the gate. Non-residents can use the pool (daily 6am–6pm) for about JD5. ⑧.

Mövenpick [3] (☎03/215 7111, fax 215 7112, email *petramph@go.com.jo*). The best hotel in Jordan by quite a long way. Superbly designed in Damascene style right down to the last exquisite detail, the rooms are immaculate, service is calm, friendly and efficient and the location ideal. ⑨.

Petra Palace [7] (☎03/215 6723, fax 215 6724, email *ppwnwm@go.com.jo*). Impressive pile on the main tourist strip down by the gate, lavish and sparkling new. ⑤–⑥.

Resthouse and Hotel [1] (☎03/215 6266, fax 215 6977, email *petrafh@nets.com.jo*). Owned by the *Forum* – and with the same reservation system – this has less good, but still perfectly acceptable, rooms which overlook the ticket gate. In the forecourt, a Nabatean tomb known as al-Khan has been rather tackily converted into a bar. ⑥.

Sela [16] (☎03/215 7170, fax 215 7173). Flamboyantly draped rooms are super-clean, cosy and reasonably priced. A solid quality choice. ④.

Taybet Zaman (☎03/215 0111, fax 215 0101, website *www.jtic.com*). Award-winning luxury hotel built on the old Ottoman quarter of the village of Taybeh, 11km from Wadi Musa; see the box on p.237 for more information. All the spacious renovated cottages feature distinctive interior design and are equipped with every facility; you couldn't want for anything more. ⑨.

Eating and drinking

For **eating in Wadi Musa**, most travellers stick with whatever's on offer in their hotel, although a couple of town diners are worth checking out, and the *Mövenpick*'s buffet has to be seen to be believed. As usual, the only places for **drinking alcohol** are in the big hotels or a couple of specifically designated bars in town. All places listed are keyed on the map on pp.234-5.

Cleopetra restaurant [f]. Not to be confused with the *Cleopetra* hotel, this is an OK diner, empty during the day but often crowded with *shwarma*-munching locals at night. Avoid the buffet meals, however. Daily 6am–midnight.

Fresh Food [c]. Excellent sweet and savoury pastries and *mana'eesh*, along with a few other staples. Daily 6am–11pm.

Mövenpick. The hotel sports two different restaurants. The *al-Saraya* (daily noon–3.30pm & 7–10.30pm) has a lavish buffet, from fresh vegetables stir-fried as you watch through superb kebabs to proper Black Forest gateau, everything top quality. Lunch is JD11.400 and dinner JD15 – but the unmissable bargain of Wadi Musa is their all-you-can-eat soup-and-salad bar for a mere JD4.200, with free gourmet breads. Several notches up the scale, *al-Iwan* (daily 7–10.30pm) offers seriously sophisticated à la carte dining for JD30 and up. In addition, their bakery shop (daily 9am–7pm) boasts not only delicious fresh-baked wholegrain, nut and crusty white loaves, but also the best croissants this side of Beirut and a real espresso machine. If all this is beyond you, settle for an ice-cream in the stunning atrium.

Papazzi [a]. Down near the gate, with pretty good pizza and pasta dishes for around JD4. Daily 10am–11pm.

Petra Pearl [e]. The best little diner in town, perfect for cheap breakfasts and simple Arabic fare. Daily 6am–midnight.

EATING INSIDE PETRA

The only facilities for **eating** once you get **inside Petra** are expensive and low-quality. There are a handful of **tent cafés** along the path from the theatre to the Qasr al-Bint offering meagre buffets and very inadequate "boxed lunches" (little more than bread, cheese and an orange) – poor sustenance for the amount of walking you're likely to be doing. The canteen-style *Forum Basin* **restaurant** (daily 8.30am–5pm or so, depending on the weather conditions), opposite the Qasr al-Bint, is the only proper restaurant inside Petra, and necessarily pricey considering they have to truck everything in. Very ordinary buffet lunch comes in at JD7.200, although JD3.600 for salads or pasta is less galling.

By far your best option is to carry supplies with you for the day. Supermarkets and vegetable stalls in the centre of Wadi Musa can provide simple **picnic fare**, but nothing so energy-sustaining as nuts or dried fruit, which you should bring from outside. The local bakers are up before dawn at the little place just below the Shaheed Roundabout doing the normal range of Arabic breads; for something very different, try the Mövenpick's bakery shop (see opposite). Bear in mind that in the summer you'll need to be drinking at least five litres of **water** a day (over three bottles), possibly much more. Unless you can carry it all, you should budget on shelling out JD1 at the tent cafés for water or a soft drink to keep yourself hydrated.

Rose City Restaurant [b]. Close to the gate, a basic, inexpensive diner with an all-day buffet and a handful of à la carte staples. Daily 6.30am–11pm.

al-Shamia Flower, aka Family Sweet [d]. Friendly place serving simple, good-quality Arabic food. Daily 6.30am–11pm.

Wadi Petra [g]. OK food, but more notable as the diviest, sleaziest bar in town. Daily 6.30am–midnight.

Listings

American Express The agent is International Traders, in the *Silk Road Hotel* building, near the ticket gate (daily except Fri 8am–1pm & 4–7pm; ☎03/215 7711; 24-hr mobile ☎079/84510). They can sell travellers' cheques – to Amex card-holders only – but don't cash them.

Banks You can change cash, travellers' cheques and get Visa advances at the Arab Bank (daily 8am–noon) in the Visitors' Centre. Much the same services are offered at the Housing Bank (daily except Fri 8.30am–1pm & 3.30–5pm), just above the Shaheed Roundabout in Wadi Musa, where you can also use a Visa/Plus ATM. The big hotels offer poor rates or charge hefty commissions.

Clinic If you're afflicted with something serious, get to the Petra Emergency Clinic (daily 8am–8pm) in the car-park of the *Forum* hotel; they have beds, X-ray equipment and a small operating theatre, and can whisk a specialist to tend to you within minutes.

Email, fax and Internet access The *al-Nabatee* computer shop (Mon–Thurs, Sat & Sun 9am–2pm & 5–8pm, Fri 1–8pm), next to the *al-Janoub* restaurant in town, offers access, although not cheaply: JD6/hr for email, a little more to surf. Their good-value email-to-fax service can get a page to the US, for example, for JD1.500.

Pharmacy The Modern Petra Pharmacy (daily 8.30am–11pm), next to *al-Shamia Flower* restaurant, has friendly, qualified English-speaking staff who give sensible advice. They also stock items not common in other towns, such as tampons and condoms.

Police In emergency, dial ☎191. Police are on 24-hr, highly visible duty at Ain Musa and in all parts of the Petra ruins. Headquarters is off the Police Roundabout in Wadi Musa, and

MOVING ON FROM WADI MUSA

Moving on is not as easy as you might think. Buses to **Amman**'s Wihdat station depart only in the early mornings, roughly between 6 and 8am. See p.233 for information about the bus service JETT used to run to Amman; to find out if it happens to be running, ask a day ahead of time at Jeff's Bookshop, one of the souvenir stalls near the Petra ticket gate. Buses to **Aqaba** also generally leave between 6 and 8am, with one afternoon departure at around 4pm. One bus leaves for **Wadi Rum** at about 6.30am. These few routes are all very popular, and this is the only time in Jordan where you actually have to **book seats in advance** for a normal minibus. Ask your hotel manager the night before to reserve you a place on a bus for the next morning: most of the more switched-on hotels can do this as a matter of course, but if yours can't, the *Mussa Spring, Twaissi* and *al-Anbat* know what's what. All buses start from the Shaheed Roundabout, but if you've reserved a seat the bus should come to your hotel's door. The few *service*s to Amman (Wihdat) operate on their usual first-come first-served basis from the same roundabout, also in the early morning.

If you miss any of these, buses leave hourly during the day from the Shaheed Roundabout for **Ma'an**, which has connections to Amman, Aqaba, Karak and Rum; and **Shawbak**, which has no connections to anywhere but which is a good place to start a hitch up the King's Highway to Qadsiyyeh and beyond.

A **taxi** can get you to Rum for about JD22, Aqaba for JD25, Karak for JD35 and along the King's Highway to Amman for JD50 or more.

there are police offices next to the ticket gate and at al-Habees overlooking the Qasr al-Bint. English-speaking tourist police are available 24hr in their main office directly opposite the Visitors' Centre, and they're also on duty at the Visitors' Centre during opening hours.

Post There are three post offices in Wadi Musa, all open the same hours (Mon–Thurs, Sat & Sun 8am–5pm, Fri roughly 8am–1pm). The main office, which is the cheapest place to make international calls in Petra (there are no cardphones), is just off the Shaheed Roundabout, and there's a branch office up at Ain Musa. Both of these give small Wadi Musa postmarks, but the office 50m from the ticket gate is the only one to whack a nice big "PETRA" postmark onto everything.

Taxis Wadi Musa's two companies are al-Anbat (☎03/215 6777) and Petra (☎03/215 6600), and there are always plenty of taxis sharking around the streets. Standard flat rate for a ride anywhere in town – from the ticket gate to Ain Musa or anywhere in between – is JD1.

Turkish bath At least two places offer the chance to steam the day's dust out of your pores in a *hammam*. In the middle of town, the rather frenetic *Salome* (daily 3–10pm; ☎03/215 7342; JD10–15) can bring you from your hotel to undergo the full sauna, massage, hot and cold shower treatment and take you back again. For an entirely different class of experience, check out Taybet Zaman's stained-glass, five-star *hammam* (daily 10am–10pm; JD12), infinitely more elegant, regal and relaxed.

PETRA

After you've finished coping with the practicalities of bed and board in Wadi Musa, **PETRA** comes as an assault on the senses. As you leave the ticket gate behind, the sense of exposure to the elements is thrilling; the natural drama of the location, the sensuous colouring of the sandstone, the stillness, heat and clarity of light – along with a lingering, under-the-skin quality of supernatural power that seems to seep out of the rock – make it an unforgettable adventure.

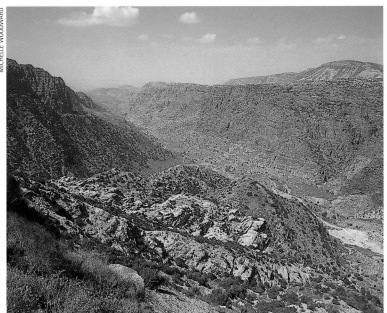
Wadi Dana

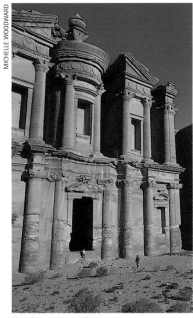
The Monastery, Petra

The hot waterfalls at Hammamat Ma'in

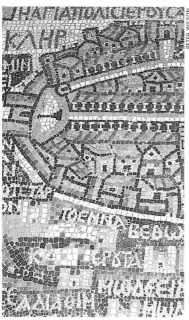

PETER WILSON

The mosaic map at Madaba

MICHELLE WOODWARD

Eroded facade at Petra

MICHELLE WOODWARD

Aqaba, with Eilat in the background

The mountains fringing Wadi Araba

The Treasury, Petra

King Hussein

Bedouin "house of hair"

Rock bridge at Umm Fruth, Wadi Rum

Wadi Rum landscape

HIGHLIGHTS

There's enough to explore in Petra that you could easily spend days in the place. Shelling out JD20 for a single day will have you running around like crazy to get value for money; if your pockets are deep enough, paying JD30 for four days buys time to pace yourself and explore to your heart's content.

Major **highlights**, which count as unmissable, are the Siq, the Treasury, the High Place of Sacrifice, the Monastery, a walk up the Colonnaded Street, and the Royal Tombs. With a break for lunch, and a little time for personal exploration, this would occupy a pretty exhausting ten-hour day.

If you have even one extra day, your options widen considerably. Choosing an entry or exit route other than the Siq for one trip – via Madras, Wadi Muthlim/Mataha or Wadi Turkmaniyyeh – can give you a feel for outlying landscapes. Depending on your taste for archeology or nature, you could then devote more time to exploring the city centre slopes and the East Cliff, or choose one or two of the many hikes and climbs. You should also budget some down-time to take in the extraordinary late-afternoon views from the Qasr al-Bint up the Colonnaded Street towards the fiery East Cliff.

With Siq al-Berid ("Little Petra") being free-entry, you should wait to take your half-day excursion to Wu'ayra, al-Berid and, possibly, Baydha until the morning after your Petra ticket has expired.

Whether you're in a group or alone, you'd do well to branch off the main routes every now and again. These days, Petra sees somewhere around half a million visitors annually – over two thousand daily, on average; the place is physically large enough to absorb that many people (although archeologists and environmentalists are both lobbying for controls on numbers), but the central path that runs past the major sights gets very busy between about 10am and 4pm. Taking a ten- or fifteen-minute detour to clamber around the rocks to either side of the path or explore interesting-looking side valleys is a good idea, since not only does it instantly get you out of the crush, but it's also liable to yield previously unseen views and fascinating little carved niches or facades – all over Petra, the Nabateans carved for themselves paths and signposts, shrines and houses in what seem to us remote and desolate crags.

For advice on **eating and drinking** in Petra, see the box on p.239.

Information and admission

The **Petra Visitors' Centre** (daily 7am–10pm; ☎03/215 6020), 50m from the gate, is the main office for help and information, with efficient and friendly staff, and the tourist police on hand. This is where you can hire a professional, accredited **guide**, at fixed prices (current rates are posted on the wall): a basic JD8 for a simple tour of the major sights, plus extra sums for sights a little off the beaten track (for example, an extra JD9 up to the Monastery, or JD6 to the High Place). JD35 hires a guide for a full, dawn-to-dusk day, whether you stay on the path or head into the mountains. A prominent notice in the centre warns that you should venture to Sabra, the Snake Monument, Jebel Haroun or Jebel Nmayr only with a guide "as they are far and steep"; for the first two, it's possible to take this with a pinch of salt and still stay this side of foolhardiness. However, there are plenty

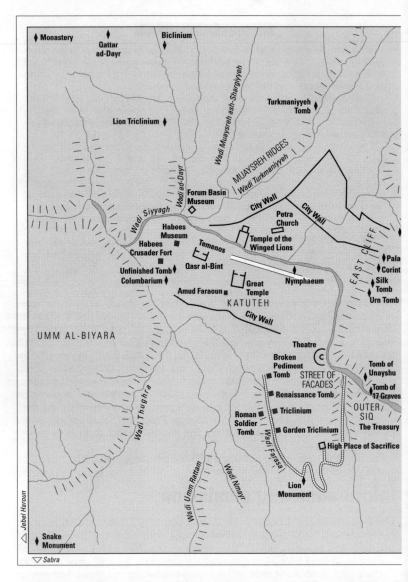

of places in Petra where you definitely shouldn't venture without a guide, and we've mentioned this in the account below where relevant. Aside from the dangers of twisted ankles or worse scrambling around rocky cliffs, once you leave the main routes it's easy to lose the path.

The Visitors' Centre is also where you can request and pay for a **horseback** ride down to the Siq entrance, although at JD7 for a 900-metre walk, it's no thrill.

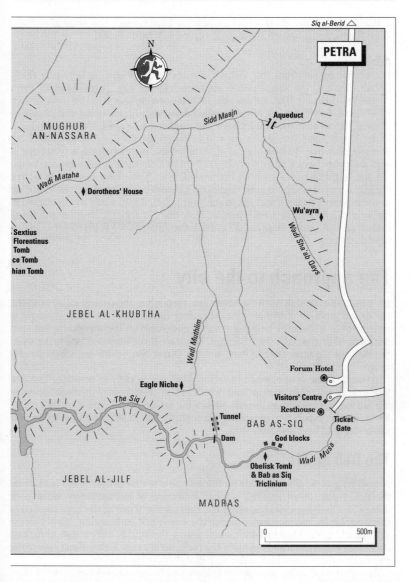

It's forbidden to ride horses through the Siq, but a **horse and carriage** seating two – supposedly only for the elderly and infirm – can be taken all the way through the Siq to the Treasury for JD20 (round-trip). If you see a horse or donkey in **discomfort**, you can call or visit the Brooke Hospital for Animals (daily except Fri 8am–3pm; ☎03/215 6379), an English-run charity located to the left of the gate.

Within the Centre there's also a **shop** for books, maps and souvenirs (daily 7am–10pm), and a branch of the Arab Bank (daily 8am–noon).

Admission

Round the corner from the Visitors' Centre is the **Petra ticket gate** (daily 6.30am–sunset), the single public entrance into the site. **Admission** to Petra costs a jaw-dropping JD20 for one day, JD25 for two days, or JD30 for three or four days; this refers to blocks of consecutive days, with no chopping and changing allowed. Archeologists, researchers and students all pay full whack, children under 12 pay half-price, Jordanians and foreign residents pay JD1, and only King Hussein goes free. Tickets are dated, stamped and non-transferable (you have to sign multi-day passes and carry ID), and they're checked at the entrance to the Siq and at varying points within Petra itself; even if you hike several kilometres out of the way to avoid the gate, there's no guarantee a police officer won't pop up in some remote location and ask to see your ticket. A minuscule sop is offered in the form of a **free map** to each person. Note that Siq al-Berid, Baydha and, for all intents and purposes, Wu'ayra fall outside the (undefined) ticketed area, and so have free entry.

The approach to the city

It's a walk of over 3km from the ticket gate through to the central valley of Petra, the gentle gradient of five percent concealing the fact that the drop in height is equivalent to a 35-storey building – barely noticeable on the way down, but murder for tired thighs on the way back up. There are three main sections to the walk: the **Bab as-Siq** area, the **Siq** itself and the **Outer Siq**, which leads into the city centre.

If you have the option, you'd do well to start out as early as possible. The first tour groups set off by 8.30 or 9am, which brings them noisily through the echoing Siq to the Treasury as the sun strikes the facade (which you shouldn't miss). However, the experience of walking through the Siq in silence and alone is definitely worth at least one 6am start.

The Bab as-Siq

A modern gravel path – one side for horses, the other for pedestrians – leads from the ticket gate down through a lunar landscape of extraordinary white rock domes and looming cliffs known as the **Bab as-Siq** (Gate of the Siq); the bed of the Wadi Musa, carrying water during the winter and early spring, curves alongside. In all but the bleached-out midday hours, the light is soft enough to pick up earth tones of browns and beiges in the rock, but it's only with the last rays of the sunset that there's any hint of the pink that Petra is famous for.

Almost immediately, you can see evidence of Nabatean endeavour: three huge **god-blocks**, six-to-eight metres high, loom next to the path just round the first corner, carved probably to serve as both representations of and repositories for the gods to stand sentinel over the city's vital water supply. Twenty-five such god-blocks exist in Petra, deemed by the locals to have been the work of *jinn*, or genies, and so also termed **jinn-blocks**; another name is **sahrij**, or water-tanks (ie tanks holding divine energy next to flowing water). The middle one has shaft

NABATEAN RELIGION

As much as they created a blend of Arab culture with Mediterranean, the Nabateans also blended inherited elements of the ancient **religions** of Egypt, Syria, Canaan, Assyria and Babylon with elements of the Greek and Roman pantheons, to create specifically Petran forms of worship.

Central to their religion was **rock**. Jehovah, the god of the Israelites, for example, was said to inhabit a blank rock called Bet-El, the House of God. This insistence on non-figurative representation was shared by many Levantine and Arabian peoples, and was passed on to the Nabateans (in stark contrast to the Egyptians' and Assyrians' lavish portrayals of gods and goddesses). Concepts such as "the Lord is my rock" also appear many times in the Old Testament, implying an extension of the "House of God" idea so that the rock actually represents the deity itself. Nabatean deities were thus often represented simply by squared-off rocks, termed **"god-blocks"**. In addition, a later development gave the rock a third aspect: that of the altar, the contact point between the divine and the material.

At the head of the Nabatean pantheon was **Dushara**, "He of the Shara" (the mountains around Petra), later identified with the Greek god Zeus and the Syrian Hadad. The fact that his name is so closely tied to the locality indicates that he may originally have been an Edomite, rather than a Nabatean, god. To the Nabateans, Dushara was the sun, the primordial Light of the World, the Creator, and he was often represented by an obelisk – the visual materialization of a beam of light striking the earth. With the mingling of Semitic and Mediterranean ideas, Dushara also came to be associated with Dionysus, god of wine, and so began to assume human form, bedecked with vines and grapes (as at the Nabatean temple on Jebel Tannur).

At Dushara's side were **Atargatis**, the goddess of fertility, of grain, fruit and fish; **Allat** (which means simply "The Goddess"), who represented the moon; **Manat**, the goddess of luck and fate, suggested to have been the patron deity of Petra and possibly the goddess worshipped at the Treasury; and **al-Uzza** (The Mighty One), assimilated with the Egyptian goddess Isis, and the Roman goddesses Diana, deity of water and fertility, and Venus, embodied by the evening star and representing spiritual and erotic love. Allat, al-Uzza and Manat are all mentioned by name in the Quran, implying that their cult was still active and popular in Mecca as late as the seventh century, the time of the Prophet Muhammad.

The Nabateans also had a plethora of smaller gods, including **al-Kutbay**, god of writing; **She'a-al-Qawm**, the patron deity of caravans; **Qos**, originally an Edomite god; and **Baal-Shamin**, a Phoenician god especially popular in northern Nabatea, who had a temple somewhere near the modern mosque in the centre of Wadi Musa town.

graves cut into it, implying that it may also have served as some kind of funerary monument. Opposite the god-blocks are some caves, one of which has an obelisk carved in relief, representing the soul, or **nefesh**, of a dead person. Such carved shrines abound in every corner of Petra's mountains, and, for those with time to explore, the small side valleys off this section of the Bab as-Siq are filled with tombs, water channels, niches and shrines: behind the blocks, the area of domes known as **Ramleh** is cut through by parallel wadis (one of which is Wadi Muthlim; see p.246) and is equally explorable.

The Obelisk Tomb and Bab as-Siq Triclinium

The first major Nabatean monuments are a few metres further on, and – being on an exposed corner – badly eroded. Although apparently the upper and lower halves of a single monument, the **Obelisk Tomb** and **Bab as-Siq Triclinium** may be separate entities, carved at different times. Above, four huge obelisks guard the entrance to a cave in the rock; such free-standing obelisks, as opposed to the *nefesh* in relief, are much like the god-blocks, both representing a god and storing divine energy in a material form. Between the four is an eroded figure in a niche, and the cave behind holds graves. The *triclinium*, or dining room, below is a single chamber with stone benches on three walls, for holding banquets in honour of the dead. On the opposite side of the path, 5m off the ground, is a bilingual **inscription** in Nabatean and Greek, recording that one Abdmank chose this spot to build a tomb for himself and his children, although it's not certain that this refers to the monuments opposite.

Just past the Obelisk Tomb is a path leading to the hidden Petran suburb of **Madras**, tucked into the hills to the left (south), from where it's possible to cross the hilltops over the Jebel al-Jilf plateau, avoiding the Siq, to the top of the high, narrow Danqur al-Khazneh valley leading down to the Treasury; the views are stunning, and the sense of isolation is worth the scramble if you've already seen the Siq. However, the route is far from clear, relying on worn Nabatean rock-cut stairs, and you'll need a guide.

The dam and tunnel

Back on the path, the curving northern bank of the wadi is liberally pock-marked with caves and niches, round to the point where the path is taken over the wadi bed by a bridge and the Wadi Musa itself is blocked by a **dam**; this is almost exactly the same configuration as was built by the Nabateans in about 50 AD, and for the same reasons: to divert the floodwaters of the Wadi Musa away from the Siq so that the principal entry into the city could remain clear year round. It's here, at the mouth of the Siq, that all horse riders must dismount and that entrance tickets will be checked. On the opposite bank of the wadi are four *nefesh* obelisks, one mentioning a man who lived in Reqem (Petra) but died in Jerash.

To the right, the Nabatean-carved, eight-metre-high **tunnel** – guarded by another, solitary god-block – enabled the floodwaters to feed into the Wadi Muthlim leading north around the gigantic Jebel al-Khubtha; today, this is an alternative way into Petra.

The Wadi Muthlim route

Although you should definitely follow the Siq into Petra at least once – and probably more than once, at different times of day – if you've allocated several days to a visit, the beautiful **Wadi Muthlim** is a wonderful alternative entry route through stunning scenery, peaceful and considerably easier than the twisting Madras path, but taking no less than two hours to deliver you to the Nymphaeum in the city centre. Due to the very real danger of flash floods, you shouldn't attempt it at all during the rainy season – roughly October to March – and even as late as May, there may be difficult-to-avoid standing pools of water harbouring water snakes: wading would be a big mistake.

Before beginning the walk, you can take a small detour from the dam to the **Eagle Niche**, set in the rocks 400m to the northwest. Cross the wadi over the roof of the tunnel, and head left up the second side valley; it's a short scramble over the smooth, hot rock up to a set of small niches carved in the right-hand wall, one of which features a strikingly carved eagle with wings outspread.

Returning to the tunnel to begin the walk, Wadi Muthlim – full of oleanders, but with high walls cutting out all sound bar the occasional birdsong – is easily passable up to the remains of another Nabatean dam; beyond here, the path gets steadily narrower, until you reach a point where a massive boulder all but blocks the way. It's possible to squeeze past, and the path continues to narrow until, with the wadi floor no wider than your foot, you reach a T-junction; arrows on the solid walls all around will point you left. This cross-wadi is the **Sidd Maajn**, equally narrow, but beautifully eroded by flowing water. As you proceed, seemingly moving through the heart of the mountain, you'll notice the Nabateans were here before you: there are dozens of carved niches, some featuring pediments, other curving horns. It is around here that the way might be blocked by rockpools. Eventually, you'll emerge into the open **Wadi Mataha** (see p.268), about 600m northeast of Dorotheos' House, and the best part of 2km northeast of the Nymphaeum.

The Siq

From the crowded, horse-smelly bridge, the path drops sharply down over the lip of the dam into Petra's most dramatic and awe-inspiring natural feature – the **Siq** gorge, principal entrance into the city, yet invisible until you're almost upon it. Overhead, the path was originally framed by an ornamental **arch**, which collapsed in 1896 although its abutments survive, decorated by the smoothed-out remnants of niches flanked by pilasters. All the way along the left-hand wall is a Nabatean rock-cut **water-channel**, and on the right-hand wall further along are the remains of terracotta pipes for water, both probably dating from the same time as the reorganization of the city water supply that prompted the building of the dam. At various points, you'll come across worn patches of the road which originally paved the Siq along its entire length; work is currently under way to consolidate the now stony path, and, unfortunately, shiny new paving is a very real threat in the future.

The Siq was formed when tectonic forces split the mountain in two. The waters of the Wadi Musa subsequently found their way into the fault, laying a bed of gravel and, helped by the cool winds that blow in your face all the way down, eroding the sharp corners into curves as smooth as eggshell. The path along the wadi bed twists and turns between high, bizarrely eroded sandstone cliffs for 1200m, sometimes widening to form broad, sunlit open spaces in the echoing heart of the mountain, dotted with a tree or two and the cries of birds; in other places, the looming 150-metre-high walls close in to little more than a metre apart, blocking out sound, warmth and even daylight. All the way down, high, narrow wadis feed in from either side, but most of them have been recently blocked by nasty modern walls to limit both flood danger and unauthorized exploration: once you're in the Siq, the only way is onward or backward. Dotted along the walls at many points are small **votive niches**, some Greek-style with pediments, others with mini god-blocks. After about 350m, a small **shrine** has been carved on the downhill side of a free-standing outcrop of rock, with two god-blocks, the larger of which is carved with eyes and a nose. A little further on, on the left-hand wall at a sharp right-hand bend, is a merchant in Egyptian-style dress leading two large **camels** – the water channel originally ran behind all five sets of legs, and it's just possible to trace the worn outline of the camels' humps in the rock wall.

PETRA COLOURS

One of the most breathtaking aspects of Petra – for many people superseding even the architecture – is its **colours**, encapsulated in a delightful incident below the East Cliff almost 150 years ago. As the artist Edward Lear strolled up the Colonnaded Street on a visit in 1858, coolly noting "the tint of the stone … brilliant and gay beyond my anticipation", his manservant and cook, Giorgio Kokali, burst out in delight, "Oh master, we have come into a world of chocolate, ham, curry powder and salmon!" Agatha Christie preferred to see the rocks as "blood-red", and a character in her *Appointment with Death*, set in Petra, comes out with a line describing the place as "very much the colour of raw beef".

Unfortunately for posterity, however, the most famous lines on Petra's colours have become rather less endearing. In 1845, John William Burgon, later to become Dean of Chichester, wrote in his poem *Petra*:

It seems no work of Man's creative hand,
By labour wrought as wavering fancy planned;
But from the rock as if by magic grown,
Eternal, silent, beautiful, alone!
Not virgin-white like that old Doric shrine,
Where erst Athena held her rites divine;
Not saintly-grey, like many a minister fane,
That crowns the hill and consecrates the plain;
But rose-red as if the blush of dawn
That first beheld them were not yet withdrawn;
The hues of youth upon a brow of woe,
Which Man deemed old two thousand years ago,
Match me such a marvel save in Eastern clime,
A rose-red city half as old as Time.

It's a shame this trite last line has such a ring to it, since it's stuck to the place like glue: you'll be sick of reading the words "rose-red city" on every map, poster and booklet by the time you leave. Tellingly, Burgon had never been to Petra when he wrote it; he finally went sixteen years later, and at least then had the humility to write, if only in a letter to his sister, "there is nothing rosy about Petra, by any means."

In fact, over the centuries wind has rubbed away at the soft sandstone of Petra's cliffs to reveal an extraordinary array of colours streaking through the stone like watered silk. The most colourful facades in Petra are the Silk Tomb and the Carmine Tomb, both on the East Cliff; the cafés on the path below are set in caves no less breathtaking. Elsewhere, the lower walls of the Wadi Farasa are streaked with colour, and the Siq cliffs are striped with everything from scarlet to yellow to purple to brown; add the green foliage on the trees, the pink of the oleander flowers, and shreds of blue sky, and there's a rainbow of colours to appreciate, aside from the geological drama. The one place in Petra that's truly "rose-red" is the Treasury, lit in the afternoons by low reflected sunlight off the pinkish walls.

When you think the gorge can't possibly go on any longer, there comes a dark, narrow defile, framing at its end a strip of extraordinary classical architecture. With your eye softened to the natural flows of eroded rock in the Siq, the clean lines of columns and pediments come as a revelation. As you step out into the daylight, there is no more dramatic or breathtaking vision in the whole of Jordan than the facade of the Treasury.

The Treasury

Perfectly positioned opposite the main route into Petra, the **Treasury** was designed to impress, and, two thousand years on, the effect is undiminished. What strikes you first is how well preserved it is; carved deep into the rockface and concealed in a high-walled ellipse of a valley (known as Wadi al-Jarra, "Urn Valley"; see box below), it has been protected from wind and rain from day one. The detailing of the capitals and pediments on the forty-by-thirty-metre facade is still crisp. The best times to view the Treasury are when the sun strikes it directly, between about 9am and 11am, and late in the afternoon, around 5 or 6pm, when the whole facade is suffused with a reflected reddish-pink glow from the walls all around.

The **carvings** on the facade, though much damaged by iconoclasts, are still discernible and show to what extent Nabatean culture was an amalgam of elements from the Hellenistic and Middle Eastern worlds. The Treasury is normally dated to the first century BC, possibly to the reign of King Aretas III Philhellene ("the Greek-lover"), who brought architects to Petra from the centres of Hellenistic culture throughout the Mediterranean. Atop the broken pediments, framing the upper storey, are two large eagles, symbols of the Nabateans' chief male deity, Dushara (see box on p.245). In a central position on the rounded *tholos* below the urn is what's been identified as a representation of Isis, an Egyptian goddess who equated with the Nabatean goddess al-Uzza; in the recesses behind are two Winged Victories, although the remaining four figures, all of whom seem to be holding axes aloft, haven't been identified. Two lions, also symbolizing al-Uzza, adorn the entablature between the two storeys. At ground level, the mounted riders are Castor and Pollux, sons of Zeus. The parallel marks up the side of the facade, which occur in a couple of other places in Petra, may well have been footholds for the sculptors and masons.

Inside the doorway – unlike the scene in *Indiana Jones and the Last Crusade*, when Indy finds stone lions and Crusader seals set into the floor – there's only a blank **square chamber**, with smaller rooms opening off it, the entrance portico flanked by rooms featuring unusual round windows above their doors. The function of the Treasury is unknown, but a significant clue is the recessed **basin** on its threshold with a channel leading outside, clearly for libations or ritual washing. None of Petra's tomb-monuments has this feature, but the High Place of Sacrifice does, suggesting that the Treasury may have been a place of worship, possibly a tomb-temple.

TARGET PRACTICE

The name "Treasury" is not Nabatean, and derives from the local name for such a seemingly inexplicable construction – *Khaznet al-Faraoun*, or Pharaoh's Treasury. Unaware of classical history, and unable to fathom why anyone should carve such a monument, the bedouin of Wadi Musa tagged it as the work of the pharaoh, lord of black magic. In pursuit of the Israelites after the Exodus (the legend goes), the pharaoh was slowed down by having to carry all his treasure, so he created the Treasury at a stroke and deposited his riches in the urn at the very top of the facade, out of human reach. For centuries after Petra's abandonment, bedouin marksmen tried to shatter the urn, and so release the treasure, but to no avail: their only success was in blasting chunks off the solid urn.

One column is obviously new, a brick-and-plaster replacement for the original which fell in antiquity. This neatly demonstrates one of the most extraordinary features of Nabatean architecture. A normal building that lost a main support like this would probably have come crashing down soon after; these Nabatean columns, though, support nothing. Like all of Petra's monuments other than the Qasr al-Bint, the entire Treasury "building" was sculpted *in situ*, gouged out of the unshaped rock in a kind of reverse architecture.

To the left of the facade, a set of stairs come down into the valley from the Danqur al-Khazneh area. Off to the right, a wall blocks the narrow north end of the Wadi al-Jarra; if you climb over the wall then double back to scramble up the rocks you'll reach a small, jutting plateau, with a perfect view from above of the Treasury and the whole bustling plaza in front of it.

The Outer Siq

From the Wadi al-Jarra, the path – known here as the **Outer Siq** – broadens and is lined with tombs in varying states of erosion. Steps lead up to a large cavern on the right, lined with benches inside and rather smelly. Opposite is a line of tombs at different heights, showing how the wadi floor rose during Nabatean occupation of Petra; most are badly eroded and give the peculiar impression that the classical facades are trying to push forward out of the soft rock but only half succeeding. One has the crow-step ornamental design that originated in Assyria and was adapted by the Nabateans to reappear in dozens of Petra's facades – a band of rising and falling zigzags running horizontally across the top of the facade. As the path broadens, in the corner of the right-hand cliff – pointed to by the terracotta pipe that has emerged from the Siq – the **Tomb of 17 Graves** is being restored behind scaffolding, but if you look up and to the left of it, you'll spot one of the clearest examples of Nabatean facade-building; the Tomb of Unayshu presents a sharp profile of a clean classical facade facing left carved from a rough outcrop of rock behind that looks barely capable of supporting it.

The path then opens out to the left to expose the **Street of Facades**, an agglomeration of dozens of facades carved side by side out of the rock on at least four different levels. Most are simple, cornice-free designs, probably some of the earliest carving in Petra. It's around here that you'll come across the first of Petra's many tent-cafés, all of which offer water, shade and soft drinks.

The theatre

A few metres ahead sits Petra's massive **theatre**. Obviously classical in design and inspiration, it's nonetheless been dated to the first century AD, before the Romans annexed Nabatea but at a time when links between the two powers must have been strong. The Romans refurbished the building after they took over in 106, but the basic design was still Hellenistic, with seats coming right down to the orchestra's floor level. As many as 8500 people could be accommodated, more even than in the vast theatre at Amman. Aside from the stage backdrop and the ends of the banks of seating, the entire edifice was carved out of the mountainside; one whole street of facades was wiped out to form the back wall of the auditorium, leaving some of their interiors behind as incongruous gaps. Much renovation work has been done here in recent years, in particular to build up the stage area, with its niches in front and elaborate *scaenae frons* behind (tumbled in the earthquake of 363), the high back wall of which would have sealed off the theatre from the street outside.

THE BEDOUIN NAMED FOR CHANGING

From time immemorial, the caves and dens of Petra have been occupied by one of Jordan's poorest and most downtrodden tribes, the **Bdul**. Surrounded by tribes living traditional lifestyles – the Saidiyeen to the south and west, the Ammareen to the north, and the Liyathneh and *fellaheen* (peasants) to the east – the Bdul remain a community apart, looked down upon for their poverty, their small numbers (only about three hundred families) and their cave-centred lifestyle.

Most bedouin tribes can trace their lineage back to a single founding father (whether real or fictitious), but mystery surrounds the origin of the Bdul. Some Bdul, naturally enough, claim descent from the Nabateans, but this may just be wishful thinking. Most claim that the name Bdul derives from the Arabic word *badal*, meaning to swap or change, and was given to the tribe after the handful of survivors of a massacre at the hands of Moses and the Israelites had agreed to convert to Judaism; at some point in the centuries following, the tribe converted again, this time to Islam. Much more plausible is the possibility that the Bdul earned their name from being a nomadic tribe that decided to settle in the ruins of Petra, changing their habits to suit a more stable existence.

The tribe comprises five branches. The **Judaylat** – meaning the stubborn or primitive – live around Jebel Haroun, many working as shepherds for the Saidiyeen. It was the Judaylat that Burckhardt stumbled on when he passed through Petra; he wrote that their tents "were the smallest I had ever seen, about four feet high and ten in length. The inhabitants were very poor, and could not afford to give us coffee; our breakfast and dinner therefore consisted of dry barley cakes, which we dipped in melted goat's grease." The **Fuqara** – meaning the poor – are the source of the tribe's shamans, and are held to possess healing powers: they have the distinguished role of custodians of the shrine of Haroun. The other branches are less well demarcated. The **Mawasneh** and **Jamadat** are closely related to the Fuqara, and the **Samaheen** comprise a few families living in and around Mughur an-Nassara.

The Bdul were slow to benefit from the growth in tourism in Petra, largely because of cut-throat competition with the more cosmopolitan and better-educated Liyathneh of Wadi Musa. When the Resthouse opened in the 1950s, Liyathneh were hired as construction workers, hotel staff, book- and postcard-sellers and even to provide horses for rides into Petra, and their near-monopoly on tourist facilities in Wadi Musa has persisted to this day. Adding insult to injury, a USAID report dating from the establishment of Petra as a National Park in 1968 acknowledged that the Bdul held traditional rights over park lands, but nonetheless recommended that they be resettled elsewhere. This sparked a fifteen-year battle to oust the Bdul from Petra, which saw the tribe's traditional lifestyle of agriculture and goat-herding decimated, income instead dribbling in from the refreshment cafés within Petra and the few individuals offering crafts and antiquities – real and fake – to tourists. In the mid-1980s, tempted by the carrot of some material comforts in the new, purpose-built village of Umm Sayhoun, many Bdul families finally submitted to the stick of resettlement, and left the caves of Petra for the breezeblock houses on the ridge. Some still herd a few goats, others cultivate small plots, but most Bdul are refocusing their energies on making an income providing services to tourists. You'll meet Bdul adults and kids in all corners of Petra, running the tent-cafés or offering tea and trinkets in the hills, and often happy to chat (in surprisingly fluent English). The "bedouin named for changing", as archeologist Kenneth Russell dubbed them, are embracing change yet again.

For more on the Bdul, surf to *corp.arabia.com/DesertLand/bedintro.html*.

The path continues past cafés on both sides and even a public toilet built into a beautifully colourful and tree-shaded cave, down to a point at which the Wadi Musa turns sharp left (west) into the city centre (see p.256). Way up to the right, a row of some of Petra's grandest monuments has been etched into the East Cliff (see p.255), while straight ahead the valley opens up towards Baydha, with the Wadi Mataha (see p.268) coming in from the northeast.

The High Place of Sacrifice route

A little before you reach the theatre, a set of steps leading south up a rocky slope to one side of a deep valley gives access to the **High Place of Sacrifice**, a diversion off the main path, but an unmissable part of a visit. Even if you have only one day in Petra, this is still worth the 170-metre climb, about thirty or forty minutes with safe steps at all tricky points – there's no scrambling or mountaineering involved. Steps also lead down off the back of the mountain into **Wadi Farasa**, forming a long but interesting loop that delivers you (after about two and a half hours) to the Qasr al-Bint. The breathtaking views and some of Petra's most extraordinary rock-colouring in themselves make the hike worthwhile, quite apart from the wealth of Nabatean architecture at every turn and the dramatic High Place itself. The path is well travelled, and you're unlikely to find yourself alone for more than a few minutes at a time.

The route from the Outer Siq

The steps up are clearly marked, guarded by several god-blocks, and wind their way into the deep cleft of the lush and beautiful Wadi al-Mahfur – at several points, the Nabatean engineers took their chisels to what were otherwise impassable outcrops and sliced deep-cut corridors through the rock to house the stairs. The sign that you're reaching the top, apart from one or two impromptu cafés beneath bamboo shelters, is the appearance on your left of two very prominent **obelisks**, both over 6m high. As in the Bab as-Siq and elsewhere, these probably represent the chief male and female Nabatean deities, Dushara and al-Uzza, although far more extraordinary is to realize that they are solid – far from being placed there, this entire side of the mountain-top was instead levelled to leave them sticking up. The ridge on which they stand is still marked on modern maps with the bedouin name of *Zibb Attuf*, the Phallus of Mercy (often adapted to *Amud Attuf*, the Column of Mercy), implying that the notion of these obelisks representing beneficial fertility was somehow passed down from the Nabateans to the modern age unchanged. Opposite stand very ruined walls, the last remnants of what could have been a **Crusader fort** or a Nabatean structure; broken steps lead beside it up to the summit.

The High Place of Sacrifice

As you emerge onto the hand-levelled platform atop the ridge, the sense of exposure after the climb is suddenly liberating. The **High Place of Sacrifice** – *al-Madhbah* in Arabic – is one of the highest easily accessible points in Petra, perched on cliffs that drop almost sheer to the Wadi Musa below. It's just one of dozens of High Places perched on ridges and mountain-tops around Petra, all of which are of similar design and function. A platform about 15m long and 6m wide served as the venue for the religious ceremonies, oriented towards an **altar**, set up on four steps, with a basin to one side and a socket into which may have slotted a stone representation of the god. Within the courtyard is a small dais, on which probably stood a table of (bloodless) offerings. What exactly took place up here – probably in honour of Dushara – can only be guessed at, but there were almost certainly libations, smoking of frankincense and animal sacrifice. What is less sure is whether **human sacrifice** took place, although there is much evidence: boys and girls were known to have been sacrificed to al-Uzza elsewhere; the second-century philosopher Porphyrius reports that a boy's throat was cut annually at the Nabatean town of Dunat, just 300km from Petra; and at Hegra, a major Nabatean city in the Arabian interior, an inscription states explicitly "Abd-Wadd, priest of Wadd, and his son Salim ... have consecrated the young man Salim to be immolated to Dhu Gabat. Their double happiness!" If such sacrifices took place in Petra, the High Place would surely have seen at least some of them. It's also been suggested that Nabatean religion incorporated ritual exposure of the dead, as practised among the Zoroastrians of Persia; if so, the High Place would also have been an obvious choice as an exposure platform. You can survey the vastness of Petra's mountain terrain from here, and the tomb of Aaron atop Jebel Haroun is in clear sight in the distance.

The ridge extends a short distance north of the High Place, nosing out directly above the theatre, with the tombs of the Outer Siq minuscule below. From here, it's easy to see that the city of Petra lay in a broad valley, about a kilometre wide and hemmed in to east and west by mountain barriers; north the valley extends to Baydha, south to Sabra. Although it looks tempting, there is no easily manageable path down the front of the ridge.

The Wadi Farasa route

Although it's easy to go back the way you came, the route down the western cliff of the Attuf ridge via **Wadi Farasa** (Butterfly Valley) is far preferable. The route leads directly away from you (south) as you scramble down past the ruined Crusader walls, keeping the bamboo café on your right. After 50m you'll come to stairs winding downward to your right along the valley wall; the way is often narrow and steep but always clear. Note that it's also possible to descend via **Wadi Nmayr**, parallel to Wadi Farasa, but this is a very difficult, concealed path and should only be attempted with a knowledgeable guide.

The Lion Monument and Garden Triclinium

Part of the way down into the Wadi Farasa you'll come to the **Lion Monument** carved into a wall. This may have been a drinking fountain, since a pipe seems to have fed water to emerge from the lion's mouth. The creature itself, as on the Treasury facade, represented al-Uzza, and the monument was probably intended both to refresh devotees on their way up and prepare them for the ceremonies about to be held at the High Place. The precipitous stairs beyond, which give views of the monuments below, bring you down to the **Garden Triclinium**, a simple monument overlooked by a huge tree in a beautiful, hidden setting, which got its name from the carpet of green that sprouts in springtime in front of the portico. Two free-standing columns are framed by two engaged ones; within is a small square shrine. Stairs to the right of the facade lead to a huge cistern on the roof, serving the Roman Soldier Tomb below.

The Roman Soldier Tomb

A beautiful set of rock-cut stairs to the left of the Garden Triclinium brings you down to the complex of the **Roman Soldier Tomb**. Although not immediately apparent, the two facades facing each other across the wadi formed part of a unified area, with an elaborate colonnaded courtyard and garden between them, long vanished. The tomb itself is on your left, an orthodox classical facade with three framed niches holding figures probably representing those buried within; the interior chamber has a number of recesses for the dead. Opposite the tomb, with an eroded but undecorated facade, is a startlingly colourful **triclinium**, unique in Petra for having a carved interior. The walls have been decorated with fluted columns and bays, all worn to show streaks of mauves, blues, pinks, crimsons and silver. Why this *triclinium* was decorated so carefully, and who was buried in the tomb opposite, isn't known; even the name is only a supposition from the middle of the tomb's three figures, a headless man wearing a cuirass.

Stairs lead down over the lip of a retaining wall to the wadi floor, and it is around here that the colouring in the rock is at its most gorgeous. Plenty of tombs crowd the lower reaches of the wadi; one of the most interesting is the **Renaissance Tomb**, topped by an urn and with an unusual arch above its doorway also carrying three urns. Nearby is the **Broken Pediment Tomb**, above the level of the path, displaying an early forerunner of the kind of broken pediment found on Petra's grandest monuments, the Treasury and the Monastery.

Zantur, Katuteh and Amud Faraoun

As you emerge from the wadi into the open, you should bear in mind that you're still the best part of half an hour from reaching the main routes again. From here onwards, though, there's not a scrap of shade – you're exposed to the full force of the sun and are quite often walking in stifling breezeless dips between hills. In addition, the path isn't initially clear. You should bear a little right, initially keeping out of the wadi bed, and aim for the left flank of the smooth rounded hill dead ahead. This hill is **Zantur**, Petra's rubbish dump, and it crunches underfoot with fragments of pottery: as well as coarse, crudely decorated modern sherds, there are countless chips of beautiful original Nabatean ware – very thin, smooth pottery that's been skilfully painted. As long as you don't start digging, you can take whatever you like.

Within metres are the remains of the house of a wealthy Nabatean merchant at **Katuteh**, suddenly abandoned for some reason (possibly as a result of having the city's garbage dumped in the back garden). The path eventually curls around to the western flank of the hill and **Amud Faraoun**, called *Zibb Faraoun* (Pharaoh's Phallus) by the bedouin. This standing column, which must have formed part of the portico of a building – part-visible buried in the rubbly hill behind – now serves as a useful landmark and resting-spot. Paths converge here from all sides; to the southwest (see p.265) is the main route into Wadi Thughra towards Umm al-Biyara, Jebel Haroun and Sabra; to the west is a path accessing a route up al-Habees (see p.262); to the northwest is the Qasr al-Bint (see p.261) and the tent-cafés; and to the northeast a path runs behind the markets area of the city centre (see p.260) parallel to the Colonnaded Street.

The East Cliff

About 250m beyond the theatre, just before the Wadi Musa makes its sharp left turn, solid, modern steps lead to the **East Cliff**, looming up to the right above the whole of the city centre. This whole elbow of Jebel al-Khubtha is ranged with some of Petra's most impressive facades, collectively known as the **Royal Tombs**. If you have anything more than half a day in the city, you should fit them in; the climb is easy and the views are marvellous. From down below, in the direct, reddish light of late afternoon, the entire cliff seems to glow with an inner translucence, and is one of the sights of Petra. However, it's probably best to aim to be up here in the morning shadows, with the sun lighting up the valley and the mountains opposite.

From right to left, the first tomb on the cliff – separate from the big ones, and missable if you're short of time – is the **Tomb of Unayshu**, viewed in profile from the Outer Siq and easiest to get to by scrambling up the rocks opposite the High Place staircase. This is part of a complete Nabatean tomb complex, and features a once-porticoed courtyard in front, with a *triclinium* to one side.

The Urn Tomb

Heading north from Unayshu above the main path, past another well-preserved tomb facade, you join the modern steps leading from below up to the soaring facade of the **Urn Tomb**, with its very large colonnaded forecourt partially supported on several storeys of arched vaults. The Bdul know the tomb as *al-Mahkamah*, "the Court", dubbing the vaults *as-Sijin*, "the Jail". Whether it was later used in this way or not, the whole structure would seem originally to have been the tomb of somebody extremely important, quite probably one of the Nabatean kings – but who exactly, isn't known. Set into the facade high above the forecourt between the engaged columns are spaces for three bodies; this is a unique configuration in Petra, since such *loculi* are normally inside the monument, and they seem to have been placed here as an indication of the importance of their occupants. The central one – possibly that of the king himself – is still partially sealed by a stone which formerly depicted the bust of a man wearing a toga. The urn which gave the tomb its name is, as always, right at the top.

Due, no doubt, to its dominating position in the city's landscape, the tomb was later converted into a major church – possibly Petra's **cathedral**; the large interior room features, near the left-hand corner of the back wall, a Greek inscription in red paint recording the dedication of the church by Bishop Jason in 447 AD. Probably at the same time, two central recesses of the original four were combined to make a kind of apse, and myriad holes were drilled in the floor to support all the relevant ecclesiastical furniture: chancel screens, a pulpit, maybe a table, and so on. The view from the forecourt, which takes in the full sweep of the valley (and even the urn atop the Monastery) is one of Petra's best.

The Silk Tomb, Corinthian Tomb and Palace Tomb

Working your way around the cliff, the next facade is the **Silk Tomb**, unremarkable but for its brilliant colouring. The facade of the nearby **Corinthian Tomb** was being consolidated at the time of writing, and an area in front was fenced off.

Something like a hybrid and ramshackle Treasury, it has the Treasury's style on the upper level – a *tholos* flanked by a broken pediment – but below it's a mess, the symmetry thrown out by extra doors on the left, and it's also suffered badly at the hands of the wind. However, such an exposed position on the corner of the cliff – directly in line with the Colonnaded Street – points to the fact that, like the Urn Tomb, this may well have been the tomb of another Nabatean king, visible from everywhere in the city.

Adjacent is an even more ramshackle mess, the very broad **Palace Tomb**, boasting one of Petra's largest, and least comprehensible, facades. There are at least five different storeys, the top portions of which were built of masonry because the cliff turned out to be too low, and so subsequently collapsed. The unevenly spaced line of engaged columns on the second row clashes nastily with the orthodox lower level. Protected by the cliff, the extreme right-hand edge of the facade still has some sharply carved detail surviving.

The Sextius Florentinus Tomb, Carmine Tomb and the Khubtha High Places

From the Palace Tomb, tracks lead west towards the city centre, and northeast hugging the cliff round to the beautiful and peaceful **Sextius Florentinus Tomb**, positioned facing north where a finger of the cliff reaches the ground. Sextius Florentinus was a Roman governor of the Province of Arabia who died about 130 AD, and must have chosen to be buried in Petra rather than in the provincial capital of Bosra. The facade of his tomb, with a graceful semicircular pediment, is one of the most pleasing in the city. A few metres north, behind a tree, is the spectacular **Carmine Tomb**, girt with breathtaking bands of colour, but, by virtue of its position, hardly ever noticed. Wadi Zarnug al-Khubtha, which divides the two, holds a path which gives reasonably easy, if steep, access to unvisited High Places and a few scattered ruins perched atop the massive **Jebel al-Khubtha**, the main barrier standing between Petra and Wadi Musa town. Needless to say, the views from on top are tremendous – especially of the theatre – but you'd have to be keen (and sure-footed) to try it.

The path beyond Sextius Florentinus along the Wadi Mataha is described on p.268.

The city centre

As you round the corner of the path leading from the theatre, the **city centre** of Petra, focused along the Cardo Maximus, or **Colonnaded Street**, stretches out ahead, framed by the barrier range of mountains – and the flat-topped giant Umm al-Biyara – behind. Although there are excavations continuing on the flat, rounded hills to either side, the overall impression is of barrenness and rocky desolation; however, in Petra's prime, the landscape in all directions was covered with buildings – houses big and small, temples, marketplaces – all of them long since collapsed. Many archeologists are theorizing that much of Petra is in fact still hidden beneath the dusty soil, and that all the facades and what few buildings have so far been exposed are the tip of the iceberg.

Until you reach the **Temenos** at the far end, the only monument actually on the Colonnaded Street is the **Nymphaeum**, although both the **northern** (right-

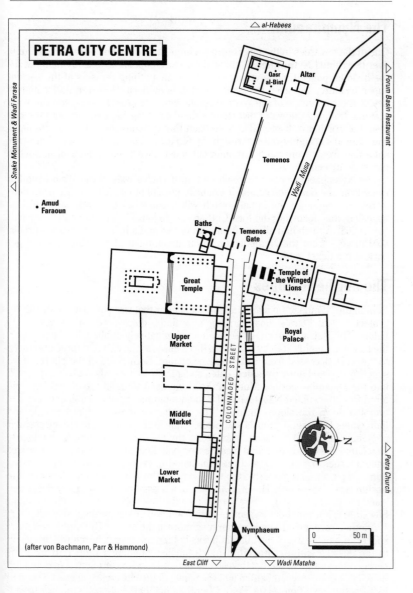

PETRA CITY CENTRE

△ al-Habees

Qasr al-Bint

Altar

Temenos

Wadi Musa

△ Snake Monument & Wadi Farasa

△ Forum Basin Restaurant

• Amud Faraoun

Baths

Temenos Gate

Great Temple

Temple of the Winged Lions

Upper Market

Royal Palace

COLONNADED STREET

Middle Market

N

Lower Market

△ Petra Church

Nymphaeum

| 0 | 50 m |

(after von Bachmann, Parr & Hammond)

East Cliff ▽   ▽ Wadi Mataha

hand) and **southern** (left-hand) slopes hold plenty of interest. Petra's main **museum** is just beyond the Temenos. Looming over the city centre from the west is a pinnacle of rock known as **al-Habees**, separate from the huge mountains behind and featuring, partway up, another small museum and – on the summit – a crumbling Crusader fort and some of the most fantastic views in all of Petra.

The Nymphaeum

One of the few trees in the city centre – a huge, lush pistachio – stands out a mile over the ruined **Nymphaeum**, these days more popular as a shady hangout for the bedouin police than anything else. Virtually nothing remains of the ancient superstructure, and even the retaining wall is modern. However, its location is key, at the confluence of the Wadi Musa, flowing from east to west, and the Wadi Mataha, bringing the water diverted by the dam at the Siq entrance into the city from the northeast. It may also have been the terminus for the terracotta pipes and channels bringing water through the Siq itself. The sight and sound of water splashing freely from such a monument must have been wonderful in such a parched city centre.

The Nymphaeum is where you'll end up if you've walked the Wadi Muthlim route from the dam (see p.246); it's equally possible to walk the route from here in reverse, although the initial stretch will be down in the wadi bed, and less appealing than following the East Cliff around to join Wadi Mataha further north (see p.268). You should allow a minimum of two and a half tough hours – preferably three – from the Nymphaeum to circumambulate Jebel Khubtha and get back to the ticket gate.

The northern slopes

Behind the Nymphaeum stands a modern shelter that was constructed in 1997 to protect one of Petra's most thrilling new finds, discovered only seven years before. The **Petra Church**, as it's been unimaginatively dubbed, is a large tripartite basilica, roughly 26m by 15m, with three apses to the east and three entrances to the west, accessed from a stone-paved atrium. Both aisles of the church have superbly detailed **floor mosaics**, dated stylistically to the early sixth century, well into the Byzantine period. Much of the stone used to build the church was pilfered from the ruined Nabatean and Roman monuments all around, and now lies tumbled down the slopes in front. The north-aisle mosaics depict people and indigenous and exotic animals and birds, while in the south aisle are spectacular personifications of the seasons, the Ocean, the Earth and Wisdom. Archeologists also found thousands of gilded glass tesserae, indicating that lavish wall mosaics once adorned the church, and they managed to reconstruct from more than a hundred pieces a huge marble tub with panthers for handles (this now sits in the Forum Basin Museum). The presence of such a large church so richly decorated – and the discovery of the Petra scrolls (see the box opposite) – merely highlight how little is known about Byzantine Petra, and how much awaits discovery.

Another recent find sheds a glimmer more light on the Byzantine period. A short climb to the top of the hill that peaks behind the Petra Church will bring you to the austere **Ridge Church**, a much smaller building (some 18m by 13m) perched on a ridge at the northwestern edge of Byzantine-era Petra, overlooking the Wadi Turkmaniyyeh behind and the whole of the city centre in front. Dated to roughly the same time as the Petra Church, much of the church's interior paving survives, but there's no decoration. What's most interesting about the place is that archeologists found almost no remnants of the building's superstructure nearby, although they did find a hoard of water-washed stones in the church courtyard brought up from the wadi below. From this confusing evidence, they came up with an elaborate theory for the church's destruction. At a time of

THE PETRA SCROLLS

One of the most significant recent archeological finds in the entire Middle East was made by accident in a storage room at the northeast corner of the Petra Church on December 4, 1993: archeologists stumbled on a cache of 152 **papyrus scrolls**, tumbled higgledy-piggledy from the shelves that presumably once carried them, which had lain buried beneath four metres of rubble. At the time of writing, analysis of the scrolls is still incomplete, but the preliminary results give tantalizing glimpses of life in Byzantine Petra, a period that is rarely accounted for.

The whole archive seems to have belonged to one Theodore, born in 514, who married at the age of 24 a young woman from a family already connected with his own by marriage in a previous generation. Theodore became archdeacon of the "Most Holy Church of NN in the metropolis" – presumably the Petra Church. Most of the documents date from a sixty-year period, roughly 528 to 588, and comprise property contracts, out-of-court settlements and tax receipts – not immediately gripping stuff, but providing a wealth of detail about everyday life. Transfers from one family to another of vineyards, arable land, orchards, living quarters and stables within a 50km radius of Petra were all dutifully recorded. One man's will specifies that after his mother's death, all her assets were to be donated (presumably whether she liked it or not) to the "House of Aron", undoubtedly the Byzantine monastery newly identified atop Jebel Haroun. Farmers, tailors, doctors, slaves and soldiers are all mentioned by name, including one Abu Karib ibn Jabala, known to have been a military commander of the Arab tribes. However Petra was decisively Christian at this time, and monks and priests feature prominently, not least a Bishop Theodore, who may have been the same Theodore who took part in a synod at Jerusalem in 536. Another reference is to a priest "of her, our All-Holy, Praised Lady, the Glorious God-Bearing and Eternally Virgin Mary", indicating that there may be a church to Mary yet to be uncovered in Petra. Only once the content of the scrolls has been published can investigation proceed any further, but this is just another sign that archeologists have only just begun to scratch Petra's surface.

increasing political instability, they postulate, the Petrans deliberately dismantled the church – which lay hard up against the city wall – in order to use its stones as missiles against invaders approaching from below. When the church had been razed, they collected more stones from the wadi to hoard against future attacks, but these were forgotten as, possibly, the city was overrun from a different direction. Any truth in this tale has yet to be confirmed.

The Temple of the Winged Lions

Overlooking the Temenos Gate west of the Petra Church, the principal building of the northern slope, the **Temple of the Winged Lions**, was haphazardly fenced off at the time of writing awaiting restoration. It was named for unusual column capitals featuring winged lions (one of which is in the Forum Basin Museum), but would have been more appropriately named the Temple of al-Uzza, for it seems to have been dedicated to her. Approximately dated to the early first century AD, the building – which must have been a major focus of the city's religious life – was approached via a bridge across the Wadi Musa, parts of which you can still see on the banks. The worshipper would have proceeded across ascending terraces, an open colonnaded courtyard and a portico into the temple itself, featuring close-packed columns and an altar platform. The floors were paved in contrasting black, brown and white marble, and the walls decorated with painted plaster; appropriately enough, archeologists uncovered both a painter's workshop – with paints and pigments still in their ceramic pots – and a marble-cutter's workshop adjoining the temple. One of the most spectacular discoveries, also now on display in the Forum Basin Museum, was a small rectangular stone idol, complete with a stylized face and a hole between the eyes (possibly for a set of horns, the symbol of the goddess Isis, to be inserted); the inscription along the base reads "Goddess of Hayyan son of Nybat". Adjacent to the temple to the east is a large unexcavated area of rubble deemed to have been a royal palace, also with a bridge over the wadi, but no work has as yet been done on it.

The southern slopes

From the Nymphaeum all the way along the paved Colonnaded Street westwards, columns on your left (south) stand in front of what have been dubbed Petra's **Upper, Middle and Lower Markets**, but these remain in the very preliminary stages of digging. It seems that ranged along street level in front of the markets, to either side of the grand staircases, were small shops, which may have been refitted in the Byzantine period, but, at the time of writing, the stairs themselves were fenced off and work was proceeding to excavate the market floors and outbuildings.

The Great Temple

Almost adjacent to the Temenos Gate at the western end of the street, a set of steps lead up to the **Great Temple**, or Southern Temple, an extremely grand affair, one of the largest complexes in the city. Excavation work only began in 1993, and is also far from finished; you may be able to explore only part of the building. Worshippers originally climbed a staircase from street level through a now tumbled gateway onto the hexagonally paved lower precinct, featuring triple colonnades to east and west culminating in semicircular benched alcoves. The temple itself stands some 25m above street level, fronted by four enormous columns which were originally stuccoed in red and white. Within the *cella*, archeologists very recently came across what seems to be a small Nabatean theatre, about 7m in diameter, which would have seated at least three hundred people, although much still remains to be unearthed. The whole building is extremely complex, with stairs and corridors leading every which way. In addition, tumbled columns and chunks of architectural elements (many of them beautifully carved) all point to the fact that this was one of Petra's most important monuments. As yet, though, not even the deity who was worshipped here is known.

The Temenos

In most Roman cities, the main east–west and north–south streets ploughed straight furrows from city gate to city gate; however, as at Bosra, the heterodox Nabateans blocked off Petra's main street at one end and turned the area beyond – hard up against the mountain cliffs – into a **Temenos**, or sacred temple precinct. Framing the western end of the Colonnaded Street stands the partially reconstructed remains of the **Temenos Gate**, marking the end of the commercial sector of Petra and the entrance to the main area of worship. Sockets in the threshold indicate that great doors once closed off all three entrances of the gate; the floral frieze which survives on the easternmost facade of the gate was originally framed by free-standing columns which stood just in front and to either side.

As you pass through the gate, the impression remains of having left the city behind; the courtyard – occupied at the far end by, on one side, camels and on the other the bulk of a temple – is huge, paved and open, and at times of religious celebration, would have been thronged with people. Low walls enclosed the Temenos on both sides, although the northern one has been eroded away by the waters of the Wadi Musa. Just inside the Temenos Gate to the south are three domed rooms tentatively identified as **baths**, but only partially excavated. All along the south wall is a double row of stone benches, some 73m in length, leading almost up to the main feature of the Temenos, the Qasr al-Bint, the only free-standing monument as yet uncovered in the whole of Petra.

The Qasr al-Bint

The **Qasr al-Bint al-Faraoun** – the "Palace of Pharaoh's Daughter" – is nothing of the sort. Its name derives from another far-fetched bedouin tale of the pharaoh, who, it's said, after stashing his riches in the Treasury, and still desperate to let nothing slow him down in his pursuit of the Israelites, stashed his daughter away here for safekeeping. Interestingly enough, though, an inscription, probably from the base of a statue, naming Suudat, daughter of the Nabatean king Malchus II (40–70 AD), was found on the steps, indicating that some link between the *qasr* and the daughter of a powerful man may not be so fanciful after all.

The building is a huge, square Nabatean temple, dating from the late first century BC, oriented to the north and facing a huge, free-standing altar, some 13m by 12m and at least 3m high. The altar, clad in marble, showed a blank wall to the north, and was originally approached by steps from in front of the temple. From here looking back, the four gigantic columns of the temple portico, standing at the head of a broad staircase wider than the building, and topped by an architrave and pediment, would have made a deeply impressive sight. The huge arch that survives today was probably only a relieving arch for a lower, horizontal lintel of the doorway into the *cella*, which spanned the width of the building and was lit by windows high up in each wall. Behind, the holy of holies was divided into three separate chambers, or *adyta*; the central one is slightly raised, has engaged columns along the walls and another relieving arch overhead, and this is where the god-block or cult statue would have stood. The temple's dedication is unknown, but Dushara is the most obvious candidate.

The Forum Basin Museum

Tent-cafés and camel drivers crowd the area in front of the Qasr al-Bint, and this is the main area for gathering strength before you continue to explore or start the long walk back (a full hour uphill by the most direct route to the ticket gate through the Siq). In front of the *qasr*, a path crosses the Wadi Musa; to the right leads the Wadi Turkmaniyyeh dirt road (see p.267), but 50m ahead is the *Forum Basin Restaurant* and adjacent **Forum Basin Museum** (daily 8am–3.30pm), definitely worth a quick look if only to give yourself a break from all the imposing architecture. There are excellent informative noticeboards on Petra's history and geography (including a fascinating digression into the frankincense trade), as well as stacks of information about the Nabateans. Plenty of finds are on display from all periods of occupation at Petra, stretching right back to Neolithic times, among which Nabatean coins, pottery and some beautiful and delicate jewellery are by far the most engaging. Specific pieces that stand out are the small but extraordinarily powerful idol from the Temple of the Winged Lions, statues of Aphrodite and Dionysus, and the massive panther-handled marble tub from the Petra Church.

al-Habees

The modern building next to the Qasr al-Bint – now used by the Department of Antiquities – is known as Nazzal's Camp, and was formerly Petra's sole hotel, built in the 1940s on the site of Thomas Cook's old campground: early tourists were offered the option of sleeping in one of the caves cut into **al-Habees** looming overhead. These caves are used now as storage areas and offices for the police, but one has been converted into a small **museum** (Mon & Wed–Sun 8am–3.30pm; sometimes also closed Fri), accessed up stairs in front of Nazzal's Camp and well worth a look. The chamber is crammed full of marvellous statuary; above the door is a bust of a curly-headed figure, and there are other busts of various Roman gods, an eagle with outspread wings perched on a thunderbolt (symbol of Zeus), and a headless statue of Hercules recovered from the theatre.

From the museum it's possible to follow the path around the mountain a little way on the initial stretches of a processional way to the summit. A little way around is an open area overlooking the beautiful Wadi Siyyagh, with plenty of rock-cut caves – whether they're tombs or houses isn't certain – as well as a small **High Place**, in perfect isolation above a prominent crow-step facade and sunken courtyard in the **Convent Group** of monuments. Beyond, though, the Nabatean stairway is worn and dangerous, and the best way up to the summit is now via a staircase on the southern flank of the mountain, for which you must return to Nazzal's Camp.

Wadi Siyyagh

Just to the north of al-Habees, **Wadi Siyyagh** – which takes the waters of the Wadi Musa down to Wadi Araba – was formerly one of the most gorgeous and quiet short walks you could make in Petra. This was once an exclusive residential neighbourhood of the city, enclosed between high walls, and there are plenty of houses and tombs, a Nabatean quarry and a well to explore. However, the wadi is now a short-cut for local people driving their pickups, and a cave near the eastern end is home to a generator that keeps the *Forum Basin Restaurant* and the Department of Antiquities offices operational; the insane roar of the thing echoes for a good half-hour down the wadi, the first 150m of which are now also covered with litter.

The Unfinished Tomb and Columbarium

If you scramble up the rubbly hill behind Nazzal's Camp and hug the foot of the eastern wall of al-Habees, you'll soon spot one of Petra's most interesting monuments, the **Unfinished Tomb**. This is what it says, and shows how Nabatean craftsmen worked from the top down, scooping out the interior as they went. A little further uphill is the **Columbarium**, a strange monument covered inside and out with hundreds of tiny square niches that had an unknown function: the name literally means "dovecote", but no dove could roost here, and they seem too small to hold funerary urns, as has also been suggested.

The al-Habees Crusader fort

To reach the **Crusader fort** on the top of al-Habees, you should continue south from the Columbarium, and follow a sign pointing right, even though it appears to point at the blank rubbly cliffside. As you get nearer, you'll spot the modern, restored stairs which take you up to the summit; it's an easy fifteen-minute climb, although there is one wooden footbridge without railings on the way. A gate with a rock-cut bench marks the approach to the fort, after which you'll have to scramble over loose stones up to a gatehouse. From here, you must find your own way the last little bit to the top; steps rise at one point over the barrel vault of a small room. The layout of the ruined fort itself – only occupied for a few decades in the twelfth century – is jumbled and confusing, but the 360-degree views are quite stunning.

The Monastery

Petra's most awe-inspiring monument is also one of the most taxing to reach. The **Monastery** (*ad-Dayr* in Arabic) boasts a massive facade almost fifty metres square, carved from a chunk of mountain nearly an hour's climb northwest of the city centre, 220m above the elevation of the Qasr al-Bint. Daunting though this sounds, there are well-trodden steps the whole way, as well as plenty of places to rest; a tranquil holy spring two-thirds of the way up is almost worth the climb by itself. Even if you've had your fill of facades, the stupendous views from the mountaintop over the entire Petra basin and the Wadi Araba make the trip essential. Whether you want to ride a donkey to the summit or not (prices are *very* negotiable), you'll most likely have to beat off the hordes of kids riding alongside offering them as "Air-condition taxi, mister?" On two feet or four hooves, by far the best time to attempt the climb is in the afternoon; not only is the way up mostly in shadow by then, but the sun has moved around enough to hit the facade on the summit full-on.

The route up to the Monastery

The route passes in front of the *Forum Basin* restaurant and museum, and leads dead ahead into the soft sandy bed of the Wadi ad-Dayr. The steps begin after a short distance, and soon after there's a diversion pointed left to the **Lion Triclinium**, a small classical shrine in a peaceful bushy wadi, named for the very worn lions that flank its entrance. A small round window above the door and the doorway itself have been eroded together to form a strange keyhole shape. The frieze above has Medusas at either end, and to the left of the facade is a small god-block set into a niche.

The processional way up to the Monastery is broken after another patch of steps by a sharp left turn where the Wadi Kharrubeh joins from in front; a little way along this wadi – off the main path – you'll find on the right-hand side a small **biclinium**, a ceremonial dining room with two stepped benches facing each other. Returning to the path, after a step-free patch the climb recommences. Some twenty or thirty minutes from the Forum Basin, where the steps turn sharp left, you can branch right off the main path into a narrow wadi; double-back to the left, follow a track up and then right onto a broad, cool, protected ledge overlooking a deep ravine below. This is the **Qattar ad-Dayr**, an enchanted mossy grotto enclosed by high walls, completely silent but for the cries of wheeling birds and the continual dripping of water and a perfect spot for a picnic. Here, the one place in Petra where water flows year-round, the Nabateans built a *triclinium* and cisterns, and made dozens of carvings, including a spectacular two-armed cross.

As the steps drag on, the views begin to open up, and you get a sense of the vastness of the mountains and valleys all around. With tired legs, it's about another twenty minutes to a small sign pointing right to the **Hermitage**, a sheer-sided pinnacle of rock featuring a less-than-gripping set of caves carved with crosses. Another ten minutes, after a squeeze between two boulders and a short descent, and you emerge onto a wide, flat plateau, where you should turn right for the Monastery.

The site

The **Monastery** facade is so big that it seems like an optical illusion – the doorway alone is taller than a house. A local entrepreneur has thoughtfully set up a refreshments stall in a cave opposite, and there's a bench you can sink down on to take in the full vastness of the view. At first glance, the facade looks much like the Treasury's, but it's much less ornate; indeed, there's virtually no decoration at all. The name "Monastery" is again a misnomer, probably suggested by some crosses scratched inside; this was almost certainly a temple, possibly dedicated to the Nabatean king Obodas I, who reigned in the first century BC and was posthumously deified. Inside is a single chamber, with the same configuration of double staircases leading up to a cultic niche as in the Qasr al-Bint and the Temple of the Winged Lions. The flat plaza in front of the monument isn't natural: it was levelled deliberately, probably to contain the huge crowds that gathered here for religious ceremonies. You can pick out traces of a wall and colonnade in the ground to the south of the plaza, near where you entered. The opposite side (the left flank of the monument as you face it) has a scramble-path which can take you up to the **urn** on the top of the facade, which is no less than 10m high. Leaping around on the urn is a test of mettle for the local goat-footed kids, and some even shimmy to the very top; follow them with your life in your hands.

There are dozens more monuments and carvings to explore around the Monastery, not least of which is a cave and stone circle directly behind the refreshments cave. At any point, once you climb off ground level, the views are breathtaking. The cliff to the north (left) of the facade is punctuated for well over 100m with Nabatean caves, tombs and cisterns; some 200m or so north of the Monastery, you'll stumble onto a dramatically isolated High Place, with godlike views over the peaks down to the far-distant Wadi Araba, 1000m below.

The only route back into Petra from the Monastery is the way you came up. Like all these descents, it's too rocky and isolated even to think about attempting it after sunset.

Further afield

If you have time, there are plenty of sites of interest beyond Petra's central valley to explore. Although they're more difficult to reach, and generally have less striking architecture once you arrive, just the experience of hiking through Petra's incredible landscape is thrilling enough: all of these walks involve getting well off the popular tour-group routes, and it's quite possible the only people you meet will be local Bdul families. You'll need guides only for the climbs; the hikes – as long as you're carrying sufficient food and water for a full and strenuous day – are easily manageable alone. Sites within striking distance are ranged along Petra's main valley to either side of the city, so we've divided this section into treks **southwest** and **northeast** of Petra's city centre. **Siq al-Berid** and **Baydha**, some 9km north of Petra, are treated separately; they're easily accessible on foot across country, but you're more likely to want to get to one or both of them on a half-day taxi excursion.

Southwest of Petra

Walking routes to the southwest of Petra begin from the Amud Faraoun; a path from there drops down to follow the main **Wadi Thughra** along the base of the cliffs, from which all the following sights can be reached. **Umm al-Biyara** is the numinous flat-topped mountain overlooking the whole of Petra; a tough climb up steps delivers you to Nabatean ruins, the remains of a seventh-century BC Edomite settlement and vertiginous panoramas few people other than mountaineers ever get to experience. The **Snake Monument**, a single block carved as a huge snake, is over 2km southwest of Petra but on the flat. From there, a path branches out to the steps leading up the holy mountain **Jebel Haroun**, on the summit of which is the little white shrine visible from just about everywhere in Petra and Wadi Musa, the tomb of Moses' brother Aaron. Beyond the Snake Monument, **Sabra** is a southern suburb of Petra, mostly unexcavated and featuring a semi-ruined amphitheatre, a full day's hike on the flat through gorgeous open countryside.

Umm al-Biyara
Petra's hardest climb (other than off-route scrambling) is up **Umm al-Biyara**, likely to take a full hour from base to summit and requiring something of a head for heights: a couple of exposed scrambles might give you the flutters. You definitely need a guide, and should only make the climb in the afternoon when the east face of the mountain is in shadow.

About 350m southwest of the Amud Faraoun, Wadi Umm Rattam comes in from the left; keep straight and, a little beyond, branch right (west) on a path directly towards a gully on the western edge of the massif, itself dotted all the way along with facades at different levels. The initial stages of the Nabatean processional way have collapsed, but a little to the south you'll find some modern steps, which lead you round to join the Nabatean path again higher up, part original, part restored. A little further is a sweeping hairpin ramp, deeply gouged out of the rockface to form a high corridor. Beyond here, the way is often eroded and although there are some cairns to mark the way, the drops are precipitous. You emerge at the south edge of the **summit plateau**, a scrubby slope that rises another thirty metres to the highest point on the northwest. The Edomite settlement is dead ahead, with many high dry-stone walls and corridors excavated; from the evidence of lamps, jars and looms, it seems that this community was a quiet, peaceful one, but it must have been important enough to receive a letter from Qaush-Gabr, king of Edom around 670 BC – his seal was discovered in the ruins. *Biyara* means "cisterns", and there are plenty up here, probably Nabatean. All along the eastern rim are ruins of Nabatean buildings commanding spectacular bird's-eye views over the Petra basin, 275 sheer metres below; the mountain vistas to the west, from the highest point of the plateau, are no less stunning. There are only two ways down: the fast way, and the way you came up.

The Snake Monument

The path to the Snake Monument is the same as for Umm al-Biyara in the initial stretches, except instead of branching off the Wadi Thughra, you should keep going ahead through the undulating countryside. This was (and is) the main road into Petra from the south. After around thirty minutes or so you'll see a very prominent, top-heavy **god-block** atop an area of caves and tombs which has been dubbed "The Southern Graves"; these caves are still inhabited by Bdul, so you shouldn't be exploring too inquisitively without being invited in. Poised above and to the left of the god-block, not immediately apparent, is the **Snake Monument**, a worn block carved with a huge, coiled serpent overlooking the tombs and houses below. If you head another five minutes or so along the valley, you'll come to a flat area with trees that's been fenced around and cultivated; it's here that paths divide – south to Sabra, southeast towards the foot of Jebel Haroun.

Jebel Haroun

Jebel Haroun – Aaron's Mountain – is the holiest site in Petra and one of the holiest in Jordan, venerated by Muslims as the resting place of Prophet Haroun, as they know him, as well as by Christians and Jews. Although much less of an issue than in former years, there persists some local resistance to tourists casually climbing the mountain simply for the views, or to gawk: you should bear in mind that this is a holy place of pilgrimage. The trip there and back takes at least six hours from Petra city centre, involving a climb of almost 500m (a donkey can take you for all but the last twenty minutes), and you shouldn't attempt it without a guide, six to eight litres of water, some food, respectable clothing and a sense of humility. Don't bother if you're expecting an impressive shrine (it's small and unremarkable) or outstanding views (they're equally good from the Monastery and Umm al-Biyara). If you choose to visit, you should consider bringing a sum of money with you to leave as a donation.

Rosalyn Maqsood, in her excellent book on Petra (see p.354), explained the power of Jebel Haroun well:

> *Believers in the "numinous universe" accept that certain localities can be impregnated with the life-giving force of some saint or hero – transforming the sites into powerhouses of spiritual blessing. Traces of their essential virtue would cling to their mortal leavings even though their spirits had passed to another and better world. Holiness was seen as a kind of invisible substance, which clung to whatever it touched. So the virtues (the Latin word* virtu *means "power") of saints would remain and be continually renewed and built up by the constant stream of prayer and devotion emanating from the pilgrims who found their way there. These places are visited to gain healing, or fertility, or protection against dangers psychic and physical, or to gain whatever is the desire of the heart. Jebel Haroun is such a place. ... There is nothing there, really, and no one to watch you – so why should you remove your shoes, or leave an offering? Only you can answer this.*

From the cultivated area near the Snake Monument, a path leads down into the Wadi Magtal ad-Dikh. A little beyond a cemetery on the right-hand side, and past a rock ledge called **Settuh Haroun** (Aaron's Terrace) at the foot of the mountain, where pilgrims unable to climb make an offering (Burckhardt slaughtered his goat here), there is a reasonably clear path up the mountain. You should check in the tent at the bottom of the mountain whether the guardian will be around to open the shrine at the top; if not, you should collect the keys from him before you head up.

As recently as 1997, archeologists revealed that a plateau just below the summit was the location of a **Byzantine monastery** dedicated to Aaron; excavations are proposed in the future. The small domed **shrine of Haroun** on the peak was renovated by the Mamluke sultan Qalawun in 1459, replacing earlier buildings which had stood on the same site. Up until then, the caretakers had been Greek Christians, and it was in the late sixth century that the Prophet Muhammad, on a journey from Mecca to Damascus, passed through Petra and climbed Jebel Haroun with his uncle. The Christian guardian of the shrine, a monk named Bahira, prophesied that the boy – then aged ten – would change the world. Today, pilgrims bedeck the shrine with rags, twined threads and shells – the Muslim equivalent of lighting a candle to the saint.

Sabra

At the zenith of its economic power, Petra must have been processing goods from dozens, possibly hundreds, of caravans, and it was obviously not desirable to have hordes of foreign merchants – not to mention camels, random travellers and all the hangers-on associated with the caravan trade – pouring into the city centre. The Nabateans therefore built for themselves "suburbs" on all the main routes into the city, where business could be done, camels fed and watered, and goods stored well away from the sensitive corridors of power. Bir Mathkoor (see p.303) in Wadi Araba was the western suburb dealing with trade to and from Gaza; Siq al-Berid (see p.269) the northern, for trade with Palestine and Syria; al-Khan (the area of the Petra Resthouse near the ticket gate) may have been the eastern, receiving goods from the Arabian interior; and the southern suburb – with goods arriving from the Red Sea and Hejaz – was **Sabra**. Little has been excavated here, and the walk from Petra could take two and a half hours, much more appealing as a day-long round-trip hike in open country than a ruin hunt.

There are two routes down to Sabra, both on the flat the whole way. The first, and more open, goes from the cultivated area near the Snake Monument, around the humped Ras Slayman hill and through the Ragbat al-Btahi pass between peaks before dropping to the sandy wadi floor; shortly after, Wadi Sabra joins from the left. As an alternative, you could head southwest from Amud Faraoun, then after 350m turn left (southeast) along Wadi Umm Rattam, which crosses to hug the eastern side of the valley below Jebel Nmayr; after a little less than an hour, aim right (southwest) to follow Wadi Sabra which is eventually joined by the first path. The ruins are a little ahead, set in beautifully green and rolling countryside well watered by the Ain Sabra spring. On the left is a large rock-cut **theatre**, with, above the auditorium, a large cistern that was used to provide a head of pressure for flooding the place so that the Nabateans could apparently indulge in mock sea battles. Ruinous evidence of the size of Nabatean Sabra is everywhere around – houses, monumental buildings, niches and several temples.

Northeast of Petra

There are two main walking routes northeast from Petra, following the two wadis that join the Wadi Musa in the city centre. On the western side of the valley is the quiet **Wadi Turkmaniyyeh** – also often called **Wadi Abu Ullaygeh** – along the bank of which runs the only driveable track into and out of Petra (forbidden to the general public without written permission in advance from the Wadi Musa tourist police – granted only *in extremis*). On the eastern side of the valley, the rocky **Wadi Mataha** hugs the east face of Jebel al-Khubtha, giving access to strenuous walking routes out to Wadi Musa town which avoid the Siq. Set in the heart of the lunar-looking domes behind the *Forum Hotel* is the ruined Crusader fort of **Wu'ayra**.

The Wadi Turkmaniyyeh route

Joining the Wadi Musa between the Qasr al-Bint and the *Forum Basin Restaurant*, **Wadi Turkmaniyyeh** is a very pleasant walking route to take out of Petra to the north, a small sandy valley with the hundred-metre-high jagged mountains on your left contorted into weird shapes. There are two groups of tombs and facades along the way: if you enter the **Wadi Muaysreh ash-Shargiyyeh**, which joins Wadi Turkmaniyyeh on the left barely five minutes from the restaurant, after about 350m you'll come to a dense gathering of facades; and five minutes further northeast along Wadi Turkmaniyyeh you'll see, ranged up on the **Muaysreh Ridges** to your left, a whole stack of fascinating carved facades, with niches, double-height courtyards and a tiny High Place dotted amongst them. Either of these areas would repay scrambled exploration, well away from the crowds.

About 1km along Wadi Turkmaniyyeh from the restaurant you'll see the facade of the **Turkmaniyyeh Tomb** on the left, with the entire bottom half broken away; at the time of writing, there was scaffolding in front for renovation work. Between the two pilasters is the longest inscription in Petra in Nabatean, a dialect of Aramaic, dedicating the tomb and the surrounding property to Dushara. All the gardens, cisterns and walls mentioned in the inscription must have been swept away by the floodwaters of the wadi, as, indeed, the facade almost has been.

From here, the road begins 1500m of tight switchbacks as it climbs the ridge to the police post on the outskirts of **Umm Sayhoun**, the breezeblock village constructed for the Bdul in the 1980s. Buses shuttle regularly from the village into Wadi Musa, about 4km away; they follow the road to the right, curling around the head of the valley and south past Wu'ayra to the *Mövenpick Hotel*.

The Wadi Mataha route

From the Sextius Florentinus Tomb (see p.256), a path hugs the Jebel al-Khubtha northeast along the broad **Wadi Mataha**. After 300m or so, you'll spot a complex of rock-cut dwellings known as **Dorotheos' House** set into the cliff on your right, named because "Dorotheos" occurs twice in Greek inscriptions within a large, airy *triclinium* here. Opposite, on the western side of the wadi, are **Mughur an-Nassara** – the "Caves of the Christians" – a still-populated rocky crag dotted with dozens of tombs and rock-cut houses, many of which are carved with crosses (thus the name). The whole outcrop is worth exploring and commands an excellent view of Petra from the north.

About 600m northeast from Dorotheos' House is the point at which the narrow **Sidd Maajn** joins the larger Wadi Mataha from the east. There are two routes back to civilization from here, neither of them particularly easy. First – and less complicated – is to follow the Wadi Muthlim route (see p.246) in reverse; this brings you to the dam at the mouth of the Siq. The other route is tricky and takes you into the heart of the mass of rocky domes west of Wu'ayra, where it's easy to get lost; from the Wadi Mataha, you should be certain you have at least two hours of good daylight left, or you may find dusk falling with you stranded in a hundred-metre-high blind gorge and no one in earshot. From the Sidd Maajn junction, continue north only another 100m or so along Wadi Mataha, and scale the dark rusty rocks to your right. This ridge gives you a view down into the Sidd Maajn from above, and along the parallel wadis leading south away from you into the mountain. As you walk left (east) you'll spot – like an enchanted bridge – a Nabatean **aqueduct**, gracefully spanning a wadi below. You need to aim for the wadi which leads south-southeast into the domes from a point directly at the foot of the aqueduct; make a wrong move at this point, and you'll have trouble later on extricating yourself. This is **Wadi Sha'ab Qays** and, like all of them hereabouts, is long, straight and perfectly still; tracks and fresh goat droppings are good signs that you're going roughly in the right direction. You'll have to scrape past woody oleanders rooted in the sandy bed, but the going is easy enough until you reach a gigantic boulder (featuring an endearing little niche) all but blocking the way. There's just enough room to squeeze through on the right. Much further along, you'll come across a Nabatean water channel, which you can follow all the way out of the domes and towards the *Forum Hotel*.

Wu'ayra

On the edge of the domes, only about 200m east of Wadi Sha'ab Qays but utterly inaccessible from it, stands the Crusader fort of **Wu'ayra**. The ruins themselves are only of passing interest, but the location of the place is fairytale stuff, balanced on a razor-edge pinnacle of rock with sheer ravines on all sides and a single bridge giving access.

After King Baldwin led the Crusaders into Transjordan in 1115, founding their headquarters at Shawbak, his forces rapidly set about consolidating their defences; Wu'ayra (called by them *Li Vaux Moise*, or "Moses' Valley") was one outpost constructed the following year, al-Habees another, with forts also going up at Aqaba and Tafileh. Wu'ayra was only briefly in Frankish hands, though; after some tussling over possession, Salah ad-Din seized control for good only seventy years later.

The fort is only accessible off the road towards Umm Sayhoun about 1km north of the *Mövenpick Hotel*, the spot handily marked out by a gaping rectangular tomb to the left of the road. Aim for a gap in the rocks about 10m left of the tomb, and you'll find the straightforward path down to where the **bridge** spans the chasm. The **gatehouse** on the other side, with benches and a graffitied niche, gives into the castle **interior**, rough, rocky and ruined.

Siq al-Berid and Baydha

Petra's northern suburb of **Siq al-Berid** is often touted to tourists as "Little Petra" – which, with its short, high gorge and familiar carved facades, isn't far wrong; however, although it's now consequently seeing its share of tour buses, the place retains an atmosphere and a stillness that have largely disappeared from the central areas of Petra. Adding in its location in gorgeous countryside and its proximity to **Baydha** – a rather less inspiring Neolithic village – it's well worth half a day of your time. Most travellers choose to visit by taxi, combining the two places with a quick peek at Wu'ayra (see above) on the way; the going rate for a full car from Wadi Musa there and back, with a wait included, is JD8.

Siq al-Berid

The route follows the road north from the *Mövenpick Hotel*, through Umm Sayhoun and on through flat, cultivated uplands that are breathtakingly beautiful after Petra's barren rockscapes. About 8km from the Mövenpick, a T-junction signs Shawbak to the right (this is a rough back-route to the King's Highway), and the entrance to the

Siq al-Berid is about 800m to the left. This whole area was a thriving community in Nabatean times, and there's evidence in almost every cranny of Nabatean occupation. Just before you reach the Siq entrance, there's a particularly striking facade on the right, with a strange, narrow passage for an interior.

As you enter the Siq, you'll realize why this was dubbed the "Cold Siq" – almost no sun can reach inside to warm the place. It's only about 350m long, with alternating narrow and open sections, and differs from most areas of Petra firstly in the density of carved houses, temples and *triclinia* – there are very few blank areas – and secondly in the endearingly quaint rock-cut stairs which lead off on all sides, turning it into a multi-storey alleyway that must have once hummed with life. Feel free to explore on all sides; there are a few highlights, but every corner has something worth seeing. In the first open area is what was probably a **temple**, fronted by a portico, below which is a very explorable little rock-cut house. The second open area has four large **triclinia**, which could well have been used to wine and dine merchants and traders on their stopover in Petra. A little further on the left, stairs climb up to the **Painted House**, a *biclinium* featuring one of the very few Nabatean painted interiors to have survived the centuries, although much damaged. You might just be able to make out, on the ceiling at the back, a winged cupid with a bow and arrow; just above is a bird, to the left of which is a Pan figure playing a flute. The third open area culminates in rock-cut stairs which lead through a narrow gap out onto a wide flat ledge; the path drops down into the wadi (Petra is to the left), but you can scramble up to the right for some excellent views.

Baydha

If you emerge from the Siq al-Berid and head right on a track that hugs the cliff all the way round, after fifteen minutes or so you'll come to the Neolithic ruins of **Baydha**, which date from around nine thousand years ago, when the first experiments in settled agriculture were happening. There are two main levels of occupation; the first, from about 7000 BC, involved building a wall around what was formerly a temporary camping ground. The round stone houses inside were partly sunk into the ground and supported on a framework of vertical wooden posts (now rotted away). The occupants seemed to have farmed goats and possibly other animals, as well as cultivating a wide variety of cereals and nuts: querns, tools and stones for grinding and flints are dotted all over the site. After a fire sometime around 6650 BC, the village was rebuilt with "corridor houses", characterized by long, straight walls and large communal areas in addition to smaller rooms. Sometime around 6500 BC, and for a reason as yet unknown, Baydha was abandoned. Although the Nabateans later farmed the site, no one lived here permanently again.

travel details

Buses, minibuses and *services* to and from Wadi Musa simply depart whenever they are full, with no fixed timetables.

Buses, minibuses and *services*

Taybeh to: Wadi Musa (25min).

Umm Sayhoun to: Wadi Musa (15min).

Wadi Musa (Shaheed roundabout) to: Amman (Wihdat station; 3hr); Aqaba (1hr 45min); Ma'an (40min); Shawbak (30min); Taybeh (25min); Umm Sayhoun (15min); Wadi Rum (1hr 30min).

CHAPTER SIX

THE SOUTHERN DESERT AND AQABA

T he huge eastern deserts of Jordan are mostly stony plains of limestone or basalt, but much of the southern desert to the south and southeast of Petra is sand, presaging the dunes and vast emptinesses of the Arabian interior. The principal town of the south, Ma'an, is eminently missable, but you shouldn't leave Jordan without having spent at least some time in the incredible desert moonscape of Wadi Rum, the haunt of Lawrence of Arabia and starting point for camel treks into the red sands. At the southern tip of the country, squeezed onto Jordan's only stretch of coastline, the peaceful town of Aqaba is much less impressive than the breathtaking marine flora and fauna which thrive in the warm Red Sea waters just offshore.

Two of the three north–south highways connecting Amman with Aqaba are desert roads, and really only of interest as access routes to and from the south, so we've included them in this chapter. The easternmost of the three, the so-called **Desert Highway**, follows the line of the Hejaz Railway and serves as a demarcation line between well-watered hills to the west and the open desert. In an utterly remote location east of the highway is the majestic but ruined **Qasr Tuba**, the most isolated of the Umayyads' "Desert Castles". The westernmost of the three north–south routes is the fast **Wadi Araba road** which hugs the Israeli border and the Dead Sea shore. The middle route of the three and by far the most interesting – the King's Highway – is covered in detail in Chapter 4.

Transport is very straightforward. Plenty of buses run along the Desert Highway to Ma'an and Aqaba, and you can get connections from both of them to

---

HOTEL PRICE CODES

Throughout this guide, hotels have been categorized according to the **price codes** given below, which indicate the normal price for the **cheapest double room** in a particular establishment during the **high season** (excluding the ten-percent tax and ten-percent service charge levied in all hotels of ③ and above). **Single rooms** can cost anything between seventy and a hundred percent of the double-room rates. Where a hotel offers beds in **shared rooms**, the price per person to share has been given; if a price code has also been included, this indicates that private rooms are also available. For a fuller explanation, see p.39.

① under JD10	④ JD30–40	⑦ JD65–80
② JD10–20	⑤ JD40–50	⑧ JD80–95
③ JD20–30	⑥ JD50–65	⑨ over JD95

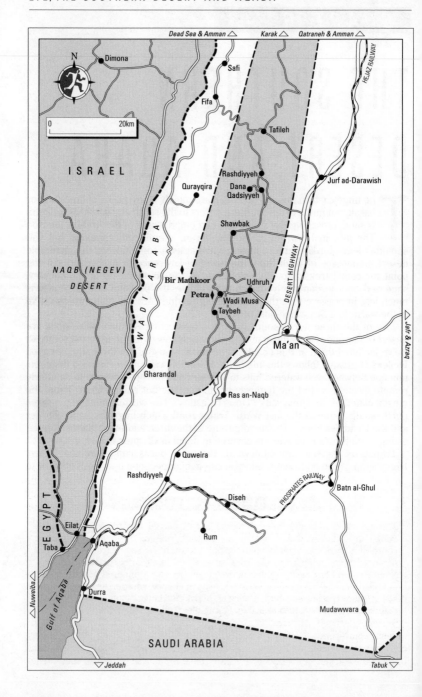

all other destinations in the region. Aqaba is also a major entry point into the country, with a land crossing to and from Israel and a ferry port serving Egypt, as well as an airport near the town. The Wadi Araba road has only a handful of buses between Karak or Tafileh and Aqaba, and Qasr Tuba is inaccessible without a 4x4.

Destinations in the south are often less appealing than the journeys to get to them, and the freedom a **rental car** gives really comes into its own when you're travelling in the desert here. Being able to stop and walk even 100m away from the highway, to get a first-hand experience of the wide open vistas rather than having them just skim past a dirty window, can give you a taste of an incredible natural environment.

The Desert Highway

The **Desert Highway** via Ma'an is the least romantic of the three routes linking Amman and the south of Jordan. Nonetheless, it's the favoured route of almost all public transport and can whisk you from the capital to Petra and beyond in a fraction of the time the same journey would take on the langorous King's Highway – but with a fraction of the interest. For the most part, the journey south is framed by bleached-out desert hills rolling off into the distance, the monotony broken only by feeder roads branching west at regular intervals to link the highway with – in north-to-south order – Dhiban, Karak, Tafileh, Dana, Shawbak and Wadi Musa on the King's Highway (all described in Chapter 4).

However, this route is older than it appears, as the highway was built along the line of the **Hejaz Railway** (see p.82), which itself shadowed earlier Ottoman **pilgrimage** routes through the desert from Damascus to Mecca. During the sixteenth century, the Ottoman authorities positioned tiny *hajj* forts roughly a day's journey apart all down the length of the route to guard local water sources and to serve as accommodation for the pilgrims; some survive today, but almost all are ruined and/or inaccessible, the preserve of kestrels and archeologists.

Qatraneh

After swishing past the Mamluke fort at Jiza – now a bedouin police station – and the infamous desert prison at Suwaqa, most buses from Amman take a break at **QATRANEH**, some 95km south of the capital. This small, dusty town has made a living out of introducing pitstop culture to Jordan, and a handful of generally decrepit and overpriced snack bars now line the highway, exploiting nod-and-wink understandings with bus operators to fleece hungry passengers. Rather than submit to the delights of stewed lamb or dry biscuits, you'll probably prefer to tighten your belt, or if you have your own transport, make instead for the upstart *Baalbaki Tourist Complex* (☎03/398090, fax 398156), 8km north of Qatraneh. Sparkling new and superbly equipped, this boasts the cleanest public toilets in the country, a basic canteen-style restaurant, supermarket, *Pizza Hut*, crafts from Bani Hamida, Beit al-Bawadi and others, a bookshop, and nine comfortable, en-suite **motel rooms** (③).

Within Qatraneh, the small *hajj* **fort** off to the west of the road, built under the mid-sixteenth-century Ottoman sultan Suleiman the Magnificent, is atmospherically situated and in well-preserved condition, but locked. The road to Karak branches west just beyond. There's little more to distract you from the journey south, other than the phosphate mines around Hasa (50km from Qatraneh) and the turnings to Tafileh (69km), Rashdiyyeh (83km) and Shawbak (92km).

Qasr Tuba

Way off any road in the depths of the desert, about 110km southeast of Amman, **Qasr Tuba** is the most southerly of the Umayyads' "Desert Castles" (see p.164), and, though ruined, the only one which still has its original atmosphere of a grand estate reached after a long and difficult journey. However, you won't make it without a 4x4 and a reliable guide – either someone from Qatraneh who knows Tuba, or a nature or archeology specialist from Amman or Azraq who's been there before. A road branching east off the Desert Highway about 14km north of Qatraneh signposts Tuba, but the tarmac runs out after about 30km, leaving you to negotiate the last 40km or so across the desert. Rougher tracks also lead to Tuba 47km south from Hraneh (see p.185) and about 30km west from the Azraq–Jafr road (see p.177). As you get close, keep an eye out for the **barrel vaults** of the buildings, visible from some way off on the south side of the Wadi al-Ghadaf.

Although utterly remote these days, Tuba was intended to be a **caravanserai** on the route between Syria, the Hawran, Azraq, Jafr and northern Arabia. It was begun around 743 AD, the same time as Mushatta (see p.187), and in a similar style, with bricks built up on a stone foundation. Tuba's bricks, though, are of sun-baked mud, unique among the Desert Castles. The complex is very large and was originally planned as two seventy-metre-square enclosures linked by a corridor, but only the northern half was completed. You can still make out **towers** around the external wall, and around the entrance there are corridors, courtyards, passageways and rooms still surviving. The arched **doorways** are particularly striking, even if all the beautifully carved stone lintels have been smashed or taken away.

Birders who take the trouble to get to Tuba will probably also want to head some 35km due east from the *qasr*, into the stark and roadless desert close to the Saudi border. This area, known as **Thlaythwat**, is the sole Jordanian nesting place of the very rare Houbara Bustard, an improbable kind of wild chicken that can, by half-flying and half-running, outpace a saluki hound.

Ma'an

MA'AN, some 124km south of Qatraneh, is the capital of the southern desert, a dyed-in-the-wool bedouin town at the meeting point of highways from Amman, Iraq, Aqaba and Saudi Arabia, as well as countless smaller roads and tracks from settlements dotted around the desert. A frontier staging post from its earliest days, Ma'an only began to assert itself after the **Hejaz Railway** came through in 1904, transforming an isolated desert encampment into a thriving settlement. Farmers come in from all over the region to do business in the markets, and an outpost of Karak's Muta University brings a little student colour to the streets, but for the most part Ma'an is still a pretty lacklustre place. The Desert Highway bypasses the town, and there's little reason to visit other than to grab a bite or to change buses. If you've got time to burn, you might also fancy a wander into the **old quarter**, not far south of the bus station, where Hejazi-style mudbrick houses cluster around palm-laden wadis, and lush, shady gardens – sealed off from the outside world behind crumbling walls – make a wonderfully cool retreat in such a hot, dry city.

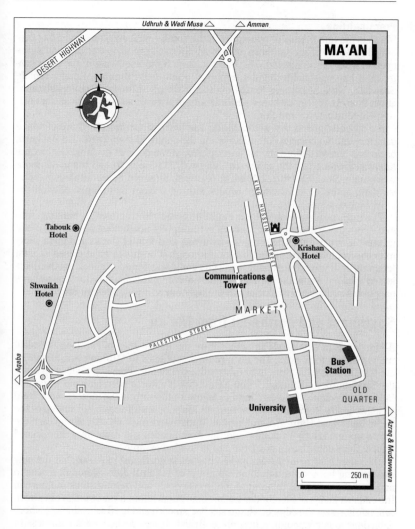

Surprisingly enough for a blue-blooded, conservative town, Ma'an has often been the focus of **civil unrest** in recent decades. In 1970, during Black September, the town was the scene of skirmishing between Palestinian fighters and the Jordanian army, and it was the setting for major riots in 1989 and 1996 over rising bread prices. In 1998 rioting again flared, ostensibly to demonstrate support for Iraq amidst tension over UN weapons inspections, but in fact equally strongly rooted in an expression of general discontent at rising poverty and unemployment. On this occasion, having flouted a government ban on public assembly, Ma'anis found their town sealed off for a week under military curfew; only an appeal for calm from King Hussein was able to restore order.

Practicalities

Ma'an is the hub of **public transport** in the south, and if you can't find a bus running directly from one southern town to another you can almost always find a connection from Ma'an instead. The bus station is 500m southeast of the town centre, and has reasonably regular services to and from Amman, Karak, Tafileh, Shawbak, Wadi Musa and Aqaba, although things slow down noticeably after about 2pm. Less regular buses serve Diseh, near Rum, as well as the desert outposts of Mudawwara and Jafr.

For those stranded overnight, Ma'an has four spartan **hotels**, three of which pass muster. Best placed is the *Krishan* in the centre of town (☎03/213 2043; ①), basic but comfortable, with an atmospheric verandah but no fans. Out on the highway feeder road, the grimy *Tabouk* (☎03/213 2452; ①) and the much more welcoming *Shwaikh* (☎03/213 2428; ①) exist to serve Saudi families passing through, and both offer decent rooms with or without bathrooms, all with the advantage of a fan.

The main produce **market**, on Palestine Street, is crammed to bursting with excellent-quality fruit and veg, and it's in the streets nearby that life in Ma'an is at its most active, with a scattering of **shwarma and falafel** stands and pizza joints in between clothes shops and banks. Although it seems to have closed at least temporarily, if you have an hour to kill you could wander up to check out the dilapidated *Khoury Resthouse* on the Amman feeder road, famous for the owner's psychedelic collection of clocks and the only **bar** in a very Muslim town.

Southeast and northeast from Ma'an

A junction 5km east of Ma'an town centre marks the start of two long, desolate roads through the desert. The main route is southeast to **Mudawwara**, and there are few reasons to venture onto this road if you're not actually intending to cross the Saudi border – although if you have a 4x4, it's worth searching out a guide to help you navigate the long, hard-to-follow route across the desert west from Mudawwara to Rum. Some 80km beyond Ma'an is a well-preserved station of the Hejaz Railway at **Batn al-Ghul**, and at Mudawwara itself an old railway carriage blown up in 1917 by Lawrence and the Arab armies still rests near the disused tracks. Occasional buses run from Ma'an to Mudawwara.

The other road from the Ma'an junction leads northeast to **Azraq**, but the only buses along here terminate some 50km out of Ma'an at **Jafr**. Although trucks to and from Iraq do pass this way, nobody else does, and getting stuck out here in the endless Plains of Flint under a scorching sun without a ride wouldn't be much fun. Jafr is set on the edge of a huge salt flat, smooth and hard as a tabletop, where – incongruously enough – in 1997 a British team clocked up an impressive 869kmh in the world's fastest car, ThrustSSC, before going on to the Nevada desert to set a new world land speed record of 1228kmh.

Southwest from Ma'an

Some 22km southwest of Ma'an on the southern continuation of the Desert Highway is the start of the "**Scenic Road**" running to Wadi Musa and Petra via Taybeh. A little further, the Desert Highway becomes a narrow, single-lane road, and stays so from here all the way to Aqaba, by far the most dangerous stretch of road in Jordan (and possibly the world). Dozens of heavy, slow-moving articulated trucks – many loaded with flammable oil and petrol – jostle for position on the narrow blacktop in a hair-raising slalom with reckless tourist buses, speeding taxis and crawling farmers' vans. Add in a potholed road surface, cliffs and treacherous wadis on both flanks with no crash barriers, and stupendous views over the desert from the edge of the plateau at **Ras an-Naqb**, and it's small wonder that this heavily skid-marked highway sees more horrendous crashes than anywhere else in the country. Until work is completed on upgrading the road, you'd be well advised to do all you can to avoid driving here, especially at night.

Once out of the hills, the highway scoots across the sandy floor of the southern desert, with the sheer mountains of Rum clearly visible off to the left of the road for much of the way. Some 41km from the Ras an-Naqb viewpoint and a little beyond the village of Quweira, a clearly marked left turn at a handful of shacks known as Rashdiyyeh points the way to Rum.

Wadi Rum

One of the most spectacular natural environments in the Middle East, the desert scenery of **WADI RUM** is a major highlight of a visit to Jordan. The wadi itself is one of a sequence of parallel valleys in the sandy desert south of the Shara mountains that are oriented almost perfectly north–south, shaped and characterized by giant granite, basalt and sandstone **mountains** rising up to 800m sheer from the desert floor. The rocky landscape has been weathered over the millennia into bulbous domes and weird ridges and textures that look like nothing so much as molten candle-wax, but it's the sheer bulk of these mountains that awes – some with vertical, perfectly smooth flanks, others scarred and distorted, seemingly dripping and melting under the burning sun. The level corridors of soft red sand between only add to the image of them as monumental islands in a dry sea. Split through by networks of **canyons** and ravines, spanned by naturally formed **rock bridges** and watered by hidden **springs**, the mountains offer opportunities galore for scrambling and rock climbing, where you could walk for hours or days without seeing another soul.

However, the place is far from depopulated. Wadi Rum has abundant fresh water, and, aside from the tents of semi-nomadic bedouin scattered in the desert, there are a handful of modern villages in the area, including **Rum** itself in the heart of the wadi. There's also extensive evidence of past cultures, with plenty of **rock-carved drawings** and ancient **Thamudic inscriptions** still visible and a single, semi-ruined **Nabatean temple**.

T.E. Lawrence (see the box on p.279) waxed lyrical about the Rum area, describing it as "vast, echoing and godlike", and, appropriately enough, much of the epic *Lawrence of Arabia* was filmed here in the early 1960s, prompting tourists to visit in dribs and drabs during the years after. However, until very recently, Rum village was still mostly tents, its one phone line serving the lone Desert Patrol fort. Then, in 1984, a British climber, Tony Howard, was invited by the Ministry of Tourism to explore the possibilities for serious **mountaineering** in and around Wadi Rum, and an excellent book on trekking and climbing resulted which brought the area into the forefront of mainstream tourism for the first time.

Since then, the bedouin have established a co-operative to organize tourism, and with the proceeds have built breezeblock houses and a school at Rum, and bought buses to link the village with Aqaba and Wadi Musa. The mid-1990s saw

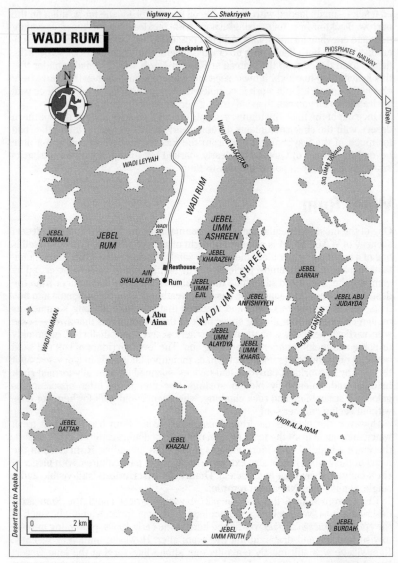

a tourist boom that has shown no signs of abating, and in the peak months of March, April, September and October, the Resthouse on the edge of Rum village is thronged with visitors, a strange mix of budget backpackers, well-heeled groups bussed in on whirlwind tours, and serious professional climbers. You'll probably quickly find that escaping into the desert is infinitely more rewarding than staying to try and cope with the Resthouse hubbub.

In our account, we've outlined a handful of the more popular and accessible sights around Rum in enough detail for most general readers, and also given a few pointers for hikers to get off the beaten track. However, if you intend to stay in Rum for some time, or if you're at all serious about trekking or climbing, you should seek out two excellent **books** on Rum, both written by Tony Howard, *Walks & Scrambles in Wadi Rum* and *Treks and Climbs in Wadi Rum Jordan* (see p.354). A new book by Howard focusing on trekking in Rum, Petra and Dana is in the pipeline.

LAWRENCE OF ARABIA

Very few of the events concerning T.E. Lawrence and the Arab Revolt can be pinned down with any accuracy. The Arab protagonists left no record of their actions and motivations, and the single account of the Revolt is Lawrence's own, his famous *Seven Pillars of Wisdom*, written after the war, lost, rewritten from memory and published in 1926. By then, though, the image of Lawrence as a true British hero was firmly in place; he was almost universally seen as a soldier of integrity, a brilliant strategist, honest and courageous, who acted with genuine altruism in leading the Arabs to victory and was betrayed by his own officers. The image is a beguiling one, and stood the test of dozens of biographies. Even one of his closest friends describing him as "an infernal liar" didn't crack the facade.

But with the gradual declassifying of British war secrets – and dozens more biographies – elements of a different truth have slowly been taking hold. Lawrence was undoubtedly close to British Intelligence; indeed, even in his early twenties, Lawrence's work on an archeological dig in northern Syria may have been a front, enabling him to photograph engineering work on the nearby Berlin–Baghdad railway. His supposed altruism during the Arab Revolt seems to have been firmly rooted in a loyalty to his own country and a hatred of the French. During the Revolt, Lawrence was well aware of the Sykes-Picot Agreement that was to carve up the Levant, and seems to have wanted to establish Arab self-rule mostly to stop the French gaining any control. Although his own conscious betrayal of the Arabs racked him with guilt, he justified himself on the grounds that it was more important to defeat Germany and the Ottomans. Details have also emerged of Lawrence's dishonesty and self-glorification. Biographers who have compared *Seven Pillars* to documentary evidence have regularly come up against inconsistencies and outright lies perpetrated by Lawrence, often for his own self-aggrandizement.

Lawrence is much less highly regarded in Jordanian eyes than in the West. He is today seen as an imperialist, who sought to play up his role in what was essentially an Arab military victory, achieved and led by Faysal. Although he pretended to have Arab interests at heart, in fact – as was shown by the events after the Revolt – his loyalty to British interests never wavered.

Nonetheless, as the years pass and the biographies pile up, the myth persists of Lawrence the square-jawed, blue-eyed buccaneering English bedouin as portrayed by David Lean's 1962 film epic *Lawrence of Arabia*. But in 1919, Lawrence's friend Colonel Richard Meinertzhagen recorded a conversation they had about the text of *Seven Pillars*: "He confesses that he has overdone it, and is now terrified lest he is found out and deflated. He told me that ever since childhood he had wanted to be a hero. And now he is terrified at his brazen imagination. He hates himself and is having a great struggle with his conscience." This seems as appropriate an epitaph as any to a life still shrouded in mystery.

Practicalities

There's only one **road** into Wadi Rum, signposted off the Desert Highway 41km south of Ras an-Naqb and 42km north of Aqaba. This road, shadowed by a railway transporting phosphates from desert mines to Aqaba port, skirts the mountains for some 17km to a checkpoint; Diseh and a handful of other villages lie to the left, while the road ahead bends right into the long avenue of Wadi Rum itself, ending 11km further on at the Resthouse on the outskirts of Rum village. The only **buses** into Wadi Rum are from Aqaba and Wadi Musa, although they run largely on demand. Buses run more regularly from Aqaba to Rashdiyyeh and Quweira, and these can drop you at the highway junction; hitching into Rum isn't hard. Buses to Diseh from Ma'an can drop you at the checkpoint at the head of Wadi Rum.

As you enter the village from the north, Jebel Rum rises to the right, Jebel Umm Ashreen to the left. The standard **entry fee** of JD1 (more for 4x4 vehicles) goes to the Rum village co-operative, and entitles you to a welcoming tea or coffee in the bedouin tent behind the Resthouse.

Currently, all the practicalities of organizing a stay in Rum – from jeeps and camel treks to a starlit dinner-for-two on the desert sands – can be done at the **Resthouse** (☎03/201 8867, fax 201 4240), government owned but privately run. If you're proposing any trips out of the ordinary, especially during the spring and autumn high seasons, or if you have special requirements, you should co-ordinate your plans with them well in advance. There's an office of the **tourist police** (☎03/201 8215) in the Resthouse.

Accommodation

There is only one style of **accommodation** at Rum: rough. Aside from the plausible chance of being invited to stay with a bedouin family, the least expensive option is dossing down on a mattress on the **Resthouse** roof (JD2 including blankets). You can pitch your own tent on the sand behind the Resthouse for JD2 per person, or use one of the dozens of tents already there; a tent costs JD3 per person empty, JD5 including a mattress and blankets, JD8.800 also including breakfast, JD13.200 if you add dinner. The small campsite at **Abu Aina** is run on an ad hoc basis, charging something like JD3 per person in the bedouin tent already pitched there (blankets extra). Bear in mind also the extremes of temperature: although it may be killingly hot during the day, nights even in summer can be chilly and, in winter, a dusting of frost isn't uncommon.

THE FUTURE FOR RUM

By mid-1998, plans were well advanced to establish an RSCN-run **nature reserve** in Rum and the whole of the surrounding area. Such plans are likely to become a reality during 1999 and will, eventually, completely change the way visitors get to experience the Rum desert, including controls placed on the numbers permitted to camp, the marking out of specific jeep routes in the open desert in order to limit environmental damage, and construction of an ecologically sound visitors' centre in the village. Hotel-style accommodation is also a possibility. Changes are likely to be made slowly, at least in the initial stages of establishing the reserve, but by 2000, you'd be advised to contact the RSCN in Amman (see p.39) for up-to-date information about the practicalities of staying in Rum and travelling in the desert.

Eating and drinking

As for **eating and drinking**, the Resthouse offers a good and substantial breakfast for JD4, and buffet lunch and dinner for JD6 each (JD3 without meat). They also have less pricey à la carte options. You can pick up expensive mineral water, beer and soft drinks here. Across the road, the *Wadi Rum Bedouin Restaurant* is cheaper and nastier. Otherwise, the only option is to bring in your own supplies for picnicking; there is a small shop in the middle of the village selling cans, dry biscuits and some basic veg, but you'd do better to calculate your food needs for however long you intend to stay, and buy in Aqaba, Wadi Musa or Ma'an before you arrive. Your water needs while hiking and scrambling in this arid desert are of paramount importance (see p.19); if you carry nothing else, carry water.

Organizing trips

Aside from **walking** solo, the only way to get out into the desert and see the sights is in a 4x4 or a **jeep** driven by a local, or on a **camel**. If you've rented a 4x4 yourself, you really shouldn't head off into the sands hoping to navigate by maps alone – ours or anyone else's. To a foreign eye, Rum's mountains, dunes and valleys soon all begin to look alike, and it's very easy to get confused and lost, to say nothing of becoming bogged in soft sand.

With the exponential growth in visitors to Rum since the 1980s, the local bedouin have almost completely given up keeping goats, and now make their living predominantly by providing **guide and driving services** to visitors. The huge majority of the drivers are friendly, professional and knowledgeable, both about Rum and about what's fun to see. The area around the Resthouse has become a bustling jeep- and camel-park, and at all times of day there are locals ready to drive you out to any spot you name or to suggest places you might like to see. Before you open discussions, you should check the latest **government-fixed prices** for the different trips around the area, posted on the wall of the police office in the Resthouse (bear in mind also that most jeeps can hold up to six passengers). The Resthouse staff are very happy to discuss your plans and explain to a driver what you want to see, but although the Resthouse acts as a kind of clearing house, putting travellers in touch with drivers, it can't enforce prices and doesn't own any jeeps or camels itself. Few drivers, however – generally those who are less competent or have less knowledge of the area – are willing to bargain down from the posted prices.

To give an idea of cost, at the time of writing **prices** to three of the more popular sights (by jeep/camel) were: Khazali JD15/16, Burdah JD32/40, Barrah JD45/60. All these include intermediate sights along the way such as Abu Aina, small rock bridges, carvings or inscriptions, dunes and sunset spots. Camels are more expensive only because they're slow: by jeep, the trip of 40km to Burdah and back can be done in four hours; by camel, the same thing is a two-day journey involving a night's camping out in the desert. Aside from local trips, it's quite possible to negotiate for journeys much further afield; in general, a full dawn-to-dusk day costs JD45 in a jeep, JD20 on camel-back (but by camel you should factor in food and drink for the long journey and also paying for getting the camels back to Rum from wherever you leave them). The most popular long-haul ride is to **Aqaba**, the 50–70km covered in a day by jeep, two or three by camel. Longer trips obviously have more appeal on camel-back, and it's possible to reach Mudawwara this way in about four days, Petra or Ma'an in five or six.

MOVING ON FROM RUM

Buses out of Rum are few and far between. There are generally two departures a day to Aqaba (roughly 7.30am and 1.30pm) – only one on Fridays – and a single bus to Wadi Musa (roughly 8.30am). Otherwise, hitching a ride out to the highway isn't difficult, from where buses pass reasonably frequently, south to Aqaba and north to Ma'an and Amman.

The easy-to-overlook downside of jeep trips, and, to a lesser extent, camel treks is that neither allows you to soak up the silence and isolation of the desert at your own walking pace. Hiring someone to drive your gear out to a camping spot in the desert while you take your time and walk, or arranging for a **one-way ride** by jeep or camel (either back to the Resthouse from a pre-agreed landmark, or out to a particular spot from where you walk back) mean you can both have your cake and eat it.

Sights and walks close to Rum

There are plenty of interesting places to visit within easy reach of the Resthouse that require neither a jeep nor a camel to get to. Lawrence's Spring, for example, is wonderful, and simple to get to, but you needn't feel restricted to just visiting named sites: if you have a couple of hours to spare in Rum there's nothing to stop you striking out across the sands in whichever direction you fancy. Crossing to the east side of Wadi Rum immediately transfers you from the Resthouse frenzy into stillness and solitude, and following the cliffs of the massif south or north for a few minutes will give you a more intimate flavour of the desert environment than a bouncing two-hour jeep ride ever could.

If you're travelling in an ordinary rental car, as opposed to a 4x4, another way to lose the bustle is to drive out of Rum to the checkpoint, and then follow the Diseh road east, past the villages of Twayseh and Mensheer. The desert out here is just as explorable – and the views just as awesome – as in and around Wadi Rum itself, but remains virtually unmarked by foreign feet.

Jebel Rum

If you walk alongside the telephone poles that lead away behind the Resthouse, within five minutes you'll come to a small **Nabatean temple** dating from the first or second centuries AD tucked up against the daunting cliffs of **Jebel Rum**, with Nabatean inscriptions on the walls and columns overlaid by later Thamudic graffiti (the Thamud were a tribe, cousins of the Nabateans, who lived as nomads in the deserts of southern Jordan and northern Arabia). From here, a modern water tank is in plain view a little way south; a safe and easy track leads from the tank up the hillside and around the cliffs above the mouth of a little valley, past springs lush with mint. On the south side of the valley, at the head of a Nabatean rock-cut aqueduct, is **Ain Shalaaleh**, known as **"Lawrence's Spring"**, a beautiful and utterly tranquil spot cool with water and shaded by ferns and trees. Nabatean (and modern) inscriptions are all around and there are stunning views out across Wadi Rum. Taking your time, you could devote a relaxing half-day to visiting these two places alone.

From the spring, it's not hard to work your way east around an outcrop and south over a pass onto a path above the desert floor; about 500m further on, another pass to the right will deliver you to the bedouin tent and spring at **Abu Aina** – also easily reachable on a simple one-hour valley-floor walk 3km south from the Resthouse. One part of the tent is for tourists to stay here overnight, but you should arrange this ahead of time with the Resthouse.

A much longer and more serious undertaking is to **circumnavigate Jebel Rum** – from the Resthouse to Abu Aina, then north, passing to the east of Jebel Rumman and across a saddle into Wadi Leyyah – but this could take nine hours or more and is only for the fit (the route is described in detail in Tony Howard's *Walks & Scrambles*). A much easier prospect is walking northwest from the Resthouse along the small, well-watered **Wadi Sbakh**, between the cliffs of Jebel Rum and the outcrop of **Jebel Mayeen**; you'll eventually have to make a short scramble over a saddle into the tiny, narrow **Wadi Sid**, often dotted with pools, from where you can easily join the road a little north of Rum, making a peaceful three-hour round-trip.

Jebel Umm Ashreen

The west face of **Jebel Umm Ashreen** – the "Mother of Twenty", named (depending on whom you talk to) for twenty climbers killed on the mountain, or twenty hikers swept away in a flash flood, or a crafty woman who killed nineteen suitors before marrying the twentieth – is pierced by a number of explorable ravines and canyons. Northeast of the Resthouse, between the highest peak of the Umm Ashreen massif and Jebel Kharazeh, is **Makhman Canyon**, explorable for about a kilometre along its length.

The enormous ravine splitting Jebel Kharazeh from Jebel Umm Ejil, directly east of the Resthouse, is negotiable all the way through the mountain, although once you're standing at the foot of the cliffs, the way in isn't easy to spot. A very short distance to the right of the bushes which crowd the mouth of the ravine is the so-called **Goat's Gully**, marked by an overhang to its right; you might want to ask someone from the village to walk over with you to point this out, since if you miss it you'll find no other way in. Once up and over the gully, you emerge on a hidden plateau dotted with wind-eroded towers and framed by looming molten cliffs. Diagonally left is **Kharazeh Canyon**, and you can work your way along it for some distance before the cliffs close in. From the plateau, another path continues on into **Rakabat Canyon**, which after much scrambling and complex manoeuvring (detailed in *Walks & Scrambles*) delivers you out to **Wadi Umm Ashreen**, from where you could walk south around the massif back to the Resthouse, completing a full and energetic day.

A different circumnavigation of Jebel Umm Ashreen – which avoids difficult scrambling but could involve as much as ten hours of hiking, some on soft sand – can be done by heading 8km north from Rum to **Wadi Siq Makhras**, which narrows as it cuts southeast through the massif to eventually deliver incredible views over the vast and silent Wadi Umm Ashreen. The twelve-kilometre walk from here south around the massif and back to the Resthouse can be shortened by navigating Rakabat Canyon from west to east. Other routes of 10 to 12km from the eastern opening of Wadi Siq Makhras involve heading northeast through Siq Umm Tawagi (see p.285) to get picked up in Diseh village, or southeast to camp overnight in Barrah. As with all these walks, your imagination (and the terrain) are the only constraints, and if you don't fancy such long hikes, you can arrange in advance to be picked up at any identifiable intermediate spot by jeep or camels for the return journey.

Longer trips from Rum

For those with more time to spend in the area, there are literally dozens of possible jaunts, whether you're into climbing and scrambling or would prefer to investigate inscriptions. The following gives an idea of what to expect from the more impressive sites, but again Tony Howard's *Walks & Scrambles* cannot be recommended too highly for its clear and detailed route descriptions. These sights are far enough away from Rum that you'll almost certainly prefer to rent transport: by jeep, a three- or four-hour excursion could whisk you round most of them and still leave time for the sunset; a stately tour by camel would take days.

South of Rum

About 8km south of Rum, on the desert track to Aqaba, rises **Jebel Qattar**, the "Mountain of Dripping" – origin of several freshwater springs. A short walk up the hillside brings you to the largest spring, Ain Qattar, which was converted by the Nabateans into a well. Stone steps in an area of lush greenery descend into a hidden, underground pool of cold, sweet water, drinkable if a little mossy. South and west of Qattar, just off the Aqaba track in the beautiful hiking area around **al-Maghrar** are a handful of "sunset sites" (the places that give the best sunset views change according to the seasons), very popular spots for afternoon jeep excursions from the Resthouse.

The titanic chunk of mountain opposite Qattar is **Jebel Khazali**, standing over the trails north through Wadi Rum and Wadi Umm Ashreen and south and east from Arabia. It's supposedly named for a criminal, Khazal, who was pursued up to the summit and, with nowhere to run, leapt off, whereupon he miraculously floated to earth and landed unharmed. The mountain's north face is split by a mammoth canyon, entered by a ledge on the right, the inner walls of which are covered at different heights with stylized **Thamudic rock drawings** of people, horses and pairs of feet. It's possible to scramble your way up through the cool, narrowing ravine, dodging the pools of stagnant water, for about 200m until you meet unscaleable rock.

The area east and south of Khazali is full of small domes and outcrops, with a cat's-cradle of wadis and hidden valleys running through and between the peaks. To the south, a small, easily climbed rock bridge rises from the desert floor at **Jebel Umm Fruth**, but the major highlight of the area – and, possibly, of the whole of Wadi Rum – is the large and impressive rock bridge perched some 80m off the desert floor on the north ridge of **Jebel Burdah**. Best photographed from the east, the bridge is best scaled from the west; it's an easy but slightly taxing climb, especially if you're not that good with heights and, as *Walks & Scrambles* advises, it should only be done in the company of a guide. The sense of achievement at reaching the bridge, though, is marvellous, and the views are stupendous. A final, crowning glory would be to climb Jordan's highest mountain, **Jebel Umm ad-Daami** (1830m), some 40km south of Rum on the Saudi border; but, by all accounts, it's harder to find a driver who knows the way than it is to reach the summit.

East and north of Rum

East of Wadi Umm Ashreen is an area of soft sand, with some scramblable **red dunes** rising to 20m or more against the north face of Jebel Umm Alaydya. Very close by, some of the best Thamudic carvings can be seen on **Jebel Anfishiyyeh**, including a herd of camels – some ridden by hunters, others suckling their calves – and some strange circle-and-line symbols. A little southeast, **Jebel Umm Kharg** has on its eastern side a small Nabatean structure, named – rightly or wrongly – Lawrence's House, which commands spectacular panoramic views out over the desert.

Further east lie Jebel Barrah and Jebel Abu Judayda, divided by the sandy, easily negotiable and deeply atmospheric **Barrah Canyon**, which winds between the cliffs for some 5km; this is an often-used overnight camping stop, the journey from the Resthouse best done with camels. North of Barrah, between a group of three peaks, the hidden valley of **Siq Umm Tawagi** features plenty of Thamudic rock drawings, and is a good second-day route from Barrah to a pick-up point in Diseh village, about 15km north. From Barrah, it's also possible to round the Umm Ashreen massif and return to Rum.

For obvious reasons Rum has cornered the trade in desert adventuring in Jordan, but the wild landscape north of the nearby villages of Diseh and Shakriyyeh is just as impressive and half as well known. Two easily accessible sites stand out to give a taste of the area, although you should be warned that many Rum drivers don't know their way around here; the Resthouse can get hold of someone for you who does, or you could go straight to Diseh and negotiate with the jeep drivers who hang out there. About 6km north of Shakriyyeh are some amazing Thamudic drawings at **Abu al-Hawl**; the name means "father of terror" and suits well the extraordinary experience of coming across two-metre-high figures with stubby outstretched limbs carved into a remote desert cliff. About the same distance again north is a breathtaking rock arch at **Jebel Kharaz**. You could either take a half-day drive out to these two spots, or treat them as stop-offs on a long desert journey northwest to Petra or northeast to Ma'an.

Aqaba

At the southern tip of the country, glorying in the balmiest of climates and a paradisiac setting on the shores of the Red Sea, **AQABA** is a perfect place to spend a few days underwater. Some of the best diving and snorkelling in the world is centred on the unspoiled **coral reefs** which hug the coast just south of the town. Whether you're an experienced pro or a novice paddler, getting into the clear blue water is a major priority: the sun-dappled vistas of coral and swarms of multicoloured fish cavorting inches below the surface are far more engaging than the rather pedestrian town in the open air above.

The huge industrial **port** is what drives Aqaba, not the beach, and, although it's one of the few places in the Arab world where local men can be seen wearing shorts, the town's proximity to – and historical links with – Saudi Arabia make it actually one of the more conservative urban centres in Jordan. Another factor that works against on-land Aqaba is its extreme **heat and humidity**; during the four mild months around the New Year, a few days in Aqaba can pleasantly warm the chill of Amman from your bones (not for nothing does King Hussein keep a

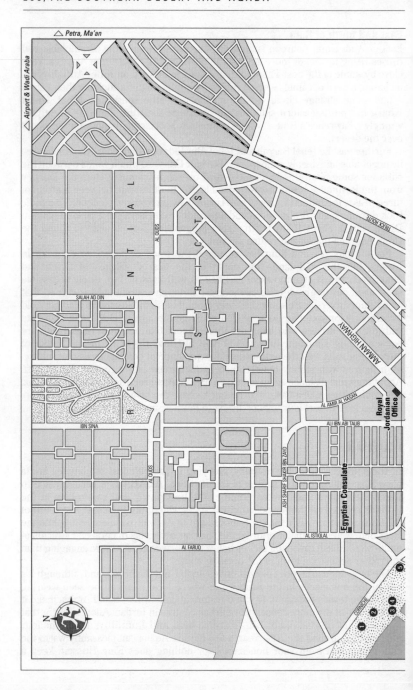

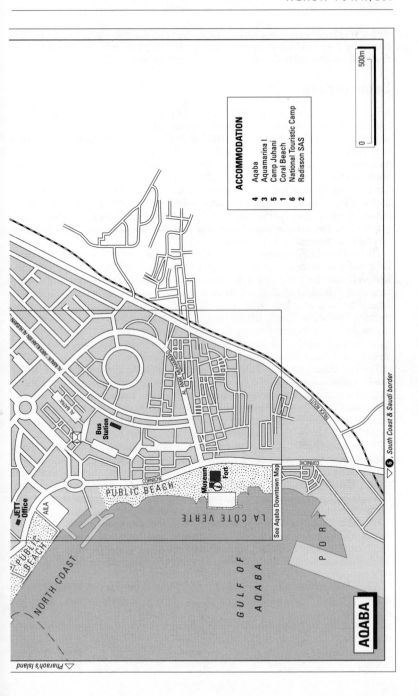

ACCOMMODATION

4 Aqaba
3 Aquamarina I
5 Camp Juhani
1 Coral Beach
6 National Touristic Camp
2 Radisson SAS

500m

AQABA

GULF OF AQABA

NORTH COAST

PUBLIC BEACH

AILA

JETT Office

Bus Station

AL BATRA

CORNICHE

Museum
Fort

LA CÔTE VERTE

PORT

CORNICHE

See Aqaba Downtown Map

POLICE ROUTE

AL NAMIR ABDULLAH IBN HUSEIN

AL WAHDA

△ Pharaoh's Island

▽ **6**, *South Coast & Saudi border*

winter residence here), but for the rest of the year, daytime temperatures damply soar. The four months of summer can be stifling, with July and August's fifty-degree days and thirty-degree nights too much to bear.

Some history

Aqaba is these days utterly overshadowed by its huge Israeli neighbour Eilat, founded in 1949 on what used to be arid desert and clearly visible sprawling around the opposite shore of the Gulf of Aqaba. However, Aqaba's location is much more naturally favoured than Eilat's: a series of freshwater springs barely a metre or two below the beaches has ensured almost continuous habitation of the shore at least since Nabatean times, although the town in or near Aqaba's position has confusingly changed names many times. In biblical times it was called Elot; through the Roman and Islamic periods this was adapted variously into Aela, Ailana or Aila. *Aqaba* means "alley", and is a shortening of the title "Aqabat Aila", referring to the narrow Wadi Yitm pass that was the only route into the town through the mountains to the north.

One of the earliest references to the area comes in the Old Testament (I Kings). King Solomon built a large port at Ezion Geber "beside Elot on the shore of the Red Sea" both for trade and also to house his new navy. During the 1930s, excavations at **Tell al-Khaleifeh**, a little west of Aqaba, seemed to indicate occupation around the time of Solomon, but archeologists – hampered by construction of the modern Jordanian–Israeli border fence – later pinpointed occupation to have begun during the eighth century BC, much later than Solomon. Ongoing investigation is suspended while the *tell* lies in a militarily restricted zone, but nonetheless the real Ezion Geber must have been very close by.

The **Nabateans** controlled a series of ports from Aqaba all down the eastern Gulf coast. Aqaba's fresh water also ensured that the town became an important caravan stop for merchants arriving from Arabia, with routes leading north to Petra and Syria, northwest to the Mediterranean coast at Gaza and west across the Sinai desert into Egypt. A new highway constructed by the Roman emperor **Trajan** in 111–14 AD led from his provincial capital at Bosra (Syria) to the sea at Aqaba.

Not much is known about Aqaba during the **Byzantine** period, although recent excavations have revealed some fragments of buildings below the sands, and the town is known to have been the seat of a bishopric. Aqaba was the first prize to fall to the **Muslims** on their military advance northwards in 630, and flourished throughout the early Islamic period, hosting an acclaimed theological seminary. By the tenth century, Aqaba was an important stop on the pilgrimage route to Mecca.

On their push into Transjordan after 1115, the **Crusaders** built a castle at Aqaba, although no trace of it survives. In response, the Muslim resistance fortified a small offshore island, known to the Crusaders as the Ile de Graye (today dubbed Pharaoh's Island), and within a century Salah ad-Din had retaken Aqaba on a campaign which eventually led to Jerusalem.

A small **Mamluke** fort on the shore was rebuilt in the early sixteenth century just before the **Ottoman** seizure of power, and its remains survive today. For three hundred years, Aqaba became again an important caravan stop, but the opening of the Suez Canal in 1869 dealt a death blow. For the first time, seaborne trade around the region, and between Europe and Asia, became an economically viable alternative to the camel caravans; equally, for Turkish and Syrian Muslims, making the pilgrimage to the Holy Places by sea through Suez was infinitely preferable to the arduous journey through the desert via Aqaba. The town's fortunes rapidly declined, and during the 1917 **Arab Revolt**, the forces of Faysal and Lawrence were able to surprise the small Ottoman garrison by approaching through the desert from the north: with all defensive artillery directed towards the sea, Aqaba fell with barely a skirmish.

Modern Aqaba

The sleepy fishing village of Aqaba was only dragged into modernity following a 1965 readjustment of the international border: Saudi Arabia got a patch of interior desert in exchange for Jordan gaining an extra few kilometres of coastline south of Aqaba. This made room for construction of full-size **port** facilities, and since then Aqaba has seen a resurgence in overland trade, although the camel caravans of antiquity have been replaced by a continuous stream of juggernauts: as well as being the sole outlet for Jordan's principal export, phosphates, Aqaba port has also become the transit point for goods trucked to and from sanctions-bound Iraq.

In 1998, in a bid to lend a slightly more appealing face to Aqaba's **tourist industry** – which for years had played a hopeless game of catch-up with slick Eilat next door – plans were approved for the construction of a lavish tourist village centred on an inland lagoon west of the town, to be mirrored to the south of town by at least seven large beach hotels plus golf course and theme park. The whole project, due to commence in 1999, is slated to take up to twenty years to complete, but – in a potentially disastrous oversight – no detailed studies have yet been completed on the likely impact on the coral reef just offshore and the fragile marine ecosystems that depend upon it. Time will tell whether such massive development will pay off.

Arrival, orientation, local transport and information

The **highway** entering Aqaba from the north winds sinuously along the line of the Wadi Yitm, still today, as in antiquity, the only negotiable route through the craggy mountains that seal Aqaba off from the rest of the country. This road is often clogged with huge and slow-moving trucks, but two bypasses ensure that Aqaba town itself is free of them; the first leads behind the mountains direct to the Saudi border at Durra, and the second – just before entering the town itself – diverts trucks south to the port facilities. The highway heads on into the centre of town, connecting with the **Corniche**, or coast road; this hugs the shore west to Aqaba's North Coast, lined with hotels; and east to the longer South Coast, currently home to the port, the Royal Diving Centre and some isolated beaches but slated as the location for imminent luxury-hotel development.

Buses from Amman, Wadi Musa, Ma'an, Quweira and Rum all arrive at the bus station, opposite the police station in the heart of town; those from Karak (via Safi) and Tafileh terminate 100m south in a rundown residential neighbourhood, still within walking distance of the hotels. **JETT** buses from Amman stop at the JETT office, on the Corniche about 500m north of the centre.

Ferries and catamarans from Nuweiba in Egypt dock at the passenger terminal, 9km south of town. Arrival is straightforward, as is purchase of visas, and taxis and *service*s gather outside the gates of the building to whisk passengers into town for JD1 per person. There are some banks in the terminal building, but you'd do better to change money in the town-centre banks or exchange bureaux.

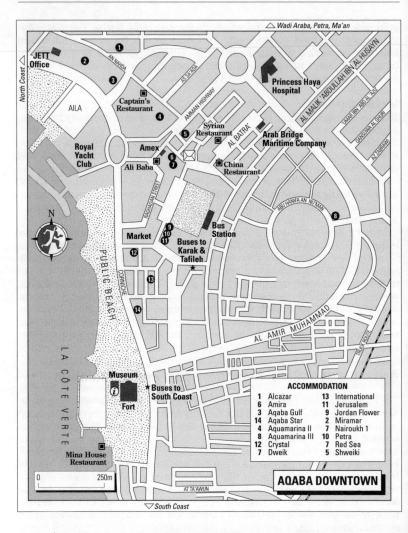

△ Wadi Araba, Petra, Ma'an

ACCOMMODATION

1	Alcazar	13	International
6	Amira	11	Jerusalem
3	Aqaba Gulf	9	Jordan Flower
14	Aqaba Star	2	Miramar
4	Aquamarina II	7	Nairoukh 1
8	Aquamarina III	10	Petra
12	Crystal	7	Red Sea
7	Dweik	5	Shweiki

AQABA DOWNTOWN

▽ South Coast

The **Arava border** between Israel and Jordan is 5km north of the city, off the Wadi Araba road. The border formalities are simple, and *service*s do the run into town for JD1 per person. Alternatively, the **border tourist office** (daily except Fri 8am–2pm), as well as supplying maps and information, can order a taxi to whisk you directly to Petra (JD25) or Wadi Rum (JD15).

Aqaba airport is about 9km north of the city, also off the Wadi Araba road. To cope with the prevailing northerly winds blowing down the huge wadi, all flights have to circle over the city in order to approach the runway from the south, in the process conveniently alerting Aqaba's taxi-drivers that business is to be done. Plenty gather to meet arriving planes, and the fare into the centre is JD4–5.

Although there is a system of city *service*s, the routes tend to serve only far-flung residential suburbs, and by far the simplest way to **get around town** is on foot. Walking the length of the Corniche (from the *Coral Beach* hotel to the fort) takes around half an hour. If it's too hot to walk, you need only lift a finger for a meterless **taxi** to screech to a stop for you; an ordinary in-town ride shouldn't be more than 500 fils. To reach the South Coast, **minibuses** depart regularly from the Corniche outside the fort to Durra on the Saudi border, running past the ferry terminal, the aquarium, the *National Touristic Camp* and the Royal Diving Centre on the way.

Aqaba's super-friendly **tourist office** (daily 7.30am–1.30pm; ☎03/201 3731) is in the same building as the museum, adjacent to the fort just above the public beach, with free maps and plenty of information.

Accommodation

Aqaba's conservatism leads to very definite divisions of price and service among the town's **hotels**. Bottom of the range – **camping** aside – are sweaty dosshouses catering mostly to Egyptian workers on long stays; a handful of ② hotels look to Western backpackers; the huge number of ③ hotels get the majority of their trade from middle-income Saudi families on holiday; and the soulless and generally rather rundown "luxury" market is targeted specifically at Western tour groups. This results in different **high seasons** in different price brackets, and **booking in advance** is advisable. Winter and spring are when most tour groups come to Aqaba, so hotels of ⑤ and above fill up fast. Spring and autumn are when most backpackers come through, while late spring and summer is the main Saudi holiday season. The *hajj* – currently in March – is an added complication, with thousands of Egyptian and North African pilgrims stopping off in Aqaba on their way home.

Whatever your budget, a major concern is how to combat the stifling **heat** of Aqaba's spring, summer and autumn nights. Even the cheapest dives should offer some kind of fan, and any hotel of ② and above that doesn't have **air conditioning** isn't worth paying for.

Camping

There are a few spots in and out of town to **camp**, but none is particularly appealing and all suffer from a lack of shade. On the beach some 11km south of town, the *National Touristic Camp* (☎03/201 6750) charges JD1 per person to pitch a tent, and offers nose-wrinkling toilets and showers. Even more squalid, the fenced-off square of dirt entitled *Camp Juhani* (no phone) charges JD1.500 per person, but has the advantage of being beside the *Aqaba Hotel* in town. Staff at the *Aqaba Hotel* itself – their rates set by the government – hang their heads in shame as they ask for an absurd JD6 per person to pitch a tent in their front garden.

Budget and midrange hotels

Aqaba has a good choice of **budget** accommodation, most staff well used to the foibles of Westerners. **Midrange** hoteliers have gone to town on their lobby decor, but do less well when it comes to the rooms: in many of these places, a four-star reception desk preludes one-star facilities. Furthermore, sometimes as much as JD15 can separate rooms with a **seaview** from those facing the mountains; however, be aware that a beautiful view westwards towards Eilat and the water carries with it exposure to the scorching force of the sun for the entire afternoon.

To add to the confusion, prices are subject to wild fluctuations depending on the season and current room occupancy. All hotels other than ① offer en-suite rooms.

Amira, near the post office (☎03/201 8840, fax 201 2559). Simple rooms are light, airy, without frills and sensibly priced. One of four hotels in this price range within 20m of each other (the others are the *Dweik*, *Nairoukh 1* and *Red Sea*). ②.

Aqaba Star, Corniche, town centre (☎03/201 6480, fax 201 8147). Comfortable en-suite rooms with balconies overlooking the sea – and, unfortunately, the street as well. ③.

Dweik, near the post office (☎03/201 2984, fax 201 2985). Sizeable rooms are cleaner than the *Red Sea*'s and marginally better value. ②.

International, behind the *Aqaba Star* (☎ & fax 03/201 3445). Clean, well-furnished rooms that are comfortable, cosy and very good value. ③.

Jerusalem, next to *Petra* (☎03/201 4815). About as low as you'd want to go; basic, hot and grimy. JD2 to share. ①.

Jordan Flower, next to *Petra* (☎03/201 4377, fax 201 4378). Recently renovated rooms aren't bad, but it's still runner-up to the *Petra*. ①.

Miramar, Corniche, beside *Aqaba Gulf* hotel (☎03/201 4340, fax 201 4339). Dim, spacious rooms are nothing outstanding, but pretty good value considering the location. ③.

Nairoukh 1, near the post office (☎ & fax 03/201 9284). A friendly choice, but with little to differentiate it from its spitting-distance neighbours. ②.

Petra, town centre (☎03/201 3746). Longstanding backpackers' favourite, with understanding staff and a lift. Rooms are clean, and many have balconies with superb views; they'll turn on the air con for an extra JD7. The shaded rooftop sleep-in (JD2) is a good choice for hot nights. ①.

Red Sea, near the post office (☎ & fax 03/201 2156). OK, with a range of different rooms, well managed and popular with a backpacking clientele – but not such great value. ②.

Shweiki, town centre near *Aquamarina II* (☎03/202 2657, fax 202 2659). Very large rooms are spotless and have good facilities. ③.

Expensive hotels

The fair number of more **expensive** hotels is no reflection of their quality: most are old, unrenovated and distinctly seedy. Hotels on the beachfront charge considerably more than those set back in town, whether their rooms are better or not. True luxury is only to be had at the *Radisson*, although currently going up next to the *Aqaba Gulf* is Mövenpick's latest creation, occupying both a beachfront site and a plot set back some way, the two linked by a bridge over the Corniche. If their Wadi Musa palace is anything to go by, it should be an eye-opening edifice when complete. All the hotels listed below accept major credit cards.

Alcazar, behind *Aqaba Gulf* (☎03/201 4131, fax 201 4133, email *alcsea@alcazar.com.jo*). Individually decorated carpet-free rooms are cool, airy and pleasant, set around an open atrium. Aside from the homely, friendly atmosphere, further attractions include snooker in the pub, the Sea Star inhouse diving centre and the biggest pool in town (JD3 to non-residents). ⑤.

Aqaba, Corniche, North Coast (☎03/201 4090, fax 201 4089). Excellent-value, government-owned place, with surprisingly comfortable, large rooms and dozens of less worthwhile bungalows ranged along its stretch of beach. ⑥.

Aqaba Gulf, Corniche, north of the centre (☎03/201 6636, fax 201 8246). Landmark hotel which sees a lot of tour-group business, but the smallish, unprepossessing rooms are priced sky-high for no apparent reason. ⑦.

Aquamarina I, Corniche, North Coast (☎03/201 6250, fax 201 4271). Good-value beachfront hotel, with generally pleasant and comfortable rooms of varying size, some with balconies over the sea. Also sports its own patch of beach with bars galore, a diving centre and watersports facilities. Its popularity – both with tourist groups and with US Navy crews on shore leave – means that it's often full. ⑥–⑧.

Aquamarina II, aka *City Hotel*, town centre (☎03/201 5165, fax 201 5169). Set back from the beach, with spacious, comfortable rooms that are better value than *Aquamarina I*. Guests can use all facilities of all three *Aquamarina* hotels. ⑥.

Aquamarina III, east of the centre (☎03/201 9425, fax 201 3569). High above the town with good views, but a pretty laboured variation on the thin *Aquamarina* theme. ⑥.

Coral Beach, Corniche, North Coast (☎03/201 3521, fax 201 3614). Quiet, low-rise, beach-front place next to the Royal Palace that's dowdy – though far from unpleasant – and over-priced. ⑦.

Crystal, Corniche, town centre (☎03/202 2001, fax 202 2006). Classy choice in the heart of the town-centre action, very clean, with a range of large rooms and excellent facilities. ⑤–⑥.

Radisson SAS (formerly *Holiday Hotel*), on the beachfront, Corniche, North Coast (☎03/201 2426, fax 201 3426). Aqaba's only slice of genuine luxury. Seaview or landview rooms are all luxurious to a fault, and service is swift and courteous. Until renovations are complete, rooms in the old wing are slightly more affordable. ⑨.

The Town

Aqaba town centre is a dense network of streets and alleys clustered around the junction of the Corniche and the main highway from the north. Here you'll find the bulk of the town's smaller hotels, dozens of cafés and restaurants, the main produce market, access to the public beach and all of Aqaba's promenading, street-based nightlife. Sights within the town are limited to a **Mamluke fort** and small **museum** to the south of the centre, and the open excavations of Islamic-period **Aila** to the north. All are worth checking out, although you'd do well to do any investigations early in the morning, before the sun has had a chance to turn up the heat. Aside from beach-bumming, Aqaba's only other land-based attraction is an **aquarium**, well south of the town in the Marine Science Station, housing examples of the local, bizarrely colourful underwater fauna.

The fort

Set in the midst of the palm-laden beach known as *La Côte Verte* (The Green Coast), Aqaba's Mamluke **fort** (daily 7.30am–sunset) is an atmospheric place for an hour's wander, cool, shady and cut off from the Corniche traffic behind thick walls.

The impressive entrance is flanked by semicircular **towers** each bearing a cal-ligraphic invocation to Allah; the arch that currently spans the gap between them is much narrower than the original, the line of which can still be traced. Overhead is a panel bearing the Hashemite coat of arms, installed following the ousting of the Ottomans in 1917. Inside the gloomy cross-vaulted entranceway, a long **inscription** runs around the walls, celebrating the construction of the fort by the penultimate Mamluke sultan Qansawh al-Ghawri ("slayer of the unbelievers and

---

SUNSET IN AQABA

The big question in Aqaba is where to be as the burning sun finally sinks majesti-cally behind the mountains. Photographers should install themselves on the roof of the *Petra* hotel well ahead of time to capture probably the most romantic twilight views in Jordan. For those who prefer late-afternoon contemplation fuelled by a quiet beer or three, the bar at the very end of the *Aquamarina*'s pier is perfect. A less dreamy, but equally mellow, toes-in-the-water experience can be had courtesy of the hubbly-bubbly cafés under the palm trees on the public beaches.

the polytheists, reviver of justice in the universe") in either 1504–05 or 1514–15. A roundel commemorates rebuilding work in 996 H (1587 AD), by which time the Ottomans were in power.

Through a dark passageway (with mysterious rooms off to either side) lies a domed area, beyond which opens the large, airy interior **courtyard**, dominated by a huge eucalyptus. This fort was the main focus of Aqaba's caravan trade for centuries, and rooms all around the walls – some of which have been restored – testify to its more hospitable function as caravanserai for much of its later life. The ruined section to the right as you enter the courtyard was destroyed mostly by shells fired from British gunboats during the Arab Revolt. Opposite the entrance is a concrete-and-plaster mosque, and steps to the right and left of it can bring you up onto the highest point of the walls for a dreamy view through the palm trees and over the blue gulf waters.

The museum

Next to the fort is a small building housing both the tourist office and Aqaba's small **museum** (daily except Tues 8am–1pm & 3–5pm; JD1), currently undergoing refurbishment. Worth a short wander, the museum's collection demonstrates Aqaba's reliance on international trade over the centuries, with coins and pottery from Egypt, Iraq, Ethiopia and China, a section of fresco from Islamic-period Aila, Byzantine inscriptions and milestone one of the Roman emperor Trajan's *Via Nova Traiana* highway, discovered on the beach and inscribed "from the borders of Syria to the Red Sea".

This pleasantly shady building also served for a short time as the **House of Sheikh Hussein bin Ali**, Sharif of Mecca and the present King Hussein's great-grandfather. He spent six months here during 1924, in an attempt to dissuade his son, Emir Abdullah, from acceding to divisive British policy in the region; the 1923 Anglo-Jordanian Treaty had not only separated Transjordan from both Palestine and the Hashemite heartland of the Hejaz, but had also formally instituted Abdullah as emir over his father's claims. One room off the museum courtyard contains interesting remnants of Hussein's stay – huge *mensaf* plates, coffee grinders and pots, camel saddles and copperware.

Aila

Opposite the *Miramar* hotel, north of the town centre, the open site of the Islamic-period city of **Aila** lies in an unromantic location, sandwiched between the Royal Yacht Club, the new *Mövenpick* hotel, the Corniche road and the public beach. A wadi runs through the middle of the site, and the fenced-off grounds of the yacht club enclose most of the southeastern corner of the city, but the relatively small remaining area within the excavated city walls is well described on good information boards and worth a short wander.

A low reconstructed wall runs along the Corniche roughly in the position of the original – you enter the site through an open gateway which is also more or less where the original **Syrian Gate** would have met the road from the northeast. To the right, the foundations of towers projecting out of the city wall have been cleared; these can be followed down to the **Egyptian Gate**, the history of which reflects the history of the whole city. In the early Islamic, pre-Umayyad period, the gate was about three metres wide, flanked by the two semicircular towers still apparent and featuring a round arch overhead. A stump in front is the remnant of a central column, built some time in the eighth century to narrow the arch. A century or two followed during which Aila was at its zenith; however, debris and rubbish from the burgeoning population dumped outside the walls caused the ground level to rise, the flanking towers were used as storerooms and shops further swamped the gate. Rebuilding work resulted in the current smaller, pointed arch over the gate, but Aila's days were numbered, and eventually the gate was sealed, serving only as a drain.

The street leading into the city from the Egyptian Gate has now been cleared, and walking along it – well below current beach level – is a great way to get a feel for Aila, with simple shops and houses flanking the street (many bread ovens were discovered in the small residences here). Some 50m along the street, at the centre of the city, is the **Pavilion Building**, formerly a tetrapylon at the junction of four axial streets, later converted, during the ninth or tenth century, into a grand, two-storey residence (though the rooms seem tiny today). The minuscule square room in the nearest corner was a bath, and the interior of the building was a courtyard framed by rooms and open *iwan*s.

AQABA'S BEACHES

All the **beaches** in town, whether privately owned or public, are slim stretches of sand jammed with bodies from dawn to well after dusk; for peace and quiet, you'll have to head south. On all private beaches sunbeds cost JD1–2.

Aqaba's cleanest beach, and the one place where foreign women will get no hassle whatsoever, is at the Royal Diving Centre (see p.298). A little north of the RDC, but still well out of town, the *National Touristic Camp* beach (500 fils) is clean-ish and offers some snorkelling opportunities. The best of the town's hotel beaches is at the *Aquamarina I* (free); the adjacent *Aqaba* pointlessly charges JD2.200 for access to the same beach, and suffers from gangs of lads from the public beach next door swimming around the wall to check out the latest bikini fashions. Both the *Radisson* and the *Coral Beach* are quieter and more comfortable, but both charge JD6.

The public beach, stretching from the *Aqaba* hotel to the Côte Verte, is free, and the best place to soak up a slice of local life, with radios blaring, women sitting in the shallows fully clothed, hubbly-bubbly smoke wafting over everything, and square-eyed families glued to top-volume TVs balanced within a metre of the lapping waves. Needless to say, this is not the place either for a relaxing spot of sun worship or for women to take a dip wearing anything less than an overcoat.

The best place to head for **watersports** is the *Aquamarina I*: they offer a short zip round on water-skis for JD4, windsurfing for JD5/hr, or you can ask to be dragged around in a "tube" or "banana" behind a speedboat for JD2 a time. There are also dozens of **glass-bottomed boats** chugging around the public beach sharking for customers, and they can be a mildly diverting way to check out the underwater scenery while still enjoying the wind in your hair. Plenty of people can fit on board, although it's worth checking how sturdy the boat actually is when weighed down by fifteen or so bodies. A full complement of passengers should pay no more than JD10/hr, although this may require some bargaining skills. For a much better level of service, the *Aquamarina I* and *Aqaba* hotels offer boats for around JD14/hr, but the glass-bottomed bargain of Aqaba is the *Red Sea Hotel*'s seven-hour excursion for JD18 including lunch and snorkelling equipment.

A wadi cuts across the city just beyond the Pavilion Building, but the road from the Egyptian Gate would have continued straight across to the **Hejaz Gate**, now in the grounds of the yacht club opposite. Another road led from the Pavilion Building right to the **Sea Gate** and left to the Syrian Gate. Towards the Corniche, also on the banks of the wadi, lies a large building, anonymously termed on the noticeboards "The Large Enclosure" but recently determined to be a congregational **mosque**. Much rebuilding work makes it difficult to tell what's what, but a *mihrab* and a double row of columns along the south wall indicate a covered prayer hall, and the line of the external walls of the rectangular building can be traced. The huge size of this mosque relative to the area of the city shows the importance of Aila in its heyday, both in terms of its population and also as a centre of Islamic study.

The Marine Science Station aquarium

Some 10km south of the town, between the ferry terminal and the Royal Diving Centre, is the Marine Science Station (run by the University of Jordan and Irbid's Yarmouk University), the only part of which open to the public is a small **aquarium** (daily 8am–5pm; JD1). Handy if you're unable to dive or snorkel, this gives the chance to check out first-hand the kind of fishy life that teems below the surface, although it is a little sad that these characters get to live out their days circling a grimy tank while the vast clear gulf waters are merely a finstroke away. The staff are happy to talk you through the varied collection, and you could easily spend a half-hour or so nose-to-nose with lionfish, parrotfish, moray eels and more, although the highlight (and a useful reference point if you intend to dive later on) is checking out a tank full of lethally poisonous stonefish – if you can tell them apart from the stones, that is.

Diving and snorkelling

Some of the best **diving and snorkelling** to be had in the world is packed along the slim 27km of coastline between Aqaba and the Saudi border, and a handful of professional dive centres can provide technical assistance and a helping hand to pros and novices alike. If you've never been snorkelling before, Aqaba is an easier, and more instantly attractive, place to start than nearby Eilat (Israel) or Dahab (Egypt), and diving beginners can go down accompanied by an instructor in complete safety. For those with an internationally recognized diving qualification, there are some thirteen dive sites along the coast to choose from, with entry generally from the shore, although boat entries are possible; all the diving centres can bus you to the site of your choice.

The major advantage of diving in Jordan rather than Egypt's Sinai coast, or the handful of sites off Eilat is the almost untouched condition of the **coral**. Fish abound in greater densities elsewhere in the Red Sea (although you're still likely to come face-to-face with more marine life than you could shake a stick at), but Aqaba was a relatively slow and careful starter in specialized diving tourism, and so has managed to avoid severe deterioration of the reefs. The visionary **Red Sea Marine Peace Park** was set up by Jordan in 1995 – and soon joined by Israel – to protect the marine flora and fauna of the entire Gulf of Aqaba in an intended multinational co-operative effort. Coral conservation guidelines concerning correct diving procedures are already in place, and safe mooring buoys have been set up at all major dive sites to halt damage from boat anchors. International funding is forthcoming, and all that has to follow is Egyptian and Saudi implementation, and good will.

Currently, wherever you choose to dive or snorkel off Aqaba, wide fields of near-perfect soft corals stretch off into the startlingly clear blue water, huge bommies of stony corals growing literally as big as a house. Fish life is also thrillingly diverse, with endless species of small and large multicoloured swimmers goggling back at you from all sides. Butterflyfish, angelfish, parrotfish and groupers are all common, as are shoals of damselfish, jewelfish and even moray eels. Those who have had some previous experience of diving should grab the chance to go down at **night** with both hands.

The dive sites

There are thirteen dive sites off Aqaba's South Coast, although, confusingly, different dive centres use different names for the same sites, and sometimes divide one site into two areas. We're copying the names used by the Royal Diving Centre (RDC). If you intend diving or snorkelling, you should always consult with a dive centre in advance about the latest conditions; these notes – which cover the sites from north to south – are for general guidance only and are not meant to be exhaustive.

Just south of the Marine Science Station's fenced-off area, the *National Touristic Camp* controls access to the **Prince Abdullah Reef**, which extends for several hundred metres offshore and is good for snorkelling as well as diving; close by is the steeply sloping **Black Rock**, with a wide variety of massive hard corals and the added attraction of occasional turtle sightings. Some 4km north of the RDC (see p.298) and barely 50m from the shore lies the **wreck of the Cedar Pride**, a Lebanese cargo ship deliberately sunk here in 1986 as an artificial reef. Lying in 30m of water, it's now covered in soft corals. Very close by is the gently undulating **Hussein Reef**, colourful and good for snorkellers. A little further south, two of the most attractive sites in the whole Red Sea are the unmissable **Gorgonion I** and **II**, the reef gently inclining down to 30m or so with spectacular fish life and perfectly preserved coral growth of all kinds stretching off to all

---

PHARAOH'S ISLAND

Some 17km southwest of Aqaba – and 250m off the Egyptian coast – lies a small rocky island known to Jordanians and Egyptians as **Pharaoh's Island** (*Jezirat Faraoun*), to Israelis as Coral Island, and to twelfth-century Crusaders as the Ile de Graye. On their sweep south through Transjordan in 1115, King Baldwin's army built a castle at Aqaba, and, to counter the Frankish presence, Salah ad-Din's Muslim resistance fortified this barren islet at the head of the Gulf of Aqaba. Rising impressively from the craggy island, the **castle's** towers and passageways have been restored, but the main reason for coming is to **dive or snorkel** in the maze of reefs off the northeastern tip of the island. Currents are strong and the reefs labyrinthine, so it's best to be accompanied by a guide.

Pharaoh's Island lies in Egyptian waters and and – since private sailing is forbidden in the gulf for security reasons – the only way to get there is with the day-trips run by the *Aquamarina I* hotel. You need to reserve a place with them two days in advance to give time to organize a group visa. When enough people show interest, a boat departs from the hotel at around 9.30am; the trip to the island takes about 45 minutes and you're back in Aqaba by 5pm. The JD24 price includes transport, visas, a full lunch, snorkelling equipment and a quick tour of the castle. It's not possible to leave from the island to the Egyptian mainland.

sides. A much-ignored site is the **Canyon**, with a shallow slope leading off for several hundred metres to a drop-off plunging over 45m, the whole slope split from the shallows outwards by a steep-sided ravine. **Blue Coral**, named for a blue-ish lacework coral found here, is a little south. Just north of a fenced-off nature reserve, **Moon Valley** offers an undulating reef framed by sandy beds, and is also the entry point for the 700-metre **Long Swim**, taking divers or experienced snorkellers south beyond the reserve fence to the RDC's jetty, past patches of dense coral interspersed with sandy valleys. From the jetty itself, the **Aquarium** (to the north) and the **Garden** (to the south) are both superb for divers and novice snorkellers alike. Aqaba's southernmost dive site is appropriately known as the **Saudi Border**, only 300m north of the international frontier; once beyond the inshore shallows, you'll discover superbly preserved hard and soft corals, although the best of the reef is beyond snorkelling range.

Dive centres

There are a handful of small **dive centres** dotted around town, but the following are the three biggest and most professional, with knowledgeable staff and well-maintained equipment.

Aquamarina I hotel, Corniche, North Coast (daily 8am–5pm; ☎03/201 6250, fax 201 4271). The *Aquamarina* is more of a beach-bum magnet than the other diving centres, and its location – on the sandy North Coast beach – means that, even to do a spot of snorkelling, you have to be bussed (or boated) out to the coral reefs down the coast a way. Hiring a mask, fins and snorkel for the day is JD7.200; boat transport for the day (minimum eight people) is JD4.800. One dive, including cylinder, weight belt and transport, is JD16.800, or with full equipment JD48. Taking a five- or six-day PADI beginners' diving course costs JD276, but novices are likely to feel less intimidated elsewhere.

Royal Diving Centre, 17km south of Aqaba (daily: March–Oct 9am–5pm, Nov–Feb 9am–4pm; entrance JD2; ☎03/201 7035, fax 201 7097). A private RDC minibus (JD1) picks up from the big hotels around 9am, and returns to town at 5pm; alternatively, a taxi one way is around JD3. The only dive centre actually located on the reefs, the RDC is expertly run, friendly, well equipped and far and away the best of the bunch, whether you want to just hang out on their private beach, snorkel or dive. They have lockers, changing rooms, a pool and a snackbar, and government ownership leads to significantly lower prices than elsewhere. Hiring a mask, fins and snorkel for the day costs JD3, and they have a small jetty projecting out over breathtaking coralscapes for the simplest of water entries. A trial dive for beginners (by appointment only) is JD25; for those who are qualified, one dive including all transport, cylinder and weight belt, is JD10, two in a day JD17. Complete diving equipment costs JD5 per dive. Night dives – when possible – cost JD20, plus JD5 for a torch. It's also possible, with advance reservation, to train for an international diving certificate (BSAC, PADI or CMAS), costing JD215 for the four-day beginners' course, more for advanced courses.

Sea Star, at *Alcazar* hotel, behind *Aqaba Gulf* hotel (daily 9am–5pm; ☎03/201 4131, fax 201 4133). Friendly, professional and long-established centre. A simple snorkelling excursion is JD7. One or two dives with full equipment are JD30 per dive, three to ten dives JD18 per dive, with a sliding scale giving good value rates for more dives. Diving at night adds JD10. A trial dive – including morning instruction, practice and an afternoon in the water – is JD50; a PADI or BSAC five-day beginners' course JD280. They can also give more advanced diving courses.

Eating and drinking

Aqaba shakes a leg when the sun goes down, and many **restaurants and cafés** have tables either on balconies or out on the street for open-air evening consumption. Although there's quite a few choices of places to eat (the best restaurants are recommended below), there's not that great a choice of dishes. The obvious thing to plump for when you're by the sea is **fish** – and there are plenty of places to oblige – but, although the creatures themselves are very fresh, so are the prices. A plate of good, but unspectacular fried fish is rarely less than JD6 anywhere, and can be much more expensive.

At the bottom end of the market, the *Syrian Restaurant*, 200m east of the centre, is the best Arabic **diner** in town, although there are plenty of others clustered around the alleys in the middle of town; the one built around a white-painted eucalyptus tree beside Mecca Exchange is particularly appealing. Opposite the *Crystal Hotel* are a handful of burger-style fast food stalls, though they're none of them much good; the best *shwarma*s and street cafés are opposite the *Aquamarina II*, where you'll also find a familiar *Pizza Hut* and two manageable but uninspiring chicken tikka diners. Raghadan Street in the middle of town is shoulder-to-shoulder Arabic restaurants serving simple kebab/chicken dishes (JD2–3 for a meal) with not much to choose between them. The two best are the *Syrian Palace* and the *al-Shami* (aka *Upstairs*), but there're half a dozen more to check out.

Ali Baba, town centre. The most varied menu in Aqaba, with a full complement of OK *mezze* and Arabic main courses, as well as a good fish selection – the fish curry is a lot better than it sounds. Simple fare can be had for simple prices, but larger dishes can push the bill up to JD8–10 per person. Serves beer. Daily 9am–11pm.

Captain's Restaurant, beside *Aquamarina II* (☎03/201 6905). Housed in tiny boat-like premises – so often full – with good fish, as well as pasta and all the normal Arabic staples at moderate prices. Daily 9am–11.30pm.

China, 100m east of the centre. Climb to the top of the building for a surprisingly good Chinese, with a range of excellent soups and all the usual meat, chicken and veg dishes – plus sweet-and-sour fish. Good value at JD3–4. Daily 11.30am–3pm & 6.30–11pm.

Mina House, a tiny boat moored beside the fishing harbour south of the museum (☎03/201 2699). Aqaba's only floating restaurant, in a perfect, peaceful location in shallow water and specializing in fish, squid and lobster. You pay extra for the location (upwards of JD9 per person) but the food is good; not the place for a cosy, private dinner, though. Daily noon–midnight.

Royal Yacht Club, off the main Corniche roundabout in the town centre (☎03/202 2404). The best restaurant in Aqaba, calm, comfortable and air-con, owned and catered by *Romero's* of Amman (which is a high recommendation). Superb pasta and well-prepared fish dishes are padded out with *mezze*, but a meal could stay under JD8. Also has a terrace overlooking the marina. Accepts credit cards. Restaurant daily 11.30am–3.30pm & 7.30–11.30pm; adjacent pool (JD5) and bar both daily 11am–midnight.

Juice bars, cafés and ice cream

A little up from the *Crystal Hotel* are a handful of **juice bars**, complete with pavement tables, that can quench the most raging of thirsts with anything from plain orange juice to sensational mango-guava-strawberry-banana concoctions. Dozens of ordinary tea- and **coffee-houses** all over town come into their own in the evening, when every empty car-park and patch of waste ground is laid with chairs and a TV for locals to while away the twilight hours with coffee and a hubbly-bubbly or two. Cafés down on the public beaches give much the same service, with added palm trees and gulf views. After dark, half a dozen parlours on the honky-tonk strip in front of the *Petra Hotel* do a roaring trade in cups of super-sweet, strangely elastic Day-Glo **ice cream** that tastes a whole lot better than it sounds.

Moving on from Aqaba

Suitably enough for a town at the end of the country, **transport** connections out of Aqaba are many and varied. As well as a good selection of buses around **the south**, there are fast bus connections and daily flights to **Amman**, ferry and catamaran services to nearby **Egypt** and an easily accessible overland crossing point into **Israel**. The bus services which formerly ran from Aqaba into Saudi Arabia are currently suspended.

Domestic destinations

Several fast air-con JETT **buses** depart daily to **Amman** from the JETT office (☎03/201 5222) near the *Miramar* hotel – the first at 7am, the last at 4pm. It's advisable to book in person a day in advance for these services. Ordinary buses depart from the bus station in the middle of town to Amman's **Wihdat** station and **Ma'an**, and roughly four times a day to **Wadi Musa** (8am, 10.30am, 12.30pm & 3pm, although these timings depend on demand). There are also, in theory, four daily departures to **Rum** (5am, 6.30am, noon & 3pm), but if you miss these you could take one of the regular Ma'an or Quweira buses and hitch into Rum from the highway junction at Rashdiyyeh. Buses to **Tafileh** and **Karak** depart from a residential street 100m south of the bus station and head up the Wadi Araba road, the latter scooting past both Lot's Cave and Bab adh-Dhraa (see p.216).

Royal Wings, with an office at the airport (daily 6am–3pm & 7–11pm; ☎03/201 4477), has two or three **flights** daily from Aqaba to Amman (JD30), stopping first at Queen Alia airport, although at least one continues on to the better-placed Marka airport close to Downtown. You can buy tickets ahead of time at the Royal Jordanian office on the Amman highway beyond the Haya hospital, but it's normally no problem to turn up at the airport and buy as you board. Make sure to get a seat on the left-hand side of the plane for some spectacular Dead Sea views.

To Egypt

There are two options for getting into Egypt from Aqaba. Seemingly the most straightforward – daily ferry and catamaran services to Nuweiba – can in practice be horrendously frustrating and time-consuming. Crossing overland to Taba via Eilat in Israel is easier, but, with a huge Israeli departure tax, not any cheaper. Irregular charter flights do exist, but are impossible to plan for.

The Arab Bridge Maritime Company operates the ferry and catamaran to **Nuweiba** on Egypt's Sinai coast, the only passenger services out of Aqaba port. You can buy tickets for all services from the company's offices, either at the town-centre branch (daily 7am–midnight; ☎03/201 3237) near the *China* restaurant, or up to an hour before departure at the port itself (daily 24hr; ☎03/201 3240), some 9km south of town. Local buses to the Saudi border from the Corniche outside Aqaba's fort run past the passenger terminal, or a taxi could whisk you down there for JD2 or so. There is a handful of ticket agents along the Corniche in town, but they offer no advantages over going straight to the horse's mouth.

Despite published timetables, the ferry and the catamaran are notoriously unpunctual, and both are especially chaotic around the Muslim *hajj* pilgrimage (currently March). The slow **ferry** (April–Sept Mon, Tues, Fri & Sat noon & 6pm, Wed, Thurs & Sun 3pm; Oct–March daily 3pm) takes up to three hours to do the seventy-kilometre crossing, and costs US$19 or JD14 in ordinary class, US$27 or JD20 in first class. Grotty air-con cabins are available for an extra US$5/10. The **catamaran** (daily 10.30am & 2.30pm) takes an hour and costs US$27 or JD20. You should add a 200 fils charge and the port **departure tax** of JD6 onto all prices. The catamaran is people-only, but you can take onto the ferry a bicycle (free), motorbike (US$20 or JD14) or private car (US$100 or JD71). Although it's possible to get an **Egyptian visa** on the boat, getting one ahead of time in Amman or Aqaba (see below) will save endless bureaucratic chaos on arrival. Taxi-drivers at Nuweiba port do the eight-kilometre run into town for £E20 or whatever they can get. There's plenty of accommodation there or you can take a bus straight to Cairo or Dahab, among other places.

Crossing **overland** into Egypt via Eilat (see the next section) can be much less time-consuming. The border, 6km south of Eilat, is open daily 24 hours, but a size-able Israeli departure tax (currently NIS106 or US$34) and a small Egyptian entry tax (£E7) are disincentives to cross this way, as is the anodyne border town of **Taba** – 70km north of Nuweiba and dominated by a huge *Hilton* hotel and casino. Buses run from Taba to all major Sinai destinations, as well as Suez and Cairo.

Royal Wings operates charter **flights** between Aqaba and numerous Egyptian airports, most popularly Cairo, Luxor and Sharm el-Sheikh. These can be good value but they tend to come and go, so you should check with RW's office at Aqaba airport (☎03/201 4477) for latest information.

To Israel

The **Wadi Araba** border crossing into Israel (Mon–Thurs & Sun 6.30am–10pm, Fri & Sat 8am–8pm) – also euphemistically known as the "southern crossing point" – is down a side road off the Wadi Araba highway about 5km north of Aqaba. *Service*s (marked "Southern Pass Service") run regularly from the bus station to the border for JD1 per person. Procedures are simple and straightforward – there's a JD4 **departure tax** – and the Israeli side, where free visas are issued on arrival, has city bus #16 (NIS4) departing regularly to Eilat's Central Bus Station (only about 2km away) and on down the coast to the Egyptian border at Taba. Note that during the Jewish *shabbat* – from Friday 2pm until Saturday dusk – all Israeli public transport and many services shut down.

Listings

American Express The agent is International Traders (daily except Fri 8am–1pm & 4–7pm; ☎03/201 3757), near the *Ali Baba* restaurant. They can sell travellers' cheques – to Amex card-holders only – but, curiously, don't cash them. Mail for card-holders, c/o American Express, PO Box 136, Aqaba 77110, is held for three months.

Books and newspapers The Yamani and the Redwan bookshops (both daily 8.30am–2pm & 5–9pm), within 10m of each other opposite the post office, have good ranges of English-language books and international newspapers.

Car rental and petrol stations As well as international agencies, there's a handful of good local operators, but prices across the board are higher than in Amman. Most agencies offer 4x4s, but, depending on size, age of the car and whether you want limited or unlimited kilometres, you could pay anything from JD35 to JD65. Rum (☎ & fax 03/201 3581), opposite the post office, is the longest-established local outfit, but the staff at Oryx (☎03/201 1333, fax 201 8288), at the *Miramar* hotel, inspire more confidence by their attitude. Another good place to compare is Moon (☎03/202 2232, fax 201 9734), on the Corniche past the *Crystal* hotel. Avis (☎ & fax 03/202 2883), a few doors from Moon, and Hertz (☎03/201 6206, fax 201 6125), opposite the *Aquamarina II*, both offer much better deals on one-way rentals to Amman (minimum three days). The 24hr petrol station at the junction of the Amman highway and the truck route has *soober.*

Egyptian consulate Istiqlal St, 15 minutes' walk north of JETT office (☎03/201 6171). Visa application Mon–Thurs, Sat & Sun 9.30am–noon; collection same day noon–2pm. One photo needed. Quiet and efficient. One-month single-entry "tourist visas" cost JD12, while one-month "Sinai-only" visas, valid only for travel along the east Sinai coast as far as Sharm el-Sheikh (including St Catherine's), are free. All these are extendable in Egypt, and they're also all available to Western nationalities on arrival at Nuweiba or Taba, but then you can pay only in US dollars or Egyptian pounds, and prices and validities may be different.

Email and Internet access A single PC in the lobby of the *Alcazar* hotel is available for access at JD5/hr (daily 7–10pm). Uniquely, you can also use an Internet phone here.

Medical emergencies The Princess Haya hospital (☎03/201 4111), on the roundabout just north of the *Aquamarina II*, is one of the best in the country; as well as a 24hr emergency room, it's equipped with a modern, six-person recompression chamber and has professionally trained staff to deal with diving accidents.

Police In emergency, dial ☎191. Headquarters of the tourist police are at the Wadi Araba border (☎03/201 9717), and you can generally also find them on duty at the museum. The main police directorate (☎03/201 2411) is on the highway north out of town, but a more convenient office to attempt visa extension is opposite the bus station.

Post and phones The post office (Mon–Thurs, Sat & Sun 7.30am–7pm, Fri 7.30am–1pm) and the phone office (daily 8am–10.30pm) are next to each other in the middle of town. There are plenty of Alo and JPP cardphones just outside. The post office has a poste restante service. For sending valuables, you'd do better to trust international couriers such as Aramex (☎03/201 5352) or DHL (☎03/201 2039).

The Wadi Araba road

The road running due north from Aqaba along the floor of the vast **Wadi Araba** is much overlooked as a fast route back to Amman, but if you have your own transport it's in many ways much preferable to the rather tedious and traffic-bound Desert Highway. However, you should bear in mind that there are only three turns off this road – after 179km to Tafileh, 224km to Karak, and 278km to Amman – and one petrol station at Safi, 202km from Aqaba. The only buses to use the road run between Aqaba and Tafileh or Karak.

Aside from **Lot's Cave** and some hot springs at **Zara**, there are few sights to enjoy other than the scenery, which, at least in the southern parts, is about as sandy as Jordan gets. Local bedouin tend to let their families of camels graze freely beside the road, and the dunes and the camels, interspersed with acacia trees and framed by giant mountains on both sides, make a picturesque scene. At some points, the border fence with Israel is right next to the road, and traffic on the mirror-image Israeli highway on the other side is sometimes clearly visible, as are the fields of irrigated land cultivated by a string of desert kibbutzes.

From Gharandal to Mazra'a

At **Gharandal**, some 70km north of Aqaba, the Chinese company who built this road left behind a pagoda as a memento; although a notice says "Gharandal

Tourist Park", the incongruous object has since been turned into the weirdest police station you're likely to see. Some 48km further, a sign points to **Bir Mathkoor**, which was the westernmost caravan suburb of Petra, tucked away in the mountains to the east of the road (you can spot the white shrine atop Jebel Haroun from here). The Bir Mathkoor ruins, however, are likely to inspire only the most enthusiastic of archeologists. About 20km further, the turn to Fidan and Qurayqira is passable in a 4x4 all the way to the ancient copper-smelting site of **Faynan**, at the western end of the Wadi Dana; there is a campsite here (see p.223) and hiking trails galore around the area and up to Dana village.

Another gently rising 35km of highway brings you to the edge of a scarp with the whole of the Dead Sea plain stretching in front. This natural hothouse is one of the most intensively farmed areas of Jordan, with bananas, tomatoes and other fruits as staple irrigated crops. The adjacent southernmost portion of the lake has been corralled into huge evaporation pans for Jordan's phosphate and chemical industries. The lush farming village of **Fifa** at the foot of the scarp heralds the turnoff to Tafileh, and, a little further, **Safi** is phosphate capital of Jordan, although – under the name Zoar – it also has a history as one of the five biblical "cities of the plain" along with Sodom and Gomorrah. **Lot's Cave** (see p.216) is close by. The turnoff to Karak (and Bab adh-Dhraa) is 1km south of **Mazra'a**, a small town located on the Dead Sea's Lisan Peninsula, which, with the ecological damage being wrought, is now a belt of dry land across the lake. Although exploring the peninsula isn't encouraged by the Arab Potash Company, it's still possible to turn off at the company's sign, drive out a little way and then venture into the ankle-deep soft white sand on foot. Although giving directions is impossible, you might stumble upon one of the many old monasteries that lie ruined here, unexcavated, in an eerie landscape forever muggy and thick with haze.

From Mujib to Swaymeh

From here northwards, the Dead Sea maintains a shimmering, piercingly blue presence, the winding road hugging the salt-spattered shore below arid, rocky cliffs. Some 24km north of Mazra'a is a bridge spanning the outflow of **Wadi Mujib** (see p.209); although the river itself is off-limits – it's part of a protected nature reserve – you can splash around in the refreshing sweet water between the bridge and the lake. On Fridays in particular, this is a hugely popular picnic spot for locals.

Some 15km north, in the area known as **Zara**, is a series of wadi outflows, most of them warm or hot; upstream a little way are the scalding waterfalls of Hammamat Ma'in (see p.204). Zara's secluded valleys are also popular with daytrippers, but women should be careful to show their skin only within the small, all-female shack close to the shore: splashing around in public in the river is the preserve only of the fully clothed or male. A fraction south of Zara are the remains of King Herod's baths and port at **Callirhoë**, although there's little left to see other than a handful of column drums and the remnants of a harbour wall. A few kilometres north and you'll come to the *Dead Sea Spa Hotel* (see p.125) and the resort of **Swaymeh** (see p.124).

travel details

Since most buses and all minibuses and *services* simply depart whenever they are full, regularity of service is indicated only when a fixed timetable is in operation.

Buses, minibuses and *services*

Aqaba to: Amman (JETT office; 6–8 daily; 4hr); Amman (Wihdat station; 4hr); Durra (20min); Karak (3hr); Ma'an (1hr 30min); Quweira (45min); Safi (2hr); Tafileh (2hr 30min); Wadi Musa (1hr 45min); Wadi Rum (1hr).

Diseh to: Ma'an (1hr 20min).

Durra to: Aqaba (20min).

Jafr to: Ma'an (40min).

Ma'an to: Amman (Wihdat station; 2hr 30min); Aqaba (1hr 30min); Diseh (1hr 20min); Jafr (40min); Karak (2hr); Mudawwara (1hr); Shawbak (30min); Tafileh (1hr); Wadi Musa (40min).

Mudawwara to: Ma'an (1hr).

Quweira to: Aqaba (45min).

Wadi Rum to: Aqaba (1hr); Wadi Musa (1hr 40min).

Domestic flights

Aqaba to: Amman (Marka airport; 1 daily; 50min); Amman (Queen Alia airport; 1 daily; 50min).

International ferries/catamarans

Aqaba to: Nuweiba, Egypt (3–4 daily; 1–3hr).

THE
CONTEXTS

THE HISTORICAL FRAMEWORK

The history of Jordan is a history of occupation. Never the seat of an empire, the country – known in the past as "Transjordan" (ie the land across the Jordan river) – has been stamped with the footprints of foreign armies and merchants since the pharaohs. Aside from brief flurries of political power in antiquity, the indigenous population, largely comprising bedouin tribes, tended to live under the thumb of governors sent from Transjordan's larger and more powerful neighbours until independence in the mid-twentieth century.

Only relatively small parts of the country – the well-watered northern highlands and Jordan Valley – have ever been able to support large populations. Since prehistoric times, huge tracts of land to the south and east have received very little rainfall and have no rivers; only tiny populations of nomadic or semi-nomadic bedouin have been able to live there. Thus the history of Jordan revolves largely around the history of the fertile north and west; the history of the desert survives only in the culture and oral traditions of the bedouin themselves.

THE STONE AGE: UP TO 3200 BC

During the **Paleolithic** period (c.500,000–17,000 BC), Jordan's climate was a good deal wetter than it is today, and what is now desert was then semi-fertile savannah. The local population of hunter-gatherer hominids, as well as foraging for wild plants, preyed upon the area's native big game, which included lions, elephants, bears and gazelle. Flint and stone handaxes from this time have been found all over the country, most significantly in enormous quantities at the **Azraq oasis** in the eastern desert.

Some time around 17,000 BC, at the beginning of the **Epipaleolithic** period, major changes took place in Transjordan. The previously nomadic hunter-gatherers began to make seasonal camps, broadened their diet to include small mammals and – most importantly – learnt how to domesticate goats and cultivate some wild grains, both of these advances providing a diet that was not only stable and assured but also nutritionally rich. These new proto-farmers, who used complex tools such as sickles and pestles and mortars, have left evidence of their building work all over Jordan: small, circular enclosures and huts solidly built with subterranean foundations.

From about 8500 BC onwards, during the **Neolithic** period, there were three profound shifts which fundamentally altered the pattern of life. First, responding to the introduction of new food sources from agriculture and animal husbandry, people began to opt for the certainties of community life, giving up their semi-nomadism and establishing permanent villages such as at **Baydha**, near Petra. The large Neolithic settlement at **Ain Ghazal**, northeast of Amman, was made up of many rectangular, multi-roomed houses, some with plastered floors. From the discovery here and across the region of skulls covered with plaster, their eye sockets stuffed with bitumen, it seems that one aspect of the new, comfortable Neolithic village life was veneration – or even worship – of the dead. The oldest statues in the world, dating from around 6000 BC, were recently uncovered at Ain Ghazal: one-metre-high androgynous figures with huge, painted eyes, now on display in the National Archeological Museum in Amman.

A second shift resulted from changing weather patterns: as temperatures rose, the eastern savannah dried out and became virtually uninhabitable. Desertification marked a clear distinction between Transjordan's arid east and fertile west, forcing most people to congregate in the western areas that, today, still hold the greater population.

But the most important innovation of Neolithic times was the discovery of how to make **pottery**. Around 5000 BC, potters arrived in Transjordan from the more advanced civilizations of Mesopotamia (the area between the rivers Tigris and Euphrates, in modern Iraq), and earlier Transjordanian efforts at making vessels from plaster were promptly abandoned as the new skill spread. By 4000 BC or so, during the **Chalcolithic** period, copper had been smelted for the first time for use in fashioning hooks, axes and arrowheads, and the new metal began to be used in conjunction with older technologies of pottery and flint-working to considerably improve the quality of life. People slowly began to turn their attention away from subsistence hunting and towards planned cultivation: olives, lentils, dates, barley and wheat were all common, as was sheep- and goat-breeding. The area's principal copper deposits were at **Faynan** in Wadi Araba, but the largest Chalcolithic village discovered in Jordan is at **Teleilat Ghassul** in the Jordan Valley, where mud-brick houses with roofs of wood, mud and reeds were constructed around large courtyards. Here, people used well-made, decorated pots and wove strong baskets. From the evidence of the village's huge and mysterious murals of masked figures, stars and geometric motifs, it seems that Ghassulian women decorated themselves with necklaces of shells and stones, and their men took some pride in their tattoos.

THE BRONZE AGE: 3200–1200 BC

Capitalizing on the success and security of earlier villages, Transjordanian people developed more and more complex settlements in many areas of the country. Towns from the **Early Bronze Age** (c.3200–1950 BC) – although still relying on copper ("Bronze Age" is a misnomer from the early days of archeology) – often included the strongest defensive fortifications yet built, probably to keep the marauding nomadic tribes of the open countryside away. The tentative new technology of water management led to channelling and some storage of supply against drier times. New customs of burial also developed, sometimes involving the digging of deep shaft tombs: at **Bab adh-Dhraa** in Wadi Araba, archeologists have uncovered over

twenty thousand such shafts, perhaps containing up to a quarter of a million corpses in total. Other burial customs – possibly brought from Syria or Anatolia – involved the construction of dolmens (two or more huge stone slabs standing side by side and capped by another slab), which are now found dotted all over the hills and valleys of Jordan.

Elsewhere in the region at this time, the extraordinary innovation of **writing** was leading to the development of highly sophisticated civilizations. To the south, Egypt was unified into one kingdom, while to the north and east, Anatolia and Mesopotamia saw the rise of equally complex urbanized cultures. Occupying the area midway between the three, the simpler people of the Levant, who wouldn't start to use writing themselves for another millennium or so, fell into the role of merchant middlemen, and the first significant commerce began to flow between the great powers.

Around 2300 BC, many of the fortified towns in Transjordan were destroyed, although there is some controversy as to whether this was due to conquest by a new people, the Amorites, or simply an earthquake. A decrease in rainfall levels, though, coupled with a general rise in temperature, almost certainly played its part, and the fragile network of city states across the region may simply have fallen victim to changes in climate and the regional power balance.

The years after 2000 BC – known as the **Middle Bronze Age** (c.1950–1550 BC) – saw trade between Egypt, Arabia and the great city states of Syria and Palestine continuing to flow through Transjordan, generating wealth and facilitating the spread of ideas and culture. It was during this period that artisans mixed copper with tin for the first time; the resulting metal, **bronze**, made much harder and more durable tools and weapons than before. Transjordanian towns, such as Amman, Irbid and Pella (as well as Jericho, on the western bank of the river), built massive, banked earth ramparts, implying a need for security – as borne out by the eighteenth-century BC conquests of the Hyksos who overran much of the Levant. The Hyksos, who were probably nomadic herders from Central Asia, interrupted the steady indigenous cultural growth of Transjordan, replacing it with new, foreign elements. As well as importing a more graceful and technically accomplished style of pottery, they also introduced both horses and chariots to the Middle East.

Following the expulsion of the Hyksos around 1550 BC by the Egyptian Seventeenth Dynasty, Transjordan – and the rest of the Levant – saw an expansion of Egyptian influence during the **Late Bronze Age** (c.1550–1200 BC), especially under Pharaoh Tuthmosis III. Despite conflict further north, occupied Transjordan remained relatively peaceful and prosperous, and the presence of pottery from Mycenean Greece and Cyprus indicates strong trade links across the Mediterranean and Aegean at this time.

By 1200 BC, however, the peace and prosperity of the entire eastern Mediterranean had been shattered, probably by the arrival of unknown invaders collectively termed **"Peoples of the Sea"**, one group of whom, the Philistines, settled around Gaza, giving Palestine its name. The principal cities of Greece and Cyprus fell to these foreigners, the Hittite Empire in Anatolia collapsed, wealthy city states in Syria were razed, and the Egyptian occupiers of Transjordan retreated to face the onslaught at home. In addition, events surrounding a group of tribes known as the Israelites – about which ample, if contradictory, records survive – began to alter the power balance in Transjordan and Palestine.

BIBLICAL ACCOUNTS OF THE BRONZE AGE

At some undetermined time probably well before 2000 BC, Genesis records that **Abram**, a native of the city of Ur, in modern-day Iraq, travelled with his wife and extended family to Canaan (Palestine). After some years, the land – already home to existing tribes of Canaanites and others – was unable to support so many people, and bickering ensued between Abram's tribe and that of his nephew **Lot**. In an attempt to broker peace, Abram offered a separation: Lot would be given the choice of taking his tribe and flocks either east or west of the River Jordan, and whichever direction he chose, Abram and his tribe would go the other way. Lot chose to go east and pitched his tents at the southeastern corner of the Dead Sea. Abram went west and eventually settled near Hebron, meanwhile having a vision of God granting him in perpetuity the land that Lot had spurned.

After the adaptation of Abram's name to Abraham following another vision, Lot's home city of Sodom – and others nearby – were destroyed (see p.217) in a cataclysm visible from Hebron. The only survivors were Lot and his two daughters, who lived for a time in a cave in the desert. Fearful that their tribe would die out since no man had escaped with them other than their father, the elder of Lot's two daughters hatched a plan to get their father so drunk he wouldn't be able to tell who they were, whereupon they would seduce him and thus preserve the family. Everything worked to plan and both daughters gave birth to sons; the elder named her child **Moab**, and the younger Ben-Ammi, or "father of **Ammon**".

Meanwhile Abraham had had two sons, the first – **Ishmael** – by his Egyptian mistress Hagar, and the second – **Isaac** – by his wife Sarah. On Sarah's insistence, Hagar and Ishmael were banished to the desert, and the biblical record concentrates on Isaac's two sons, Esau and Jacob. (The Quran, though, concentrates on Ishmael, who had twelve children and died at the age of 137; Muslims view him as their forebear and the *hajj* pilgrimage centres on commemoration of Hagar and Ishmael's banishment.) Jacob persuaded Esau to sell his inheritance for some food and, by dint of trickery, also gained the blessing of his father to rule over his brother; the two then separated, Jacob fleeing to an uncle's house and after a series of visions changing his name to **Israel**. Esau married into Ishmael's family and settled in the southern part of Transjordan, known as the land of **Edom**. Its southern neighbour **Midian** (modern Hejaz), and its northern neighbours **Moab** and **Ammon**, as well as Edom itself, were all established kingdoms by soon after 2000 BC.

The Bible makes no further mention of Transjordan until the **Exodus**, which occurred several centuries after Esau, although much controversy remains as to its exact date. The most accepted chronology places it during the reign of Pharaoh Merneptah (c.1236–1217 BC), but it may have been over two centuries earlier. The book of Numbers records that, after expulsion from Egypt and several generations of wandering in the Sinai, the Israelites, an extended group of twelve related tribes descended from Abraham's grandson, Israel, arrived in the southern Palestinian desert near Aqaba, on a journey towards the lands west of the Jordan that had been granted by God to the tribal patriarch Abraham. The Israelite sheikh

Moses and his brother Aaron had a vision from God instructing them to speak to a rock to produce water for their tribes; however, Moses instead struck the rock, and for this transgression both he and his brother were denied future entry to the Promised Land.

After Aaron's death on **Mount Hor** (possibly Jebel Haroun near Petra – see p.266), the Israelites apparently followed the route of the present Desert Highway northwards. A little way north of modern Qatraneh, the Israelites defeated the **Amorites** in battle and destroyed their cities, including Hesban, Dhiban and Madaba. They proceeded north to Dera'a (just over the modern Syrian border), defeated King Og and returned to make camp in "the plain of Moab" opposite Jericho, probably near modern Shuneh al-Janubiyyeh. Much alarmed at the presence of such powerful newcomers on his borders, the king of Moab made a military pact with the kings of Midian, but after a seer prophesied only victory for the Israelites, the combined Moabite-Midianite forces lost heart, and were attacked and routed. Three Israelite tribes occupied Transjordan from Dhiban as far north as Gilead (the hills around modern Jerash) and the Jawlan (Golan) north of Umm Qais. Moses then had several visions and, sometime probably around 1200 BC, at the age of 120, died on top of **Mount Nebo** near Madaba (see p.202). Soon afterwards, his successor Joshua led the Israelite tribes across the Jordan into the Promised Land.

THE IRON AGE: 1200–332 BC

With the bulk of the Israelite forces safely on the other side of the Jordan, the years after 1200 BC saw a consolidation and development of the Transjordanian kingdoms of Ammon, Moab and Edom, all three of which lay on the lucrative Arabian–Syrian trade route for gold, spices and other precious goods. However, the times were anything but peaceful, and the three were constantly tussling among themselves and with the Israelites.

By about 1000 BC, though, the Israelites were strong enough to declare a united Kingdom of Israel; under **King David**, they expanded military control to encompass virtually the entire Levant and won several victories in Transjordan (see p.73). Edom managed to regain some

independence following David's death in 960 BC, but it wasn't until David's son **Solomon** died some thirty years later that the Israelite empire fell. The last vestiges of Israelite control in Transjordan were erased during the mid-ninth century BC, partly by the efforts of Mesha, apparently king of Moab, who recorded his victories on a basalt stone, the "**Mesha Stele**" (see p.208), set up in the Moabite capital, Dhiban. To the north, Ammon, centred on modern Amman, prospered, while to the south, Edom had developed great skill in mining and smelting copper and had major settlements near Busayrah, Petra and Aqaba, although much of the Edomite population may have been nomadic or semi-nomadic.

Just as Mesha was subduing the Israelites, in central Syria the **Assyrian** army's advance southwards had been halted – only temporarily though, since by the mid-eighth century BC Assyrian forces had captured both Damascus and portions of Israel. It was only by paying tribute that Ammon, Moab and Edom managed to retain their independence and continue to exploit the north–south flow of trade.

Barely a century later, in 612 BC, the Assyrians were themselves defeated by an alliance of Medes (from modern Iran) and **Babylonians** (from Iraq); the latter then took control in the Levant, considerably limiting the independence of the Transjordanian kingdoms and, in 587 BC, destroying Jerusalem and deporting thousands of Jews. Some fifty years later, chaotic Babylonian rule was overrun by the **Persian Empire**, the largest yet seen in the region. The Persians released the Jews from captivity in Babylon and permitted them to rebuild their temple at Jerusalem. The indignant Ammonites and Moabites took this to be a declaration of sovereignty and attacked, only to be repulsed by the direct intervention of the Persian leadership.

Two centuries of relatively stable Persian rule were brought to a swift end by the military adventures of the Greek general known as **Alexander the Great**. In 333 BC, at the age of 21, he defeated the Persian army in southeastern Turkey and proceeded to conquer the entire Levant and Egypt before heading east. At his death in Babylon in 323 BC, Alexander controlled an empire stretching from Greece to India.

THE GREEKS AND THE NABATEANS: 332–64 BC

Alexander's conquest of the Persian capital Persepolis in 332 BC confirmed **Hellenistic** control over the formerly Persian lands of the Levant, and ushered in a period of dominance over Transjordan by Alexander's successors that lasted, with some turmoil, for three centuries. On Alexander's death, his generals **Seleucus** and **Ptolemy** divided the eastern part of his empire between them: Palestine, Transjordan and southern Syria went to Ptolemy, while Seleucus took northern Syria and Mesopotamia. Predictably, neither rested on his laurels, and bitter struggles for the upper hand ensued, with much of Transjordan caught in the crossfire. After more than a century of fighting, the Seleucids finally wrested Transjordan away from the Ptolemies in 198 BC. Meanwhile, many new and rebuilt Transjordanian cities had been flourishing, including Philadelphia (Amman), Gerasa (Jerash), Pella and Gadara (Umm Qais). Unfortunately, later Roman, Byzantine and Islamic rebuilding at all these sites obliterated much of the Hellenistic work, and virtually the only Hellenistic monument to survive in the region is a lone palace in the countryside west of Amman, **Qasr al-Abd**.

Long before these events, and possibly as early as the sixth century BC, a nomadic tribe of Arabs had wandered out of the deserts to the south and taken up residence in and around Edom. Slowly these **Nabateans** had abandoned their nomadic ways and founded a number of settlements in southern Transjordan, northern Arabia and the Naqb (Negev) desert of modern Israel, probably using their position to plunder the caravans heading out of Arabia loaded with luxury goods. The Roman historian Diodorus Siculus, writing much later, describes "Arabs who are called Nabatei" occupying **Petra** around 312 BC (for more on Petra's history, see p.225). The Nabateans switched from plundering caravans to providing them with safe passage, and managed to remain largely independent throughout the Seleucid–Ptolemaic power battles raging all around.

With the Seleucid victory of 198 BC, trade again prospered in Transjordan and the Nabateans consequently began to expand their sphere of influence, absorbing as they went many Hellenistic influences which worked their way into the art and architecture both of Petra and of the outlying regions that fell under Nabatean influence. By 150 BC – and co-existing alongside Seleucid rule in western Transjordan – the independent **Kingdom of Nabatea** extended along a strip of eastern Transjordan as far north as the Hawran, and south into the Hejaz. The Nabateans were accumulating vast profits from trade across the Middle East in everything from Indian silks and spices to Dead Sea bitumen. The jewel in the Nabatean crown, though, and their greatest source of wealth, was a monopoly over trade in frankincense and myrrh. Both essences were central in religious ceremonies throughout the West and both were produced only in southern Arabia; transport overland from the Arabian coast terminated at the sole taxation and international distribution centre at Petra.

While the Nabateans were quietly amassing fabulous wealth, riots were breaking out in Judea to the west against Hellenistic rule. In three successive years – 167 to 165 BC – Jewish rebels defeated the Greek army four times. The Jewish leader **Judas Maccabeus** then invaded northern Transjordan. Although the Seleucids eventually won the area back, their empire was in terminal decline and, less than a century later, Judas' successor was occupying the whole of Transjordan as far south as Wadi Hasa, although the Nabatean kingdom – by now distended to Damascus but still confined only to a slice of the country east of the King's Highway – remained independent. With nothing appearing likely to put a stop to the growth of Nabatean wealth and influence, and faced by an increasingly unstable political situation, the generals of **Rome** decided that the time had come to impose some law and order in the east.

ROME AND THE NABATEANS: 64 BC–324 AD

In 64 BC, the Roman general **Pompey** took Damascus and ordered Nabatean forces to pull back from the city. After proceeding to annex most of the region, Pompey showed his hand by sending a force to Petra specifically to subdue the Nabateans, but the Nabatean king was able easily to repulse the attack and dip into his treasury to pay the Romans off.

Pompey turned his attention elsewhere. The group of Hellenized northern Transjordanian cities that included Gerasa, Gadara, Philadelphia and Pella had been badly damaged under the Jewish occupation; Pompey restored their infrastructure and granted them some local autonomy. With shared cultural and economic ties, these cities – in a region of Transjordan known as the **Decapolis** ("Ten Cities"; see p.129) – agreed to pay taxes to the Romans and so retained complete independence.

In 44 BC, Julius Caesar was assassinated in Rome and the power of the Romans flickered. The **Parthians** – based in Mesopotamia and Persia – took the chance to attack, and the Nabateans sided with them; following Rome's reassertion of its power, the Nabatean king was forced to dip into his treasury again to placate the generals. The local Roman placeman, Herod the Great, twice attacked the Nabateans to ensure consistent payments, seizing control in 31 BC of a swathe of the Nabatean kingdom in Syria. By the time of Herod's death in 4 BC, Rome was in control of the region, with Transjordan divided into three spheres of influence: to the north, the Decapolis remained independent; Palestinian Jewish puppet-kings ruled central Transjordan (although Philadelphia remained part of the Decapolis); the south comprised the rump Kingdom of Nabatea, still nominally independent, though coming under increasing imperial pressure to submit to Rome.

Possibly as a tactical ploy, Herod the Great's successor, Herod Antipas, married a daughter of the Nabatean king Aretas IV, but soon afterwards divorced her, and married his brother's wife instead. Unable to ignore such an insult, Aretas sent an army against Herod and won, but showed magnanimity in withdrawing peacefully. A local holy man, John the Baptist, condemned Herod's incestuous marriage, was imprisoned at the royal palace at **Machaerus** and, at the behest of Herod's step-daughter Salome, beheaded.

Jewish uprisings in Palestine during the mid-first century AD gave a chance for the Nabateans to weigh in militarily and so restore amicable relations with Rome. The Nabatean king was personally present at the Roman capture of Jerusalem in 70 AD. Many Palestinian Jewish rebels sought refuge at Machaerus, but the Roman army razed the palace in 72 AD and slaughtered everyone inside.

It was clear to the Nabateans by this stage that their days of independence were numbered. A new trading centre far to the north, **Palmyra** – positioned on Roman-sponsored routes that were growing in popularity – was chipping away at Petra's business, and the Nabatean king Rabbel II, seeing Roman dominance all around, almost certainly made a deal permitting the Romans to annex the Nabatean lands peacefully. In 106, on Rabbel's death, the whole of Transjordan – with the exception of the Decapolis – was incorporated into the new Roman **Province of Arabia**, under **Emperor Trajan**, with a new capital at Bosra, in Syria.

Almost immediately, Roman city planners, engineers and construction workers moved into Transjordan. Large forts were built near Karak, Petra and in the north to house the massed legions; Petra itself, along with Philadelphia, Gerasa, Gadara and other cities, was renovated and Romanized; and, by 114 AD, a massive new fortified road – the **Via Nova Traiana** – was in place, running from Bosra right the way through Transjordan to the Red Sea at Aila (Aqaba). Trajan's successor, Hadrian, paid the province a visit in 130, and, although he passed through Petra, his main port of call was **Gerasa**, by this time one of the most splendid of Rome's provincial cities. During the second and third centuries, Transjordan gained new social and cultural sophistication under the Romans, and prosperity rose to an unprecedented level. In 199, the emperor Septimius Severus toured the province with his Syrian wife; although many overland trade routes from Arabia had been diverted to Palmyra and seaborne trade along the Red Sea was flourishing, Petra was still important enough to merit a visit, and his family connection prompted Severus to devote extra energy to the upkeep of roads and infrastructure throughout the province. It was around this time that **Azraq**, at the head of a major route to and from the Arabian peninsula, was fortified for the first time.

Nonetheless, the desert fringes of the empire remained open to infiltration, and in 260, Persian **Sassanians** invaded from the north. Six years later, the Roman military commander of the region, based in Palmyra, was murdered, precipitating a rebellion throughout Syria led by Queen Zenobia. The strategic situation in the east was perilous enough to force **Emperor Diocletian** (284–305) to take drastic measures. Retaining overall command from his base in Turkey, Diocletian split the empire into eastern and western administrations under separate emperors, and then proceeded to strengthen the infrastructure of the eastern fringes, building forts and new roads, among them the **Strata Diocletiana** linking Azraq with Damascus. Meanwhile, with Palmyra's predominance annulled through its association with rebellion, trade through Transjordan once again began to flourish, and the Red Sea port of Aila took on a new importance.

On top of the military setbacks, a new force was beginning to make itself felt throughout the empire. The influence of **Christianity** went much deeper than the extent of its practice (by a mere 14 percent or so of the empire's population) might show. The new religion – with its attractive doctrine of the equality of every individual soul – was uniquely popular, and **Emperor Constantine** had already converted by 324 when he made Christianity the official religion of the eastern empire. Six years later, he confirmed the eclipse of Rome by founding a new Christian imperial capital called Constantinople – today's Istanbul – in the east.

THE BYZANTINE PERIOD: 324–636

The **Byzantine** period – so named because Constantinople had been built over the ancient Greek colony of Byzantium – drew together existing strands in the empire: long-lived Roman institutions coexisted with the new Christian faith, which flourished within a broadly Greek culture. In Transjordan, the period was characterized by a steady growth of population coupled with energetic construction projects and important artistic development.

Constantine's mother, Helena, started a trend of **pilgrimage** by journeying to Jerusalem in 326. It was around this time that the first church on Mount Nebo was built to commemorate Moses' death, and the area around Nebo and Madaba became the focus for pilgrimage in Transjordan. As Christianity became the mainstream religion of the country following the final divorce between Rome and Constantinople in 395, an enormous number of churches went up, often on the foundations of Roman temples and often decorated with ornate **mosaics**. Madaba, in particular, was a flourishing centre for mosaicists, especially during the reign of **Justinian** (527–65). Church building and mosaic art in Transjordan (see p.194) entered a golden age.

However, twin disasters were to bring both artistic development and, indirectly, the empire itself to an end. The first was **plague**, which struck Transjordan during Justinian's reign and wiped out much of the population. However, a far more sustained, if equally lethal, threat came from the dogged Persian **Sassanians**, who, in the sixth century, launched a series of raids against the Euphrates frontier, breaking through to sack Antioch (modern Antakya) in 540. There followed over eighty years of titanic, but inconclusive, struggle in Syria between Byzantium and Persia – Transjordan remaining quiet throughout – which was only ended by **Emperor Heraclius'** recapture of Syria in 628.

During the struggles – and unknown to either combatant – far to the south an Arab holy man named **Muhammad** had been gathering around himself a large band of followers following a series of divine visions. Initial sorties northwards had won over a few desert tribes on the southern frontiers of Transjordan but the **Muslims**, as they styled themselves, actually lost their first battle with Byzantium, near Karak in 629. Muhammad himself died in Mecca in 632, but his armies, led by Abu Bakr, the first caliph ("successor"), and fired by the zeal of a new religion, pushed northwards again, seizing Damascus from Heraclius in 635. On the banks of the River Yarmouk the following year, they defeated a Byzantine army exhausted from decades of war.

THE EARLY CALIPHS OF ISLAM: 636–1250

After the Yarmouk victory, it took the Muslim armies barely ten years to entirely dismantle Byzantine control over the Levant, although the Byzantine Empire itself limped on for another eight hundred years. By 656, though, the whole of Persia and the Middle East was ruled from the Muslim capital at Medina. That year, the third caliph, Othman, was murdered; when his successor, Ali, dismissed many of Othman's appointees – including Muawiya, governor of Syria – civil war broke out among the Muslims, brought to an end only by negotiations held probably at Udhruh near Petra in 659. Ali was subsequently assassinated, and Muawiya, a member of the **Umayyad** clan, was acclaimed caliph in 661. This marked a schism in Islam, which persists today, between the **Sunnis** – the orthodox majority who accept the Umayyad succession – and the minority **Shi'ites**, who believe the succession should have passed instead to Ali, a relative of Muhammad's, and his descendants.

THE UMAYYADS: 661–750

Muawiya's first, and most significant, decision was to relocate the Muslim capital away from the arid desert of Arabia to the vibrant metropolis of Damascus. At one stroke, Transjordan was transformed: not only was it on the direct pilgrimage route between the imperial capital and the holy sites in Mecca and Medina, but it also suddenly lay at the heart of a rapidly expanding empire, which, at its fullest extent, reached from India virtually to the Pyrenees. The Umayyad caliphs almost immediately began a vigorous campaign of extraordinarily accomplished monument building throughout the Levant, which included both the Dome of the Rock in Jerusalem and the Great Mosque of Damascus. At heart, however, they were desert people, and their most enduring legacy to Transjordan is a series of buildings in the eastern desert, now known as the "Desert Castles": some, such as **Qasr Hraneh**, served as focuses for negotiation with the bedouin tribes of the area, while others – **Qusayr Amra**, **Qasr Mushatta** – were lavish country mansions or hunting lodges. Motivated less by adherence to Islamic orthodoxy than by older Arab notions of honour, loyalty and rule by negotiation, the Umayyads saw themselves as inheritors of the cosmopolitan Roman and Byzantine imperial legacy and had a lively aesthetic sense, valuing intellectual curiosity, poetry and wine in roughly equal quantities. Christianity was widely tolerated, and churches were still being built in Transjordan up to the middle of the eighth century.

ABBASIDS AND FATIMIDS: 750–1097

However, followers of stricter interpretations of Islam eventually gained the upper hand, possibly aided by a devastating earthquake which struck the region in 747. Three years later, Damascus fell to a new dynasty, the **Abbasids**, who immediately shifted the Muslim capital eastwards to Baghdad, a symbolic move embodying a fundamental rejection of the liberal Umayyad – and Mediterranean – spirit in preference for straighter-laced Persian and Mesopotamian methods. Transjordan – instantly reduced to a provincial backwater – fell into obscurity.

During the ninth century, internal dissent whittled away at the power of the Abbasid caliphate, and by 969 a breakaway rival caliphate had been proclaimed in Cairo by the Tunisian **Fatimid** dynasty, who took control of Palestine, Transjordan and southern Syria soon after, destroying many churches and harassing Christian pilgrims. In 1037, Seljuk Turks took power in the Abbasid empire and within fifty years, ruling from Baghdad as sultans, had defeated both the Fatimids and the Byzantines to regain Transjordan for orthodox Islam.

These tides of Muslim conquest and reconquest sweeping the Holy Land, coupled with the anti-Christian feeling aroused by the Fatimids and, more particularly, a Byzantine request for military aid against the Seljuks, didn't go unnoticed in the West. In 1095 Pope Urban II, speaking in France, launched an appeal for a European force to intervene in the chaos in the Middle East, to restore Christian rule in Palestine and, above all, to liberate Jerusalem. This holy war was termed a **crusade**.

CRUSADERS AND AYYUBIDS: 1097–1250

In 1097, an army of some 100,000 – comprising seasoned troops and peasant rabble alike – arrived at Constantinople; two years later, they seized Jerusalem, slaughtering every man, woman and child in the city. Within forty years, there was a strip of Crusader-held territory running from southern Turkey to Aqaba, part of it incorporating the Lordship of Oultrejourdain (Transjordan) with its two impressive castles at **Karak** and **Shawbak** (for more on the Crusaders in Transjordan, see p.212). In 1144, local Muslim forces started to eat into Crusader realms in northern Syria, inspiring a wave of strong Muslim resistance to the invaders, led after 1176 by a Kurdish officer named **Salah ad-Din al-Ayyubi** – or, to European tongues, **Saladin**. Having already disposed of the Fatimids in Cairo (and by doing so uniting the Muslim world) Salah ad-Din turned his attention to the common enemy, routing the Crusaders on the battlefield in 1187 and rapidly retaking Jerusalem, coastal Palestine and Transjordan. After his death in 1193, his dynasty, the **Ayyubids**, ruled the Muslim forces from their power base in Cairo. Undaunted, waves of Crusaders continued to arrive from Europe over the next decades, and rule of Levantine coastal areas shifted to and fro.

The Ayyubids came increasingly to rely for their military strength upon a band of highly disciplined and trained slave-troops, known as "the owned ones". Most of these **Mamlukes** were Turks or Caucasians from southern Russia who had been bought at market; once trained, they were lavished with property, goods and women, their lack of local tribal allegiance guaranteeing loyalty to their master. In 1250, however, the worm turned: with the Ayyubid sultan on his deathbed, the Mamlukes seized power for themselves.

MAMLUKES AND OTTOMANS: 1250–1915

The Mamlukes faced their first challenge less than a decade after taking control. In 1258, a **Mongol** army under Genghis Khan's grandson Hulagu destroyed Baghdad and swept westward through Transjordan to Galilee, where they were halted by a Mamluke army. The victorious general, **Baybars**, claimed the title of sultan and proceeded methodically to eject the last remaining Crusaders from the Levant.

During the fourteenth century, the Mamluke unification of Syria and Egypt provided a period of relative peace for the embattled Transjordanian population, who resorted to their tried and trusted roles of facilitating north–south commerce and providing shelter to Muslim pilgrims. Another Mongol invasion in 1400 under Tamerlane overran much of Syria; Mamluke finances – which relied on the Red Sea shipping trade – were further undermined by the Portuguese discovery of a new sea route to India which circumnavigated Africa. Meanwhile, in northwestern Turkey a new dynasty had been gathering power for more than a century, and, in 1453, these **Ottomans** seized Constantinople, erasing what was left of the Byzantine Empire. In a short campaign begun in 1516, the Ottoman leader **Selim the Grim** occupied Damascus, Transjordan and Jerusalem in quick succession, eventually suspending the last Mamluke sultan from the gallows in Cairo.

Ottoman expansion throughout the Mediterranean continued apace (halted only at the gates of Vienna in 1683) but although imperial architects lavished care and attention on Damascus and Jerusalem, Transjordan was seen as important only for being the area through which the road to Mecca passed; apart from small inns built along the pilgrimage route, the infrastructure of the country was allowed to fall into decline. Not so much governed as merely occupied, the people of Transjordan were largely left to themselves. Western European merchants, who had long been established within all the important trading towns and ports around the region, quietly but efficiently siphoned wealth away from the imperial coffers, and the empire slowly and majestically crumbled.

In 1798, **Napoleon Bonaparte** invaded Egypt, but lost power less than a decade later. In the 1830s, the new Egyptian ruler Ibrahim Pasha embarked on a military adventure through Transjordan and the Levant which looked poised to overthrow Ottoman rule altogether but for the intervention of the British, who preferred the presence of a feeble and ineffective sultan to that of an enthusiastic and powerful young general. Trade on the Red Sea was revivified by the opening of the Suez Canal in 1869, but the canal itself, which represented the fastest sea route from Europe to India, remained under sole control of the British, who were by now firmly installed in Egypt and nurturing imperialist designs on Palestine.

In the 1870s, Russian persecution of Muslims in the Caucasus region east of the Black Sea led to waves of refugees putting themselves at the mercy of the Ottoman authorities in Turkey, who dumped them more or less wholesale onto ships bound for Levantine ports. These **Circassian** and **Chechen** farmers settled throughout the region, working their way inland to godforsaken Transjordan and colonizing the long-abandoned ruins at Amman, Jerash and elsewhere, not without some initial conflict with local bedouin. In a separate but contemporary development, Russian persecution of **Jews** in modern Poland and Lithuania led a few to seek refuge in the Levant, but this time exclusively in Palestine. Spurred on by the dynamism of these emigrés, Jewish thinkers and activists codified a philosophy of organized Jewish settlement of Palestine – **Zionism**.

THE DECLINE OF THE OTTOMAN EMPIRE: 1900–1915

By the turn of the twentieth century, there was a spate of railway building around the Levant. The

French were establishing a network in Syria; the German Berlin–Baghdad railway had reached Aleppo; and in Palestine, the British had long been operating a line from Jaffa to Jerusalem. To counter this European influence, and in a dramatic bid to bolster his waning religious authority, the sultan announced the construction of an Ottoman-sponsored **Hejaz Railway** (see p.82), to run from Damascus south through Transjordan, terminating at the holy city of Mecca. Ostensibly, the railway was to serve as a means of transporting Muslim pilgrims, but the sultan also had an eye on facilitating the rapid mobilization of Ottoman troops should the Arab nationalism that was beginning to stir in the Hejaz come to a head. Transjordanian Circassian and Chechen labour was vital in the construction of the line – as were the thick forests around Ajloun and Shawbak, felled indiscriminately for fuel. By 1908, the track had reached Medina, 400km short of Mecca, but a coup in Constantinople the following year led to seizure of Ottoman power by a group of secular Turkish nationalists, and the railway got no further.

On the outbreak of **World War I**, the puppet sultan sided with the Germans, bringing the Ottoman Empire into conflict with both Britain – eagerly eyeing the newly discovered oilfields in Iraq and Persia – and France. Turkification was proceeding apace, with a ban on the use of Arabic in schools and offices, arrests of Arab nationalist leaders in Damascus and Beirut, and, in 1915, the first of the twentieth century's genocides, when over a million Armenians were exterminated and thousands more dispersed throughout the Levant. Observing from Cairo, the British conspired on the best way to foment ill-will towards Turkish authority into full-scale rebellion. Negotiations with opposition leaders in Cairo and Damascus to involve Arab forces in a revolt against the Turks broke down, but contact with Sharif Hussein, the ruler of Mecca and self-styled "King of the Arabs", was more fruitful. Its consequences, and the events surrounding the end of World War I, have directly caused almost a century of war in the Middle East, and profound trauma, dislocation and conflict for the peoples of Transjordan and its neighbours.

BRITISH PROMISES AND THE ARAB REVOLT: 1915–1918

When the Ottoman Empire entered World War I, the sultan had declared a *jihad* (an Islamically

sanctioned struggle) against the Western powers. Alarmed at the possible repercussions of this in Muslim areas under their control, the British were keen to enlist for their side the support of Sharif Hussein, an authoritative religious dignitary and direct descendant of the Prophet Muhammad. In 1915, ten letters, known as the **McMahon Correspondence**, passed between Sir Henry McMahon, British High Commissioner in Egypt, and Hussein, in which Britain pledged to support Arab claims for independence if Hussein sparked a revolt against Turkish authority. Hussein's initial claims were for an independent Arab state stretching from Aleppo to the Yemeni coast, but McMahon specifically countered this by stating that Arab claims were excluded from three areas: the districts of Basra and Baghdad in Iraq (which the British wanted for themselves), the Turkish Hatay region around modern Antakya, and – most significantly – "portions of Syria lying to the west of the districts of Damascus, Homs, Hama and Aleppo". Sharif Hussein took this clause to refer to Lebanon, and accepted the terms. Confident of British backing, he proclaimed Arab independence on June 16, 1916, and declared war on the Turks.

Meanwhile, the British had other ideas. Following negotiation with France and Russia, the secret **Sykes-Picot Agreement** of May 1916 carved up the Middle East into areas of permanent colonial dominance, riding roughshod over the promises made to Sharif Hussein about Arab independence. Under the agreement, France was handed power in southeastern Turkey, Lebanon, Syria and northern Iraq, Britain in a belt of land stretching from Haifa to Baghdad and the Gulf, with most of Palestine to be administered by an international body. The colonial powers told nobody of their plans (Sharif Hussein only learnt of them more than a year later). Also in 1917, in a letter addressed to a leader of Britain's Jewish community, which came to be known as the **Balfour Declaration**, the British Foreign Secretary Arthur Balfour wrote that "His Majesty's Government view with favour the establishment in Palestine of a national home for the Jewish people." Hussein had specifically agreed in the McMahon Correspondence to Arab claims being excluded from the "portion of Syria lying to the west of Damascus", and, in an attempt to cover their backs, British ministers later claimed that this clause referred not, as maps indicate, to Lebanon, but rather to Palestine. The Balfour Declaration thus completed an astonishing triangle of mutually incompatible promises and agreements made by the British government between 1915 and 1917.

THE ARAB REVOLT: 1917–1918

Meanwhile, still assuming wholehearted British support, Sharif Hussein – aided by two of his sons, Abdullah and Faysal – had launched the **Great Arab Revolt**. A ragtag army of some thirty thousand tribesmen quickly seized Mecca and Jeddah from Ottoman forces, and, in January 1917, local notables, as well as Britain, France and Italy, recognized Sharif Hussein as "King of the Hejaz", leader of the first independent Arab state. In its initial stages, the British lent their support to the Arab Revolt principally in the form of Second Lieutenant **T.E. Lawrence**, later mythologized as "Lawrence of Arabia" (see p.279). Charged with assessing the Arab leadership, Lawrence picked out **Faysal** as being the ablest of Sharif Hussein's sons. Leaving Abdullah to pin down a forlorn Turkish garrison in Medina, Faysal led an army northwards to the port of Aqaba, a strategic prize through which the Arabs would be able to receive weaponry and material support from the British Army in Egypt. Ottoman defences in the town, protected on two sides by arid mountains, focused all their attention on attack from the sea. Holed up to the south, Lawrence instead planned a looping overland route through the desert, and with a small force emerged from the mountains to launch a surprise attack on the town from the north. The plan worked, and Aqaba fell to Faysal on July 6, 1917.

Faysal's Arab forces then came under the command of the British general **Allenby**, who was leading several divisions from Egypt towards Jerusalem. The Arabs and the British worked their way northwards in concert, the Arabs using the old castle at **Azraq** as a base during the winter of 1917–18. After Jerusalem fell to the British, the Arab armies skirmished up the newly laid Hejaz Railway line, taking Ma'an, Shawbak, Tafileh and Karak. Amman fell in the late summer of 1918, and the way was clear for the final assault on Damascus, launched that September from Azraq. On October 1, Faysal and Lawrence entered Damascus victorious, both of them instrumental in ending Ottoman rule in the Levant.

ESTABLISHMENT OF THE EMIRATE: 1918–1923

By now, the French (working to the Sykes-Picot Agreement) had designs on Syria and Lebanon, while both the British and Zionist Jewish immigrants (working to the Balfour Declaration) had designs on Palestine. When, in 1920, elected Arab delegates to the government in Damascus declared the Levant independent under King Faysal, and Iraq independent under the absent King **Abdullah**, both Britain and France came out in sharp denunciation. Within six weeks, administrative control – termed a "**mandate**" – over the Middle East was awarded by an international conference to the colonial powers, forming borders within the Levant for the first time and splitting Palestine and Iraq (awarded to Britain) away from Syria and Lebanon (handed to France). Faysal was forcibly ejected from Damascus by the French, and the British spent £40 million suppressing open rebellion in Iraq (more than four times the expenditure of the entire Arab Revolt). In Mecca, the stunned Sharif Hussein realized the extent of the betrayal. "I listened to the faithless Englishmen," he muttered to a group of confidants. "I let myself be tempted and won over by them."

Amidst the tussling over Palestine and Syria, the position of Transjordan remained unclear for some time. Britain informed a meeting of sheikhs at Salt that it favoured self-government for Transjordan, but then did little to foster it. Further south, Arab discontent was growing at British and French duplicity, and, in late October, Abdullah left Mecca with an army of five hundred intending to liberate Damascus from the French. On November 21, 1920, he arrived in Ma'an to a rousing reception of Transjordanian sheikhs and Arab nationalists.

From Ma'an, Abdullah's path lay through British-held Transjordan, still neither part of the Palestine Mandate nor fully autonomous. To try and nip the rebellion in the bud, the British laid detailed plans for the **military occupation** of Transjordan, plans that were scotched only by a Finance Committee in London ruling on expenditure. With an army now grown to three thousand, Abdullah proceeded north without hindrance, arriving in the village of Amman on March 2, 1921, to cheering crowds of mounted tribesmen. Confronted by a *fait accompli*, but obligated to prevent attack on the French from

British territory, the new British Colonial Secretary, Winston Churchill (accompanied by his special adviser T.E. Lawrence) proposed a separate British mandate to be established in Transjordan; in exchange for Abdullah's abdication of the throne of Iraq in favour of the exiled Faysal, Britain would offer Abdullah the temporary title of Emir (Prince) of Transjordan, until "some accommodation" could be made with the French in Damascus. With the knowledge that he was being brought to heel, Abdullah attempted at least to secure the unification of Palestine with Transjordan, but was told that Britain had other plans for Palestine which took account of Jewish national aspirations. Well aware that Transjordan was the best he and the Arabs were likely to get for the moment, Abdullah accepted.

The territory that Abdullah took control of in April 1921 was rugged, undeveloped and in a state of anarchic chaos. The borders drawn by Churchill were more or less arbitrary, frequently cutting across tribal areas and grazing grounds in the far desert. The three existing Transjordanian governments – centred in Irbid, Salt and Karak – had virtually no authority and were overlaid by a patchwork of unstable local sheikhdoms jockeying for position with each other. The population numbered about 230,000, of which over 200,000 were Muslim Arabs, the remainder Christian Arabs and Muslim Circassians. Over half were **fellaheen**, or landowning tribal village-dwellers (there were only four towns holding more than ten thousand people); a quarter were semi-nomadic bedouin concentrated in the north and west, and the remaining quarter – some fifty thousand people – were fully nomadic, relying on their livestock and on raiding the *fellaheen*, pilgrimage caravans and each other for survival. Amman was a village of some 2400 people. Political loyalties were rooted in tribalism, and although the population at large tended towards common aims – desire for an Arab ruler, hatred of the French for their destruction of the Kingdom of Syria, distrust of the British for their double-dealing – they had no leader and lacked a collective voice. When Abdullah arrived, apart from a brief challenge from some petty potentates in Salt, he was accepted without question as a unifying leader.

For their part, the British wrote Transjordan out of the Palestine Mandate. On May 15, 1923, under an **Anglo-Jordanian Treaty** replacing the mandate provisions, the British formally recognized Abdullah as head of the new **Emirate of Transjordan**, describing it as a national state being prepared for full independence under the supervision of the British High Commissioner in Jerusalem.

CONSOLIDATION OF THE EMIRATE: 1923–1928

To the south, in Mecca, the fury of Abdullah's father Sharif Hussein at being supplanted was uncontrollable, and in January 1924, he left his power base in the Hejaz for Aqaba, where he ignored his son's, and British, authority and started to rule in his own right. It rapidly became apparent, though, that his dream of becoming sole king of the Arabs was as much in tatters as the Arab heartland itself. Syria was controlled by the French, who had carved Lebanon out of it; Iraq was ruled by one son, Faysal, Transjordan by another, Abdullah; Palestine was under the thumb of the British; and late in 1924 the Hejaz was invaded by forces of a fundamentalist central Arabian tribe led by **Abdul Aziz al-Saud**, who shortly afterwards established the Kingdom of Saudi Arabia. As a crowning ignominy, the British insisted that Hussein be kept from interfering any longer, and the old man spent his last years in exile on Cyprus.

Meanwhile, Abdullah, free of his father's influence, set about consolidating power in his newly chosen capital of **Amman** (favoured over the fractious Salt). The 1920s and 1930s saw the forging of a cohesive political unity from among the disparate tribes, with one of Abdullah's earliest acts being the creation of an authoritative centralized security force; clinging to notions of pan-Arabism, he pointedly omitted any mention of its being Transjordanian, instead naming it the **Arab Legion**.

Throughout this period, a series of Anglo-Jordanian treaties guaranteed British funding for central government, with the payback of British advisers maintaining intimate contacts with Abdullah in the running of the country. A pragmatist, as visionary as he was realistic, Abdullah knew that the British still called the shots, and that without Britain – specifically, without military assistance and money – the emirate could never survive. By choosing his battles, and compromising where necessary,

Abdullah was able to maintain progress towards his ultimate goal of independence, though his concessions to the British were profoundly to tarnish his reputation among Arab nationalists.

Some of the earliest challenges to his authority came from urbanized Syrians who had fled Damascus in 1920 to form **Hizb al-Istiqlal** (the Independence Party), intent on stoking in Transjordan a hotbed of nationalist activity against the French. Sophisticated and well-educated, they were scathing in portraying Abdullah as a British lackey, yet he actively sought to co-opt them into power, partly because at the time few Transjordanians had the calibre of education for governmental office, but partly because his pan-Arabist notions of Transjordan as the "country of all Arabs" didn't allow him to reject any element of Arab opinion. During 1926 and 1927, Abdullah gave refuge to many Syrian Druzes fleeing insurrection against the French, yet received stinging criticism from nationalists for his lack of material support for the rebellion (despite the British grip on control of the Arab Legion). By militantly opposing compromise with the French ten years before, such hardline nationalists had been the downfall of his brother Faysal in Damascus, and Abdullah was far too astute a diplomat to pay their carping much heed. Indeed British and popular Transjordanian hostility towards the "foreigners" installed in Amman led him to reshuffle *Istiqlal* party members out of power in favour of the newly formed, exclusively Transjordanian **Hizb al-Shaab** (People's Party). To assuage growing popular discontent with the status quo, Abdullah rapidly promulgated the **first Transjordanian constitution** in 1928 and, a year later, representative elections to a legislative council placed Transjordanians in real power for the first time, quietening the mood in the country.

With his domestic affairs stable, Abdullah was able to turn his attention further afield – specifically to the increasingly fraught situation in Palestine.

ABDULLAH AND PALESTINE: 1920–1939

Like most other Arab countries, Palestine had always had a small native Jewish community, resident for the most part in the towns, Arabic-speaking and culturally Palestinian. Since the 1880s, however, Jews from central and eastern Europe had been arriving in Palestine, many of them tough-minded nationalistic **Zionists**, for whom the area was not simply a holy land to be shared amongst religious communities but the rightful national homeland of the Jews of the world. As it became obvious that the Balfour Declaration was to become official mandate policy in Palestine, a **militant Arab reaction** to Zionism developed, denouncing both the mandate in general and Britain's perceived right in particular to hand the country over to the Jews. In Amman, Abdullah quickly grasped the political reality – principally that Britain was in a position to dictate its will and that at least some degree of Jewish immigration to Palestine was inevitable. He put forward the pragmatic proposal that if the Jews were prepared to accept the extension of his own rule over Palestine, they would be left free to govern themselves with all civil rights guaranteed; this would not only secure the Jewish position in Palestine with minimum cost to the existing local population, but it would also enable Jews to settle in Transjordan, where they could contribute much-needed money and skills to the country's development.

However, amidst the increasingly hot-headed politics of the time, such a practical vision was doomed to failure. The Jews wanted more in Palestine than mere political autonomy under a Muslim king, and rejected his proposals. Mainstream Arab opinion viewed Abdullah's plan as overly concessionary, and from this time on, doubts were laid in Palestinian minds as to Abdullah's rectitude and motives. Popular reservations were fuelled by the paramount leader of the Palestinians, **Hajj Amin al-Husseini**, *mufti* of Jerusalem. A strict hardliner who refused to compromise an inch with the Jews, Hajj Amin led persistent calls for a complete ban on Jewish immigration and land purchase, ahead of a termination of British mandatory rule and declaration of Palestinian independence; grotesquely enough, he was aided by a silent, unholy alliance with the British, who had no desire to see Abdullah extending influence over a land he wasn't supposed to be ruling. Amman became the focus for the Palestinian opposition to Hajj Amin, which believed that the only way of saving Palestine for the Arabs was to cultivate British goodwill and offer limited concessions to the already entrenched Zionist settlers.

Throughout the 1920s and 1930s, anti-Zionist feeling among Palestinian Arabs exploded into violence, put down with increasing harshness by the British. Meanwhile, with the coming to power of the Nazis in Germany in 1933, Jewish immigration to Palestine increased dramatically, as did Arab attacks on both Jewish and British targets. From 1933 onwards, Abdullah began to appoint Palestinians to positions of power in Amman, but in such a charged political atmosphere, his pragmatism in backing both Arab dialogue with the Jews and Arab concessions to British dominance merely fanned Palestinian distrust of his motives. In 1936, Hajj Amin called a **general strike** and repeated demands for a ban on Jewish immigration. In no mood to be dictated to, the British demanded the strike be called off before negotiations could proceed. Hajj Amin stood firm, but the British simply ignored him and Jewish immigration continued. The following year, a **Royal Commission** arrived from London to assess the political situation; the Palestinian leadership immediately boycotted the Commission's proceedings, and under threat of arrest, Hajj Amin fled to Lebanon.

THE BUILDUP TO WORLD WAR II: 1937–1939

War in Europe looked increasingly likely, and Britain now embarked on an attempt to secure its position in the Middle East, an area commanding vital land and water routes and, most important, harbouring oil. However, a good working relationship with the Arabs had to be restored if the British weren't to be exposed to possible rebellion. As an initial gambit, the Royal Commission report of 1937 recommended **partitioning** Palestine between Arabs and Jews, but this was rejected by the all-or-nothing Palestinian leadership. With war imminent, the British ruled out partition and instead, in May 1939, offered a sudden, dramatic turnaround in policy. On the table was **full independence** for Palestine after ten years, with severe limitations in the meantime on land transfers to Jews and with Jewish immigration permitted only subject to Arab approval. Victims of a mercenary U-turn, the Jews immediately rejected the proposal. In Amman, Abdullah hailed it as the best the Palestinian Arabs could ever hope to get, but his credibility in mainstream Palestinian opinion had been eroded too far. From exile,

Hajj Amin denounced the deal as a British ploy, and his authority won the day.

Seeing reason dissipating before him, Abdullah wrote, with his usual perspicacity: "The pillars of Zionism in Palestine are three: the Balfour promise; the European nations that have decided to expel the Jews from their lands; and the extremists among the Arabs who do not accept any solution. So behold Palestine, breathing its last."

INDEPENDENCE AND THE LOSS OF PALESTINE: 1939–1952

World War II had little impact in Transjordan, other than to delay advances towards independence. However, Abdullah's Arab Legion served loyally and effectively alongside the British elsewhere in the Middle East, helping to retake Baghdad from the Axis powers in 1941 (which paved the way for the British victory at Alamein the following year), and helping to eject the Vichy French from Syria and Lebanon. Abdullah deserved reward, and what he hoped for – as he had done for decades – was the throne of a new Greater Syria. However, neither the Syrians nor the Lebanese would accept anything other than independence now the French had been removed from power; and the king of Saudi Arabia, already faced by a strong Hashemite monarchy in Iraq, had no desire to see another on his northern borders (Britain and the United States were both aware by now of the vast oil reserves in Saudi Arabia, and were willing to bend over backwards to avoid upsetting King Saud). Syria and Lebanon were both granted independence, but Transjordan remained under British mandate until the 1946 **Treaty of London**, which granted the emirate independence, albeit with Britain maintaining a controlling presence. In May, the Transjordanian cabinet switched Abdullah's title from emir to king, and officially changed the name of the country to the **Hashemite Kingdom of Jordan**.

Meanwhile, the situation in Palestine had been getting worse and worse, with a flood of post-Holocaust Jewish immigration into the country and a simultaneous campaign of terror by underground Jewish groups aimed at the British. Early in 1947, Britain announced that it would unilaterally pull out of its Palestine mandate; in November, the UN approved a plan to partition Palestine into a Jewish and an Arab state, with Jerusalem administered internation-

THE HASHEMITES

The aristocratic **Hashemite** dynasty, headed by Jordan's **King Hussein**, traces its genealogy back at least to the Prophet Muhammad. An Arab chieftain **Quraysh**, claimed to be a descendant of Ishmael, and thus of Abraham himself, is said to have first arrived in Mecca in the second century AD. By 480, his family ruled the city. One of his descendants, **Hashem**, was the great-grandfather of the Prophet Muhammad, who was born into the tribe of Quraysh in Mecca around 571.

Muhammad's daughter had two sons, and the direct descendants of the elder son have been known as "**Sharifs**" (nobles) since that time. Different Sharifian families ruled the Hejaz from 967 onwards, with King Hussein's own branch ruling Mecca itself from 1201 right through to 1925, when the Saudis seized control from Sharif Hussein. King Hussein himself is the forty-second-generation direct descendant of the Prophet Muhammad.

ally. The Jews were unhappy, having been denied Jerusalem, and mainstream Arab opinion was outraged at the whole idea of conceding any kind of Jewish state in Palestine. On May 15, 1948, the last British troops departed from Haifa. Highly efficient Jewish forces immediately declared an independent **State of Israel**, and woefully disorganized Arab armies, led by Jordan's Arab Legion, simultaneously entered the region intent on taking the land allotted to the Jews by the UN. By the time fighting ended in July, Jordan had occupied a swathe of the interior of Palestine, as well as the eastern districts – and Holy Places – of Jerusalem, although the entire Galilee region and the valuable fertile coastal strip, including the large towns of Haifa, Jaffa, Lydda and Ramle, had been lost to Israel. Hundreds of thousands of Palestinians fled, or were forcibly ejected, from towns and villages throughout the country and most sought refuge in the Jordanian-held sector, known as the **West Bank**.

Immediately following the hostilities, Abdullah came under severe criticism from around the Arab world, both for compromising with Israel on the West Bank armistice border and for his perceived desire to incorporate the Jordanian-occupied part of Palestine into his kingdom. A short-lived Government of All Palestine was set up in Egyptian-occupied Gaza to block Abdullah's claims, but, with the continued advance of Jewish forces, was forced to flee to Cairo and soon dissolved. In December 1948 Abdullah convened a meeting in Jericho of Palestinian notables to proclaim the absorption of the Jordanian-occupied West Bank into Jordan proper. In April 1950, Jordan formally annexed the West Bank under the guise of

"**uniting the two banks**". Before the Israeli war, the kingdom's population had stood at around 435,000; four years later, it was 1.5 million, of whom two-thirds were Palestinian (including more than half a million refugees living in temporary camps).

Following 1948, the newly formed **Arab League** had ruled that Arab countries should not grant citizenship to Palestinian refugees, lest the disowned and displaced should then lose their claim to their homeland. To this day, Palestinians who sought refuge in Lebanon, Syria and Egypt remain stateless and without rights. Jordan, though, was the only Arab country to go against this policy; it formally resettled its Palestinian refugees, granting them (and, in fact, any Palestinian living anywhere in the world) full Jordanian citizenship and civil rights. Abdullah's policy enabled Palestinians in Jordan to pick up their lives again and start afresh, but it ran entirely against mainstream Arab thinking that refused to accept the fact of Israel's existence in Palestine. Citizenship notwithstanding, most Palestinians – in Jordan and elsewhere – felt betrayed by Abdullah's policies from as far back as the 1920s, and particularly by his perceived eagerness to absorb Arab Palestine under the Hashemite banner. On July 20, 1951, as Abdullah was about to enter the al-Aqsa mosque in Jerusalem for Friday prayers, a young Palestinian stepped up and shot him dead. A bullet intended for Abdullah's fifteen-year-old grandson, Hussein, ricocheted off a medal on the boy's chest.

On Abdullah's assassination, the throne passed automatically to the Crown Prince, Abdullah's forty-year-old son **Talal**, who at the time of his accession, was in Switzerland receiving treatment for schizophrenia. Talal returned to Amman and took up his constitutional duties, but his increasingly erratic behaviour made it rapidly clear that he was unfit to rule. In 1952, under guidance from the Jordanian parliament, Talal abdicated the throne in favour of his eldest son, Hussein.

KING HUSSEIN'S EARLY YEARS: 1952–1967

Born in 1935, **King Hussein** was educated in Britain, at Harrow School and Sandhurst military academy. He succeeded to the throne before his seventeenth birthday, and was crowned king in May 1953. At this time, the Cold War was well established, and the new king found himself caught between a powerful Egyptian-Syrian-Saudi bloc on the one hand, closely allied with the Soviets, and on the other, the controlling British presence at the heart of his government pushing him towards the pro-Western Baghdad Pact (a British-designed defensive treaty against Soviet aggression, subscribed to by Iraq, Turkey, Iran and Pakistan). In addition, the events of 1948 had utterly changed the character of Jordan, and had thrown a cosmopolitan, well-educated and urbanized Palestinian population into the arms of an outnumbered Transjordanian population with an entirely different, rural- and bedouin-based culture. Most of the Palestinians yearned to return to their lost homeland, and were unwilling to follow the generally conciliatory and pro-Western Hashemite line; many favoured instead the **Pan-Arabism** espoused

by the charismatic Egyptian leader, **Nasser**.

1955 and 1956 were crisis years for Hussein. In nine months, five prime ministers came and went; Jordan's initial declaration of Cold War neutrality wavered under British pressure to join the Baghdad Pact, but violent street protests in Amman in response prompted Hussein to peremptorily dismiss the English commander-in-chief of the Jordanian Armed Forces, **Glubb Pasha** (see the box below), and replace him with a Jordanian. Nonetheless, anti-Western feeling continued to run high, especially after the British-French-Israeli invasion of Egypt during the **Suez Crisis** of 1956. A few months later, Jordan's pro-Soviet prime minister **Suleiman Nabulsi** terminated the 1948 Anglo-Jordanian treaty, and the British subsidy to Jordan was replaced instead by contributions from Saudi Arabia, Syria and Egypt (although the last two soon defaulted). British troops left Jordan for good in July 1957. To make up the financial shortfall, Hussein then requested aid from the US, which was granted; outraged, Nabulsi unsuccessfully attempted a coup. After accepting Nabulsi's resignation, Hussein took control of army appointments and ordered political parties and trade unions to be suppressed; all parliamentary elections – right through until 1989 – were conducted only under strict controls. The US weighed in with a declaration of its determination to preserve Jordan's independence, and when Syria overtly allied itself with the USSR in September 1957, US forces sent a large airlift of arms to Amman.

GLUBB PASHA

The name of **General Sir John Bagot Glubb** is generally much better known and better respected in Jordan than T.E. Lawrence: there are still old-timers in Amman who remember him with some affection as an upstanding soldier and asset to the young emirate – though many other Jordanians indelibly associate his name with the colonialist treachery of the British.

Glubb was instrumental in establishing and developing the Arab Legion, as the British-officered Transjordanian army was known. From 1918, he served first in British-controlled Iraq, famously halting incursions of bedouin fighters from the desert by establishing a loyal bedouin counteractive force. In 1930 he was posted to Transjordan, which was suffering from similar

tribal raids. Glubb set up the bedouin **"Desert Patrol"**, which, after subduing the raids, went on to evolve into an elite army unit, serving in World War II and the 1948 war with Israel. In 1939, Glubb took over supreme command of the Arab Legion and became known as **"Pasha"**, an honorific title awarded to senior Jordanian officers. However, with the rise of Arab nationalism and the ascension to the throne of the young King Hussein in 1953, Glubb began to appear increasingly outdated, and, worse, a tool of British imperialism. He was dismissed in 1956, but went on to write dozens of well-respected books on Jordan and Arab history, including his autobiography *A Soldier with the Arabs*. He died in England in 1986.

Egypt and Syria were both revolutionary republics, and throughout the 1950s they both kept up a bombardment of anti-Hashemite propaganda, with Nasser's **Radio Cairo** particularly vocal in its championing of the cause of Pan-Arabism to the denigration both of the Jordanian government and of King Hussein himself. Diplomatic representation between Egypt and Jordan was suspended, and, instead Hussein travelled east to consolidate relations with his Hashemite cousins in Baghdad. On February 1, 1958, Egypt and Syria announced – to wild celebrations on the streets of Jordan as everywhere in the Arab world – their merger in a **United Arab Republic** (UAR); as a counter-move, two weeks later, the Hashemite monarchies of Jordan and Iraq announced their own merger in an **Arab Federation**. The latter body was to survive barely five months, however, the entire Iraqi royal family being slaughtered in a military coup in July. Tensions in Lebanon had meanwhile led to open Muslim insurrection in that country, supported by the new UAR, against a Christian-led and staunchly pro-American government. Anti-Western feeling in the Middle East was at its height, and the only obstacles most observers saw standing in the way of Pan-Arab unity were the Lebanese Christians and Jordan's Hashemite monarchy. Few gave the latter much chance of survival.

The American response to the crisis was to bomb Lebanon and, in July, land Marines in the country. Meanwhile, the US administration had received a request for help from Jordan, which had run out of oil. However, with the revolutionary forces in Syria and Iraq sealing off their borders with Jordan, and the Saudi king in thrall to Nasser's popularity, the only remaining direction by which the US could deliver oil to Jordan was over **Israeli airspace**. Amazingly, Hussein applied to Israel for permission, which was granted, and the airlift commenced, to a barrage of scorn from all Arab sides. Soon after, to match the US landings in Lebanon, Britain flew troops into Amman to bolster the regime; they too arrived over Israel and the insults flew once again. Nonetheless, in Jordan, democracy had been sacrificed for stability, and Hussein's **security services** kept a tight lid on the simmering discontent. Palestinian-planted bombs exploded in Amman, and, in 1960, the prime minister, **Hazza al-Majali**, was assassinated, but a coup and repeated attempts on the king's life were foiled.

Opposition to Hussein slowly died down, not least because US financial aid – and substantial remittances from Jordanians working in the Gulf countries – were fostering tangible **economic development**: Jordan's key potash and phosphate industries were taking off, modern highways were being built for the first time, unemployment was down as construction teams greatly expanded East and West Bank cities, and Christian tourism to Jordanian Jerusalem, Bethlehem, Hebron and the West Bank, as well as the East Bank sites, was bringing in much-needed hard currency. Mutual ties with the Saudi Arabian monarchy were also strengthening in the face of strident Arab nationalism and communism elsewhere. Perhaps most important of all, Hussein came to the decision, albeit reluctantly, to approve the creation of a separate political entity to represent the Palestinians, the **Palestine Liberation Organization (PLO)**, founded in 1964. Its charter, in a specific rebuff to Jordanian claims on the West Bank, stated that it was to be the "only legitimate spokesman" for the Palestinian people. From the outset, however, King Hussein refused to permit the PLO to raise funds from Palestinians resident in Jordan, or the military units of the Palestine Liberation Army to train on Jordanian soil, indirectly pushing them towards pro-Soviet Syria.

THE SIX-DAY WAR AND BLACK SEPTEMBER: 1967–1974

During late 1966, relations with Syria deteriorated dramatically, and Jordan suspended support for the PLO, accusing its secretary of pro-communist activity. Syria and the PLO both made direct appeals to ordinary Jordanians to revolt against King Hussein. Clashes followed on the Jordanian-Syrian border, and PLO-laid bombs exploded in Amman. At the same time, skirmishes with Israeli troops and cross-border raids led Jordan to introduce conscription; the prospect of war with Israel seemed inevitable, but rather than isolate himself even more from his Arab neighbours, Hussein flew to Cairo in May 1967 to throw in his lot with Egypt and Syria. On June 5, Israel launched a pre-emptive strike against its Arab neighbours. By the end of the **Six-Day War**, Jordanian losses were devastating: Israel was occupying East Jerusalem and the entire West Bank. From Syria it had seized the Jawlan (Golan Heights); from Egypt, the Gaza Strip and Sinai Peninsula as far west as Suez. In the eyes of the entire Arab world, this was an utter catastrophe: Egypt and Syria had lost relatively small areas of strategic importance, but Jordan had lost fully half its inhabited territory, a third of its population, its prime agricultural land and – perhaps most ignominious – control over the Muslim and Christian holy sites in Jerusalem. Up to a quarter of a million refugees crossed to the East Bank, putting the government, economy and social services under intolerable pressures.

The defeat was crushing, giving Palestinians in Jordan cause to believe that King Hussein and the other Arab leaders were unable or unwilling (or both) to liberate their homeland. King Hussein rapidly included equal representation from the East and West Banks in the National Assembly, but this was never going to satisfy Palestinian demands. The rift grew between the government and the Palestinian guerrilla organizations in Jordan, principally the Fatah organization, led by **Yasser Arafat**, chairman of the umbrella PLO. After 1967, these groupings – funded by the oil-rich Gulf states and receiving arms and training from Syria – assumed effective control in Jordan's refugee camps, backed also by widespread grassroots support from Jordan's majority Palestinian population. A **fedayeen** ("martyrs") movement developed within the camps, which took on the appearance of a state-within-a-state, intent on liberating Palestine by their own independent efforts. The *fedayeen* took for granted their ability to overrule King Hussein in his own country, and launched military operations against Israel. The ensuing reprisals, however, caused extensive damage to the border areas – now Jordan's only remaining agricultural land – and seriously undermined any possibilities for a peace settlement with Israel, on which the country's long-term future depended.

BLACK SEPTEMBER AND ITS AFTERMATH: 1970–1974

Fedayeen opposition to the Hashemite regime, rooted in revolutionary socialism, remained implacable. Confrontations flared in 1968, leading to serious street battles, and in June 1970, the Jordanian army entered Amman to assert authority over the guerrilla movements. Arafat – although threatened by extremist splinter groups within his own organization – squeezed

major concessions from King Hussein, who was forced to dismiss prime movers of the anti-*fedayeen* bloc from the army and cabinet; nonetheless, tension remained high, and there was at least one attempt on the king's life. In September, *fedayeen* **hijacked** three international aircraft to Amman, ostensibly demanding the release of imprisoned comrades, but equally intent on embarrassing King Hussein in the eyes of the world and forcing the issue of the Palestinian revolution in Jordan. Once emptied of passengers and crew, all three aircraft were spectacularly blown up; the *fedayeen* then took over Irbid proclaiming a "people's government", and the country exploded into violence. By the end of **"Black September"**, full civil war was raging, with thousands dead and injured, and the *fedayeen* claiming complete control of the north of Jordan. Despite agreement between Hussein and Arafat to end the war in October, sporadic outbursts continued for months. Egypt, Syria and Algeria all issued protests at the Jordanian government's attempts to "liquidate" the *fedayeen*; nonetheless, by April, the Jordanian army had pushed them out of Amman, and, three months later, after a violent offensive on Palestinian positions around Jerash and Ajloun, forces loyal to the king were back in control. The *fedayeen* fled to Lebanon to continue their fight (within four years, civil war had broken out in Lebanon as well). Meanwhile, Iraq and Syria both closed their borders with Jordan in protest, Algeria withdrew diplomatic relations, and Egypt, Libya, Sudan and North and South Yemen all bitterly criticized Jordan. Palestinian commandos made three unsuccessful attempts to hijack Jordanian aircraft, and, in September 1971, members of the Black September faction of Fatah assassinated the Jordanian prime minister, Wasfi at-Tall. Within Jordan, internal social divisions between Transjordanians and Palestinians were profound, and suspicion and resentment ran high on both sides.

King Hussein made an immediate attempt to regain Palestinian political credibility by announcing in March 1972 his plans for a United Arab Kingdom, a **federation** of Jordan and Palestine, both regions to be near-autonomous but ruled by him from Amman. Criticism of the plan was almost universal, from Israel, from the exiled Palestinian organizations and from Egypt, which broke off diplomatic relations. A military coup in November was only just averted, and, in February 1973, leaders of Fatah were arrested on charges of infiltrating Jordan and sentenced to death (later commuted by the king to life imprisonment). Jordan's isolation in the Arab world was almost complete. Nonetheless, Hussein attended a **reconciliation summit** soon afterwards with presidents Sadat of Egypt and Assad of Syria – condemned by Fatah, among others – which resulted in a general amnesty for all political prisoners in Jordan, including those Fatah activists sentenced months before. Jordanian security services and intelligence organizations were beefed up to deter dissident activity; political parties remained banned and the country had no elected parliament. Jordan stayed out of the 1973 Egyptian-Syrian **October War** against Israel, but gathered little kudos for doing so.

THE RABAT SUMMIT AND CAMP DAVID: 1974–1980

Throughout 1974, King Hussein attempted to preserve his claim over the West Bank, flying in the face of intense pressure from other Arab states and the increasing power and prestige of the PLO (in an unprecedented move, Yasser Arafat had that year been invited to address the UN General Assembly). In October 1974, at the **Arab Summit Conference** in Rabat, Morocco, twenty Arab heads of state passed a resolution recognizing the PLO as the "sole legitimate representative of the Palestinian people", and confirming its right to establish a national authority over any liberated Palestinian lands. King Hussein reluctantly agreed to this, thus effectively ceding Jordan's claims both to represent the Palestinians and to reincorporate the West Bank into the Hashemite realm. His authority, and what was left of his appeal, among West Bankers plummeted.

In 1974, both Egypt and Syria had signed disengagement agreements with Israel over the Sinai and the Jawlan respectively; in 1975 and 1976, King Hussein held secret talks with Israel over the West Bank, which later collapsed due to Israel's proposal to retain control over thirty percent of the territory. Post-Rabat, Jordan's relations with Syria were meanwhile improving, with trade and diplomatic links flourishing, but the new realities were thrown into turmoil by Egyptian President Sadat's peace initiative in visiting Jerusalem in 1977; Hussein tried to stand as an arbiter between Egypt and the rejectionist Arab states (led by Syria), while still demanding Israel's complete withdrawal from East Jerusalem, the West Bank and Gaza. Jordan joined the rest of the Arab world in scorning the US-sponsored Egypt–Israel **Camp David accords** of 1978, and, as a reward, was promised $1.25 billion annually by wealthy Iraq. Just prior to the formal signing of an Egypt–Israel peace treaty in 1979, King Hussein chose to demonstrate instead his commitment to the PLO by inviting Yasser Arafat on an official visit.

Throughout the 1970s, and despite virulent anti-Jordanian propaganda emanating from Baghdad, economic relations between Jordan and **Iraq** improved, with Iraq funding the expansion of Aqaba port and construction of major highways within Jordan. However, relations with Syria simultaneously soured, with Syria suspicious of Jordanian-Iraqi ties, as well as accusing Jordan of allowing the Muslim Brotherhood – a populist politico-religious organization with branches throughout the region – to foment treason in Syria. When Iraq invaded Iran in September 1980, launching the bloody **Iran–Iraq War**, King Hussein's immediate unwavering support for Iraq on Arab nationalist principles further alienated Damascus; nonetheless, Jordan benefited greatly from the passage of goods through Aqaba bound for Iraq.

THE PALESTINIANS AND THE INTIFADA: 1980–1989

Since Black September, the PLO's bid for authority over Palestinians on the East Bank had – bizarrely – reinforced the stand both of Transjordanian and of Israeli hardliners. The former had never viewed the Palestinians as true Jordanians anyway; the latter saw the Hashemite monarchy as the sole obstacle to annexation of the West Bank by Israel, and, under the slogan **"Jordan is Palestine"**, pressed for a Palestinian revolution east of the Jordan, offering to help it along by expelling Palestinians *en masse* from the West Bank. Needless to say, this rapidly dampened Palestinian opposition to King Hussein in Jordan, and led to something of a *rapprochement*. From Rabat onwards, Hussein's relations with the PLO markedly improved, adding greatly – as did his support for Iraq – to his regime's status in the Arab world.

In 1982, the PLO was summarily ejected from its Beirut headquarters by the **Israeli invasion of Lebanon**, and sent into further exile in Tunis; humiliated, Arafat looked to King Hussein for some way to challenge Israeli hegemony. A series of talks between the two men took place during 1983; in the next year, Hussein reconvened the National Assembly, comprising representatives from both banks of the Jordan, for the first time since 1967, as a forum for discussion of moderate Palestinian opinion away from the extremist intransigence of the Syrian position. Israel even permitted West Bank deputies to travel to Amman. In March 1984, the first **elections** in Jordan for seventeen years (and the first in which women could vote) took place, although political parties were still banned and the eight seats up for grabs were East Bank only.

Less than a year later, in opposition to a widely denounced peace plan put forward by US President Reagan (who refused to talk to the PLO), Hussein and Arafat agreed to allow Jordan to start direct negotiations with Israel under UN auspices, on the basis of Hussein's formula of **"land for peace"** – that is, the return of lands occupied by Israel in 1967 in exchange for a comprehensive Arab-Israeli peace. Were this to have gone ahead, though, hardline Syria would have been completely marginalized in the region; Damascus therefore forced Hussein to drop the initiative, partly by a number of assassinations of Jordanian diplomats abroad, and partly by uniting the Abu Nidal Palestinian guerrilla organization with Arafat's main PLO rival, George Habash, to attack the accord. At the end of 1985, Hussein and Syria's President Assad issued a joint statement rejecting any direct peace negotiations with Israel; Hussein's motivation for this was also to put pressure on Arafat to accept **UN Resolution 242**, without which the PLO could gain no international credibility. "242" had been a thorn in the side of the Arabs since 1967, since it called ambiguously for Israeli to withdraw from "occupied territories" (which could be taken to mean whatever anyone wanted) and referred to the Palestinians as "refugees", thus implying a denial of the existence of a Palestinian nation and the right of Palestinians to self-determination, and accepting the right of Israel to exist. Hamstrung by extremist attitudes embedded within the PLO, Arafat couldn't stop the PLO Executive Committee reiterating its opposition to 242 in December 1985. The following February, King Hussein severed political links with the PLO.

Meanwhile, US unwillingness to halt illegal Israeli settlement on the West Bank persisted, and an increasingly frustrated Hussein turned instead to the USSR, buying up defences for the woefully under-equipped Jordanian air force. Reagan could offer Jordan only a paltry $250m of economic aid, spread over two years.

Although rumours of secret talks between Hussein and the Israeli Prime Minister Shimon Peres persisted through the mid-1980s, publicly Jordan continued to reject Israeli proposals for peace talks which excluded PLO participation. In November 1987, King Hussein managed to convene in Amman the first full meeting of the Arab League for eight years; the summit unanimously expressed solidarity with Iraq in the continuing Iran-Iraq War, and King Hussein, acting in the interests of Arab unity, was able to draw Egypt back into the fold after its expulsion for making peace with Israel. Following a two-year hiatus, co-operation between Jordan and the PLO recommenced.

THE INTIFADA AND JORDAN'S WEST BANK PULLOUT: 1987–1989

In December 1987, an incident in the Gaza Strip sparked a widespread violent Palestinian uprising against Israeli occupation of the West Bank and Gaza, termed the **intifada**, or "shaking-off". Despite brutal security measures, Israel was unable to suppress the uprising, and, alarmed at the possibility of demonstrations turning violent, the Jordanian security services enforced their own clampdown on any shows of solidarity. The intensity of the revolt, as well as the Israeli response to it and the news that emerged of horrendous living conditions among Palestinians under Israeli occupation, alerted world opinion to the necessity of a comprehensive settlement in the Middle East. The US Secretary of State, George Shultz, shuttled around the region, but could only come up with a plan that not only refused participation by the PLO, but also neglected to address the Palestinian right to self-determination. This effectively guaranteed the plan's rejection by every Arab state; potentially threatened by a Palestinian backlash in his own country, King Hussein had no option but to reject what he termed "partial or interim solutions".

In a momentous decision on July 31, 1988, with the *intifada* in full swing, Hussein announced the **severing** of all legal and administrative links between Jordan and the West Bank, stressing his adherence to the Rabat formula of the PLO as "the sole legitimate representative of the Palestinian people". By doing so, he effectively ended Hashemite claims to Arab Palestine which had been playing beneath the surface of political machinations in the region since 1917. Hussein dissolved the half-Palestinian House of Representatives and dismantled Jordanian public services in the West Bank (Jordan had been paying teachers and civil servants there since 1967). The 850,000 Palestinians on the West Bank welcomed the clean break. However, with the departure of Jordanian staff, Israel immediately began restricting the activities of West Bank Palestinian institutions. Anti-Hashemite opinion cynically suggested that Hussein wanted to demonstrate the inability of the PLO to run public services and conduct international diplomacy without the backing of Jordan.

Shortly afterwards, on November 15, the PLO made the equally historic announcement of the establishment of an independent **State of Palestine**, endorsing UN Resolution 242 and thus implicitly recognizing the right of Israel to exist (within its pre-1967 frontiers). Jordan and sixty other countries recognized the new state. The following month, Yasser Arafat renounced violence on behalf of the PLO in front of the UN General Assembly.

DEMOCRACY AND THE GULF WAR: 1989–1991

In Jordan, the pullout from the West Bank caused the value of the dinar to fall dramatically, and the austerity measures that followed resulted in **price rises** of up to fifty percent on basic goods and services. In April 1989, anti-government **riots** broke out in depressed southern towns such as Karak and Ma'an, particularly alarming because of these areas' traditional loyalty to the establishment (Jordan's Palestinians remained on the sidelines). The prime minister and the entire cabinet resigned, and King Hussein announced that a full **general election** would be held for the first time since 1967.

The free election, held in November 1989, was contested mostly by independents, since the ban on political parties had not been lifted. Some 52 percent of the electorate voted – Jordanians of Palestinian origin were particularly under-represented – and 34 of the 80 seats went to Islamist candidates; a further 18 went to perceived "leftists". This strength of support for the opposition was surprising, not least because there had been some gerrymandering to ensure disproportionately large representation among traditionally loyal bedouin rural areas.

Despite apparently improving political health, 1990 was a year of desperate crisis for Jordan. The dinar had lost two-thirds of its value in the two years since the pullout from the West Bank, and unemployment was running at twenty percent. Fraud and embezzlement had been uncovered at the country's second largest bank, and the scandal had spread to the national airline and some 37 other companies. In addition, a huge influx of Jews into Israel from the former Soviet Union was resulting in ever more settlements going up on the West Bank and a consequent flood of Palestinians crossing the river into Jordan; with the West Bank Palestinians under almost continuous curfew, the *intifada* seemed to have fizzled out. Nonetheless, in July, the Muslim Brotherhood called on the government to arm the people for protection against Israel.

THE GULF WAR: 1990–1991

As the 1980–88 Iran–Iraq war juddered to a halt, it became clear that Iraq, which had received substantial loans from the Gulf states, was now in no position to repay them. President Saddam Hussein campaigned to have the loans cancelled, but **Kuwait** stood out by refusing to accede. This quarrel was complicated by a long-standing border dispute between the two countries – and by the fact that the disputed area was rich in oil. Penurious Iraq then also accused Kuwait and the UAE of producing oil above its quota and of thus deliberately depressing global prices. Retaining his pan-Arab stance, King Hussein pressed for a resolution to the crisis by Arab mediation before an international crisis flared, but before steps could be taken, Iraq suddenly **invaded** Kuwait on August 2, 1990. An attempt to set up a pro-Iraqi regime failed, and Saddam Hussein quickly proclaimed the annexation of Kuwait to Iraq.

The UN Security Council imposed **economic sanctions** on Iraq four days later, precipitating a further crisis in Jordan. Thousands of Jordanian refugees returned destitute from Iraq and Kuwait, ending substantial foreign remittances to the kingdom and placing a huge burden on the country's social services; petroleum prices rose sharply, as Jordan's supply of free Iraqi oil (in return for loans during the Iran–Iraq war) dried up; fully a quarter of Jordan's export trade had been to Iraq, and this was terminated; and business at Aqaba port was cut overnight, as the road to Iraq was closed to trade.

It was clear, politically and militarily, that Saddam Hussein's actions flouted international law. However, Jordan differed from other Arab states and the international community in pressing for the matter to be resolved among **regional partners**. King Hussein attempted to get the Arab League to mediate in the crisis, but he was countered by Saudi Arabia, Egypt and Syria leading calls for international action to proceed. The king's stance was perceived in the West as being pro-Iraq, yet it chimed with Arab popular opinion outside the Arabian Peninsula – especially in Jordan – which held that the US-led coalition was pursuing double standards, condemning Iraqi aggression against Kuwait, yet condoning Israeli aggression in the occupied territories; that the Gulf states were greedy, unwilling to share their new-found oil wealth with other Arabs; and that the West, by weighing in against Iraq, was supporting the oil-rich states against the poorer Arab states.

In August, King Hussein started a round of peacemaking, intent on avoiding conflict in the Gulf. On September 23, he gave a televised address to the US Congress, urging withdrawal of the multinational force in Saudi Arabia. In November, he warned the World Climate Conference of the potentially disastrous environmental effects of war – borne out by Iraq's later ignition of Kuwaiti oil installations. The next month, he proposed a peace plan linking the Iraq–Kuwait dispute with the Arab–Israeli conflict, and advocating dialogue amongst Arab leaders.

His efforts proved fruitless: on January 16, 1991, **hostilities** began, sparking widespread anti-Western and anti-Israel demonstrations throughout Jordan. Saudi Arabia had halted oil supplies to Jordan in September 1990, and petrol rationing was introduced, which only bolstered pro-Iraqi sentiment. In Jordan, as in all Arab countries outside the peninsula, the war was generally seen to be an **anti-Arab crusade**, and King Hussein was highly regarded for being the only leader to articulate this opinion fully, although he was lambasted for it in the West. Consequently, after hostilities ceased in March, the US Congress cancelled an aid programme in punishment for the king's stance. Kuwait regarded its sizeable Jordanian and Palestinian community as collaborators with the Iraqis, and expelled them all – about 300,000 people – to Jordan, a further burden on the country's social infrastructure.

PEACE AND CRISES: 1991–1998

In 1991, the Royal Commission set up to regulate political life in Jordan drafted a new **National Charter**, endorsed by the king in June: as well as improving openness within government and easing bureaucracy, the charter lifted the ban on political parties, which had been in effect since 1963, in return for their pledge of allegiance to the crown. Martial law, which had been in force since 1967, was repealed. Jordan's first one-person one-vote, multiparty elections were slated for November 1993.

New moves in the Middle East **peace process** were initiated by the US in Madrid in October 1991, and Jordan enthusiastically participated in a joint delegation with the Palestinians, thus relieving some of the US's lingering opprobrium. Soon after inception, the peace talks hit deadlock, but, unknown even to King Hussein, Israel's new left-wing government and the PLO were engaged in secret talks in Oslo throughout the first half of 1993. That September, they emerged with a **Declaration of Principles** regarding Palestinian self-rule in the occupied territories. Soon after, King Hussein insisted that Jordan and the PLO sign agreements on economic and security co-operation, closely bonding the ongoing Israeli–Palestinian and Israeli–Jordanian peace talks together into a single framework. Jordan's **election** of November 8, 1993, saw a 68 percent turnout, with by far the majority of candidates independent centrists loyally backing the king, although the Islamic Action Front (the political arm of the Muslim Brotherhood) gained strong support.

On July 25, 1994, in Washington, King Hussein and Israeli Prime Minister Yitzhak Rabin formally ended the state of war that had existed between their two countries since 1948. A full **peace treaty** followed in October, opposed both by Syria and by Islamists within Jordan; President Clinton, however, immediately wrote off Jordan's outstanding debt to the US of $700 million. A clause in the treaty acknowledging King Hussein as the custodian of the Holy Places in Jerusalem initially brought complaints from the PLO that it undermined Palestinian claims to the city, later mollified.

In August 1995, two sons-in-law of Iraqi President Saddam Hussein fled to Jordan and were granted political asylum (they later voluntarily returned to Baghdad, and were killed). Since then, King Hussein has become more openly critical of the Iraqi regime, while still pressing for UN sanctions to be lifted and simultaneously providing Iraq with a vital economic link with the outside world.

In August 1996, under intense pressure from the International Monetary Fund to institute austerity measures, the government ended **subsidies** on grain which were producing a ballooning economic deficit. The result was an immediate doubling of bread prices, and discontent, especially strong in the poorer towns of the south, flared into open **rioting**, which rapidly spread also to Amman. King Hussein suspended parliament and sent troops and tanks into Karak and elsewhere to suppress the disturbances, but the austerities remained.

The election in 1996 of an extreme rightwing government in Israel, headed by **Binyamin Netanyahu**, brought the entire Middle East peace process to a grinding halt. The Israeli–Palestinian Oslo Accords stipulated a final agreement between the two sides to be in place by December 1998, but that is now impossible; in many ways, the cause of Middle East peace is at a lower ebb now than in 1991, principally due to the policies and actions of Netanyahu's government. Vital issues of water sharing between Israel and Jordan – enshrined in the 1994 peace treaty – have still not been fully addressed, and within Jordan much resentment has been inspired towards Israel as a result.

CRISIS AFTER CRISIS: 1997–1998

For many Jordanians, 1997 was a year of shattered self-images, as the country was exposed to a series of domestic and regional crises. Early in the year, a Jordanian soldier opened fire on Israeli schoolgirls visiting **Baqoura**, in northern Jordan, killing seven. King Hussein attempted to mend ties with Israel by personally visiting the bereaved families, a gesture which inspired much admiration in Israel and much contempt in the Arab world (no bereaved Arab families have ever been consoled by an Israeli leader, the argument ran). Anti-Israel feeling surged in Jordan, and the soldier was spared the death penalty on the grounds of mental instability. The prime minister, Abdul Karim Kabariti, was particularly vocal in his criticism of Israel, and shortly afterwards was asked to resign by the king over a domestic scandal. In July, nine major political parties announced their intention to **boycott** the November parliamentary election, as a sign of their opposition to normalizing relations with Israel and as a stand against the election law, which, through gerrymandering, gave overrepresentation to the tribal and rural populations and underrepresentation to Jordanians of Palestinian origin.

Diplomatic relations with Israel were almost terminated in September 1997, after a botched **assassination attempt** in Amman by Mossad, the Israeli intelligence service, on Khaled Mishal, an official of the Palestinian opposition group Hamas. As a concession in the wake of the fiasco, Israel released from jail the spiritual leader of Hamas, **Sheikh Ahmed Yassin**, and transferred him to Jordan. Yasser Arafat and the Palestinian leadership protested strongly, believing Jordan to be undermining its authority, and King Hussein transferred Yassin back to Gaza.

Days before the Jordanian elections in November, Human Rights Watch issued a damning report on the state of **human rights** in Jordan. The May 1997 press law – which had forced the closure of thirteen weekly newspapers and magazines – came in for particular criticism. The **elections** themselves were held to be a whitewash, with extremely low voter turnout (just twenty percent in some Amman districts). Out of the 80 seats, 62 were won by pro-government or independent centrist candidates. Of the 524 candidates who stood for office, only 19 were **women** and none was elected; the king later appointed three women to the Senate. Nonetheless, a UNICEF report found that in Jordan six percent of top-level government positions were held by women in 1997, a fraction below the world average of seven percent (and way ahead of Jordan's neighbours at two percent). A separate report from Jordan University showed unemployment in the country to stand at a crippling 22–27 percent, double the official estimate.

Riots broke out again across the country in February 1998 after a rise in tension in Iraq over UN weapons inspections; a crowd of several thousand in Downtown Amman protested the US-led military buildup, and riot police were sent in to disperse them. Ma'an, a hotbed of dissent, was sealed off by tanks and placed under military curfew for several days.

At the time of writing, Jordan's response to the August 1998 **US air strikes** against Afghanistan and Sudan hadn't been formulated – not least because, days before, Prime Minister Majali had been asked to resign by the king due to a scandal over water supply. The unilateral US air strikes threw Jordan onto the horns of a dilemma. The country's overriding foreign policy priority is to stay on friendly terms with the West, and above all with the US; yet anti-American feeling among Jordanians and Palestinians is likely to rise significantly at the sight yet again of Arabs and Muslims being the target of US aggression. Pro-Iraqi feeling in Jordan, fuelled by popular compassion at the impact of UN sanctions and by outrage at the

weapons-inspection imbroglio, is also running high, and the real possibility of an overtly anti-American axis developing, centred on Iraq, Sudan and Afghanistan but encompassing many more Arab and Muslim countries, would add a third horn to Jordan's dilemma.

Last but not least, concern has been bubbling under Jordanian politics for a number of years about the **health of the king**. In August 1992, one of his kidneys was removed during an operation for cancer; spring 1996 saw an operation for an enlarged prostate, and during summer 1998 he underwent chemotherapy for lymph cancer. All these procedures were done in the US, his youngest brother, **Crown Prince Hassan**, being sworn in as regent on each occasion. King Hussein is 63 in 1998, and has been in power for 46 years – one of the longest-serving executive heads of state in the world. His succession – to Hassan – is assured, but his death or incapacity could well pitch the entire region into new crisis; no Middle East leader has Hussein's vision, or his political and diplomatic expertise. Hassan is known for his clarity of analysis and commitment to dialogue, but it would take him some time to build up the level of trust commanded in the West, in Israel and in the Arab world by King Hussein.

ISLAM

It's almost impossible to make any sense out of the Middle East – and especially out of Jordan – without knowing something of Islam. Around 94 percent of Jordan's population are Muslim, and the practice and philosophy of Islam permeate most aspects of daily life. What follows is the briefest of backgrounds; more detail can be found in the books cited on p.359, and the websites on p.26.

THE BASICS

Islam was the third of the great monotheistic religions to originate in the Middle East, and places itself firmly in the tradition begun by Judaism and Christianity: Abraham is seen as the first Muslim, and Islam itself is defined as a reaffirmation, correction and consummation of the earlier faiths.

Islam was propagated in the seventh century AD by a merchant named **Muhammad** from the city of Mecca, in the Hejaz region of what is now Saudi Arabia. Muhammad is seen as the last of a series of prophets sent by God to earth; among earlier prophets were Abraham, Noah, Moses, Solomon, Job, John the Baptist and Jesus, whose messages, for whatever reason, had been lost or corrupted over the centuries. Muhammad was sent to revive and refine the words of past prophets.

The basic principles of Islam are that there is one God (in Arabic, *Allah*), and he must be worshipped; and that Muhammad is his final prophet. The main sources of the religion are the Quran (or Koran) – the revelation Muhammad received during his lifetime – and Muhammad's own actions.

THE QURAN

Muslims regard the **Quran** (literally, "recitation") to be the word of God, as revealed by the Angel Jibril (Gabriel) to Muhammad from about 610 AD, when Muhammad was about forty, until his death in 632. There is a noticeable difference in the style of the Quran between the early portions – which have the ring of soothsaying about them, arising from Muhammad's early role as mystic – and the later portions, which go into detail about the conduct of Muslim life, as befits Muhammad's status as the leader of a large group of followers.

The principal emphasis of the Quran is on the **indivisibility of God**. Human duty is to demonstrate gratitude to God by obedience and worship – *Islam* itself means "submission" – for he will judge the world on the Day of Resurrection. Islamic concepts of heaven, as reward, and hell,

THE ISLAMIC CALENDAR

The **Islamic calendar** is dated from sunset on July 15, 622 AD, the start of the *hijra* (migration) of the Prophet Muhammad from Mecca to the nearby city of Medina; thus 1999 AD starts out in the Islamic year 1419 (AH 1419). Whereas the Western calendar is solar, the Islamic one (like the Jewish) is lunar, and thus one Muslim year contains 354 days, 8 hours, 4 minutes and 48 seconds. The effect of this is that Muslim religious festivals move in a slow cycle backwards through the seasons, each one arriving eleven days earlier, in relation to the

Western calendar, than it did the previous year. A rough conversion from an Islamic year number to a Western one is to divide it by 1.031, then add 621 or 622 (depending on which month you're in); an easier option is to surf to *www.solat.net*.

The names of the Islamic **months** are: Muharram (30 days), Safar (29), Rabia Awwal (30), Rabia Thaani (29), Jumada Awwal (30), Jumada Thaani (29), Rajab (30), Shaaban (29), Ramadan (29), Shawwal (30), Dhul Qida (29) and Dhul Hijja (29 or 30).

as punishment, are close to Christian ideas, although the way they are described in the Quran is very physical, even earthy. God sent the prophets to humankind in order to provide the guidance necessary to attain eternal reward.

The Quran is divided into 114 chapters, or **suras**. The first *sura* is a prayer which Muslims recite frequently: "Praise be to God, Lord of the Worlds, the Compassionate, the Merciful, King of the Day of Judgement. We worship you and seek your aid. Guide us on the straight path, the path of those on whom you have bestowed your Grace, not the path of those who incur your anger nor of those who go astray." After this, the *sura*s are in approximate order of length, starting with the longest and ending with the shortest. They are not in chronological order, and in fact many are patched together from passages revealed to Muhammad at different periods of his life.

According to traditional Islamic belief, the Quran is the word of God which has existed forever. It is unique, and it is the miracle which Muhammad presented to the world to prove his prophethood. However, not everything the Quran reveals is comprehensible; the book itself declares that it contains "clear" verses and "obscure" verses. On occasions, it appears to contradict itself. As a result, an elaborate literature of **interpretation** of the Quran developed, and early specialists put forward the idea that some revelations were made for a particular place or time and were cancelled out by later revelations.

THE HADITH

The Quran provided a basic framework for the practices and beliefs necessary for Muslims, but it didn't go into much specific detail: of 6616 verses, only 80 concern issues of conduct. For precise guidance, Muslims also look to the example and habitual practice (*sunna*) of the Prophet Muhammad himself, as well as his words and actions. These were remembered by those who had known him, and transmitted in the form of reports, **hadith**, handed down within the Muslim community – *hadith* is generally translated into English as **"traditions"**.

Although Muhammad himself didn't claim any infallibility outside revealing the Quran, Muslims around him seem to have collected these *hadith* from a very early time. Scholars soon began categorizing them by subject. It was obvious, though, that many of the reports of what the Prophet said or did weren't authentic; tales wove their way into his legend, and some of those who transmitted reports of his doings undoubtedly invented or exaggerated them. Scholars therefore developed a science of *hadith* criticism, requiring both specific content of what the Prophet is supposed to have said or done, and, more importantly, a traceable chain of transmission back to the Companion of the Prophet who had originally seen or heard it. Biographical dictionaries – to ascertain just how reliable a transmitter was – rapidly became a distinctive feature of Arabic literature. Two particularly refined collections of *hadith* from the late ninth century are generally held to have an authority second only to that of the Quran.

THE PILLARS OF ISLAM

Drawn both from the Quran and the *hadith*, there are five basic religious duties every Muslim must perform.

STATEMENT OF FAITH

Firstly, and most simply, is the **statement of faith** (*shahada*): "I testify that there is no god but God, and that Muhammad is the Messenger of God." If you say this with sincerity, you become a Muslim.

PRAYER

A Muslim must perform **formal prayer** (*salat*) five times a day. Since the day begins at sunset, the five times are sunset (*maghrib*), evening (*isha*), dawn (*fajr*), midday (*suhr*) and afternoon (*asr*), the exact times set in advance by the religious authorities. Before performing the *salat*, a Muslim must be in a state of **ritual purity**, achieved by rinsing out the mouth, sniffing water into the nostrils, washing the face, head, ears, back of the neck, feet, and lastly the hands and forearms. All mosques, big or small, have ablutions fountains adjacent for worshippers to cleanse themselves.

The faithful are summoned to prayer by the **muezzin**; in previous centuries, he would climb the minaret of the mosque and call by shouting, but almost everywhere in Jordan this has now been overtaken either by a taped call to prayer or by amplification. Nonetheless, the sound has a captivating beauty all its own, especially down in the echoing valleys of Amman when dozens of mosques are calling simultaneously, repeating in long, melodious strings: "God is most great! (*Allahu akbar!*) I testify that there is no god but God. I testify that Muhammad is the Messenger of God. Come to prayer, come to salvation. God is most great!" The dawn call has another phrase added: "Prayer is better than sleep."

Although it's preferable for men to pray together in the mosque, it's not obligatory, and you'll see many men throughout Jordan instead laying down a small **prayer mat** in their shops, or by the side of the road, to mark out a space for them to pray alone. Women almost always pray at home. Unlike in some Islamic countries, non-Muslims are permitted to enter mosques in Jordan, but only at the discretion of the officials of that particular mosque; however, you must always be dressed suitably modestly. If you're not praying, you don't have to go through any ritual ablutions.

Once worshippers have assembled in the mosque, another call to prayer is given. Prayers are led by an **imam**, and are performed in a **ritualized cycle** facing towards Mecca without shoes on: standing with hands slightly raised, bowing, prostrating, sitting on one's haunches, and prostrating again. During the cycle, worshippers recite verses of the Quran, particularly the opening *sura*. Repetition of the cycles is completed by everyone turning and wishing peace on each other.

The midday prayer on Fridays is a special congregational prayer, and Muslims are expected to attend a large mosque of assembly, where a religious or political **sermon** is also given. The sermon must include a mention of the legitimate ruler – in fact, one of the traditional ways to bestow legitimacy on a ruler. If the mosque is controlled by the government, the sermon is often used to endorse government policy; if it is independent, the Friday sermon can be used as a means to incite rebellion among the faithful. This is part of the reason why many political demonstrations in the Muslim world begin from the mosque after the midday prayer on a Friday.

One way in which Islam differs crucially from Christianity and Judaism is that it has **no priests**. The *imam* who leads the prayers has no special qualification to do so, other than enough knowledge of the Quran to enable him to recite, or perhaps some standing in the local community. Anyone may lead prayers, and there is no claim to special religious knowledge or holiness marking out an *imam* from any other Muslim.

A very common sight in Jordan is to see men holding strings of "worry beads", passing them rhythmically through their fingers in an almost unconscious action as they walk or sit quietly. The beads – *tasbih* or *subhah* – are **prayer beads**, and they always come in strings of 33 or 99, representing the 99 revealed names of God. As one passes through the fingers, the prayer is *subhanallah* ("Glory to God"); the next one is *al-hamdulillah* ("Thanks be to God"), the next *Allahu akbar* ("God is most great"), these three being repeated in a mantra until the cycle of 99 has been completed.

ALMS

All Muslims who are able to do so should pay one-fortieth of their own wealth for purposes laid down in the Quran: for the poor, for those whose hearts need to be reconciled, for the freeing of slaves, those who are burdened with debts, for travellers, for the cause of God, and so on. This payment of alms is called *zakat*, literally **purification**, and is primarily regarded as an act of worship – the recipients are less important than the giving, which is always done anonymously.

FASTING IN THE MONTH OF RAMADAN

Ramadan is the ninth month of the Muslim year, and was the time at which Muhammad received his first revelation; it's a particularly holy month, during which all Muslims must **fast** from sunrise to sunset each day. All forms of consumption are forbidden during daylight hours, including eating, drinking and smoking, and any form of sexual contact. However, this is only the outward show of what is required; one *hadith* says: "There are many who fast all day and pray all night, but they gain nothing but hunger and sleeplessness." Ramadan is a time of spiritual cleansing.

As the Muslim calendar is lunar, Ramadan doesn't fall in a specific season each year: summer Ramadans, when the days are fourteen or fifteen hours long and the heat draining, can be particularly taxing, but Ramadan is an intense month at any time of year. Shops, offices and public services all operate limited hours. Families get up together before dawn for a quick breakfast (many people then go back to bed for another few hours' sleep). During the day, particularly late in the month, tempers can fray; there are even special judicial exemptions from certain criminal actions during Ramadan, which is seen as a time of particular stress. As sunset approaches, people hurry home to be with their families to break the fast, and after dark, a hectic round of socializing over large meals often brings distant relatives together for the only time in the year. Jordan is much quieter than, say, Egypt (where Ramadan nights involve huge, festive street parties), but nonetheless a special mood of excitement grips people all over the country. The month ends with a three-day festival, *Eid al-Fitr*, also a time for family get-togethers.

PILGRIMAGE

Mecca was a sacred place long before the time of Muhammad, its central feature the **Kaaba**, a fifteen-metre-high stone cube inset with a smaller, holy black stone. Islam incorporated both the Kaaba and a set of rituals involved with pagan worship at Mecca into its own set of rituals around the *hajj*, or **pilgrimage**, which takes place in the twelfth month, Dhul Hijja (although a lesser pilgrimage, known as the *umrah*, can be undertaken at any time of year). Every Muslim who has the means must make the pilgrimage to Mecca at least once in his lifetime. These days, over two million descend each year on Mecca for the *hajj* from all over the world, and the Saudi Ministry of Pilgrimage has an organizational budget of some $300 million.

The Kaaba, now in the central precinct of the vast Grand Mosque at Mecca, is held to have been built by Abraham and his son Ishmael on the ruins of a shrine built by Adam, the first human. Male pilgrims wear only two strips of plain, unsewn cotton cloth (symbolizing the equality of all before God); women veil their hair but must leave their faces uncovered, to express confidence and an atmosphere of purity. Everybody circumambulates the Kaaba seven times, emulating the angels who circle the throne of God, and kisses the black stone. They go to the Well of Zamzam, discovered by Ishmael, and run between two small hills, commemorating the frantic running in search of water by Hagar, Abraham's concubine and Ishmael's mother, after Abraham had left them both in the desert. One day is spent on the arid Plain of Arafat, listening to sermons, praying and standing on the Mount of Mercy. All the pilgrims go to Mina, a suburb of Mecca, and hurl stones at three pillars, symbolically stoning the Devil. The *hajj* ends with the four-day festival of *Eid al-Adha*, celebrated throughout the Islamic world, when all who are able slaughter a sheep to commemorate Abraham's sacrifice – he was

JIHAD

One of the buzzwords that has been latched onto by the Western media when reporting seemingly inexplicable acts of violence committed by Muslims is *jihad*. This is most often translated, with dramatic inaccuracy, as **"holy war"**; in fact, *jihad* simply means "striving". Early Islamic jurists divided the world into the domain of Islam (*dar al-Islam*) and the domain of war (*dar al-harb*) and posited that there could be truces between the two but never permanent peace. The Quran stipulates that it's the duty of every able-bodied Muslim to defend the *dar al-Islam* from attack, and *jihad* was thus applied in history to struggle by Muslims against unbelievers; in World War I, for instance, the Ottoman caliph declared a *jihad* to defend the Islamic countries from the advancing British forces. True Islamic *jihad* is explicit in forbidding killing for the sake of religion; wars of aggression, to force people to adopt Islam or over border disputes or nationalisms, explicitly do not come under the banner of Islamically sanctioned *jihad*.

In addition, military action is only the most extreme form of *jihad*, even if this is currently the most common way by which the word filters through to the West, in association with acts of violence committed by extremists claiming religious authority. Within the mainstream religion, *jihad* most often refers to a daily internal striving towards individual moral or spiritual goals, and is an entirely peaceful and reflective action. Sufis – mystical Islamic philosophers – even broke the idea down, placing emphasis on the "greater *jihad*", a struggle against one's base instincts, and downgrading the "lesser *jihad*", a struggle against unbelievers.

about to kill his son but God stopped him and provided a ram instead (Jews and Christians hold the victim was to have been Isaac, but Muslims believe it was Ishmael).

There are often parties and celebrations to welcome home those who have returned from the *hajj*, and you'll sometimes see murals painted by pilgrims on the outside walls of their houses, depicting the mosque at Mecca – with the Islamic symbol of the crescent often prominent – the Kaaba and other details of what they saw and experienced on their journey.

MODERN ART

Jordan has an active contemporary arts scene, something of a surprise to many Western visitors. Darat al-Funun in Amman is one of the Arab world's leading centres for contemporary art and stands at the epicentre of efforts to nurture Jordanian artists in all fields.

ORIGINS

The origins of modern art in Jordan – and, indeed, in all the Ottoman-ruled areas of the Levant – can be traced back to the **1798 invasion of Egypt** by the armies of Napoleon Bonaparte. For the first time since the Crusades, a European power invaded an Arab country not only militarily, but with a full complement of artists, writers and intellectuals in tow, introducing a completely new, European aesthetic to Cairo's – and the region's – urban intellectual elite, and, equally importantly, laying the foundations for a Western obsession with all things "oriental" that was to continue for the best part of two centuries. In 1867, **Sultan Abdul Aziz** visited Europe, the first Ottoman sovereign to cross the boundaries of his empire for a purpose other than war. The first-hand knowledge he gained of European art, and the invitations to Istanbul he subsequently extended to a number of European artists, resulted in the opening, in 1883, of the Academy of Fine Arts in Istanbul, the first of its kind in the Islamic world.

However, little of the Istanbul enlightenment filtered down to Transjordan. At this time the area was still populated almost entirely by nomadic bedouin, the regional capital Jerusalem was a town of a few thousand people, and Salt, the only settlement of any size east of the Jordan, was barely more than a village. The introduction during the 1880s by the **Ottoman army** of courses in drawing and topographical perspective for all officers as part of their training – although instrumental in introducing Western aesthetic styles to cadets from Iraq, Syria and Lebanon, who then returned to sow the seeds of modern art movements in their home countries – had little impact in the impoverished agricultural and desert areas south of Damascus.

ART IN THE EMIRATE: 1921–1950

Jordan's modern art movement began with the nascent emirate in the 1920s, when a handful of artists came to live and work in Amman, their ideas and practice slowly attracting students. The first, a Lebanese painter named **Omar Onsi**, came in 1922 to visit his cousin; he eventually stayed five years, but, although a key figure in modern Lebanese art, Onsi was young and untrained at the time of his stay in Transjordan and painted only a sequence of watercolours.

The first figure to have a significant impact on Jordanian art – and the first to live entirely as a professional artist – was a former officer in the Ottoman army, **Ziyaeddin Suleiman**, who moved to Amman in 1930 and spent the last fifteen years of his life in Transjordan. He had almost certainly taken art classes during his military training in Turkey – and possibly during a stay in Paris – and his unruffled, impressionistic style attracted much attention in the small world of Amman at that time. He mounted the city's first-ever solo exhibition, in 1938. Other individual artists such as **George Aleef** and **Ihsan Idilbi**, who drifted into the city at various times during the 1940s, gathered a small coterie of artists around them and ideas began to spread. The royal family were active patrons, acquiring many works by these early artists, and, through Onsi and Suleiman, art found its way for the first time into the homes of Transjordan's noble families.

One result of the first **Arab-Israeli war** of 1948 was a blurring of the boundaries between specifically Jordanian and Palestinian art movements. Following the establishment of the State of Israel in Palestine in 1948, and the union two years later of the West Bank with the Emirate of Transjordan, many refugees from Palestine – artists among them – crossed into the territory of the newly expanded kingdom and either took Jordanian citizenship or began to consider themselves Jordanian. Artists resident on the West Bank often exhibited their work in Amman; those resident on the East Bank equally often in Jerusalem or Nablus. In addition, the Jordanian government employed a number of Palestinian artists to teach at schools, and some were given grants to study at art academies in Arab countries and the West.

EXPERIMENTATION AND DISASTER: 1952–1967

In 1952, a group of artists – among them Ihsan Idilbi, Muhanna Durra, Rafiq Lahham and Valeria Sha'aban – founded the **Jordanian Art Club**, both to spread awareness of art among the general public and to encourage the growing number of amateur artists. In the same year, the Institute of Music and Painting was set up with similar aims. Although both institutions proved to be short-lived, their influence took hold, and foreign cultural centres in both Amman and Jerusalem began to exhibit works by local and foreign artists. A significant feature of the rapidly developing art scene at this time was the sizeable number of **women** involved, notably Afaf Arafat, Rebecca Bahu, Fatima Muhib and Wijdan Ali. Indeed, Arafat was the first Jordanian artist sent by the government to study abroad, at Bath in England.

During a stay in Damascus in 1955, Ihsan Idilbi had met and worked with the pioneer of Syrian **impressionism**, Michel Kirsheh, and on Idilbi's return to Amman, impressionism began to take hold as the dominant style. As the decade progressed, and more artists returned from academies in the West and, increasingly, from art schools in cosmopolitan Arab capitals such as Cairo, Baghdad and Damascus, **abstraction**, largely dependent on line and mass, began to take hold.

During the 1960s, the government began exhibiting the work of Jordanian artists abroad, most notably at the New York International Fair of 1965. However, the **Six-Day War** of 1967 fell like a hammer blow on Jordan and its maturing cultural scene. The West Bank was separated from the rest of the country; many

Palestinian artists chose to emigrate and those who stayed became isolated. Amman and the whole of the East Bank area was flooded with semi-destitute refugees, and the bulk of governmental energy and funding was diverted to programmes of social welfare. Across the Arab World, subject matter in art shifted towards the expression of overtly **nationalistic** messages opposing the occupation, and with the intrusion of politics and military defeat into the everyday lives of the Jordanian population, art necessarily took a back seat.

POST-WAR DEVELOPMENT: 1967–1989

It took fully five years for the Jordanian art scene to revive itself after the 1967 disaster. In 1972, the Department of Arts and Culture – headed by the long-established and influential artist **Muhanna Durra** – set up the first two-year foundation course in painting, sculpture and graphic art. Other well-established artists, including Durra and Rafiq Lahham, gave private instruction to students at their studios; in this undramatic way, Mahmoud Taha taught students how to use a kiln and single-handedly reintroduced **ceramic art** to Jordan after a gap of several centuries.

During the 1970s, art began to enter the mainstream of Jordanian society and to receive greater and greater recognition, aided by the decision of the renowned **Fahrelnissa Zeid** to move – at the age of 74 – from Paris to Amman. Zeid had studied and exhibited throughout Europe since the 1920s and was an artist of recognized talent; on her arrival in Jordan she became tutor to eight women, of whom four – Suha Shoman, Rula Shuqairy, Hind Nasser and Ufemia Rizk – went on to pursue art as a career. The **Royal Society of Fine Arts** was set up in 1979 as a private, non-profit organization to promote the visual arts in Jordan and the wider Islamic world: its principal achievement was the founding of the first art museum in the country, the **National Gallery of Fine Arts** (see p.97), which opened in 1980 and remains the premier establishment showcase for contemporary art in the country. The 1980s also saw art exhibitions travelling outside Amman for the first time, with shows in all corners of the country that allowed bedouin and peasant farmers their first opportunities to view Western-style art. One of the breakthrough

A HIT LIST OF JORDANIAN ARTISTS

Nawal Abdallah (b.1951). Partly trained by Muhanna Durra, Abdallah is one of the leading lights of Jordan's contemporary art scene, her dynamic, abstract style based on the interplay of forms and dimensions.

Wijdan Ali (b.1939). A motivator of Jordanian art since the 1960s, Princess Wijdan was the recipient of London University's first-ever PhD in Islamic Art. Her best-known works, from the 1980s, are a series of shimmering desertscapes.

Omar Bsoul (b.1951). While still working as a barber in Irbid, Bsoul has carved a niche as one of the few naive painters in Jordan, producing strikingly patterned evocations of traditional life.

Muhanna Durra (b.1938). The pioneer of modern Jordanian art, responsible for introducing and developing cubist and abstract elements through his early works and studio classes. Although known for his character portraits, his later abstract work relies on shifting masses of colour.

Ali Jabri (b.1943). Mainly working in gouaches, watercolour, pencil and charcoal, Jabri has roamed the country to record in perfectionist and idiosyncratic style on large diptychs and triptychs mundane details of city and wilderness.

Ammar Khammash (b.1960). One of Jordan's leading architects and photographers, Khammash designed the Resthouses at Dana and Pella and renovated Darat al-Funun, Madaba's *Haret Jdoudna* and the Umm Qais Resthouse (among others) using traditional methods and materials, often featuring his own wrought-iron, wood and stone furniture. He is also an accomplished watercolourist of city, village and rural landscapes.

Khalid Khreis (b.1956). A widely travelled painter, who has gathered research and experience from Cairo, Barcelona, New York and Mexico, Khreis's abstract and symbolic work is often lent a mystical quality by the use of calligraphy.

Rafiq Lahham (b.1932). A pioneer colleague of Durra, Lahham has experimented throughout his career with different styles and techniques, the most striking being a series of works on Jerusalem mixing arabesque figures with folk motifs and calligraphic script.

Larissa Najjar (b.1957). Born and educated in Moscow, Najjar works in sandstone, producing stylized and mellifluous sculpture portraits.

Ahmad Nawash (b.1934). A leading Jordanian painter of Palestinian origin, Nawash has a distinctive, almost infantile style, figures floating around the canvas in an often disturbingly sombre and despairing ambience.

Annie Sakkab (b.1969). A member of the new wave, painting monochromatic abstractions characterized by a sense of balance and design.

Mona Saudi (b.1945). The best known abroad of all Jordanian artists, Saudi's speciality is abstract sculpture in stone, marked by smooth, intertwining figures often charged with emotion. A number of her works are displayed in public areas in Jordan, and one is on permanent display outside the *Institut du Monde Arabe* in Paris.

Suha Shoman (b.1944). From a family of artists, Shoman has concentrated since the 1980s on depicting Petra in an acclaimed series of expressively coloured abstract works.

Mahmoud Taha (b.1942). The leading Jordanian ceramicist; he also studied calligraphy in Baghdad and combines both skills in a blend of prehistoric, Islamic and contemporary design.

Fahrelnissa Zeid (1901–91). A cornerstone of Jordanian art, best known for her massive oil portraits and many large works in ink lovingly characterized by much intricate detail.

achievements of the Royal Society was a 1989 exhibition in London, which showed over two hundred works from the National Gallery of Fine Arts' collection.

CONTEMPORARY ART: THE 1990S

With greater and greater numbers of art students electing to work in Jordan, coupled with a meteoric rise in graphic and computer-aided design, Jordanian art has expanded and diversified greatly during the 1990s, due also to the efforts of the charitable Shoman Foundation and, specifically, **Suha Shoman**, formerly a student of Fahrelnissa Zeid and a painter in her own right. After establishing a gallery and information centre in the late 1980s, the foundation inaugurated **Darat al-Funun** (see p.97) in 1992, now the leading centre for the arts in the Arab world, comprising diverse exhibition halls, reference libraries and studios. In order to maintain a dialogue between Jordanian and foreign artists, each summer a different graphic artist takes up residence at the Darat, holding workshops and masterclasses. Pressure for exhibition space has also resulted in a boom in the number of **galleries** in and around Amman, and Jordan's major banks and corporations have competed with each other to buy up works by local artists for exhibition in their headquarters and branch offices around the world.

Coming to maturity in an era where specific schools of style have been largely replaced worldwide by a spirit of individuality and personal experimentation, **contemporary Jordanian art** has few unifying stylistic features. The cosmopolitan nature of Jordanian society itself, coupled with the creative drive of a relatively small number of artists who feel themselves still to be pioneers, instead results in a wide spread of differing styles, with only occasional stylistic touches – such as the use of Nabatean motifs – identifying the work as Jordanian. The Islamic injunction against figurative art has shaped, but not cramped, Jordanian style, and you can find both abstract and representational contemporary art on show in Amman's galleries.

WRITING FROM JORDAN

Before the 1970s, very little Jordanian writing had been translated for publication in the West. Cairo and Beirut were the centres of literary debate in the Arab world and Amman was a backwater. However, with the surge of scholarly interest in the West in Arabic literature that began in the mid-1980s, far more writing from Jordan is now being translated into English, much of it under the aegis of PROTA (the Project for the Translation of Arabic), founded in 1980 by the Palestinian poet and critic Salma Khadra Jayyusi.

Native Jordanian literary traditions are oral for the most part, rooted in poems sung to a musical accompaniment and tales of tribal history; even today, research into this jealously guarded body of traditions – and attempts to catalogue and transcribe it – is in its infancy. By contrast, Jordanians of Palestinian origin draw on a rich written Palestinian literary culture stretching back to the beginning of the century.

ABD AL-RAHMAN MUNIF

Abd al-Rahman Munif was born in Amman in 1933. After working for many years as an economist in the oil industry, he published his first novel in 1973. He is best known in English for his trilogy Cities of Salt *(1984–89), depicting the evolution of a desert kingdom resembling Saudi Arabia. In 1992, he was awarded the Sultan al-Uways Award, the Arabic equivalent of the Nobel Prize for Literature.* Story of a City: A Childhood in Amman *was published in Arabic in 1994, and has been translated into several major European languages.*

Amman, the city and its people, was discovered by the child through the shock of death. … The monotonous sound of church bells in the morning created a sense of sadness and ending, affecting not only the dead person's family, or the religious community to which he belonged, but everyone, both Muslim and Christian. Muslim children had early memories of the questions they used to ask when they heard those bells: "Who is dead?", "Why did he die?", "Where do dead people go?"

When the ceremonies were over, the old, tired feet of the mourners would slowly trudge up the left side of al-Misdar hill [Jebel al-Ashrafiyyeh], accompanied by children, candles, the pale and weak ringing of the cemetery church bell and the priest, who shook with grief or out of habit. All this painted a heavy, cruel picture of death, affecting everyone in Amman, irrespective of religion.

The Muslim graves lay on the opposite side, across the road, visibly sloping to the west. They were more numerous and humbler than the Christian graves, with a few exceptions. Funeral processions used to arrive there more speedily, as though the pallbearers felt it necessary to carry out their duties as fast as possible, exactly as someone entrusted with a burdensome item would want to return it with the utmost haste. Despite the speed and simplicity of Muslim funerals, which expressed the inevitability and even the necessity of death, they struck fear into the hearts of children. Although that fear was concealed and the children pretended that they were unafraid, the terror did not disappear or wear off. Some would have nightmares and be jolted out of their sleep in panic. Others would hallucinate, screaming and crying.

Mothers and grandmothers were worried by such occurrences, dreading them. They would bring water to the children, saying prayers and reciting holy verses over their heads. They would insist that the child recite a *sura* from the Quran. If the child was too young to do this, he would be asked to repeat a few prayers, then say the name of God until he fell asleep.

The next day, the Cup of Terror had to be brought. A search for it would take place in neighbouring homes. It would usually be found in one of the Damascene homes. After being made to drink water from the cup three times, the terror of the previous night would disappear and things would return to how they had been before the nightmare.

Independence day was memorable in Amman. People went into the streets early. Those who found space on King Faisal Street near the spot where a platform had been erected at its intersection with Rida and Sa'adeh streets were lucky. When delegations from other areas and Arab countries arrived, the overcrowding, joy, goodwill and singing surged to unimaginable levels. ... People's faces and behaviour resembled those of children. They laughed and at times cried simultaneously. They were quietly dazed, then their shouting exploded for no clear reason. They were highly excited as memories, emotions and hopes which had formed in some mysterious way combined within their thoughts. ...

It was an exceptional day in the life of Amman. It was rarely repeated, and it said a great deal about people's dreams and ambitions, and also about their suffering.

The mounds of Jaffa oranges piled high in the vegetable market and other places during winter were a familiar sight in the 1940s. When the trucks arrived from Palestine and emptied their loads of oranges, a deliciously intoxicating smell permeated the souk, and everything was covered by the golden-yellow colour. Huge quantities arrived and anyone watching the sight of people buying and carrying vast numbers to their homes would imagine that they ate nothing but oranges. ...

When Grandmother saw oranges being brought home in large quantities, she looked at them happily. She would pick up an orange, rub it with a tender firmness and smell it as a mother does her newborn child. Before eating it, she would shake her head several times as she recollected, going on a journey in her mind, laughing as her face clouded over. Whenever she saw oranges she would ask herself aloud, "The scent of orange flowers gladdens the heart. If God does not prove me wrong, there is no better smell in the world. Why do the people of Amman not plant orange trees like the people of Baghdad?" ...

As for marjoram, thyme, olive oil soap, *k'naffy*, the sea, the Mountain of Fire in Nablus, they were all simply synonyms for the other side of the River Jordan. As soon as one of them was mentioned, it would evoke a series of endless associations. When the word "mujahideen" was spoken, an image leapt up of men with half-covered faces, living mostly in the countryside and in caves. Late at night, they moved from one place to another to fight the English and the Jews, who surrounded them completely. Those men were so strong, heroic and self-denying that every child hoped to be like them or to become one of them when he grew up.

The names of the cities across the River Jordan were many and ever-present, and they stirred the imagination. Sometimes, the names of cities in the other Arab countries were confused with one another or not easily remembered, but all the hands of all the students would shoot up when the teacher asked who could name five cities in Palestine. Voices competed, drowning each other out: Jerusalem, Jaffa, Haifa, Gaza, Lydda, Ramlah, Acre, Safad, Ramallah, Hebron ... Every student had more names!

Palestine was more than just a land and a people. In the mind of every Arab individual, it is a constellation of meanings, symbols and connotations which have accumulated and filtered down through several generations. In addition to its collective common significance, it also has a private significance to each person which may be mysterious and different but is very powerful. ...

Even before going to school, children were more familiar with the name "Palestine" than any other, as though they had imbibed it with their mother's milk. It had a special effect and evoked many shades of meaning. The first games improvised by the children were soldiers and robbers, and Arabs and Jews. The outcome of those games was always predetermined. The soldiers beat the robbers and the Arabs defeated the Jews. ... At school, during the earliest lessons and songs, patriotism in its highest form was embodied by the attitude to Palestine. Whatever differences people had, they did not disagree about the Palestinian cause.

[By June 1948, Amman] had already received thousands of refugees. It had not been nervous or frightened, but its anger had grown. It had waited for mid-May eagerly, the date on which the British forces would withdraw [from Palestine] and the Arab forces would go in. Amman licked its wounds, hid its pains and waited. The refugees themselves, despite their weariness and suffering, were full of confidence and optimism as they waited for that date. But after what happened, after the new losses and tragedies, after cities had fallen and large amounts of territory were occupied, great numbers of new refugees poured in and an atmosphere of misery, ill-will and suspicion prevailed. At the end of spring, Amman was full of wounds and bitterness. The horror and harshness of the shock left nothing untouched. No one could believe what had happened and life resembled a nightmare. Every individual was angry. ...

From that time onwards, the city became different. Its mood, the number of its inhabitants, its size and the depth of the anxiety and fear holding the city in its grip all changed. Events such as these cause people to grow old in a short, if not a record, time. Even the young boys, after these events, turned into men bowed down by worries and filled with questions. The adults, who had been contented and confident, suddenly became confused.

The tragedy left deep wounds. If some of them could be healed by time, the wounds of the spirit would never heal. They might disappear for some time, they might be forgotten, but they still exist, deep down. They continue to bleed, causing excruciating pain, tormenting body and soul. The torment cannot end unless the injustice is removed, the mistakes are rectified and relations are governed by justice, logic and the good of the generations to come.

Palestine is more than just a land and it is larger than one generation. It transcends armies fighting wars in which one army defeats another. Palestine does not concern only those who inhabit it, and is not an issue that can be determined by who defeats whom, or which side is more cunning than the other. Others from far away who are strong can intervene to change the course of things at one time or another. But those who are far away and are strong today cannot continue to be the deciding power, nor can they remain strong for ever. They cannot act for others, or substitute the movement of life, the strength of history and the power of geography. That is as impossible as trying to control the sun or the ebb and flow of the tide, or attempting to change the direction of the wind, the movement of the waves and the times of night and day.

Perhaps the Jews, using the Old Testament as their main argument, were able to "create" and impose a situation, benefiting from the advantages they had gained from the societies they came from, and from their relations with others. They capitalized on the weakness of the opposite side in the conflict. Although it remains weak and dazed, overwhelmed by backwardness and the harshness of the regimes that govern it, the other side will not remain weak for ever. It will not remain indefinitely servile, and its rulers will not be able to continue to impose whatever they want. The Arab side bases its claim on facts that are stronger than old papers and scrolls, and will not submit or surrender to the power that now prevails and the *de facto* situation that it is trying to impose.

The generation born into the eye of the storm may be carried by its winds towards this choice or that. The winds may blow it off course, especially since the older generation was not aware of what was being plotted and did not make ready. But the next generation, and the one after it, must take a look back, re-evaluate and learn from the mistakes of their predecessors, and from their anger as well, so that the balance can be changed and things can be corrected. Large-scale wars may be started, as they have been in many parts of the world during different eras, due to persistence of injustice and degradation. The coming generations will have to pay for the mistakes of those who preceded them, and blood will be the law that rules the region for a long time to come.

From Story of a City: A Childhood in Amman
by Abd al-Rahman Munif,
published by Quartet Books Limited in 1996.
Translated from the Arabic by Samira Kawar.
Reprinted with the permission of the publisher.

JANSET BERKOK SHAMI

Janset Berkok Shami was born in Istanbul and began to learn English when she was 12. She studied English literature at Ankara University and Queen Mary College in London, and has lived in Amman since 1951. More than twenty of her short stories have appeared in magazines in Britain and the United States, and her first novel, Cages On Opposite Shores, *was published in 1995 by Interlink (New York). The following story,* Waiting, *first appeared in* Mid-American Review, *Vol XI No 2, 1991, and has since been translated into Arabic, Turkish and Swedish.*

We are sitting in a coffee house one evening, every evening, in the dry, dusty well of central Amman surrounded by mountains and thinking. Thinking about the Israelis. What will they do next? Thinking about the Americans. Waiting for the calm face of their President to invade the television screen, waiting for his cautiously worded speeches. Waiting for help from our wealthier brethren, the other Arab nations.

Trying to figure out a way of putting two pennies over two pennies. Trying to discover a way of holding onto the two pennies, until we earn the next two pennies. The weight of four pennies in the pocket! Ya Allah!

I am a musician, so I need money to buy instruments. Without money, no instruments. Without instruments, no money. Similarities and contradictions interest me, because I am an Arab, a philosopher. I am an Arab because I am a philosopher. The daily parades of ruminating mouths on the television screen demonstrate that not all philosophers are Arabs. What is the world coming to?

The other night our group, "Pals from Palestine", had a piece of luck. A boy I knew from the Jebel Hussein refugee camp came up to our smoky table and said, "Look here, Yousef, I am going to get married tonight. How about some noise?"

He put it so aptly, that refugee boy who is all grown up now. What else do we do besides noise? Noise, noise, dusty noise all around!

What else can we do? See, I study accounting at a community college; I have no free time to practice during the day. Salah, the handsome keyboard man with the large head of curly hair, is a tile-fitter's helper. He mixes cement in the yards and carries it indoors. Each metal container he carried on his shoulder weighs ten kilos or more. Our drummer is an electrician. His big feet at the end of his skinny legs shuffle up and down his ladder all day long. He bores holes in walls and stretches wires through narrow tunnels inside them.

So, I tally and add other people's money on the strings of my guitar, at nights. Ali hits his sticks steadily on the same spots on his drums. The thin sticks are heavy hammers and the drumskins are newly painted walls behind the closing eyelids of his sleepy eyes. Salah's hands drop like blocks on the keyboard. The grey cement he carries stiffens his fingers and accumulates under his fingernails.

We go and set up our equipment on the flat roof of the two room house. The roof is a drop of water in a sea of refugee roofs. The refugee roofs of 1948 and the refugee roofs of 1967 extend to the edge of the hill rippling with their slightly alternating heights.

Our transistor size singer, Sameer, comes half an hour before the party starts, wearing his hundred percent polyester silk scarf. He lowers the stand of the microphone to his height and bends the goose neck down. He caps the microphone with an orange coloured sponge, a windscreen, to tone down the hoarse sound which comes out of his throat when he sings. I line up my pedals side by side, starting from left to right: noise gate, screamer, distortion, phaser.

The Arab-disco music we play involves no risks. Our equipment protects us from listeners of yesterday and of today. The listeners fail to estimate our true musical competence. "How well he distorts the sound of his guitar," a young listener says about my playing. You see, my music is naturally distorted. But it is my prominently displayed distortion-effect pedal which makes the listener say that. My worn out guitar, covered by stickers of various music companies, is a Fender. A Fender by Fender, Made In Taiwan. It is a genuine imitation of the Fender of the USA.

The keyboard is a Hammond. An American instrument constructed in the up-to-date factories of the war-torn Korea of the past. Salah hands over most of what he earns from carrying buckets of cement as payments to the proprietor of the music store who sold him the keyboard. If he decides to get married within the coming three years, which he might as he already has a sexy girlfriend, the expenses of the wedding and setting up a house will stop the monthly payments. The proprietor of the music store will present the unpaid bills to the lawyer who takes care of such matters, and Salah will be taken to court. That will not change the situation much. If anything, it will help. He will pay nothing as the court sessions progress and the judge takes his time in reaching a decision. When it is over, he will be ordered to pay the total sum, but *Allah Kerim!* God is generous!

Ali's drum set was cheap. He bought it second hand, and paid in cash. Anyway Ali is an electrician. He makes more money than any of us.

We start our noise. First it whirls around, whirring like the new Jewish spy planes. That is the special trick of my guitar. Then the drum takes over, bringing heaven and earth over the heads of the unsuspecting listeners.

Suddenly, having spotted the approach of the bride on the arm of the groom, Sameer's booming voice joins in and the noise we produce becomes louder. The female relatives circle the couple. Inside the beaded decollete dresses provided by the groom, their middle-aged breasts quiver visibly as they let out their customary ululations. Their ululations complement our music. Our music complements their ululations. We are one happy, unhappy, noisy family trying to forget tomorrow as we wait for miracles.

Then we start eating from the trays of *mansaf.* The groom, the boy of yesterday, tells us that he works at a foreign institute as a messenger. The building of this institute is next to another one. The objectives of both institutes seem almost identical to him. There is a narrow alleyway between them. Mahmoud carries important documents and reports from one building to the other. They pay him three hundred dollars a month for this service. He stresses the fact: they pay him in dollars. America is a great country, dollars never lose value! We, the musicians, including our singer, listen to him. We suppress the envy in our hearts as best we can. We congratulate him.

The colour of the lately grown-up, tall and handsome groom's suit is dove grey. Its material is a mixture of nylon and shiny polyester. His patent leather shoes with large plastic buckles remind me of those worn by pageboys in European television plays. His long black hair is parted in the middle. It is pasted to his head and cheeks with an oily pomade. His nose which appears from that flattened surface is sharp and shapely as the tip of an iceberg.

The dinner invigorates our music. Its pulsating rhythm lifts the young women out of their chairs, and brings them to the little circle of the dance arena. They tie colourful scarves around their hips and wiggle and shake everything moveable in their comely bodies. Their abandon to gaiety pushes from our minds the uncertainties of the future. Their sparkling eyes woo us from the alleyways of the past. Captured by the moment, imprisoned in the hollows of pairs and pairs of brown eyes, we breathe again. We rest in the present as long as the spirited dance keeps us whirling. Ali smiles with one gold tooth at the side of his mouth. Salah smiles with his even teeth and pink gums. I skip a note or two on my guitar while I desperately call self-control to my aid and hold my lips tightly clamped over a mouthful of stained teeth.

I miss the grand entry of the five policemen through the opening leading to the roof. But I witness the face-down fall of the tall policeman on the unevenly cemented floor. What tripped him were the water pipes which are laid out haphazardly on the roof. No harm comes to him. He stands up clutching the popped button of his tight uniform.

The other four policemen walk toward us with measured, dignified steps, and shout. First their leader shouts, then they shout in chorus. They take us by the arms and carry us off to some distance from our equipment.

People come up to the neighbouring roofs. "You were keeping us awake," murmur some voices apologetically. I try to figure out under which roof the guilty telephone hides. I try to imagine its colour. Red? Who put in the call? The father? What did he say to the policeman who answered the call?

The groom leaves his bride's side and comes to our rescue. He lunges at the tall policeman who still holds the button in his clasped hand. He sends him sprawling once again to the floor which loosens his grip on the button. This time it disappears. Does it go down the drain pipe? Perhaps! Who knows? Only Allah knows!

Two policemen grab the groom and push him towards us. His forcefully induced steps carry him right into the midst of our tightened front and his dove grey, nylon silk suit exposes our secondhand, *rababikia* clothes like a neon light.

The five of us, the musicians and the groom, and the five of them, the policemen of different sizes and the tall one with the missing button, march briskly to the police station. The five of us go further; we are taken on a journey to the crowded jail. They release us, the musicians, the next day, but they keep the groom. The groom who paid us for the noise we made, the groom who bought the dresses for the baby-faced bride's numerous sisters and aunts, remains in jail.

He sits in his small cell and thinks about the Israelis. What will they do next? He thinks about the Americans. What deflated words will come from the thin lips of their President? When he speaks, whenever he speaks, when he starts, "Peace in the Middle East is…", "is" is the only word he cares about. The word is a present tense form of "to be". Mahmoud was top of his class in English. He knows how to conjugate verbs.

I am a messenger.

You are a president.

Prophet Muhammad is the messenger of God.

We are the victims.

You are indifferent.

They are killing us. They are killing us with their rubber bullets. They are killing us with their tear gas. They are killing our youth. They are killing our dignity!

No help comes from conjugating the verb. No help comes from thinking about his babyfaced bride. So, he confines his thoughts to everyday concerns. He tries to figure out a way of putting two pennies over two other pennies. Who knows what the future will bring? He stops all kinds of thoughts and waits for his release. He waits.

His babyfaced bride serves coffee to her mother-in-law and listens to the old woman's nostalgia stream alongside her tears.

"Our tall wheat sways gently, in the past. Our heavy oranges pull the branches low, in the past. The harvest of our youngest olive tree fills knee-high jars, in the past. Our girls sing and dance, our young men curl their moustaches, in the past. Palestine glows, Palestinians thrive, in the past."

Sighs follow sighs, sighs follow sighs. A pair of dry hands draws circles and triangles in the air. Cones and pyramids in the air. The old woman waits for her son's return. She waits for a future which will twinkle like a million stars in Palestine's clear skies, in the past.

Reprinted with the permission of the author.

FADIA FAQIR

Fadia Faqir was born in Amman in 1956. She gained her BA in English literature, MA in creative writing and doctorate in critical and creative writing at Jordan University, Lancaster University and the University of East Anglia respectively. Her first novel, Nisanit, *dramatizing the Arab-Israeli conflict through the eyes of a Palestinian guerrilla, the woman in love with him and an Israeli interrogator, was published in 1987. This extract is taken from her second novel,* Pillars of Salt. *She is at present working on her third novel and teaching Arabic literature at Durham University in the UK.*

"Imam Rajab will ask you some questions. You answer yes," Daffash said as he twisted his moustache between thumb and forefinger.

I looked at the solemn faces of the men of the tribe.

Imam Rajab stood up with difficulty and said loudly, "Maha, daughter of Nimer, will you accept Sheikh Talib as a husband?"

My body grew lighter and lighter and began rising up, up towards the sky. I saw my mother's smiling face, my father's stick and Harb's arm. I would only place my head on Harb's strong arm. Daffash was rubbing his clenched fists. My voice was weak and thin when I said, "I want a sip of water."

Imam Rajab smiled, showing uneven brown teeth. Dark words could grind your teeth and tint them. "Daffash, she is shy. Let her have some water." I turned my back on them and went to the house, found a cup, marched out of the house, threw the cup on the soil, stuck the end of my robe in my trousers and ran, ran to the orchard.

Nasra was leaning on one of the orange trees talking to Murjan. She grabbed my hand and said in her shrill voice, "Quick, the mountains." The soles of my feet were blazing hot, Mubarak's crying filled the valley, the men would shoot me between the eyes if they caught me. Then, I could only hear the noise of my lungs rasping for air. Thorn shrubs, grass, dry soil and bugloss sped under my feet. Sweat trickled down my nose. We took one of the footpaths leading to the top of the mountain. Nasra was pulling me forwards. I felt very hot although the air was getting cooler. Murjan was right behind us. When we reached the top, I stopped and shouted to the wind, to the sick light of dusk. "No." I would not accept Sheikh Talib as a husband.

The jaws of Abu Auqab's cave were wide open. A lion ready to devour his prey. We entered the cave and threw ourselves on the rug-covered ground. My lungs felt as if they had been slashed by a dagger. Murjan and Jawaher had prepared the cave for us. A clay jar, a lamp, bread and some butter and dates. "Enough for a few days," Murjan said. "Close the entrance with the rock outside. I will keep an eye on the path leading to the cave. If you hear any noise, run south towards the Dead Sea. Do not stay here. If you hear voices, sneak quietly out of the cave."

"May Allah lengthen your life, my son," I gasped. Nasra brought a cup of water and told me to drink.

The foxes' barking and the howling of dogs besieged us in our cave. Nasra's face twitched under the dwindling light of the lamp. Sleep was far away from me. My heart quivered beneath my ribs. Mubarak. Would Tamam feed him, undress him, wipe his tears? I rocked and swayed my body to try to go to sleep. The rounded rock they pushed to lock the mouth of the cave seemed to crouch upon my chest. From now on, fear and exhaustion would be my sisters, my companions in the land of my tribe. No arrivals at all. The cave was dark, the rug I covered my body with was cold, my luck was scattered flour.

I was floating lightly between hazy clouds when Nasra shook my shoulder. "Wake up. Voices." We stood up and placed our ears on the ground. Faint sounds vibrated through soil and stone. "We must go." We pushed the rock slowly to one side and left the cave. A procession of torches climbed up the mountain like a glowing snake.

"Run."

Following the sounds of waves, we dashed to the south towards the hollow of the sea. Swishing waves crashed on the shore with all their might then retreated. My muscles ached, my eyes watered and the soles of my feet were bleeding. The running blood would leave a trace on the soil, would make it easy for the men of the tribe to find us. The salt covering the pebbles on the seashore rubbed into my cuts, inflaming them. Fire, fire, fire. The mother of Hulala was licking the soles of my bare feet. Nasra's back was stiff my feet barely touched the ground, and the only sign of my being alive and running was the deep sound of drawn breath. The wings of darkness hid our figures, protected them, enveloped us like a kind mother.

The sky was a cloud of black smoke suspended over the open plain of the sea. Nasra guided me to a spring of fresh water flowing into the sea. "We will spend the night here." A warm breeze carrying the smell of carbon hit my damp face. Some faint lights were reflected in the water over on the other bank. Darkness and heat swathed the vast salt flats. I placed my head between my legs to let the blood stream down and push out the dizziness. When I closed my eyes I saw the smiling face of Harb, his warm hands pulling me closer and the water lapping my body gently. Had I – Maha the Indian

fig, bitter like colocynth but patient – had I run away from my house? Was I really sitting on the salty stones, looking at the awesome hollow of the Dead Sea without the twin of my soul, without Harb, my beloved and the father of my son? Why did I leave my son with Tamam? Why did I…?

The darkness of the clouds descended and enveloped Nasra and me. The land-locked water held its breath and nothing moved on that vast coast except water from the mineral springs which gurgled out then glided down the cliffs to the black mirror. Mist lined the water, the rocks, the springs, making breathing impossible. The stink of acids and minerals rose up to the sky. I placed my head on a flat stone and tried to listen to the sound of fresh water streaming down to meet its death. A drop of fresh water in the vast salty sea. The sapless cloak of death shrouded the low land, the tops of mountains and even Jerusalem with its high minarets. I would try to go to sleep, I would try to shut my eyes like Nasra; I would try to forget about the pillars of salt under the water and the vipers lurking in the dark.

The sun rose, lighting up the white sky, scattering flickering beams on the surface of the calm water. The dawn transformed every grain of salt into a sparkling jewel, a precious stone. The sound of water swishing and hissing in the wind ebbed and swirled. Nasra was still asleep on top of the flat rock. In her black robe, she looked like a thin black lining of the rock. I filled my cupped hands with water and splashed my face. The bitter taste of minerals stuck to my tongue, to the rims of my eyes. A contraction in my chest told me that my son was crying. Whenever I thought about him, I felt it in my breasts. I stroked my nipples. He must be hungry. He must be crying. His tiny feet must be searching for a crack in the cliffs to fit into. Curse my heart which caught fire as easily as dry palm leaves.

Nasra woke up, stretched her hands and looked at the sky. Dangling her legs, she started blowing into her reed-pipe. She played sharp, bouncy tunes as a greeting to the morning.

"Nasra, sister, I want you to go to the village and bring me some news."

"Bring food?"

I looked at the dusty shrubs bravely sprouting on the banks of mineral springs. "Yes." Nasra leapt off the rock and washed her face. She stuck the end of her robe into her trousers and walked away. I watched her negotiate her way between the shrubs. When she had become just a crawling ant in the distance, I sighed and sat down. The heat started rising under the rude glare of the sun. My black robe absorbed the heat, stored the heat, baking my body inside. The swishing and hissing of the cool water filled my ears.

The translucent hands of the water waved to me, pulled me, held my wrists. The call of the sea was deep, husky, sad. My past. I untied my headband, flung the veil on a stone, then undid my plaits. I took off my tatty black robe, my trousers and my petticoat then stretched my naked body. My feet when plunged into the water welcomed the pleasant coolness. Whenever I dived in the Dead Sea my eyes hurt. The acids and minerals seemed to attack the tender tissues of my body. Must endure it till pleasure overtook the pain and I could see again. Fresh tears would wash out the salt. The lapping water, the wet hair and the bitter taste of minerals brought Harb back. First he kissed the right corner of my mouth, then the left corner, then the centre of my lips. I grabbed his shoulders and moved closer to him. When I enveloped him, curled around him with my being, he started crying like a baby. His expression was tender, was full of response. Receiving him was like coming home after a long sweaty day. My body tuned into a light pestle swiftly grinding coffee and cardamom in a mortar. Whispers and swishes. "Mistress of my soul, deer-eyes." I hugged myself tightly. Tears, emptiness and love. I dived to hold him, then floated. Murky green puddles followed by fresh air and dazzling light.

I thought I saw the crooked figure of Hakim. I wiped the water from my face. Yes, by the grey hair of my grandmother. He stopped, put his goat on the ground, then waved to me. His step when he continued walking was light as if he were only twenty years old. Holding his goat, he disappeared behind one of the high cliffs. I cried at the top of my voice, "Hakim." Nothing except the echo of my voice and the swishing of the waves. Maybe he could, with his rare herbs, cure my tired heart. "Hakim." Nothing except the echo of my voice breaking on top of the mountains.

The sun unchained its scalding flames and turned them loose in the plain of the Dead Sea.

Sweat trickled down my face and my back. Two blurred crawling ants. Murjan and Nasra. Bearers of good news, I prayed.

"Peace be upon you," said Murjan.

"And upon you, my son," I said.

"Fine, Mubarak," said Nasra.

"Maha, my mother, your brother Daffash has taken possession of the orchard, the house and your son."

"Rooted out your vegetables, Daffash."

Grains of Dead Sea bitter salt lined my throat, stuck to my tongue, rimmed my eyes. "I am thirsty." Murjan handed me the waterskin. I gulped some water. Nasra offered me dates. I shook my head.

My orchard, the gem hanging on the valley's forehead. The golden dawn gently fingered the citrus trees and lifted them up, up to the sky and suspended them there. The icy water running in the old canal split the orchard in two and filtered into the soil, blunting the edges of the dry grains, making the whole area cool and damp. The scent of the blossoms carried me smoothly to another world. The cloud of perfume filled the valley. The clear water ran to the depth of my heart, wiped my tired soul clean and left me fragile, transparent.

Shielding my eyes, I looked at the sun. What was I, Maha, daughter of Maliha, daughter of Sabha doing there? How could I leave my son and house? I must fight Daffash. Slowly, slowly, I turned round and said in a determined voice, "I am going back to the village."

Nasra started slapping her cheeks and crying, "Crazy, Maha?"

Murjan gazed at the sea and said as if talking to the waves, "Do whatever you feel is right."

Straight backed, head held high, chin quivering, I marched across the vast plain. The few palm trees were like drops of fresh water in a salty sea. They could not change the plain to kind green. The forces of the pale desert triumphed over the bright green spots. A camel and a calf chewed and chewed the cud. Bringing the food back from the stomach and chewing it was useless for me. The banana plantation was the shortest cut to the village. A thorn pricked the sole of my foot. Nasra and Murjan tried to catch up with me.

Daffash, my brother, the son of my mother Maliha, my father Sheikh Nimer and the grandson of my grandmother Sabha swallowed the farm and the house. I should have killed Daffash in the cave as he mounted Salih's wife. I should have pulled the trigger and shot him in the heart. I should have killed him before Nasra's tunes had lost their warmth. I should have shot Daffash before Nasra had lost her earring and the brilliance of her green eyes.

I pushed the headband up, wiped my sweat and continued marching towards the forgotten village which clung to the mountainside like a leech. Only two days and the village seemed older. Gloomy brown. Mud domes, mud walls, mud ears and eyes. I left the Dead Sea behind, roaring in its low land. The land belonged to me. Mubarak was my son, a piece of my heart. I planted the lemon and orange shoots, waited for three years, watered them until they threw their first crop. My fingernails were lined with soil, with dung and mud. I had dug, cleaned, uprooted. My brother's hands were clean, were never plunged into mud. The land was mine. It was better to be shot between the eyes than see the orchard withering away. I would prefer to lie in peace under the ground, entangled with the roots of my orange trees.

From Pillars of Salt *by Fadia Faqir,*
published by Quartet Books Limited in 1996.
Reprinted with the permission of the publisher.

JORDANIAN-PALESTINIAN POETRY

Of all Arab countries, Jordan has the closest links with Palestine and Palestinian culture, and many writers chose or were forced to take refuge in Jordan after the wars of 1948 and 1967. Following are four poems (all translated from the Arabic) by Palestinian writers with some close connection with Jordan – either as their birthplace, or as their present or former country of residence. All share common themes, evoked by Salma Khadra Jayyusi in her introduction to the Anthology of Modern Palestinian Literature*:*

"Modern Palestinian experience is harsh, unrelenting and all-penetrating; no Palestinian is free from its grip and no writer can evade it. It cannot be forgotten and its anguish cannot be transcended. Whether in Israel, or in the West Bank and the Gaza Strip, or in the diaspora, Palestinians are committed by their very identi-ty to a life determined by events and circumstances arising out of their own rejection of captivity and national loss, as well as by other people's intentions, suspicions, fears and aggressions. There is no escape. For the writer to contemplate an orientation completely divorced from political life is to belie reality, to deny experience; for to engross oneself for too long in "normal" everyday experiences is to betray one's own life and one's own people. This means that Palestinian writers have little scope for indulging in escapism; they are compromised by the events of contemporary history even before they are born. The luxury of choosing one's past, of selecting memories, of re-arranging relations that transcend events and external circumstances, is not theirs; they have become permanent exiles, the prototype of the strangers of all times, struggling against obstacles of every kind and magnitude. But the greatest struggle and the greatest triumph of Palestinian writers lies in their refusal to become humanity's cringing victims during the second half of the twentieth century. While never ceasing to be aware of the particular predicament of their people, they exhibit a resilience that transcends tragedy and overcomes necessity. This has coloured contemporary Palestinian literature and directed its intention and tone."

HAYDAR MAHMOUD

Haydar Mahmoud was born in Haifa in 1945 and has been general director of culture and arts in Jordan and Jordan's ambassador to Tunisia. His collected poetry was published in 1990. This poem, "Two-in-One", was translated by Salwa Jabsheh and John Heath-Stubbs.

One part of me is not
from the other part estranged,
although the whole wide world
against myself is ranged.

How can I cancel out
details of what I am
How can my pulse deny
pulse of its own bloodstream?

How can I myself
from my own self separate
when what within me is one
with that which is without?

One with myself, my eye
gazing sees only me
wherever I may go
it is myself I see.

MUREED BARGHOUTHY

*Mureed Barghouthy was born in 1944 and has
spent all his life living outside Palestine. He left
Egypt in 1979 after the signing of the peace
treaty with Israel, and has since been living in
Amman. This poem, "The Tribes", was translated by Lena Jayyusi and W.S. Merwin.*

Our tribes regain their charm:

Tents and more tents
tents of tranquil stone, their pegs are tile and
marble
inscriptions on the ceiling, velvet paper covering the walls
the family portraits and "La Gioconda"
facing a tablet with inscriptions
to repel the evil eye
beside the diploma of a son
framed in gold, coated with dust.
Tents, and a glass window
it is the trap for young girls, who look out
from it and tremble for fear
their young sister or brother might tell the
grown-ups.
Vapour rises from the tea, whiskey and soda
and "I do not like wine" and "excuse me"
"did you manage with the fourth wife?"
Tents and more tents
the chandeliers illuminate opulent furnishings
flies of speech dance through them
in and out of brass gates draped with chains
Our tribes retain their charm
now that the tribes are out of date!

ABD AL-RAHEEM UMAR

*Abd al-Raheem Umar was born near Tulkarm,
Palestine, in 1929, and has spent much of his
life in Amman, as a poet, playwright and political journalist. This is an extract from "The
Siege", which was translated by Sharif Elmusa
and Naomi Shihab Nye.*

The fathers would have built
a great wall between us and the road,
the waves of the vanquished sea
would have turned into stone,

had they known we'd become refugees.
Who could know our tents would be strewn
across the sands?

Long times passed, longer, long.
During nights of exile,
conquerors filed into our world.
Could our slender bodies ward them off?
Could we really have sung in such
interminable dark? We learned
the low hum of exile, nothing more.

Now Abel lies among ruins,
disintegrating, while a crow tells the tale
of a brother who killed his own.
Long times passed, longer, long
Conquerors filed past—
Kufr Qasim, Sabra, Shateela.*
And our own brothers, the ones
who speak our mother tongue,
had forsaken us.
Between the ocean and the gulf,
the gulf and the ocean,
between the weak and the strong,
the strong and the weak,
stretches the long arm of our siege.

*In 1956, Israeli soldiers imposed a curfew on
the village of Kufr Qasim while its inhabitants
were out working in the fields; when the villagers returned home unaware of events, the
soldiers killed them for breaking the curfew.
Sabra and Shateela are the names of two slum
areas in south Beirut, whose Palestinian inhabitants were massacred during Israel's 1982
invasion by Lebanese Christian militias operating with the connivance of the occupying Israeli
army.*

IBRAHIM NASRALLAH

*Ibrahim Nasrallah was born in the Wihdat
refugee camp in South Amman in 1954, and
still lives and works in Amman as a journalist
and poet. His acclaimed novel* Prairies of Fever
*(1985) has been translated into English (see
p.352). This poem, "The Hand", was translated
by Lena Jayyusi and Jeremy Reed.*

It is the hand
day's beautiful branch
blossoming with fingers,
soft as the dove's cooing,
that neither catches the wind,

nor arrests the water.
But it takes in space
and embraces the earth
from the wild flower
to the palm tree.
It is the hand
comforts us when we are broken,
consoles us when we cry,
offers solace to our tiredness.
It is the hand
dream's miracle
legend of creation
columns of light
or a handful of embers
that quicken or subside.
It is the hand
a field, and a posy of children's songs,
and a planet.

The hand isn't a book, or lines.
Don't scrutinize the details

Don't read its silence
nor its contours
you will find nothing.
All the lines that have invaded it
all the bends
are our fault
from the first aberrations
to the advent of misery.
It is the hand
do not read it
read what it will write
read what it will do
and raise it
raise it
till it becomes a sky.

All poems, and the prose excerpt in the
introduction, are from
Anthology of Modern Palestinian Literature,
ed. Salma Khadra Jayyusi
© 1992 Columbia University Press.
Reprinted with the permission of the publisher.

BOOKS

It can be difficult to find books focused on Jordan. Countless millions of words have been written about Palestine, Israel, Lebanon, Egypt and Syria, but Jordan is all too often relegated to patchy later chapters or a series of mentions in passing.

The selection of recommendations below is a personal one, and necessarily omits much. Lawrence's *The Seven Pillars of Wisdom* has appeal far beyond its worth, but if you want **fiction**, Fadia Faqir's tale of bedouin women *Pillars of Salt*, or Mahmoud Darwish's lyrical account of Beirut under Israeli siege *Memory for Forgetfulness* are both gripping. The best twentieth-century **history** is Kamal Salibi's super-clear *Modern History of Jordan*, but – especially if you're travelling throughout the Middle East – Albert Hourani's magisterial *History of the Arab Peoples* is unmissable. For history that reads like fiction, you should certainly make time for Amin Maalouf's marvellous *The Crusades through Arab Eyes*. The best one-stop take on why the region's **politics** is such a mess is Avi Shlaim's *War and Peace in the Middle East*. John L. Esposito's lively *Islam: The Straight Path* gives much readable insight into **Islam**.

In Britain, there are two excellent **booksellers** specializing in the Arab world: al-Saqi, 26 Westbourne Grove, London W2 5RH (☎0171/221 9347, fax 229 7492, email *alsaqibooks@compuserve.com*); and al-Hoda, 76 Charing Cross Rd, London WC2H 0BB (☎0171/240 8381, fax 497 0180, email *alhoda@alhoda.com*, website *www.alhoda.com*). Saqi, in particular, has a diverse and fascinating catalogue; both shops do worldwide mail order. In the US, Interlink Books, 99 Seventh Ave,

Brooklyn, NY 11215, publish a lot of translated Arabic fiction. Otherwise, your best hunting grounds are the massive Internet bookstores, premier among them *amazon.com*, but also including *barnesandnoble.com* and *borders.com*.

In most of the reviews following, **publishers** in the UK and US are listed; where they differ, they're given in the form "UK publisher; US publisher". Books published in Amman are generally available only in Jordan. "UP" stands for University Press, "o/p" signifies out-of-print.

LITERATURE

With the paucity of Jordanian literature currently available in English, we've expanded horizons slightly in this section, not least because there's so much more available in English from Palestinian writers. As well as including some general anthologies of Arab writing, we've outlined works from three of the most important Palestinian authors, Ghassan Kanafani, Sahar Khalifeh and Mahmoud Darwish.

GENERAL

Inea Bushnaq (ed), *Arab Folktales* (Pantheon, US). Delightful collection of translated tales, including a section of bedouin stories entitled "Tales Told In Houses Made of Hair".

Mahmoud Darwish, *Memory for Forgetfulness: August, Beirut, 1982* (University of California Press, US). Startling prose-poems, written as the Israeli army was laying siege to the city. Darwish is acknowledged as the greatest living Arab poet, and has published more than a dozen collections of poetry (his work appears in the two Columbia anthologies in this section); this, though, is perhaps the easiest way into his extraordinarily visceral and moving style.

Nur and Abdelwahab Elmessiri, *A Land of Stone and Thyme* (Quartet, UK). Digestible and well-chosen anthology of Palestinian short stories from the 1960s onwards, with all the big names present, including Liana Badr, Emile Habibi and Ghassan Kanafani.

Salma Khadra Jayyusi (ed), *An Anthology of Modern Palestinian Literature* (Columbia UP, US). What it says, with poetry, fiction and personal narratives from Palestinians writing all over the world. Four poems by Jordanian-Palestinian writers from the anthology are reprinted on pp.348-50.

Salma Khadra Jayyusi (ed), *Modern Arabic Poetry: An Anthology* (Columbia UP, US). Extensive selection, translated from poets in all Arab countries over the last century; most of these poems appear in English in this anthology for the first time.

Ghassan Kanafani, *Men in the Sun* (Three Continents, US). Perhaps the best-known short story ever written in Arabic, about a journey across the desert from Amman to Kuwait, here translated along with six more. Kanafani was spokesman for the Popular Front for the Liberation of Palestine (and was assassinated at the age of 36), but his stories, far from being political diatribes, are tender, lyrical and superbly plotted.

Sahar Khalifeh, *Wild Thorns* (Al Saqi Books/Interlink). Modern classic of Palestinian fiction, and a devastating view of life under Israeli occupation in the West Bank. A young Palestinian returns from abroad eager to take it all out on the occupiers, only to discover the reality of life among his compatriots is rather different from what he was expecting.

MODERN JORDANIAN FICTION

Diana Abu-Jaber, *Arabian Jazz* (Harcourt Brace, US). Feisty, funny and touching first novel from Abu-Jaber, a Jordanian-American, about the life and daughters of a Jordanian widower transplanted to a poor white community in upstate New York.

Fadia Faqir, *Nisanit* (Penguin). Powerful dramatization of the Arab-Israeli conflict through the voices of a guerrilla, his girlfriend and an interrogator, written in a raw, fractured style, describing violence, fanaticism and degradation through gritted teeth. Exhausting, and not easy to read.

Fadia Faqir, *Pillars of Salt* (Quartet/Interlink). Exceptionally skilful and lyrical novel set in the cities and countryside of mandate-period Jordan, which manages simultaneously to champion both the rights of women and the traditional values of bedouin culture. Two women, one from the city, the other from a bedouin tribe, end up in Fhays Mental Hospital after abuse at the hands of their male relatives; the fluid and compelling story traces the elements of their resistance to domination. See p.345 for an extract.

Abd al-Rahman Munif, *Story of a City: A Childhood in Amman* (Quartet, UK). Rambling tales of life in Amman in the 1940s, recalling the city passing from a period of bucolic innocence through World War II and the tragic loss of Palestine. Barely counting even as oral history, this is closer to fireside remembrances, padded out with digressions and family tales. See p.340 for an extract.

Abd al-Rahman Munif, *Cities of Salt*; *The Trench*; *Variations on Night and Day* (all Vintage). Highly acclaimed trilogy of novels chronicling the disruption, and subsequent corruption, in a fictional Gulf state caused by the discovery of oil. Munif's own close links with the oil industry, and his years working in the Gulf, give a uniquely insightful slant to his fictional indictment: all three novels were banned in Saudi Arabia and elsewhere.

Ibrahim Nasrallah, *Prairies of Fever* (Interlink, US). Intense and bewildering postmodern novel. The protagonist, a young teacher hired to work in a remote part of the Arabian peninsula, is pronounced dead on page one; from then on, his struggle to keep a grip on his life shifts from past to future, from reality to hallucination, from human to animal.

Mu'nis Razzaz, *Alive in the Dead Sea* (Ministry of Culture, Amman). Poorly translated early novel from this doyen of Jordanian journalists, charting the disillusionment of an intellectual departing his birthplace, Amman, for the city of his dreams, Beirut, only to find his hopes shattered by the actions of his compatriots. If you can see through the lumpiness of the English version, there's some beauty beneath, but the author's mingling of wakefulness, dreaming and hallucination doesn't aid the struggle.

Janset Berkok Shami, *Cages on Opposite Shores* (Interlink, US). A longtime resident of Amman, Shami here concentrates on her native Istanbul during World War I. A modern Turkish woman, caged in an indeterminate present in a city symbolically divided between Europe and Asia, discovers diaries which reveal her grandmother's Armenian identity. In shimmering confident, poetic prose, the novel traces her exploration of her emotional and ethnic roots and her journey to the "opposite shore". See p.342 for one of Shami's short stories.

TRAVEL

EARLY TRAVELLERS

Thomas J. Assad, *Three Victorian Travellers* (Routledge). Short, accessible digest of the lives and travels of Blunt, Doughty and Burton, with extracts from their writings.

Gertrude Bell, *The Desert and the Sown* (Virago/Beacon). Hard-to-read account of a 1905 journey from Jerusalem to Antioch, strewn with grating cultural assumptions about the people Bell meets. Although concentrating on the more populated and engaging lands in Syria, the book contains some interesting vignettes from Transjordan.

John Lewis Burckhardt, *Travels in Syria and the Holy Land* (Darf, UK). Recent reprint of the original 1822 text, describing a massive jaunt around the Levant by a pioneer traveller and explorer (see p.230), who, partway through his journey, stumbled upon Petra. His style is surprisingly and refreshingly upbeat, bringing the wildness of Transjordan in this period very much to life.

Charles M. Doughty, *Travels in Arabia Deserta* (Dover). Reprint of Doughty's ponderous nineteenth-century, two-volume trek on the *hajj* to Mecca, much harder to read than Burckhardt.

Hon. Charles Irby and James Mangles, *Travels in Egypt and Nubia, Syria and Asia Minor* (Darf, UK). Venerable tome from 1823, reprinted complete, in which two British naval captains make their no-nonsense way through the Middle East, via Petra and Palmyra.

Selah Merrill, *East of the Jordan* (Darf, UK). Reprint of one of the first truly comprehensive early modern surveys of the antiquities and peoples of Transjordan, conducted in 1875–77.

MODERN TRAVELLERS

Michael Asher, *The Last of the Bedu* (Penguin). Engrossing tales of epic desert travel, seeking to illuminate the myths surrounding bedouin culture across the whole Middle East from Syria to Oman to Sudan. A rather treacly style and disappointingly skimpy look at the Bdul and Howeitat of Jordan don't detract from the author's uniquely insightful empathy with his subject.

Annie Caulfield, *Kingdom of the Film-Stars* (Lonely Planet). Possibly the only travel book ever written solely about Jordan, and a light, chatty read. The author is whisked around the country to all the important places and some interesting family gatherings, against a background of her falling in love with a Jordanian man.

Jonathan Raban, *Arabia* (Picador, UK). Engaging and deeply insightful tales of the Gulf states, Yemen, Egypt and Jordan in 1978 at the height of oil wealth, and before the Lebanese civil war and attempts at peace with Israel had had much impact on the Arab world. Much more than mere travelogue, the book is perceptive, fluently written and sympathetic, as relevant today as when it first appeared.

Bettina Selby, *Like Water in a Dry Land* (HarperCollins). The famed solo traveller rides her bike quickly through Syria and Jordan in order to get to Israel. An occasionally acerbic manner doesn't detract too much from the freewheeling readability.

SPECIALIST GUIDES

Iain Browning, *Jerash and the Decapolis* and *Petra* (both Chatto & Windus, UK). Incomparably strong investigations into every aspect of the architecture, history and culture of Jordan's two premier ancient sites. In prose that's always very accurate but never turgid, Browning, an architectural historian, communicates a deep understanding and knowledge with zest, and the illustrations of what crumbling monuments might have looked like when new enhance sitewanderings enormously. *Jerash* hasn't been revised since 1982, less of a drawback than the fact that *Petra* is in a badly outdated 1989 edition.

Guy Buckles, *The Dive Sites of the Red Sea* (New Holland, UK). Thoroughly comprehensive full-colour coverage of every site from Aqaba to Eritrea, packed with sensible advice, clear assessment of each location and some interesting background.

Herbert Donner, *The Mosaic Map of Madaba* (Kok Pharos, Kampen, The Netherlands). Slim but intricately detailed analysis of the map, covering every inscription and place name and giving fascinating insight into context, history and sources. Available in Jordan.

Lankester G. Harding, *The Antiquities of Jordan* (Jordan Distribution Agency, Amman). Overview of all known sites, written in 1959 by the British director of the Department of Antiquities. The histories of different sites are engagingly well written and photographs often show that ancient sites have crumbled faster in the last few decades than in the previous few centuries.

Tony Howard, *Treks and Climbs in Wadi Rum, Jordan* (Cicerone, UK; 1997 edition). Written by a professional climber with years of experience in Rum, and containing detailed rock-face plans and precise descriptions of equipment-assisted ascents, this is an invaluable guide for dedicated pros, in a full-length paperback. However, for most general wandering in and around Rum, the excellent booklet *Walks & Scrambles in Wadi Rum* (by Tony Howard and Diana Taylor; al-Kutba, Amman), available only in Jordan, is indispensable.

Rami Khouri, *Jerash: A Frontier City of the Roman East* (Longman o/p). Handy, detailed little book concentrating solely on Jerash, although now a bit outdated.

Rami G. Khouri, *The Antiquities of the Jordan Rift Valley* (al-Kutba, Amman). Guide to every *tell* and wadi on the east bank from Shuneh ash-Shamaliyyeh to Aqaba, all with minute attention to detail. Authoritative, knowledgeable and specialized.

al-Kutba Jordan Guides, *Amman; The Desert Castles; Jerash; Madaba, Mt Nebo; Pella; Petra; Umm el-Jimal; Umm Qais* (all al-Kutba, Amman). Series of stapled, pocket-sized booklets giving solid archeological and historical information for most major sites in the country. *Madaba, Umm el-Jimal* and *Umm Qais* are written by the archeologists who excavated the sites, and thus give a particularly enthusiastic insight.

Rosalyn Maqsood, *Petra: A Travellers' Guide* (Garnet, UK; 1996 edition). Vivid and entertaining guide to Petra, featuring detailed walking tours and a comprehensive history, with much careful detail devoted to the religious and spiritual culture of the place. Highly recommended.

K.E.M. Melville, *Stay Alive in the Desert* (Lascelles, UK). Thoroughly sensible and practical guide to all aspects of desert survival, although few travellers will be as far off the beaten track as to have to recognize edible cactus or die.

Michele Piccirillo, *Mount Nebo* (Custodia Terra Santa, Jerusalem). Only available in the Moses Memorial Church itself, this is an excellent and well-illustrated guide to Siyagha, Mukhayyat and Ayoun Musa, with detailed and learned explication of the mosaics interspersed with biblical passages referring to Nebo, accounts of early pilgrims, maps, plans and photographs.

ART, ARCHITECTURE AND LOCAL CRAFTS

Wijdan Ali, *Modern Art in Jordan* (Royal Society of Fine Arts, Amman). The first and only book on the subject, a learned, first-hand history lavishly illustrated with work from 72 Jordanian and Palestinian artists. The author, as well as being an artist in her own right, is a world authority on classical and contemporary Islamic art.

The Crafts of Jordan (al-Kutba, Amman). Introductory booklet guide, with good explanation of different techniques for everything from weaving and embroidery to sand bottling.

Ammar Khammash, *Notes on Village Architecture in Jordan* (Arabesque Int., Amman). The university thesis of this pioneering Jordanian architect (see p.338), but not half as intimidating as that sounds – this is actually light and interesting reading, exploring methods and styles of building and pottery design in small villages throughout the country.

Madaba: Cultural Heritage (American Center of Oriental Research, Amman). Incredibly detailed account of a complete archeological and architectural survey of all buildings in Madaba, their history, past usage and present ownership. Accounts from early travellers to the town and information gleaned from old-timers build a complete picture of life in Madaba in the 1920s, 1930s and 1940s.

Tess Mallos, *The Complete Middle East Cookbook* (Landsdowne, Australia). Perhaps the only book in the world to enthuse over Jordanian cuisine. All your favourite *mezze* are here, plus a recipe for *mensaf*; the photos are as mouth-watering as the text.

Michele Piccirillo, *The Mosaics of Jordan* (American Center of Oriental Research,

Amman). Eminently learned explication of every mosaic to have been uncovered in Jordan, with large, clear photographs of every one and massive historical detail. A huge and lavish volume, with a JD100 price tag to match.

Peter Vine, *Jewels of the Kingdom: The Heritage of Jordan* (Immel, UK). Superb survey of the country, well illustrated if a little old by now (1987). The history section is outstanding, and the section on Jordan's flora and fauna is far and away the best introduction currently available; there are also very strong overviews both of cultural traditions and of more than twenty reproductions of Jordanian works of modern art. The best single bite at the whole country.

COFFEE-TABLE BOOKS

The Holy Sites of Jordan (TURAB, Amman). Full details –lavishly presented – of all Jordan's holy sites, Muslim and Christian, ranging from sacred trees in the far desert to shabby city-centre shrines, and backed up by quotes and stories from the Quran and the Bible.

Jordan: A Land for all Seasons (Queen Alia Fund for Social Development, Amman). Stunningly beautiful panoramic images of Jordan's countryside taken by the royal photographer, Zohrab, and embellished with quotes from world literature. Reverentially beautiful, but not at all easy to get hold of – try calling the Queen Alia Fund in Amman (☎06/582 5241).

Old Houses of Jordan (TURAB, Amman). Fascinating stories, and nice photographs, of the country's old emirate-period villas, concentrating on Amman, but with Salt and other places getting a look-in as well. Aside from the beauty of the architecture, and the gorgeous interiors, this also gives interesting background on the highest of Jordan's high society then and now.

Jane Taylor, *Petra* and *High above Jordan* (Hodder & Stoughton, UK). Written and photographed by an English expat now living in Amman, these give some interesting new angles on the Jordanian landscape – the aerial shots in particular – but are neither stunningly beautiful nor particularly insightful. *Petra* is well written, with some engaging tales from the place, and is probably the better of the two.

JORDAN: HISTORY, POLITICS AND SOCIETY

Raouf Sa'd Abujaber, *Pioneers over Jordan: The Frontier of Settlement in Transjordan 1850–1914* (I.B. Tauris). Interesting but dry account of the first decades of settled life in Transjordan for centuries, drawn from first-hand accounts of life on the Abujaber estate south of Amman (now the tourist village of Kan Zaman).

Musa S. Braizat, *The Jordanian-Palestinian Relationship* (British Academic Press, UK). Subtitled "The Bankruptcy of the Confederal Idea", this is a thorough and learned trawl through the whole notion of confederacy between the two countries and its lack of appropriateness for 1998 and beyond. For dedicated politicos only.

Uriel Dann, *King Hussein and the Challenge of Arab Radicalism* (Oxford UP, UK). Concise and pleasantly readable account of the turbulent years 1955–67, as Hussein scrabbled for a safe foothold in his own kingdom.

Graeme Donnan, *The King's Highway* (al-Kutba, Amman). Slim and worthwhile general introduction to the history of Jordan from pre-history to the Arab Revolt, with well-sketched outlines of major events and some illustrations.

Jean Hannoyer and Seteney Shami (eds), *Amman: Ville et Societé: The City and Its Society* (CERMOC, Beirut). Bilingual study that's mostly of interest to sociologists, but nonetheless there are precious few other books that examine Amman as it is today.

Joseph Nevo, *King Abdullah and Palestine* (Macmillan/St Martin's). An exposé of Abdullah's ambitions to place the crown of a Greater Syria on his own head.

Kamal Salibi, *The Modern History of Jordan* (I.B. Tauris). Outstanding and very readable account of the founding and development of the country from the Arab Revolt to the Gulf War. Salibi is one of the foremost historians of the Middle East, both Professor of History at the American University in Beirut and director of the Royal Society for Inter-Faith Studies in Amman: his political and religious insights make this book the first stop for those wanting a better understanding of Jordan's past and present role in the Middle East.

Avi Shlaim, *The Politics of Partition: King Abdullah, the Zionists and Palestine 1921–51* (Oxford UP, UK). Abridged paperback version of *Collusion across the Jordan*. Absorbing chronicle, in minute detail, of Abdullah's secret dealing with his neighbours to the west from the founding of the emirate to his assassination, that doesn't shirk from pointing fingers. Rarefied, but of unique historical interest.

Andrew Shryock, *Nationalism and the Genealogical Imagination: Oral History and Textual Authority in Tribal Jordan* (University of California Press, US). Surprisingly accessible anthropological tome examining the bedouin's transition from oral traditions to written history, and the contradictions embodied in trying to pin tales down that have never needed pinning down before, while simultaneously not letting the mask of honour slip from the tribal visage. The implications for Jordanians' self-image run deep.

Adaia and Abraham Shumsky, *Bridge across the Jordan* (Arcade, US). Engaging tale based on personal memoirs of the friendship that developed between a Jewish master carpenter and Emir Abdullah, when the former was invited to Amman in 1937 to work at the Royal Palace.

Mary C. Wilson, *King Abdullah, Britain and the Making of Jordan* (Cambridge UP, UK). This has become the standard work on Abdullah's role in the establishment of the emirate, a political biography showing the emir searching for a role beyond the confines of Transjordan.

THE MIDDLE EAST AND THE ARAB WORLD

GENERAL HISTORY

A.A. Duri, *The Historical Formation of the Arab Nation* (Croom Helm). Duri is a professor at the University of Jordan and expert on Islamic history; this is a suitably scholarly and detailed work on Arab history since Muhammad.

David Fromkin, *A Peace to End All Peace: Creating the Modern Middle East 1914–22* (Penguin). Lucid dissection of the Great Powers' carve-up of the Ottoman Empire.

Philip K. Hitti, *A History of the Arabs* (Macmillan/St Martin's). Authoritative classic tome, updated from the first half of the century, though not recommended for carrying while on the road.

Albert Hourani, *A History of the Arab Peoples* (Faber/Warner). Essential reading – Hourani's wonderfully articulate and highly erudite prose draws threads through centuries of history, yet remains easily readable.

Terry Jones and Alan Ereira, *Crusades* (Penguin–BBC Books, UK). If you don't know anything about the Crusades, this is by far the best place to start. Funny, sharp and only two hundred pages long, it covers everybody and everything, with at least one interesting nugget of digression on every page.

Elie Kedourie, *England and the Middle East: The Destruction of the Ottoman Empire 1914–21* (Penguin). Authoritative and unsentimental assessment of British fingers in Middle Eastern pies.

T.E. Lawrence, *The Seven Pillars of Wisdom* (Penguin). The old chestnut itself. Certainly not history, it is nonetheless the only first-hand account of the Arab Revolt, and is valuable for that. Otherwise, it's really rather dull, with Lawrence's pompous style showing its age badly, and his day-by-day recounting of battles and discussions and fights and intrigues wearing very thin very fast.

Amin Maalouf, *The Crusades through Arab Eyes* (Al Saqi Books). Fascinating new take on all the noble stories of valiant crusading normally touted in the West. Drawing on the extensive chronicles kept by Arab historians at the time, Maalouf paints a picture of a developed and civilized Arab society, riven by internal dissent, suddenly having to face the violent onslaught of a bunch of European barbarians fresh out of the Dark Ages. Superbly readable and endlessly intriguing.

Alan Palmer, *The Decline and Fall of the Ottoman Empire* (John Murray, UK). Comprehensive and very well-researched overview of the breakup of the empire across the region.

F.E. Peters, *The Hajj: The Muslim Pilgrimage to Mecca and the Holy Places* (Princeton UP, US). Engaging look at the history of the *hajj* from the earliest written records through fascinating early photographs up to recent times.

Steven Runciman, *A History of the Crusades* (Penguin). Standard three-volume work by the pre-eminent Western historian of the period, though probably a little stodgy to count as general background.

CONTEMPORARY POLITICS AND SOCIETY

Elizabeth Warnock Fernea and Robert A. Fernea, *The Arab World: Forty Years of Change* (Anchor). Intelligent and highly readable accounts of meetings with kings, sheikhs and ordinary people across the region over forty years of academic research. Part travelogue, part social commentary, part oral history, the authors – both eminent anthropologists – give a marvellously human insight into daily life in the Arab world.

Thomas L. Friedman, *From Beirut to Jerusalem* (Fontana). Thick memoir from Pulitzer Prize-winning New York Times journalist subtitled "One Man's Middle Eastern Odyssey". Friedman's description of his work first in Beirut (1979–84), then Jerusalem (1984–88), is human, funny, accessible but ultimately unsatisfying; his knowledge of political causes is profound, but he seems so much the estranged onlooker that little real insight filters through. Nonetheless, his evocation and analysis of the social diversity of Israel is startlingly good.

Charles Glass, *Tribes with Flags* (Secker & Warburg/Atlantic). Huge tome describing a 1987 journey which was meant to take Glass – an American journalist with Christian Lebanese ancestry – from Turkey to Aqaba, but which was truncated in West Beirut when he was kidnapped. The first two-thirds of the book, detailing endless conversations over cups of tea from Alexandretta to Damascus is worth skimming to get more quickly to the empathetic and genuinely insightful account of Christian Lebanon during the turmoil of war. The first-hand description of kidnapping and escape is, of course, gripping.

Fred Halliday, *Islam and the Myth of Confrontation* (I.B. Tauris). Trenchant rejection of the prevailing notion among Western commentators that a "clash of civilizations" between Islam and the rest is nigh.

Jochen Hippler and Andrea Lueg (eds), *The Next Threat: Western Perceptions of Islam* (Pluto, UK). The blurb on the back says it all: "Enemy images tell more about those who produce them than about the real other." Fascinating insight into the consequences of Western governments' attitudes towards the Middle East, both for the perceived and, tellingly, the perceiver.

Fatima Mernissi, *Islam and Democracy* (Addison-Wesley, US). One of the leading Arab feminists currently writing, and an outspoken voice in sociology and politics in the Arab world, Mernissi dissects why democracy hasn't taken root in the Middle East. Far from dry analysis, though, her writing – although translated – is engaging and empathetic. A compelling overview of the main issues.

Edward Said, *Covering Islam* (Vintage; 1997 edition). Shrewd investigation into how the Western media portray Islam, and where they got their ideas from about Islam being repressive and extreme.

Edward Said, *Orientalism* (Penguin; 1995 edition). Seminal study of Western attitudes towards the Arab and Islamic worlds that is both breathtakingly erudite and beautifully fluent. Said expertly picks apart preconception after preconception, taking Western ideas about the Arab East back to their foundations and exposing a tangle of shabby roots – not simple to read, but endlessly rewarding.

Avi Shlaim, *War and Peace in the Middle East* (Penguin). Superb concise modern history of the region in 150 pages, concentrating on the period 1948–95. The perspective Shlaim brings to picking apart the clichés and rhetoric in order to get down to the plain sequence of events, and the plain motivations that led to them, is refreshing and illuminating.

WOMEN'S ISSUES

Margot Badran and Miriam Cooke (eds), *Opening the Gates* (Virago, UK). Excellent one-stop anthology of Arab feminist writing over the last century.

Geraldine Brooks, *Nine Parts of Desire: The Hidden World of Islamic Women* (Penguin). Hack dons a chador for a romp through the "closed" world of Middle Eastern women, on the way bumping into several notable figures, Queen Noor of Jordan among them. The interesting social criticism and details of a solo woman's journey, all catalogued with a journalistic eye, can't quite dispel the air of tabloidery.

Elizabeth Fernea, *Middle Eastern Muslim Women Speak* (University of Texas Press, US). Collection of biographical and autobiographical writings demonstrating a commitment to what the title says, and managing to come up with masterly social and cultural history. One of the stories is from a woman in a Bani Hassan bedouin family settled in Amman.

Elizabeth Warnock Fernea (ed), *Women and the Family in the Middle East* (University of Texas Press, US). Wide-ranging collection of documents, essays and stories, gathered from all over the region, gripping for the opportunity to hear voices never normally heard.

Haifaa A. Jawad, *The Rights of Women in Islam* (Macmillan/St Martin's). Slim but forceful debunking of supposed Islamic sanctioning of the repression of women. Close analysis of both the Quran and *sunna* shatters many myths.

Judy Mabro, *Veiled Half-Truths: Western Travellers' Perceptions of Middle Eastern Women* (I.B. Tauris). Fascinating analysis of orientalist writings from the eighteenth and nineteenth centuries, examining the ways in which visiting Westerners portrayed Middle Eastern women – mostly in appallingly demeaning ways – and drawing lines towards more recent portrayals. Mabro's introduction to the subject is worth the cover price alone.

Fatima Mernissi, *The Veil and the Male Elite* (Addison-Wesley, US). Convincing, lucid argument that the Quran and Muhammad himself stipulated direct, participatory equality between the sexes. Mernissi's *Beyond The Veil* (Al Saqi Books) – surveying Islamic attitudes towards female sexuality – is, if anything, even more gripping.

Wiebke Walther, *Women in Islam: From Medieval to Modern Times* (Markus Wiener, US). A stirring overview of the historical roles played by women in Islam, from the earliest warriors through slaves, concubines and "boygirls" to the present.

PALESTINIAN POLITICS AND SOCIETY

Ebba Augustin (ed), *Palestinian Women* (Zed). Wide-ranging survey of women's post-*intifada* writings in the West Bank and Gaza, giving a vivid picture of contemporary Palestinian life.

Laurie A. Brand, *Palestinians in the Arab World* (Columbia UP, US). Unique political history of the Palestinians in Jordan (and elsewhere in the diaspora) after 1948 as they built social and political institutions that later underpinned the drive towards statehood. Minutely detailed, and of highbrow appeal only, but no less interesting for it.

Dick Doughty and Mohammed El Aydi, *Gaza: Legacy of Occupation* (Kumarian, US). Articulate and accessible account of three months spent living amongst Palestinian families in the Gaza Strip in 1993 by an American photojournalist; narrated with refreshing humanity and the clarity of a photographer's eye – invaluable for its insight into the nature of Palestinian society.

Edward Said, *The Politics of Dispossession* (Vintage). Just one of Said's many books on Palestine, all of them unrivalled in the quality of their research and lucidity of presentation. This one is more accessible than most, a collection of his political essays charting the Palestinians' struggle for self-determination from 1969 to 1994.

Edward Said, *After the Last Sky* (Vintage). Lovingly detailed look at Palestinian lives and culture just before the *intifada* changed everything. Nonetheless, Said's prose outlining the Palestinians' ongoing dispossession is marvellous, and the accompanying photos benefit the book tremendously.

Graham Usher, *Palestine in Crisis: The Struggle for Peace and Political Independence after Oslo* (Pluto, UK; 1997 edition). Succinct and highly acclaimed overview of post-Oslo disillusionment among Palestinians, written to an extremely high quality by a renowned Middle East journalist.

REFERENCE

Dilip Hiro, *Dictionary of the Middle East* (Macmillan/St Martin's). Knowledgeable and generally impartial outlines of everything and everybody to do with the region, from "aal" to "Zoroastrianism".

T. Mostyn and Albert Hourani (eds), *The Cambridge Encyclopedia of the Middle East and North Africa* (Cambridge UP, UK). Weighty tome delving into every aspect of society, culture and politics in the region. Don't go looking for up-to-date material – the book was published in 1988 – but extensive sections on Islam and modern Islamic thinkers; Christians and Jews under Islam; Arabic, Persian, Turkish and Hebrew literature; Islamic art and architecture; and even Islamic garden design make for excellent library browsing.

Peter Sluglett and Marion Farouk-Sluglett (eds), *The Times Guide to the Middle East* (Times Books, UK; 1996 edition). Admirably succinct and informed political surveys country by country, putting all recent events into a nutshell, but never neglecting context.

ISLAM

John L. Esposito, *Islam: The Straight Path* (Oxford UP, UK). The best-written and most intelligent handbook to what Islam means, where it came from and where it seems to be going.

Majid Fakhry (trans.), *The Quran: A Modern English Version* (Garnet, UK). One of the most accessible of the many translations of the Quran. The ubiquitous Penguin version, translated by N.J. Dawood, is also good, but lacks some clarity.

Ruqaiyyah Maqsood, *Teach Yourself Islam* (Hodder & Stoughton). The fundamentals of the religion presented in an admirably clear and accurate way, everything from pilgrimage and dietary laws to Green Islam and women's rights.

Maxime Rodinson, *Muhammad* (Penguin). Fascinating and superbly researched secular account of the life and works of the Prophet, exploding many myths and giving Islam the kind of intelligible, human face it lacks in much Western writing. Recently removed from the curriculum of the American University in Cairo under direct pressure from the highest authorities of Sunni Islam, who tagged it blasphemous. Unmissable and unputdownable.

Faruq Sherif, *A Guide to the Contents of the Quran* (Garnet, UK). Remarkably clear and sensible compendium of themes in the holy book, designed for novices to get a handle on what the Quran actually says.

LANGUAGE

Many people in Jordan are surprisingly fluent in English, and many more have at least some grasp of the basics. However, plain communication isn't necessarily the only consideration. Jordanian culture is deeply rooted in the verbal complexities of the Arabic language (see also p.56 on "Behaviour and attitudes"), and being able to exchange pleasantries in Arabic, or offer the appropriate response to a greeting, will endear you to people more than anything else. The most halting "*assalaamu alaykoom*" is likely to provoke beams of joy and cries of "You speak Arabic better than I do!"

Arabic is phenomenally hard for an English-speaker to learn. There are virtually no familiar points of contact between the two languages: the script, written in cursive from right to left is unrelated; there's a host of often guttural sounds which don't appear in English and which take much vocal contortion to master; and the grammar, founded on utterly different principles from English, is proclaimed as one of the most pedantic in the world. It's said that, starting from scratch, Arabic can take seven times as long to master as French.

Briefly, the three forms of Arabic are:

• **Classical** – the language of the Quran, with many words and forms which are now obsolete.

• **Modern Standard** (*fuss-ha*) – the written language of books and newspapers, and the Arabic spoken in news broadcasts and on formal occasions. Identical throughout the Arab world and understandable from Morocco to Kuwait. Although most people can read *fuss-ha*, few ordinary people are completely fluent in it.

• **Colloquial** (*aamayya*) – umbrella term for the many dialects of spoken Arabic. In Jordan, as in all other Arabic-speaking countries, the colloquial language has no proper written form (although dialogue in plays and novels is sometimes transcribed from *aamayya*). Pronunciation varies not only from country to country but district to district, and people from Irbid may have difficulty understanding an Aqaba accent. Furthermore, the vocabulary and verb forms of Jordanian Arabic can be markedly different from the related Palestinian, Syrian and Iraqi dialects. Once you move further afield, Tunisian Arabic is about as incomprehensible to Jordanian-speakers as it is to English-speakers. If there is a *lingua franca*, it's Egyptian Arabic, radically different from other dialects but instantly understandable throughout the Arab world because of the prevalence of movies and TV soap operas emanating from Cairo.

There are no **phrasebooks** dedicated to Jordanian or Levantine Arabic, but as a handy second-best *The Rough Guide to Egyptian Arabic* covers essential expressions in Arabic script with phonetic equivalents, as well as dipping into grammar and providing a fuller vocabulary in dictionary format (English–Arabic and Arabic–English). Of **teach-yourself courses**, *Colloquial Arabic (Levantine)* by Leslie J. McLoughlin (Routledge; book and cassette) is almost the only one to concentrate specifically on the spoken dialect of Jordan. Well presented, manageable and very helpful, it needs two or three months of study end-to-end. *Nasr's Pocket English–Colloquial Arabic Dictionary* (Librarie du Liban, Beirut) is an indispensable little **dictionary** that gives everything only in phonetic transliteration from Levantine dialect. However, it's not at all easy to find, either in Jordan or internationally. Far and away the clearest introduction to **writing** and recognizing Arabic script is *The Arabic Alphabet* by Nicholas Awde and Putros Samano (Al Saqi Books; Lyle Stuart); with everything explained simply and carefully from first principles, this slim volume is invaluable for getting a handle on how the language works.

PRONUNCIATION

Throughout this book, Arabic has been transliterated using a common-sense what-you-see-is-what-you-say system (see the introduction). However, Arabic **vowel-sounds** in particular often cannot be rendered accurately in English letters, and **stress patterns** are a minefield – both really need to be mimicked. Where two **consonants** fall together, pronounce them both– *hammam* means bathroom, but *hamam* means pigeon. The following are four of the most difficult common sounds:

kh represents the throaty rasp at the end of the Scottish "loch";

gh is the same sound as *kh*, but voiced – it sounds like the gargled French "r";

q represents a very guttural *k* sound made far back in the throat; Palestinians often change this into an unsounded glottal stop, while bedouin change it into a straightforward hard *g;*

aa is especially tricky: constrict your throat muscles tightly like you're about to retch, open your mouth wide and make a strangulated "aaah" sound. Ridiculous as it feels, this is about as close as an English-speaker can get, and won't make Jordanians laugh. To keep things simple, the sound hasn't always been transliterated (it stands at the beginning of "Amman", for instance).

In this book, *ay* has been written where the Arabic rhymes roughly with "say". Arabic *f* and *s* are always soft, and *r* is heavily trilled. Generally pronounce *h* – *ahlan* (welcome) features a clear and definite exhalation of breath, as does *mneeh* (happy); *Allah* (God), though, doesn't. The subtleties between the two different kinds of *s, t, d, h* and *th* are too rarefied to get into here. However, it's useful to know that the definite article *al* is elided into certain letters, known as "sun" letters: broadly *t, th, d, r, z, s, sh* and *n*. Thus *al-salaam* becomes *as-salaam*. All the rest are "moon" letters, and *al* remains unchanged in front of them.

A good rule of thumb for coping with Arabic stress patterns is to place stress exactly where you wouldn't expect to in English. *Allah* and *sabah* (morning) are stressed on the second syllable; *moutabbel* (a sesame dip) and *dishdasha* (a man's robe) on the middle syllable. The only way to get it is to copy the locals.

JORDANIAN ARABIC

Where the form of a word or phrase differs depending on whether the speaker is male or female, we've shown this with (m) and (f): to say "I'm sorry", a man says "*mitaasef*", a woman says "*mitaasfeh*". Where the form differs depending on who you're speaking to, we've shown the two separated by a slash, with the form for addressing a man first, thus: "*allah yaafeek/ yaafeeki* (to a woman)". Note also that all words and phrases ending -*ak* are for addressing a man; if you're addressing a woman, substitute -*ik*.

STANDARD FORMS OF GREETING

The following greetings are often said in long strings, barely waiting for a response, while pumping your interlocutor's hand, and – if you're the same sex – looking him/her in the eyes. Old friends might also indulge in a complex ritual of double and triple kisses on both cheeks, but as a foreigner you won't be roped into this.

Greetings

assalaamu alaykoom	"peace be upon you"; all-purpose greeting in any situation, formal or informal	keef sahtak?	"how's your health?"
		keef shughulak?	"how's your work?"
		keef al-awlad?	"how are the kids?"
		keef hal ahlak?	"how's the family?"
sabahl-khayr	"good morning" (literally, "morning of abundance")	al-afyeh	"wellbeing/good health"
		gawak	"your strength"; only in rural dialects
masa il-khayr	"good afternoon/evening"		
shoo akhbarak?	"what's your news?"	shlawnak	"what's your colour?" ie "how are you?"; only in rural dialects
keefak	"how are you?"		
keef halak?	"how's your status?" (also *keef il-hal?*)		

Continues over

marhaba	"hello"; said by one already settled to someone arriving from outside; generally connotes speaking from a higher status to a lower status	salaam	"hi"
		tisbah/ tisbahi (to a woman) ala-khayr	"good night"
		ma assalaameh	"goodbye" (literally, "go with peace")
ahlan	"welcome"; generally formal		

Responses

wa alaykoom assalaam	"and upon you be peace"; the response to *assalaamu alaykoom*	maleeh (m)/ maleeha (f)	"I'm well"; spoken mostly in rural dialects
ahlan feek or beek (ahlan feeki or beeki to a woman)	it's you who are welcome"; the response to *ahlan*"	(kulshee) kwayyis (m)/kwayyseh (f)	"(everything's) good"
marhabtayn or ahlayn	"two hellos/welcomes [back to you]"; responses to *marhaba*	(kulshee) tamam	"(everything's) perfect"
		tayyib (m)/taybeh (f)	"I'm doing fine"
		maashi il-hal	"I'm OK [but only OK]"
hamdulillah	"thank God"; all-purpose response to any of the variations on "how are you?"; covers a range of moods from "everything's great!" to "can't complain" or even "not so good really"	allah yaafeek/ yaafeeki (to a woman)	"May God give you health"
		sabahn-noor sabahl-werd sabahl-full	"morning of light"; "morning of roses"; "morning of fragrance"; responses to *sabahl-khayr*
		masa en-noor	"afternoon/evening of light"; the response to *masa il-khayr*
hala	no translation; simply an acknowledgment of having been greeted	wa inta/inti (to a woman) min ahlo	the response to *tisbah/ tisbahi ala-khayr*
mneeh (m)/ mneeha (f)	"I'm well"	allah ysalmak	"God keep you safe"; the response to *ma assalaameh*

THE BASICS

yes	naam	Canadian/ Australian/ New Zealand	canadee/ ostraalee/ noozeelandee; if you're a woman, add -yyeh to all of these
no	leh		
OK	maashi		
thank you	shukran		
you're welcome	afwan		
please	minfadlak	I don't speak/ understand Arabic	mabahki/mabafham arabee
excuse me both used to attract someone's attention. afwan is also a casual apology (eg if you bump into someone)	afwan; or lao samaht/ samahti (to a woman)	I understand a little Arabic	ana bafham shwayyet arabee
		I don't understand	ana mish fahem (m)/ fahmeh (f)
I'm sorry	mitaasef (m)/mitaasfeh (f)	I partly understand	ana fahem (m)/f ahmeh (f) shwayy
hopefully, God willing	insha'allah	what's the meaning of that in English?	shoo manato bil ingleezee?
what's your name?	aysh ismak?	could you write it for me, please?	mumkin tooktoobliyaha, lao samaht?
my name is ...	ismi ...	never mind/forget it/it's OK/ don't worry	maalesh
do you speak English/French?	btihki ingleezee/faransi?		
I'm British/Irish/ American/	ana biritanee/irlandee/ amerkani/		

no problem	*mafee mushkelah*	let's go	*yalla*
as you like	*mittel ma biddak*	it's none of your business	*ma dakhalak*
I'm 25 years old	*ana khamsa wa-ashreen senneh*	get your hands off me	*eem eedak*
I'm (not) married	*ana (mish) mitjowez* (m)/ *mitjowzeh* (f)	leave me alone	*utruknee le-halee*
we're getting married next year	*rah nitjowez essenneh al-jay*	go away	*rooh*
		I don't know	*mabaaraf*
congratulations!	*mabrook!*	I can't (do that)	*mabagdar (aamalo)*
God bless you	*allah ybarrak feek/feeki* (to a woman); the response to *mabrook,* but also used widely to acknowledge someone's kindness to you	slowly/quickly	*shwayy-shwayy/bsooraa*
		immediately	*hela*
		enough/finished/ stop it	*khalas*
		it's impossible	*mish mumkin*
		I'm tired	*ana taaban* (m)/*taabaneh* (f)
I have no children	*maandi awlad*	I'm unwell	*ana mareed* (m)/ *mareedeh* (f)
I have 1/2/3 children	*aandi walad/waladayn/ thalaath awlad*	get me to a doctor	*khuthni ala al-doktor*

DIRECTIONS AND TRAVEL

where is Hotel Petra?	*wayn funduq Betra?*	where's the post office?	*wayn maktab al-bareed?*
where's the bus station?	*wayn al-mujemma al-bussat?*	open/closed	*maftooh/msekker*
where's the train station?	*wayn al-mahattat al-sikkat al-hadeed?*	when will it be open?	*imta rah yiftah?*
where's the nearest *service* stop?	*wayn agrab mawqaf lal-servees?*	where's the police station?	*wayn makhfar al-shurtah?*
left/right/ straight on	*shmal/ymeen/dooghri*	where's the bank?	*wayn al-bank?*
		I want to change dollars/British pounds	*biddi asruf dollarat/ masari ingleeziyyeh*
near/far	*gareeb/baeed*		
here/there	*hawn/hunac*	money/cash	*masari*
when does the first/last bus leave to …?	*imta bitrik awwal/ akher bus lal …?*	travellers' cheques	*shikaat siyahiyyeh*
		how many JDs will I get?	*kam dinaar rah aakhoud?*
does this bus go to …?	*hadal-bus birooh ala …?*	is there a commission?	*fee comishon?*

SHOPS AND HOTELS

do you have the Jordan Times?	*andak Jordan Times?*	double-bed/ hot water/ an en-suite bathroom/ a fan	*takht mizwej/ my sukhneh/ hammam bil-ghurfeh/ marwaha*
I want something else	*biddi ishi thaani*		
better than this/ cheaper/like this	*ahsan min hada/ arkhas/zay hada*	it's not clean, show me another one, please	*hada mish mutheef, ferjeenee wahad thaani, lao samaht*
big/small	*kbir/zgheer*		
bigger/smaller	*akbar/azghar*		
do you have a room free?	*andak ghurfeh fadiyyeh?*	is there a toilet here?	*fee hammam hawn?*
for one person	*le-shakhs wahad*	how much for one night?	*gadaysh al-layleh?*
for two people/ three people	*le-shakhsayn/ le-thalaath ashkhas*	how much is it?	*gadaysh hada?*
can I see the room please?	*bagdar ashouf al-ghurfeh lao samaht?*	it's too expensive	*ktir ghali*
is there a balcony?	*fee balconeh?*	I don't want this	*mabiddi hada*
			Continues over

NUMBERS

zero	*sifr*	twenty-one	*wahad wa-ashreen*
quarter	*rubé*	thirty	*thalatheen*
half	*nuss*	forty	*arbaeen*
one	*wahad*	fifty	*khamseen*
two	*ithnayn*	sixty	*sitteen*
three	*thalaatheh*	seventy	*sabaeen*
four	*arbaa*	eighty	*thamaneen*
five	*khamseh*	ninety	*tisaeen*
six	*sitteh*	a hundred	*miyyeh*
seven	*sabaa*	a hundred and one	*miyyeh wa-wahad*
eight	*thamanyeh*	126	*miyyeh wa-sitteh wa-ashreen*
nine	*tisaa*		
ten	*ashra*	two hundred	*meetayn*
eleven	*hidash*	three hundred	*thalaath miyyeh*
twelve	*ithnash*	four hundred	*arbaa miyyeh*
thirteen	*thalaatash*	one thousand	*elf*
fourteen	*arbatash*	two thousand	*elfayn*
fifteen	*khamstash*	2594	*elfayn wa-khamesmiyyeh wa-arbaa wa-tisaeen*
sixteen	*sittash*		
seventeen	*sabatash*	three thousand	*thalaath alaaf*
eighteen	*thamantash*	four thousand	*arbaa(t) alaaf*
nineteen	*tisatash*	million	*milyon*
twenty	*ashreen*		

TELLING THE TIME

what time is it?	*gadaysh se'aa?*	10.30	*ashra wa-nuss*
it's ten o'clock	*se'aa ashra*	10.35	*ashra wa-nuss wa-khamseh*
10.05	*ashra wa-khamseh*	10.40	*hidash illa-toolt*
10.10	*ashra wa-ashra*	10.45	*hidash illa-rubé*
10.15	*ashra wa-rubé*	10.50	*hidash illa-ashra*
10.20	*ashra wa-toolt*	10.55	*hidash illa-khamseh*
10.25	*ashra wa-nuss illa-khamseh*		

DAYS AND MONTHS

day	*yom*	Tuesday	*al-thalaatha*
night	*layl*	Wednesday	*al-arbé'a*
week	*isbooa*	Thursday	*al-khamees*
month	*shahr*	Friday	*al-juma*
year	*senneh*	January	*kanoon thaani*
yesterday	*imbaarih*	February	*shbaat*
today	*al-yom*	March	*athaar*
tomorrow	*bukra*	April	*nisaan*
this morning	*essubbeh*	May	*ayyar*
this afternoon	*baad edduhr*	June	*huzayran*
this evening	*al-messa*	July	*tamooz*
tonight	*al-layleh*	August	*aab*
tomorrow night	*bukra bil-layl*	September	*aylool*
Saturday	*essebt*	October	*tishreen awwal*
Sunday	*al-ahad*	November	*tishreen thaani*
Monday	*al-ithnayn*	December	*kanoon awwal*

STREET NAMES

For making sense of street names (where they exist), it helps to memorize some basic Arabic terms. *Sharia* is "street" and always precedes the name. Both *duwaar* (circle) and *maydan* (square) are used to mean "traffic intersection". Many streets are named after members of the royal family and the same titles keep cropping up: *al-Malek* is "King" and *al-Malka* or *al-Malekah* is "Queen". Similarly, *al-Amir* or *al-Ameer* is "Prince" and *al-Ameera* is "Princess" (so Prince Muhammad Street translates as *sharia al-Amir Muhammad*).

NUMERALS

١	1	١٠	10	١٩	19	٨٠	80
٢	2	١١	11	٢٠	20	٩٠	90
٣	3	١٢	12	٢١	21	١٠٠	100
٤	4	١٣	13	٢٢	22	٢٠٠	200
٥	5	١٤	14	٣٠	30	٣٠٠	300
٦	6	١٥	15	٤٠	40	٤٠٠	400
٧	7	١٦	16	٥٠	50	١٠٠٠	1000
٨	8	١٧	17	٦٠	60		
٩	9	١٨	18	٧٠	70		

GLOSSARY

The first list is a glossary of Arabic terms in common usage in Jordan. Common alternative spellings, as well as singulars and plurals, are given where appropriate in brackets. Afterwards is a list of English terms used in the guide to describe features of architecture.

ARABIC TERMS

ABU Literally "Father of" – used as a familiar term of respect in conjunction with the name of the man's eldest son, as in "Abu Muhammad".

AIN (AYN, EIN) Spring.

ARJILEH (ARGILEH, NARJILEH, NARGILEH) Floor-standing water-pipe designed to let the smoke from the tobacco – which is kept smouldering by small coals – cool before being inhaled through a chamber of water. The sound of the smoke bubbling through the water gives the pipe its common name in Jordan of "hubbly-bubbly". To use the Victorian English term "hookah" is to imply the smoking of hashish as opposed to tobacco, unheard of in Jordan. Variants on the basic style include the very common use of sweet, moist tobacco flavoured with honey or apple; and, in a handful of Christian-run places, the use of *araq* instead of water to cool and alcoholize the smoke.

BADIA The desert plains of eastern Jordan.

BAHR Sea.

BALAD Nation or city.

BALADI Countryfied, rural.

BALQA (BALKA, BALGA) The fertile hill-country around Salt, west of Amman.

BANI (BENI) Tribe.

BAYT (BEIT, BAIT; pl. BYOOT) House.

BEDOUIN (also BEDU) Generally refers to nomadic or semi-nomadic people who live in desert areas within a tribal social structure. Some Jordanian bedouin tribes, however, have long been settled in towns and cities and, although taking pride in their bedouin culture and ancestry, are indistinguishable in dress and lifestyle from urbanized Jordanians. To signify their claim to being the original inhabitants of the Middle East, bedouin often refer to themselves simply as "Arabs".

BILAD ASH-SHAM Literally "countries of the north"; more or less synonymous with *Mashriq*.

BINT (pl. BANAT) Girl or daughter.

BIR (BEER) Well.

BIRKEH (BIRKA, BIRKET) Reservoir, pool, lake.

BURJ Tower.

DARAJ Flight of steps.

DARB Path or way – "Darb al-Hajj" is the ancient pilgrimage route from Damascus to Mecca, following the present Desert Highway.

DAYR (DEIR) Literally monastery or convent; by extension, a catch-all term for any ancient ruin of unknown usage.

DIWAN Formal architectural space, not necessarily within a house, intended for tribal discussions; by extension, the action of debating.

DUWAAR Circle (ie traffic intersection).

FELLAHEEN (FELLAHIN; sing. FELLAH) Settled peasant farmers.

GHOR "The sunken land", ie the Jordan Valley.

HAJJ (HAJ, HADJ; fem. HAJJEH) The holy Muslim pilgrimage to Mecca and Medina; by extension, a title of respect, like "sir", either for one who has literally made the pilgrimage, or – more commonly – simply for one who is of advancing years and thus deserving of honourable treatment.

HAMMADA Stony desert.

HAMMAM Turkish steam-bath; by extension, a bathroom or toilet.

HAMMAMAT Natural hot springs.

HAWRAN (HAURAN) The basalt desert plains around Mafraq.

HIJAB Veil or head-covering worn by women.

IMAM Prayer leader of a mosque, cleric.

IQAL (IGAL) Circular black cord keeping a *keffiyeh* in place.

IWAN (LIWAN) Arched reception area at one end of a courtyard in traditional Arab architecture.

JAHMEH "Place of assembly", ie a large, congregational mosque.

JAHMYAA University.

JAWLAN Arabic equivalent for the Hebrew *Golan*, referring to the area of high ground lying north of Umm Qais which was captured by Israel from Syria in 1967 and annexed in 1981.

JEBEL (JABAL; pl. JIBAL) Hill or mountain.

JELLABIYYEH Ankle-length outer robe worn by men.

JISSR Bridge.

KEFFIYEH (QUFFIYEH, KAFIYA, etc) Patterned headscarf worn by men.

KHALEEJ The Gulf.

KHALIFA Caliph (literally "successor", ie to the Prophet Muhammad); the spiritual leader of orthodox Islam. The post was abolished by Turkey in 1924.

AL-KHALIL Literally "the friend" (refers to Abraham, "the friend of God"); the Arabic name for the West Bank town of Hebron, first settled by Abraham.

KHIRBET Ruin.

K'NEESEH Church.

MAGHRIB (MAGHREB) The Arabic name for Morocco; also a collective term for the Arab countries of North Africa which share a common culture – Morocco, Algeria and Tunisia and, by extension, Libya and Mauritania.

MAHATTA "Station", as in train or petrol (ie a building or identifiable landmark, different from *mujemma*).

AL-MAMLAKEH AL-URDUNIYYEH AL-HASHMIYYEH The Hashemite Kingdom of Jordan, often abbreviated to "HKJ".

MANARA Minaret, the tower attached to a mosque, from which the call to prayer sounds.

MASHRIQ Collective term for the Arab countries bordering the eastern Mediterranean which share a common culture: Syria, Lebanon, Palestine and Jordan. The English near-equivalent is "the Levant".

MASJID "Place of prostration", ie a small, everyday mosque.

MASR The Arabic names for both Egypt and Cairo.

MAYDAN (MIDAN) Public square, or traffic intersection.

MIHRAB Niche in the wall of a mosque indicating the direction of Mecca, and thus the direction of prayer.

MINBAR Pulpit in a mosque, from which the Friday sermon is given.

MUALLIM Literally "teacher"; used as a term of two-way respect between those serving and those being served.

MUEZZIN (MUETHTHIN) The one who gives the call to prayer.

MUJEMMA "Assembly point", used to describe a bus or *service* station (ie an open area, different from *mahatta*).

NABULSI Native of Nablus.

NAHR River.

QA Topographical depression, pan.

QALA'A (KALAA) Fortress, citadel.

QASR (KASR; pl. QUSOOR) Palace, mansion; by extension, castle, fortress or a catch-all term for any ancient ruin of unknown usage.

QIBLA The direction in which Mecca lies, and therefore the direction in which Muslims pray.

QUBBA Dome; by extension any domed building.

AL-QUDS Literally "the holy"; the Arabic name for Jerusalem.

QURAN (KORAN) The holy book of Islam.

QUSAYR (KUSEIR) Diminutive of *qasr*.

RAMADAN Holy month in the Muslim calendar – see p.333.

RIWAQ Colonnade.

SAHARA General term for desert; can also refer to sandy desert in particular.

SA'ID Mister, as in "*al-sa'id* John Bull".

SHAM (SHUM) The popular Arabic name for Damascus; also *Dimashq*.

SHAMAGH Southern Jordanian term for a *keffiyeh*.

SHARIA Street or way; by extension, a set of laws based on Quranic precepts.

SHEBAB Literally "youth", but used most commonly where English uses "guys", as a casual term of greeting to peers.

SHEIKH (SHAYKH) Tribal leader; consequently, mayor of a town or village.

SIDI Literally "my master"; term of respect for holy men. Used in everyday speech roughly in place of the English "sir".

SOUQ (SUQ, SOUK) Market or bazaar.

TARIQ Direction or road.

TELL (TAL, TALL) Hill; by extension, an artificial mound concealing ancient remains, resulting from the continuous collapse and rebuilding of settlements, one on top of another.

UMM (UM, OUM) "Mother of" – used as a term of respect in conjunction with the name of the woman's eldest son, as in "Umm Muhammad". Women sometimes prefer to take the name of their eldest daughter instead.

USTAZ Literally "teacher"; used as a term of deference to one who has greater knowledge than you. Used commonly in the same way as *muallim*.

WADI Valley or watercourse (also refers to dry or seasonal riverbeds).

WAHA Oasis.

WALAD (pl. AWLAD) Boy or son; by extension, child.

WATAN Homeland.

YA The vocative prefix; no translation in English. Used before names to attract attention, as in "*Ya Muhammad!*", or before terms of respect for added emphasis, as in "*Naam ya sidi*" (which translates literally as "Yes, O my master", but connotes no more deference than "Certainly, sir").

ARCHITECTURAL TERMS

APSE Semicircular recess behind the altar of a church.

ARCHITRAVE Lintel resting on columns or piers, forming the lowest part of an entablature.

ATRIUM Open inner courtyard of a Roman villa; also the court in front of a Byzantine church.

BASILICA Rectangular, apsed building; the earliest style of church.

BICLINIUM Room with two benches, often a banqueting hall.

CARDO Colonnaded main street of a Roman city; usually running north–south.

CELLA Inner sanctum of a classical temple.

CORBEL Projection from the face of a wall supporting a horizontal beam.

CORNICE The upper part of an entablature; also a moulding running along the top of a wall.

DECUMANUS Main street of a Roman city; usually running east–west.

ENGAGED COLUMN Column attached to or partly set into a wall.

ENTABLATURE Element of Roman architecture positioned between the columns and the pediment; consists of architrave, frieze and cornice.

FRIEZE Part of an entablature between the architrave and cornice, often decorated with figures.

GLACIS Slope below the walls of a castle, designed to be difficult to scale.

HYPOCAUST Roman heating system allowing hot air to circulate beneath a floor raised on small pillars.

MACHICOLATION A projecting parapet of a castle or fort – often above a doorway – with holes below through which to pour boiling oil, etc.

NARTHEX In a church, an area spanning the width of the building at the end furthest from the altar.

NAVE Central part of church, normally flanked by aisles.

NYMPHAEUM A Roman public fountain dedicated to water nymphs and decorated with statues.

ORCHESTRA In a classical theatre, the semicircular area in front of the stage.

PEDIMENT The shallow triangular gable over a door, window etc.

PROPYLAEUM Monumental entrance gateway to a temple precinct.

SQUINCH Small arch which spans the right angle formed by two walls, thus supporting a ceiling dome.

TEMENOS Sacred enclosure of a temple.

TETRAPYLON Monumental four-sided structure supported on arches, usually at an important intersection of streets.

THOLOS Round section of building surrounded by columns.

TRICLINIUM Roman dining hall, most often with three benches.

INDEX

A

Abila 155
accommodation 39
airports
  Amman (Marka) 79, 109
  Amman (Queen Alia) 78, 108
  Aqaba 290, 300
Ajloun 142
alcohol 45–48
Allenby Bridge *see* King
  Hussein Bridge
AMMAN 71–118
  Abdali station 79, 109
  Abu Darwish mosque 98
  accommodation 85–89
  Ahl al-Kahf 98
  airline offices 108
  airports 78, 108
  arrival 78
  bars 104
  books 107
  cafés 99
  Cave of the Seven Sleepers 98
  changing money 115
  cinema 105
  Citadel 94
  city transport 83
  coffee-houses 99
  consulates 110, 116
  crafts 106
  cultural centres 116
  Darat al-Funun 97, 338
  Downtown 90–96
  eating and drinking 99–104
  email 116
  embassies 110, 116
  film 105
  Folklore Museum 91
  Gold Souq 55, 93
  Hejaz train station 83
  history 72
  hospitals 117
  Husseini Mosque 92
  information 78
  Jebel al-Ashrafiyyeh 98
  Jebel al-Lweibdeh 97
  Jebel al-Qala'a 94
  JETT office 79, 109
  juice bars 99
  Kan Zaman 102, 107

  King Faysal Street 93
  libraries 116
  mosaics 91, 98
  Museum of Popular Traditions 91
  music 105
  National Archeological Museum
    94
  National Gallery of Fine Arts 97,
    337
  nightlife 104
  Nymphaeum 92
  Odeon 91
  pharmacies 117
  Raghadan station 82, 109
  Rainbow Street 97
  restaurants 101
  Roman Theatre 90
  Saqf Sayl 92
  service routes 84
  shopping 106
  Souq Sukkr 92
  supermarkets 104
  Swayfiyyeh church mosaic 98
  Temple of Hercules 95
  transport to Cairo 114
  transport to Damascus 111
  transport to Israel 113
  transport to Jerusalem 112
  transport within Jordan 109
  Umayyad Palace 95
  visa extensions 17, 118
  Wihdat 98
  Wihdat station 79, 109
apartment rental 89
Aqaba 285–302, 317
Arab Revolt 219, 279, 317
Arabic, xii, 64, 360, 366
Arava crossing *see* Wadi Araba
  crossing
archeology 64
architecture 368
Ariha 209
arjileh 45, 106, 366
Asaykhin 181
Ayoun Musa 203
Azraq 173–182, 276, 307, 312,
  317

B

Baa'idj 170
Bab adh-Dhraa 216, 308
Bani Hamida tribe 106, 206
Baqaa 134
Baqoura 155
bargaining 66

Battle of Fahl 158
Battle of Hattin 212, 213
Baydha 270, 307
Bdul tribe 251
beaches 123, 295
bicycles 37
Bir Mathkoor 267, 303
Black September 160, 275, 324
books 350
Burckhardt, J.L. 131, 230, 251
Burqu 172
buses 33

C

Callirhoë 205, 303
camels 38, 281
camping 38, 125, 134, 144,
  159, 173, 177, 196, 209, 223,
  280, 291
car rental 35, 115, 301
changing money 29
children 66, 115
Church of the Map 199
Circassians 74, 93, 119, 131,
  315, 318
coffee 44
contraceptives 67
costs 32
credit cards 30
Crusaders 189, 210, 212, 223,
  230, 263, 269, 288, 297, 314
customs 17

D

Dana 107, 219, 338
Dayr Alla 160
Dayr al-Kahf 170
Dayr al-Kinn 170
Dead Sea 123–126, 303
Decapolis 73, 129, 149, 312
dehydration 19
departure taxes 67
Desert Castles 164, 274, 314
Desert Highway 273
Dhiban 208, 210, 310
Dibbeen National Park 144
Diseh 285
diving 296
dress codes 56
driving 34–37, 117, 301
drugs 63

E

ecotourism 7, 38, 171, 219, 280
Egypt, travel to and from 15, 83, 114, 300
email 52, 116, 147, 239, 302
embassies
  foreign in Amman 110, 116
  foreign in Aqaba 302
  Jordanian abroad 17
embroidery 54

F

fax 52
Faynan 223, 303, 308
Faysaliyyeh 204
ferries 15, 289, 300
Fhays 120
flat rental 89
flights
  from Australia 11
  from Britain 3
  from Egypt 16
  from Ireland 3
  from Israel 15
  from New Zealand 11
  from North America 8
  within Jordan 3, 37, 110, 300
food 41
frescoes 155, 183

G

Gadara see Umm Qais
gay travellers 59
Gerasa see Jerash
gestures 60
Gharandal 303
glossary 366
Glubb Pasha 322
Golan Heights see Jawlan

H

Halawa 144
Hallabat 166
Hammam as-Srah 166
Hammamat Afra 219
Hammamat Ma'in 204
Haret Jdoudna 201, 338
Hawran 167
health 18
Hejaz Railway 82, 273, 276, 316
Himmeh 154

history of Jordan 307
hitch-hiking 34
hospitality 61
hospitals 21, 117, 239, 302
hotels 39
hubbly-bubbly see arjileh

I

insurance 22
Internet access see email
invitations 61
Iraq al-Amir 119
Irbid 145–148
Islam 49, 309, 313, 331–335, 359
Israel, travel to and from 15, 83, 113, 148, 301
Israeli border stamps 114

J

Jafr 276
Jawa 170
Jawlan 153, 366
Jebel Haroun 228, 266, 310
JERASH 130–142
  agora 137
  arrival 134
  Baths of Placcus 141
  Birketayn 141
  Cardo 137
  Cathedral 140
  Church of Bishop Genesius 141
  Church of Bishop Marianos 136
  Church of SS Cosmas and Damian 141
  Church of St Theodore 141
  eating 134
  festival 135
  Fountain Court 140
  Glass Court 140
  guides 134
  Hadrian's Arch 135
  Hippodrome 135
  history 130
  mosaics 141
  museum 137
  North Decumanus 139
  North Gate 140
  North Theatre 139
  Nymphaeum 138
  Oval Plaza 136
  Propylaeum Church 138
  Sacred Way 138
  Sarapion passage 141
  South Decumanus 137

  South Gate 136
  South Theatre 136
  Stepped Street 141
  Synagogue Church 141
  Temple of Artemis 138
  Temple of Zeus 136
  Tomb of Germanus 141
  Umayyad mosque 139
  Visitors' Centre 134
  West Baths 139
Jerusalem, travel to and from 14, 79, 112
Jesus Christ 151, 160, 202
JETT buses 33, 79, 109, 204, 240, 300
jewellery 55
jihad 316, 334
Jiza 273
John the Baptist 160, 206, 312
Jordan Valley 155, 156–160, 307

K

Kafrayn 160
Kallirhoë see Callirhoë
Karak 210–216, 314
Karameh 160
Khirbet al-Mukhayyat 203
Khirbet as-Samra 165
Khirbet Tannur 218
King Hussein Bridge 14, 112
King's Highway 189–224
Kraymeh 159

L

language 360
Lawrence, T.E. ("of Arabia") 175, 178, 279, 317
lesbian travellers 59
literature 340, 350
Lot's Cave 216, 303, 309

M

Ma'an 274
Ma'in 204
Machaerus 205, 312
Madaba 192–201
Mafraq 167
mail 50
maps 27
Mazar 218
medical treatment 21

Mesha stele 208, 310
modern art 336–339
Mosaic Map of the Holy Land 196
mosaics 91, 98, 141, 194, 196, 199, 200, 207, 258, 313
Moses 202, 203, 228, 310
Moses Memorial Church 202
Mount Nebo 202, 310
Mshare'a 159
Mudawwara 276
Muhammad, Prophet 218, 267, 313, 331
Mukawir 205
Mukhaybeh 154
Muqat 172
Museum of Jordanian Heritage, Irbid 145
Muta 218
Muwaggar 187

N

Nabateans 189, 218, 228, 282, 288, 311
nargileh see arjileh
nature reserves 144, 179, 180, 209, 219, 280, 296
newspapers 53

O

opening hours 48

P

Pella 157, 338
PETRA 225–270
  accommodation 233
  Ain Musa 233
  Amud Faraoun 254
  arrival 232
  Bab as-Siq 244
  Bab as-Siq Triclinium 245
  Baydha 270
  Bdul tribe 251
  Broken Pediment Tomb 254
  Carmine Tomb 256
  changing money 239
  City centre 256
  Colonnaded Street 256
  Columbarium 262
  Corinthian Tomb 255
  Crusaders 263, 269
  dam 246
  Dayr *see* Monastery

Dorotheos' House 268
Eagle Niche 246
East Cliff 255
eating 238
email 239
Garden Triclinium 253
god-blocks 244, 245, 246, 266
Great Temple 260
guides 241
Habees 262
High Place of Sacrifice 252
history 225
human sacrifice 253
Jebel Haroun 266
Jebel al-Khubtha 256
Katuteh 254
Lion Monument 253
Lion Triclinium 263
Little Petra 269
Madras 246
Monastery 263
mosaics 258
Muaysreh Ridges 268
Mughur an-Nassara 268
museums 261, 262
Nymphaeum 258
Obelisk Tomb 245
Outer Siq 250
Palace Tomb 256
Petra Church 258
Petra scrolls 259
post 240
Qasr al-Bint 261
Qattar ad-Dayr 263
Renaissance Tomb 254
Ridge Church 258
Roman Soldier Tomb 254
Royal Tombs 255
Sabra 267
Scenic Road 233, 237
Sextius Florentinus Tomb 256
Sidd Maajn 247, 268
Silk Tomb 255
Siq 247
Siq al-Berid 269
Snake Monument 266
Street of Facades 250
Taybeh 237
Taybet Zaman 237
Temenos 260
Temple of the Winged Lions 259
Theatre 250
Tomb of 17 Graves 250
Tomb of Unayshu 255
Treasury 249
Turkmaniyyeh Tomb 268
Umm al-Biyara 265
Umm Sayhoun 232, 251, 268
Unfinished Tomb 262
Urn Tomb 255

Visitors' Centre 241
Wadi Abu Ullaygeh *see* Wadi Turkmaniyyeh
Wadi Farasa 253
Wadi al-Jarra 249, 250
Wadi Mataha 247, 268
Wadi Muaysreh ash-Shargiyyeh 268
Wadi Muthlim 246, 268
Wadi Sha'ab Qays 269
Wadi Siyyagh 262
Wadi Thughra 265
Wadi Turkmaniyyeh 268
Wadi Umm Rattam 267
Wu'ayra 269
Zantur 254
Pharaoh's Island 297
phones 50
photos 67, 117
poetry 348
police 63, 117
post 50
press 26, 53
public holidays 49

Q

Qadsiyyeh 222
Qala'at ar-Rabadh 142
Qasr 209
Qasr al-Abd 119, 311
Qasr Azraq 178
Qasr Burqu 172
Qasr Hallabat 166
Qasr Hraneh 185, 314
Qasr Kharana *see* Qasr Hraneh
Qasr Mushash 187
Qasr Mushatta 187, 314
Qasr Tuba 274
Qatraneh 273
Qusayr Amra 182, 314
Quweira 277
Qwaylbeh 155

R

Rabba 209
radio 53
Ramadan 42, 48, 333
Ramtha 148
Ras an-Naqb 277
Rashdiyyeh (Dana) 221
Rashdiyyeh (Wadi Rum) 277
Red Sea Marine Peace Park 296

religious holidays 49
River Jordan *see* Jordan Valley
rugs 54, 106, 201, 206
Rum 277–285
Ruwayshid 172

S
Safawi 171
Safi 125, 217, 303
Salt 121
service charges 32, 40
services 33
sexual harassment 57
Shaumari Wildlife Reserve 180
Shawbak 223, 314
Sheikh Hussein Bridge 15, 114, 148
Shuneh al-Janubiyyeh 110, 125, 160
Shuneh ash-Shamaliyyeh 155
Siyagha *see* Mount Nebo
snorkelling 296
Sodom 216, 309
sport 67, 118, 295
studying Arabic 64
Suf 134
Swaymeh 124, 303
sweets 44
Syria, travel to and from 13, 79, 111, 148

T
Tabqat Fahl 159
Tafileh 219
tax 32, 40
taxis 36, 84
Taybet Zaman 237

tea 45
teaching English 64
telephones 50
Tell Dayr Alla 160
Tell as-Sa'idiyyeh 159
terrorism 63
tipping 32
tour operators
  in Australia 13
  in Britain 7
  in Jordan 39
  in New Zealand 13
  in North America 10
tourist guides 68
tourist information
  abroad 25
  in Jordan 78
trains 14, 37, 82, 112
travel agents
  in Australia 12
  in Britain 5
  in Ireland 6
  in Jordan 108, 300
  in New Zealand 12
  in North America 9
TV 53

U
Umm al-Jimal 167
Umm Qais 149–153, 338
Umm ar-Rasas 206

V
vegetarians 43
Via Nova Traiana 73, 165, 170, 294, 312
visa extensions 17, 118
visas 16, 110, 301

W
Wadi Araba crossing 15, 301
Wadi Araba road 125, 302
Wadi Butm 182
Wadi Dana 219
Wadi Hasa 218
Wadi Hidan 208
Wadi Kharrar 160
Wadi Mujib 126, 208, 303
Wadi Musa 232–240
Wadi Qwaylbeh 155
Wadi Rum 277–285
Wadi Seer 118
Wadi Shuayb 123
Wadi Sirhan 173, 175
Wadi Wala 208
Wadi al-Yabis 144
Wadi Zerqa Ma'in 204
Websites 26
welcome 61
wildlife reserves 144, 179, 180, 209, 219, 280, 296
wiring money 31
work 64
writing 340

Y
Yarmouk Gorge 155
Yarmouk University 145, 296

Z
Zai National Park 123
Zara 126, 303
Zerqa 165
Zubia 144

Stay in touch with us!

ROUGHNEWS **is Rough Guides' free newsletter.
In three issues a year we give you news, travel
issues, music reviews, readers' letters and the
latest dispatches from authors on the road.**

I would like to receive ROUGH*NEWS*: please put me on your free mailing list.

NAME . . . .

ADDRESS . . . .

Please clip or photocopy and send to: Rough Guides, 62–70 Shorts Gardens, London WC2H 9AB,
England or Rough Guides, 375 Hudson Street, New York, NY 10014, USA.

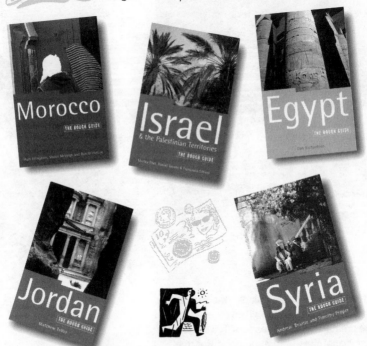

Know Where You're Going?

Wherever you're headed, **Rough Guides** show you the way, on and off the beaten track. We give you the best places to stay and eat on your **budget**, plus all the inside background and info to make your **trip** a great experience.

ROUGH GUIDES

Travel Guides to more than 100 destinations worldwide from Amsterdam to Zimbabwe.

AT ALL BOOKSTORES • DISTRIBUTED BY PENGUIN

Departure time?

Just say when.

Tel. No. 4891994 **FAX** 4893902 or contact
any Royal Jordanian office
email: info@arabwings.com.jo
website: http://www.arabwings.com.jo

For your executive travel,
air ambulance and priority
cargo needs, our crew is ready
to fly you at any time.
To any destination you have
in mind. Anywhere in the
world. Aboard a selection of
Sabrelinre, Falcon 50 or
Boeing 727 aircraft.
So just decide when you'd like
your flight.
We're ready for take off.

Fly At Will.

Arab Wings

YELLOW, BLUE, GREEN, ORANGE, RED SEA

We'll show you every shade of
the Red Sea experience. Royal
Wings fly you to Aqaba, your
gateway to amazing Petra, and
awesome Wadi Rum. Get to
know Jordan with the airline that
knows its home region in depth.

Royal Wings
AIRLINES

AT HOME IN THE HEART OF THE LEVANT

AMMAN • AQABA • HAIFA • TEL AVIV • REGIONAL CHARTER FLIGHTS
TEL. 4875201 **FAX** 4875656 SITA AMMYRRJ AMMAN - JORDAN
email: info@royalwings.com.jo **Website**: http://www.royalwings.com.jo

What is the RSCN?

The Royal Society for the Conservation of Nature (RSCN) is a non-governmental organization of international standing devoted to the conservation of Jordan's natural environment. Created in 1966 under the patronage of His Royal Majesty King Hussein, the RSCN has been given responsibility by the Jordanian government to protect the country's wildlife and wild places.

What can the RSCN offer to visitors?

The nature reserves of Jordan offer visitors a chance to experience some of the country's most beautiful landscapes, including the spectacular sandstone cliffs of Dana, the flowing rivers of Mujib, the oak woodlands of Zubia, the desert grassland of Shaumari and the marshes of Azraq.

Beauty without crowds

In order to protect the environment within the nature reserves, the number of visitors allowed to enter each day is limited and cars are required to park outside, so you get a real chance to experience the wonders of nature in peace and quiet.

Learn about nature

RSCN offers trained guides to accompany visitors during their visit who can tell them all about the wildlife, landscape and history of the area.

Explore unspoiled landscapes

There are hiking trails in all the reserves, which enable visitors to discover beautiful places and experience the special character of each reserve. Some can be self-guided; others need a tour guide to lead the way.

A sense of adventure

For small groups seeking a challenge, adventure treks can be arranged in the more dramatic and remote wild places of Jordan.

Support the conservation of wildlife

All the money visitors contribute through entrance fees, accommodation charges and buying crafts is used to further the work of the RSCN and help it protect the wildlife and wild places of Jordan.

Help local people

RSCN has a policy to employ local people wherever possible and to try and create opportunities for them to earn income from the nature reserves. Tourism is one of the main ways by which local people can improve their standard of living, and this is borne out by the success of the Dana reserve.

ANIMAL ADOPTION PROGRAMME!

Adopt a Nubian ibex or a gazelle for just JD30 per year, a roe deer or an onager for JD40, an ostrich for JD50, or a majestic Arabian oryx (which graces our logo) for just JD60. Contact the RSCN for more information, and details of how to pay.

For more information on the animal adoption programme, how to join the RSCN, or anything to do with Jordan's natural environment, please contact:

The Royal Society for the Conservation of Nature
PO Box 6354, Amman 11183, Jordan.
Tel: (+962) (0)6 533 4610 or 533 7931 or 533 7932. Fax: 534 7411.
Email: tourism@rscn.org.jo

A Resort Vacation in Natural Environment

Taybet Zaman, *Global Winner of the British Airways Tourism for Tomorrow Award 1996;*
Recipient of Green Globe Commendation Award 1997 and EIBTM Green Award 1998.

Sales Office Tel **(962 6) 553 7677** Fax **(962 6) 552 6785** Amman, Jordan
Taybet Zaman Tel **(962 3) 215 0111** Fax **(962 3) 215 0101** Petra, Jordan

---

"A good place for any trip planner to begin..."
— Gourmet Magazine

TRAVELLER'S BOOKSTORE

75 Rockefeller Plaza
(22 W. 52nd Street—lobby)
New York, NY 10019

TRAVELLER'S BOOKSTORE offers a FREE color, mail-order
catalogue to bring you a selective, personal look at the latest in
travel literature and guidebooks. Our vast collection includes:

- Well-known and hard-to-find guidebooks
- Worldwide road and city maps • Adventure travel guides
- Travel writing, non-fiction and fiction • Travel accessories
  - Children's travel books • Picture books and gifts

**Call 1-800-755-8728 for our FREE mail-order
catalogue, or fax 212-397-3984**

www.travellersbookstore.com

11:00 a.m.
Radisson SAS
Resort Aqaba

By the end of his vacation, this kid will think "Radisson SAS" is French for "fun."

R E S O R T   A Q A B A
The difference is genuine.

The location's as old as history. Our four-star facilities are brand new. It's a magical mix - the past with the best of the present for today's generation. Relax on the beach. Visit ancient Petra and the awe-inspiring Wadi Rum desert. Dive into the fascinating undersea world of the Gulf of Aqaba. Wind-down in our pool and view the Red Sea from our beach bar and grill. To us, holidays are a real family affair.

KINGS BOULEVARD • P.O. BOX 215 • AQABA 77110 • JORDAN
(962) 3 2012426 • FAX (962) 3 2013426
For reservations call (962) 3 2012426,
visit us at www.radisson.com or contact your travel professional

STANFORDS MAPS CHARTS BOOKS

Est.1852

World Travel starts at Stanfords

Maps, Travel Guides, Atlases, Charts
Mountaineering Maps and Books, Travel Writing
Travel Accessories, Globes & Instruments

Stanfords
12-14 Long Acre
Covent Garden
London
WC2E 9LP

Stanfords
at Campus Travel
52 Grosvenor Gardens
London
SW1W 0AG

Stanfords
at British Airways
156 Regent Street
London
W1R 5TA

Stanfords in Bristol
29 Corn Street
Bristol
BS1 1HT

International Mail Order Service
Tel: 0171 836 1321 **Fax**: 0171 836 0189

The World's Finest Map and Travel Bookshops

RENT A **RELIABLE** CAR
اصالة

لتأجيــر السيــارات السياحية

COMPETITIVE PRICES

 **BRAND NEW CARS**

ONE-WAY RENTAL

**FREE DELIVERY AND COLLECTION
AT QUEEN ALIA AIRPORT**

 ANY DRIVING LICENSE

FULL COMPREHENSIVE INSURANCE

Tel: ++ 962 6 5929676 Fax: ++ 962 6 5929676
E-mail:Reliable@nets.com.jo / Jormed@go.com.jo
Mobile : ++ 962 79 21358
P.O.Box : 960643 Amman 11196 Jordan
Abdoun 19 Fawzi Al-Qaweqji St.

HILLAWI
Desert Services

Handling • Jeep Safari • Camel Tours • Camping

Wadi Rum Resthouse
tel (+962-3) 201 8867   fax 201 4240
PO Box 114, Aqaba 77110, Jordan

Our Holidays Their Homes

Exploring New Destinations?
Ever wondered what that means to the locals?
Ever seen things you're uncomfortable with?
Ever thought of joining Tourism Concern?

Tourism Concern is the only independent British organisation seeking ways to make tourism just, participatory and sustainable – world-wide.

For a membership fee of only £18 (£9 unwaged) UK, £25 overseas, you will support us in our work, receive our quarterly magazine, and learn about what is happening in tourism around the world.

We'll help find answers to the questions.

Tourism Concern, Stapleton House, 277-281 Holloway Road, London N7 8HN
Tel: 0171-753 3330 Fax: 0171-753 3331 e-mail: tourconcern@gn.apc.org

A heavyweight insurance for those who travel light.

For details call

Our 'hassle-free' insurance includes instant cover, medical, personal liability, legal expenses, cancellation, passport and much more.

0171-375 0011

Lines open: 8am-8pm Mon-Fri, 9am-4pm Sat.

COLUMBUS DIRECT
TRAVEL INSURANCE

2 MINS FROM LIVERPOOL STREET STATION
Visit us at 17 DEVONSHIRE SQUARE, LONDON EC2M 4SQ

Take the Rough with the smooth.

The London Heathrow to Jordan service

Check out your Rough Guide. Add the comfort and convenience of our non-stop service to Amman, and your visit to Jordan will go smoothly from start to finish.

To book please contact your travel agent, British Airways Travel Shop or call British Airways anytime on (+44) 0345 222111.

Service operated by the independent carrier British Mediterranean Airways Ltd.

BRITISH AIRWAYS
The world's favourite airline

www.british-airways.com